A SURVEY OF THE
NEW TESTAMENT

4TH EDITION

A SURVEY OF THE
NEW TESTAMENT

ROBERT H.
GUNDRY

ZONDERVAN™

GRAND RAPIDS, MICHIGAN 49530 USA

ZONDERVAN™

A Survey of the New Testament, Fourth Edition
Copyright © 1970, 1981, 1994, 2003 by Robert H. Gundry

Requests for information should be addressed to:

Zondervan, *Grand Rapids, Michigan 49530*

Library of Congress Cataloging-in-Publication Data

Gundry, Robert Horton.
    A survey of the New Testament / Robert H. Gundry. — 4th ed.
      p. cm.
    Includes bibliographical references and indexes.
    ISBN 0-310-23825-0
    1. Bible. N.T. — Textbooks.   I. Title.
  BS2535.2G85 2003
  225.6'1—dc20

This edition printed on acid-free paper.

Credits and permissions for illustrations and maps are indicated on pages iv–xi, which hereby become a part of this copyright page.

Interior design by Sherri L. Hoffman

Printed in China

04 05 06 07 08 09 /❖ HK/ 10 9 8 7 6 5 4

CONTENTS

ILLUSTRATIONS, MAPS, AND CHARTS

Illustrations

Permissions and credits:

PLBL: Pictorial Library of Bible Lands, vols. 1–8, CD-ROM, copyright ©
     2001 by Todd Bolen. www.bibleplaces.com
ZIA: Zondervan Image Archives, copyright © 1995–1999 by Zondervan
Copyright © The Granger Collection, 381 Park Avenue South, New York,
     NY 10016. www.granger.com
Copyright © Corbis, 15395 SE 30th Place, Suite 300, Bellevue, WA 98007
     http://pro.corbis.com
Copyright © by Zev Radovan, Jerusalem, Israel
Copyright © by Carta, Jerusalem, Israel. www.carta.co.il
Copyright © by Hugh Claycombe
Other photos provided either by the author or by Zondervan

Maps

Permissions and credits:

Map on page 10 copyright © 2001 by Zondervan
Maps on page 317 copyright © 1986 by Zondervan
Relief map on pages 192–93 copyright © by Hugh Claycombe
All other maps provided by John R. Kohlenberger III and Zondervan

Charts

PRONUNCIATION KEY

a	cat	n	not
ah	father	ng	sing
ahr	lard	o	hot
air	care	oh	go
aw	jaw	oi	boy
ay	pay	oo	foot
b	bug	*oo*	boot
ch	chew	oor	poor
d	do	or	for
e, eh	pet	ou	how
ee	seem	p	pat
er	error	r	run
f	fun	s	so
g	good	sh	sure
h	hot	t	toe
hw	whether	th	thin
i	it	*th*	then
i	sky	ts	tsetse
ihr	ear	tw	twin
j	joke	uh	ago
k	king	uhr	her
kh	ch as in German *Buch*	v	vow
ks	vex	w	weather
kw	quill	y	young
l	love	z	zone
m	mat	zh	vision

Syllables with primary accent are shown in capital letters. Secondary emphasis is indicated by an accent mark.

Adapted from William O. Walker Jr., ed., *The HarperCollins Bible Pronunciation Guide* (San Francisco: HarperSanFrancisco, 1989), xiii.

ACKNOWLEDGMENTS

Apart from very occasional references to the King James Version (KJV) and the New International Version (NIV) of the Bible, I take responsibility for the English versions of biblical passages and the following: *Didache* 8:1; *Letter to Diognetus* 5:3, 5–6, 9; Eusebius, *Church History* 3.39.1–16; *2 Enoch* 44:1–2; *Testament of Levi* 18:1–14; *Community Rule* (1QS) 6:1, 20–21, 24–25; 7:15–19; 9:9–11; 10:17–18; *Damascus Document* (CD) 1:10–11; 2:7–8; 10:22; 11:9–10, 14–15; 13:7–9; *Melchizedek Text* (11Q Melch) 1–26; *Sectarian Manifesto* (4QMMT) C, 26–32; *Thanksgiving Hymns* (1QH) 5:22–23; Mishnah, *Avot* 3:16 and *Yadayim* 4:7; Babylonian Talmud, *Qiddushin* 30b and *Yevamot* 77a,b; *Targum Pseudo-Jonathan* on Exodus 7:11; the Theodotus Inscription; Aratus of Soli in Cilicia, *Phaenomena* 2–5; Aristotle, *Nicomachean Ethics* 8.9.1–2; Diogenes, Letter 47 (to Zeno); Epictetus, *Discourses* 4.1.1; Homer, *Odyssey* 17.483–87; Letter of Heraclitus to Amphidamas number 5, lines 15–21; Musonius Rufus, "Is Marriage a Handicap for the Pursuit of Philosophy?" 2–11; Oxyrhynchus Papyrus 1296; Paris Papyrus 574; Cologne Papyrus 7921; and Pliny the Younger, *Letters* 10.97.

As for remaining translations, those of the Old Testament Apocrypha come from the New Revised Standard Version; of the Old Testament Pseudepigrapha from *The Old Testament Pseudepigrapha* (ed. J. H. Charlesworth; 2 vols.; Garden City, N.Y.: Doubleday, 1983, 1985); of the New Testament Apocrypha from *New Testament Apocrypha* (ed. E. Hennecke, W. Schneemelcher, and R. McL. Wilson; 2 vols.; Philadelphia: Westminster and Louisville: Westminster John Knox, 1964, 1991); of the *Gospel of Thomas* from *Synopsis Quattuor Evangeliorum* (K. Aland; 14th ed.; Stuttgart: Deutsche Bibelgesellschaft, 1995); of the *Apocryphon of John* and *Gospel of Truth* from *The Nag Hammadi Library in English* (ed. J. M. Robinson; 3d ed.; San Francisco: Harper & Row, 1988); of the Paris Magical Papyrus from A. Deissmann, *Light from the Ancient East* (New York: Doran, 1927), 254–63; of the Mishnah from H. Danby, *The Mishnah* (Oxford: Clarendon, 1933); of the Babylonian Talmud, *Sanhedrin* 90b, 91b, from Jacob Neusner, *The Talmud of Babylonia: An American Translation: XXIIIC: Tractate Sanhedrin, Chapters 9–11* (Chico: Scholars Press, 1985); of the church fathers from *A Select Library of the Ante-Nicene Fathers of the Christian Church* (ed. A. Roberts and J. Donaldson; Grand Rapids: Eerdmans, 1971–77 reprint), *A Select Library of the Nicene and Post-Nicene Fathers of the Christian Church,* First Series (ed. P. Schaff; Grand Rapids: Eerdmans, 1974–76 reprint), and *A Select Library of the Nicene and Post-Nicene Fathers of the Christian Church,* Second Series (ed. P. Schaff and H. Wace; Grand Rapids: Eerdmans, 1974–76); of Stobaeus,

Anthologium 3, 417 (= III 10, 37), from *Hellenistic Commentary to the New Testament* (ed. M. E. Boring, K. Berger, and C. Colpe; Nashville: Abingdon, 1995); of Tebtunis Papyrus 276 from B. P. Grenfell, A. S. Hunt, and E. S. Goodspeed, *Tebtunis Papyri II* (London: Oxford University Press, 1907); of Cleanthes, Chrysippus, and Zeno from E. R. Bevan, *Later Greek Religion* (London: Dent, 1927); of *Corpus Inscriptionum Latinarum* 1.2.1211 from S. B. Pomeroy, *Goddesses, Whores, Wives, and Slaves: Women in Classical Antiquity* (New York: Schocken, 1995); and of other papyri and Greek and Latin classical authors, Josephus, and Philo from the Loeb Classical Library (Cambridge, Mass.: Harvard University Press).

Some of these translations have been adjusted slightly for clarity, up-to-dateness of spelling, style, and diction, and fidelity to the original languages. For example, "elders" substitutes for "presbyters," "immediately" for "straightway," "ought not to be" for "ought to be not," "allowed" for "suffered," "from then on" for "henceforth," "regularly" for "was wont to," "unburden" for "disburden," "house" for "home" for consistency with "house" elsewhere in the passage, the addition of "also" to "but" to complement "not only," the addition of "yet" for the otherwise untranslated Greek conjunction *alla*, some repositioning of words and phrases, and some repunctuation for correspondence to present standards. A blank space before the first in a series of four dots signals an ellipsis of words ending a sentence, so that the fourth dot is a period. The lack of a preceding blank space signals a sentence-ending period followed by an ellipsis. To conserve space, ellipses are frequent; but care has been taken to avoid distortion of meaning. These quotations fall within the limits of fair use.

My thanks to the staff at Zondervan, especially to supervising editor Jim Ruark, copy editor Laura Weller, compositors Sherri Hoffman and Beth Shagene, and proofreaders Becky Danley and Todd Sprague, for their work in the production of this volume.

Robert H. Gundry
Westmont College
Santa Barbara, California

PREFACE

A textbook surveying the New Testament should bring together the most salient items from New Testament background, technical introduction, and commentary. Nearly all surveys of the New Testament suffer, however, from a deficiency of comments on the biblical text. As a result, study of the survey textbook often nudges out a reading of the primary and most important text, the New Testament itself.

Reading the New Testament Itself

Since many beginning students have never read the New Testament systematically or thoroughly, if at all, the present survey prompts them to read it by carrying on a continual dialogue with it. This dialogue takes the form of comments on and references to the New Testament sections assigned for reading. By tracing the flow of thought from section to section, students will gain a sense of logical progression. By this means it has also proved possible to move at least some of the background material concerning intertestamental history, Judaism, and other matters, which seem tortuous to many students, from the first part of the book to later parts, where such material elucidates the biblical text directly. This procedure reduces the discouragingly long introduction to the typical academic course in New Testament survey, better enables students to see how background material helps interpret the text, and above all keeps the textbook from supplanting the New Testament.

INTRODUCTORY MATERIAL To be sure, the procedure demands brevity in the treatment of intertestamental and Roman history. But brevity is the soul of wit for the beginning student, for at least we do not obscure the big picture by dwelling on the unessential details of Hasmonean family squabbles, political intrigues within the Herodian household, and similarly incidental matters.

LAYOUT OF THE MAIN MATERIAL After the necessary introductory material, then, the four Gospels receive separate treatments suitable to their individual emphases. Even though not the first books of the New Testament to be written, they come under consideration first because their subject matter provides the basis for all that follows. To avoid discontinuity, the study of Acts proceeds without interruption. The Letters of Paul, Hebrews, the Catholic Letters, and Revelation follow in roughly chronological order (so far as that can be determined) with indications of their relation to events in Acts. Throughout, comments on the biblical text (in addition to introductory discussions) do not merely summarize or rehearse what is self-evident but concentrate on what is not readily apparent to uninitiated readers.

Special Features

Overviews and study goals introduce chapters to invite expectancy, induce right questioning, and launch thinking into proper channels. Sectional and paragraph headings keep students oriented. In the body of the text, bolded expressions highlight important topics and italics emphasize instructions for reading. Outlines systematize the scriptural material. Sidebars and photographs add illustrative collateral material. Questions and lists of items to remember aid not only a review of the material, but also its application to the contemporary scene. Suggestions for further investigation include commentaries and other standard works, ancient primary sources, topical works, and related literature.

Standpoint

The theological and critical standpoint of this textbook is evangelically Christian. In a survey, considerations of space and purpose rule out a full elaboration of presuppositions and method as well as a complete consideration of opposing views. Nevertheless, frequent note is taken of those views; and literature of different persuasions often appears among the suggestions for further reading. Instructors will be able to guide their students in evaluating those supplementary sources. Grateful acknowledgment is made to the publishers Charles Scribner's Sons and Harper & Row for permission to quote from works duly noted in the following pages.

Fourth Edition

A good reception of the third edition of this textbook has seemed to imply the inadvisability of radical changes. The present, fourth edition includes then an updating of bibliographies, the upgrading of maps and pictures, and pronunciations of important terms that many beginning students are unlikely to know, as well as the already mentioned sidebars and other added features. The pronunciations are given on the first occurrence of terms, are gathered together in a glossary near the end of the book and, with few exceptions, follow *The HarperCollins Bible Pronunciation Guide* (ed. William O. Walker Jr.; San Francisco: HarperSanFrancisco, 1989).

Readers will notice from the list of Illustrations, Maps, and Charts that almost half of the photographs in this edition come with permission from the *Pictorial Library of Bible Lands*. Teachers and serious students will find in this library a rich resource at economical cost. The CDs that make up the resource contain very many more high-resolution photographs than are included here—all usable with a monitor, a projector, or a printer, all ready for use in Microsoft Powerpoint, and all editable. For more details, consult www.BiblePlaces.com.

INTRODUCTION

Approaching the New Testament

AN ANTHOLOGY The New Testament consists of twenty-seven books of varying lengths and forms part 2 of the Bible but has only one-third the bulk of part 1, the Old Testament. The Old Testament covers thousands of years of history, the New Testament only one century. This century, the first one A.D., formed the crucial era during which according to Christian belief the fulfillment of messianic prophecy began, the divine outworking of human salvation reached a climax in the coming of God's Son, Jesus Christ, and the new people of God, the church, came into existence—all on the basis of the new covenant, under which God forgives the sins of believers in Jesus Christ by virtue of his ↓vicarious death and bodily resurrection.

TITLE In fact, the title "New Testament" means "new covenant" and contrasts with the Old Testament, or "old covenant," under which God forgave sins provisionally by virtue of animal sacrifices. Those sacrifices anticipated the truly adequate self-sacrifice of Christ (Hebrews 9:11–14; 10:1–18). His self-sacrificial death inaugurated the new covenant and made possible a full remission of sins (1 Corinthians 11:25; Hebrews 9:15–17).

Authorship

Early church tradition ascribes the books of the New Testament, written in Greek about A.D. 45–95, to **the apostles Matthew, John, Paul, and Peter** and to **their associates Mark, Luke, James, and Jude,** the last two also being half brothers of Jesus. In our Bibles the New Testament books do not appear in the chronological order of their writing. With the possible exception of James, for example, Paul's early Letters, not the Gospels of Matthew, Mark, Luke, and John, were the first to be written. Even in the grouping of Paul's Letters, the order does not follow chronology, for Paul wrote Galatians or 1 and 2 Thessalonians well before Romans, which stands first because it is the longest; and among the Gospels Mark, not Matthew, appears to have been written first.

Arrangement

The order of books, then, follows a certain logic and developed as a matter of Christian tradition. The **Gospels** appear

"The Hebrew Bible"

Old Testament and New Testament are Christian, not Jewish, designations, since Jews accept only the Old Testament as Scripture. Today the Old Testament is often called "the Hebrew Bible" because, unlike the New Testament, it was originally written in the Hebrew language (with the exception of Ezra 4:8–6:18; Daniel 2:4b–7:28, written in a sister language, ↓Aramaic).

Definitions

covenant = an agreement, here imposed by God alone rather than reached by negotiation between parties

vicarious = taking the place of others, substitutionary

remission = dismissal, forgiveness, pardon

at the beginning because they narrate the momentous events of **Jesus' career.** Matthew appropriately comes first because of its length and close relation to the immediately preceding Old Testament. (Matthew often cites the Old Testament and begins with a genealogy that reaches back into the Old Testament.) After the Gospels comes the triumphant aftermath of Jesus' life and ministry in the **Acts of the Apostles,** a stirring account of the **successful upsurge and outreach of the church** in Palestine and throughout Syria, Asia Minor, Macedonia, Greece, and as far as Rome, Italy. (Literarily, Acts follows up Luke to form the second volume in a two-volume work, Luke-Acts.) Acts is the last of the historical books of the New Testament.

The **Letters** and **Revelation** explain the **theological significance** of the foregoing redemptive history and spell out implications for **Christian conduct.** Among the Letters, Paul's stand first; and within that group the order is one of decreasing length, first for the subgroup of those addressed to churches, then for the subgroup of those addressed to individuals. The longest of the non-Pauline Letters, Hebrews (author unknown), comes next, then the so-called Catholic, or General, Letters by James, Peter, John, and Jude. Finally, the book that looks forward to Christ's return, Revelation, draws the New Testament to a fitting climax.

Definitions

early church tradition = material that appears in early Christian writings subsequent to the books of the New Testament, that is, from the late first or early second century onward for several centuries

apostles = the specially chosen, closest followers of Jesus during his earthly lifetime (see page 135)

redemptive (in this context) = liberating from sin and its dreadful consequences

catholic = having a general or universal rather than specific, very limited address (not Roman Catholic)

Purpose of Study

But why study such ancient documents as the New Testament contains? The **historical reason** is that in the New Testament we find an explanation for the phenomenon of Christianity. The **cultural reason** is that the influence of the New Testament has permeated Western and, increasingly, global civilization to such an extent that one cannot be well-educated without knowing what the New Testament says. The **theological reason** is that the New Testament consists of divinely inspired accounts and interpretations of Jesus' redemptive mission in the world and forms the standard of belief and practice for the Christian church. The **devotional reason** is that the Holy Spirit uses the New Testament to bring people into a living and growing personal relation with God through his Son Jesus Christ. All reasons enough!

PART 1

Political, Cultural, and Religious Antecedents

CHAPTER
1

INTERTESTAMENTAL AND NEW TESTAMENT HISTORICAL BACKGROUND

Overview:

- The Greek Period and Preliminaries
- The Maccabean Period
- The Roman Period
- Summary

Study Goals—Learn:

- What political events took place in the Middle East from the end of the Old Testament period through the intertestamental and New Testament periods
- How the Jews fared
- What cultural developments took place
- What religious questions arose out of the political events and cultural developments
- What factions the political events, cultural developments, and religious questions produced among Jews
- Who the leaders were in these developments and what they contributed to the sweep of this history

Harbor at Ptolemais on the Mediterranean coast in Palestine

3

The Greek Period and Preliminaries

From the Old Testament to Alexander the Great

In Old Testament times the kings Saul, David, and Solomon ruled over all twelve tribes of Israel. Then the nation split into the ten-tribe northern kingdom of Israel and the southern kingdom of Judah, with the tribe of Benjamin absorbed into the tribe of Judah. The **Assyrians** conquered the northern kingdom and took most of its inhabitants as exiles into Assyria. Next, the **Babylonians** took control of the Middle East from the Assyrians, conquered the southern kingdom of Judah, and took most of its inhabitants as exiles into Babylonia. The **Persians** then took control from the Babylonians and let exiled peoples, including Jews, return to their native lands if they so wished. Some did. Others did not. Under the Persians there began the **intertestamental period**, sometimes called "the four hundred silent years" because of a gap in the biblical record (though nonbiblical records have survived). During this gap Alexander the Great came from Greece-Macedonia and conquered the Middle East by inflicting successive defeats on the Persians at the battles of Granicus (334 B.C.), Issus (333 B.C.), and Arbela (331 B.C.).

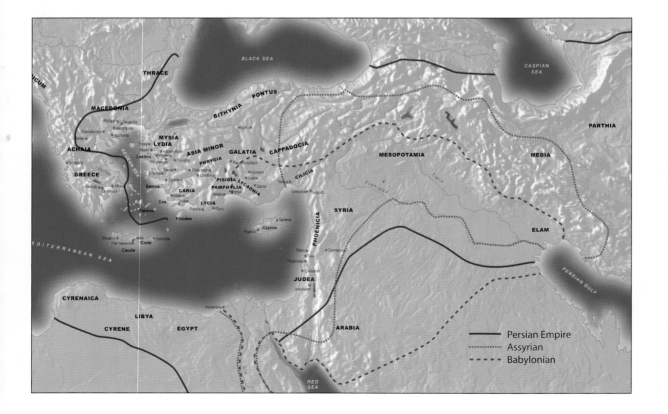

↓*Hellenization*

The Greek culture, called ↓**Hellenism**, had been spreading for some time through Greek trade and colonization, but Alexander's conquests provided far greater impetus than before. The **Greek language** became the ↓*lingua franca*, or common trade and diplomatic language. By New Testament times Greek had established itself as the street language even in Rome, where the indigenous proletariat spoke Latin but the great mass of slaves and freedmen spoke Greek (compare Paul's writing his Letter to the Romans in Greek). Alexander founded seventy cities and modeled them after the Greek style. He and his soldiers married oriental women. Thus the Greek and oriental cultures mixed.

Battle scene on the sarcophagus of Alexander the Great

Hellenization: hel´-uh-n*i*-ZAY-shun ■ Hellenism: HEL-uh-niz´uhm ■ lingua franca: LING-gwuh FRANG-kuh

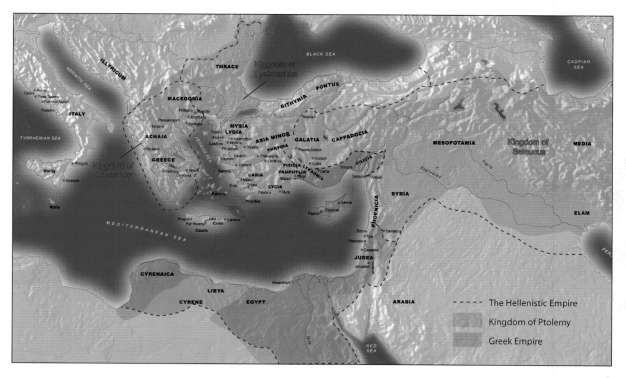

- - - - - The Hellenistic Empire
Kingdom of Ptolemy
Greek Empire

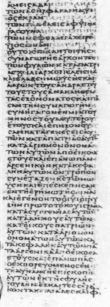

Portion of the Septuagint in Codex Vaticanus

↓Diadochi

When Alexander died in 323 B.C. at the age of thirty-three, his leading generals (called *diadochi*, Greek for "successors") divided the empire into four parts. Two of the parts are important for New Testament historical background, the ↓Ptolemaic and the ↓Seleucid. The Ptolemaic Empire centered in Egypt. Alexandria was its capital. The series of rulers who governed that empire are called the Ptolemies, after the name of the first ruler, Ptolemy. Cleopatra, who died in 30 B.C., was the last of the Ptolemaic dynasty. The Seleucid Empire centered in Syria. ↓Antioch was its capital. A number of its rulers were named ↓Seleucus, after the first ruler. Several others were named ↓Antiochus, after the capital city. Together they are called the Seleucids. When the Roman general ↓Pompey made Syria a Roman province in 64 B.C., the Seleucid Empire came to an end.

Because it was sandwiched between Egypt and Syria, Palestine became a victim of rivalry between the Ptolemies and the Seleucids, both of whom wanted to collect taxes from its inhabitants and make it a buffer zone against attack from the other. At first the Ptolemies dominated Palestine for 122 years (320–198 B.C.). Generally, the Jews fared well during this period. Early tradition says that under Ptolemy Philadelphus (285–246 B.C.) seventy-two Jewish scholars began to translate the Hebrew Old Testament into a Greek version called the ↓Septuagint. Translation of the ↓Pentateuch came first. Remaining sections of the Old Testament came later. The work was done in Egypt, apparently for Jews who understood Greek better than Hebrew and, contrary to the tradition, probably by Egyptian rather than Palestinian Jews. For parts of the translation betray a knowledge of Hebrew so poor as to indicate that the translators had less familiarity with Hebrew than with Greek, as would be probable if they lived, not in Palestine, but in Egypt. The Roman numeral **LXX** (seventy being the nearest round number to seventy-two) has become the common symbol for this version of the Old Testament.

Coin identifying Antiochus Epiphanes as "God manifest"

---

diadochi: dee-AH-doh-khī´ ■ Ptolemaic: tol´uh-MAY-ik ■ Seleucid: si-LOO-sid ■ Antioch: AN-tee-ok ■ Seleucus: si-LOO-kuhs ■ Antiochus: an-TI-uh-kuhs ■ Pompey: POM-pee ■ Septuagint: SEP-too-uh-jint ■ Pentateuch: PEN-tuh-tyook

"So they built a gymnasium in Jerusalem, according to Gentile custom, and removed the marks of circumcision, and abandoned the holy covenant. They joined with the Gentiles and sold themselves to do evil" (1 Maccabees 1:14–15).

Definitions

intertestamental history = "the four hundred silent years" = the period between the end of Old Testament history and the start of New Testament history

Hellenism = Greek culture

Hellenization = the spread of Greek culture, including especially the Greek language, so as to mix with other cultures

lingua franca = the language shared by different peoples even though their native languages might differ

indigenous proletariat = people of low class and native to a region; here, Romans of low class

dynasty = a succession of rulers belonging to the same family

Septuagint = a translation of the Old Testament from Hebrew into Greek

Pentateuch = the first five books of the Old Testament, traditionally ascribed to Moses: Genesis, Exodus, Leviticus, Numbers, and Deuteronomy

THE SELEUCIDS Seleucid attempts to gain Palestine, both by invasion and by marriage alliance, repeatedly failed. But success finally came with the defeat of Egypt by Antiochus III (198 B.C.). Among the Jews two factions developed, "the house of ↓Onias" (pro-Egyptian) and "the house of ↓Tobias" (pro-Syrian). Antiochus IV or ↓Epiphanes (175–163 B.C.) replaced the Jewish high priest Onias III with Onias's brother Jason, a Hellenizer who started making Jerusalem into a Greek city. A gymnasium and an adjoining race track were built. There, to the outrage of strict Jews, Jewish lads exercised in the Greek fashion—nude. Track races opened with invocations to pagan deities. Even Jewish priests attended these events. Such Hellenization also included attendance at Greek theaters, the adoption of Greek dress, surgery to disguise circumcision when exercising in the nude, and the exchange of Hebrew names for Greek names. Jews who opposed this paganization of their culture were called ↓Hasideans, "pious people," roughly equivalent to "Puritans."

Before launching an invasion of Egypt, Antiochus Epiphanes replaced his own appointee in the Jewish high priesthood, Jason, with ↓Menelaus, another Hellenizing Jew, who had offered to collect for Antiochus higher taxes from his subjects in Palestine. Jewish priests were supposed to have descended from Aaron, the elder brother of Moses, but Menelaus may not have belonged to a priestly family. In any case, pious Jews resented the selling of their most sacred office of high priest to the highest bidder, especially when the money was to come from their own pockets.

DIPLOMATIC DEFEAT Despite initial successes, Antiochus's attempt to annex Egypt failed. Ambitious Rome did not want its main source of grain taken over by the Seleucids nor the Seleucid Empire to increase in strength. Outside Alexandria, therefore, an envoy of the Roman senate drew a circle on the ground around Antiochus and demanded that before stepping out of the circle he promise to leave Egypt with his troops. Antiochus had learned to respect Roman power during twelve earlier years as a hostage in Rome, so he acquiesced.

Onias: oh-NI-uhs ■ Tobias: toh-BI-uhs ■ Epiphanes: i-PIF-uh-neez ■ Hasideans: has´uh-DEE-uhnz, also "Hasidim," HAS-uh-dim (sometimes spelled with "Ch," pronounced kh, at the beginning) ■ Menelaus: men´uh-LAY-uhs

"For example, two women were brought in for having circumcised their children. They publicly paraded them around the city, with their babies hanging at their breasts, and then hurled them down headlong from the wall.... The king fell into a rage, and gave orders to have pans and caldrons heated [for seven brothers and their mother, already tortured with whips and thongs for refusing to eat pork, forbidden by the law of Moses]. These were heated immediately, and he commanded that the tongue of their spokesman be cut out and that they scalp him and cut off his hands and feet, while the rest of the brothers and the mother looked on. When he was utterly helpless, the king ordered them to take him to the fire, still breathing, and to fry him in a pan. The smoke from the pan spread widely, but the brothers and their mother encouraged one another to die nobly" (2 Maccabees 6:10; 7:3–5; there follow the similarly gruesome martyrdoms of the remaining brothers and their mother, the father and husband having already been killed by being stretched apart on a rack and beaten).

Dionysus, god of wine, with grapes and a goblet

PERSECUTION BY ANTIOCHUS EPIPHANES Meanwhile, a false rumor reached the displaced high priest Jason that Antiochus had been killed in Egypt. Jason immediately returned to Jerusalem from his refuge in Transjordan and with his supporters seized control of the city from Menelaus. The embittered Antiochus, stung by his diplomatic defeat at the hands of the Romans, interpreted Jason's action as a revolt and sent soldiers to punish the rebels and put Menelaus back into the high priesthood. In the process they ransacked the temple and slaughtered many Jerusalemites. Antiochus himself returned to Syria.

Two years later, in 168 B.C., he sent his general ↓Apollonius with an army of 22,000 to collect taxes, outlaw Judaism, and enforce paganism as a means of consolidating his empire and replenishing his treasury. The soldiers plundered Jerusalem, tore down its houses and walls, and burned the city. Jewish men were killed, women and children enslaved. It became a capital offense to practice circumcision, observe the Sabbath, celebrate Jewish festivals, or possess scrolls of Old Testament books. Many such scrolls were destroyed. Pagan sacrifices became compulsory, as did processional marching in honor of ↓Dionysus (or ↓Bacchus), the Greek god of wine. An altar to the Syrian high god, identified as ↓Zeus, was erected in the temple. Animals abominable according to the Mosaic law were sacrificed on the altar, and prostitution was practiced right in the temple precincts.

Apollonius: ap´uh-LOH-nee-uhs ■ Dionysus: di´uh-NI-suhs ■ Bacchus: BAK-uhs ■ Zeus: *zoos*

"For the temple was filled with debauchery and reveling by the Gentiles, who dallied with prostitutes and had intercourse with women within the sacred precincts" (2 Maccabees 6:4).

The ↓Maccabean Period

Revolt

Jewish resistance came quickly. In the village of ↓Modein (or Modin, as it is also spelled) a royal agent of Antiochus urged an elderly priest named ↓**Mattathias** to set an example for the villagers by offering a pagan sacrifice. Mattathias refused. When another Jew stepped forward to comply, Mattathias killed him, killed the royal agent, demolished the altar, and fled to the mountains with his five sons and other sympathizers. Thus the Maccabean Revolt began in 167 B.C. under the leadership of Mattathias's family. We call this family the ↓**Hasmoneans**, after Hasmon, great-grandfather of Mattathias, or the **Maccabees**, from the nickname "Maccabeus" ("the Hammer") given to Judas, one of Mattathias's sons.

Judas Maccabeus led the rebels in highly successful guerrilla warfare until they were able to defeat the Syrians in pitched battle. The Maccabean Revolt also triggered a civil war between pro-Hellenistic and anti-Hellenistic Jews. The struggle continued even after the death of Antiochus Epiphanes (163 B.C.). Ultimately, the Maccabees expelled the Syrian troops from their citadel in Jerusalem, regained religious freedom, rededicated the temple, and conquered Palestine.

Independence

After Judas Maccabeus was killed in battle (160 B.C.), his brothers **Jonathan** and then **Simon** succeeded him in leadership. By playing contestants for the Seleucid throne against each other, Jonathan and Simon gained concessions for the Jews. Jonathan began to rebuild the damaged walls of Jerusalem and its other structures. He also assumed the high-priestly office. Simon gained recognition of Judean independence from ↓**Demetrius II**, a contestant for the Seleucid throne, and renewed a treaty with Rome originally made under Judas. Proclaimed as "the great high priest and commander and leader of the Jews,"

Maccabean: mak´uh-BEE-uhn ■ Modein: MOH-deen ■ Mattathias: mat´uh-TH*I*-uhs ■ Hasmoneans: haz´muh-NEE-uhnz ■ Demetrius: di-MEE-tree-uhs

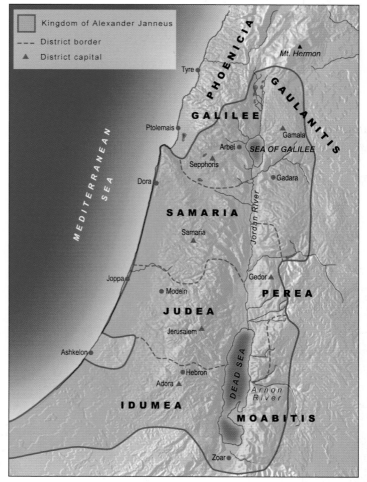

The Hasmonean Kingdom 76 B.C.

Kingdom of Alexander Janneus
--- District border
▲ District capital

PHOENICIA
Mt. Hermon
Tyre
GALILEE
GAULANITIS
Ptolemais
Gamala
Arbel SEA OF GALILEE
Sepphoris
Dora
Gadara
MEDITERRANEAN SEA
Jordan River
SAMARIA
Samaria
Joppa
Gedor
PEREA
Modein
JUDEA
Jerusalem
Ashkelon
DEAD SEA
Hebron
Adora
Arnon River
IDUMEA
MOABITIS
Zoar

Simon officially united in himself religious, military, and political headship over the Jewish state.

The subsequent history of the **Hasmonean dynasty** (142–37 B.C.) tells a sad tale of internal strife caused by ambition for power. The political aims and intrigues of the Hasmoneans alienated many of their former supporters, the religiously minded Hasideans, who split into the ↓**Pharisees** and the ↓**Essenes**. Some of the Essenes produced the Dead Sea Scrolls from ↓**Qumran** (see pages 60–61, 65–67). The aristocratic and politically minded supporters of the Hasmonean priest-kings became the ↓**Sadducees**. Finally, the Roman general **Pompey** subjugated Palestine (63 B.C.). Throughout New Testament history, then, Roman power dominated Palestine.

The Roman Period

The Rise of Rome

The eighth century B.C. saw the founding of **Rome**, and the fifth century B.C. the organization of a republican form of government there. Two centuries of war with the North African rival city of ↓**Carthage** ended in victory for Rome (146 B.C.). Conquests by **Pompey** in the eastern end of the Mediter-

Pharisees: FAIR-uh-seez ■ Essenes: ES-eenz ■ Qumran: KOOM-rahn ■ Sadducees: SAD-joo-seez ■ Carthage: KAHR-thij

The Roman Empire

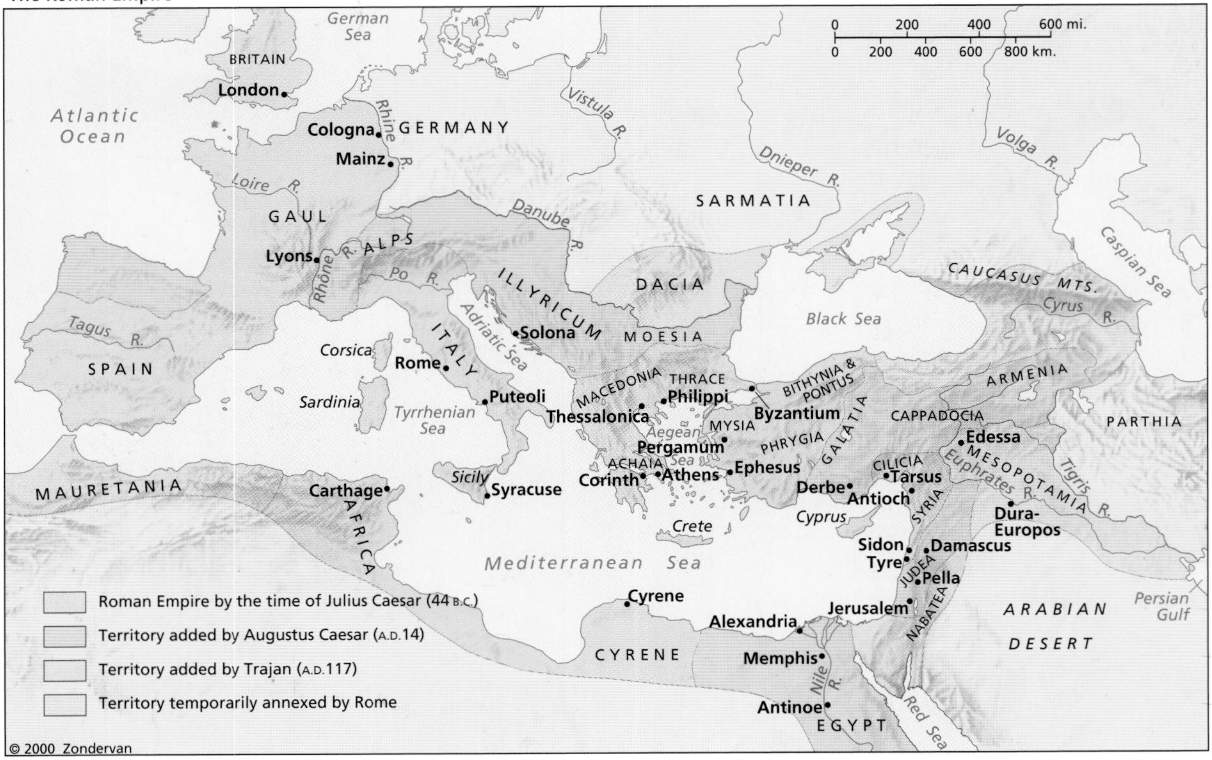

© 2000 Zondervan

ranean Basin and by **Julius Caesar** in Gaul (roughly equivalent to modern France) extended Roman domination. After Julius Caesar's assassination in the Roman senate, ↓**Octavian**, later known as ↓**Augustus**, defeated the forces of his rival **Antony** and the Ptolemaic queen **Cleopatra** in a naval battle off the coast of ↓Actium, Greece (31 B.C.), and became the first Roman emperor. Thus Rome passed from a period of expansion to a period of relative peace, known as the ↓*Pax Romana.* The province of Judea broke the peace with major revolts that the Romans crushed in A.D. 70 and 135. Nevertheless, the prevailing unity and political stability of the Roman Empire facilitated the spread of Christianity when it emerged.

> *Pax Romana* is Latin for "the Roman peace," but Calgacus, a Caledonian chief defeated by the Romans about A.D. 85, bitterly remarked in view of their plunder, butchery, and robbery, "They make a wasteland and call it peace" (Tacitus, *Agricola* 30).

ROMAN ADMINISTRATION Augustus set up a provincial system of government designed to keep proconsuls from administering foreign territories for their own aggrandizement. There were two kinds of provinces—senatorial, and imperial. ↓Proconsuls answered to the Roman senate, which appointed them over senatorial provinces, usually for terms of only one year. Alongside the proconsuls stood ↓procurators, appointed by the emperor, usually over financial matters. ↓Propraetors governed the imperial provinces. Also appointed by the emperor, they answered to him and exercised their civil and military authority by means of standing armies.

Roman Emperors

Touching the New Testament story at various points are the following Roman emperors, who do not make up a complete list even for the first century:

Bronze equestrian statue of Octavius Augustus

Augustus (27 B.C.–A.D. 14), under whom occurred the birth of Jesus, the census connected with his birth, and the beginning of emperor worship

↓**Tiberius** (A.D. 14–37), under whom Jesus publicly ministered and died

↓**Caligula** (A.D. 37–41), who demanded worship of himself and ordered his statue placed in the temple at Jerusalem, but who died before the order was carried out

---

Octavian: ok-TAY-vee-uhn ∎ Augustus: aw-GUHS-tuhs ∎ Actium: AK-ti-uhm ∎ *Pax Romana:* pahks roh-MAH-nuh ∎ proconsuls: proh-KON-suhlz ∎ procurators: PROK-yuh-ray´tuhrz ∎ propraetors: proh-PREE-turz ∎ Tiberius: *ti*-BIHR-ee-uhs ∎ Caligula: kuh-LIG-yuh-luh

Nero

"Therefore to scotch the rumor [that he had set fire to Rome], Nero substituted as culprits, and punished with the utmost refinements of cruelty, a class of men loathed for their vices, whom the crowd styled Christians. . . . They were covered with wild beasts' skins and torn to death by dogs; or they were fastened on crosses and, when daylight failed, were burned to serve as lamps by night. Nero offered his gardens for the spectacle" (Tacitus, *Annals* 15.44).

↓**Claudius** (A.D. 41–54), who expelled Jewish residents from Rome, among them Aquila and Priscilla (Acts 18:2), for civil disturbance

↓**Nero** (A.D. 54–68), who persecuted Christians, probably only in Rome, and under whom Peter and Paul were martyred

↓**Vespasian** (A.D. 69–79), who as a general began to crush a Jewish revolt, returned to Rome to become emperor, and left completion of the military task to his son Titus, whose army destroyed Jerusalem and the temple there in A.D. 70

↓**Titus** (A.D. 79–81), who may have been ruling at the time the book of Revelation was written

↓**Domitian** (A.D. 81–96), who some think persecuted the church and thus provided a background for the book of Revelation

Herod the Great

The Romans allowed natives of Palestine to rule the country under them. One was Herod the Great, who ruled from 37 to 4 B.C. His father, ↓Antipater, having risen to power and favor with the Romans, had thrust him into a military and political career. The Roman senate approved the kingship of Herod, but he had to gain control of Palestine by force of arms. Because of his ↓Idumean ancestry, the Jews resented him. (An Idumean was an ↓Edomite, a descendant of ↓Esau, the elder brother and rival of Jacob, who was also called Israel, the father of the twelve sons from whom the twelve tribes of Israel descended and took their names.) Scheming, jealous, and cruel, Herod killed two of his own wives and at least three of his own sons. So because Herod did not eat pork (presumably he wanted to avoid offending his Jewish subjects), Augustus said that it was better to be Herod's pig

Claudius: KLAW-dee-uhs ■ Nero: NIHR-oh ■ Vespasian: ves-PAY-zhuhn ■ Titus: TI-tuhs ■ Domitian: duh-MISH-uhn ■ Antipater: an-TIP-uh-tuhr ■ Idumean: id´yoo-MEE-uhn ■ Edomite: EE-duh-mit ■ Esau: EE-saw

than his son (a wordplay, since the Greek words for pig, ↓*hus*, and for son, ↓*huios*, sound very much alike). According to Matthew 2:16–18, Herod had the infants in Bethlehem slaughtered shortly after Jesus' birth there.

But Herod was also an efficient ruler and clever politician who managed to survive

"Thus, in the fifteenth year of his reign, he restored the Temple and, by erecting new foundation-walls, enlarged the surrounding area to double its former extent. The expenditure devoted to this work was incalculable, its magnificence never surpassed" (Josephus, *Jewish War* 1.21.1 §401).

struggles for power in the higher echelons of Roman government. For example, he switched allegiance from Mark Antony and Cleopatra to Augustus and successfully convinced Augustus of his sincerity. Secret police, curfews, and high taxes, but also free grain during famine and free clothing in other calamities, characterized the administration of Herod. Among many building projects, his greatest contribution to the Jews was **beautification of the temple in Jerusalem.** This beautification did not represent his sharing of their faith (he did not share it), but an attempt to please them. The temple, decorated with white marble, gold, and jewels, became proverbial for its splendor: "Whoever has not seen the temple of Herod has seen nothing beautiful." As best we can tell, Herod died of dropsy, Fournier's gangrene, and kidney disease or intestinal cancer in 4 B.C. He had commanded a number of leading Jews to be slaughtered when he died, so that

hus: hyoos ■ *huios:* hyoo-ee-AWS

Herodian masonry alongside a first-century street in Jerusalem. Note the characteristic indentation around the perimeter of the stone's face.

"The fever that he had was a light one . . . . He also had a terrible desire to scratch himself because of this . . . . There was also an ulceration of the bowels and intestinal pains that were particularly terrible, and a moist, transparent suppuration of the feet. And he suffered similarly from an abdominal ailment, as well as from a gangrene of his private parts that produced worms. . . . He also had convulsions in every limb that took on unendurable severity" (Josephus, *Jewish Antiquities* 17.6.5. §§168–69).

"While the temple blazed, the victors plundered everything that fell in their way and slaughtered wholesale all who were caught. No pity was shown for age, no reverence for rank; children and greybeards, laity and priests, alike were massacred. . . . The roar of the flames streaming far and wide mingled with the groans of the falling victims; and, owing to the height of the hill and the mass of the burning pile, one would have thought that the whole city was ablaze. . . . There were the war-cries of the Roman legions sweeping onward in mass, the howls of the rebels encircled by fire and sword, the rush of the people who, cut off above, fled panic-stricken only to fall into the arms of the foe, and their shrieks as they met their fate. . . . You would indeed have thought that the temple-hill was boiling over from its base, being everywhere one mass of flame, but yet that the stream of blood was more copious than the flames and the slain more numerous than the slayers. For the ground was nowhere visible through the corpses; but the soldiers had to clamber over heaps of bodies in pursuit of the fugitives" (Josephus, *Jewish War* 6.5.1 §§271–76).

although there would be no mourning *over* his death, at least there would be mourning *at* his death. But the order died with him.

HEROD'S DYNASTY Lacking their father's ability and ambition, the sons of Herod ruled over separate parts of Palestine: ↓**Archelaus** over Judea, Samaria, and Idumea; **Herod Philip** over Iturea, Trachonitis, Gaulanitis, Auranitis, and Batanea; and **Herod** ↓**Antipas** over Galilee and Perea (see the map on page 16). John the Baptist rebuked Antipas for divorcing his wife to marry ↓**Herodias**, the wife of his half brother. When in retaliation Herodias induced her dancing daughter to demand the head of John the Baptist, Antipas yielded to the grisly request (Mark 6:17–29; Matthew 14:3–12). Jesus called him "that fox" (Luke 13:32) and later stood trial before him (Luke 23:7–12). **Herod** ↓**Agrippa I**, grandson of Herod the Great, executed James the apostle and son of ↓Zebedee and imprisoned Peter (Acts 12:1–19). **Herod Agrippa II**, great-grandson of Herod the Great, heard Paul's self-defense (Acts 25–26).

Roman Governors and Revolts

The misrule of Archelaus in Judea, Samaria, and Idumea led to his removal from office and banishment by Augustus (A.D. 6). According to Matthew 2:21–23, this same misrule had influenced Joseph to settle with Mary and Jesus in Nazareth of Galilee when they returned from Egypt. Except for brief periods, Roman governors ruled Archelaus's former territory. One of those governors, ↓**Pontius Pilate**, sat in judgment on Jesus. The governors **Felix** and ↓**Festus** heard Paul's case (Acts 23–26). And a raiding of the temple treasury by the governor ↓**Florus** ignited the Jewish revolt of A.D. 66–74, which reached a climax with the Romans' **destruction of Jerusalem and the temple in** A.D. 70.

Mopping-up operations lasted several years till the capture of ↓**Masada**, a fortress on the west side of the Dead Sea. There the last rebels and their families, numbering more than nine hundred, committed mass suicide just

Archelaus: ahr´kuh-LAY-uhs ■ Antipas: AN-tee-puhs ■ Herodias: hi-ROH-dee-uhs ■ Agrippa: uh-GRIP-uh ■ Zebedee: ZEB-uh-dee ■ Pontius Pilate: PON-shuhs PI-luht ■ Festus: FES-tuhs ■ Florus: FLOR-uhs ■ Masada: muh-SAH-duh

Side view of Masada

before the Romans entered. The Jews had suffered even greater loss of life at the destruction of Jerusalem. Both that destruction and the capture of Masada were preceded by long sieges. Apart from such events and in spite of the Herods and the Roman governors, however, Jewish priests and Jewish courts controlled most local matters of daily life.

FROM THE FIRST JEWISH WAR TO THE SECOND Worship at the temple and its sacrificial system ceased with the destruction of Jerusalem in A.D. 70. As a substitutionary measure Jewish rabbis established a school in the Mediterranean coastal town of ↓Jamnia (also spelled Jabneh or Yavneh) to expound the ↓Torah, the Old Testament law, more intensively. Unsettled conditions continued in Palestine until Emperor ↓Hadrian erected a temple to the Roman god Jupiter where the Jewish temple had stood. He also prohibited the rite of circumcision. The Jews revolted again, this time under the leadership of ↓Bar Kokhba, hailed by many of them as the Messiah (A.D. 132). The Romans crushed this uprising in A.D. 135, rebuilt Jerusalem as a

Jamnia: JAM-nee-uh ■ Torah: TOH-ruh ■ Hadrian: HAY-dree-uhn ■ Bar Kokhba: bahr KOHK-buh

A Kokhba Is a Cochba Is a Kosiba Is a Koziba

Kokhba is also spelled Cochba, pronounced the same. The man's real name was Simon bar Kosiba, "Simon son of Kosiba." But the famous rabbi Akiba believed him to be the Messiah and therefore nicknamed him Bar Kokhba, "son of the star," an allusion to Numbers 24:17, which compares David, after whom the Messiah was to be modeled, to a rising star. Because Bar Kokhba did not turn out to be the Messiah, other rabbis nicknamed him Bar Koziba, "son of a lie," that is, a liar.

THE HERODIAN KINGDOMS
After A.D. 6 the territory formerly
allotted to Archelaus was ruled
by successive Roman governors.

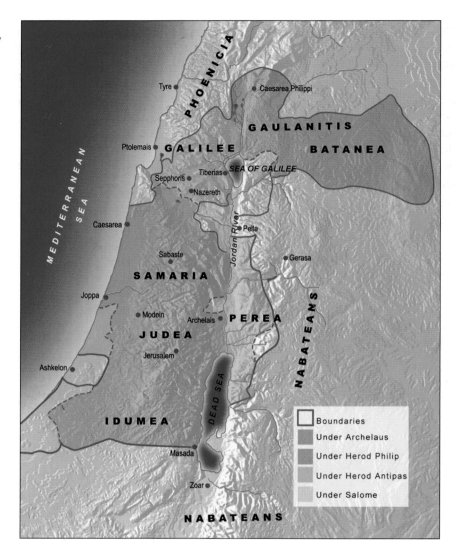

THE HERODIAN KINGDOMS
After A.D. 6 the territory formerly allotted to Archelaus was ruled by successive Roman governors.

Roman city, and banned Jews from entering it. Thus the Jewish state ceased to exist until its revival in 1948.

Summary

Toward the end of Old Testament history the Assyrians took northern Israel into exile. Next, the Babylonians took southern Judah into exile. Then the Persians allowed the exiles to return to the land of Judah if they wished to do so, and some did. The intertestamental period of four hundred years ensued. During that time Alexander the Great conquered the Middle East and spread the Greek culture. His successors the Ptolemies, based in Egypt, treated the Jews in Palestine relatively well. Other successors of Alexander, the Seleucids of Syria, gained control of those Jews and tried to impose on them the Greek culture, including its pagan religion. Pious Jews rebelled under the leadership of a family called the Maccabees, or Hasmoneans. The success of the rebellion led to independence under Maccabean rulers. Just before the start of the New Testament period, the Romans conquered Palestine. Roman domination continued throughout that period. Under their jurisdiction, the Romans allowed rulers native to Palestine to rule it, though because of misrule, Roman governors were eventually sent to Judea. In A.D. 70 a Jewish revolt was crushed with the destruction of Jerusalem and the temple. Another Jewish revolt was crushed in A.D. 135, not long after the close of the New Testament period.

REVIEW OF LATE OLD TESTAMENT, INTERTESTAMENTAL, AND NEW TESTAMENT HISTORY

Century	Dominant Power	Important Events
B.C. 8th (700s)	Assyria	Exile of the northern kingdom of Israel with the destruction of its capital city, Samaria, in 722–21 B.C.
7th (600s)	Babylonia	Exile of the southern kingdom of Judah with destruction of Jerusalem and the first temple in 587–86 B.C.
6th (500s)	Persia	Return of some Jews to Palestine to rebuild their nation, temple, and Jerusalem from 537 B.C. onward
5th (400s)		
4th (300s)	Greece-Macedonia	Conquest by Alexander the Great and an upsurge of Hellenization throughout the Middle East
		Death of Alexander the Great in 323 B.C. and the division of his empire
	Egypt	Ptolemaic domination of Palestine, 320–198 B.C.
3d (200s)		Beginning of the Septuagint with translation of the Pentateuch from Hebrew into Greek
2d (100s)	Syria	Seleucid domination of Palestine, 198–167 B.C.
		Development of Hellenistic and Hasidic parties within Jewry
		Failure of Antiochus Epiphanes' attempt to annex Egypt
		Antiochus Epiphanes' violent attempt to force complete Hellenization, or paganization, on the Jews in 168 B.C.
		Outbreak of the Maccabean Revolt in 167 B.C. and the gaining of Jewish independence under the successive leadership of Mattathias, Judas Maccabeus, Jonathan, and Simon
	Jewish Independence	Hasmonean dynasty, 142–37 B.C.
1st (100–1)		Internal strife
		Development of Jewish sects: Pharisees, Essenes, and Sadducees
	Rome	Subjugation of Palestine by the Roman general Pompey in 63 B.C.
		Rise to power in Palestine of Antipater and his son Herod the Great
		Assassination of Julius Caesar

		Augustus's rise to Roman emperorship (27 B.C.–A.D. 14) at the expense of Mark Antony and Cleopatra
		Birth of Jesus about 6 B.C.
		Death of Herod the Great in 4 B.C.
A.D. 1st (1–100)	Rome	Tiberius's emperorship (A.D. 14–37); Pilate's governorship
		Public ministry, death, and resurrection of Jesus (A.D. 26–30 or 29–33)
		Beginnings of the Christian church under the leadership of Peter, Paul, and others
		Caligula's and Claudius's emperorships (A.D. 37–41 and 41–54)
		Expansion of the Christian church
		Beginnings of New Testament literature
		Nero's emperorship (A.D. 54–68)
		Persecution of Christians on a limited scale
		Martyrdoms of Peter and Paul (A.D. 64–68)
		First Jewish War (A.D. 66–74)
		Short-lived emperorships of Galba, Otho, and Vitellius (A.D. 68–69)
		Vespasian's emperorship (A.D. 69–79)
		Destruction of Jerusalem and the second temple by Titus in A.D. 70
		Titus's emperorship (A.D. 79–81)
		Domitian's emperorship (A.D. 81–96)
		Reconstitution of Judaism at Jamnia with almost total emphasis on the Torah because the temple had been destroyed
		Final production of New Testament literature with the Johannine writings
		Beginnings of further Roman persecution of the church
2d (100s)		Nerva's and Trajan's emperorships (A.D. 96–98 and 98–117)
		Hadrian's emperorship (A.D. 117–138)
		Second Jewish War under the rebel leader Bar Kokhba (A.D. 132–135)
		Rebuilding of Jerusalem as a Roman city with a ban against Jewish entrance

People to Remember

Alexander the Great	Judas Maccabeus	Pompey	Vespasian
Antiochus Epiphanes	Mattathias	Pontius Pilate	
Bar Kokhba	Nero	Tiberius	
Herod the Great	Octavian/Augustus	Titus	

Places to Remember

Alexandria, Egypt	Idumea	Perea
Antioch, Syria	Jamnia (Jabneh, Yavneh)	Rome
Carthage	Jerusalem, Palestine	Samaria
Galilee	Judea	
Greece	Modein (Modin)	

Terms to Remember

diadochi	lingua franca	Seleucid Empire
Hasideans (Hasidim)	Maccabees/Hasmoneans	Septuagint/LXX
Hellenism/Hellenization	Pax Romana	
intertestamental period	Ptolemaic Empire	

How Much Did You Learn?

- What foreign powers dominated Palestine, with one interruption, from the end of the Old Testament period through the end of the New Testament period?
- What was the interruption?
- What cultural phenomenon accompanied the conquests of Alexander the Great?
- Why did many of the Palestinian Jews rebel against Antiochus Epiphanes?
- Trace the rise and fall of the Hasmonean family.
- What important events occurred in Palestine during the first and second centuries A.D.?

For Further Discussion

- In what providential ways did the events of the intertestamental period prepare for the coming of Christ and the rise of the church?
- What parallels may be drawn between the controversy of the Hasideans with Hellenistic Jews and similar controversies within the church, especially in recent church history?
- What comparisons may be made between the Hasidic movement and Maccabean Revolt, on the one hand, and current Islamic fundamentalism and its activities on the other hand?

For Further Investigation

Primary Materials

1 and 2 Maccabees. In *The New Oxford Annotated Apocrypha*. Edited by B. M. Metzger and R. E. Murphy. New York: Oxford University Press, 1991.

Barrett, C. K. *The New Testament Background: Selected Documents*. 2d ed. San Francisco: Harper & Row, 1989. Especially pages 1–22, 135–76, 269–75, 290–98, 306–8.

Josephus. *Jewish Antiquities*. 7 vols. Loeb Classical Library. Cambridge, Mass.: Harvard University Press, 1930–65.

_____. *The Jewish War*. 2 vols. Loeb Classical Library. Cambridge, Mass.: Harvard University Press, 1927–28.

Kee, H. C. *The Origins of Christianity*. Englewood Cliffs, N.J.: Prentice-Hall, 1973. Especially pages 10–53.

Polybius. *Histories* 29.27. On the meeting between Antiochus Epiphanes and the Roman envoy outside Alexandria.

Yadin, Y. *Herod's Fortress and the Zealots' Last Stand*. New York: Random House, 1967. For archaeological discoveries confirming Josephus's dramatic account of the Zealots' last stand at Masada toward the close of the first Jewish revolt.

_____. *The Finds from the Bar Kokhba Period in the Cave of Letters*. Jerusalem: Israel Exploration Society, 1963. For technical description of an archaeological dig and discoveries in a cave that yielded letters from Bar Kokhba during the second Jewish revolt.

Modern Treatments

Avi-Yonah, M. *The Holy Land. From the Persian to the Arab Conquests (536 B.C. to A.D. 640): A Historical Geography*. 2d ed. Grand Rapids: Baker, 1970.

Bruce, F. F. *New Testament History*. Garden City, N.Y.: Doubleday, 1972.

Collins, J. J. *Between Athens and Jerusalem: Jewish Identity in the Hellenistic Diaspora*. 2d ed. Grand Rapids: Eerdmans, 2000.

Gowan, D. E. *Bridge Between the Testaments*. Pittsburgh: Pickwick, 1976.

Hengel, M. *Jews, Greeks, and Barbarians: Aspects of the Hellenization of Judaism in the Pre-Christian Period*. Philadelphia: Fortress Press, 1980.

_____. *Judaism and Hellenism*. 2 vols. Philadelphia: Fortress Press, 1974.

The Jewish People in the First Century. Vol. 1. Edited by S. Safrai et al. Philadelphia: Fortress Press, 1974.

Niswonger, R. L. *New Testament History*. Grand Rapids: Zondervan, 1988.

Richardson, P. *Herod*. Columbia: University of South Carolina Press, 1996.

Schürer, E. *The History of the Jewish People in the Age of Jesus Christ (175 B.C.–A.D. 135)*. Vol. 1. Revised and edited by G. Vermès and F. Millar. Edinburgh: T. & T. Clark, 1973.

Witherington, B., III. *New Testament History: A Narrative Account*. Grand Rapids: Baker, 2001.

CHAPTER
2

THE SECULAR SETTINGS OF THE NEW TESTAMENT

Overview:

- Demography
- Languages
- Transportation, Commerce, and Communication
- Public Conveniences
- Housing
- Food
- Clothing and Styles
- Social Classes
- The Family
- Honor and Shame
- Morals
- Entertainment
- Business and Labor
- Science and Medicine
- Summary

Study Goals—Learn:

- How people in the first century lived, thought, spoke, worked, ate, dressed, traveled, learned, and entertained themselves
- What differences existed between daily life inside Palestine and daily life outside Palestine

Colonnaded street in Gerasa, Jordan

Demography

It is impossible to know with certainty how many Jews lived in the Roman Empire during New Testament times. Perhaps 2 million to 3 million people lived in Palestine; but we can be fairly sure that more Jews lived in Syria than in Palestine, more in Alexandria, Egypt, than in Jerusalem. Even Rome had a Jewish quarter. On the other hand, a sizable number of Gentiles lived in parts of Palestine, such as Galilee, where Jesus grew up; and they out-numbered Jews in the nearby ↓Decapolis. Gentiles were to be found particularly in major cities.

Languages

Latin was the legal language of the Roman Empire but was used mainly in the West, though even there Greek was widely used. In the East, generally speaking, Greek predominated. Jews living in Palestine, such as Jesus and his first disciples, spoke not only Greek but also and mostly Aramaic and perhaps some Hebrew. The Jews had picked up Aramaic, a sister language to their traditional Hebrew, during the exile. Estimates of literacy vary widely. Those that depend on modern social anthropological studies put the rate at 10 to 30 percent, city folk and men toward the high end, country folk

Decapolis: di-KAP-uh-lis

Hellenistic architecture in Gerasa of the Decapolis

and women toward the low end. But the large numbers of ancient graffiti and nonliterary papyri, plus lists of graduates from elementary schools, suggest a higher rate of literacy, in places perhaps as much as 80 percent of the population, including women and slaves.

"When they [a crowd of Jews in Jerusalem] heard him [Paul] speak to them in Aramaic, they became very quiet" (Acts 22:2).

Transportation, Commerce, and Communication

In transportation, commerce, and communication, Palestine was relatively undeveloped. Nevertheless, several main roads deserve mention. One led southwest from Jerusalem past Bethlehem through ↓Hebron to ↓Gaza and northeast from Jerusalem past Bethany to ↓Jericho, then north up the Jordan Valley and the west side of the Sea of Galilee toward ↓Capernaum. To avoid ↓Samaria, whose inhabitants the Jews despised, Jews often traveled this road in going between Galilee and ↓Judea. Another road led from Jerusalem straight up through Samaria to Capernaum. It was along this road that Jesus talked with a Samaritan woman by Jacob's well. Another road branched east from Jericho to Philadelphia, turned north, and went through ↓Gerasa to Damascus. Paul was traveling this road when he received his transforming vision of Christ. Yet another road went up the Mediterranean coast from Gaza to ↓Tyre. A branch on which the risen Jesus conversed with two disciples went from the southern coast past ↓Emmaus to Jerusalem. Finally, a road led from the northern coast past Nazareth and Capernaum to Damascus.

Although the Palestinian road system was comparatively poor, throughout much of the Roman Empire the roads were justly famous. They were as straight as possible and durably constructed. Early Christian missionaries used them to full advantage, and the imperial post carried governmental dispatches over them. Private businesses had their own couriers to carry messages. People traveled by foot, by donkey, by horse or mule, and by

Road system in Roman Palestine

Hebron: HEE-bruhn ■ Gaza: GAH-zuh ■ Jericho: JER-uh-koh ■ Capernaum: kuh-PUHR-nay-uhm ■ Samaria: suh-MAIR-ee-uh ■ Judea: joo-DEE-uh ■ Gerasa: GER-uh-suh ■ Tyre: tir ■ Emmaus: i-MAY-uhs

Model of an Alexandrian merchant ship

"There the centurion found an **Alexandrian ship** sailing for Italy and put us on board.... After three months we put out to sea in an **Alexandrian ship** that had wintered in the island" (Acts 27:6; 28:11).

carriage or litter. Because roadside inns were usually squalid, bedbugs being a particularly annoying problem, people of better means depended on friends for lodging; and even ordinary people could depend on the Middle Eastern law (more like an obligatory custom) of showing hospitality to strangers. One could buy tourist maps in manuscript form and even guidebooks for tourists.

Water offered the primary means of commercial transport. Since Egypt served as breadbasket for the Roman Empire, Alexandria provided the main port and outlet for Egyptian grain. Alexandrian ships reached almost 200 feet in length, had sails, and carried oars for emergencies. One large ship could transport several hundred passengers in addition to cargo. Paul was aboard an Alexandrian ship when he suffered shipwreck, and he finished his voyage on another Alexandrian ship. Warships were lighter and faster. Galley slaves labored at the oars, of which there were two to five banks, sometimes more. Barges plied the rivers and canals.

A Roman road

Roads, rivers, and the Mediterranean Sea supplied lines of communication. Papyrus, ostraca (broken bits of pottery), and wax tablets were used as writing materials for letters and other documents. For important manuscripts, leather or parchment was used. Most news was spread by word of mouth, by town criers, and by public notices posted on bulletin boards.

> "When you come, bring the cloak that I left with Carpus at Troas, and the **scrolls**, especially the **parchments**" (2 Timothy 4:13).

Public Conveniences

Public bathroom in Sardis

Alexandria had a well-developed school system. The city library contained well over half a million volumes. Excavations have shown that the city of Antioch, Syria, had two and one-half miles of streets colonnaded and paved with marble and a complete system of night lighting. Serving major cities of the empire were underground sewage disposal systems. Bathhouses featured large pools and served the general public. The Greeks had invented shower baths long before New Testament times.

Remains of a bathhouse in Troas, with a view to the sea

Housing

Most housing was cramped, so that people—especially men—spent the majority of their waking hours out of doors and in workshops and public spaces. Fortunately, the weather was usually mild. Houses in the western part of the Roman Empire were built of brick or concrete, at least in cities. Poorer sections and rural areas had frame houses or huts. In the eastern part of the empire, houses usually consisted of stucco and sun-dried brick. Few windows opened onto the street, because cities lacked proper police forces to keep thieves from roaming the streets at night and breaking into houses through windows. More expensive houses had double-door front entrances, sometimes with knockers. A vestibule led to the door, beyond which lay a large central court called an ↓*atrium*. Roofs were tile or thatch. In the kitchen an open hearth, or an earthen or stone oven, served for cooking. Oil lamps provided lighting. Plumbing and heating were well developed. A central furnace heated some houses, pipes conveying the warm air to different rooms. Many Roman lavatories had running water, and ↓Pompeian houses had at least one toilet convenience, sometimes two. Murals decorated walls. In larger cities lower- and middle-class people often rented flats in multi-storied tenements. The upper classes might enjoy expensive villas in the countryside as well as luxurious dwellings in the city.

> "And there was a certain young man named Eutychus, sitting in a window and sinking into a deep sleep as Paul talked on and on. When he had fallen sound asleep, he fell down from the **third story**" (Acts 20:9).

Palestinian towns and houses differed somewhat from their Greco-Roman counterparts and were comparatively backward. One entered a town through a gate in the wall. Inside the gate an open square provided a public place for trade and for social and legal interchange. Jesus must have preached often in these town squares. The houses were low and flat-roofed, sometimes with a guest chamber perched on top. The building material for these houses consisted of bricks made of mud and straw baked in the sun or of small stones and blocks of basalt. The typical low-class Palestinian had an apartment in a building containing several apartments, all on ground level. Some apartments had only one room, part of which was on a slightly higher level than

An ancient apartment building in Ostia, Italy

---

atrium: AY-tree-uhm ■ Pompeian: pom-PAY-uhn (from "Pompeii," a town located on the Bay of Naples, Italy, and destroyed by the eruption of Mount Vesuvius in A.D. 79)

Old village of Yata, neighboring Hebron and preserving the structure of typical villages in ancient Palestine

the rest. Beds, chests for clothes, and cooking utensils were located on the higher level. Livestock and other domestic animals inhabited the lower level; or, when the animals were outside, children played there. Branches laid across rafters and plastered with mud formed the flat roofs. Rain caused leakage; so after each rain the mud had to be rolled to seal the holes. A parapet around the edge of the roof kept people from falling off, and a flight of stairs on the outside of the house led up to the roof. The housetop was used for sleeping in hot weather, drying vegetables, ripening fruit, and, in devout homes, for praying. The floors consisted of the hard earth or, in better houses, of stone. The beds were merely a mat or a coverlet laid on the floor. Only well-to-do homes had bedsteads. People slept in their day garments.

> "About the sixth hour . . . Peter went up **on the roof** to pray" (Acts 10:9).

> "Jesus says to him, 'Get up! Pick up your mat [KJV: "bed"] and walk'" (John 5:8).

A Mud-Plastered Roof

"And since they could not bring him to Jesus because of the crowd, they made an opening in the roof above Jesus and, after **digging through it,** lowered the mat that the paralyzed man was lying on" (Mark 2:4).

A Tiled Roof

"And not finding any way to bring him in because of the crowd, going up on the **roof** they lowered him with his mat through the **tiles** into the middle of the crowd, in front of Jesus" (Luke 5:19).

"And during the evening meal . . . . one of his disciples, the one whom Jesus loved, was reclining next to Jesus' chest. . . . So leaning against Jesus' chest, he says to him, 'Lord, who is it?'" (John 13:2, 23, 25).

Food

Romans ate four meals a day. An average diet consisted of bread, porridge, lentil soup, goat's milk, cheese, vegetables, fruit, olives, bacon, sausage, fish, and diluted wine. Jews ate only two meals a day, one at noon, another in the late afternoon or evening. The Jewish diet consisted mainly of bread, fruits, and vegetables. Meat, roasted or boiled, was usually reserved for festivals. Since sugar was unknown, raisins, figs, honey, and dates supplied sweetening. Fish, often in the form of a relish, substituted for meat. At formal meals people reclined on cushions; for informal meals they sat.

Clothing and Styles

Next to their skin men wore ↓tunics, a shirt-like garment extending from the shoulders to the knees. They also wore a longer outer garment. A belt or sash, called a "girdle" in some translations of the New Testament, was worn around the waist, coarse shoes or sandals on the feet, and a hat or a scarf on the head. In cold weather a mantle or heavy cloak gave additional warmth. These garments were usually white. Women wore a short tunic as an undergarment and a sometimes brightly colored outer garment extending to the feet. The more fashionable used cosmetics lavishly, including lipstick, eye shadow, and eyebrow paint, and for jewelry wore earrings and nose ornaments. Women's hairstyles changed constantly. Men wore their hair short and shaved with straight razors. Dandies had their hair curled and used large amounts of hair oil and perfume. Both men and women dyed their hair, often to cover up the gray. False hair added to the coiffure, and both sexes wore wigs. In Palestine men grew beards and let their hair grow somewhat

"And if someone wants to sue you and take your tunic, let him have your cloak as well" (Matthew 5:40).

Woman wearing a tunic and cloak

tunics: TOO-niks

"Zenon's trunk in which are contained: 1 linen wrap, washed, 1 clay-colored cloak, for winter, washed, and 1 worn . . . 1 white tunic for winter, with sleeves, washed . . . 3 for summer, white, new . . . 1 coarse mantle . . . 2 pairs of socks, clay-colored, new . . ." (Zenon Papyrus 59092, a list of clothes).

longer, but still not so long as portrayed in traditional pictures of biblical people. Generally, Palestinian styles leaned toward conservatism for both sexes.

Social Classes

Classes were sharply stratified in pagan society. Aristocratic landowners, politicians, government contractors, and others lived in luxury. A strong middle class did not exist, because slaves did most of the work. Now dependent on government support, the more or less middle class of previous times had become home-

Cosmetic equipment, including a comb, glass ointment bottle, Kohl stick, and palettes

less, foodless mobs in the cities, often worse off than slaves, who at least had job security. The leveling influence of Judaism tended to reduce stratification in Jewish society; but the religious and political elite, concentrated in Jerusalem, formed an upper class. Farmers, artisans, small-business owners, and their families made up a majority of the population, living mostly in rural villages.

Among the Jews, tax collectors—traditionally called "publicans"—became special objects of class hatred. They collected poll taxes, property taxes, road use taxes, and sales taxes. Other Jews despised the tax collectors because they handled currency with blasphemous pagan inscriptions and ↓iconography and cooperated with Roman overlords. These overlords auctioned the job of collecting taxes to the lowest bidder, that is, to the one who bid the lowest rate of commission for a contract. A collector would gather not only the tax and his commission, but also whatever he could pocket illegally. Bribery of tax collectors by the rich increased the financial burden on those who were barely scraping by. As a result, the masses deeply resented the collectors. People who could not scrape by resorted to begging or banditry. Lacking the economic support of a husband, widows often sank into destitution; and because they had usually been married off to men older than they were, their number was disproportionately high.

> "A man was there by the name of Zacchaeus; he was a chief tax collector and was wealthy.... All the people saw this and began to mutter, '[Jesus] has gone to be the guest of a "sinner"'" (Luke 19:2, 7).

> "Sarapion has paid the 1% tax for toll dues of the Oasis on 1 donkey-load of barley and 1 donkey-load of garlic. The 2nd year of Vespasian the emperor, 7th day of Mecheir" (Oxyrhynchus Papyrus 1439, a toll receipt).

iconography: i´kuh-NOG-ruh-fee (the depiction of images, here on coins)

A Paternalistic Society

- "For women are evil, my children, and by reason of their lacking authority or power over man, they scheme treacherously how they might entice him to themselves by means of their looks. And whomever they cannot enchant by their appearance they conquer by a stratagem. Indeed, the angel of the Lord told me ... that women are more easily overcome by the spirit of promiscuity than are men.... Accordingly, ... order your wives and your daughters not to adorn their heads and their appearance so as to deceive men's sound minds. For every woman who schemes in these ways is destined for eternal punishment" (*Testament of Reuben* 5:1–3, 5).
- "Women or slaves or minors may not be included [to make up the number of three needed] for the Common Grace [thanks for food at a meal]" (Mishnah, *Berakot* 7:2).
- "He who loves his son will whip him often, so that he may rejoice at the way he turns out.... Pamper a child, and he will terrorize you; play with him, and he will grieve you.... Give him no freedom in his youth, and do not ignore his errors.... beat his sides while he is young, or else he will become stubborn and disobey you" (Sirach 30:1, 9, 11–12).

There were exceptions and variations from place to place, but as a general rule women—especially Jewish women—lived under severe restrictions. They were largely uneducated. Males dominated them in the home and in religious and political institutions. Similarly, children lived under the almost unlimited authority of their fathers.

Especially in cities, slaves may have numbered nearly as many as free people. Slavery was not racially based. It had been common to condemn criminals, debtors, and prisoners of war to slavery; but by the first century most slaves were born as such. Many of Jesus' sayings and parables imply that slavery existed in the Jewish culture of his time, though Jews tended not to enslave other Jews; and Paul's letters reflect the presence of slaves in Christian households. Some slaves—doctors, accountants, teachers, philosophers, managers, clerks, copyists—had greater skill and education than their masters had. Other slaves worked on construction projects and in households, workshops, and mines. A fair number of slaves bought their freedom, sometimes in the name of a god of the temple where they had banked their savings (a procedure known as ↓**sacral manumission**). Or they were set free by their masters, though in this case usually not till the slaves had outlived their useful service. Then they found it difficult to make ends meet, while their former masters no longer had to support them. To pay their debts or gain economic security, some people sold themselves into slavery, perhaps for a contractually limited period of time. Masters ranged from kind to cruel and considered their slaves, including young boys and girls, legitimate objects of sexual exploitation. Often they castrated their male slaves.

"From Sosibius of Amphissa [a slave owner] the Pythian [god] Apollo purchased a female slave named Nicaea to free her ... at a price of 3-1/2 silver minas" (a deed of sacral manumission inscribed on a wall of Apollo's temple at Delphi, Greece).

sacral manumission: SAY-kruhl man´yoo-MI-shuhn

Originally, slaves who had turned criminal were the only ones to be executed by crucifixion. Later, however, free people who had committed heinous crimes also suffered this fate. During the siege of Jerusalem in A.D. 70, Titus's soldiers crucified as many as five hundred Jews in a day just outside the city walls, in plain view of the people still inside. Execution by beheading and burning at the stake was also practiced. At other times condemned men were forced to fight as gladiators in the arena. Whole groups might kill one another in staged warfare.

A man and his family

The Family

As would be expected, the family formed the basic unit of society. Some factors tended to break down the family, however, such as the high number of slaves and the training of children by slaves rather than by parents. On the other hand, nuclear families were not the norm; extended families were. They included not only the husband and wife and their unmarried children, but also their married sons, daughters-in-law, grandchildren, and any slaves belonging to the household. They all lived under the same roof or in nearby dwellings. The most senior male acted as head of the family.

Ties of kinship were very strong, then, so strong that marriages to first cousins on the father's side were most preferred, though not always possible. (The marriage of two people more closely related than cousins fell into the category of incest, prohibited.) ↓**Endogamy**, the technical term for marriage between relatives, kept property and other forms of wealth within the clan. Thus marriages were arranged in the economic and other interests of the families involved, so that romance seldom played a part. Brides were purchased, and weddings featured an in-house ceremony and celebration without religious rite.

The typical Greco-Roman family had a low birth rate. To encourage larger families, the government offered special concessions to parents of three or more children. Bachelorhood appears to have been taxed. By various means, both contraception and abortion were practiced.

Good and Bad Women

- "This is the unlovely tomb of a lovely woman. Her parents named her Claudia. She loved her husband with her whole heart. She bore two sons.... She was charming in conversation, yet her conduct was appropriate. She kept house, she made wool" (from *Corpus Inscriptionum Latinarum* 1.2.1211).

- "Ah, women, why do you dig out your child with sharp instruments and administer harsh poisons to your children as yet unborn?... Neither the tigress has done this in the jungles of Armenia, nor has the lioness had the heart to destroy her unborn young. Tender woman does it, though, but does not go unpunished. Often she who slays her own in her uterus dies herself" (Ovid, *Loves* 2.14.27–38).

endogamy: en-DAW-guh-mee

Large families were common in Palestine. The birth of a boy brought joy; that of a girl, disappointment. On the eighth day after birth a Jewish boy was circumcised and named. The naming of a girl could wait a month. People with the same name were distinguished by the mention of their father ("Simon the son of Zebedee"), their religious or political conviction ("Simon the Zealot"), their occupation ("Simon the tanner"), or their place of residence ("Simon of ↓Cyrene"). At the death of a person the surviving family performed formal acts of grief, such as rending their garments and fasting, and also hired professional mourners, usually flutists and women skilled at wailing. In addition, the family could enlist the services of a professional undertaker. Skeletal remains from the Roman period in Greece show an adult longevity of about forty years for men, thirty-four years for women.

Honor and Shame

Marriages were arranged not only for economic reasons, but also to enhance family honor. The concern for honor spread far beyond marriage and family, however, and exceeded the concern for wealth, even for life itself (compare the often fatal dueling, practiced to preserve honor, that lasted until fairly recent times). Shame consisted in concern for one's honor. To lack such concern was to be shameless. Honor consisted in public recognition of one's status in society, whatever that status was. Ascribed honor came from the givens of one's ancestry, gender, locality, and so on. Acquired honor came from one's benevolence, heroism, athletic victories, political and religious advancements, and various other attainments.

The wealthy financed the construction of public buildings, the laying of pavement, and the holding of sporting events—all to acquire honor. They were rewarded with public accolades in the form of proclamations, inscriptions, and statues of themselves. For recognition, even the giving of charity to the poor was done in the most conspicuous way possible. What others thought of you counted more than what you thought of yourself, so that there resulted what scholars call a ↓**dyadic personality**, one determined largely by others rather than highly individualistic (contrast "being your own person" and "doing your own thing").

To gain and preserve honor, especially within one's peer group, boasting was considered normal and appropriate; humility, abnor-

Sidewalk advertisement for a brothel in Ephesus

Cyrene: *si*-REE-nee ■ dyadic: *di*-AD-ik

mal and mistaken. For honor, like all other goods, was thought to be in short, limited supply. What you lost, another gained; and vice versa. Therefore interpersonal and intergroup relations became competitive. Even a dinner invitation or the giving of a gift challenged the honor of the recipient, since a failure to reciprocate in equal measure would bring dishonor on the recipient. A refusal or rejection would, of course, bring dishonor on the giver and invite retaliation through slander and defamation of character, among other means.

Morals

In the New Testament Letters, sexual sins usually head a list of prohibited vices. Every conceivable kind of immorality was attributed to the pagan gods and goddesses. Prostitution by both men and women was a well-recognized institution. Slave girls often fell victim to this debauchery. To gain money, some men prostituted their own wives and children. Most of society accepted pederasty and other homosexual behavior. As we know from excavations at

Rampant Immorality

- "Isis and Osiris were enamored of each other and had sex together in the darkness of the womb before their birth. Some say that Arueris came from this union" (Plutarch, *Moralia,* "Isis and Osiris," 12).
- "And the women . . . sit along the passageways [of a pagan temple], burning bran for incense. When one of them is led off by one of the passers-by and is taken to bed by him, she derides the woman next to her, because she was not as attractive as herself" (Letter of Jeremiah 6:42–43).

"Even if he happens to be poor everyone rears a son, but exposes a daughter even if he is rich" (Stobaeus, *Flor.* 77.7).

A street in Pompeii, the stepping stones spaced so as to allow the passage of wheeled vehicles and a flow of rain water

Pompeii, obscene pictures and carvings often decorated the exterior walls of houses.

Divorce was easy, frequent, and acceptable. In fact, divorce documents are among the most numerous of papyrus remains. Murder was common. Gentile parents often "exposed" their infant daughters, that is, abandoned them in the city forum, on a hillside, or in an alley. One letter from a husband to his wife reads, "If by chance you bear a child, if it is male, let it live. If it is female, throw it out" (Oxyrhynchus Papyrus 744). Many exposed girls were picked up to be reared as prostitutes. In fairness it should be added that despite the prevalence of low morality, decent people were not wholly lacking in the Greco-Roman world.

Entertainment

A risqué stage reflected the immorality of the day, sexual acts sometimes being performed right on stage. But not all entertainment had sunk into sensuality. The Olympic games had long provided sporting pleasure of a wholesome sort. Worthy music and literature uplifted the human spirit. Children amused themselves with toys such as baby rattles, dolls with movable limbs, miniature houses with furniture, balls, swings, and

"During his stay at Caesarea, Titus celebrated his brother's birthday with great splendor, reserving in his honor for this festival much of the punishment of his Jewish captives. For the number of those destroyed in contests with wild beasts or with one another or in the flames exceeded 2,500" (Josephus, *Jewish War* 7.3.1 §§37–38).

Gladiators

games similar to hopscotch, hide-and-seek, and blindman's buff.

Chariot races corresponded to modern automobile races. Betting was common. Naturally, the public idolized winning charioteers. But gladiatorial shows provided the most spectacular form of entertainment. Gladiators might be slaves, captives, criminals, or volunteers. Once an entire arena was flooded and a naval battle staged. As many as ten thousand died in a single performance. The sand in the arena became so soaked with blood that it had to be replaced several times during the day.

Such shows often featured beasts. On one occasion three hundred lions were killed. At the opening of Titus's amphitheater, five thousand wild beasts and four thousand tame beasts were slaughtered. Elephants, tigers, panthers, rhinoceroses, hippopotamuses, crocodiles, and snakes fought each other.

Vomitorium (tunnel to and from banks of seats) at the theater in Miletus

Business and Labor

Small businesses dotted the main streets and marketplaces of cities. They were owned by butchers and bakers, grocers and barbers, cobblers, tentmakers, leather workers, carpenters, blacksmiths, launderers, and other shopkeepers. Big industry was virtually unknown, because the transportation of goods to distant places was prohibitively expensive. Besides, caravans were slow and subject to plunder, and shipping on the Mediterranean Sea could take place only during the summer months of calm weather. Foreshadowing modern labor unions, trade guilds charged dues for membership, had officers and patron deities, followed rules of order in their meetings, engaged in politicking, extended aid to members in distress, gave benefits to widows and orphans of deceased members, and formed one kind of **voluntary association**. (Other such associations included religious clubs, burial societies, and philosophical schools.) In Palestine they regulated days and hours for working.

In some respects agriculture was surprisingly advanced. Farmers practiced seed selection according to size and quality and soaked grain seeds in

"For a certain silversmith named Demetrius, a maker of silver shrines of Artemis, was providing no little business for the craftsmen. He called them together, along with the workmen in related trades" (Acts 19:24–25).

chemical mixtures to protect them from insect pests. They also used different kinds of fertilizer and practiced crop rotation.

Private companies carried on banking much as it is done today with borrowing, lending, discounting of notes, exchanging of foreign currency, and issuing of letters of credit. The ordinary interest rate varied from 4 to 12 percent.

Much business took place by way of **brokers'** bringing **patrons** and **clients** together for mutual benefit. Clients were people in need. Patrons were people who could provide the goods, funds, and services to meet the needs of clients in return for the clients' honoring them with public praise, voting for them in elections, and otherwise championing them. Having personal contacts with both sides enabled brokers to act as middlemen. All in all, success depended not so much on hard work or what you knew, but on whom you knew—or came to know.

Science and Medicine

Though Jews had little interest in science during the New Testament period, science had already made a beginning. In the third century B.C., for example, ↓Eratosthenes, librarian at Alexandria, taught that the earth is spherical and calculated its size at 24,000 miles in circumference (only 800 miles short of the modern estimate) and the earth's distance from the sun at 92 million miles (the modern estimate is 93 million miles). He also conjectured the existence of the American continent.

Medicine, or at least surgery, had advanced more than we might have guessed—a relevant bit of information since one of the New Testament writers, Luke, acted as Paul's private physician. Surgeons performed amputations, operations on the skull, and tracheotomies (incisions into the windpipe). Knowledge and use of anesthetics were limited, however, so that "a surgeon ought to be young, or, at any rate, not very old; his hand should be firm and steady, and never shake; he should be able to use his left hand as readily as his right; . . . he should be so far subject to pity as to make him desirous of the recovery of his patient; but not so far as to suffer himself to be moved by his cries; he should neither hurry the operation more than the case requires, nor cut less than is necessary but do everything just as if the other's screams made no impression on him."[1]

A variety of medical instruments were used, such as lancets, stitching needles, an elevator for lifting up depressed portions of the skull, different kinds of forceps, catheters, spatulas for examining the throat, and ratcheting instruments for dilating passages in the body for internal examination. Dental work included the filling of teeth with gold. False teeth came from

1. Quoted by A. C. Bouquet, *Everyday Life in New Testament Times* (New York: Scribner, 1953), 171. This book is a source for some other material in the present chapter.

Eratosthenes: er´uh-TOS-thuh-neez

the mouths of deceased people or animals. People sometimes used tooth powder for brushing and polishing their teeth.

And so a sampling of the first-century Greco-Roman world shows that though they lived before the age of modern science and technology, the people of New Testament times, no less intelligent and gifted than we, had developed a society and culture in many respects surprisingly close to our own. This similarity was less in Palestine, where Christianity began, but greater outside Palestine, where Christianity rapidly spread.

Surgical instruments and jars for ointment

Summary

In the first century more Jews lived outside Palestine than inside. Those living inside spoke Aramaic, but also Greek and perhaps some Hebrew. Though well-constructed roads ran far and wide in the Roman Empire, the road system in Palestine remained relatively poor. Most people traveled overland by foot, but ships provided a fairly advanced means of sea travel and commerce. We do not know how many could read and write. The primary writing material was papyrus. Large cities featured public facilities of various sorts. Private homes ran a gamut from the large and luxurious to the cramped and squalid. Diet was mainly meatless, clothing robe-like. Hairstyles and the use of cosmetics resembled modern Western customs. Society lacked a strong, numerous middle class. Tax collectors formed a small but especially despised class, and slaves were numerous. Roman crucifixion had expanded from a slave's punishment to a punishment for heinous criminals of other classes too. Family values competed with easy divorce and widespread immorality. Extended families were the rule, and males ruled the roost. Competition for honor affected interaction between families, between groups, and between individuals. Much entertainment reflected the immorality of society and fed on blood-lust in the gladiatoral games. Tradesmen organized themselves into voluntary associations, as did others of common interests; but industry was confined to small shops. Methods of agriculture and banking foreshadowed modern methods; and business depended on brokers' bringing patrons and clients together. Science and medicine were still in their infancy but already showed signs of what was yet to come.

Terms to Remember

Aramaic	honor	sacral manumission
broker	ostraca	shame
client	papyrus	tunic
endogamy	patron	voluntary association
exposing	publican	

How Much Did You Learn?

- Describe living conditions in the first-century Roman world.
- Identify the languages used and the whereabouts of their use.
- Describe working conditions.
- Identify social classes.
- Describe customs of dress and diet, standards of morality, and means of travel and entertainment.
- Identify precursors of modern agriculture, business, science, and medicine.
- Trace the road system in first-century Palestine.

For Further Discussion

- What cultural preparation for the coming of Christ and the rise of the church can you see in the Greco-Roman world?
- Why did Palestinian Jewry tend to be culturally backward?
- Does the Christian church likewise tend to be culturally backward? If so, is it for similar or for different reasons? If not, why not, in view of the fact that Christianity arose out of Judaism?

For Further Investigation

As the Romans Did: A Source Book in Roman Social History. Edited by J.-A. Shelton. New York: Oxford University Press, 1988.

Bailey, A. E. *Daily Life in Bible Times.* New York: Scribner, 1943.

Barrett, C. K. *The New Testament Background: Selected Documents.* 2d ed. San Francisco: Harper & Row, 1987. Especially pages 38–50 for quotations from primary sources.

Bouquet, A. C. *Everyday Life in New Testament Times.* New York: Scribner, 1953.

Corswant, W. *A Dictionary of Life in Bible Times.* Completed and illustrated by E. Urech. New York: Oxford University Press, 1960.

Daniel-Rops, H. *Daily Life in the Time of Jesus.* New York: Mentor, 1964.

deSilva, D. A. *Honor, Patronage, Kinship & Purity: Unlocking New Testament Culture.* Downers Grove, Ill.: InterVarsity Press, 2000.

Dictionary of New Testament Background. Edited by C. A. Evans and S. E. Porter. Downers Grove, Ill.: InterVarsity Press, 2000.

Everyday Life in Bible Times. 2d ed. National Geographic Society, 1976.

Freyne, S. *The World of the New Testament.* Wilmington, Del.: Michael Glazier, 1980.

Jeffers, J. S. *The Greco-Roman World of the New Testament Era: Exploring the Background of Early Christianity.* Downers Grove, Ill.: InterVarsity Press, 1999.

The Jewish People in the First Century. Vol. 2. Edited by S. Safrai et al. Philadelphia: Fortress Press, 1976.

Jones, C. M. *New Testament Illustrations.* New York: Cambridge University Press, 1966.

Keener, C. S. *IVP Bible Background Commentary: New Testament.* Downers Grove, Ill.: InterVarsity Press, 1993.

Malina, B. J. *The New Testament World: Insights from Cultural Anthropology.* 3d ed. Louisville: Westminster John Knox, 2001.

Millard, A. *Reading and Writing in the Time of Jesus.* New York: New York University Press, 2000.

Osiek, C. *What Are They Saying About the Social Setting of the New Testament?* 2d ed. New York: Paulist Press, 1992.

Stegemann, E. W., and W. Stegemann. *The Jesus Movement: A Social History of Its First Century.* Minneapolis: Fortress Press, 1999.

Stembaugh, J. E., and D. L. Balch, *The New Testament in Its Social Environment.* Philadelphia: Westminster, 1986.

Tidball, D. *The Social Context of the New Testament: A Sociological Analysis.* Grand Rapids: Zondervan, 1984.

Women's Lives in Greece and Rome: A Source Book in Translation. Baltimore: Johns Hopkins University Press, 1982.

THE RELIGIOUS AND PHILOSOPHICAL SETTINGS OF THE NEW TESTAMENT

Overview:

- Paganism
- Judaism
- The Literature of Judaism
- The Theology of Judaism
- Sects and Other Groups within Judaism
- Jewish Education
- Greco-Roman Education
- Summary

Study Goals—Learn:

- The religious beliefs and practices—esoteric, mythological, superstitious, philosophical—among pagans in the Greco-Roman period
- How Jewish religious institutions and beliefs developed from Old Testament to New Testament times
- What ways the pagan and Jewish religious settings contributed to the birth of Christianity

Temple of Zeus in Athens, the largest temple in ancient Greece

Paganism

Mythology

Atop the Greek pantheon or hierarchy of gods sat **Zeus**, son of ↓Cronus. According to myth, Cronus, who had seized dominion of the world from his father, ↓Uranus, ordinarily devoured his own children as soon as they were born. But the mother of Zeus saved her infant by giving Cronus a stone wrapped in baby blankets to swallow. On reaching adulthood, Zeus overthrew his father and divided the dominion with his two brothers, ↓**Poseidon**, who ruled the sea, and ↓**Hades**, who ruled the underworld. Zeus himself ruled the heavens. The gods had access to earth from their capital, **Mount Olympus** in Greece.

Zeus had to quell occasional rebellions by the gods, who exhibited the human traits of passion and lust, love and jealousy, anger and hate. In fact, the gods excelled human beings only in power, intelligence, and immortality—certainly not in morality. A very popular god was ↓**Apollo**, son of Zeus and inspirer of poets, seers, and prophets. He played many other roles as well. At ↓**Delphi**, Greece, a temple of Apollo stood over a cavern out of which issued fumes thought to be his breath. A priestess seated on a tripod over the opening inhaled the fumes, fell into a trance, and muttered words that were written and vaguely interpreted by priests in answer to inquiring worshipers.

Zeus

State Religion

Roman state religion incorporated much of the Greek pantheon and mythology. Roman gods came to be identified with Greek gods: **Jupiter** with Zeus, **Venus** with ↓Aphrodite, and so on. The Romans also added new features, such as a priesthood in which the emperor himself acted as *pontifex maximus* (chief priest). The all-too-human traits of the gods destroyed many people's faith in the Greco-Roman pantheon, but for others this faith persisted through the New Testament period.

Cronus: KROH-nuhs ■ Uranus: YOOR-uh-nuhs ■ Poseidon: poh-SI-duhn ■ Hades: HAY-deez ■ Apollo: uh-POL-oh ■ Delphi: DEL-fi ■ Aphrodite: af´ruh-DI-tee

"You, O Zeus, are to be praised above all gods. Your names are many, and yours is all power forever" (Cleanthes, *Fragment* 537, "Hymn to Zeus").

Temple of Apollo at Delphi

Emperor Worship

Following the long-established practice of ascribing divinity to rulers, the Roman senate started the emperor cult by deifying—after their decease—Augustus and subsequent emperors who had served well. Because they had long regarded their living rulers as divine, enthusiastic loyalists in the eastern provinces sometimes anticipated this postmortem deification. But first-century emperors who claimed deity for themselves while still alive failed to receive the senatorial honor even at death. They were Caligula, Nero, and Domitian. The insane Caligula ordered his statue erected for worship in the temple of God at Jerusalem. Fortunately, the more sensible Syrian legate (governor) delayed carrying out the order. He knew the Jews would revolt. Meanwhile, Caligula was assassinated. Domitian made the first concerted attempt to force worship of himself. The refusal of Christians to participate in what most others considered a patriotic duty and unifying pledge of allegiance to the emperor as a god brought increasing persecution.

Mystery Religions

Much has been written about the widespread popularity and influence of Greek, Egyptian, and oriental mystery religions in the first Christian century: the cults of ↓Eleusis, ↓Mithra, ↓Isis, Dionysus, ↓Cybele, and many

---

Eleusis: i-*LOO*-sis ■ Mithra: MITH-ruh ■ Isis: *I*-sis ■ Cybele: SIB-uhl-ee´

An Initiation

"About midnight I saw the sun shine brightly. I likewise saw the gods celestial and the gods infernal, before whom I presented myself and worshiped them. . . . When morning came and the solemnities were finished, I came forth sanctified with twelve stoles and in a religious habit . . . . In my right hand I carried a lighted torch, and on my head was a garland of flowers with white palm-leaves sprouting out on every side like rays. Thus I was adorned like the sun" (Apuleius, *The Golden Ass* 11.23–24).

local cults. These promised purification and immortality of the soul and often centered on myths of a goddess whose lover or child was taken from her, usually by death, and later restored. The mysteries also featured secret initiatory and other rites involving ceremonial washing, blood-sprinkling, sacramental meals, intoxication, emotional frenzy, and impressive pageantry by which devotees were supposed to gain union with the deity.

On the other hand, not until the second, third, and fourth centuries of the Christian era do we get detailed information concerning the beliefs held by devotees of the mysteries. Therefore, though nobody doubts the pre-Christian existence of mystery religions, their pre-Christian beliefs remain largely unknown. Where their later beliefs look slightly similar to Christian beliefs, the direction of borrowing may have gone from Christianity to the mystery religions rather than vice versa, especially since pagans were notoriously assimilative (see the following discussion of "Syncretism") and early Christians exclusivistic. Besides, similarities are often more apparent than real, and even where real they do not necessarily imply borrowing in either direction.

In particular, the myths of **dying and rising gods** do not really correspond to the New Testament accounts of Jesus' death and resurrection. In the first place, the deaths of the gods were not thought to purchase redemption for human beings. Furthermore, the story of Jesus' death and resurrection had to do with a recent historical figure; the myths usually had to do with personifications of vegetational processes (the annual dying and renewal of plant life) and thus did not move on the plane of history at all, much less recent history. Finally, the mythological gods did not rise in full bodily resurrection, but revived only in part or merely in the world of the dead. When the fourteen pieces of the dismembered corpse of ↓Osiris were reassembled, for example, he became king of the dead in the underworld. And all that Cybele could obtain for the corpse of ↓Attis was that it should not decay, that its hair should continue to grow, and that its little finger should move. Yet the story of Cybele and Attis, who according to the myth died because of self-castration, is sometimes cited as a significant parallel to the story of Jesus' death and resurrection! As a matter of fact, the very thoughts of death by crucifixion and of physical resurrection were abhorrent to ancient pagans, who associated crucifixion with slaves and criminals and often thought of the body as a prison for the soul and as the seat of evil. If Christians had borrowed their beliefs from popular mystery religions, you would have to wonder why the pagans widely regarded the Christian gospel as foolish and incredible and Christians as deserving of persecution.[1]

---

1. See the discussions in J. G. Machen, *The Origin of Paul's Religion* (Grand Rapids: Eerdmans, 1947), chapters 6–7; J. S. Stewart, *A Man in Christ* (New York: Harper, n.d.), 64–80.

Superstition and ↓Syncretism

Superstition had a stranglehold on most people in the Roman Empire. Use of magical formulas; consultation of horoscopes and oracles; augury or prediction of the future by observing the flight of birds, the movement of oil on water, or the markings on a liver; and the hiring of professional exorcists (experts at casting out demons)—all these superstitious practices and many more played a part in everyday life. Jews numbered among the most sought-after exorcists, largely because it was thought they alone could correctly pronounce the magically potent name ↓*Yahweh* (Hebrew for "LORD"). Correct pronunciation and secrecy were considered necessary to the effectiveness of an incantation. In a practice known as **syncretism**, pagan people simply combined various religious beliefs and superstitious practices, much as many modern people diversify their investments and buy multiple insurance policies. If one fails, another may take up the slack. The images of

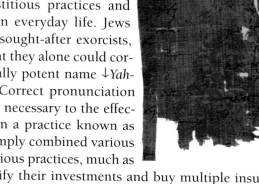

A magical text

syncretism: SIN-kruh-tiz´uhm ■ *Yahweh:* YAH-weh

An Exorcistic Text

"For those possessed by demons, an approved charm by Pibechis: Take oil made from unripe olives, together with the plant mastigia and lotus pith, and boil it with marjoram (very colorless), saying, 'Joel, Ossarthiomi, Emori, Theochipsoith, Sithemeoch [there follow further nonsensical tongue-twisters] .... Come out of so-and-so.' But write this phylactery on a little sheet of tin, 'Jaeo, Abraothioch, Phtha . . . ,' and hang it around the sufferer. It is for every demon a thing to be trembled at, which he fears. Standing opposite, adjure him. The adjuration is this: 'I adjure you by the god of the Hebrews Jesu, Jaba, Jae, Abraoth, Aia . . . . Let your angel descend . . . and draw into captivity the demon . . . .' But when you are adjuring, blow, sending your breath from above [to the feet] and [bouncing back] from the feet to the face, and he [the demon] will be drawn into captivity. Be pure and keep it [the formula] secret" (excerpts from the Paris Magical Papyrus).

An Astrological Text

"Jupiter in triangular relation to Mars or in conjunction makes great kingdoms and empires. Venus in conjunction with Mars causes fornications and adulteries. . . . If Mars appears in triangular relation to Jupiter and Saturn, this causes great happiness, and a man will make great acquisitions" (Tebtunis Papyrus 276).

birds, dogs, bulls, crocodiles, beetles, and other creatures filled the idol shelves of pagan households.

↓Gnosticism

Plato's dualistic contrast between the invisible world of ideas and the visible world of matter formed a substratum of Gnosticism, which started to take shape late in the first century and equated matter with evil, spirit with good. Out of these equations came two opposite modes of conduct: (1) **asceticism**, the suppression of bodily passions because of their connection with evil matter; and (2) **libertinism** or **sensualism**, the indulgence of bodily passions because of the transience and consequent unimportance of matter. In both modes, oriental religious notions mixed with Platonic philosophy. Physical resurrection seemed abhorrent so long as matter was regarded as evil. Spiritual immortality seemed desirable, however, and attainable through the knowledge of **secret doctrines** and **passwords** by which at death one's departing spirit could elude hostile demonic guardians of the planets and stars on its flight from earth to heaven. Under this view the human problem does not consist in guilt, which needs forgiveness, so much as in ignorance, which needs replacement with knowledge. In fact, Gnosticism comes from ↓*gnōsis*, the Greek word for **knowledge.** To keep the realm of supreme deity pure, later Gnostics separated it from the physical and therefore evil universe by a series of lesser divine beings called "↓aeons." Thus an elaborate angelology developed alongside demonology.

Gnostic ideas seem to stand behind certain heresies attacked in later New Testament literature; but the contents of a Gnostic library discovered in the 1940s at ↓**Nag Hammadi, Egypt,** give evidence that full-blown Gnostic mythology did not yet exist at the time Christianity arose. In the first century, Gnosticism was still developing out of an aggregate of loosely related philosophical and religious ideas and had yet to turn into highly organized systems of doctrine.

> "When you **know** yourselves, then you will be **known**; and you will **know** that you are the sons of the living Father" (*Gospel of Thomas* 3).

Gnosticism: NOS-tuh-siz´uhm   ■   *gnōsis:* NOH-sis   ■   aeons: EE-uhns   ■   Nag Hammadi: nahg huh-MAH-dee

Nag Hammadi books

Philosophies

The intelligentsia were turning to purer forms of philosophy. ↓Epicureanism taught pleasure (not necessarily sensual) as the chief good in life. ↓Stoicism taught dutiful acceptance of one's fate as determined by an impersonal Reason that rules the universe and of which all human beings are a part. ↓Cynicism regarded the supreme virtue as a simple, unconventional life in rejection of the popular pursuits of comfort, affluence, and social prestige. Skepticism was relativistic, so that its followers abandoned belief in anything absolute and succumbed to doubt and conformity to prevailing custom.

Greek philosopher depicted on a sarcophagus

With the partial exception of Stoicism, however, these and other philosophies did not determine the lives of very many people. Superstition and

Epicureanism: ep´uh-kyoo-REE-uhn-iz-uhm ■ Stoicism: STOH-i-siz´uhm ■ Cynicism: SIN-uh-siz´uhm

Examples of Stoicism:

- "The General Law, which is Right Reason, pervading everything, is the same as Zeus, the Supreme Head of the universe" (Zeno, *Fragment* 162).
- "He is free who lives as he wishes . . . whose choices are unhampered, who gets what he wants to get and avoids what he wants to avoid" (Epictetus, *Discourses* 4.1.1).
- "Man, you have been a citizen in this World-City, what difference does it make to you whether for five years or a hundred? For what is in conformity with the laws is just for all. . . . Depart then with good grace" (Marcus Aurelius, *To Himself* 12.36).
- "The Stoics say that when the planets return . . . to the same relative positions . . . they had at the beginning . . . , this produces the conflagration and destruction of everything that exists. Then the world is restored anew in a precisely similar arrangement as before. The stars move again . . . without any variation. Socrates and Plato and each individual human being will live again with the same friends and fellow citizens. They will go through the same experiences and the same activities . . . over and over again— indeed to eternity without end. . . . For there will never be any new thing . . . but everything is repeated down to the minutest detail" (Chrysippus, *Fragment* 625).

syncretism characterized the masses. Thus, Christianity entered a religiously and philosophically confused world. The old confidence of classical Athens had run out. The enigmatic universe defied understanding. Philosophy had failed to provide satisfactory answers. So also had the traditional religions. People felt helpless under the fate of the stars and planets, which they regarded as angelic-demonic beings. Gloom and despair prevailed.

Judaism

Synagogues

More important for New Testament study than the pagan religious and philosophical milieu is the Judaism out of which Christianity arose. This Judaism, known as **Second Temple Judaism**, originated toward the close of the Old Testament period. The prophets had predicted exile as punishment for the idolatry practiced by the people of Israel. Fulfillment of the prediction cured them of idolatry. Loss of the temple at the beginning of the Babylonian exile gave rise to increased study and observance of the Old Testament law (the Torah) and at least ultimately to establishment of the synagogue as an institution. It is debatable whether synagogues originated during the exile, during the restoration from it, or during the intertestamental period. But a reasonable conjecture is that since the Babylonian conqueror ↓**Nebuchadnezzar** had destroyed the first temple (Solomon's) and deported most of the Jews from Judea, they established local centers of worship called synagogues ("assemblies"). Once established as an institution, synagogues remained and multiplied even after the second temple was built under the leadership of ↓**Zerubbabel** (see Ezra 3–6; Haggai; Zechariah 1–8 for the rebuilding of the temple).

At first not very elaborate, the typical synagogue came to consist of a rectangular room perhaps having a raised speaker's platform behind which rested a portable chest or shrine containing Old Testament scrolls. The congregation sat on stone benches running along two or three walls and on mats and possibly wooden chairs in the center of the room. In front, facing the congregation, sat the ruler and elders of the synagogue. Singing was unaccompanied. The speaker stood to read from an Old Testament scroll and sat to preach. Everyone stood for prayer. The **typical synagogue service** consisted of the following:

- Antiphonal recitations of the ↓**Shema** (the "golden text" of Judaism) and of the ↓**Shemone Esreh** (a series of praises to God)

The Power of the Torah

"Even so did the Holy One, blessed be he, speak to Israel, 'My children, I created the evil impulse, but I [also] created the Torah as its antidote. If you occupy yourselves with the Torah, you will not be delivered into the power of the evil impulse. But if you do not occupy yourselves with the Torah, then you will be delivered into the power of the evil impulse'" (Babylonian Talmud, *Qiddushin* 30b). The Hebrew word *torah* has a wider meaning than "law." It also connotes guidance, teaching, and divine revelation in toto and refers variously to the Ten Commandments, the Pentateuch, the whole Old Testament, and the oral law or traditional interpretations of the Old Testament by rabbis.

Nebuchadnezzar: neb´uh-kuhd-NEZ-uhr ■ Zerubbabel: zuh-RUHB-uh-buhl ■ Shema: SHEE-muh, shuh-MAH ■ Shemone Esreh: sheh-MOH-neh ES-reh

Mosaic in the synagogue at Sardis

- Prayer
- Singing of psalms
- Readings from the Hebrew Old Testament Law and Prophets interspersed with a ↓**Targum**, that is, a loose oral translation into Aramaic (or Greek), which many Jews understood better than Hebrew
- A sermon (if someone competent to preach was present)
- A blessing or benediction

There was freedom in the wording of the liturgy. The whole congregation joined in an "Amen" at the close of prayers. The elected ruler of the synagogue presided over meetings, introduced strangers, and selected different members of the congregation to lead recitations, read Scripture, and preach. Qualified visitors were likewise invited to speak, a practice that opened many opportunities for Jesus and Paul to preach the gospel in synagogues. A synagogue attendant took care of the scrolls and furniture, lighted the lamps, blew a trumpet announcing the Sabbath, stood

Targum: TAHR-guhm

Recited in the Synagogue

- The Shema: "Hear, O Israel: The Lᴏʀᴅ is our God, the Lᴏʀᴅ is one" (Deuteronomy 6:4, later expanded by verses 5–9; 11:13–21; Numbers 15:13–41). Shema is the Hebrew word behind "Hear."
- Shemone Esreh means "eighteen," but in fact the exact number of benedictions has varied from time to time. Here is the seventh benediction: "Look on our affliction and plead our cause, and redeem us speedily for your name's sake. For you are a mighty redeemer. Blessed are you, O Lord, the Redeemer of Israel."
- *Targum Pseudo-Jonathan* of Genesis 1:1–2, with additions to the original Hebrew in boldface type: "At the beginning God created the heaven and the earth. And the earth was waste and void, **desolate without the sons of men, and empty of animals.** And darkness was upon the face of the deep, and the spirit **of mercies from before God blew** on the face of the waters."

beside readers to ensure correct pronunciation and accurate reading of the sacred texts, and sometimes taught in the synagogue school. A board of elders exercised spiritual oversight of the congregation. Erring members faced punishment by whipping and excommunication. Alms taken into the synagogue were distributed to the poor. Early Christians, mainly Jews, naturally adopted synagogal organization as a basic pattern for their churches.

"Theodotus . . . built the synagogue for the reading of the law and for the teaching of the commandments, and the guest-house and the rooms and the supplies of ritual water as an inn for those who have need when they come from a foreign country" (an ancient inscription from a synagogue in Jerusalem).

Not only was the synagogue a center for religious worship every Sabbath (Saturday). During the week it also became a center for the administration of justice, political meetings, funeral services, the education of Jewish lads, and study of the Old Testament. This study made the teaching of the law important. As a result its teachers began to wield an influence that vied with that of priests, whose base of power lay in the temple.

The Second Temple

The Mosaic law prescribed that sacrifices should be offered only at a central sanctuary. The second temple continued to be important, therefore, until its destruction in A.D. 70. The urging of the prophets ↓Haggai and ↓Zechariah had spurred its building during the Old Testament period of

Haggai: HAG-*i* ■ Zechariah: zek´uh-R*l*-uh

Model of Herod's temple

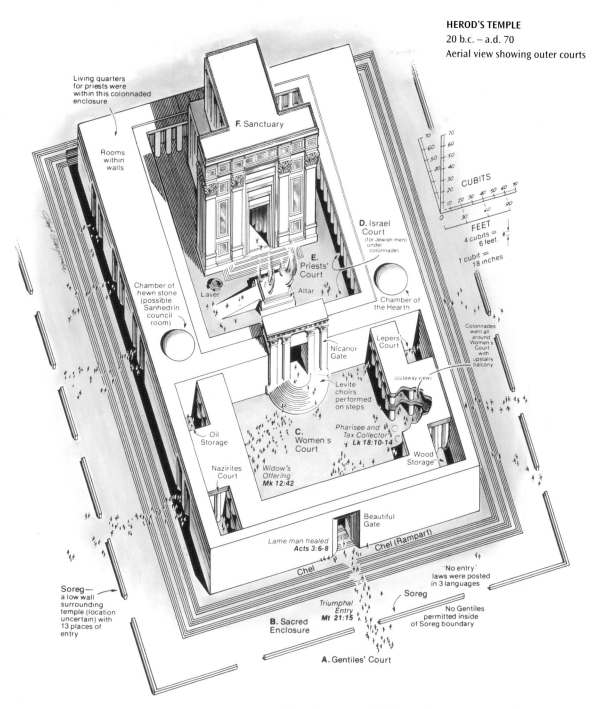

HEROD'S TEMPLE
20 b.c. – a.d. 70
Aerial view showing outer courts

Living quarters for priests were within this colonnaded enclosure

Rooms within walls

F. Sanctuary

D. Israel Court
(for Jewish men) under colonnades

CUBITS

FEET
4 cubits = 6 feet

1 cubit = 18 inches

E. Priests' Court

Chamber of hewn stone (possible Sanhedrin council room)

Laver

Altar

Chamber of the Hearth

Nicanor Gate

Lepers' Court

Colonnades went all around Women's Court with upstairs balcony

(cutaway view)

Levite choirs performed on steps

Oil Storage

C. Women's Court

Pharisee and Tax Collector
Lk 18:10-14

Wood Storage

Nazirites Court

Widow's Offering
Mk 12:42

Beautiful Gate

Lame man healed
Acts 3:6-8

Chel (Rampart)

Chel

Soreg— a low wall surrounding temple (location uncertain) with 13 places of entry

Triumphal Entry
Mt 21:15

Soreg

"No entry" laws were posted in 3 languages

No Gentiles permitted inside of Soreg boundary

B. Sacred Enclosure

A. Gentiles' Court

Dimensions are stated in history (Josephus and the Mishnah) but are subject to interpretation, and all drawings vary.

Jerusalem during the ministry of Jesus

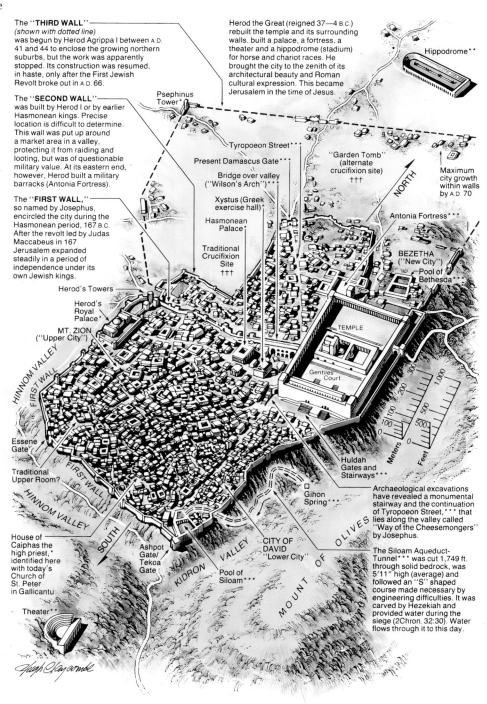

The "THIRD WALL"
(shown with dotted line)
was begun by Herod Agrippa I between A.D.
41 and 44 to enclose the growing northern
suburbs, but the work was apparently
stopped. Its construction was resumed,
in haste, only after the First Jewish
Revolt broke out in A.D. 66.

The "SECOND WALL"
was built by Herod I or by earlier
Hasmonean kings. Precise
location is difficult to determine.
This wall was put up around
a market area in a valley,
protecting it from raiding and
looting, but was of questionable
military value. At its eastern end,
however, Herod built a military
barracks (Antonia Fortress).

The "FIRST WALL,"
so named by Josephus,
encircled the city during the
Hasmonean period, 167 B.C.
After the revolt led by Judas
Maccabeus in 167
Jerusalem expanded
steadily in a period of
independence under its
own Jewish kings.

Herod the Great (reigned 37—4 B.C.)
rebuilt the temple and its surrounding
walls, built a palace, a fortress, a
theater and a hippodrome (stadium)
for horse and chariot races. He
brought the city to the zenith of its
architectural beauty and Roman
cultural expression. This became
Jerusalem in the time of Jesus.

Hippodrome**

Psephinus
Tower*

Tyropoeon Street***

Present Damascus Gate***

Bridge over valley
("Wilson's Arch")***

Xystus (Greek
exercise hall)*

Hasmonean
Palace*

Traditional
Crucifixion
Site
†††

"Garden Tomb"
(alternate
crucifixion site)
†††

NORTH

Maximum
city growth
within walls
by A.D. 70

Antonia Fortress***

BEZETHA
("New City")

Pool of
Bethesda***

Herod's Towers

Herod's
Royal
Palace*

MT. ZION
("Upper City")

TEMPLE

Gentiles
Court

HINNOM VALLEY

FIRST WALL

300
1,000
500
100
500
0
0
Meters
Feet

Essene
Gate*

Traditional
Upper Room?

FIRST WALL

HINNOM VALLEY

SOUTH

Huldah
Gates and
Stairways***

Gihon
Spring***

Archaeological excavations
have revealed a monumental
stairway and the continuation
of Tyropoeon Street,*** that
lies along the valley called
"Way of the Cheesemongers"
by Josephus.

House of
Caiphas the
high priest,*
identified here
with today's
Church
of St. Peter
in Gallicantu

Ashpot
Gate/
Tekoa
Gate

Pool of
Siloam***

CITY OF
DAVID
"Lower City"

KIDRON VALLEY

MOUNT OF OLIVES

The Siloam Aqueduct-
Tunnel*** was cut 1,749 ft.
through solid bedrock, was
5'11" high (average) and
followed an "S" shaped
course made necessary by
engineering difficulties. It was
carved by Hezekiah and
provided water during the
siege (2Chron. 32:30). Water
flows through it to this day.

Theater**

* Location generally known, but style of architecture is unknown;
    artist's concept only, and Roman architecture is assumed.

** Location and architecture unknown, but referred to in written
    history; shown here for illustrative purposes.

*** Ancient feature has remained, or appearance has been
     determined from evidence.

Buildings, streets and roads shown here are artist's concept
only unless otherwise named and located. Wall heights
remain generally unknown, except for those surrounding
the Temple Mount.

restoration from the exile. Plundered and desecrated by Antiochus Epiphanes in 168 B.C., it had been repaired, cleansed, and rededicated by Judas Maccabeus three years later. Then, at much expense, Herod the Great beautified it even beyond the glory of the first temple, which had been built in grand style more than nine hundred years earlier by King Solomon, son of King David. The outer retaining walls jutted up as much as 100 feet from street level. Some of its stones reached 150 feet in length, and they were all neatly fitted together without mortar. The two-door gate towered 45 feet high, each door 22 feet wide.

Much of the temple proper was overlaid with gold. It stood in the middle of courts and cloisters covering about twenty-six acres. Gentiles could enter the outer court; but inscriptions in Latin and Greek warned them on pain of death not to enter the inner courts, reserved for Jews alone. Just outside the temple proper stood an altar for burnt offerings and a ↓laver, which was a large basin full of water that the priests used for washing. Inside the first room, or **holy place**, curtained from the outside with a heavy veil, stood three pieces of furniture: (1) the ↓menorah, a seven-branched golden lampstand that burned olive oil mixed with other substances; (2) a table stocked with bread that represented God's providential presence; and (3) a small altar for the burning of incense. Another heavy veil curtained off the innermost room, the **holy of holies**, which the high priest entered once a year, alone, on the Day of Atonement. The ark of the covenant, the only piece of furniture placed in the holy of holies during Old Testament times, had long ago disappeared in the upheavals of invasion and captivity. Besides private sacrifices, daily burnt offerings for the whole nation were sacrificed at midmorning and midafternoon in conjunction with the burning of incense and with prayers, priestly benedictions, the pouring out of wine as a libation (liquid offering), the blowing of trumpets, and chanting and singing by choirs of ↓Levites to the accompaniment of harps, lyres, and wind instruments. Sabbaths, festivals, and other holy days featured additional ceremonies.

The Religious Calendar

Closely related to worship in the temple were religious **festivals** and **holy days.** The Jewish civil year began approximately in September–October, the Jewish religious year approximately in March–April (see the Jewish religious calendar on page 58). Because of differences in calendrical systems, the equivalents in our months are only approximate. The Mosaic law prescribed the first six items on the calendar: Passover–Tabernacles (see Leviticus 23:4–43 for details). The remaining two, Hanukkah and ↓Purim, arose later and apart from scriptural command. **Pilgrims** thronged to Jerusalem from elsewhere in Palestine and also from foreign countries for the three main festivals: **Passover-Unleavened Bread, Pentecost,** and **Tabernacles.**

---

laver: LAY-vuhr ■ menorah: muh-NOR-uh ■ Levites: LEE-vits ■ Purim: PYOO-rim

THE JEWISH RELIGIOUS CALENDAR

Feast of		Dates
Passover and Unleavened Bread	Commemorating the exodus from Egypt and marking the beginning ("first fruits") of the wheat harvest	Nisan (Mar.–Apr.) 14 15–21
Pentecost, or Weeks	Marking the end of the wheat harvest	Iyar (Apr.–May) Sivan (May–June) 6 Tammuz (June–July) Ab (July–Aug.) Elul (Aug.–Sept.)
Trumpets, or Rosh Hashanah	Marking the first of the civil year and the end of the grape and olive harvests	Tishri (Sept.–Oct.) 1–2
Day of Atonement, or Yom Kippur	For national repentance, fasting, and atonement (not called a "feast")	10
Tabernacles, or Booths, or Ingathering	Commemorating the Israelites' living in tents on their way from Egypt to Canaan—a joyous festival, during which the Jews lived in temporary shelters made of branches	15–22
Lights, or Dedication, or Hanukkah	Commemorating the rededication of the temple by Judas Maccabeus, with brilliant lights in the temple precincts and in Jewish homes	Heshvan (Oct.–Nov.) Kislev (Nov.–Dec.) 25– Tebet (Dec.–Jan.) 2 or 3
Purim	Commemorating the deliverance of Israel in the time of Esther, with public readings in the book of Esther in synagogues	Shebet (Jan.–Feb.) Adar (Feb.–Mar.) 14

The Literature of Judaism

Old Testament

The Old Testament existed in three linguistic forms for Jews of the first century: the original **Hebrew,** the **Septuagint** (a Greek translation), and the **Targums** (oral paraphrases into Aramaic that were just beginning to be written down). The Targums also contained traditional, interpretive, and imaginative material not found in the Old Testament itself.

↓Apocrypha

Written in Hebrew, Aramaic, and Greek and dating from the intertestamental and New Testament periods, the apocryphal books of the Old Testament contain mainly history, fiction, and wisdom. The Jews and the

Apocrypha: uh-POK-ruh-fuh

earliest Christians did not generally regard these books as sacred Scripture. Thus *apocrypha,* which originally meant "hidden, secret" and therefore "profound," came to mean "noncanonical." The apocryphal books include the following:

1 ↓Esdras
2 Esdras (or 4 Ezra, apocalyptic in content; see the next paragraph on the nature of apocalyptic)
↓Tobit
Judith
Additions to the book of Esther
Wisdom of Solomon
↓Ecclesiasticus, or the Wisdom of Jesus the Son of ↓Sirach, or simply Sirach
↓Baruch
Letter of Jeremiah
Prayer of ↓Azariah and the Song of the Three Young Men
Susanna
Bel and the Dragon
Prayer of ↓Manasseh
1 Maccabees
2 Maccabees

Fragments of nonbiblical Jewish books discovered among the Dead Sea Scrolls

↓*Pseudepigrapha and ↓Apocalyptic*

Other Jewish books dating from the same era are labeled *pseudepigrapha* ("falsely inscribed"), because some of them were written under the falsely assumed names of long-deceased Old Testament figures to achieve an air of authority. Some pseudepigraphal writings also fall into the class of apocalyptic literature, so called because they claim "to reveal" (Greek: ↓*apokalyptein*) in highly symbolic and visionary language the true course and end of human history with the coming of God's kingdom on earth. By promising the soon arrival of that kingdom, apocalyptists encouraged the Jewish people to endure persecution. Repeated disappointment of the hopes built up in this way eventually stopped the publication of apocalyptic literature.

The pseudepigraphal literature, which has no generally recognized limits, also contains anonymous books of legendary history, psalms, and wisdom. A list of better-known pseudepigraphal books follows:

1 Enoch
2 Enoch

Esdras: EZ-druhs ■ Tobit: TOH-bit ■ Ecclesiasticus: i-klee´zee-AS-ti-kuhs ■ Sirach: SI´-ruhk ■ Baruch: BAIR-uhk ■ Azariah: az´uh-RI-uh ■ Manasseh: muh-NAS-uh ■ Pseudepigrapha: soo´duh-PIG-ruh-fuh ■ apocalyptic: uh-pok´uh-LIP-tik ■ *apokalyptein:* ah-paw´kah-LYOOP-tayn

2 Baruch, or Syriac Apocalypse of Baruch
3 Baruch, or Greek Apocalypse of Baruch
↓Sibylline Oracles
Testaments of the Twelve Patriarchs
Testament of Job
Lives of the Prophets
Assumption of Moses
Martyrdom of Isaiah
↓Paralipomena of Jeremiah
Jubilees
Life of Adam and Eve
Psalms of Solomon
Letter of ↓Aristeas
3 Maccabees
4 Maccabees

There are also apocalypses attributed to Adam, Abraham, Elijah, and ↓Zephaniah, and testaments attributed to Adam, Abraham, Isaac, Jacob, Moses, and Solomon, plus various other books. Roman Catholics call the pseudepigrapha the Apocrypha, and they accept what Protestants call the Apocrypha into their Scripture as deuterocanonical books. Others call the pseudepigrapha the Outside Books. The Eastern Orthodox and Ethiopic Scriptures include some of the pseudepigrapha as well as the Apocrypha.

Dead Sea Scrolls

In addition, the approximately eight hundred scrolls discovered in caves near the ruins of **Qumran** just off the northwest shore of the Dead Sea contain literature similar to the traditional pseudepigrapha:

Damascus (or ↓Zadokite) Document (fragments of which were known before)
Community Rule, or Manual of Discipline
War Between the Sons of Light and the Sons of Darkness
Description of the New Jerusalem
Temple Scroll
Copper Scroll
Thanksgiving Hymns
Genesis Apocryphon
Psalms of Joshua
↓Melchizedek Text
pseudo-Jeremianic literature

Sibylline: SIB-uh-leen ■ Paralipomena: pair´uh-li-POM-uh-nuh ■ Aristeas: air´is-TEE-uhs ■ Zephaniah: zef´uh-NI-uh ■ Zadokite: ZAY-duh-kit ■ Melchizedek: mel-KIZ-uh-dek

apocryphal Danielic literature

various commentaries on the Old Testament books of Psalms, Isaiah, ↓Hosea, Micah, ↓Nahum, ↓Habakkuk, and Zephaniah

various books of laws, liturgies, prayers, blessings, mysteries, wisdom, and astronomical and calendrical calculations

↓Talmud

Rabbinic case decisions about interpretive questions stemming from the Old Testament law formed a memorized oral tradition in New Testament times. This tradition grew during the succeeding centuries until the Jewish Talmud enshrined it in writing. A **Palestinian edition** came out in the fourth century; a **Babylonian edition**, about three times longer and encyclopedic in length, in the fifth century. Chronologically, the Talmud consists of the ↓**Mishnah**, or **oral law**, developed by rabbis through the second century, plus the ↓**Ge-marah**, which contains **comments** on the Mishnah by rabbis living from the third through the fifth centuries. Topically, the Talmud consists of the ↓**ha-lakah**, or strictly legal portions, and the ↓**haggadah**, or nonlegal portions

---

Hosea: hoh-ZAY-uh ■ Nahum: NAY-huhm ■ Habakkuk: huh-BAK-uhk ■ Talmud: TAL-mood ■ Mishnah: MISH-nuh ■ Gemarah: guh-MAH-ruh ■ halakah: hah´lah-KAH ■ haggadah: huh-GAH-duh

Qumran Caves 4a and 4b

(stories, legends, explanatory narratives). By eventually asserting that the oral law dates back to Moses at Mount Sinai, the rabbis elevated their conflicting interpretations of the Old Testament to a position of greater practical importance than the Old Testament itself. Two famous schools of rabbinic interpretation existing already in the first century were the usually moderate school of ↓**Hillel** and the usually strict school of ↓**Shammai**, though even the moderate school seems very strict by prevailing modern standards.

The Theology of Judaism

Jewish beliefs sprang from the **acts of God in history** as recorded and interpreted in a collection of sacred books (the Old Testament), not as in paganism from mythology, mysticism, or philosophic speculation, though later legendary material, mystical practices, and philosophic speculation did make their way into Second Temple Judaism. The Old Testament emphasized the fate of Israel, the nation God had chosen for his own and with whom he had made a covenant. So the doctrine of individual resurrection did not appear often. The intertestamental period saw an increased emphasis on the fate of the individual and therefore on the doctrine of individual resurrection, especially for the redressing of martyrdom suffered at the hands of Antiochus Epiphanes. Nationalism and the awareness of being God's chosen people had by no means died out, however.

> "By three things the world is sustained: by the law, by the temple service, and by deeds of loving-kindness" (Mishnah, *Avot* 1:2).

Messianic Hope

Jews were looking for the Messiah to come. Indeed, some of them awaited a variety of messianic figures—prophetic, priestly, and royal. But they did not expect the Messiah to be a divine as well as human being, or to suffer, die, and rise from the dead for their salvation from sin. Some have interpreted a fragment among the Dead Sea Scrolls to indicate a belief at Qumran in the Messiah's suffering, but this interpretation is neither the only one possible nor the most likely one. The Jews looked, rather, for God to use a purely human figure in bringing military deliverance from Roman domination. Or God himself would deliver his people, they thought, and then introduce the Messiah as ruler. It is probable that characterizations of the Messiah as a preexistent higher being, as in the "Similitudes" of 1 Enoch and in 2 Esdras, postdate the rise of Christianity and developed out of the Jewish troubles with Rome during A.D. 66–135 and perhaps also in imitation of the high Christian view of Jesus.

Hillel: HIL-uhl   ■   Shammai: SHAM-*i*

Until the Messiah Comes

- "See, Lord, and raise up for them their king, the son of David, to rule over your servant Israel in the time known to you, O God. Undergird him with the strength to destroy the unrighteous rulers, to purge Jerusalem from Gentiles who trample her to destruction; in wisdom and in righteousness to drive out the sinners from the inheritance.... He will gather a holy people, whom he will lead in righteousness, and he will judge the tribes of the people that have been made holy by the Lord their God.... He will distribute them upon the land according to their tribes; the alien and the foreigner will no longer live near them.... There will be no unrighteousness among them in his days, for all will be holy, and their king will be the lord Messiah" (*Psalms of Solomon* 17:21–23, 26, 28, 32).
- "They shall not deviate from any counsel of the law so as to walk in the complete stubbornness of their heart, but instead shall be governed by the original directives with which the men of the Community began to be taught—until the Prophet comes, and also the Messiahs of Aaron and Israel" (*Community Rule* 9:9–11).

"**This present age,**" evil in character, was to be followed by the utopian "**days of the Messiah**" or "**Day of the Lord,**" indeterminate or variously calculated as to length. Afterwards, "**the coming age**"—that is, the eternal future—would begin. Occasionally in Jewish thinking, the messianic kingdom merged with the eternal age to come.

Sects and Other Groups within Judaism

Pharisees

The Pharisees ("separated ones" in a ritualistic or derogatory sense) originated shortly after the Maccabean Revolt as an outgrowth of the Hasideans, who had objected to the Hellenization of Jewish culture. Middle-class laymen for the most part, Pharisees made up the largest of Jewish religious sects but still numbered only about six thousand in the time of Herod the Great. They scrupulously observed the rabbinic as well as Mosaic laws. Dietary restrictions attained such importance that a Pharisee could not eat in the house of a "sinner" (a flagrant violator of the law) but might entertain a sinner in his own house. Yet he had to provide clothes lest the sinner's own clothes be ritually impure. The concern for ritual purity loomed large throughout Judaism but with special prominence in Pharisaism.

Observance of the Sabbath was similarly scrupulous. Some rabbis in the Pharisaical tradition forbade spitting on

"Jewish philosophy takes three forms, in fact. The followers of the first school are called Pharisees; of the second, Sadducees; of the third, Essenes. The Essenes have a reputation for cultivating peculiar sanctity.... The Pharisees ... are considered the most accurate interpreters of the laws and hold the position of the leading sect.... The Sadducees, on the contrary, are—even among themselves—rather boorish in their behavior and ... as rude as to aliens" (Josephus, *Jewish War* 2.8.2, 14 §§119, 162, 166).

A *mikveh,* or pool for ritual washing, in Jericho

[handwritten margin notes: No work on a loophole Sabbath; believe in angels, spirits, immortality of the soul, + resurrection of the body]

the bare ground during the Sabbath lest the action disturb the dirt and thus constitute plowing, which would break the prohibition of working on the Sabbath. A woman should not look in the mirror on the Sabbath lest she see a gray hair, be tempted to pluck it out, yield to the temptation, and thereby work on the Sabbath. It became a moot question whether one might lawfully eat an egg laid on a festival day. Were such eggs tainted even though hens lack an awareness of festival days?

But Pharisaically minded rabbis devised legal loopholes for their and others' convenience. Though a man should not carry his clothes in his arms out of a burning house on the Sabbath, he could put on several layers of clothing and bring them out by wearing them. One should not travel on the Sabbath more than three-fifths of a mile from the town or city where he lived.

> "R. Akiba said, '... The tradition is a fence around the law [that is, scribal interpretation protects the law by keeping people from even coming close to breaking it]'" (Mishnah, *Avot* 3:14).

But if he wished to go farther, on Friday he might deposit food for two meals three-fifths of a mile from his home in the direction he wished to travel. The deposit of food made that place his home-away-from-home, so that on the Sabbath he could travel yet another three-fifths of a mile. Jesus and the Pharisees repeatedly clashed over the artificiality of such legalisms. Nevertheless, average Jews admired Pharisees as paragons of virtue; indeed, they considered them the mainstays of Judaism.

Sadducees

The aristocratic Sadducees were heirs of the intertestamental Hasmoneans. Though fewer than the Pharisees, they wielded more political influence because they controlled the priesthood. "Sadducees" may originally have meant "members of the supreme council," reinterpreted by the Sadducees to mean "righteous ones." Others relate the term to ↓Zadok, a leading priest under David and Solomon. Contacts with foreign overlords tended to diminish the Sadducees' religious devotion and carry them further in the direction of Hellenization. Unlike the Pharisees, they regarded only the first five books of the Old Testament (the Pentateuch, Mosaic law, or Torah) as fully authoritative and denied the oral law of the nonpriestly rabbis. They did not believe in divine foreordination, angels, spirits, or the immortality of the soul and resurrection of the body, as did the Pharisees. Though strict, the Pharisees were in one sense progressive, for they kept applying the Old Testament law to new and changing circumstances of daily life. But the comfortably situated Sadducees wanted to maintain the status quo and therefore resisted any contemporizing of the law lest they lose their favored positions of affluence and wealth. Because the center of priestly power, the temple, was destroyed in A.D. 70 along with large numbers of the Sadducees themselves, the Saducean party disintegrated. The Pharisees survived to become the foundation of orthodox Judaism in later centuries.

> "The Sadducees say, 'We complain against you, O you Pharisees, because you declare clean an uninterrupted flow of liquid.' The Pharisees say, 'We complain against you, O you Sadducees, because you declare clean a stream of water that flows from a burial ground'" (Mishnah, *Yadayim* 4:7).

Essenes

A small sect of Essenes numbered about four thousand. Like the Pharisees, they evolved from the Hasideans who had become disgruntled with the increasingly political aims of the Hasmoneans. Some of the Essenes lived in monastic communities, such as the one at Qumran, which produced the Dead Sea Scrolls. Admission required a three-year probation and relinquishment of private property and wealth

> "And God observed their deeds, that they sought him with a perfect heart; and he raised up for them a Teacher of Righteousness to guide them in the way of his heart" (*Damascus Document* 1:10–11).

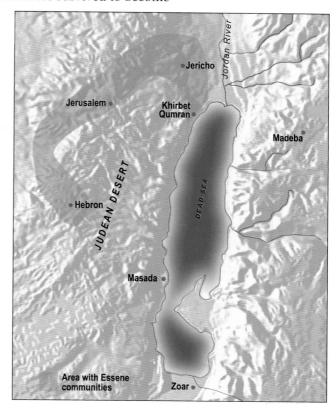

Zadok: ZAY-dok

to a communal treasury. Either the stricter ones refrained from marriage, or they all stopped cohabiting with their wives after several years of marriage. The Essenes' punctilious legalism exceeded that of the Pharisees. For this reason it is doubtful they contributed significantly to the rise of Christianity, as has been suggested by some modern writers. If Jesus denounced Pharisaic legalism, he certainly could not have owed very much to the even more legalistic Essenes; and his mingling with sinners contrasted sharply with Essene withdrawal from society.

The Essenes did not offer animal sacrifices in the temple at Jerusalem, because they regarded it as polluted by a corrupt priesthood. To maintain ritual purity, they even refrained from bowel movements on the Sabbath; and to symbolize that purity they wore white robes. The sect regarded itself as the elect remnant living in the last days. They looked for the appearance of several eschatological figures—a great prophet, a royal messiah, and a priestly messiah—and prepared themselves for a forty-year war that they expected to culminate in the messianic kingdom. A former leader called the **Teacher of Righteousness** exerted a profound influence on their beliefs and practices but hardly occupied the position of divine and redemptive prominence given to Jesus in Christian belief.

Ruins of the Essene settlement at Qumran

Some Regulations at Qumran

- "If one of them has knowingly lied in matters of property, he shall be excluded from the pure food of the Many for one year and shall be sentenced to one quarter of his bread . . . . And whoever spits during a meeting of the Many shall do penance for thirty days. . . . And whoever guffaws inanely shall do penance for thirty days. . . . But whoever slanders the Many shall be expelled from their midst and never return" (*Community Rule* 6:24–25; 7:15–19).
- "No one shall eat on the Sabbath day except what has been prepared beforehand. . . . No one shall wear perfumes while going and coming on the Sabbath. . . . No one shall stay in a place near Gentiles on the Sabbath" (*Damascus Document* 10:22; 11:9–10, 14–15).

Herodians and Zealots

The ↓Herodians seem to have been a small minority of influential Jews—probably centered in Galilee, where Herod Antipas ruled—who supported the Herodian dynasty and, by implication, the Romans, who had put the Herods in charge. Contrasting with the Herodians were revolutionaries dedicated to the overthrow of Roman power. They refused to pay taxes to Rome, regarded acknowledgment of loyalty to Caesar as sinful, and sparked several uprisings, including the Jewish revolt that led to the destruction of Jerusalem in A.D. 70. During that revolt some of them came to be known as "Zealots" (formerly a nonpolitical designation—Acts 21:20; 22:3; compare Luke 6:15; Acts 1:13). Modern scholars have sometimes identified these Zealots with the ↓Sicarii ("assassins"), who carried concealed daggers; but the Sicarii may have formed a branch of Zealotry or an originally separate group that fused with the Zealots.

Scribes and Disciples

The scribes were neither a religious sect nor a political party, but a professional class. *Lawyer, scribe,* and *teacher (of the law)* are synonymous terms in the New Testament. To these must be added *rabbi* (literally, "my great one"), a term of respect for teachers as well as for deserving others. Originating with Ezra, according to tradition, the scribes interpreted and taught the Old Testament law and delivered judicial pronouncements on cases brought to them. Application of the law to daily life necessitated their interpretive task. What constituted working on the Sabbath, for example? The disciples ("learners") of the scribes followed behind them wherever they went and learned by observation and rote memory the minutiae of the Old Testament and of rabbinic lore. The scribes taught in the temple

Herodians: hi-ROH-dee-uhnz ■ Sicarii: si-KAHR-ee-*i*

precincts and synagogues and occasionally debated in the presence of their disciples.

By Jesus' time most of the scribes probably belonged to the Pharisaical sect, though not all Pharisees possessed the theological expertise required of scribes. Since scribal activity was gratuitous, scribes depended on a trade to support themselves. For example, Paul, who had received rabbinic training, made tents (Acts 18:3). Though he lacked formal theological education, Jesus was called "Rabbi" and gathered disciples around himself. He regularly taught in easy-to-remember rhythmic structure, sententious sayings, and vivid parables. His teaching carried the weight of his own authority ("Truly I say . . ."; compare Matthew 7:28–29). In contrast, the scribes endlessly quoted opinions of past rabbis.

↓Sanhedrin

The Romans allowed Jews to handle many of their own religious and domestic matters. As a result, numerous sanhedrins—that is, local courts—existed. Outranking them all was the Jewish supreme court, the Great Sanhedrin in Jerusalem. This Sanhedrin even commanded a police force. The high priest chaired meetings of the court. The New Testament refers to the Great Sanhedrin by the terms "council," "chief priests and elders and scribes," "chief priests and rulers," and simply "rulers."

People of the Land

In Palestinian Jewry the masses of common people, called "the people of the land," remained unaffiliated with the religious sects and political parties. Because of their ignorance of and indifference to the fine points of Old Testament law and scribal regulations, the Pharisees held these people in contempt; but they criticized Jesus most of all for mingling with those known for flagrant violations of the Mosaic law.

↓Diaspora

Outside Palestine the Jews of the Diaspora ("Dispersion") fell into two classes: (1) **Hebraists**, who retained not only their Judaistic faith but also their Jewish language and customs and thereby incurred Gentile hatred for their standoffishness, and (2) **Hellenists**, who adopted the Greek language, dress, and customs while retaining their Judaistic faith in varying degrees. An outstanding example of Hellenistic Judaism was ↓**Philo**, a first-century Jewish philosopher and resident of Alexandria. He combined Judaism and Greek philosophy by allegorizing the Old Testament and thus making it teach Greek philosophy in symbolic form. Doubtless, Judaism outside

Sanhedrin: san-HEE-druhn ■ Diaspora: di-AS-puh-ruh ■ Philo: FI-loh

Palestine tended to be less strict and more influenced by Gentile modes of thinking than was Judaism in Palestine. But we must not overdraw the differences, for Hellenistic influences had so pervaded Palestine that Judaism there was much more variegated than the Talmud (which represents a later and more monolithic stage of Judaism) might lead us to believe. After the failure of revolts against Rome in A.D. 70 and 135, Palestinian Judaism consolidated itself increasingly around a deapocalypticized Pharisaism emphasizing the Torah; for the Sadducees had lost their base of influence in the temple, and the Romans had defeated the hopes of smaller, apocalyptically minded sects such as the Essenes.

Proselytes and God-Fearers

Despite its intensely nationalistic spirit, Judaism attracted Gentile proselytes, who were full converts, and—in larger numbers—God-fearers, who were Gentiles willing to practice Judaism in part but, if male, unwilling to undergo circumcision and observe the stricter Jewish taboos. All proselytes had to baptize themselves in the presence of witnesses and go to the temple in Jerusalem, if possible, to offer a sacrifice there. It may be that the requirement of self-baptism came after the destruction of the temple in lieu of

> "But from now on if you eat the forbidden fat of cattle, you will be excommunicated. If you profane the Sabbath, you will be stoned" (a warning to proselytes in the Babylonian Talmud, *Yevamot* 47a,b).

offering a sacrifice there. Proselytes and God-fearers found Jewish theology superior to pagan polytheism and superstition, for the Jews emphasized their monotheistic belief in one God and opposed idolatry even in their own temple. Unconverted pagans, on the other hand, could not comprehend a temple without an idol. Why build a temple if not to house an idol? The Jewish emphasis on moral behavior also appealed to the conscience of Gentiles offended by the immorality of the pantheon as described in pagan mythology and of the devotees of those gods and goddesses.

Jewish Education

Jewish children received their first lessons in Hebrew history and religion, practical skills, and reading and writing from their parents. The Mosaic law and Proverbs in the Old Testament contain many injunctions concerning this parental responsibility, which included the employment of physical punishment for failure to learn properly. Jewish boys entered local synagogue schools at about six years of age. There they used the Old Testament as a textbook at least for reading and possibly for writing as well. Lessons also included simple arithmetic, extrabiblical Jewish tradition, and religious rituals. Besides this narrow academic training, every Jewish boy learned a trade. To become an advanced scholar in the Old Testament, a Jewish young man attached himself as pupil to a rabbi. Before Paul's Christian

Library of Celsus in Ephesus

conversion, for example, he studied under the famous rabbi ↓**Gamaliel** (Acts 22:3).

Greco-Roman Education

By contrast, Greco-Roman education was liberal in scope. Slaves supervised boys in their earlier years by giving them their first lessons and then leading them to and from private schools until they graduated into adulthood with a great deal of ceremony. Even girls and young slaves might attend these elementary schools. After graduation, young men could attend universities in Athens, Rhodes, Tarsus, Alexandria, and other cities to study philosophy, rhetoric, law, mathematics, astronomy, medicine, geography, and botany. Or they could attend the lectures of ↓peripatetic philosophers, so called because these philosophers dispensed their wisdom as they walked around. Graffiti and papyrus remains show that education was fairly common, so that people often carried small notebooks for jotting down grocery lists, appointments, and other memoranda. Occasionally, shorthand was used.

And so a wide range of literature, including extrabiblical writings as well as the New Testament, helps us reconstruct the pagan and Jewish religious and philosophical backgrounds necessary for a reasonably complete understanding of the New Testament. The Judaism out of which Christianity arose was a monotheistic faith with cross currents of religious and political thought and with various religious and cultural institutions.

Gamaliel: guh-MAY-lee-uhl ■ peripatetic: per´i-puh-TET-ik

Summary

Traditional pagan religion featured a pantheon of gods who, according to the myths about them, often behaved badly. Roman emperors also were elevated to divine status and worshiped; and secret religions, called mysteries, became increasingly popular. Superstitious practices flourished. Pagans were syncretistic in that they combined these practices and religions rather than following one to the exclusion of others. The ideas that later formed full-blown Gnosticism were beginning to jell, ideas such as the inherent evil of the physical world and superior knowledge as the means of salvation for the religiously elite. Philosophical notions were peddled widely. Stoicism in particular enjoyed some popularity.

Jews of the period had forsaken idolatry. Obedience to the Mosaic law came to the fore. Religious and other meetings were held in local synagogues. There nonsacrificial worship took place each Sabbath day. Sacrificial worship took place daily and only at the temple in Jerusalem, where annual religious festivals and holy days were also celebrated. The Old Testament provided a sacred text as the basis for Jewish beliefs and practices. This text gave an account of salvation history, among other things, and existed in the original Hebrew, a Greek translation, and mainly oral paraphrases into Aramaic. But Jewish authors had written, and were still writing, other religious books containing various sorts of material that add to our knowledge of the Judaism then current. Teachers' oral interpretations of the Old Testament law were written in the Talmud only later.

Judaism attracted high-minded Gentiles, both full converts (proselytes) and half converts (God-fearers), but Judaism remained very nationalistic. Belief in bodily resurrection was gaining ground. So too were messianic expectations, which, however, varied. Yet the messiahs or Messiah was not expected to be divine as well as human, nor to die for the sins of others.

Pharisees were strict; Essenes, stricter; Sadducees, loose, upscale, centered in Jerusalem, and destined to disintegrate as a sect with the destruction of Jerusalem and the temple in A.D. 70. The Herodians supported Herod's family in power. Zealots opposed the Roman power, represented by the Herods and Roman governors. Scribes taught and applied the Old Testament law. Though limited in jurisdiction, Jewish courts handled most questions of daily life. The Sanhedrin in Jerusalem met as a kind of supreme court. The mass of common folk belonged to none of these sects or classes and were designated "people of the land." Jews living outside Palestine formed the Diaspora, or Dispersion, and divided into traditionalists (Hebraists) and progressives (Hellenists). Jewish education was narrow in scope; Greco-Roman education, wide.

People to Remember

Gamaliel	Philo	Teacher of Righteousness
Hillel	Shammai	

Places to Remember

Delphi	Nag Hammadi
Mount Olympus	Qumran

Terms to Remember

apocalyptic	Great Sanhedrin	Pseudepigrapha
Apocrypha	haggadah	rabbis
asceticism	halakah	Sabbath
the coming age	Hebraists	Sadducees
cynicism	Hellenists	salvation history
the days of the Messiah/	Herodians	scribes
the day of the Lord	laver	Second Temple Judaism
Dead Sea Scrolls	libertinism/sensualism	Shema
Diaspora/Dispersion	menorah	Shemone Esreh
disciples	Mishnah	Sicarii
emperor cult	monotheism	Skepticism
Epicureanism	mystery religions	Stoicism
Essenes	pantheon	synagogue
exorcist	people of the land	syncretism
Gemarah	Pharisees	Talmud
gnōsis	polytheism	Targum
Gnosticism	the present age	Yahweh
God-fearers	proselytes	Zealots

How Much Did You Learn?

- Characterize the gods of the pantheon according to the myths about them.
- Compare the mystery religions with traditional paganism and Christianity.
- Compare Gnostic ideas with the various current philosophies.
- How did synagogues and the temple in Jerusalem differ in their functions?
- Distinguish from one another the Old Testament, the Apocrypha, the pseude-pigrapha-apocalyptic literature, the Dead Sea Scrolls, and the Talmud.
- Draw contrasts between the Pharisees, Essenes, Sadducees, and "people of the land."
- Contrast the Herodians and the Zealots.
- Give synonyms for "scribes" and for "the Great Sanhedrin."
- Identify the two classes of Jews in the Diaspora/Dispersion.
- Distinguish Gentile proselytes and God-fearers from each other.
- Contrast Jewish and Greco-Roman education.

For Further Discussion

- In the times just before the New Testament, what religious and philosophical developments prepared for the coming of Christ and the rise of Christianity?
- Do modern people hold to mythological, superstitious, and syncretistic beliefs and practices? If not, why not? If so, what are those beliefs and practices—and why have modern science and technology failed to banish them?
- What parallels as well as differences may be drawn between Gnosticism and current philosophies of education?
- What counterparts to the Pharisees, Sadducees, Essenes, Herodians, and Zealots might be found in Christendom today?
- To which of those groups would you have joined yourself, and why? If to none of them, give your reasons.
- In what ways have educational practices in Western culture combined traits characteristic of both Jewish and Greco-Roman educational practices?

For Further Investigation

Primary Materials

The Ancient Mysteries: A Sourcebook. Edited by M. Meyer. San Francisco: Harper-Collins, 1987.

Barrett, C. K. *The New Testament Background. Selected Documents.* 2d ed. San Francisco: Harper & Row, 1989. Especially pages 31–38, 51–134, 157–62, 177–268, 279–89, 298–349.

Cotter, W. *Miracles in Greco-Roman Antiquity: A Sourcebook for the Study of New Testament Miracle Stories*. New York: Routledge, 1999.

deSilva, D. A. *Introducing the Apocrypha*. Grand Rapids: Baker, 2002.

Foerster, W. *Gnosis*. 2 vols. Oxford: Clarendon, 1972–74.

Kee, H. C. *The Origins of Christianity*. Englewood Cliffs, N.J.: Prentice-Hall, 1973. Especially pages 54–261.

Martinez, F. G. *The Dead Sea Scrolls Translated*. Leiden: Brill, 1994.

Nag Hammadi Texts and the Bible: A Synopsis and Index. Edited by C. A. Evans, R. L. Webb, and R. A. Wiebe. Leiden: Brill, 1993.

The New Oxford Annotated Apocrypha. Edited by B. M. Metzger and R. E. Murphy. New York: Oxford University Press, 1991.

The Old Testament Pseudepigrapha. Edited by J. H. Charlesworth. 2 vols. Garden City, N.Y.: Doubleday, 1986.

Robinson, J. M., et al. *The Nag Hammadi Library in English*. 2d ed. San Francisco: Harper & Row, 1990.

Vermès, G. *The Dead Sea Scrolls in English*. 3d ed. New York: Penguin, 1987.

Wise, M., M. Abegg Jr., and E. Cook. *The Dead Sea Scrolls: A New Translation*. San Francisco: HarperCollins, 1996.

Modern Treatments

Binder, D. B. *Into the Temple Courts: The Place of the Synagogues in the Second Temple Period*. Atlanta: Society of Biblical Literature, 1999.

Collins, J. J. *The Scepter and the Star: The Messiahs of the Dead Sea Scrolls and Other Ancient Literature*. New York: Doubleday, 1995.

Grabbe, L. L. *Judaic Religion in the Second Temple Period: Belief and Practice from the Exile to Yavneh*. New York: Routledge, 2000.

Jeremias, J. *Jerusalem in the Time of Jesus*. Philadelphia: Fortress Press, 1969.

Jobes, K. H., and Moisés Silva. *Invitation to the Septuagint*. Grand Rapids: Baker, 2000.

Jonas, H. *The Gnostic Religion*. 2d ed. Boston: Beacon, 1963.

Levine, L. I. *The Ancient Synagogue: The First Thousand Years*. New Haven: Yale University Press, 2000.

Martin, L. H. *Hellenistic Religions: An Introduction*. New York: Oxford University Press, 1987.

Moore, G. F. *Judaism*. 3 vols. Cambridge, Mass.: Harvard University Press, 1927–30.

Neusner, J., W. S. Green, and E. S. Frerichs. *Judaisms and Their Messiahs at the Turn of the Christian Era*. New York: Cambridge University Press, 1987.

"Qumran and the Dead Sea Scrolls: Discoveries, Debates, the Scrolls and the Bible." *Near Eastern Archaeology* 63, no. 3 (September 2000), 120–78. Includes many photographs.

Religions of Antiquity. Edited by R. M. Seltzer. New York: Macmillan, 1989. Pages 237–304.

Religious Diversity in the Graeco-Roman World: A Survey of Recent Scholarship. Edited by D. Cohn-Sherbock and J. M. Court. Sheffield: Sheffield Academic Press, 2001.

Rudolph, K. *Gnosis.* San Francisco: Harper & Row, 1987.

Sanders, E. P. *Judaism: Practice and Belief 63 BCE–66 CE.* Philadelphia: Trinity Press International, 1992.

Schürer, E. *The History of the Jewish People in the Age of Jesus Christ* (*175 B.C.–A.D. 135*). Vol. 2, revised by G. Vermès et al. Edinburgh: T. & T. Clark, 1979.

VanderKam, J. C. *The Dead Sea Scrolls Today.* Grand Rapids: Eerdmans, 1994.

Williams, M. A. *Rethinking "Gnosticism": An Argument for Dismantling a Dubious Category.* Princeton: Princeton University Press, 1996.

Yamauchi, E. M. *Pre-Christian Gnosticism.* Grand Rapids: Eerdmans, 1973.

PART 2

Literary and Historical Materials

CHAPTER 4

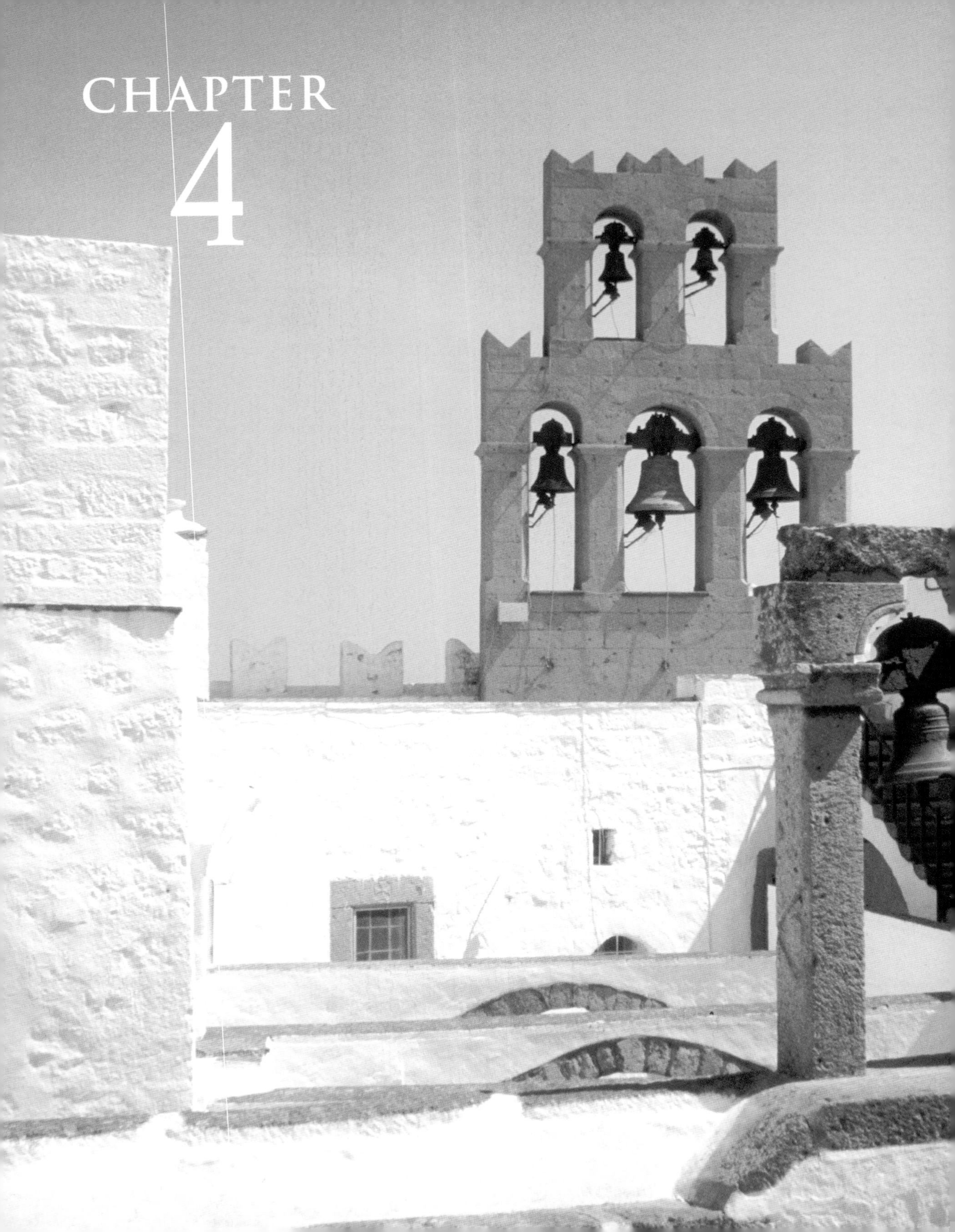

THE CANON AND TEXT OF THE NEW TESTAMENT

Overview:

- The Canon
- The Text
- Summary

Study Goals—Learn:

- How the early church managed at first without the New Testament
- How the New Testament then came to be considered by the church as an authoritative collection of books
- How we know that our New Testament accurately represents what its authors originally wrote

The fortified Monastery of St. John on Patmos, noted for its library of 900 manuscripts, including a sixth-century manuscript of Mark

The ↓Canon

The New Testament canon consists of books accepted by the early church as divinely inspired. The term **canon** originally meant "measuring reed" but developed the metaphorical meaning "standard" (compare the literal and metaphorical meanings of "yardstick"). As applied to the New Testament, canon refers to those books accepted by the church as the standard that governs Christian belief and conduct.

The Precanonical Period

At first, Christians did not have any of the books contained in our New Testament. They depended therefore on the **Old Testament**, on **oral tradition about Jesus' words and deeds**, and on **messages from God spoken by Christian prophets**. Even after having been written, many of the New Testament books were not distributed geographically throughout the church. And before the books were gathered into the New Testament, Christian writers had produced still other books—some good, some inferior. Books such as Paul's Letters and the Gospels received canonical recognition quickly. We call them the ↓*homolegoumena* (Greek for "confessed"). Because of their brevity and limited circulation, other books simply did not become known widely enough for rapid acceptance into the canon. Uncertain authorship caused Hebrews to be questioned for a while, and the early church hesitated to adopt 2 Peter because its Greek style differs from that in 1 Peter and thus raised doubts about its claim to authorship by the Apostle Peter. We call such books the ↓*antilegomena* (Greek for "contradicted").

Canonization

Quotations of New Testament books as authoritative by the early church fathers help us recognize what books they regarded as canonical. Later the church compiled formal lists, or canons. An early Gnostic heretic named ↓**Marcion** may have played a provocative role. He taught that a harsh God of the Old Testament and Judaism and a loving God oppose each other; that Jesus came as a messenger of the loving God; that Jesus was killed at the instigation of the harsh God; that Jesus entrusted to the twelve apostles his message from the loving God; that they failed to keep it from corruption; and that Paul turned into the sole preacher of the uncorrupted message. To

Before the New Testament

- "These things happened to them [the Israelites] as examples and were written down [in the Old Testament] to instruct us [Christians]" (1 Corinthians 10:11).
- "And I will not hesitate to append to the interpretations all that I ever learned well from the elders and remembered well . . . . For I did not suppose that information from books would help me so much as the word of a living and surviving voice" (Papias as quoted by Eusebius, *Church History* 3.39.3–4).
- "And we entered the house of Philip the evangelist . . . . Now this man had four virgin daughters who prophesied" (Acts 21:8–9).
- "What good will I be to you unless I speak to you by way of revelation or knowledge or prophecy or teaching?" (Paul in 1 Corinthians 14:6).

canon: KAN-uhn ■ *homolegoumena:* ho´muh-leh-GOO-meh-nah ■ *antilegomena:* ahn´tee-leh-GAW-meh-nah ■ Marcion: MAHR-shuhn

support this teaching Marcion selected only those books he considered free from and contrary to the Old Testament and Judaism: Luke (with some omissions) and most of Paul's Letters. This canon dates from about A.D. 144. The reaction of orthodox Christians against its omission of other Christian books now in the New Testament shows that the church as a whole had already accepted or was in the process of accepting those books that Marcion rejected. By the fourth and fifth centuries, all our New Testament books were generally recognized and others excluded. Church councils of those centuries formalized existing belief and practice concerning the New Testament canon.

The idea of a canon implies that God guided the early church in its evaluation of various books, so that truly inspired ones gained acceptance as canonical and those not inspired, whatever of lesser value they might offer, did not gain acceptance as canonical. The process of canonization took time, and differences of opinion arose. But we may be grateful that the early church did not accept books without evaluation and, at times, debate. Most readers who will compare the **subapostolic writings** and the **New Testament apocrypha** with the canonical books of the New Testament will heartily endorse the critical judgment of the early Christians.

CRITERIA Various criteria for canonicity have been suggested, such as edifying moral effect and agreement with the oral tradition of apostolic doctrine. But some edifying books failed to achieve canonical status. So also did some books that carried forward the oral tradition of apostolic doctrine. More important—in fact,

> "Marcion expressly and openly used the knife, not the pen, since he made such an excision of the Scriptures as suited his own subject matter" (Tertullian, *On Prescription Against Heretics* 38).

Subapostolic Writings

Subapostolic writings are books written in the period immediately following that of Jesus' twelve apostles by the "apostolic fathers," who themselves did not belong to the Twelve but who succeeded them in leadership of the church:

1 and 2 Clement
Letters of ↓Ignatius
Letter of ↓Polycarp to the Philippians
↓Didache, or Teaching of the Twelve Apostles
Letter of ↓Barnabas
Shepherd of ↓Hermas
Martyrdom of Polycarp
Letter to ↓Diognetus
Writings of ↓Papias (extant only in fragments)

Sample passages:

- "This teaching of theirs [Christians] has not been discovered by the intellect or cogitation of busy people, nor do they advocate a human dogma, as some do. . . . They live in their own fatherlands, but as sojourners. They share all things as citizens, and endure all things as foreigners. Every foreign country is their fatherland; and every fatherland, a foreign country. They marry, as all do, but they do not expose their offspring. . . . They pass their time on earth, but have their citizenship in heaven" (*Letter to Diognetus* 5:3, 5–6, 9).

- "I am dying willingly for God's sake, if you do not hinder it. . . . Allow me to be eaten by the beasts, through which I can attain to God. I am God's wheat, and I am ground by the teeth of wild beasts that I may be found pure bread of Christ. Rather, entice the wild beasts that they may become my tomb . . . . Then I will truly be a disciple of Jesus Christ" (*Letter of Ignatius to the Romans* 4:1–2, on the way to martyrdom).

Ignatius: ig-NAY-shuhs ■ Polycarp: POL-ee-kahrp ■ Didache: DID-uh-kay ■ Barnabas: BAHR-nuh-buhs ■ Hermas: HUHR-muhs ■ Diognetus: di-OG-ni-tuhs ■ Papias: PAY-pee-uhs

The New Testament Apocrypha

The New Testament Apocrypha differ from the Old Testament Apocrypha, consist of fanciful and sometimes heretical books, and do not enjoy acceptance as canonical by any major branch of the Christian church. Sample passages:

- "Even so my mother, the Holy Spirit, took me by one of my hairs and carried me away onto the great mountain Tabor" (Jesus in the *Gospel of the Hebrews,* according to Origen, *Commentary on John* 2.12.87).

- "And on the first day we arrived at a lonely inn . . . we were trying to find a bed for John . . . . But when he lay down he was troubled by the bedbugs; and since they became more and more troublesome to him and it was already midnight, he said to them in the hearing of us all, 'I tell you, bedbugs, to behave yourselves . . . .' John went to sleep . . . . Now as the day was breaking I got up first, and Verus and Andronicus with me. And we saw by the door of the room . . . a mass of bedbugs collected. . . . And when he [John] woke up . . . he looked at them and said, 'Since you have behaved yourselves and listened to my correction, go back to your own place.' And when he had said this and got up from the bed, the bugs came running from the door to the bed and climbed up its legs and disappeared into the joints" (*Acts of John* 60–61).

crucial—was the criterion of **apostolicity**, which means authorship by an apostle or by an apostolic associate and thus also a date of writing within the apostolic period.

Mark associated with both of the apostles Peter and Paul. Luke accompanied Paul. And whoever authored Hebrews exhibits close theological contacts with Paul. James and Jude were half brothers or stepbrothers of Jesus and associates of the apostles in the early Jerusalem church. Traditionally, all other authors represented in the New Testament were themselves apostles: Matthew, John, Paul, and Peter. Modern criticism casts doubt on some of the traditional ascriptions of authorship. Such questions receive individual attention in later sections of the present book. But even under negative critical views it is usually affirmed that books not written by apostles were at least written in the apostolic tradition by followers of the apostles.

RATIONALE Jesus himself affirmed the full authority of the Old Testament as Scripture but made his own words and deeds equally authoritative and promised the apostles that the Holy Spirit would remind them of his ministry, teach them its significance, and reveal to them further truth. The canon of the New Testament consists, then, of the authoritative record and interpretation of God's self-revelation through Jesus Christ—an interpretive record predictively authenticated by Jesus himself, whose view of his own words and deeds, now written and expounded by the apostles and their associates, did not fall below his view of the Old Testament as God's Word. The closing of the canon by limiting it to apostolic books arose out of a recognition that God's revelation in Christ needs no improvement.

The Text

Writing

↓**Papyrus** supplied the writing material for most, and perhaps all, books of the New Testament. Most and perhaps all New Testament authors used **scrolls**, though a few may have used ↓**codices** (plural of **codex**, a book with

---

papyrus: puh-PI-ruhs ■ codices: KOH-duh-seez

Papyrus plants

pages bound together in the modern style), and for copies the codex quickly gained popularity among Christians. Commonly, an author dictated to a writing secretary called an ↓**amanuensis**. Sometimes the author gave the amanuensis greater or lesser freedom in the choice of words.

Copying

The original documents, none of which are extant, go by the term *autographs*. At first copies were made one by one when private individuals and churches wanted them. But as demand increased, a reader dictated from an exemplar to a roomful of copyists. Gradually, errors of sight and sound, inadvertent omissions and repetitions, marginal notes, and deliberate theological and grammatical "improvements" slipped into the text. Concern for textual purity led to the checking of some manuscripts

amanuensis: uh-man´yoo-EN-sis (plural: -es, -eez)

God's Word, Old and New

- In Mark 7:6–13 Jesus equates what "Isaiah prophesied" and what "Moses said" with "the commandment of God" and "the word of God" (see also Matthew 5:17–19a; John 10:35b).

- In the Sermon on the Mount Jesus said, "You have heard that it was said to the ancients [there follows an Old Testament quotation or paraphrase] . . . . But I tell you [there follows Jesus' own teaching]" (Matthew 5:21–22, 28–29, 31–32, 38–39, 43–44; compare Mark 1:22, 27; Luke 4:32, 36).

- "But the Counselor, the Holy Spirit, whom the Father will send in my name, will teach you all things and will remind you of everything I have said to you" (John 14:26; see also 16:12–15).

The Greek text, written in uncial (majuscule) letters, of Luke 16:16–21 in a Bodmer papyrus

against other manuscripts. Nevertheless, the number of errors kept multiplying.

As the church grew richer and increasingly regarded the text of the New Testament as sacred, more durable writing materials, such as **vellum** (treated calfskin) and **parchment** (treated sheepskin), came into use. Earlier manuscripts were usually written all in capital (↓**uncial**, or ↓**majuscule**) letters, later manuscripts in cursive, small (↓**minuscule**) letters. Word divisions, punctuation marks, and chapter and verse divisions were lacking at first—in fact, these did not come till much later. The earliest manuscripts in the possession of modern scholars date from the second century, the very earliest being the ↓Rylands Fragment of John from about A.D. 135. Most of the **variant readings**, or differences, in early manuscripts have to do with spelling, word order, the presence or absence of "and" and "the," and other relatively inconsequential items.

TEXTUAL CRITICISM The exercise of determining the original wording of the New Testament is called textual criticism. Making up our primary sources for this exercise are **Greek manuscripts**, **early versions** (that is, ancient translations, especially Syriac and Latin), and **quotations** in the writings of the **early church fathers** and in **lectionaries** (readings from the New Testament in ancient liturgies). By comparing these, scholars can usually decide among variant readings with a fair degree of certainty. Among their most important rules for evaluation are preferences for

- The reading in the oldest, most carefully copied, geographically widest spread manuscripts and versions
- The reading that reflects the author's style and theology as seen elsewhere and that best explains the development of other readings
- The more difficult reading (since it is more probable that copyists made an expression easier to understand than harder to understand)
- The shorter reading (because copyists were more liable to add to the text than to delete, except where the omission appears to have been accidental)

For example, since angels regularly speak but eagles do not, an original "eagle" would explain a shift in some texts to "angel" at Revelation 8:13; but for the same reason a shift from "angel" to "eagle" would hardly have occurred. With regard to God's granting of prayer requests, some texts of

uncial: UN-shuhl ▪ majuscule: muh-JUHS-kyool ▪ minuscule: mi-NUHS-kyool ▪ Rylands: RI-luhndz

Mark 11:24 read the present tense "you receive" or the future tense "you will receive" (compare Matthew 21:22), because the past tense of the original "you received" seemed too bold. Some texts add "paralytics" at the end of John 5:3, apparently because the self-description of the man whom Jesus is about to heal makes you think of paralysis. In 1 Corinthians 10:19 some texts seem to have accidentally skipped from the first "is" to the second "is" and thus omitted Paul's question about whether an idol is anything.

Materials for determining the original text of the New Testament are far more numerous and ancient than those for the study of any of the old classical writings. Thanks to the labors of textual critics, remaining uncertainties about the text of the Greek New Testament are not serious enough to affect our understanding of its fundamental teachings. Deserving special mention for putting textual criticism on a firm footing are two British scholars of the nineteenth century, B. F. Westcott and F. J. A. Hort.

Translations into English

So far as English versions of the New Testament are concerned, **John ↓Wycliffe** produced his translation from Jerome's Latin Vulgate in 1382, and **William ↓Tyndale** translated from the original Greek in 1525. Following a succession of further English Bibles, the Roman Catholic ↓**Douay Version** appeared in 1582 and the vastly influential **King James** (or **Authorized**) **Version** in 1611. But the earliest and best manuscripts of the New Testament had not yet been discovered, and the following centuries saw great advances in scholarly knowledge concerning the kind of Greek used in the New Testament. A large contribution has come from the study

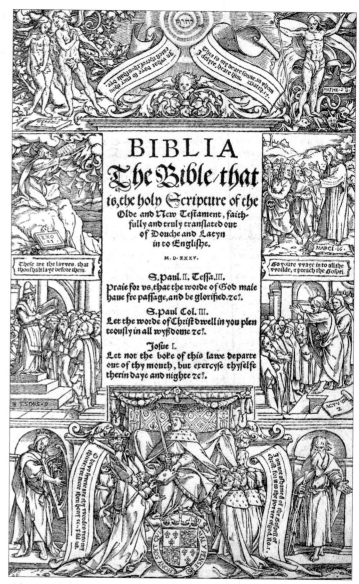

Title page of Coverdale's Bible, the first complete English translation of the Bible to be printed in England (1537)

Chapter and Verse

Stephen Langton (d. 1228) divided the biblical text into chapters, Robert Stephanus into verses in his printed edition of 1551.

Wycliffe: WIK-lif ■ Tyndale: TIN-duhl ■ Douay: DOO-ay

KING JAMES VERSION	NEW INTERNATIONAL VERSION
"For there are three that bear record in heaven, the Father, the Word, and the Holy Ghost: and these three are one. And there are three that bear witness in earth, the Spirit, and the water, and the blood: and these three agree in one." (1 John 5:7–8)	"For there are three that testify: the Spirit, the water and the blood; and the three are in agreement." (1 John 5:7–8)

Note not only alternative expressions but also the NIV's omission of copyists' additions to the original text, which is represented by earlier, better manuscripts as yet unknown to translators of the KJV.

of numerous papyri found during the last 150 years. As a result, numerous versions have appeared in recent times, for example, the **English Revised Version** (1881), the **American Standard Version** (1901), the **Revised Standard Version** (1946), the **New English Bible** (1961), the **New American Standard Bible** (1963), the **Jerusalem Bible** (1966), **Today's English Version** (1966), and the **New International Version** (1978), plus updates of some of these versions and various individual efforts. Of special interest to advanced students is the **NET Bible** (www.netbible.com).

Summary

As a canon, the books of the New Testament provide an authoritative guide for Christian belief and behavior. These books were written over the latter half or so of the first Christian century. Despite initial doubts concerning some of them, eventually Christians recognized all of them to have divine authority mediated through Jesus' Spirit-inspired apostles and their associates.

Through hand copying, errors crept into the text of the original documents. As a result, it has become necessary to do textual criticism, that is, to decide between differences of wording in early Greek manuscripts, translations, and quotations of the New Testament for what its authors are most likely to have written. Fortunately, we have an abundance of materials to perform this task; and there is large-scale agreement on the original wording. Recent English translations have capitalized on the labors of textual critics, so that we now have a more reliable understanding of the New Testament than was possible before the discovery of its earliest and best manuscripts.

People to Remember

F. J. A. Hort	William Tyndale	John Wycliffe
Marcion	B. F. Westcott	

Terms to Remember

amanuensis	homolegoumena	Rylands Fragment of John
antilegomena	King James Version	scroll(s)
apostolicity	lectionary(-ies)	subapostolic writings
autograph(s)	majuscule	textual criticism
canon	minuscule	uncial
codex (codices)	New Testament Apocrypha	variant reading(s)
cursive	papyrus	vellum
Douay Version	parchment	version(s)

How Much Did You Learn?

- What is the meaning of the word *canon* as applied to the New Testament?
- On what did the earliest Christians depend for their beliefs and practices before the books of the New Testament were written?
- Into what two categories did the New Testament books fall during the period of canonization?
- Why did some Christians doubt at first the canonicity of certain books that became part of the New Testament?
- Describe the possible role of Marcion in the history of canonization.
- On what basis were some Christian books canonized whereas others were not?
- Outline the rationale for adding the New Testament to the Old Testament.
- Why is textual criticism necessary?
- Describe the materials and manner of writing and copying the New Testament books.
- What criteria do textual critics use?
- Name several of the most important English translations of the Bible.

For Further Discussion

- Try to reconstruct a typical church service as it was before the New Testament was formed as a basis for preaching and teaching. Also reconstruct an early Christian's private devotional life without the New Testament.
- What evidences of continuing Marcionism are still apparent?
- How and why are Christian classics such as Augustine's *Confessions,* John Bunyan's *Pilgrim's Progress,* and some of Charles Wesley's hymns to be distinguished from the canonical books of the New Testament?
- Why did the church close the canon? Or is it still open? If an apostolic book—say, a long lost letter of Paul to the Corinthian church besides the letters to that church that we already have—came to light and was verified as apostolic, should the church add it to the New Testament?
- For practical purposes, does translation of Scripture take away the benefit of inspiration by removing readers one step from the original text?
- What are the advantages and disadvantages of a single accepted translation of the New Testament and of many different translations?

For Further Investigation

Primary Materials Containing Translations of the Subapostolic Writings and New Testament Apocrypha

The Apostolic Fathers: Greek Texts and English Translations. Edited by M. W. Holmes. Grand Rapids: Baker, 1999.

Grant, R. M., et al. *The Apostolic Fathers.* 6 vols. New York: Nelson, 1964–68. With extensive introductions and notes.

Hennecke, E. *New Testament Apocrypha.* Edited by W. Schneemelcher. 2d ed. 2 vols. Louisville: Westminster John Knox, 1993. With technical introductions and notes.

James, M. R. *The Apocryphal New Testament.* New York: Oxford University Press, 1924.

Lake, K. *The Apostolic Fathers.* 2 vols. Loeb Classical Library. New York: Putnam's, 1930. With Greek text as well as English translation.

General

Gamble, H. Y. *Books and Readers in the Early Church: A History of Early Christian Texts.* New Haven: Yale University Press, 1995.

Harrop, C. *History of the New Testament in Plain Language.* Waco: Word, 1984.

Richards, E. R. *The Secretary in the Letters of Paul.* Tübingen: Mohr, 1991.

Modern Discussions of the Canon

Bruce, F. F. *The Canon of Scripture.* Downers Grove, Ill.: InterVarsity Press, 1988.

Gamble, H. Y. *The New Testament Canon: Its Making and Meaning.* Philadelphia: Fortress Press, 1985.

McDonald, L. M. *The Formation of the Biblical Canon.* Nashville: Abingdon, 1988.

Metzger, B. M. *The Canon of the New Testament.* New York: Oxford University Press, 1992.

Ridderbos, H. N. *Authority of the New Testament Scriptures.* Nutley, N.J.: Presbyterian & Reformed, 1963.

Modern Surveys of Textual Criticism

Aland, K., and B. Aland. *The Text of the New Testament.* 2d ed. Grand Rapids: Eerdmans, 1990.

Black, D. A. *New Testament Textual Criticism: A Concise Guide.* Grand Rapids: Baker, 1994.

Ehrman, B. D. *The Orthodox Corruption of Scripture: The Effect of Early Christological Controversies on the Text of the New Testament.* New York: Oxford University Press, 1993.

Greenlee, J. H. *An Introduction to New Testament Textual Criticism.* 2d ed. Peabody, Mass.: Hendrickson, 1995.

Holmes, M. W. "Textual Criticism." In *New Testament Criticism and Interpretation.* Edited by D. A. Black and D. S. Dockery. Grand Rapids: Zondervan, 1991. Pages 101–34.

Metzger, B. M. *The Text of the New Testament: Its Transmission, Corruption and Restoration.* 3d ed. New York: Oxford University Press, 1992.

Parker, D. *The Living Text of the Gospels.* Cambridge: Cambridge University Press, 1997.

The English New Testament

Bruce, F. F. *History of the Bible in English.* 3d ed. New York: Oxford University Press, 1978.

CHAPTER
5

The Jordan River

THE STUDY OF JESUS' LIFE

Overview:

- Sources
- Higher Criticism
- The Study of Jesus' Life
- Summary

Study Goals—Learn:

- Whether there are literary sources for the life and teaching of Jesus outside the New Testament—and if so, what they are and what their value might be
- Whether the Gospels are independent or interdependent—and if interdependent, what their relationships might be
- What sources, if any, lie behind the Gospels
- How reliable the Gospels are in the information they give about Jesus
- How the Gospels came to be written and the main modern understandings of their portraiture of Jesus

Sources

Biblical and Extrabiblical

Though not the first documents of the New Testament to have been written (some of the Letters—also called Epistles—were written earlier), the Gospels of **Matthew, Mark, Luke,** and **John** fittingly stand first as our main sources for reconstructing the life of Jesus. The few non-Christian notices concerning him—for example, by the first-century Jewish historian ↓**Josephus,** in the Babylonian Talmud, and by the Roman writers ↓**Pliny the Younger,** ↓**Tacitus,** ↓**Suetonius,** and ↓**Lucian**—are so brief as to be almost valueless for a reconstruction. They do confirm, however, that Jesus lived, became a public figure, and died under Pontius Pilate, and that within a dozen years of his death the worship of him had spread as far as Rome.

↓**AGRAPHA** Some sayings of Jesus are recorded outside the four Gospels. For example, Paul quotes a ↓dominical saying otherwise unknown: "It is more blessed to give than to receive" (Acts 20:35). These *agrapha*, as they are called, differ from Jesus' sayings in the Gospels but are quoted by early Christian writers and sometimes placed in the margins of ancient manuscripts of the New Testament. *Agrapha* is Greek for "unwritten." These sayings were written down somewhere, of course (otherwise we would not know them), but not in the canonical Gospels.

COLLECTIONS OF SAYINGS Most notable among other records of Jesus' sayings outside the four canonical Gospels are the ↓**Oxyrhynchus papyri** and the Coptic *Gospel of Thomas.* The latter, discovered about 1945 at Nag Hammadi, Egypt, is not really a gospel, for it does not contain a narrative thread. Nor did the Apostle Thomas write it. Both this so-called gospel and the Oxyrhynchus papyri offer sizable collections of Jesus' sayings. Some of the sayings look almost exactly like those recorded in the canonical Gospels, for example, *Gospel of Thomas* 54: "Blessed are the poor, for yours is the kingdom of heaven" (compare Matthew 5:3 and

Taking Note of Jesus

- Typical of Roman writers' short notices of Jesus is the explanation by Tacitus (about A.D. 110) that the name *Christian* originated from *Christus* (Latin for *Christ*), who "had undergone the death penalty in the reign of Tiberius, by sentence of the procurator Pontius Pilate" (*Annals* 15.44).
- The longest and most famous early extrabiblical notice of Jesus appears in the writings of Josephus. Since elsewhere they show Josephus was not a Christian, can you detect those parts of the following passage that most modern scholars think were added by Christian copyists?

"About this time there lived Jesus, a wise man, if indeed one ought to call him a man. For he was one who performed surprising feats and was a teacher of such people as accept the truth gladly. He won over many Jews and many of the Greeks. He was the Messiah. When Pilate, on hearing him accused by people of the highest standing among us, had condemned him to be crucified, those who in the first place came to love him did not give up their affection for him. On the third day he appeared to them restored to life, for the prophets of God had prophesied these and countless other marvels concerning him. And the tribe of Christians, so called after him, has still to this day not disappeared" (*Jewish Antiquities* 18.3.3 §§63–64).

Josephus: joh-SEE-fuhs ■ Pliny: PLIN-ee ■ Tacitus: TAS-uh-tuhs ■ Suetonius: swi-TOH-nee-uhs ■ Lucian: LOO-shuhn ■ agrapha: AG-ruh-fuh ■ dominical: duh-MIN-uh-kuhl, from the Latin *dominicus,* "lord, master," often used for what pertains to the Lord Jesus ■ Oxyrhynchus: ok´si-RING-kuhs

Luke 6:20). Others obviously stem from canonical sayings but have undergone changes of various sorts, for example, *Gospel of Thomas* 46b: "But I have said that whoever among you will become a little one will know the kingdom and will be greater than John" (compare Matthew 11:11 and Luke 7:28). Still others differ wholly from anything found in the New Testament, for example, *Gospel of Thomas* 82: "He who is near me is near the fire, and he who is far from me is far from the kingdom." Concerning their relationship to the New Testament, three possibilities present themselves: (1) the noncanonical records draw from the canonical Gospels; (2) the noncanonical records represent an independent tradition of Jesus' sayings; (3) both relationships hold true in a mixed way. With the exception of scholars who deeply distrust the reliability of the canonical Gospels, it is generally agreed that the Oxyrhynchus papyri and *Gospel of Thomas* reflect a largely corrupted tradition concerning the words of Jesus.

APOCRYPHAL GOSPELS Luke 1:1 mentions numerous accounts written about Jesus and antedating the third gospel, but none of these except Mark and probably Matthew have survived. Postapostolic apocryphal gospels did survive, however; and they present a motley mixture of heretical beliefs and pious imagination, especially in filling out the details of Jesus' childhood and the interval between his death and resurrection, about which the canonical Gospels are largely silent.

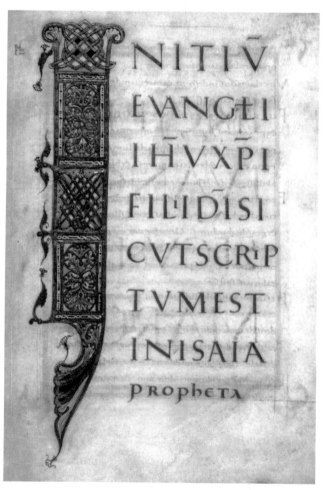

Beginning of the Gospel of Mark, ninth-century French manuscript

Higher Criticism

Alongside textual criticism, also called lower criticism and introduced in chapter 4, stands higher criticism. Whereas textual or lower critics try to answer the question of original wording, especially where ancient texts of the same document disagree, higher critics try to answer a variety of other questions concerning authorship; date, place, and purpose of writing; intended audience; possible use of comparable materials; editorial practices; and so on. Consequently, higher criticism subdivides.

Source Criticism of the Gospels

↓SYNOPTIC PROBLEM: ORAL TRADITION HYPOTHESIS As students of Jesus' life, we must go first to our primary sources, the canonical Gospels. Immediately the synoptic problem confronts us: Why are the first three (or Synoptic) Gospels—Matthew, Mark, and Luke—very much alike? (*Synoptic* comes from two Greek words meaning "seeing together.") According to the early hypothesis of oral tradition, resemblances derive from rapid crystallization of the tradition about Jesus in a more or less fixed oral form, which later came to be written down. Two Scandinavian scholars, H. Riesenfeld and B. Gerhardsson, have more recently revived this hypothesis. Their emphasis on the importance of memory in ancient Jewish culture does indeed support a high estimate of the Synoptics as historically trustworthy; but most modern scholars doubt that transmission by word of mouth could have retained so many and such minute verbal resemblances as exist among the Synoptics, especially in narrative, which is not so likely to have been memorized verbatim as possibly the words of Jesus were memorized.

On Jesus' trial before Pilate, the apocryphal *Gospel of Nicodemus* says: "Now when Jesus entered and the standard-bearers were holding the standards, the images of the emperor on the standards bowed and did reverence to Jesus. And when the Jews saw the behavior of the standards, . . . they cried out loudly against the standard-bearers. . . . They answered: '. . . We held the images; but they bowed down of their own accord and reverenced him.'"

↓GRIESBACH HYPOTHESIS Other scholars, led by W. R. Farmer, have revived the hypothesis of an eighteenth-century German scholar named J. J. Griesbach. According to him, Matthew wrote first. Then Luke used Matthew. Finally, Mark wrote an abbreviated combination of Matthew and Luke. Most contemporary scholars think the order of narratives concerning Jesus' deeds might be explained fairly adequately in this way but that Luke's disrupting the order of Jesus' teachings in Matthew and detailed changes of wording do not receive an adequate explanation under this theory.

MARCAN PRIORITY The Mark-Q documentary hypothesis has gained the greatest favor: Matthew and Luke based most of their narrative on Mark, drew most of Jesus' sayings, or teachings, from a lost document designated ↓Q, and added distinctive material of their own. Scholars marshal a number of arguments for the priority of Mark. Luke 1:1–4 states the utilization of earlier documents. This statement at least opens the possibility that Mark provided one of the documents behind Luke. More specifically, Matthew incorporates nearly all of Mark, and Luke about one-half. Both Matthew and Luke often carry the exact or nearly exact words of Mark, even in minute details. For example, both Matthew 9:6 and Luke 5:24 include the clause, "He [Jesus] said to the paralytic," that in Mark 2:10–11 leaves incomplete the statement of Jesus to his critics, "But that you may know that the Son

---

synoptic: sin-OP-tik ■ Griesbach: GREES-bahkh ■ Q, usually connected with the German *Quelle* (KVEL-eh), meaning "source"

of Man has authority to forgive sins on earth . . . ," and introduces his command to the paralytic, "I tell you, get up, take your mat and go home" (Mark 2:10–11).

Furthermore, Matthew and Luke usually carry Mark's sequence of the events in Jesus' life; they do not depart *together* from that sequence, as one would have expected them to do at least occasionally if they had not both been drawing on Mark. In other words, it appears that Mark is the anchor that keeps Matthew and Luke from drifting very far away (and never at the same time) from the order of events contained in Mark. Occasional, independent differences in sequence arise because topical considerations sometimes override chronology in the concerns of the **evangelists** (a technical term for the writers of the Gospels).

It often appears, moreover, that Matthew and Luke change the wording of Mark to clarify his meaning. For example, Luke 5:29 clears up an ambiguity in Mark 2:15 by writing that Jesus was hosted in Levi's house rather than Levi in Jesus' house. Matthew and Luke also appear to omit material that might be misunderstood—for example, by omitting Mark's story that Jesus' family thought he had gone mad, perhaps because Matthew and Luke feared their audiences might infer he really had done so. They appear to delete material unnecessary for their own purposes. For example, Matthew 8:14 and Luke 4:38 omit the names of Andrew, James, and John in Mark 1:29 and retain only Peter's name. And Matthew and Luke appear to smooth out awkward grammar (a matter of style, not of accuracy). For example, Mark 2:7 (literally translated), "Who can forgive sins except one, God?" becomes, "Who can forgive sins but God alone?" in Luke 5:21. (Mark has a rough and ready style—forceful but not elegant.) All these phenomena favor Matthew's and Luke's use of Mark.

Q HYPOTHESIS Since similarities in narrative material appear to rise from common use of the document Mark by Matthew and Luke, similarities between Matthew and Luke in sayings material not contained in Mark have led to the positing of a second document, Q, thought to be an early collection of Jesus' sayings with a minimum of narrative. Q would be something like the *Gospel of Thomas* and the Oxyrhynchus collection of Jesus' sayings or, better yet, like Old Testament prophetical books that contain the account of a prophet's call, extensive records of his preaching, sometimes bits and pieces of narrative, but no account of the prophet's death. Thus Q might be thought to begin with the baptism and temptation of Jesus (his "call"), to continue with his preaching, but to lack any account of his suffering, death, and resurrection.

As to be expected especially for a hypothetical document, Q raises some questions. For instance, why does the degree of agreement between Matthew and Luke in Jesus' teachings vary widely? Did Matthew and Luke use or make different Greek translations of an originally Aramaic Q, use different editions of a Greek Q, or use the same Greek Q? Should we doubt the very existence of Q (Why did it not survive as such?) and adopt for Jesus' teachings a theory of many short documents, or the theory of oral tradition (easier to believe for sayings than for narrative), or a combination of the two? Some believe that Luke used Matthew for many of Jesus' teachings just as he used Mark for many of Jesus' deeds (the **Mark-Matthew hypothesis** associated especially with M. Goulder); but if so, why did Luke often rearrange Matthew's order of Jesus' teachings? Or could it be that in the main, **Luke** used Mark and Q, but that he also **used Matthew**, only **subsidiarily** (a theory that would explain the so-called minor agreements of Matthew and Luke against Mark)?

ELABORATIONS OF MARK-Q Proposing a **four-document hypothesis**, B. H. Streeter added to Mark and Q a source M for the sayings of Jesus distinctive to Matthew and a source L for most of the matter distinctive to Luke. He also advanced the **Proto-Luke theory**: the first edition of Luke's Gospel consisted only of Q + L, to which Luke later added a preface and the birth stories of John the Baptist and Jesus and interspersed Marcan material. There is no general agreement on Streeter's proposals.

Marcan priority enjoys more favor than does Q, about which there is some uncertainty. Perhaps we should think of Q as a body of loose notes jotted down by Matthew. His Gospel often arranges and collects the sayings of Jesus topically instead of chronologically, as do also the other Gospels, though to a lesser degree. In contrast with Matthew, Luke may have used Mark as a supplement rather than as the backbone of his narrative; but this possibility falls far short of certainty. It does not follow that where Matthew and Luke used Mark or another common source, such as Q, their testimony is inferior. Rather, they wanted to preserve the unity of the apostolic tradition about Jesus, because that tradition was anchored in history and deserved a united testimony in its favor. Where they change Mark or any other earlier source, they do so not in misleading ways but in ways that combat misinterpretation of the earlier accounts, add further details, omit others, and elaborate so as to bring out a variety of theological implications.

Form Criticism of the Gospels

TASK The earliest Christians had none of the four Gospels, much less all four. In the first decades of the twentieth century, therefore, German scholarship set for itself the ambitious task of inferring by literary analysis what the oral tradition about Jesus was like before it came to be written down in the Gospels. For example, from the beginning of Christianity the story of Jesus' arrest, trial, and crucifixion (the passion) must have been told and retold at the Lord's Supper and in sermons. Then, as the need for instruction in Christian doctrine and conduct arose, isolated bits of tradition about the words and deeds of Jesus were recalled as an authoritative pattern for such doctrine and conduct. Should Christians marry? Divorce? Pay taxes? The oral tradition about Jesus was kept alive in the answering of these and similar questions.

METHOD Form critics try to determine the nature and content of the oral tradition by classifying individual units of the written gospel material according to their form and usage in the early church. The technical term for an individual unit is ↓**pericope**. According to form criticism, pericopes fall into different categories: (1) ↓**apophthegms**, ↓**paradigms**, or **pronouncement stories** (stories climaxing in a saying of Jesus), used for sermon illustrations; (2) **miracle stories**, used as models for the activities of Christian healers and exorcists; (3) **sayings** and **parables**, used for catechetical instruction; (4) **legends**, used to magnify the greatness of Jesus (with perhaps a core of historical truth, but greatly exaggerated); and (5) the **passion story**, used in celebrations of the Lord's Supper and in evangelistic preaching. In its more skeptical expression, this approach assumes that early Christians modified the information about Jesus greatly and invented stories and sayings to meet the needs that arose out of missionary preaching, catechetical instruction, sermonizing, formation of liturgies, doctrinal controversies, and questions of church discipline. As a result, the Gospels tell us more about the ↓*Sitz im Leben* (German for "situation in life") of the early church than about that of Jesus. To determine the truth about Jesus, form critics typically think they must strip away editorial accretions, such as geographical and chronological notations, miraculous features, and doctrinal elements supposedly dating from a period later than Jesus.

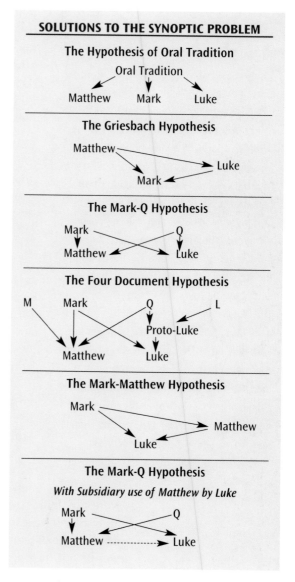

SOLUTIONS TO THE SYNOPTIC PROBLEM

The Hypothesis of Oral Tradition
Oral Tradition
Matthew   Mark   Luke

The Griesbach Hypothesis
Matthew
Mark   Luke

The Mark-Q Hypothesis
Mark   Q
Matthew   Luke

The Four Document Hypothesis
M   Mark   Q   L
Proto-Luke
Matthew   Luke

The Mark-Matthew Hypothesis
Mark
Matthew
Luke

The Mark-Q Hypothesis
With Subsidiary use of Matthew by Luke
Mark   Q
Matthew ------------→ Luke

DEVELOPMENT The Old Testament scholar J. ↓Wellhausen fostered form criticism of the Gospels. M. ↓Dibelius popularized it. K. L. Schmidt convinced many that the geographical and chronological framework in Mark came by Mark's own invention. And **R.** ↓**Bultmann** (best known of the form critics) concluded after detailed analysis that almost all of the gospel tradition was fabricated or highly distorted. A characteristic line of reasoning is

pericope: puh-RIK-uh-pee ■ apophthegm: AP-uhf-them´ ■ paradigms: PAIR-uh-dimz ■ *Sitz im Leben:* ZITS im LAY-buhn ■ Wellhausen: VEHL-houz-en ■ Dibelius: di-BAY-lee-uhs ■ Bultmann: BOOLT-mahn

Bultmann writes concerning Jesus' entry into Jerusalem on Palm Sunday that "the securing of an animal to ride on is, in this story, a manifestly legendary characteristic, indeed, . . . it is a fairy-tale motif. But the rest of the story is also legendary or at least strongly influenced by legend, and the assumption that has to be made if we are to take the story as history, the assumption namely, that Jesus intended to fulfil the prophecy in Zech. 9.9 and that the crowd recognized the ass as the Messiah's beast of burden, is absurd." Similarly, "the point of the story ['of the empty tomb'] is that the empty tomb proves the Resurrection . . . . The story is an apologetic legend . . . . Originally there was no difference between the Resurrection of Jesus and his Ascension; this distinction first arose as a consequence of the Easter legends, which eventually necessitated a special story of an ascension to heaven" (*The History of the Synoptic Tradition*, 2d ed. [New York: Harper & Row, 1968], 261–62, 290).

that since Christians believed in the deity of Jesus, they justified their belief by concocting stories in which he performed a miracle. We should, thought Bultmann, ↓demythologize the Gospels (take away the myths) to make the Christian message palatable to modern people, who from their naturalistic standpoint can no longer accept the supernatural claims of the Gospels on Jesus' behalf.

EVALUATION Form criticism has placed salutary emphasis on literary analysis as a means toward reconstructing the oral gospel tradition and on the continuing relevance of Jesus' words and deeds for the life of the early church. His openness toward Gentiles, for example, must have helped the entrance of Gentiles into the church. But utility was not the only factor. Form critics have not allowed enough room for the sheer **biographical interest** that early Christians must have had in Jesus. If those Christians really did appeal to his words and deeds to justify their beliefs and practices—as form critics themselves admit, indeed, emphasize—then the strongest motives existed for remembering him. Even the Apostle Paul, who apparently had not known Jesus, could quote no higher authority.

Nor have form critics allowed for the possibility that the gospel tradition was preserved because it was **true** as well as **useful** for Christian evangelism, teaching, and liturgy. The **single generation** between Jesus and the writing of the Gospels did not allow enough time for extensive fabrication of myths concerning him. Mythology does not normally develop in less than half a century. Yet the early Christians were proclaiming Jesus as a risen and exalted Savior-God almost immediately after his death. Moreover, during the first decades of church history the **hope of Jesus' soon return** burned brightly, so that the early Christians would not have felt much need to fabricate more information about him than was already available.

Form critics seem also to have forgotten that both Christian and anti-Christian **eyewitnesses** of Jesus' career must have deterred wholesale fabrication and distortion of information. Throughout the New Testament numerous references indicate that early Christians valued highly the factor of eyewitness in establishing testimonial reliability. For examples, see Luke 1:1–4; John 1:14; 20:30–31; 1 Corinthians 15:5–8; 1 John 1:1–4. Not only would both friendly and

"To the married I give this command—not I, but the Lord: A wife must not separate from her husband. But even if she does separate she is to remain unmarried or be reconciled to her husband. And a husband must not divorce his wife" (Paul in 1 Corinthians 7:10–11).

demythologize: dee´mith-OL-uh-jīz

unfriendly eyewitnesses have provided a restraining influence, but also their recollection of Jesus' teaching and example would have been mined for solutions to ecclesiastical and doctrinal problems, for answers to inquiries from prospective converts, and for apology in the face of malicious charges. There is more than one reason, then, not to underestimate the factor of eyewitness.

Nor must we think that all ancient people gullibly accepted every tale of the supernatural they heard. **Skepticism** in the Greco-Roman world was widespread. Even among the disciples evidence had to overcome doubt, as in the case of Thomas, who at first disbelieved the report of Jesus' resurrection. Had Jesus not been the arresting figure portrayed in the Gospels, why the great stir about him? Why was he crucified? Why did people follow him and continue to believe in him and proclaim him as Savior, even and quickly after he had died the death of a criminal? Would they have been willing to suffer and die, as they did, for a false tradition of their own making? And especially, why did Jews, trained from childhood to worship only the one invisible God, feel constrained to worship a human being whom they had seen and known? If the Gospels are not reliable, we draw a blank at the beginning of Christianity. But the **dramatic upsurge of Christianity** demands an explanation equal to the phenomenon.

Very early in the second century, probably in its first decade, the church father Papias passed on a **tradition** that Mark wrote down Peter's reminis-

"Many have undertaken to draw up an account of the things that have been fulfilled among us, just as they were handed down to us by those who from the first were eyewitnesses and servants of the word" (Luke 1:1–2).

A street in Hierapolis, where Papias was bishop

Calcified terraces at Hierapolis

cences of Jesus. There are not sufficient reasons to doubt this tradition or the reliability of the Gospels in general. On the contrary, the texts of the four Gospels contain numerous indications of authenticity. **Realistic details** abound—references to places, names, and customs unnecessary to the overall story—just as one expects in accounts deriving from eyewitnesses. Descriptions of legal practices and social conditions in Palestine vis-à-vis the Hellenistic world exhibit an amazing accuracy.[1] Later Christians would have glorified the twelve apostles (as did later Christian literature) rather than **unflatteringly portraying them** as often bumbling, thickheaded, unbelieving, and cowardly. Why would **sayings of Jesus embarrassingly difficult** to interpret have been invented? Their very difficulty implies authenticity. It is also doubtful that wholesale distortion and fabrication would have produced the large amount of Semitically parallelistic poetry evident in Jesus' teaching as recorded by the evangelists. The same thing is true concerning other traits of its **Semitic style**, which shines through even though the Gospels were written in Greek, a non-Semitic language.

The absence of **parables** from the Letters of the New Testament shows that early Christians did not use parables as a pedagogical device and are therefore unlikely to have created them in the Gospels. Similarly, the absence in the letters of the christological title "**the Son of Man**" (frequent in the Gospels) shows it to be distinctive and thus characteristic of Jesus. Conversely, the failure of the Gospels to say anything about many of the **burning issues**

1. See A. N. Sherwin-White, *Roman Society and Roman Law in the New Testament* (Oxford: Clarendon, 1963), chapter 6 and pages 186ff.

The Sayings of Jesus

- A saying of Jesus embarrassingly difficult: "No one knows about that day or hour, neither even the angels in heaven nor the Son [!], but only the Father" (Mark 13:32).
- A saying of Jesus in Semitically poetic parallelism: "Ask and it will be given to you; seek and you will find; knock and the door will be opened to you" (Luke 11:9).

reflected in Acts and the Letters (such as whether or not Gentile converts should be circumcised) shows that the early Christians did not read their own later developments of doctrine wholesale into Jesus' mouth. Paul provides a good example: He separated his own pronouncements on marriage and divorce from the Lord's (1 Corinthians 7:6, 7, 8, 10, 12, 17, 25, 26, 28, 29, 32, 35, 40). Only a positive assessment of the gospel tradition adequately explains the beginnings of Christianity and the literary features of the Gospels and Letters.

↓*Kerygma*

The prominent British scholar **C. H. Dodd** offered an alternative to skeptical form criticism by noting a common pattern in the sermons of the early chapters in Acts (especially 10:34–43) and in the Letters of Paul where Paul occasionally summarizes the gospel (for example, Romans 1:1–4; 10:9; 1 Corinthians 11:23–26; 15:3–7):

- Jesus has inaugurated the fulfillment of messianic prophecy.
- He went about doing good and performing miracles.
- He was crucified according to God's plan.
- He was raised and exalted to heaven.
- He will return in judgment.
- Therefore repent, believe, and be baptized.

This pattern Dodd called the *kerygma* (Greek for "proclamation" or "preaching"). Gradually, the bare outline of this kerygmatic pattern came to be filled with stories, sayings, and parables from Jesus' life. As eyewitnesses began to die off, the Gospels were written for a permanent record. Also, as the gospel spread geographically far from Palestine to places where eyewitnesses were not available for confirmation, the need arose for trustworthy written records to be used by Christians in their preaching about Jesus' words and deeds. Thus the Gospel of Mark is an expanded *kerygma* in written form.[2]

A common idea is that at first the Christians did not even think of writing about the life of Jesus, because they expected him to return in the immediate future. When decade after decade he failed to do so, it dawned on them that more formal and fixed accounts were needed to fill the ever-widening gap. This idea contains some truth. Nevertheless, the expectation of a nearly immediate return of Jesus is easily overestimated. Close scrutiny of relevant texts in the New Testament shows that early Christians looked for the second coming as a possibility within their lifetimes, but not as a certainty. So the books of the New Testament do not stem from embarrassment over the delay in Jesus' return. They exude far too much confidence for us ever to think so.

2. C. H. Dodd, *The Apostolic Preaching and Its Development* (London: Hodder & Stoughton, 1936).

---

kerygma: ki-RIG-muh

Redaction Criticism

After World War II, scholars began to analyze the Gospels as unified compositions carefully edited (redacted) by their authors to project distinctive theological views. A well-known example of this approach is **H. ↓Conzelmann's** hypothesis that Luke reinterpreted Jesus' ministry to be, not the final stage of history (as Conzelmann alleges early Christians believed), but the midpoint of history with the age of the church and the second coming to follow—hence Luke's addition of the book of Acts to his Gospel. Usually, the particular theological standpoint of the evangelist is attributed to an entire school of thought within the church. The contribution of redaction criticism consists in its identifying ways in which the evangelists tailored earlier materials about Jesus to the needs of their own times and circumstances. Thus his words and deeds do not appear as fossils of dead history, but as applications to contemporary life (as form critics say was already being done with individual units of tradition in the preceding oral stage). The danger of redaction criticism lies in a tendency to neglect the importance of earlier traditions as such, an importance seen in the fact that the evangelists saw those traditions as worth incorporating, tailoring, and applying.

Other Kinds of Higher Criticism

Other kinds of higher criticism jostle for attention too, though none of them has attained the prominence of the foregoing. **Composition criticism** pays attention to editorial arrangements of and additions to tradition (and as such is scarcely distinguishable from redaction criticism). **Narrative criticism** tries to establish the story line of a gospel. **Tradition criticism** traces the origin and development of theological themes present in the Gospels. **Rhetorical criticism** seeks evidence of persuasive art in the presentation of dominical tradition. **Literary criticism** studies the impact of style on the message of the Gospels. **Genre criticism**, looking for the significance of larger literary forms, asks, What is a Gospel? How does it differ from other comparable books? Why does it differ? **Canon criticism** stresses the effect on the meaning of a Gospel had by its association with other biblical books. **Tendency criticism** keeps an eye on the influence of theological conflicts in the early church. **Social science criticism** studies the influence of societal oppositions—wealth versus poverty, freedom versus slavery, honor versus shame, city versus countryside, and so forth—on Christian life and belief as represented by the Gospels. **Anthropological criticism** seeks to initiate modern readers into the culturally different ways of thinking and acting that the Gospels reflect. **Reader response criticism** examines the efforts of readers to make their own sense of the Gospels and pays special attention to reading between lines where the evangelists have left matters unexpressed or vague. **Structural criticism** examines modes of thought underlying the

---

Conzelmann: KONT-suhl-mahn

Gospels and common to human expression. **Deconstruction** tries to show that in and of itself the text of a gospel contains no meaning. These kinds of criticism have application outside the Gospels too.

The Study of Jesus' Life

Most contemporary scholars agree that a full-scale biography of Jesus is impossible, because the Gospels are very selective in the amount and kind of information they present about him. But during the nineteenth century, before this restriction was felt so keenly, several outstanding biographies of Jesus appeared. A skeptical treatment by the German scholar **D. F. Strauss** (1835) concluded that most of the material in the Gospels is mythological. **E. Renan**'s life of Christ (1863) became famous for its literary beauty. This French author portrayed Jesus as an amiable carpenter who turned into an apocalyptist. In 1883 A. ↓**Edersheim**, a converted Jew, produced his widely used and conservative *Life and Times of Jesus the Messiah* from a background of acquaintance with rabbinic literature. At the start of the twentieth century a typically liberal view—outstandingly represented by the German scholar **A. von Harnack**—saw in Jesus a good example of sacrificial service to fellow human beings and a teacher of lofty ethical ideals, but not a divine-human redeemer.

In 1906 **Albert ↓Schweitzer** shook the theological world with his *Quest of the Historical Jesus*. It was a critical survey of some modern studies of Jesus' life. Schweitzer argued that liberal treatments rested more on preconceived notions than on data in the Gospels. According to him, Jesus himself thought that God's kingdom was about to arrive on earth and that God would install him as the Messiah. In fact, Jesus told the twelve disciples that God would send him as the Son of Man (a superhuman messiah) to establish the kingdom before

Kinds of Biblical Criticism

Textual (lower) criticism = determining the original wording of the New Testament books

Higher criticism = determining the historical circumstances of the New Testament books

Source criticism = determining the use of earlier materials

Form criticism = determining the oral tradition prior to writing

Redaction criticism = determining distinctive editorial emphases

Composition criticism = determining the integration of tradition and distinctive editorial emphases

Narrative criticism = determining the story line

Tradition criticism = determining the origin and development of theological themes

Rhetorical criticism = determining the use of techniques of persuasion

Literary criticism = determining the style of writing

Genre criticism = determining the type of book

Canon criticism = determining the effect on the meaning of a biblical book from a consideration of other biblical books

Tendency criticism = determining the influence of theological conflicts

Social science criticism = determining the influence of class differences

Anthropological criticism = determining ways of thinking and acting different from those of modern readers

Reader response criticism = determining the ways readers understand the text, regardless of what the author intended

Structural criticism = determining underlying modes of thought

Deconstructive criticism = determining meaninglessness

they completed a preaching mission throughout Galilee (Matthew 10:23). When this expectation failed, Jesus became increasingly convinced that he would have to die for God to bring the kingdom.

Meanwhile, Jesus revealed the secret of his messiahship to Peter, James, and John at the transfiguration. Peter then betrayed this secret to the rest of the Twelve on the occasion of his great confession (Matthew 16:13–20; Mark 8:27–30; Luke 9:18–20). (To achieve this reconstruction Schweitzer had to switch the order of Peter's confession and Jesus' transfiguration as given in the Synoptics.) Judas then betrayed the secret to the Jewish authorities, who set in motion the events that culminated in Jesus' death. Jesus himself courageously but foolishly thought that God would raise him from the dead and immediately reveal him to the world on the clouds of heaven to establish the kingdom on earth. Such an event did not happen, of course; so for Schweitzer, Jesus became a tragic and mysterious figure, hard for moderns to understand but worthy of imitation in his selfless dedication.

Schweitzer's portrayal of Jesus has not received general acceptance. He laid too much stress on Matthew 10:23, which can be interpreted in other ways. He disregarded statements by Jesus that God's kingdom had already arrived. He failed to explain adequately why Jesus gave large amounts of ethical teaching. Someone who believed and proclaimed that God's kingdom was going to arrive in the next few weeks or months would hardly have felt the need for instructing people at length how to behave in present evil society. Schweitzer's great contribution lay, rather, in his forcing a reconsideration of the ↓eschatological teaching of Jesus and the **messianic** implications of his ministry, both of which were being passed over lightly by most liberal scholars and even now are being negated again by such scholars, sometimes with the result that the historical Jesus is portrayed as less a Jewish religious leader and as more a peasant philosopher similar to the Cynics.

In the present state of research on the life of Jesus, disparate opinions clamor for recognition. The lingering influence of Bultmann causes many to reject most of the gospel tradition. Some of Bultmann's former students, dubbed "post-Bultmannians," accepted a bit more as authentic; but the America-based and over-publicized **Jesus Seminar** has pronounced only 18 percent of Jesus' sayings recorded in the canonical Gospels as certainly or probably authentic and only 16 percent of his deeds recorded in those Gospels as certainly or probably authentic.

> "During the second phase of the Jesus Seminar . . . the Fellows examined 387 reports of 176 events, in most of which Jesus is the principal actor, although occasionally John the Baptist, Simon Peter, or Judas is featured. Of the 176 events, only ten were given a red rating (red indicates that the Fellows had a relatively high level of confidence that the event actually took place). An additional nineteen were colored pink (pink suggests that the event probably occurred). The combined number of red and pink events (29) amounts to 16% of the total (176). That is slightly lower than the 18% of the sayings [of Jesus]—primarily parables and aphorisms—assigned to the red and pink categories in *The Five Gospels* " (R. W. Funk and the Jesus Seminar, *The Acts of Jesus: The Search for the Authentic Deeds of Jesus* [San Francisco: HarperSanFrancisco, 1998], 1).

---

eschatological: es´kat-uh-LOJ-i-kuhl, "having to do with the 'end' of history"

Mediating scholars accept a larger proportion as authentic but reject the rest. Others have forsaken the quest of the historical Jesus in favor of literary, political, economic, feminist, sociological, and psychological analyses. Conservative scholars find good historical and theological reasons for full acceptance of the gospel records. Such acceptance does not imply that the evangelists always quoted Jesus verbatim and never elaborated the tradition of his words and deeds. On the contrary, differences among the Gospels imply **editorial arrangement**, **paraphrasing**, and **interpretation**, all of which can be perfectly legitimate ways to convey someone else's meaning and significance. Nor do conservative scholars insist on a complete and always chronological account of Jesus' activities. But measured by the purpose for which the Gospels were written—to proclaim the good news about him for evangelism and church life—the Gospels merit our trust.

Summary

Extrabiblical sources confirm the historicity of Jesus of Nazareth but offer few details of his life, for which the canonical Gospels provide the main source. The first three of them are called "synoptic" because they often parallel each other. Of the hypotheses suggested to explain their similarities, the most popular is that Matthew and Luke borrowed from Mark a great deal of narrative concerning Jesus' deeds and from a hypothesized collection of Jesus' teachings called Q. Individual units of the Gospels are classified according to their form in an attempt to discover the oral tradition that was circulating about Jesus before it was written down. Adoptions and revisions of earlier material are studied to discover the overall emphases of each evangelist. The telling and editing of information about Jesus raises questions about its historical reliability. These questions have received widely different answers, including an extremely skeptical one; but good reasons support the essential trustworthiness, both historical and theological, of the canonical Gospels.

People to Remember

R. Bultmann	J. J. Griesbach	Albert Schweitzer
H. Conzelmann	A. von Harnack	D. F. Strauss
M. Dibelius	Josephus	B. H. Streeter
C. H. Dodd	Lucian	Suetonius
A. Edersheim	Pliny the Younger	Tacitus
W. R. Farmer	E. Renan	J. Wellhausen
B. Gerhardsson	H. Riesenfeld	
M. Goulder	K. L. Schmidt	

Terms to Remember

agrapha	form criticism	redaction criticism
apocryphal gospels	higher criticism	*Sitz im Leben*
apophthegm	kerygma	source criticism
demythologize	Oxyrhynchus papyri	synoptic
eschatological	paradigm	
evangelists	pericope	

How Much Did You Learn?

- Identify and evaluate the major and minor sources for our knowledge of Jesus' life.
- Distinguish higher criticism from textual (lower) criticism, and compare and contrast the different subtypes of higher criticism.
- Explain the various hypotheses put forward to solve the synoptic problem. What are their strengths and weaknesses?
- Discuss the range of opinions on the Gospels' historical reliability.
- Distinguish the views of A. Schweitzer, R. Bultmann, and C. H. Dodd on the historical Jesus.
- To which of their views does the view of the Jesus Seminar most closely correspond?

For Further Discussion

- How do literary interrelationships, differences among the Gospels in wording and order, and the use and revision of source materials affect belief in the divine origin and inspiration of the Bible?
- To what extent, if any, should the Gospels be made palatable or acceptable to modern ways of thinking (a major question raised by Bultmann's program of demythologization)?
- What is a "myth"? What is its relation to history? To universal human experience?
- According to definitions, does the Bible contain myths?

For Further Investigation

The following books and articles contain extensive further bibliography.

Extrabiblical Material

Evans, C. A. "Jesus in Non-Christian Sources." *Dictionary of Jesus and the Gospels.* Edited by J. B. Green and S. McKnight. Downers Grove, Ill.: InterVarsity Press, 1992. Pages 364–68.

Extracanonical Sayings of Jesus. Edited by W. D. Stroker. Atlanta: Scholars Press, 1989.

New Testament Apocrypha. Edited by E. Hennecke and W. Schneemelcher. 2d ed. 2 vols. Philadelphia: Fortress Press, 1963, 1965.

Patterson, S. J., and J. M. Robinson. *The Fifth Gospel: The Gospel of Thomas Comes of Age.* With a new English translation by H.-G. Bethge et al. Harrisburg, Pa.: Trinity Press International, 1998.

Van Voorst, R. E. *Jesus Outside the New Testament: An Introduction to the Ancient Evidence.* Grand Rapids: Eerdmans, 2000.

On Higher Criticism of Various Sorts

The Critical Edition of Q. Edited by J. M. Robinson, P. Hoffmann, and J. S. Kloppenborg. Leuven: Peeters, 2000.

Holmberg, B. *Sociology and the New Testament: An Appraisal.* Minneapolis: Fortress Press, 1990.

Ladd, G. E. *The New Testament and Criticism.* Grand Rapids: Eerdmans, 1966.

McKnight, E. V. *What Is Form Criticism?* Philadelphia: Fortress Press, 1969.

New Testament Criticism and Interpretation. Edited by D. A. Black and D. S. Dockery. Grand Rapids: Zondervan, 1991.

Patte, D. *Structural Exegesis for New Testament Critics.* Minneapolis: Fortress Press, 1990.

Perrin, N. *What Is Redaction Criticism?* Philadelphia: Fortress Press, 1969.

Petersen, N. R. *Literary Criticism for New Testament Critics.* Philadelphia: Fortress Press, 1978.

Powell, M. A. *What Is Narrative Criticism?* Minneapolis: Fortress Press, 1990.

To appreciate some of the issues debated by source, form, and redaction critics, carefully compare Matthew's and Luke's accounts of the Sermon on the Mount/Plain (chapters 5–7 and 6:20–49, respectively), the different accounts of the Last Supper (Matthew 26:20–35; Mark 14:17–31; Luke 22:14–38; John 13–17; 1 Corinthians 11:23–26), or almost any other part of the gospel tradition.

On the Historical Jesus

Authenticating the Activities of Jesus. Edited by B. Chilton and C. A. Evans. Leiden: Brill, 1999.

Authenticating the Words of Jesus. Edited by B. Chilton and C. A. Evans. Leiden: Brill, 1999.

Blomberg, C. L. *Jesus and the Gospels.* Nashville: Broadman & Holman, 1997.

Bock, D. L. *Studying the Historical Jesus.* Grand Rapids: Baker, 2002.

Brown, C. "Historical Jesus, Quest of." *Dictionary of Jesus and the Gospels.* Downers Grove, Ill.: InterVarsity Press, 1992. Pages 326–41.

The Historical Jesus: A Sheffield Reader. Edited by C. A. Evans and S. E. Porter. Sheffield, England: Sheffield Academic Press, 1995.

Powell, M. A. *Jesus as a Figure in History: How Modern Historians View the Man from Galilee.* Louisville: Westminster John Knox, 1998.

Witherington, B., III. *The Jesus Quest: The Third Search for the Jew of Nazareth.* Downers Grove, Ill.: InterVarsity Press, 1995.

In general terms compare *The Life of Apollonius* by Philostratus, parts of which are quoted in C. K. Barrett, *The New Testament Background: Selected Documents,* 2d ed. (San Francisco: Harper & Row, 1987), pages 82–84, with the portraits of Jesus given in the Gospels; also H. C. Kee, *The Origins of Christianity* (Englewood Cliffs, N.J.: Prentice-Hall, 1973), pages 211–29.

CHAPTER

6

AN INTRODUCTORY OVERVIEW OF JESUS' PUBLIC LIFE AND MINISTRY

Overview:

- Dates
- Obscurity
- Popularity Turning into Rejection
- Excursus on the Miracles and Resurrection
- Teaching
- Summary

Study Goals—Learn:

- The possible dates of Jesus' public life
- The general developments and the ultimate outcome of his ministry
- The origins of his teaching and how he went beyond them
- The framework and primary motifs of his preaching

The hill of the Beatitudes

Dates

The dates of Jesus' public ministry remain somewhat obscure, partly because of uncertainty concerning the way Luke figured the beginning of Tiberius's reign (Luke 3:1). But the **three-and-one-half-year period** leading up to A.D. **33** is as likely as any, though many scholars prefer A.D. 30. Traditionally, this span of time has been divided into a **year of obscurity**, a **year of popularity**, and a **year of rejection**.

Obscurity

"And the child [John the Baptist] was growing and becoming strong in spirit; and he was in the desert until the day of his public appearance to Israel" (Luke 1:80).

The year of obscurity began with the heralding ministry of **John the Baptist.** He may have grown up in the Essene community at Qumran, but on his appearance in public he looks to be a lone, hermit-like prophet whose preaching to crowds and baptizing of people in preparation for the coming of God's kingdom differ from the social withdrawal of those Essenes. By the time of John it may have been required of Gentile proselytes that they baptize themselves as a rite of initiation into Judaism, but John required baptism for *Jews* as a sign of repentance from sins. Or if proselyte baptism had not yet come into Judaism (the evidence is disputed), John may have borrowed from the Essenes their practice of ritual self-washings and endowed it with new significance.[1] Under either theory of origin, John innovated by administering the rite himself. Therefore "baptism *of* John" means "baptism *by* John." Jesus received this **baptism.** Satan **tempted** him. And having resisted temptation, Jesus made his **first disciples**, started

1. See J. E. Taylor, *The Immerser: John the Baptist Within Second Temple Judaism* (Grand Rapids: Eerdmans, 1997), 64–69, and further bibliography there.

MAIN EVENTS IN JESUS' PUBLIC MINISTRY		
Year of Obscurity	**Year of Popularity**	**Year of Rejection**
Baptism	Large crowds	Peter's confession of Jesus' messiahship
Temptation	Choice of the Twelve	Predictions of passion and resurrection
Preaching and teaching	More preaching and teaching	Transfiguration
Miracle working and exorcisms	More miracle working and exorcisms	Raising of Lazarus
		Passion Week
		Triumphal Entry
		Temple cleansing
		Last Supper
		Arrest and trials
		Crucifixion
		Resurrection
		Postresurrection appearances
		Ascension

preaching, **teaching**, and performing **miracles** and **exorcisms**, mainly in Galilee but occasionally also on pilgrimages to Jerusalem.

Popularity Turning into Rejection

The activities of preaching, teaching, and performing miracles and exorcisms continued in Jesus' year of popularity. Increasingly large crowds attended him, so much so that he sought privacy for himself and his disciples, not always successfully. The year of rejection may be something of a misnomer, for large crowds kept flocking to Jesus. When able to gain some privacy, he devoted himself to teaching the disciples. Sometime during this period Peter, speaking for the rest of them, **confessed the messiahship of Jesus;** and Jesus began **predicting his death and resurrection.** The **transfiguration** occurred. The **last journey to Jerusalem** began. According to the Fourth Gospel, Jesus' **raising of ↓Lazarus** from the dead convinced members of the Sanhedrin they should eliminate Jesus and, with him, what they

Lazarus: LAZ-uh-ruhs

Old map of Jerusalem from Medeba in Moab

Rules for Trials

In capital cases, later (and possibly earlier) Jewish trial procedure required that a trial begin during the daytime; that if unfinished it be adjourned during nighttime; that a majority of only one sufficed for acquittal, but that a majority of at least two was necessary for conviction; that a verdict of acquittal might be given on the very first day, but that a verdict of guilty must be delayed until the next day so that the judges might carefully weigh a condemnatory decision overnight; that therefore no trial should be held on the eve of a Sabbath or festival day; and that the accused not be forced to witness against themselves or be convicted on their own testimony (Babylonian Talmud, *Sanhedrin* 4.1.3–5a; 5:1). It is possible that the Sadducees, who dominated the Sanhedrin in Jesus' time, lacked the consideration for accused people that characterized the later Sanhedrin, dominated by heirs of the Pharisees. On the other hand, the danger members of the Sanhedrin thought Jesus posed may well have led them to violate their normal rules of trial procedure.

thought to be the threat of a messianic revolt. According to the Synoptic Gospels, which do not mention the raising of Lazarus, Jesus' **cleansing of the temple** after his **triumphal entry** on Palm Sunday made the Sanhedrin determine to eliminate him. Judas arranged to betray him.

The Seven Last Words

- "Father, forgive them, for they do not know what they are doing" (Luke 23:34).
- "I tell you truly, today you will be with me in paradise" (Luke 23:43, spoken to the repentant criminal crucified with Jesus).
- "Woman, look—your son! . . . Look—your mother!" (John 19:26–27, spoken to Jesus' mother Mary and to the beloved disciple).
- "I am thirsty" (John 19:28).
- "My God, my God, why have you forsaken me?" (Matthew 27:46; Mark 15:34).
- "It is finished" (John 19:30).
- "Father, into your hands I commit my spirit" (Luke 23:46).

Last Supper

The Last Supper, a Passover meal, took place the following Thursday evening. The Passover liturgy included a blessing; the passing of several cups of wine around the table; a recital of the exodus story by the host; an eating of the roasted lamb, unleavened bread, and bitter herbs; and the singing of psalms. In line with the Jewish expectation of a messianic banquet, Jesus had already compared the kingdom of God to a supper. He had also described his suffering as a cup to be drunk. Furthermore, the Passover commemorated God's redeeming Israel from Egyptian slavery by virtue of the sacrifice of a Passover lamb. But Jesus had intimated that Israel was now rejected. Therefore he instituted the **Lord's Supper** to commemorate the redemption of a new people of God, the disciples, from slavery to sin by virtue of his own sacrificial death.

Death and Resurrection

The **arrest** and **Jewish trial** of Jesus took place Thursday night, the **Roman trial** early Good Friday morning, the **crucifixion** from midmorning to midafternoon, and the **burial** in late afternoon.

Jesus' sayings spoken from the cross are called "**The Seven Last Words.**" Jesus' **resurrection** occurred very early on Sunday, and Jesus appeared to his disciples a number of times during **forty days of postresurrection ministry.** Finally, he **ascended** to heaven little more than a week before the outpouring of the Holy Spirit on the Day of Pentecost.

EXCURSUS
The Miracles and Resurrection of Jesus

MIRACLES

The miracles of Jesus raise a question of the supernatural, to which people who consider themselves scientifically minded often object. But if there is a God who has acted in history, especially by revealing himself through Jesus Christ, how else may we expect him to have acted than supernaturally? If he had not, we could point to a lack of historical evidence that it really was God acting. The very fact that other religions often lay claim to the supernatural shows that people really do expect the divine to show itself in ways not subject to naturalistic explanations.

A truly scientific attitude will keep open the possibility of supernaturalism and test the claims to supernatural events in past history by searching questions: Were there eyewitnesses? If so, was their number sufficient and their character and intelligence trustworthy? How tenaciously did they maintain their testimony under pressure? Are there early written records or only late records written long after myth-making could have corrupted oral tradition? Questions like these put the claims of other religions to supernatural events in a poor light, the claims of Christianity in a favorable light. There were many eyewitnesses to Jesus' career. Those who allied themselves with him endured ostracism, torture, and even death for what they proclaimed concerning him—and they felt constrained to make proclamation even at such costs. They could have saved themselves by admitting falsehood in their testimony or simply by ceasing to testify.

Furthermore, the records of Jesus' ministry began to be written well within half a century after he lived. The very supernaturalism in the stories makes it unlikely that they were fabricated and accepted during the period when eyewitnesses were still living. Similarly, Paul would hardly have dared to argue from miracles that he had performed among the Galatians if they had never seen him do any. Thus the claim of other religions to the miraculous does not at all undercut Christianity's similar claim when both are tested by the tools of historical research in an open-minded way.[2]

2. See further C. S. Lewis, *Miracles* (New York: Macmillan, 1947); and for representative technical discussions, E. L. Mascall, *The Secularization of Christianity* (New York: Holt, Rinehart & Winston, 1966); H. van der Loos, *The Miracles of Jesus* (Leiden: Brill, 1965); L. Sabourin, *The Divine Miracles Discussed and Defended* (Rome: Catholic Book Agency, 1977); J. A. Cover, "Miracles and Christian Theism," *Reason for the Hope Within*, ed. M. J. Murray (Grand Rapids: Eerdmans, 1999).

THE RESURRECTION

That Jesus really did rise from the dead is supported by the **shortcomings of alternative hypotheses.** One is that Jesus only appeared to die, that he lapsed into a **coma** and later revived for a while. But his death is indicated by the brutal beating he endured, by the six hours of hanging on a cross, by the thrusting through of his abdomen with a spear and the resultant gushing out of watery fluid and blood, by his partial embalming and being wrapped up in grave clothes, and finally by his being sealed in a tomb.

Others hypothesize that the disciples **stole** Jesus' corpse. But to do so they would have had to overpower the Roman guards, an unlikely event, or bribe them, equally unlikely, since the guards knew they would be subject to capital punishment for failing to protect Jesus' body from theft. That the graveclothes lay undisturbed (not even unwrapped) and the turban still twirled up and set to one side militates against a hasty removal of the corpse by theft. Thieves do not usually take time to tidy up. Here they would probably have taken the body along with its wrappings.

> "So does he who supplies you with the Spirit and works miracles among you do so because of works of the law or because of hearing with faith?" (Galatians 3:5).

The surprise, even unbelief, of the disciples at Jesus' resurrection further shows that they did not steal his corpse, unless their surprise and unbelief were fabricated to make the story look convincing. But such a fabrication seems "too clever by half." It also seems unlikely that stories would have been fabricated in which the apostles are first portrayed as unbelievers in the resurrection, for the early church soon began to revere the apostles.

Yet others hypothesize that the disciples experienced **hallucinations.** But the New Testament gives evidence of Jesus' appearances in different locations at different times to different parties numbering from one to more than five hundred (1 Corinthians 15:5–8). The appearances were too many and too varied to have been hallucinations. Furthermore, the disciples were psychologically unprepared for hallucinations, since they did not expect Jesus to rise and actually disbelieved the first reports that he had risen. All that unbelieving Jews would have had to do when the report of Jesus' resurrection began circulating was to produce the corpse. But they never did.

The same objection militates against hypothesizing that Jesus' disciples came to the **wrong tomb.** Why did unbelieving Jews fail to produce his corpse from the right tomb? They must have known where it was, for they had induced Pilate to put a guard there.

Still others hypothesize that the disciples modeled Jesus' resurrection after the **dying and rising of gods** in pagan mythology. But the differences loom far greater than the similarities. History does not provide a framework for the myths as it does for the accounts of Jesus' resurrection. The New Testament draws no connection with the annual dying and reviving of nature, as in the pagan myths, associated as they are with the agricultural cycle and fertility. The matter-of-fact style of reporting in the Gospels contrasts sharply with the fantasies that abound in myths. And accounts of the resurrection appear immediately in the early church, without the lengthy interim required for an evolution of detailed mythology. Paul's triumphant statement that most of the more than five hundred people who saw Jesus at the same time and place were still alive and therefore could be asked looks unbelievably audacious if the whole story came by way of mythological development (1 Corinthians 15:6).

Something unique must have made the first Jewish disciples change their day of worship **from the Sabbath to Sunday.** Either they were deceived—then again the unbelieving Jews could have stopped Christianity by producing Jesus' corpse—or they foisted a hoax on the world—then it looks **psychologically incredible** that they willingly suffered hardship, torture, and death for what they knew to be false. It also looks inconceivable for the ancient world that fabricators would have made **women the first witnesses** of the empty tomb and the risen Jesus, for women's testimony was distrusted.

One does not have to treat the New Testament as inspired by God to feel the force of the historical evidences for Jesus' resurrection. The gospel accounts and other evidence need explanation even when they are not regarded as divinely authoritative. Making up one's mind beforehand that such a thing could not have happened forms the chief obstacle to faith in the resurrection.

Because Jesus did rise, there is a human being in heaven interceding for those who believe in him as the sacrifice for their sins. His resurrection also provides power for Christian living and guarantees both his return and the resurrection and eternal life of those who believe in him.[3]

3. For the historicity of the resurrection and criticisms of alternative theories, see J. N. D. Anderson, "The Resurrection of Jesus Christ," *Christianity Today*, 29 March 1968, 4[628]–9[633], with the dialogue and overcomment in *Christianity Today*, 12 April 1968, 5[677]–12[684]; G. E. Ladd, *I Believe in the Resurrection of Jesus* (Grand Rapids: Eerdmans, 1975); M. J. Harris, *Raised Immortal* (Grand Rapids: Eerdmans, 1985); idem, *From Grave to Glory* (Grand Rapids: Zondervan, 1990); W. L. Craig, *Assessing the New Testament Evidence for the Historicity of the Resurrection* (Lewiston: Mellen, 1989); *Jesus' Resurrection: Fact or Figment? A Debate Between William Lane Craig and Gerd Lüdemann*, ed. P. Copan and R. K. Tacelli (Downers Grove, Ill.: InterVarsity Press, 2000).

Teaching

Jesus' speech was colorful and picturesque. **Figures of speech** abounded. He often created **epigrams**, not easily forgotten, and delighted in **puns**, which usually fail to come through in translation. Many sayings are set in the **parallelistic forms** of statement characteristic of Semitic poetry.

Parables

Jesus often taught in parables, which were more or less extended figures of speech, often in story form. Interpreters used to assign allegorical meanings to every detail in the parables. The scholarly world then veered toward the view that each parable contains only one didactic point and other details are solely for realism. Now scholars are starting to recognize that no hard and fast distinction exists between a single-point parable and a multifaceted

A Classic Example of Overallegorizing a Parable

According to the early church father Augustine, in the parable of the good Samaritan (Luke 10:30–37):

The wounded man = Adam

Jerusalem = the heavenly city from which Adam fell

The robbers = the devil, who robbed Adam of his immortality

The priest and the Levite = the Old Testament law, incapable of saving anyone

The good Samaritan = Christ, who forgives sin

The inn = the church

The innkeeper = the Apostle Paul

The Golden Rule

"Therefore all things whatever you would want people to do for you, you also do thus for them" (Matthew 7:12).

parable. Allowance must then be made for some allegorism in parables, especially in the longer ones.

In the content of his teaching Jesus built on the Old Testament foundation of **ethical monotheism**, that is, of belief in one God of love and righteousness who acts redemptively and judgmentally in history according to his covenantal relations with human beings. By declaring sins forgiven, claiming to be the judge of everyone's eternal destiny, demanding utter allegiance to himself, making astounding "I am ..." statements, and introducing many sayings in a tone of ultimate authority with *amen* (translated "truly" or "verily"), Jesus put himself forward as a unique person. But he reluctantly accepted and used the term *Christ*, or *Messiah*, because of its dominantly political and militaristic overtones in first-century Judaism. He preferred to speak of himself as "**the Son of Man**" whom Daniel saw in a vision as a **superhuman** figure coming from heaven to judge and rule the whole world (Daniel 7:9–14). But Jesus also associated the **suffering** of the "**Servant of the LORD**" (Isaiah 52:13–53:12) with himself as the Son of Man. Significantly, the designation "Son of Man" occurs for Jesus almost exclusively on his own lips. Among the Jews it was largely or entirely unused in a messianic sense. As a result, Jesus could build up his own definition. The additional term "**Son (of God)**" occurs both in his claims for himself and in the words of others about him.

Jesus' consciousness of uniquely divine sonship expressed itself also in his use of the Aramaic word ↓*abba*, "**Father**," which originated as a child's stammering "Dadda" or "Daddy." Nevertheless, this address escaped over-sentimentality in that children continued to use it after they had grown up. Jesus also taught his disciples to address God as *abba* because of their relation to God through him. In earlier times God had been viewed largely as father of the Israelite nation as a whole. Thus the frequency, warmth, and individualistic emphasis with which Jesus spoke of God's fatherhood mark a distinctive feature of his teaching.

Loving God and loving one's neighbor compose the two main ethical imperatives, according to Jesus. His view of righteous living emphasized inward motivation as opposed to outward show. The **Golden Rule**, which occurs in its positive form, helps define what he meant by loving.

The Kingdom

The message of both John the Baptist and Jesus focused above all on "the kingdom." Often the two phrases "**of God**" and "**of heaven**" modify this term. The phrases are synonymous. Parallel usage occurs in the same pas-

abba: AH-buh

sage. For example, Jesus says in Matthew 19:23–24 that it is difficult for a rich man to enter the kingdom *of heaven*, so difficult, in fact, that it is easier for a camel to go through the eye of a needle than for a rich man to enter the kingdom *of God*. The phrases also alternate in parallel accounts of different gospels. For example, "to such as these [children] belongs the kingdom *of God*" (Mark 10:14) becomes ". . . *of heaven*" in Matthew 19:14. Only the Gospel of Matthew has "kingdom of heaven," because Matthew, it is usually thought, reflects the growing Jewish custom of avoiding divine names for fear of desecrating them. On the other hand, Matthew does not hesitate to use God's name elsewhere; so perhaps "kingdom of heaven" reflects Daniel 2:44 and, like that Old Testament passage, accents universality—just as heaven arches over the whole earth, so also the kingdom encompasses it. Jesus may have used both phrases, his choice depending on the audience and on the emphasis he wished to give. Or Matthew's "kingdom of heaven" represents Jesus' phrase, which the other evangelists translated into "kingdom of God" for Gentiles who might not understand the use of "heaven" for "God." Or, most likely, Jesus regularly used "kingdom of God," and Matthew substituted "kingdom of heaven."

The term *kingdom* carries two meanings: (1) a **sphere** of rule and (2) the **activity** of ruling. Because of the verbal idea in this second meaning, many scholars prefer the translation "the rule (or reign) of God." Both meanings are present in the New Testament use of *kingdom*. Context determines which of the two predominates. The activity of ruling includes the delivering of its subjects from oppression and the bringing of blessing to them as well as the exercise of authority over them.

> **Meanings of the Kingdom**
>
> • An example of "kingdom" as the activity of ruling: "The kingdom of God is within [or 'among'] you" (Luke 17:21). In other words, "God reigns within [or 'among'] you."
>
> • An example of "kingdom" as the sphere of rule: "How hard it is for the rich to enter the kingdom of God!" (Luke 18:24). In other words, "How hard it is for the rich to enter the sphere where God rules!"

REALIZED ESCHATOLOGY John the Baptist and Jesus said that the kingdom was "near" and that people must prepare for it by repenting of their sins (Matthew 3:2; 4:17; Mark 1:14–15). Once his ministry got under way, Jesus said that the kingdom had indeed come: "If I drive out demons by the Spirit of God, then the kingdom of God has come upon you" (Matthew 12:28; Luke 11:20; compare Matthew 11:12–13; Luke 16:16; 17:20–21). In other words, God's rule was invading the world in the person and activity of Jesus. One must therefore enter the kingdom by faith in him (John 3:3). Emphasis on an arrival of the kingdom in his appearance and ministry is called "realized eschatology," a phrase associated with **C. H. Dodd.**

CONSISTENT ESCHATOLOGY In another vein, Jesus also spoke about the kingdom's arrival when the present evil age comes to an end: ". . . until that day when I drink it anew in the kingdom of God" (Mark 14:25); "many will come . . . and recline [at banquet] . . . in the kingdom of heaven" (Matthew

8:11; Luke 13:28–29). The petition Jesus taught his disciples in the Lord's Prayer, "Thy kingdom come," also implies that the kingdom is yet to come. Emphasis on an arrival of the kingdom in the future, particularly in the near future, is called "consistent eschatology," a phrase associated with **Albert Schweitzer.** He himself did not hold to consistent eschatology, but he argued that Jesus held to it.

MYSTERY OF THE KINGDOM Both realized and consistent eschatology receive strong support from passages such as those just mentioned. So Jesus must have taught both present and future forms of the kingdom. Thus the "mystery" of the kingdom consists in the open secret that before God fully imposes his rule on earth when Jesus comes back, believers enjoy its **future blessings in advance.**

Through his preaching, Jesus brought God's rule to the Jews, but on the basis of repentance and faith rather than on a politico-military basis. By rejecting Jesus, most of the Jews, especially their official leaders, rejected God's rule. Consequently, God transferred it to the church (Matthew 21:42–43; compare Acts 8:12; 28:23, 28–31; Romans 14:17; Colossians 1:13) until the restoration of Israel (Matthew 19:28 parallel Luke 22:28–30).[4]

Jesus commissioned his disciples to evangelize the world in the meantime. Then he would return to judge the human race and establish God's kingdom fully and forever.

4. See further the three books by G. E. Ladd, *The Gospel of the Kingdom* (Grand Rapids: Eerdmans, 1959); *The Presence of the Future* (Grand Rapids: Eerdmans, 1974); and *Crucial Questions About the Kingdom of God* (Grand Rapids: Eerdmans, 1952); and, for a broader purview, A. J. McClain, *The Greatness of the Kingdom* (Grand Rapids: Zondervan, 1959).

Summary

Jesus' public ministry probably lasted about three-and-one-half years, either A.D. 30–33 or A.D. 27–30, and traditionally divides into a year of obscurity, a year of popularity, and a year of rejection. John the Baptist prepared the way for Jesus, whose ministry consisted in preaching, teaching, performing miracles and exorcisms, and finally in dying sacrificially for our sins and rising from the dead for our eternal life—all in the service of bringing God's kingdom to earth, that is, imposing God's rule over all the earth and drawing believers into its blessings. To the extent that Jesus' ministry succeeded among his disciples, the kingdom has been realized. To the extent that the rest of the world remains in rebellion against God, his kingdom has yet to come. This tension between the already and the not-yet makes up the mystery of the kingdom, often portrayed in the figurative language of parables. Nodal points in Jesus' public ministry were his baptism; his temptation; Peter's confession of his messiahship; his early predictions of his passion and resurrection; the transfiguration; his raising of Lazarus; his triumphal entry on Palm Sunday; his cleansing of the temple; the Last Supper; and his arrest, trials, crucifixion, resurrection, and ascension.

Terms to Remember

Abba	Golden Rule	parables
amen	kingdom of God/heaven	realized eschatology
baptism of John	Last Supper	Servant of the Lord
consistent eschatology	Lord's Supper	Seven Last Words
ethical monotheism	mystery of the kingdom	Son of Man

How Much Did You Learn?

- What are the two most probable dates of Jesus' public ministry?
- What three phrases have traditionally characterized the years of Jesus' public ministry?
- What primary activities did Jesus carry on?
- Explain the difference, if any, between "the kingdom of God" and "the kingdom of heaven."
- What are the two meanings of "kingdom"?
- Explain the difference between realized eschatology and consistent eschatology, and the meaning of the "mystery" of the kingdom.
- Delineate the style and main content of Jesus' teaching, and identify the theological meaning of his miracles and exorcisms.
- List the main events in Jesus' public ministry.
- Evaluate various hypotheses dealing with Jesus' resurrection.

For Further Discussion

- How would modern biographers differ from the evangelists in presenting the life of Jesus? What might they omit, add, emphasize, and de-emphasize? Why do the evangelists in some respects not write as modern biographers would write?
- What aspects of Jesus' life and teaching do modern people tend to find unacceptable—intellectually, aesthetically, and socially—in comparison with ancient people, and why?
- How do the startling claims of Jesus for himself square with his teaching about humility; his demand for personal allegiance with his teaching about unselfish service toward others; and his egocentricity (some would even say megalomania) with his very sanity? Or is it right to speak of his egocentricity?

For Further Investigation

From a Conservative Standpoint

Guthrie, D. *Jesus the Messiah*. Grand Rapids: Zondervan, 1972.

Hoehner, H. W. *Chronological Aspects of the Life of Christ*. Grand Rapids: Zondervan, 1977.

Stein, R. H. *Jesus the Messiah: A Survey of the Life of Christ*. Downers Grove, Ill.: InterVarsity Press, 1996.

_____. *The Method and Message of Jesus' Teachings*. 2d ed. Louisville: Westminster John Knox, 1994.

Vos, G. *The Self-Disclosure of Jesus*. Grand Rapids: Eerdmans, 1954.

From a Moderate Standpoint

Barclay, W. *Jesus as They Saw Him*. New York: Harper, 1963.

Hunter, A. M. *The Work and Words of Jesus*. Philadelphia: Westminster, 1950.

Schweizer, E. *Jesus*. Richmond: John Knox, 1971.

Stauffer, E. *Jesus and His Story*. New York: Knopf, 1960.

Taylor, V. *The Life and Ministry of Jesus*. Nashville: Abingdon, 1955.

From a Liberal Standpoint

Becker, J. *Jesus of Nazareth*. Hawthorne, N.Y.: Walter de Gruyter, 1998.

Bornkamm, G. *Jesus of Nazareth*. New York: Harper, 1960.

Braun, H. *Jesus of Nazareth*. Philadelphia: Fortress Press, 1979.

Conzelmann, H. *Jesus*. Philadelphia: Fortress Press, 1973.

Fredriksen, P. *Jesus of Nazareth, King of the Jews: A Jewish Life and the Emergence of Christianity*. New York: Knopf, 1999.

Schillebeeckx, E. *Jesus*. New York: Seabury, 1979.

PART 3

The Four Canonical Gospels and Acts

CHAPTER

7

MARK: AN APOLOGY FOR THE CRUCIFIXION OF JESUS

Overview:

- Introductory Issues
- A Rough Outline of Mark
- Reading Mark with Interpretation
- Summary

Study Goals—Learn:

- Who wrote the Gospel of Mark
- How we determine its authorship
- How close its author stood to the eyewitness tradition of Jesus' life and teachings
- When this Gospel was written and what indications we have of its date
- For what audience, from what standpoint, and with what purpose the author wrote
- What features and emphases characterize this Gospel
- What overall plan determines its movement

Headwaters of the Jordan River

Introductory Issues

Gospels

The books called *Gospels* deal with the life and ministry of Jesus. Unlike modern biographies, however, they lack contemporary historical background, analysis of character and personality, and probing of the inner thoughts of the hero. Nor do the Gospels resemble Hellenistic narratives that merely celebrate the real or supposed acts of ancient miracle workers. There is much more than narration of miracles in the Gospels. Nor do the Gospels present us with simple memoirs; rather, they give us proclamations and instructions written from theological standpoints.

Evangelists

The author of a gospel is called an *evangelist,* which means a proclaimer of good news, here in written form. Since titles were probably added to the Gospels not till some time after the original writing, we depend on early, external tradition and on internal evidence—that is, evidence within the Gospels—to answer questions of authorship. The first Gospel to have been written takes its name from **John Mark**, who appears as the companion of Paul, Barnabas, and Peter in Acts and the New Testament Letters.

MARK AND PETER Very early in the second century the church father **Papias** passed on a tradition that Mark accurately wrote down in his Gospel the **reminiscences of Peter** concerning Jesus' life and teachings, yet not with the result of a complete, close-knit account, for Peter gave his reminiscences in the form of anecdotes told here and there on various occasions. The early church fathers ↓Irenaeus, Clement of Alexandria, ↓Origen, and Jerome also support authorship by Mark in association with Peter.

ACTION With little exception, Mark's Gospel is one of action instead of lengthy discourse. In quick-moving narrative, signaled especially by the adverb "**immediately**" and its synonyms (all going back to the same Greek word), he relates Jesus' activities as the **mighty and authoritative Son of God**.

Palestine in the Time of Jesus

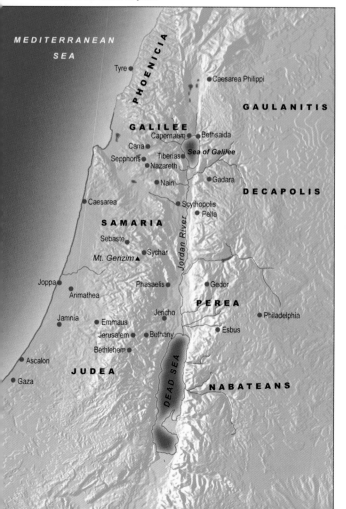

MEDITERRANEAN SEA

PHOENICIA

Tyre

Caesarea Philippi

GAULANITIS

GALILEE
Capernaum • Bethsaida
Cana
Sepphoris • Tiberias • Sea of Galilee
Nazareth
Nain • Gadara

DECAPOLIS

Caesarea • Scythopolis
• Pella

SAMARIA

Sebaste
Mt. Gerizim ▲ • Sychar

Jordan River

Joppa
Arimathea
Phasaelis • Gedor

PEREA

Jamnia
Emmaus • Jericho
Jerusalem • Bethany
Bethlehem
• Esbus
• Philadelphia

Ascalon

JUDEA

Gaza

DEAD SEA

NABATEANS

Irenaeus: *i´ruh-NEE-uhs* ■ Origen: OR-uh-juhn

ARRANGEMENT Though the order of Mark's material appears to be broadly chronological, catch words and similarity of subject matter often form the principle of arrangement for individual stories and sayings. For example, Mark 2:1–3:6 contains stories about Jesus' authority to forgive sins, to eat with tax collectors, to heal on the Sabbath, to allow his disciples to refrain from fasting, and to let them pluck and eat grain on the Sabbath. Apparently Mark strings these stories together because they all deal with Jesus' authority.

Suggested Purposes

Modern scholars have suggested a number of different purposes behind the writing of Mark:

- Some think that the evangelist writes to give new converts **catechetical instruction**. But his failure to give very much of Jesus' teaching undermines this view.
- Others think that Mark writes his Gospel for **liturgical use** in church services. But the arrangement and style lack the smoothness and symmetry that characterize liturgical documents.
- Still others think that Mark writes to **cover up a failure** by Jesus to proclaim himself the Messiah and that Mark subtly removes this embarrassment to Christian belief by inventing the *messianic secret*, that is, by putting into Jesus' mouth prohibitions against public revelation of his messiahship to make it appear that Jesus really did teach in private that he was the Messiah though he actually did not. W. ↓Wrede, who popularized the notion of a messianic secret, attributed it to Mark's predecessors whose material Mark used (*The Messianic Secret* [Cambridge: Clarke, 1971], translated from the German original of 1901).
- Others think oppositely that by inventing a messianic secret Mark was trying to **soften the political offensiveness** to Roman authorities of a ministry that was overly messianic. Both of the views that stress a messianic secret depend on hyperskepticism toward Mark's accuracy of reporting. Most readers will not gain the impression that he is embarrassed either by too little or by too much messianism in the tradition about Jesus. As we will see, moreover, Jesus' suppressions of publicity seem to have reasons that differ from one occasion to another, none of those reasons pertinent to the situation of Mark and his audience.

"On the one hand, Mark, becoming Peter's interpreter [either as an expositor or a translator], wrote as many things as he [Peter] remembered. On the other hand, he [Mark] did not write in order the things either said or done by the Lord. For he had neither heard the Lord nor followed him. But later, as I said, he had followed Peter, who was teaching with anecdotes yet not, as it were, arranging the Lord's oracles, so that Mark did nothing wrong by writing some things as he [Peter] related them from memory. For he [Mark] was thinking beforehand of one thing, to omit not a single one of the things that he had heard or to falsify anything in them" (Papias, quoting in about A.D. 110 an even earlier statement by "the elder John," identified as one of "the Lord's disciples"; ↓Eusebius, *Church History* 3.39.15).

Eusebius: *yoo-SEE-bee-uhs* ■ Wrede: *VRAY-duh*

- Or perhaps Mark writes to **encourage persecuted Christians** by showing them that Jesus also suffered and died. But why then does Mark devote the bulk of his Gospel to Jesus' miracles and exorcisms and to the authority with which he teaches and debates? And why does Mark depress and counteract as much as possible the element of suffering in the narrative of Jesus' arrest, trial, and crucifixion?

APOLOGY Crucifixion was reserved mostly for criminals and slaves and had all the connotations of a modern electric chair or gas chamber. It makes best sense to think that Mark writes for the purpose of **counteracting the shame** of the manner in which Jesus died. This counteraction takes the form of stressing his power to work miracles, to cast out demons, to teach astonishingly, to best opponents in debate, to attract crowds, to predict the future (including his own fate), and to rise from the dead. As an apology, then, Mark's Gospel is designed to convert non-Christians despite the shame of the cross.

The Supreme Disgrace

In describing crucifixion as the supreme disgrace, the Roman senator and orator Cicero says that "the very word 'cross' should be far removed not only from the person of a Roman citizen but also from his thoughts, his eyes, and his ears. For it is not only the actual occurrence of these things or the endurance of them, but also the liability to them, the expectation, even the mere mention of them, that is unworthy of a Roman citizen and a free man" (*In Defense of Rabirius* 16; see further M. Hengel, *Crucifixion* [Philadelphia: Fortress Press, 1977]).

Date

Early Christian tradition shows some uncertainty whether Mark wrote his Gospel before or after the martyrdom of Peter (A.D. 64–67) but generally favors the earlier period. Modern scholars dispute the date of Mark's writing. Those who regard "the abomination of desolation" in 13:14 as a back reference to the destruction of Jerusalem in A.D. 70 necessarily date the Gospel after that event. But this method of dating presumes that Jesus did not make a genuine prediction of the destruction and overlooks that a number of details in Mark 13 do not match Josephus's account of the destruction. Data is lacking to answer firmly the question of date. But if one accepts the phenomenon of predictive prophecy, no compelling reasons exist to deny an early date, say, A.D. 45–60. In fact, if Luke ends his book of Acts without describing the outcome of Paul's trial in Rome because the trial has not yet taken place, then Acts must be dated about A.D. 63, its preceding companion volume, the Gospel of Luke, somewhat earlier, and—if Luke's Gospel reflects Mark—Mark still earlier in the fifties or late forties.

The Gory Details

Features of the siege and destruction of Jerusalem that are missing from Mark 13:

- Cannibalism
- Pestilence
- Internecine conflict among the Jewish defenders
- Burning of the temple

See Josephus, *Jewish War* 5.1.1–5 §§1–38; 5.10.2–5 §§424–45; 5.13.1 §§527–33; 6.3.1–6.5.3 §§ 177–309; 7.1.1 §1.

Audience and Provenance

Mark probably writes for a **Roman audience**. He translates Aramaic expressions for their benefit (3:17; 5:41; 7:34; 14:36; 15:34). Even more indicatively, he explains Greek expressions by their Latin equivalents (12:42; 15:16) and uses a number of other Latin terms. Confirmation comes from the mention in 15:21 of a Rufus who, according to Romans 16:13, lives in Rome (unless the two texts refer to different men with the same name). Adding external testimony in favor of a Roman origin and address are

- The presence of Mark in Rome (symbolically called "Babylon") according to 1 Peter 5:13
- The combination of Papias's statement that Mark was Peter's interpreter with the early tradition of Peter's martyrdom in Rome
- The indication in an anti-Marcionite prologue[1] that Mark wrote his Gospel in Italy
- Further statements by Clement of Alexandria and Irenaeus

1. Anti-Marcionite prologues are early manuscript introductions supposed to have been directed against Marcionism, a brand of the Gnostic heresy (see pages 80–81).

Structure

No outline of Mark has commanded widespread agreement, probably because the Gospel echoes a desultoriness in Peter's telling of anecdotes concerning Jesus. The most that we can detect with confidence is a **loose arrangement** of materials governed mainly by the initiatory character of John the Baptist's ministry and its locale in the wilderness at the Jordan River, by the charismatic character and Galilean locale of the bulk of Jesus' ministry, by the transitional character and Transjordanian route of his journey to Jerusalem, and by the finality of his death and resurrection and their locale at Jerusalem.

A Rough Outline of Mark

Introduction (1:1–13)
  A. The ministry of John the Baptist (1:1–8)
  B. The baptism of Jesus (1:9–11)
  C. The temptation of Jesus (1:12–13)
I. The Activities of Jesus in and Around Galilee (1:14–9:50)
  A. Jesus' first preaching and call of Simon, Andrew, James, and John (1:14–20)
  B. A group of miracles (1:21–45)
    1. An exorcism in the synagogue at Capernaum (1:21–28)
    2. The healing of Peter's mother-in-law and others (1:29–39)
    3. The cleansing of a leper (1:40–45)
  C. A group of controversies (2:1–3:35)
    1. The forgiveness and healing of a paralytic (2:1–12)
    2. The call of Levi and Jesus' eating with toll collectors and sinners (2:13–17)
    3. A question about fasting (2:18–22)
    4. The plucking and eating of grain on a Sabbath (2:23–27)

A Chronological Scenario

Scenario for an early date of Mark under the assumptions that Luke used Mark, wrote Acts after writing his Gospel, and ended Acts before Paul's trial in Rome because the trial had not yet taken place:
- Mark (A.D. 50s or late 40s)
- (Matthew)
- Luke (late A.D. 50s or early 60s)
- Acts (early A.D. 60s)
- Paul's trial in Rome (c. A.D. 63)
- Destruction of Jerusalem and the temple (A.D. 70)

5. The healing of a withered hand on the Sabbath (3:1–6)
6. Jesus' withdrawal and choice of the Twelve (3:7–19)
7. The charges that Jesus is insane and possessed by Beelzebul (3:20–35)
D. A group of parables (4:1–34)
  1. The seeds and the soils (4:1–20)
  2. The lamp (4:21–25)
  3. The seed growing by itself (4:26–29)
  4. The mustard seed and others (4:30–34)
E. More miracles (4:35–5:43)
  1. The stilling of a storm (4:35–41)
  2. The exorcism of Legion from a demoniac (5:1–20)
  3. The healing of a woman with a constant flow of blood and the raising of Jairus's daughter (5:21–43)
F. Rejection at Nazareth (6:1–6a)
G. The mission of the Twelve throughout Galilee (6:6b–13)
H. The beheading of John the Baptist (6:14–29)
I. The feeding of five thousand (6:30–44)
J. Jesus' walking on the water (6:45–52)
K. Ministry at Gennesaret with controversy over ceremonial defilement (6:53–7:23)
L. More miracles (7:24–8:26)
  1. The exorcism of a demon from the daughter of a Syro-Phoenician woman (7:24–30)
  2. The healing of a deaf mute (7:31–37)
  3. The feeding of four thousand (8:1–10)
  4. The demand of Pharisees for a sign (8:11–21)
  5. The healing of a blind man (8:22–26)
M. Peter's confession of Jesus' messiahship (8:27–30)
N. Peter's notion of Jesus' messiahship and discipleship, corrected by Jesus' prediction of suffering, death, and resurrection (8:31–9:1)
O. The transfiguration (9:2–13)
P. The exorcising of a demon from a boy (9:14–29)
Q. Another prediction by Jesus of his death and resurrection (9:30–32)
R. Jesus' making a child an example for his disciples (9:33–50)

II. The Activities of Jesus on His Way to Jerusalem through Transjordan and Judea (10:1–52)
A. The question of divorce (10:1–12)
B. Jesus' blessing of children (10:13–16)
C. A rich man (10:17–31)
D. Another prediction by Jesus of his death and resurrection (10:32–34)
E. The request of James and John for places of honor and Jesus' reply concerning self-sacrificial service (10:35–45)
F. The healing of blind Bartimaeus (10:46–52)

III. The Activities of Jesus in and Around Jerusalem During the Week of His Passion, Death, and Resurrection (11:1–16:8)
   A. The triumphal entry (11:1–11)
   B. The cursing of a barren fig tree (11:12–14)
   C. The cleansing of the temple (11:15–19)
   D. The withering of a fig tree (11:20–26)
   E. Debates in the temple (11:27–12:44)
      1. The demand for a sign from Jesus (11:27–33)
      2. The parable of a vineyard (12:1–12)
      3. A question of paying taxes to Caesar (12:13–17)
      4. A question about resurrection (12:18–27)
      5. A question about the most important commandment (12:28–34)
      6. Jesus' question about the Messiah's Davidic descent and lordship (12:35–37)
      7. Jesus' warning against the scribes (12:38–40)
      8. A widow's mite versus large gifts from the rich (12:41–44)
   F. The Olivet Discourse (13:1–37)
   G. The Sanhedrin's plot against Jesus (14:1–2)
   H. The anointing of Jesus by Mary of Bethany (14:3–9)
   I. The bargain of Judas Iscariot to betray Jesus (14:10–11)
   J. The Last Supper (14:12–31)
   K. Jesus' praying in Gethsemane (14:32–42)
   L. The arrest of Jesus (14:43–52)
   M. The trials of Jesus (14:53–15:20)
      1. The trial before the Sanhedrin, with Peter's denials (14:53–72)
      2. The trial before Pontius Pilate, with the release of Barabbas (15:1–20)
   N. The crucifixion, death, and burial of Jesus (15:21–47)
   O. The resurrection of Jesus (16:1–8)

Reading Mark with Interpretation

John the Baptist

Because Mark depends on Peter's reminiscences and Peter did not associate with Jesus until Jesus' ministry, Mark's Gospel picks up at the start of that ministry. "The beginning of the good news of Jesus Christ, God's Son" refers to John the Baptist's introduction of Jesus onto the public stage and identifies Jesus as the Son of God as well as Christ. *Christ* (Greek for the Hebrew or Aramaic *Messiah*) means **"anointed"** in the sense of one chosen by God for a special task, in this case for the bringing of God's kingdom. As will become clear, "God's Son" connotes deity. *Read Mark 1:1–8.* Isaiah's "I" and "my" represent God. "You" and "your" represent Jesus. The messenger crying out in the wilderness represents John the Baptist. His preparing the way of the Lord represents his getting people ready for the appearance of the

Lord Jesus. This readiness consists in **repentance from sin**, shown by John's baptizing them in water as a sign of moral cleansing. The dress and diet of John mark him as a man of the wilderness, where he preaches and baptizes in accordance with the locale predicted by Isaiah. Powerful though John's magnetism is, he predicts the coming of someone yet more powerful, who will baptize people in an element far superior to water: **Holy Spirit.**

Jesus' Baptism

Now it comes out that John is baptizing in the Jordan River, which flows through the wilderness of Judea. There Jesus comes, gets baptized, and receives the Spirit by which he will now baptize others. This anointing with the Spirit resonates with Mark's having called Jesus "Christ." The heavenly origin of the Spirit and of the voice which assures Jesus that he is the **beloved, well-pleasing Son** likewise resonates with Mark's having called Jesus "God's Son." *Read Mark 1:9–11.* Jesus' seeing the heavens torn apart and the Spirit like a dove (regarded as a divine bird in the Hellenistic world) descending into him and the direct address of the voice to him make him aware of his power, so that he will shortly begin to exercise it.

The Temptation

But first the Spirit drives Jesus into the wilderness surrounding the Jordan River. *Read Mark 1:12–13.* The immediacy of the Spirit's driving Jesus into the wilderness confirms his reception of the Spirit. No emphasis falls on Satan's temptation as such. Mark neither details the temptation nor says whether Jesus resisted it. Emphasis falls instead on its length of time, forty days. That none less than Satan, the archdemon himself, tempted Jesus for so long, that even wild beasts did him no harm throughout the period he was with them, and that angels were serving him all constitute **acknowledgments of Jesus' status as Christ, God's Son**, by the demonic, animal, and angelic worlds in addition to the preceding declaration by God.

PREACHING AND CALLING *Read Mark 1:14–20.* Mark will explain John the Baptist's arrest in a flashback at 6:17–29, but now he turns his attention to Jesus' activity of preaching and calling the first disciples. "The good news of God" consists in the announcement that God's kingdom, or rule, has arrived. This rule demonstrates itself in the **powerful effect** of Jesus' call on Simon, Andrew, James, and John. They immediately drop their occupational activities to follow the Son of God, who is bringing God's rule. The fulfillment of Jesus' prediction that he will make Simon and Andrew "fishers of human beings" will interpret that figure of speech to mean getting people to repent, healing the sick, and casting demons out of the possessed (3:13–19; 6:7–13, 30).

EXORCISM Jesus continues to demonstrate his power as God's Son in the **astounding authority** with which he teaches and casts out a demon, here called from the Jewish point of view "an unclean spirit" (unclean in a ritualistic sense). *Read Mark 1:21–28.* The spirit's expressing a knowledge of Jesus' personal name and especially of his title "the Holy One of God" (in contrast to the uncleanness of the spirit) indicates an attempt at self-defense. Jesus' silencing this expression overcomes the attempt, and the convulsing of the possessed man and inarticulate outcry of the spirit give visual and auditory proofs of Jesus' victory.

HEALING Next, Jesus demonstrates his **power to heal** the sick as well as to exorcise demons. *Read Mark 1:29–34.* The healing of Simon's mother-in-law is proved by her serving those present. People bring their sick and demon-possessed not till after sundown because the Sabbath goes from sundown Friday to sundown Saturday, not from midnight to midnight, so that they would be breaking the Sabbath (which means "rest") had they done the work of bringing the needy before Saturday evening. But they bring them as soon as possible, so great is Jesus' magnetism. "Many" describes as numerous the "all" whom he delivers; it does not leave out some of the "all." Again, his silencing the demons thwarts their attempt to defend themselves by expressing a knowledge of his identity.

Byzantine remains over Peter's house in Capernaum

CLEANSING A LEPER So great is Jesus' magnetism that now if he wants to pray he must get up before light and go out to a deserted place. But he also widens the sphere of his powerful activity by going to towns and synagogues throughout Galilee. *Read Mark 1:35–45.* The cleansing of a leper emphasizes Jesus' ability to do what only God can do, and this with a mere touch and simple word. The immediacy of the cleansing enhances the demonstration of Jesus' ability. The immediacy and forcefulness of his thrusting out the cleansed leper emphasize the instruction to have a priest confirm the cleansing in order that the ensuing sacrifice might testify to people that a cleansing has indeed taken place (compare Leviticus 13–14). But the ex-leper does better than this instruction: He goes out and himself spreads the word, with the result that people throng to Jesus even in formerly deserted places.

Authority

A series of stories now display Jesus' authority

- To forgive sins (2:1–12)
- To eat with tax collectors and sinners (2:13–17)
- To let the disciples dispense with fasting (2:18–22)
- To let them pluck grain on the Sabbath (2:23–28)
- To heal on the Sabbath (3:1–6)

Read Mark 2:1–3:6. The four who bring a paralytic to Jesus can dig through the roof because it is made of mud-plastered branches spread over rafters. The healing of the paralytic demonstrates Jesus' authority to **forgive the sins** of the paralytic. But Jesus has this authority, a divine one, as "the Son of Man" (a phrase apparently adapted from Daniel 7:13: "one like a son of man," that is, a figure like a human being in contrast with beasts) and "on earth" (as opposed to "the clouds of heaven" with which the Danielic figure comes). To keep themselves ritually pure, Pharisees do not eat with tax collectors and sinners, those known to flout the law. But in great numbers Jesus attracts even such wicked people. His defending table fellowship with them silences the Pharisaical scribes. His presence makes his disciples so joyous that they cannot join in the fasting of John the Baptist's disciples and of the Pharisees, though the disciples of Jesus will fast in sorrow on the day of his removal. Just as an old garment could not help but rip if a patch of unshrunken cloth were to shrink after the next washing of the garment, just as old wineskins, already stretched to their limits, could not help but burst if new wine were to swell in them, so the authority of Jesus' words and deeds proves irresistible. As he does not dispute, plucking heads of grain counts as work; hence the Pharisees' question why his disciples are breaking the Sabbath. (Deuteronomy 23:25 allows the plucking of grain while going through a field; so stealing is not the issue.) Jesus answers with the example of David that the Old Testament itself teaches violation of the law in a case of human need (1 Samuel 21:1–6); and in any case, as Lord of the Sabbath, Jesus the Son of Man can let his disciples break it if he wants. And he has both the power to heal a withered hand and the authority to do so on the Sabbath, as he does despite the Pharisees' watching for such a violation, which he defends so convincingly that they plot with the Herodians against his life.

MAGNETISM Contrasting with that plot is the thronging to Jesus of a huge, admiring crowd, so that he tells the disciples to ready a boat for a hasty getaway if the crowd starts crushing him. To keep the crowd from increasing yet more at danger to his life and limb, he also orders unclean spirits to stop publicizing his divine sonship. As usual, they are trying to defend themselves; but he is concerned about the possibility of being crushed. *Read Mark 3:7–19.*

A wineskin

The Twelve Apostles

Jesus' magnetism has drawn so many that he now chooses twelve through whom he will multiply his ministry to the ever-increasing throng. Going up on a mountain, summoning "whom he wills," and exercising the prerogative of naming continue the emphasis on his authority. "Apostles" connotes being **sent to act with the sender's own authority** (compare 6:7–13). Though the number twelve corresponds to the number of Jacob's sons, ancestors of the twelve tribes of Israel, and thus suggests an intention to renew the people of God, the absence of an explanation leaves the emphasis on Jesus' authority.

THE HOLY SPIRIT VERSUS ↓BEELZEBUL But where does this authority come from? *Read Mark 3:20–35.* Jesus has the Holy Spirit, not the unclean spirit Beelzebul (another name for Satan), and therefore has authority to form a new family for himself rather than having to submit to search and seizure by his biological family. The latter are probably the ones who say he has gone berserk. Paralleling their statement is the scribes' accusation that he uses the chief demon to cast out other demons, an accusation Jesus parabolically reduces to personal, political, domestic, and physical absurdities. It is also an accusation which, he warns, constitutes an **unpardonable**

Beelzebul: bee-EL-zi-buhl

sin. (Note: by definition, believers in Jesus would never attribute his power to Satan rather than to the Holy Spirit.)

Parables

Read Mark 4:1–34. Here Jesus wields his authority by teaching a huge crowd made up of outsiders as well as his new family ("the ones around him with the Twelve"; compare the phraseology in 3:31–35). His sitting in a boat represents the usual posture of an ancient Jewish teacher, but the boat is unusually necessitated by the size of the crowd (compare 3:9–10). Though capable of many nuances, "parable" basically means "comparison." The **parable of the seeds and soils** is a parable about parables that compares the rejection of Jesus by some people and the acceptance of him by others to certain agricultural phenomena. But why does he speak in parables at all? The answer divides in two: (1) **to obscure the truth judgmentally from outsiders,** who have not responded in faith to his plain speech, and (2) with interpretation **to clarify the truth rewardingly for insiders,** who have responded in faith to his plain speech.

The mystery that God is bringing his kingdom, his rule, with words, not weapons, with deeds of mercy, not acts of violence, requires clarification. So the insiders get it in private through Jesus' interpretation, an interpretation that will help them understand the other parables too. According to this interpretation, God's rule is established in people who accept Jesus' message

Plowing a rocky field

immediately, deeply, and exclusively, rather than delaying, accepting it only superficially, and letting other concerns stifle it.

As to the other parables in this passage:

- The shining of a lamp represents Jesus' clarification.
- Nothing is hidden in a parable from outsiders that will not be revealed by him to insiders.
- People get what they deserve.
- Believers, who already have some understanding, are therefore enriched with more understanding, whereas unbelievers, who have no understanding, sink deeper into ignorance—just as in the world of investment it takes money to make money and lack of money prevents the making of any.
- The message of Jesus enlightens and enriches believers with humanly incomprehensible power, just as a seed grows to fruition in an incomprehensible way.
- What a large result from an infinitesimal beginning—like a mustard shrub grown big enough to give birds shade, though the shrub started as the smallest of seeds!

Jesus continues to speak in such parables as long as allowed by the crowd's attention span, and true to his promise he gives private explanations of all those parables to insiders, his disciples.

MIRACLES Now Mark switches from a series of Jesus' parables to a series of Jesus' deeds. The first, a nature miracle, demonstrates his power over wind and sea, representing the deadly powers of chaos. The second, an exorcism, demonstrates his power over a whole horde of demons who have made their victim dwell in the realm of death, a graveyard, and self-destructively lacerate himself. The third and fourth, a healing and a raising, demonstrate Jesus' power over the uncleanness and inevitability of death.

STILLING A STORM *Read Mark 4:35–5:43.* "The other side of the sea" is the east side of the lake called the Sea of Galilee. The onset of evening and Jesus' sleeping imply an overnight voyage. It would seem that the accompanying boats carry the crowd of his new family, those who do God's will, the twelve apostles being in the same boat with Jesus (compare 3:32–35; 4:10, 34). The details of the storm magnify his power in stilling it. The fear and unbelief of the disciples contrastively magnify his divine self-confidence. The disciples believe in him and his message in general, of course; but even his

---

Digging Deeper into a Parable

To understand the parable of the seeds and soils, you need to know that

- For lack of a sufficiently extensive road system villagers often beat pathways through fields
- Palestinian farmers often sow their seeds before plowing the soil
- Seeds from last year's thorns lie hidden in some soil
- Rocks lie hidden just below other soil
- Seed sown in thin soil sprouts first because heat absorbed by the rocks underneath speeds up germination and because the seed has only an upward direction in which to develop very much
- A yield of thirty times more seeds of grain harvested than sown is average, a yield of sixtyfold good, and of one hundredfold extraordinary (compare Genesis 26:12)

Sea of Galilee

Where Was Legion?

Early manuscripts, versions, and church fathers disagree on whether Mark writes about the country of the ↓Gerasenes, of the ↓Gergasenes, or of the ↓Gadarenes. The quality of the support for "Gerasenes" is best, but Gerasa is located about thirty miles from the nearest shoreline. Gadara is about five miles from the nearest shoreline. Gergasa is just offshore, and nearby is a steep slope such as the story of Legion mentions. Furthermore, going *away* to preach in the Decapolis (5:20) may favor Gergasa, for Gerasa and Gadara belong to the Decapolis (a league of ten cities), whereas Gergasa does not.

past miracles have not given them faith for such a threat as the present one. Fear gives way to awe, however, when wind and wave give way to utter calm.

LEGION Arrival on the other side brings Jesus and his disciples into heavily Gentile territory. The notation of earlier failures to tame a demoniac who meets Jesus makes the later exorcism performed by Jesus all the more impressive. The attempt to ward off Jesus by displaying a knowledge of his personal name ("Jesus") and title ("Son of the Most High God") provides for readers of Mark an answer to the disciples' recent question, "Who then is this one, that even the wind and the sea obey him?" (4:41). He does not succeed in the exorcism until discovery that he is dealing, not with one unclean spirit, but with many, called "Legion." They would rather have pigs as hosts than be sent out of the territory. The presence of pigs confirms its heavily Gentile character, for the Mosaic law prohibits pigs for Jews. The drowning of the pigs when Jesus lets Legion inhabit them escalates the exorcism to a destruction. The fear of the neighbors who come and see the ex-demoniac and the contrast between his present civility and his past ferocity highlight

Gerasenes: GER-uh-seenz ■ Gergasenes: GER-guh-seenz ■ Gadarenes: GAD-uh-reenz

Jesus' power. So also do the contrast between the ex-demoniac's present plea to be with Jesus and his past attempt to ward off Jesus, and the ex-demoniac's going beyond Jesus' command to report home by going away and preaching in the Decapolis.

A WOMAN AND ↓JAIRUS'S DAUGHTER The following intertwined miracles of healing and raising take place back on the more Jewish west side of the Sea of Galilee. The surreptitious behavior of the woman suffering from a chronic flow of blood is due to her ritual uncleanness according to the Mosaic law, which states that because of the flow everyone who touches either her or anything on

Steep slope near Gergasa

which she has sat or lain is rendered unclean (Leviticus 15:19–27). Heightening the power of Jesus in her healing is the worsening of her malady under the care of many physicians (she has been following the oriental custom of calling all available physicians in hope that at least one of them might cure her) and the effectiveness of mere physical contact with Jesus' clothes. Her faith has magnified his power. He calls on Jairus to exercise such faith on arrival of the news that Jairus's daughter has just died. Jesus' statement to the mourners that she is not dead but sleeping anticipates his bringing her back to life shortly, so that her death will turn out to have been a kind of nap. The mourners' scornful laughter only puts him in a better light when he proves them wrong, himself right. Her standing up and walking around demonstrate that he has brought her back to life. The command not to tell anyone but to feed her has the purpose of allowing him to get away from the large crowd outside that has been accompanying him and crushing him (5:24, 31). If the crowd hears that he has just brought the girl back to life, in their eagerness they are liable to crush him to death.

NAZARETH Back in his home town of Nazareth, Jesus teaches in the synagogue. The townspeople marvel at his wisdom and at the miracles that take place "through his hands." They cannot bring themselves to admit that a local-boy-made-good has himself performed the miracles, and they question the source and character of his wisdom and miracles. Jesus explains

Jairus: jay-*l*-ruhs

their reaction as an example of the rule that familiarity breeds contempt. Mark takes care to note that their lack of faith, not any lack of power on Jesus' part, makes him able to perform only a few miracles there. Yet even those few cause such astonishment among the townspeople that he is amazed at their refusal to believe. *Read Mark 6:1–6a.*

Mission of the Twelve

While teaching in the villages roundabout, Jesus now **extends his powerful activity through the twelve apostles,** whom he summons and sends in pairs—in pairs because the Mosaic law says that a sufficient testimony requires at least two witnesses. That they carry his authority with them is shown by their having to take no baggage: others will have to provide for the apostles as though the apostles were Jesus himself. Nonwelcome will bring judgment. The apostles go out and exercise Jesus' authority by doing what he has been doing: preaching, exorcising, and healing. Herod Antipas hears and is so impressed as to conclude that Jesus is John the Baptist risen from the dead. *Read Mark 6:6b–29.*

> "A matter must be established by the testimony of two or three witnesses" (Deuteronomy 19:15).

BEHEADING OF JOHN THE BAPTIST The flashback to John's martyrdom makes the point that stupendously mighty powers must be at work in Jesus to push a ruler into identifying him with a man whose head the ruler himself saw delivered on a platter to his own dining room, and then to his wife's dining room, and whose corpse was then interred in a different location. John had accused the ruler, not of breaking the law against adultery (though he had), but of breaking the law against marrying your brother's wife (Leviticus 18:16; 20:21).

FEEDING OF THE FIVE THOUSAND Back to the present, Jesus takes the apostles away for some rest when they return with a report of their mission; but his magnetism, now multiplied by that mission, makes their vacation no vacation at all. *Read Mark 6:30–44.* The contrast between the reasonableness of the disciples' suggestion to send the crowd away for purchase of food nearby and the unreasonableness of Jesus' command that they give the crowd something to eat highlights the miracle of feeding so vast a crowd as five thousand with only five loaves and two fish. "In groups of hundreds and fifties" probably means that the crowd sit in rows which taken together form a rectangle: longways, each row contains one hundred; sideways, fifty (100 x 50 = 5,000). The twelve baskets of leftovers show the superabundance of Jesus' power.

WALKING ON WATER ↓Bethsaida lies just east of the Jordan River on the north shore of the Sea of Galilee. *Read Mark 6:45–56.* Not as when Jesus stilled a storm (4:35–41), the adverse wind poses no danger, only difficulty. Walk-

---

Bethsaida: beth-SAY-uh-duh

ing on the sea exhibits divine power (see Job 9:8; 38:16; Psalm 77:19); so Jesus' intending to walk past the disciples is an intending to **parade his deity** before them (compare Exodus 33:19, 22; 34:5–7; 1 Kings 19:11). Their terror makes him get into the boat, however. It is the fourth watch, the last quarter, of the night. Now that Jesus has embarked, the wind dies down to provide him easy boating just as the water has provided him firm footing. The disciples are astonished because they did not even recognize a miracle in the feeding of the five thousand (note the absence of any statement of admiration at the close of 6:30–44). But Jesus' power keeps overflowing with further healings in the region of ↓Gennesaret, located off the northwest shore of the Sea of Galilee. Apparently, the adverse wind changed the direction of the voyage, which originally aimed northeast toward Bethsaida.

CLEANSING ALL FOODS The next story displays the authority of Jesus in his putting down the Pharisees and some of the scribes from Jerusalem on a question of ritual purity and in his pronouncing all foods clean (that is, ritually allowable to eat) despite the prohibition of some foods by the Mosaic law (Leviticus 11). *Read Mark 7:1–23.* The washing here in view does not have to do with personal hygiene, but with ritual purity, and not with the Mosaic law, but with traditional practices established by more recent Jewish teachers. These traditional practices, Jesus acidly notes,

First-century fishing boat from the Sea of Galilee

allow disobedience to God's command through Moses to honor your father and mother. You only have to mark an item that might be useful to them as destined for offering to God—and in the meantime keep on using the item yourself. Changing the law should run in the opposite direction, from ritual to morality. Jesus changes it that way. He has the right to.

A ↓SYRO-PHOENICIAN WOMAN Even in foreign territory Jesus' fame does not allow him privacy. During a trip through the region of Tyre, an ancient Phoenician port on the Mediterranean coast north of Galilee, a Gentile woman accosts him with a request to cast a demon out of her little daughter. To avoid publicity, Jesus tries to put her off with a statement comparing

Gennesaret: gi-NES-uh-ret ■ Syro-Phoenician: si′roh-fi-NISH-uhn

Jews, particularly his disciples, with children, and Gentiles, particularly the woman's daughter, with puppies. Jews of this period regularly called Gentiles "dogs," but Jesus is quoted as using the Greek word for "little dogs," that is, puppies, to suit the smallness of the woman's daughter. Undeterred, the woman latches onto his use of the term for puppies instead of full-grown dogs and conceives that the deliverance of her daughter might count as a mere crumb of mercy a puppy would eat under the table. In admiration of her wit, Jesus announces the demon's departure. As the woman will find out on her return home (the daughter has not accompanied her), he exorcises the demon at a distance and without a word. *Read Mark 7:24–30.*

HEALING A DEAF-MUTE A circuitous route looping north, east, and south brings Jesus back to the Sea of Galilee by way of ↓Sidon and the Decapolis. *Read Mark 7:31–37.* The extraordinary difficulty of healing a deaf-mute is indicated by Jesus' seeking privacy, using physical means, looking heavenward, groaning, and speaking a curative word. Sticking fingers into the ears mimics and thereby aids an opening of the ears to hear; and spitting, as though getting rid of something in your mouth that keeps you from talking plainly, mimics and thereby—along with the application of saliva from Jesus' well-functioning tongue to the deaf-mute's bonded tongue—aids a loosening of the bond. So astonishing is the miracle that despite Jesus' ordering them to tell no one, the people who brought the deaf-mute publicize it.

FEEDING OF THE FOUR THOUSAND Another feeding miracle takes place, but this time at a distance from towns where food might be bought; and the loaves are seven rather than five, the fish a few rather than two, the crowd about four thousand rather than five thousand, and the leftovers seven baskets full rather than twelve baskets full (contrast 6:30–44). *Read Mark 8:1–9.* Note again the lack of stated admiration for the miracle. Nobody seems to notice that a miracle has occurred.

NO SIGN FROM HEAVEN Jesus' going with his disciples by boat to ↓Dalmanutha poses somewhat of a puzzle, for Dalmanutha is not otherwise known. Since they started from the Decapolitan (that is, east) side of the Sea of Galilee, the boat trip is likely to have brought them to the Galilean (that is, west) side. Wherever the exact location, Jesus meets a challenge by the Pharisees that he produce a sign from heaven, apparently not an earthly miracle performed by himself, for they can attribute his miraculous power to Satan (3:22–30), but a heavenly display put on by God. Jesus meets this challenge, not by producing such a sign, but with a pronouncement the sheer force of which shuts down the challenge. Stressing this force are his

---

Sidon: *SI*-duhn ■ Dalmanutha: dal´muh-*NOO*-thuh

groaning in spirit, the rhetorical character of his question, the emphatic introduction to his refusal ("Truly I say to you"), and a strongly negative Hebraistic idiom in Mark's Greek text ("if to this generation a sign will be given," with the implication, "Out of the question!"). *Read Mark 8:10–21.* On the return voyage eastward, Jesus' warning against "the ↓leaven [=yeast] of the Pharisees and the leaven of Herod" makes the disciples think Jesus is alluding to their failure to bring more than one loaf of bread. They are mistaken; but Mark does not indicate what Jesus did mean, for his words turn in another direction. Jesus exposes another failure of the disciples, that is, their failure to understand he miraculously provided a superabundance of bread at the feedings of the five thousand and four thousand. So they should not imagine that their having only one loaf for the thirteen of them concerns him in the least.

HEALING A BLIND MAN Now they arrive at Bethsaida, a voyage to which was earlier thwarted by an adverse wind (6:45–56). Here Jesus confronts a case of blindness similar in difficulty to the earlier case of deaf-muteness (7:31–37). Again he seeks privacy and uses saliva as a kind of salve to perform the cure. The difficulty of this case comes out also in its taking place in two stages: (1) At first the patient can see only indistinctly; people milling about in the distance look to him like trees whose many branches and leaves are hard to distinguish from one another when waving in the wind. (2) A further application of Jesus' hands brings clear sight even at a distance. The command to go home rather than into the village is designed to demonstrate that a healing has occurred: the man no longer needs the villagers to lead him home; he can see for himself. *Read Mark 8:22–26.*

Peter's Confession

Close to ↓Caesarea Philippi, considerably north of the Sea of Galilee and different from Caesarea on the Mediterranean coast, Peter (at first called Simon—see 1:16 with 3:16) identifies Jesus as **the Christ**. Peter is representing the view of his fellow disciples too. Jesus orders them not to tell anyone. The crowds have almost crushed him to death even when thinking that he is only John the Baptist, ↓Elijah, or one of the prophets come back to earth. What might they do if convinced that he is none less than the Christ? *Read Mark 8:27–9:1.*

PASSION AND RESURRECTION PREDICTION The **human things** thought by Peter consist in expectations that Jesus will not suffer but rule as the Christ. The **things of God** that Peter fails to think consist in the necessities that Jesus will first undergo death and resurrection. The severity of Jesus' rebuke to Peter shows the strength of these divine necessities. In correspondence with them, Jesus calls on people to take up their own cross and follow him.

---

leaven: LEV-uhn ■ Caesarea Philippi: ses´uh-REE-uh FIL-i-p*i* ■ Elijah: i-L*I*-juh

"Cross" does not mean a whole cross, which would be too heavy to carry, but the cross-beam which victims often have to carry to their place of execution as crowds lining the way hurl abuse at them. So taking one's cross and following Jesus means **exposing oneself to abuse by open discipleship.** To the prediction of his own death and resurrection, which shows his divine foreknowledge, Jesus adds predictions of what will happen to those who answer his call and to those who do not. These added predictions provide reasons to answer. Finally comes a prediction that some standing right there will not die until they see—despite appearances to the contrary in the suffering of Jesus and his disciples—that God's rule has come with power.

Transfiguration

Read Mark 9:2–13. The transfiguration of Jesus fulfills his immediately foregoing prediction that some standing there at the time would see before they die that **God's rule has come with power.** Several factors here show that the upcoming suffering of Jesus and his disciples does not negate the presence of God's powerful rule: the locale on a high mountain, the glistening of Jesus' clothes, the conversation with him of Elijah and Moses (the only Old Testament figures to see God on a mountain), the disciples' terror, and the voice of God the Father declaring Jesus to be his beloved Son and telling the disciples to **listen to Jesus.** Jesus' ordering the disciples not to tell what they have seen till after his resurrection is again designed to avoid the danger of being mobbed. Because the Old Testament says that Elijah will come back before the Day of the Lord and because resurrection was expected to take place on that day, the scribes say that the return of Elijah will precede the resurrection. So the disciples perceive a possible disagreement with the prediction that Jesus will rise, apparently before Elijah's return. Jesus answers both that Elijah has already returned in the person of John the Baptist and that Elijah is yet to come, but not before Jesus suffers; for he would not have to suffer if Elijah had already restored all things, that is, introduced the world into a perfect state.

> "See, I will send you the prophet Elijah before that great and dreadful Day of the LORD comes" (Malachi 4:5).

EXORCISM *Read Mark 9:14–29.* The astonishment of a crowd who see Jesus on his descent from the Mount of Transfiguration (location unknown) suggests an afterglow on his clothes. The special difficulty of the following exorcism is shown by the disciples' failure, by the extensively described effects of the demonic possession, by the seizure on the spot, by the length of possession and the frequency of seizures, by the length of Jesus' exorcistic command, and by his saying that only prayer can effect an exorcism of this kind of demon. So strong is Jesus, however, that he has exorcised it without prayer. The shriek and severe convulsion, leaving the victim seem dead until Jesus raises him, do not add to the difficulty of the exorcism so much as they demonstrate its success and finality.

PASSION AND RESURRECTION PREDICTION Another prediction by Jesus of his death and resurrection exhibits his divine foreknowledge. The ignorance of the disciples is a foil to that foreknowledge, and their fear is a testimony to Jesus' awesomeness. *Read Mark 9:30–32.*

ICONOCLASTIC TEACHING Back at Capernaum, the divine authority of Jesus is on display in his shattering of accepted norms. He associates greatness with servanthood, firstness with lastness, children with himself and God. He affirms the possibility of allegiance to himself and to the disciples apart from following them. Better to be drowned at sea than cause a believing child to sin. Better a maimed body in heaven than a whole one in hell. The fire of judgment will rain down on everybody like salt out of a salt shaker; so be sure to have the better salt of peaceful relations as opposed to rivalry with your fellow disciples. There is no possibility of finding peace outside the community of disciples. *Read Mark 9:33–50.*

DIVORCE AND REMARRIAGE While going to Judea through Transjordan, Jesus continues to display his authority as God's Son by the shattering of accepted norms. *Read Mark 10:1–12.* What the Pharisees call a Mosaic permission of divorce Jesus calls a command, but he upsets this command by calling it an accommodation to the Pharisees' hardheartedness and by going behind Moses to God's original intention at the Creation. According to that intention, a man should not break the marital union that God has established. Thus, as Jesus later explains to his disciples, divorce followed by marriage to another constitutes adultery, which means having sex with another person's spouse. In Jewish society, only a man could divorce his wife, not a wife her husband; and a man would commit adultery against the other woman's husband, since she was considered his property, not against his own wife, also mere property. But the explanation to the disciples elevates the status of the man's own wife by directing the adultery against her and reflects (but does not defend) the right of Gentile women to divorce their husbands.

Yet again Jesus upsets norms with his authoritative pronouncements:

- Adults should imitate children in coming to Jesus and accepting God's rule.

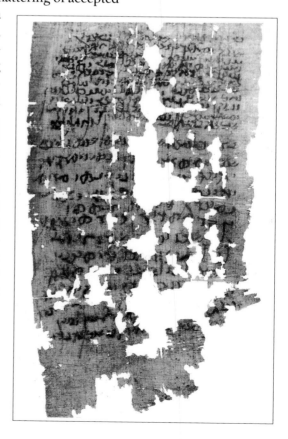

Divorce certificate from the Dead Sea Scrolls

- Wealth makes it next to impossible to enter the kingdom of God.
- Leaving your home and family for the sake of Jesus and the gospel will bring a hundred times more now as well as in eternity.
- He will be killed in Jerusalem, toward which he and other pilgrims are headed, and then rise.
- His serving others by **giving his life for their ransom** sets an example of service that will displace the disciples' vying for prominence.

Read Mark 10:13–45.

CHILDREN AND WEALTH Some children are brought to Jesus for a touch of blessing, not of healing. "Except one, [that is] God" (10:18) echoes 2:7, where Jesus acted as God in forgiving sins, so that here too Jesus is implying his deity by relating the goodness attributed to him to the exclusivity of God's goodness. That God alone is good prepares for the inadequacy of keeping even God's commandments if you want eternal life. For that, the rich man must sell all his possessions, give the proceeds to poor people, and follow Jesus. Jewish rabbis forbid selling all your possessions lest you become dependent on charity. The disciples are puzzled because they, like most people, view wealth as a blessing from God, not as a roadblock against entry into God's kingdom (see, for example, Job 1:10; Proverbs 10:22). A camel loaded with burdens cannot go through a narrow gate, much less a needle's eye; and riches are burdens that only God can unload from their victims. The community of disciples and their homes make up the hundredfold new houses, brothers, sisters, and so on of those who leave all to follow Jesus.

CUP AND BAPTISM The amazement and fear of those who are following Jesus to Jerusalem enhance Mark's portrayal of him as the Son of God as well as the Christ. Jesus has the divine foreknowledge to predict his disciples' destiny as well as his own. "Cup" and "baptism" stand for suffering and death. As a ransom, Jesus' suffering and death will liberate "many."

BLIND ↓BARTIMAEUS From Jericho the road west and a little south will lead up to Jerusalem. Usually the crowds want to see Jesus perform a miracle, but now they seem eager for him to arrive in Jerusalem for a reestablishment of the Davidic kingdom (compare 11:9–10). Surely his going ahead of them toward Jerusalem means that he is about to declare war against the Romans, crush them, and sit on David's throne (compare 10:32a). *Read Mark 10:46–52.* Following Jesus on the road contrasts with sitting on the edge of the road and offers proof that Bartimaeus is no longer blind or begging. He was begging for money from others but wanted healing from Jesus—and got it.

Bartimaeus: bahr´tuh-MEE-uhs

The Triumphal Entry

Read Mark 11:1–10. The Mount of Olives stands just across the ↓Kidron Valley to the east of Jerusalem. So the route of Jesus and other pilgrims from Galilee takes them across that mountain past ↓Bethany, on the south slope, and ↓Bethphage, probably on the west slope facing Jerusalem. In the finding of a colt Jesus' **divine foreknowledge** becomes prominent: he predicted the discovery in delicious detail. His **deity** gives him the prerogative of requisitioning the colt; and his sitting on the colt while others walk suits that deity. So also the saddle of donated garments, the paving of the road with such garments and with straw, and the acclamation by the crowd. Originally "↓hosanna" meant "save now," a prayer, but it has come to mean "Hurrah!" Even highest heaven joins in this acclamation.

A donkey and her colt

CURSING AND CLEANSING Now Jesus enters Jerusalem and the temple to inspect them. It is too late in the day to do anything about what he sees, and he knows the hostility in Jerusalem toward him (see 10:33–34); so he exits with the apostles and stays overnight in Bethany. *Read Mark 11:11–25.* The season for figs (June for early figs, then August–October) has not yet arrived, but fig trees in leaf at Passovertide (March–April) might well be expected to have edible buds, eaten by Palestinians even in modern times. Hence Jesus' cursing of the fig tree: no buds now, no fruit in June or ever after. Back in the temple he exercises his authority by driving out the traffickers who have turned the outer court, to be used for prayer by Gentiles, into an emporium for the buying of animals and doves certified as fit for sacrifice. This act and the popularity of Jesus make the Sanhedrin, who have charge of the temple, determined to kill him. Discovery next morning that the fig tree has withered, not as usually from the foliage down, but from the roots up, illustrates the power of Jesus' curse only the previous day and the impossibility of the fig tree's revival. He uses this astounding occurrence to startle the disciples further with statements about the **power of faith and prayer** and about the **necessity of forgiveness.** "This mountain" refers to the Mount of Olives, over which they are walking; and "the sea" refers to the Dead Sea, visible in the distance on a clear day. Ancient people thought that mountains reach down to the very foundation of the earth.

Kidron: KID-ruhn ■ Bethany: BETH-uh-nee ■ Bethphage: BETH-fuh-jee ■ hosanna: hoh-ZAN-uh

PARABLE OF THE WICKED TENANT FARMERS Now Jesus outwits members of the Sanhedrin, who challenge his authority to have cleansed the temple. Their challenge comes in two questions. He answers with a single question, which puts them in such an embarrassing dilemma that he then takes the initiative to tell them an accusatory parable. *Read Mark 11:27–12:12.*

- The vineyard = the Jewish people (compare Isaiah 5:1–7)
- The planter = God
- The tenant farmers = the Sanhedrin
- The slaves = past prophets
- The planter's son = Jesus the Son of God
- The murder of the son = the coming murder of Jesus
- The destruction of the tenant farmers = God's judgment on the Sanhedrin (compare 13:1–2 and the destruction of Jerusalem and the temple in A.D. 70)
- The transfer of the vineyard to others = a shift of leadership from the Sanhedrin to Jesus and his disciples
- The rejected stone's becoming the cap- or cornerstone = Jesus' exaltation, starting with his resurrection

TAXATION The battle of wits continues. To the amazement of some Pharisees and Herodians, Jesus escapes from the horns of a dilemma into which they have put him; and he exposes the ignorance of Sadducees who try to nonplus him. *Read Mark 12:13–27.* For general circulation in Palestine the Romans mint copper coins without an imperial image. But the tax to Caesar, a poll tax, has to be paid in a Roman silver coin stamped with his image and with a legend proclaiming his supposedly divine ancestry; yet the law of Moses prohibits images (Exodus 20:4–6; Deuteronomy 5:8–10), and monotheism has become the central feature of Judaism (compare Deuteronomy 6:4). So here is the dilemma: Saying that it *does* go against God's law to pay the tax would make it possible for the Herodians, supporters of Roman rule by way of the family of Herod, to charge Jesus with teaching rebellion. But saying that it does *not* go against the law of God to pay tax to Caesar would enable the Pharisees, whom the Jewish crowds respect, to undermine Jesus' popularity; for the crowds naturally resent paying the tax, and about A.D. 6 the levying of this tax provoked an outright rebellion led by Judas the Galilean (Acts 5:37). Jesus' loss of popularity would enable the Sanhedrin to arrest him without fear of crowds rising up on his behalf. A charge of rebellion would trigger the taking of action against him by Roman authorities. Jesus' answer divides the **things of God** from the **things of Caesar**. The fact that God's rule has not yet come in a political way leaves intact Caesar's authority to tax. Jesus' asking for the kind of coin with which the tax is paid embarrasses

Silver coin with the head of Tiberius Caesar

the Jews: by producing it they demonstrate their tacit acceptance of Caesar's dominion, since it is generally acknowledged that a king's domain extends as far as his coins circulate.

RESURRECTION A question of the Sadducees rests on the Mosaic law of ↓levirate marriage, according to which a surviving brother should marry the widow of his brother if that brother dies childless and, if possible, produce through her an heir for him (see Deuteronomy 25:5–10 with Genesis 38:8). But if a woman has not given birth by seven successive brothers, whose wife will she be in the resurrection? The question is supposed to make the very idea of resurrection absurd, since—polygamy being unthinkable for a woman—she will hardly be the wife of seven brothers at the same time. To defend the doctrine of resurrection, Jesus might have appealed to later passages in the Old Testament, for example, Daniel 12:2–3; but the Sadducees accept only the Pentateuch, which contains nothing explicit on the doctrine. So after pointing out the Sadducees' failure to consider the power of God to deduct marriage from life after resurrection, Jesus appeals to a passage in the Pentateuch (Exodus 3:6) and infers the resurrection from it. His statement that the resurrected will be "like the angels in heaven" (that is, unmarried) sarcastically alludes to the Sadducees' disbelief in angels on account of angels' nonappearance in the Pentateuch (apart from the angel of the Lord, an alter ego of God).

THE SON OF DAVID AND THE WIDOW'S MITE The next two paragraphs deal with scribes and a widow such as the scribes take advantage of. First, a scribe comes to recognize the truth of Jesus' teaching. Then, having weathered all questions successfully, Jesus asks his own question, based on Psalm 110:1: How can the scribes call the Christ "the son of David" when that designation never appears in the Old Testament for Christ and David himself calls the Christ "Lord" rather than his son? In the following warning against scribes, they appear to sponge off the limited resources of widows impressed by the scribes' religiosity. Contrastively, a poor widow gives her last two pennies for the upkeep of divine services in the temple. "The treasury" refers to a hall in the temple where such gifts are deposited in thirteen receptacles shaped like trumpets. Jesus' putting a higher estimate on the widow's gift than on coins of much higher value and number shows him at the business of upsetting popular norms once again. *Read Mark 12:28–44.*

The Olivet Discourse

Now Mark displays Jesus' ability to predict the fates of the **temple**, of the **world**, and of the **elect** (God's chosen, the disciples of Jesus) and **his own return** at the end of history as presently known. *Read Mark 13:1–37.* This speech is known as the Olivet Discourse, sometimes as the Little Apocalypse

levirate: LEV-uh-rit

Abomination of Desolation

"In the mountains" does not fit ↓Pella, a town at the base of foothills in Transjordan to which Christians fled from Jerusalem some time before A.D. 70, according to Eusebius (*Church History* 3.5.2–3). Nor does "the abomination of desolation" fit the setting up in the temple precincts of Roman standards with images of the supposedly divine Caesar affixed to them. That took place at the destruction in A.D. 70, and by then it was too late for flight. Originally, the abomination of desolation referred to an altar to Zeus, and perhaps his image, erected in the temple by Antiochus Epiphanes (Daniel 9:27; 11:31; 12:11). As a result, pious Jews refused to worship there until Judas Maccabeus captured, cleansed, and rededicated the temple. Compare the demand for worship of the future man of lawlessness, beast, or antichrist and his image in 2 Thessalonians 2:4; Revelation 13:11–18.

because of its similarity to the book of Revelation, also called the Apocalypse. Jesus predicts the destruction of the temple, as happened in A.D. 70, but quickly leaves that topic behind to warn his disciples not to think of the end as near merely because of false christs, wars, earthquakes, persecution, and such like. Not till they see the **abomination of desolation**, a sacrilege that causes pious Jews to stop going to the temple and thus to leave it desolate, deserted of worshipers, will the end be near. Then disciples living in the populated areas of Judea should immediately flee to the nearby wilderness of Judea, a mountainous region full of caves long used as hideaways. Pregnancy, nursing, and winter weather would hamper flight. Happily, the Lord will cut short this horrible period, known as the **great tribulation**, to save the lives of the elect. When the smoke of battle has darkened the sun and moon and meteorites have showered the earth, Jesus will come with **great power and glory**. The angels' gathering of the elect, scattered by persecution, will spell salvation. A parable teaches that those who see the abomination of desolation can be sure that Jesus is about to come, just as those who see a fig tree bud after losing its leaves for the winter know that summer is near. But exactly how near nobody knows but God the Father, for he has kept secret the amount of time that he will lop from the preceding tribulation. So all Jesus' disciples should **stay alert**.

A PLOTTING AND AN ANOINTING Now begins the fulfillment of predictions that Jesus has made concerning his passion (his suffering and death) and resurrection. *Read Mark 14:1–11.* "Not during the feast" (14:2) should probably read "not in the festal assembly." The members of the Sanhedrin do not want to risk a riot on behalf of Jesus by arresting him in a crowd of his fellow Galilean pilgrims; rather, apart from the crowd if they can catch him in such a situation. Judas Iscariot will provide them with that opportunity. In anticipation of his resultant death, Jesus interprets the perfuming of his head by a woman in the house of Simon the leper as an **advance preparation of his body for burial**. (But there is no need to suppose that she herself understood the deed as anything more than an act of devotion.) Three hundred ↓denarii amount to the annual wage of a fully employed manual laborer, and the perfume lavished on Jesus is worth even more: a tribute to his status and an amelioration of the shame of his coming crucifixion.

Pella: PEL-uh ■ denarii: di-NAIR-ee-*i*

The Last Supper

The **Thursday before Good Friday** has arrived. *Read Mark 14:12–31.* The story of making preparation for the Passover, an evening meal commemorating the exodus of Israel from Egypt (Exodus 12:1–51; Leviticus 23:4–8), serves the purpose of highlighting Jesus' divine foreknowledge with respect to two of the disciples' finding a man carrying a jar of water (as only women usually do) and finding a large upper room furnished and ready. The story of the **Passover meal** itself, traditionally called the **Last Supper**, likewise serves the purpose of highlighting Jesus' divine foreknowledge:

- He predicts that one of the Twelve will hand him over to his enemies.
- He predicts the violence of his death by separating his body and blood in the symbols of bread and a cup of wine and interpreting the violence as sacrificial on behalf of many people.
- He predicts his coming abstinence followed by a victorious celebration at the messianic banquet when God's rule takes over fully.
- He predicts with a quotation of Zechariah 13:7 that the disciples will desert him.
- He predicts that after his resurrection he will go ahead of them into Galilee.
- He predicts Peter's denials of him.

The fulfillments of these predictions will help overcome the shame of crucifixion and enhance Mark's portrayal of Jesus as the Christ, God's Son. The antiphonal singing of Psalms 113–118, constituting a hymn called the ↓**Hallel**, brings the Passover liturgy to a close.

ARREST Now the fulfillment of Jesus' predictions comes to full flower. Judas ↓Iscariot betrays him by enabling the Sanhedrin to arrest him in ↓Gethsemane apart from the crowd. The rest of the disciples flee. The Sanhedrin judge him deserving of death. And Peter denies him. *Read Mark 14:32–72.* Mark

> ### The Beginning of the Hallel
>
> Praise the LORD.
>
> Praise, O servants of the LORD,
>> praise the name of the LORD.
>
> Let the name of the LORD be praised,
>> both now and forevermore.
>
> From the rising of the sun to the place where it sets,
>> the name of the LORD is to be praised.
>
> (Psalm 113:1–3)

describes the emotional distress of Jesus to excite sympathy for him and mentions his submission to God the Father's will to excite admiration for Jesus. *Abba* is Aramaic for "Father" and indicates Jesus' sense of sonship to God. "The hour" is the hour of his betrayal (see 14:41 with 14:35), and "this cup" his death (10:38–39; 14:23–24). His strength in staying awake contrasts with the weakness of even his three closest disciples in falling asleep. Judas displays perfidy in a show of affectionate homage. Likewise, Jesus sarcastically notes, members of the Sanhedrin display an evil purpose by arresting him in

---

Hallel: HAL-el ■ Iscariot: is-KAIR-ee-uht ■ Gethsemane: geth-SEM-uh-nee

secret rather than in public as they have often had opportunity to do. Many have identified the young man who flees naked as John Mark, author of this Gospel; but no identification is given. Whoever he is, then, his escape seems to symbolize in advance the resurrection of Jesus, who will be buried in a linen cloth such as the young man has been wearing (15:46) and whose resurrection a young man will announce in the empty tomb (16:5–7).

Jewish Trial

The Sanhedrin's finding it impossible to obtain valid testimony against Jesus implies his innocence. The false testimony that he said he would destroy the man-made temple and in three days build another, God-made temple sounds like a mishmash of his predictions that the temple would be destroyed (though not by him) and that he would rise from the dead in three days. The judgment that he speaks **capital blasphemy** in answer to the high priest has to do with Jesus' prediction that at the second coming they will see him sharing the throne of God (reverentially called "the Power") just before he starts to return. Ironically, he is challenged to prophesy right as his earlier predictions are coming true. The details of the **mockery** to which he is subjected and of **Peter's three denials** this very night before the second crow of a rooster underline the exactitude of Jesus' divine foreknowledge.

Roman Trial

The train of fulfillments continues. The Sanhedrin take Jesus to **Pilate**, the Roman governor, just as Jesus said they would "give him over to the Gentiles" (10:33). Pilate does not care whether or not Jesus has blasphemed the God whom Jews worship, but he does care whether Jesus might claim to be a king rivaling the Caesar whom he the governor serves. "Are you the king of the Jews?" implies that the religious charge of blasphemy under which the Sanhedrin condemned Jesus has given way to a **political charge of insurrectionism**. His answer, "*You* are saying so," admits "the king of the Jews" as a designation given to him but rejects it as a self-designation; in other words, Jesus denies that he is an insurrectionist.

↓**BARABBAS** Read Mark 15:1–20a. Barabbas, not Jesus, is an insurrectionist— a murderer as well. Since the Sanhedrin arrested and tried Jesus in secret and brought him to Pilate early in the morning, the crowd who ask Pilate to follow his custom of releasing a prisoner to them must not have Jesus in mind.[2] It is Pilate who insinuates Jesus into the request of the crowd to find out whether Jesus' popularity is of a political sort that really does threaten the rule of Caesar, as the Sanhedrin have claimed. If the crowd want Jesus released as their king, the Sanhedrin will have been proved correct. If not,

2. On the one hand, the yearly custom of releasing a prisoner has scant support outside this story. On the other hand, the fabricating of such a custom seems unlikely in view of the well-documented fact that Romans did release prisoners occasionally— all that would be needed in the case of Jesus and Barabbas.

Barabbas: buh-RAB-uhs

Pilate will. When the crowd asks for Barabbas, Pilate knows himself to be correct in his opinion that the Sanhedrin are merely envious of Jesus' popularity, but his attempt to release Jesus wilts before the onslaught of the crowd's demand. Pilate is looking out for his own political future; he does not want the Sanhedrin to lodge a complaint with Caesar that he, Pilate, has let go a rival king. Thus the coming crucifixion of Jesus is shown to be a **miscarriage of justice**. Further mockery, this time by soldiers, returns to the fulfillment of Jesus' predictions (see 10:34). The ↓praetorium, where it takes place, is Pilate's official residence, or palace, when he visits Jerusalem from Caesarea, where he normally resides. The soldiers design the mock crown of thorns also as an instrument of torture shaped like a laurel wreath with some of the spikes pointing inward toward Jesus' head, or solely as an instrument of mockery with the spikes pointing outward in imitation of the rays of the sun.

Coin showing a radiate crown

Crucifixion

All along, Mark has been **counteracting the shame** of Jesus' coming crucifixion by noting its fulfillment of Jesus' own predictions, its benefit to others, and its stemming from the will of God the Father and at the same time from a miscarriage of human justice. In the narrative of the crucifixion itself, Mark carries forward this program by noting that

- Jesus does not have to carry his own cross.
- He is offered wine mixed with ↓myrrh (a delicacy).
- To stay awake with full sensibility, as in Gethsemane, he refuses the mixture.
- His clothes become objects of desire.
- He occupies a central position when crucified.
- Further mockery continues to fulfill his predictions (compare 10:33–34).
- He hangs on the cross only six hours (whereas victims of crucifixion normally hang there much longer, as long as several days).
- For the last three hours a supernatural darkness hides him from the leering of those who blaspheme him.
- He does not weaken bit by bit and lapse into unconsciousness before dying, but dies with a loud shout.
- With this shout the gigantic curtain of the temple—said to have measured 60 feet by 30 feet and in thickness to have matched the width of a human palm (about 5 inches)—is torn in two from top to bottom to indicate supernatural action.
- The way Jesus dies makes the centurion overseeing the crucifixion declare that truly Jesus must have been God's Son.

praetorium: pri-TOR-ee-uhm ■ myrrh: muhr

- A large number of women who followed and served him in Galilee saw the events that evoked the centurion's declaration.
- Jesus' corpse gets a dignified burial by none less than a respected, pious, and brave member of the Sanhedrin, and this despite the Roman prohibition of such a burial for those executed like Jesus under the charge of high treason.

Read Mark 15:20b–47.

DEATH AND BURIAL "The father of Alexander and Rufus" (15:21) probably implies that these sons of Simon of Cyrene are known to Mark's original audience. A rough similarity between "↓Eloi" and "↓Elian" (that is, "Elijah," 15:34–36) makes some bystanders think that Jesus is calling for help from the Old Testament prophet Elijah. Jesus does not take the sour wine offered him; he has already died with a loud shout. The shout, called the "Cry of Dereliction," derives from Psalm 22:1 and refers to God's abandoning him to die. Mark does not specify the outer rather than inner veil of the temple, but the centurion's observation requires the outer and favors the Mount of Olives, just opposite the veiled end of the temple, as the site of Jesus' crucifixion rather than the traditional site, out of eyeshot as well as on the wrong side. "Preparation" (15:42) means Friday as the day of preparing to rest on Saturday, the Sabbath. Joseph of ↓Arimathea rolled a stone against the door of Jesus' tomb to shield his corpse from the indignity of ravage by predators.

Eloi: EE-loh-*i* ■ Elian: EE-lee-ahn ■ Arimathea: air´uh-muh-THEE-uh

Tomb with a rolling stone door

Resurrection

Read Mark 16:1–7. Because of the very large size of the stone, the **women** who come to Jesus' tomb wonder who will roll it away for them only to find it already rolled away and his corpse, which they intended to honor with the application of spices (whereas Jews ordinarily applied mere oil to a corpse), absent. "A young man" recalls the young man of 14:51–52, but "clothed in a white robe" distinguishes this one, apparently an angel, from the earlier one, a human being. Sitting on the right augurs well, for the right side is the side of favor. It augurs well indeed, for the young man announces the resurrection of Jesus and promises the disciples' seeing of him in Galilee, so that his prediction at the Last Supper (14:28) will reach fulfillment.

MARK'S ENDING The best textual tradition stops with Mark 16:8. Inferior traditions add 16:9–20, called the long ending, and a shorter, unnumbered ending, both generally recognized as inauthentic. Many think that Mark intended his Gospel to end with 16:8. If so, the women's trembling and amazement, dumbfoundedness and fear, bring the Gospel to a close on the note of awe, as appropriate to Mark's portrayal of Jesus as the Christ, God's Son. On the other hand, Mark's narrating the fulfillments of all Jesus' other predictions insofar as those fulfillments had occurred during Jesus' time on earth favors that Mark went on to narrate a fulfillment of the disciples' seeing Jesus in Galilee and that the two inauthentic endings arose out of awareness that such an original ending was lost. *Read Mark 16:8.*

The Ending of Mark

The question of Mark's ending does not affect any major doctrine of the Christian faith. Biblical inspiration is certainly not at issue, only what was the original text of the Bible as opposed to later additions by copyists. The earliest and most trustworthy manuscripts of the New Testament had not yet been discovered in 1611, so that the translators of the King James Version, which contains the long ending and to whose influence more recent translations bow unfortunately often, did not know that the long ending was textually doubtful, indeed, inadmissible.

Summary

The evangelist John Mark wrote to tell the good news of Jesus Christ. Very early tradition has it that Mark got his information from the Apostle Peter's preaching. He may well have written at an early date in Rome. His narrative is loosely arranged and fast-paced, emphasizing the mighty deeds of Jesus, the authority of his teaching, and his predictive power. The narrative starts with Jesus' introduction onto the public stage by John the Baptist, proceeds to Jesus' activities in Galilee, and reaches a climax in a disproportionately long section devoted to the events of a final week in Jerusalem. A discovery of Jesus' tomb, empty because of resurrection, ends the narrative so far as we have it, though the original ending is very possibly lost. In any case, the resurrection of Jesus joins other features of Mark to erase the shame of crucifixion and thus commend the gospel of Jesus Christ to non-Christians.

People to Remember

Andrew	James	Judas Iscariot	Simon the leper
Barabbas	John	Papias	Simon Peter
Bartimaeus	John the Baptist	Pilate	
Herod Antipas	John Mark	Rufus	
Jairus	Joseph of Arimathea	Simon of Cyrene	

Places to Remember

Bethany	Decapolis	Jordan River	Transjordan
Bethphage	Galilee	Judea	Tyre and Sidon
Bethsaida	Gennesaret	Kidron Valley	upper room
Caesarea	Gethsemane	Mount of Olives	
Caesarea Philippi	Jericho	Nazareth	
Capernaum	Jerusalem	Pella	

Terms to Remember

Abba	Hallel	praetorium
abomination of desolation	Holy One of God	Preparation (as a day of the
apostle	hosanna	week)
Beelzebul	"Immediately"	Sanhedrin
Christ/Messiah/Anointed One	Last Supper/Passover	sign from heaven
Cry of Dereliction	Legion	Son of Man
cup and baptism	levirate marriage	taking a cross
evangelist (in a literary sense)	Lord's Supper	transfiguration
fishers of human beings	messianic secret	triumphal entry
Good Friday	Olivet Discourse/	unclean spirit
good news of God	Little Apocalypse	widow's mite
Gospel (in a literary sense)	other side of the sea	
great tribulation	parable	

How Much Did You Learn?

- Compare and contrast the Gospels and modern biographies.
- Discuss early church tradition concerning the writing of Mark and the origin of the material in Mark.
- Identify and evaluate the suggested purposes of Mark's writing.
- When and where did Mark write, so far as we can tell from internal and external indications?
- At what point in Jesus' life does Mark start his narrative, and in broad terms how does he develop it?
- What are the two purposes of Jesus' parables in Mark 4?
- Provide examples of Jesus' upsetting established norms in his pronouncements.
- Provide examples of Jesus' stumping his enemies in debate.
- Why the distinction between bread and wine, body and blood, in the Lord's Supper?
- Distinguish the charges brought against Jesus during his trials.
- What caused the Roman centurion to proclaim Jesus' divine sonship?
- What question plagues the ending of Mark?

For Further Discussion

- For what sort of situation is the Gospel of Mark most pertinent today?
- What kind of contemporary audience might find the Gospel of Mark appealing, and why?

For Further Investigation

Dowd, S. *Reading Mark: A Literary and Theological Commentary on the Second Gospel.* Macon: Smyth & Helwys, 2000.

Edwards, J. R. *The Gospel according to Mark.* Grand Rapids: Eerdmans, 2001.

Evans, C. A. *Mark 8:27–16:20.* Nashville: Thomas Nelson, 2000. Advanced.

Garland, D. E. *The NIV Application Commentary: Mark.* Grand Rapids: Zondervan, 1996.

Guelich, R. A. *Mark 1–8:26.* Dallas: Word, 1989. Advanced.

Gundry, R. H. *Mark: A Commentary on His Apology for the Cross.* Grand Rapids: Eerdmans, 1993. Advanced.

Hooker, M. D. *The Gospel according to Saint Mark.* Peabody, Mass.: Hendrickson, 1991.

Hurtado, L. W. *Mark.* Peabody, Mass.: Hendrickson, 1989.

Iersel, B. M. F. van. *Mark: A Reader-Response Commentary.* Sheffield: Sheffield Academic Press, 1998.

Marcus, J. *Mark 1–8: A New Translation with Introduction and Commentary.* New York: Doubleday, 2000. Advanced.

Witherington, B., III. *The Gospel of Mark: A Socio-Rhetorical Commentary.* Grand Rapids: Eerdmans, 2001.

CHAPTER

8

MATTHEW: HANDBOOK FOR A MIXED CHURCH UNDER PERSECUTION

Overview:

- Introductory Issues
- An Outline of Matthew Showing Concentric Structure
- Excursus on Fulfilled Old Testament Passages
- Reading Matthew with Interpretation
- Summary

Study Goals—Learn:

- Who wrote the Gospel of Matthew
- How we determine its authorship
- When this Gospel was written and what indications we have of its date
- For what audience, from what standpoint, and with what purpose the author wrote
- The features and emphases that distinguish this Gospel
- The overall plan that determines its movement

Sea of Galilee

Introductory Issues

↓*Logia*

The tradition passed on by Papias which says that Mark wrote down Peter's reminiscences also says that Matthew wrote *logia* (Greek for "oracles") in Hebrew or Aramaic, and that others interpreted them as they were able. In context, *logia* most naturally refers to a gospel. But we do not possess a gospel from the pen of Matthew in either of the Semitic **languages**, Hebrew and Aramaic, only the present Greek Gospel, which appears not to have been translated from a Semitic original. For example, why would Matthew give the Semitic originals and Greek translations of just a *few* terms, such as ↓*Immanuel* (1:23), if his *whole* Gospel were a translation from Hebrew or Aramaic? Some have thought that the tradition refers to a collection of messianic proof texts drawn up by Matthew in Hebrew or Aramaic and later incorporated in Greek translation into his Gospel, or to an earlier Semitic edition of Matthew not directly related to our present Greek edition. Others have thought that *logia* refers to Q (compare pages 95–96). According to yet another understanding, Papias's tradition refers to our present Greek Matthew as written in the Hebrew or Aramaic **style** rather than language and as presenting Matthew's interpretation—in the sense of **explanation**—of Jesus' life alongside Mark's interpretation. If so, there is no reference to any translation of Matthew from a Semitic original.

> "Matthew collected the oracles [*logia*] in the Hebrew [or 'Aramaic'] dialect [in the sense either of 'style' or of 'language'] and each interpreted them as best he was able" (Papias, quoting in about A.D. 110 an even earlier statement by "the elder John," identified as one of "the Lord's disciples," according to Eusebius, *Church History* 3.39.16).

Authorship

Modern scholars usually deny that the Apostle Matthew wrote the Gospel bearing his name. Following the equation of Papias's *logia* with Q, some have suggested that Matthew wrote Q and that his name became mistakenly attached to the First Gospel (in the order of our New Testament) because the unknown writer of this Gospel utilized so much of Q. But if there was a Q, adequate reasons do not exist for denying that Matthew might have written both, especially if Q consisted of, or was derived from, a body of loose notes on Jesus' teaching taken by Matthew and incorporated into his Gospel. It is argued to the contrary that an apostle like Matthew would not have borrowed narratives of Jesus' deeds from a nonapostle like Mark. But while adding his own material, Matthew may simply be **corroborating** the Petrine and therefore apostolic tradition recorded by Mark. Regardless of stature, ancient authors regularly borrowed from previous writers; no one thought that by doing so they were plagiarizing material or demeaning

---

logia: LAW-gee-ah ■ Immanuel: i-MAN-yoo-uhl

themselves. Early church tradition unanimously ascribed the First Gospel to Matthew, and false ascription to a relatively obscure apostle like Matthew seems unlikely until a later date when Christian imagination ennobled all the apostles.

The **skillful organization** of this Gospel agrees with the probable interests and abilities of a tax collector such as the Apostle Matthew had been. So also does the fact that this is the only gospel to contain the story of Jesus' paying the temple tax (17:24–27). The account of Matthew's call to discipleship uses the apostolic name Matthew rather than the name Levi, used by Mark and Luke (see the lists of apostles in 10:2–4; Mark 3:16–19; Luke 6:13–16; Acts 1:13), and omits "his," used by Mark and Luke, in describing the house where Matthew entertained Jesus at dinner (9:9–13; compare Mark 2:13–17; Luke 5:27–32). These incidental details may well give telltale indications of Matthean authorship and thus support the early church tradition.

Date

If Matthew used Mark and Mark dates from the period A.D. 45–60, Matthew probably dates from slightly later in or after that period. Denial of predictive prophecy and generally more skeptical presuppositions will force a later date in the eighties or nineties, though a number of conservative scholars prefer this later date because of other considerations, such as the argument that Matthew's interest in the **church** (he is the only evangelist to use the term, and that twice) betrays a later period when the doctrine of the church was assuming more importance as a result of the delay in Jesus' return. But the doctrine of the church already plays an important role in Paul's letters, all written well before the eighties and nineties. And if Matthew wrote especially for Jews, as is generally though not universally agreed, it seems less likely that he wrote late, after the breach between church and synagogue had widened, than early, when Jewish Christians still dominated the church and prospects for converting other Jews seemed brighter. Those who balk at predictive prophecy think that the phraseology of 22:7 ("The king was angered, sent his troops, . . . and burned their city") points back to the destruction of Jerusalem in A.D. 70, that is, takes a later vantage point. But this phraseology may instead point back to the much earlier destruction of Jerusalem in 586 B.C. and echo Isaiah 5:25 ("Therefore the LORD's anger burns against his people . . . and the dead bodies are like refuse in the streets"), as suggested by the background of Isaiah 5:1–7, which deals with the "dwellers in Jerusalem and men of Judah," for the parable immediately preceding in Matthew 21:33–46. Furthermore, a late date for Matthew would make odd the business of the temple tax, which only Matthew discusses (17:24–27), and the relative prominence of Sadducees (they appear seven times in Matthew, over against only one mention each in Mark and Luke). For the temple was destroyed in A.D. 70 and thus the Sadducees lost their base of power and, indeed, most of them their very lives.

Structure

Matthew writes his Gospel for the church as the new chosen nation, which at least for the time being has replaced the old chosen nation of Israel. The Gospel starts with the **nativity** of Jesus (chapters 1–2). The rest of the Gospel takes up **primarily Marcan narrative** (usually condensed) and inserts **five discourses** of Jesus (though some of the material in these discourses comes from Mark). The discourses consist of more or less lengthy "sermons," to which isolated sayings of Jesus have been added in appropriate places. Each discourse ends with the formula, "And it came to pass when Jesus had finished . . . ." Similarly, the formula, "From then on Jesus began to . . . ," introduces a large new section of narrative (4:17; 16:21).

Jewishness

The fivefold structure of these discourses suggests that for the benefit of his Jewish audience Matthew is portraying Jesus as a **new and greater Moses**. Like Moses, Jesus speaks part of his law from a mountain. The number of his discourses corresponds to the books of Moses, called the **Pentateuch** because they are five in number (Genesis, Exodus, Leviticus, Numbers, and Deuteronomy). By omitting the story of the "widow's mite," Matthew even welds the denunciation of the scribes and Pharisees (chapter 23) and the Olivet Discourse (chapters 24–25) into a single unit to gain this fivefold arrangement (contrast Mark 12:38–40; Luke 20:45–47).

Matthew's comparison of Jesus with Moses shows itself elsewhere too, as in the **borrowing of phraseology** from the story of Moses to describe Jesus' nativity and transfiguration (compare 2:13, 20–21; 17:2, 5 with Exodus 2:15; 4:19–20; 34:29; Deuteronomy 18:15). In the Sermon on the Mount according to Matthew, Jesus himself sets his teaching alongside the Mosaic law in a series of statements, "You have heard that it was said to the ancients [there follows a quotation or a paraphrase of the Pentateuch]. . . . But I say to you . . ." (5:21, 27, 31, 33, 38, 43; contrast Luke 6:27–35).

Besides the fivefold structure of the discourses, there are many other indications of Matthew's penchant for organization. He favors groupings of **three** and **seven**. For example, he divides the genealogy of Jesus into three sections (1:17) and gives from Jesus' teaching three examples of righteous conduct, three prohibitions, and three commandments (6:1–7:20). There are seven parables in chapter 13 and seven woes against the scribes and Pharisees in chapter 23. Even though some of these numerical groupings may go back to Jesus himself and to the events themselves, their frequency in Matthew shows his fondness for them above that of the other evangelists.

Purpose

The editorial organization of Jesus' teaching, its strongly ethical content, and its emphasis on discipleship have led to the views that Matthew writes his Gospel to provide a catechetical manual for new converts or a scholastic manual for church leaders, or that he designs his Gospel for liturgical and homiletical reading in early church services. But the Gospel gives a much stronger impression of having been written to strengthen Jewish Christians **in their suffering of persecution**, to warn them **against laxity and apostasy**, and to urge them to use their persecution as an opportunity **for the evangelism of all nations**.

Matthew's recurring stress on Jesus' **fulfillment** of the Old Testament law and messianic prophecy ("Such-and-such happened in order that what was spoken by so-and-so the prophet might be fulfilled") and his tracing of Jesus' genealogy from **Abraham**, father of the Jewish nation, through the beloved **King David** also indicate a Jewish bent. By way of contrast, Mark did not trace the ancestry of Jesus at all; his mainly Gentile readers (like most modern readers) would have little concern for it.

Still other Jewish features appear in the characteristically Jewish designation of God as the **"Father in heaven"** (fifteen times in Matthew, only once in Mark, and not at all in Luke), in the **substitution of "heaven" for God's name** (especially in the phrase "kingdom of heaven," where the other evangelists have "kingdom of God"), in the typically Jewish interest in **eschatology** (Matthew extends the Olivet Discourse by a whole long chapter, as compared with Mark and Luke), in frequent references to Jesus as the **"son of David,"** in allusions to Jewish customs **without explanation** (23:5, 27; 15:2; contrast the explanation in Mark 7:2–4), in the story of Jesus' paying the **temple tax** (17:24–27, lacking in the other Gospels), and in statements by him that have a **specially Jewish flavor** (for example, "I was sent only to the lost sheep of the house of Israel" [15:24]; "Go nowhere among the Gentiles, and enter no town of the Samaritans, but go rather to the lost sheep of the house of Israel" [10:5b–6]; see also 5:17–24; 6:16–18; 23:2–3). In telling the nativity story (chapters 1–2), Matthew stresses that Jesus was born into a Davidic family and from that standpoint, therefore, has a legitimate claim to the Jewish throne. Matthew also counters the Jewish charge that the disciples of Jesus stole away his body (28:11–15).

> Ignatius writes that Jesus was "baptized by John in order that 'all righteousness might be fulfilled by him'" (*Letter to the ↓Smyrnaeans* 1:1) and thus shows a knowledge of Matthew 3:15, a passage peculiar to Matthew's Gospel: "And answering, Jesus said, 'Permit [me to be baptized] now, for it is proper for us to fulfill all righteousness.' Then John permitted him [to be baptized]."

Universality

On the other hand, universality also characterizes the Gospel of Matthew, which reaches a climax in the Great Commission that Jesus' followers make disciples of **all nations** (28:18–20). Toward the beginning of the Gospel, the ↓magi (wise men) worship the infant Christ—they are

---

magi: MAY-*ji* ■ Smyrnaeans: SMUHR-nee-uhnz

Gentiles (2:1–12). Jesus is quoted as saying that "many will come from the east and the west and sit at table with Abraham and Isaac and Jacob in the kingdom of heaven. But the sons of the kingdom will be thrown out into the outer darkness" (8:11–12). The field is "the world" in the parable of the wheat and tares (13:38). According to the parable of the vineyard, God will transfer his kingdom from Israel to others (21:33–43). And Matthew is the only evangelist to use the word *church* (16:18; 18:17). We must describe his Gospel, then, as **Jewish Christian with a universal outlook.**

Provenance

The Jewish character of Matthew's Gospel suggests that he wrote it in Palestine or Syria, most probably **Antioch,** to which many of the original Palestinian disciples had migrated (Acts 11:19, 27). Its remarkable concern for Gentiles supports Antioch, a city with the church that sent Paul on his Gentile missions. In agreement with this view stands the fact that our oldest witness for a knowledge of Matthew's Gospel is an early bishop of the church in Antioch: Ignatius (first quarter of the second century).

An Outline of Matthew Showing Concentric Structure

An appropriate outline of the Gospel of Matthew shows a concentric structure of narrative and discourse (A-B-C-D-E-F-E'-D'-C'-B'-A').
  A. Narrative (1:1–4:25)
      1. Jesus' genealogy (1:1–17)
      2. The birth of Jesus (1:18–25)
      3. The worship of Jesus by the magi (2:1–12)
      4. The flight into Egypt for protection from Herod the Great (2:13–18)
      5. The return and residence in Nazareth (2:19–23)
      6. The preparatory ministry of John the Baptist (3:1–17)
          a. His preaching (3:1–12)
          b. His baptism of Jesus (3:13–17)
      7. The temptation of Jesus by Satan (4:1–11)
      8. Beginnings of messianic preaching and miracle working in Galilee, with the call of Simon Peter, Andrew, James, and John (4:12–25)
  B. Discourse: the Sermon on the Mount (5:1–7:29)
  C. Narrative (8:1–9:34)
      1. The cleansing of a leper (8:1–4)
      2. The healing of a centurion's servant (8:5–13)
      3. The healing of Peter's mother-in-law and others (8:14–17)
      4. Two would-be disciples (8:18–22)
      5. The stilling of a storm (8:23–27)
      6. The deliverance of two demoniacs (8:28–34)
      7. The forgiveness and healing of a paralytic (9:1–8)

      8. The call of Matthew and Jesus' eating with tax collectors and sinners (9:9–13)

      9. A question about fasting (9:14–17)

    10. The healing of a woman with a chronic flow of blood and the raising of a ruler's deceased daughter (9:18–26)

    11. The healing of two blind men (9:27–31)

    12. The deliverance of a mute demoniac (9:32–34)

D. Discourse: the commission and instruction of the Twelve (9:35–11:1)

E. Narrative (11:2–12:50)

      1. The testimony of Jesus to John the Baptist (11:2–15)

      2. Jesus' condemnation of the unrepentant (11:16–24)

      3. His thanksgiving to the Father and invitation to the weary (11:25–30)

      4. His lordship over the Sabbath (12:1–14)

        a. His defense of the disciples' plucking and eating grain on the Sabbath (12:1–8)

        b. His healing a withered hand on the Sabbath (12:9–14)

      5. His withdrawal and further healings (12:15–21)

      6. His delivering a blind and mute demoniac and defense of his exorcisms (12:22–37)

      7. His refusal to give any sign except that of Jonah, condemnation of self-righteousness, and identification of his true spiritual kindred (12:38–50)

F. Discourse: a parable about parables, plus six parables about the kingdom and a seventh about understanding (13:1–52)

      1. The sower (13:1–9)

      2. Reasons for parabolic teaching (13:10–17)

      3. An interpretation of the sower (13:18–23)

      4. The wheat and the tares (13:24–30)

      5. The grain of mustard seed (13:31–32)

      6. The leaven and fulfillment of Scripture by the parabolic method (13:33–35)

      7. An interpretation of the wheat and the tares (13:36–43)

      8. The buried treasure (13:44)

      9. The costly pearl (13:45–46)

    10. The dragnet with good and bad fish (13:47–50)

    11. The houseowner (13:51–52)

E'. Narrative (13:53–17:27)

      1. The rejection of Jesus at Nazareth (13:53–58)

      2. The death of John the Baptist (14:1–12)

      3. The feeding of five thousand (14:13–21)

      4. Jesus' and Peter's walking on water (14:22–36)

      5. Ritual versus moral defilement (15:1–20)

      6. Deliverance of the demonized daughter of a Canaanite woman and other healings (15:21–28)

      7. The feeding of four thousand (15:29–39)

      8. Another refusal to give any sign except that of Jonah (16:1–4)
      9. A warning against Phariseeism and Sadduceeism (16:5–12)
    10. Peter's confession of Jesus' messiahship and Jesus' blessing of Peter (16:13–20)
    11. A prediction by Jesus of his suffering, death, and resurrection; a rebuke of Peter for trying to dissuade him; and a call to cross-taking discipleship (16:21–28)
    12. The transfiguration of Jesus (17:1–13)
    13. The healing of a demonized boy (17:14–21)
    14. Another prediction by Jesus of his death and resurrection (17:22–23)
    15. Paying the temple tax, or "Peter's Penny" (17:24–27)

D'. Discourse: humility and forgiveness among Jesus' disciples (18:1–35)

C'. Narrative (19:1–22:46)

      1. Questions of divorce and marriage (19:1–12)
      2. Jesus' blessing the children (19:13–15)
      3. The rich young man and the cost and reward of discipleship (19:16–30)
      4. The parable of an employer and laborers (20:1–16)
      5. Another prediction by Jesus of his death and resurrection (20:17–19)
      6. A request for positions of honor by the mother of James and John for her sons (20:20–28)
      7. The healing of two blind men near Jericho (20:29–34)
      8. The triumphal entry (21:1–11)
      9. The cleansing of the temple (21:12–17)
    10. The cursing and withering of a fig tree (21:18–22)
    11. A challenge to Jesus' authority (21:23–27)
    12. The parable of an obedient son and a disobedient one (21:28–32)
    13. The parable of some wicked tenant farmers (21:33–46)
    14. The parable of a royal marriage feast and wedding garment (22:1–14)
    15. A question about paying taxes to Caesar (22:15–22)
    16. A question of the Sadducees about the resurrection (22:23–33)
    17. A question about the greatest commandment (22:34–40)
    18. Jesus' question about the Messiah's Davidic descent and lordship (22:41–46)

B'. Discourse: denunciation of the scribes and Pharisees and the Olivet Discourse (23:1–25:46)

      1. Denunciation of the scribes and Pharisees (23:1–39)
      2. The Olivet Discourse (24:1–25:46)
         a. A preview of events leading up to and including the return of Christ (24:1–31)
         b. Exhortations to watchfulness, with parables of the fig tree, the thief, the faithful and unfaithful servants, the ten virgins, and the talents (24:32–25:30)
         c. The judgment of the sheep and the goats (25:31–46)

A'. Narrative (26:1–28:20)

1. Another prediction by Jesus of his death, the plot of the Sanhedrin, and the anointing of Jesus in Bethany, with a resultant bargain by Judas Iscariot to betray him (26:1–16)
2. The Last Supper (26:17–35)
3. Jesus' praying in Gethsemane (26:36–46)
4. The arrest (26:47–56)
5. The trials (26:57–27:26)
    a. The trial before Caiaphas, with Peter's denials (26:57–75)
    b. The condemnatory decision of the Sanhedrin (27:1–2)
    c. The trial before Pontius Pilate, with the suicide of Judas and the release of Barabbas (27:3–26)
6. The crucifixion and death of Jesus (27:27–56)
7. The burial (27:57–66)
8. The resurrection (28:1–15)
9. The Great Commission (28:16–20)

EXCURSUS
New Testament Quotations of Fulfilled Old Testament Passages

Matthew's emphasis on fulfilled messianic prophecy makes appropriate here a consideration of the fulfillment motif throughout the New Testament. The writers of the New Testament and Jesus himself saw in the coming of God's rule a fulfillment of what we would distinguish in the Old Testament as **conscious predictions** and **unconscious typology.** (Typology refers to historical events, persons, and institutions divinely intended to be prefigurative, quite apart from whether or not the authors of the Old Testament were aware of the predictive symbolism.)

FULFILLMENT THEMES

Here is a summary of the main themes of both direct and typological fulfillment in Matthew and the rest of the New Testament: Jesus fulfilled the activities of **the Lord himself** as described and predicted in the Old Testament (Matthew 1:21; 3:3–4 par.;[1] 11:5 par.; 13:41; 24:31 par.; 27:9–10). Jesus was the foretold **messianic king** (Matthew 1:23; 2:6, 23; 3:17 par.; 4:15–16; 21:5; 22:44 par.; 26:64 par.), the **Isaianic Servant of the Lord** (Matthew 3:17 par.; 8:17; 11:5 par.; 12:18–21; 1 Peter 2:22–25), and the **Danielic Son of Man** (Matthew 24:30 par.; 26:64 par.; 28:18). He brought to a climax the line of **prophets** (Matthew 12:39–40 par.; 13:13–15 par., 35;

1. Par. = parallel(s) in the other Synoptics.

17:5 par.; 1 Corinthians 10:2; 2 Corinthians 3:7–18), the succession of **righteous sufferers** since Old Testament times (Matthew 21:42 par.; 27:34–35 par., 39 par., 43, 46 par., 48 par.), and the **Davidic dynasty** (Matthew 12:42 par.). He reversed the work of **Adam**, who plunged the human race into sin (Matthew 4:1–11 par.; Romans 5:12; 1 Corinthians 15:21–22, 45–49; Hebrews 2:5–9; compare Luke 3:38). He fulfilled God's **promise to Abraham** (Galatians 3:16). Since he was the **ideal Israelite**, his own personal history recapitulated the national history of Israel (Matthew 2:15, 18; 4:4, 7, 10 par.).

Melchizedek prefigured the priesthood of Christ, as did also, in an inferior and sometimes contrasting way, the ↓**Aaronic priesthood** (Hebrews 7–10). The **paschal lamb and other sacrifices** symbolized his redemptive death (John 1:29, 36; 19:36; Romans 3:25; 1 Corinthians 5:7; Ephesians 5:2; Hebrews 9–10; 1 Peter 1:19–21; Revelation 5:6–14), as well as Christian devotion and service (Romans 12:1; 15:16; Philippians 2:17). Jesus is life-giving bread like the ↓**manna** God provided in the desert during Israel's journey from Egypt to ↓**Canaan** (John 6:35; 1 Corinthians 10:3), the source of living water like the **rock** in the desert (1 Corinthians 10:4; compare John 7:37), the **serpent** lifted up in the desert (John 3:14), and the **tabernacle** and **temple** of God's abode among human beings (John 1:14; 2:18–22; compare Colossians 1:19).

John the Baptist was the predicted prophetic **forerunner** of Jesus (Mark 1:2–3). Jesus inaugurated the foretold eschatological period of **salvation** (John 6:45) and established the **new covenant** (Hebrews 8:8–12; 10:16–17). Judas Iscariot fulfilled the role of the **wicked opponents** of Old Testament righteous sufferers (Acts 1:20). The church is, or individual Christians are, the **new creation** (2 Corinthians 5:17; Galatians 6:15; Colossians 3:10), the spiritual **seed** (= offspring, descendants) **of Abraham** by incorporation into Christ (Romans 4:1–25; 9:6–33; Galatians 3:29; 4:21–31; Philippians 3:3), the **new Israel** (Romans 9:6–33; 11:17–24; 2 Corinthians 6:16; 1 Peter 2:9–10), and the **new temple** (1 Corinthians 3:16; 6:19; 2 Corinthians 6:16; Ephesians 2:20–22). The **Mosaic law** prefigured divine grace both positively and negatively (John 1:17; Colossians 2:17; Galatians). The **Deluge** (Noah's flood) stands for the Last Judgment (Matthew 24:37–39 par.) and for baptism (1 Peter 3:20–21). The passage through the **Red Sea** and the rite of **circumcision** foreshadowed baptism (1 Corinthians 10:2; Colossians 2:11–12). **Jerusalem** stands for the celestial city (Galatians 4:26; Hebrews 12:22; Revelation 21:1–22:5). **Entrance into Canaan** prefigures the entrance of Christians into heavenly rest (Hebrews 3:18–4:13). And proclamation of the gospel to all people fulfills God's **promise** to Abraham and prophetic **predictions** of Gentile salvation (Acts 2:17–21; 3:25; 13:47; 15:16–18; Romans 15:9–12, 21).

Aaronic: air-ON-ik ■ manna: MAN-uh ■ Canaan: KAY-nuhn

Text-Plots and Testimony Books

It is worth noting that the pursuit of these themes kept New Testament writers from atomizing the Old Testament. C. H. Dodd pointed out that they drew most of their fulfillment-quotations from a rather **limited set** of Old Testament passages ("text-plots") considered especially relevant to the new age.[2] Perhaps the early Christians also drew up manuals of Old Testament **proof texts**, called "testimony books" by modern scholars. Something like a testimony book has appeared among the Dead Sea Scrolls, but of course it is not Christian in orientation. Apparently the early church learned a new and holistic way of interpreting the Old Testament from Jesus himself (compare Luke 24:27).

TEXTUAL TRADITIONS The **Septuagint** provided a textual base for most of the Old Testament quotations, but variations are often evident. Matthew in particular appears to have utilized the **Hebrew** text of the Old Testament, the **Targums**, and other textual traditions in addition to the Septuagint.

HISTORICITY Sometimes it is argued that the early Christians massively invented incidents in the life of Jesus to obtain "fulfillments" of supposed messianic prophecies. It is true that the evangelists often borrow Old Testament phraseology in describing the events of Jesus' career. But the allusions to Old Testament texts are usually far too fleeting for those texts to have formed the basis of free invention of dominical tradition. Furthermore, many of the quoted Old Testament passages are so obscure that they could hardly have been the source for corruption of that tradition. The Old Testament quotations appear to be **later additions** to the tradition concerning Jesus. The tradition came first, the recognition of correspondences to ancient prophecy and typology later.

2. C. H. Dodd, *According to the Scriptures* (London: Nisbet, 1961).

Testimony Book from Qumran (4Q175), which quotes Deuteronomy 5:28–29; 18:18–19 regarding a coming prophet like Moses; Numbers 24:15–17 regarding a warring, royal Messiah to come; and Deuteronomy 33:8–11 regarding a priestly Messiah

Reading Matthew with Interpretation

Jesus' Genealogy

Matthew appeals to his Jewish Christian reading audience by starting his Gospel with a genealogy of Jesus that reaches back into the Old Testament, highlights **Abraham**, father of the Jewish people, and **King David**, prototype of the messianic king expected by the Jews, leads through David's royal descendants, and emphasizes the identity of Jesus as **the Christ**. *Read Matthew 1:1–17.* Comparison with the Old Testament shows that Matthew deliberately omits four generations of Davidic kings to get **three sets of**

fourteen generations each. These fourteens put a triple emphasis on David as prototype of the messianic king, Jesus, because David appears in fourteenth place on the genealogical list and because the numerical values of the Hebrew consonants in his name add up to fourteen: d (4) + v (6) + d (4) = D[a]v[i]d (14). (Matthew wrote before the invention of Arabic numerals and before the introduction of vowels into written Hebrew.) The third set of fourteen numbers only thirteen unless one counts Mary, the mother of Jesus, as well as Joseph, his foster father, as is perhaps intended because Jesus was born of Mary, with Joseph providing the legal but not the biological lineage. (In Jewish society at the time, legal rights passed through a father, even a foster father, not through a mother, even a biological mother.) The unusual appearance of **four women** on the list prior to Mary supplements its Jewishness with a Gentile element, for three of them were Gentiles (↓Tamar, ↓Rahab, and Ruth) and the fourth the wife of a Gentile (therefore called "the wife of ↓Uriah" rather than by her Jewish name, ↓Bathsheba). This Gentile element points forward to the discipling of all nations at the end of Matthew (28:18–20).

Nativity

Matthew tells the nativity story from the **standpoint of Joseph.** Mary conceives Jesus by the Holy Spirit during her engagement to Joseph. Engagement was so binding that Jews called the engaged couple husband and wife. Only divorce or death could break the engagement, and in case of death the survivor became a widow or widower. So on learning of Mary's pregnancy, Joseph resolves to divorce her privately; but a message from an angel of the Lord leads him to marry her instead. As a result and because of Joseph's descent from David, Jesus is born into a Davidic family and considered legally qualified to inherit David's throne. Joseph's naming Jesus indicates an acceptance of Jesus as **his legal son.** *Read Matthew 1:18–25.*

VIRGIN BIRTH "*By* the Holy Spirit" (1:18) echoes phrases used of women in 1:3, 5 (twice), 6, 16 and therefore shows that in contrast to pagan myths, according to which male gods have sexual intercourse with human mothers-to-be, the Holy Spirit does not play the sexual role of a male: there is no carnal intercourse. Nor does Joseph have intercourse with Mary till after she gives birth to Jesus. It is disputed whether Joseph resolves to divorce Mary because he thinks her unfaithful and wants to obey the law (compare Deuteronomy 22:23–24) or because he knows her to have conceived by the Holy Spirit and wants not to intrude. Favoring suspicion is the angel's telling him that she has conceived by the Holy Spirit, as though Joseph has not known this fact before. In either case, Matthew portrays him as a model of **righteousness, mercy,** and **obedience.**

Tamar: TAY-mahr ■ Rahab: RAY-hab ■ Uriah: yoo-RI-uh ■ Bathsheba: bath-SHEE-buh

"JESUS" AND "IMMANUEL" By popular etymology, *Jesus,* Greek form of the Hebrew name Joshua, means "Yahweh (the LORD) is salvation." The people whom Jesus will save from their sins are those who in the words of Isaiah 7:14, which Matthew quotes as fulfilled, will call his name "Immanuel," that is, who will recognize that he is "God with us" (compare 28:18–20).

MAGI The story of the magi portrays these astrologers from the East, probably Persia, as the vanguard of many other Gentiles who will acknowledge Jesus as the Christ (again compare 28:18–20, but also 8:10–12). *Read Matthew 2:1–12.* Bethlehem comes into the picture as the town of Jesus' birth, just as it was the town of David's origin. In accordance with Micah 5:2, the messianic king is born in the town of King David. And whatever the astronomical or nonastronomical truth (a conjunction of planets or of a planet and a star, a comet, a supernova, and so on), the star of the messianic king recalls the **star of David**. Herod the Great fears a rival in the making, and Jerusalem sides with Herod in anticipation of Jesus' later rejection in that city. The magi's worshiping Jesus and offering him gifts suit his being "God with us," but the three kinds of gifts they offer do not necessarily indicate the number of the magi.

> "A star will come out of Jacob, and a scepter will rise out of Israel" (Numbers 24:17).

SLAUGHTER OF THE INNOCENTS AND FLIGHT TO EGYPT *Read Matthew 2:13–23.* Herod's attempt to kill the infant Christ anticipates the actual killing of the adult Christ. Herod was infamous for his cruelty. The flight to Egypt and return fulfill Hosea 11:1, which originally referred to Israel's exodus from Egypt, where God had treated them as his son by preserving them from death by famine, just as now God treats Jesus as his Son by preserving him there from death by slaughter. Traditionally called "The Slaughter of the Innocents," the killing of male children under two in and around Bethlehem fulfills Jeremiah 31:15, which originally referred to the weeping of Jewish mothers on seeing their offspring taken to exile in Babylon.

NAZARETH–NAZARENE The residence of the holy family in Nazareth fulfills various prophecies that call the Messiah a **branch**, the Hebrew word for which is ↓*netzer,* which sounds something like "Nazareth" (Isaiah 11:1; also Jeremiah 23:5; 33:15; Zechariah 3:8; 6:12, where a Hebrew synonym is similarly used). The Babylonian exile cut the tree of David's dynasty down to a stump; but out of that stump of a dynasty grows a branch or shoot, reviving the dynasty in the Messiah descended from David. The very name *Nazareth* encodes this outgrowth. (Alternatively, "Nazarene" alludes to "Nazirite" in Judges 13:5, 7; 16:17, though Jesus did not at all live like a Nazirite, who had to avoid wine, grape juice, grapes, raisins, haircuts, and dead bodies [Numbers 6:1–21; contrast Matthew 11:19 par.; 9:18, 24–25], nor does this interpretation suit Matthew's Davidic Christology.)

---

netzer: NAY-tser

Ruins of Nazareth from the Roman period

The Baptist's Preaching

Read Matthew 3:1–17. "Those days" (3:1) refers to the days of residence in Nazareth (2:23). Matthew emphasizes John the Baptist's preaching of repentance and judgment. In the phrase "kingdom of heaven," which appears often in Matthew but nowhere else in the New Testament, "heaven" substitutes for "God" to put an accent on majesty and universality (compare Daniel 4:1–37). **Wheat** means kernels of wheat and stands for **repentant** people. **Chaff** means husks and straw and stands for the **unrepentant.** After the treading of oxen on a threshing floor has loosened the wheat from the husks and ground up the straw, a farmer scoops up the mixture, throws it into the air, and lets wind blow the chaff to one side. The gathering of wheat into a granary represents **salvation by baptism in the Holy Spirit.** The burning of chaff with unquenchable fire represents **judgment by baptism in fire.**

> "A shoot will spring from the stump of Jesse; and from his roots a branch [Hebrew: *netzer*] will bear fruit" (Isaiah 11:1).

Jesus' Baptism

Because of Jesus' superiority as the baptizer in the Holy Spirit and fire, John tries not to baptize Jesus; but Jesus' insistence makes him an **example** for his disciples to follow in baptism—without delay ("now," 3:15; compare 28:19); for baptism is the entirely right thing to do (the meaning of "fulfills all righteousness"). "This is my beloved Son, in whom I am well pleased" confirms to John that it was the right thing: **God has taken pleasure in Jesus because of his baptism.**

Temptation

Matthew details three temptations of Jesus by the devil. The first two urge Jesus to take personal advantage of his being God's beloved Son, as stated in the preceding story. But Jesus resists these temptations, and the third temptation as well, by citing Scripture. Thus he becomes the **model of postbaptismal obedience to the law** (compare 28:19). *Read Matthew 4:1– 11. Devil* is Greek for the Hebrew *Satan*. The terms mean "accuser" with respect to bringing before God accusations against his people. The devil tempts in the hope of being able to accuse. To **tempt** is to **test**, sometimes with hardship, at other times with enticement, and at yet other times with both. The first temptation rests on a similarity in appearance between stones and loaves of bread. The second temptation, located in Jerusalem, urges a publicity stunt; for the wilderness has many precipices off which Jesus might have jumped but for the lack of onlookers. "The highest point of the temple" may refer to the southeast corner of the temple courts dropping off into the Kidron Valley, to the lintel atop the temple gate, or to the roof of the temple proper. The devil's quotation of Psalm 91:11–12 omits "to guard you in all your ways," because that phrase points to the accidental stumbling over a stone in one's path rather than to a deliberate throwing of oneself from a high perch, as the devil is tempting Jesus to do. Given Jesus' identity as "God with us" (1:23), the devil can only leave when at the close of the third temptation Jesus tells him to be gone.

Jesus withdraws to Galilee on hearing of John the Baptist's arrest and then starts to preach, teach, heal, and make disciples in this region known for its Gentiles, which means "nations," in addition to its Jewish population. The withdrawal makes Jesus a **model of fleeing persecution so as to preach and make disciples elsewhere**, as his disciples are to do among all the nations (see 10:23 with 28:18–20). *Read Matthew 4:12–25.*

Sermon on the Mount

Now Jesus ascends a mountain, takes the seated position of a teacher, and teaches his disciples. Since he is "God with us" (1:23) and human beings are to live "on every word that comes out of the mouth of God" (4:4), what comes out of Jesus' mouth when he opens it is the very words of God, like the law of God given through Moses on Mount ↓Sinai, only perfecting that law. *Read Matthew 5:1–16.*

↓**BEATITUDES** The series of statements beginning with "Blessed" are known as the Beatitudes. The word *blessed* does not mean "happy," as is sometimes said mistakenly; for those who mourn are not happy. Otherwise they would not be mourning. *Blessed* means "congratulations to" and reflects God's estimate rather than human emotion. The Beatitudes promise compensation

---

Sinai: *SI-ni* ■ beatitudes: bee-AT-uh-tyoodz

at the Last Judgment for disciples inwardly desperate, mournful, nonretaliatory, longing for divine vindication, merciful, pure, peacemaking, and righteous in the face of persecution.

SALT AND LIGHT "The salt of the earth" means salt used in carefully measured amounts to fertilize soil and symbolizes the witness given to the world by the **good works** of Jesus' disciples, though the failure of false disciples to persevere in such works brings irreversible judgment, like the throwing away of salt that has lost its saltiness through adulteration or leaching. "The light of the world" means the sun, here an additional symbol, along with a lamp, for the witness given to the world by the good works of Jesus' disciples.

↓**ANTITHESES** After affirming the complete validity of the Law and the Prophets, the two sections of the Old Testament read in synagogues every Sabbath, Jesus contrasts his teaching with that of the Old Testament, not by way of denying that teaching, as the traditional designation "Antitheses" implies, but by way of escalating it to a level toward which it was already tending.

- The prohibition of murder escalates to a prohibition of anger and abusive speech and a command to reconciliation.

Antitheses: an-TITH-uh-seez

Mount of Beatitudes

- The prohibition of adultery escalates to a prohibition of lust.
- The command to give a divorced wife a certificate of divorce (to protect her from the false charge of desertion) escalates to warnings against making a divorcee commit adultery in marrying another man out of economic necessity and against committing adultery by marrying a divorcee.
- The command to avoid false vows and keep oaths escalates to a prohibition of all oaths.
- The command that penalties suit rather than exceed crimes (the ↓*lex talionis*, or law of retaliation: "an eye for an eye . . ." in contrast with ancient law codes that imposed severe penalties for minor crimes) escalates to a requirement of meekness and helpfulness.
- The command to love your neighbor and hate your enemy (see Psalm 139:21–22 for the latter) escalates to a command to love your enemies and pray for your persecutors.

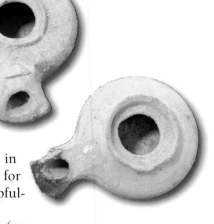

Oil lamps

Read Matthew 5:17–48. The exception of immorality in 5:32 allows a man to divorce his wife if she has had sex with another man, for then the divorce arises out of immorality instead of issuing in it (though some think that immorality here means incest, such as Leviticus 18:6–18 prohibits but Gentiles sometimes practice). Being forced to go one mile in 5:41 reflects the practice of the Romans, especially Roman soldiers, in requisitioning their subjects to carry baggage for them.

CHARITY, PRAYER, AND FASTING Comparisons with the Old Testament now fade into the distance, and Jesus teaches as a sage. He warns against showiness in religious practice, particularly in giving charity, praying, and fasting. *Read Matthew 6:1–18.* The reward of human praise is all the reward that those who seek such praise will get. Not letting your left hand know what your right hand does in the giving of charity means slipping a gift to a beggar unobtrusively with the right hand alone rather than offering it with both hands extended so as to attract the attention of onlookers. **The Lord's Prayer**, or ↓*Pater Noster* (Latin for the first words of the prayer: "Our Father"), stands here as an example of praying with an economy of words as opposed to the heaping up of empty phrases in pagan prayers. "Our debts" are moral debts owed to God, that is, our sins. Forgiving our debtors may refer to forgiving financial debts at the Year of Jubilee (Leviticus 25:8–55). "Lead us not into temptation" does not ask to avoid temptation, but means, "Do not let us succumb to temptation." The last petition reads, "but deliver us from the evil one," in reference to Satan. The familiar doxology, "For thine is the

lex talionis: leks tal-ee-OH-nis ■ *Pater Noster:* PA-ter NOS-ter

An Example of Wordiness in Pagan Prayers

"O queen of heaven—whether you are the bountiful Ceres, the primal mother of crops, who in joy at the recovery of your daughter took away from men their primeval animal fodder of acorns and showed them gentler nourishment and now dwell in the land of Eleusis; or heavenly Venus, who at the first foundation of the universe united the diversity of the sexes by creating Love and propagated the human race through ever-recurring progeny and now are worshipped in the island sanctuary of Paphos; or Phoebus' sister, who brought forth populous multitudes by relieving the delivery of offspring with your soothing remedies and now are venerated at the illustrious shrine of Ephesus; or dreaded Proserpina of the nocturnal howls, who in triple form repress the attacks of ghosts and keep the gates to earth closed fast, roam through widely scattered groves and are propitiated by diverse rites—you who illumine every city with your womanly light, nourish the joyous seeds with your moist fires, and dispense beams of fluctuating radiance according to the convolutions of the Sun—by whatever name, with whatever rite, in whatever image it is appropriate to invoke you: defend me now in the uttermost extremes of tribulation" (Apuleius, *Metamorphoses* 11.2; compare the statement in Virgil, *Aeneid* 4.510, that "with streaming hair the priestess calls in thunderous tones on 300 gods, both Erebos and Chaos and threefold Hecate, triple-faced Diana").

kingdom and the power and the glory forever," does not appear in the earliest and best manuscripts. By pouring ashes over their heads, the hypocrites made their faces *dis*appear to *appear* to others as fasting (so the wordplay in Matthew's Greek). Ancient Jews did not wash their faces and oil their heads daily for hygienic and cosmetic reasons; rather, only for joyous occasions. So Jesus says to mask your fasting, not your face, with the appearance of joy rather than with a somber look.

↓**MAMMON** The next section prohibits the building up of earthly wealth and commands the building up of heavenly wealth, because **your heart will follow your wealth**. This is not to say that building up earthly wealth is wrong *if* you have a wrong attitude toward it; rather, building it up is wrong because it will *in fact* produce a wrong attitude. By contrast, building up heavenly wealth draws your heart to heaven. *Read Matthew 6:19–34.* A healthy eye, sparkling like a lighted lamp, stands for **generosity**; an unhealthy eye, dull with disease, stands for **stinginess**. *Mammon* ("Money" in 6:24) is Aramaic for "wealth." Since God's righteousness (6:33) contrasts with your (the disciples') righteousness (5:20; 6:1), the righteousness of God that Jesus' persecuted disciples are to seek does not consist in their

---

mammon: MAM-uhn

own good works but in God's doing the right thing by them, that is, caring for them now and rewarding them at the end (compare 5:6).

SUPERIOR RIGHTEOUSNESS In 7:1–12 Jesus finishes his description of the righteousness that surpasses that of the scribes and Pharisees (note how "the Law and the Prophets" in 7:12 harks back to "the Law or the Prophets" at the start of this description in 5:17). His prohibition of judgment has to do with respect for other people's profession of discipleship (7:1–5), his prohibition of giving sacrificial meat to dogs and of throwing pearls before pigs with the danger of letting into the community of disciples people who do not even profess discipleship (7:6), and his command to keep the Golden Rule ("Therefore all things whatever you would want people to do for you, you also do thus for them") with helping one another within that community (7:7–12). *Read Matthew 7:1–12.*

Judging means taking it on oneself to declare a fellow disciple false. Only God can make that judgment, and he will make it against those hypocrites who do it themselves without noticing that their own faults exceed the faults of those they are judging. On the other hand, self-criticism will turn an otherwise condemnatory judgment into a kindly act of restoration. In the world of the New Testament most dogs were vicious street-roamers. Therefore, just as such dogs would turn on you if you whetted their appetite with a taste of sacrificial meat carelessly given them, and just as pigs would trample any pearls foolishly thrown before them, so would the imprudent admission of nondisciples into your community expose you to persecution from within. So do not let the nonjudgmentalism necessary to good community go so far as to break down that community by erasing the boundary between it and the world of nondisciples. And God's doing good for you by answering your prayers demands that you do good for one another.

NARROW AND BROAD The Sermon on the Mount concludes with warnings not to heed false prophets, but to obey the teachings of Jesus. *Read Matthew 7:13–29.* A narrow mountain road leads to the City of Salvation, impregnable atop its peak. The only way to enter is through a gate easily defended because it is narrow. The narrow road and narrow gate represent the strictures of **superior righteousness** such as Jesus demands of his disciples. A broad road leads to the City of Destruction, situated on an open plain. Its wide gate accommodates many, but by the same token beckons invaders. The broad road and wide gate represent the **lax behavior** taught by false prophets and practiced by false disciples. In the concluding parable

- The wise man = **true disciples**
- The foolish man = **false disciples**
- Building on the rock = **obedience** to Jesus' teachings
- Building on the sand = **disobedience** to them
- The storm = the **Last Judgment** conducted by Jesus on his disciples

So although lax behavior may exempt you from persecution now, it will subject you to destruction hereafter; but though superior righteousness may expose you to persecution now, it will exempt you from destruction hereafter.

Miracles

Now Matthew shifts from the teachings of Jesus to three of Jesus' miracles that add the authority of his deeds to that of his words. *Read Matthew 8:1–15.* In cleansing a **leper**, Jesus fulfills the law. In healing a **centurion's servant,** he promises believing Gentiles, like the centurion,[3] admission to the end-time banquet of salvation (the messianic feast) but says that unbelieving Jews ("the sons of the kingdom" are those who should inherit the kingdom of heaven because they belong to the chosen nation) will be thrown out of the banquet hall into the surrounding darkness of judgment. In healing **Peter's mother-in-law,** Jesus takes the initiative, uses a mere touch, and becomes the object of her service.

DISCIPLESHIP Next comes an interlude consisting of a summary, an Old Testament quotation, and two dialogues on discipleship. *Read Matthew 8:16–22.* Jesus' healings fulfill Isaiah 53:4. "Another of his disciples" (8:21) implies that the preceding "scribe" was a disciple too (see 13:52 for a scribe as a disciple). The first disciple shows his **genuineness** by expressing a determination to follow Jesus wherever Jesus goes—in an itinerant ministry, as Jesus notes. The second disciple shows his **falsity** by asking to go and bury his father before starting to follow. He probably refers to a commonly practiced secondary burial, that is, gathering the bones of his father now that the flesh has decomposed and putting the bones in a small container (called an ↓*ossuary*) so as to make room in the family tomb for a fresh corpse. Jesus' reply, "Follow me, and let the dead bury their own dead," rejects even the most sacred of filial duties (burying your father) in favor of immediate allegiance to Jesus. The dead's burying their dead is not meant to make sense (how could dead people bury one of their own?), but to dismiss the question of burial altogether.

MORE MIRACLES A second trio of miracles now comes into view. The first miracle demonstrates Jesus' authority over the **natural elements**, the second over **demons**, and the third his authority to **forgive sins**, an authority he shares with his disciples. *Read Matthew 8:23–9:8.* Matthew identifies the region where the exorcism takes place by the name of a city about five miles southeast of the shoreline. The second demoniac is missing in the parallel accounts at Mark 5:1–20; Luke 8:26–39. Do they omit a less obtrusive demoniac, or does Matthew introduce a second demoniac from the story in Mark 1:21–28; Luke 4:31–37, otherwise omitted by him? "The men" to

3. In the Roman army a centurion commanded one hundred soldiers.

ossuary: OS-yoo-er´ee

Ossuaries

whom 9:8 says God has given authority to forgive sins are "the men," that is, the disciples, who were in a boat with Jesus when he stilled a storm (8:27). Thus they declare sins forgiven and heal people to substantiate the forgiveness just as Jesus does. He is their model of forgiving and healing (compare 16:17; 18:18; John 20:23).

CALL OF MATTHEW Matthew's becoming a disciple and Jesus' instructions on fasting provide another interlude. *Read Matthew 9:9–17.* Some think that Matthew changes "Levi" (Mark 2:14; Luke 5:27, 29) to "Matthew" to gain an apostolic name (compare Matthew 10:3), others that one man bore both names, as sometimes happened. In either case, Jesus' citation of Hosea 6:6, "I [God] want mercy and not sacrifice," makes the call of Matthew an act of mercy toward outcasts such as tax collectors and notorious sinners. The preservation of both wine and wineskins accents the preservation of fasting once Jesus the bridegroom is taken away (compare 6:16–18).

YET MORE MIRACLES A third trio of miracle stories now comes into the narrative. The first story narrates a double miracle that displays Jesus' authority over the destructive effects of illness and death. The second displays his ability to heal two blind men at once. And the third displays his power to heal and deliver a man doubly afflicted with muteness and demonic possession. *Read Matthew 9:18–34.* Comparison with Matthew 20:29–34; Mark 10:46–52; and Luke 18:35–43 suggests to some that Matthew here introduces a second blind man from Mark 8:22–26, otherwise omitted by him (compare the similar possibility of his having introduced a second demoniac in 8:28–34).

Missions Discourse

Next, a short narrative introduces a long discourse. The narrative stresses Jesus' **compassion**. Out of this compassion he declares the harvest plentiful but the harvesters few and tells his disciples to ask the harvest master to send out harvesters. The harvest represents evangelism. The harvesters are the twelve apostles, who are to make further disciples by preaching the gospel. And the harvest master is Jesus, sender of the Twelve. In the end, however, they are not said to have gone and no description of their ministry is given (contrast Mark 6:12–13), so that Jesus' lengthy instructions, which shift in midstream from the Jewish setting in Galilee to a Gentile setting in the wider world, become relevant to the evangelistic enterprise of the later Christian church. Just as the Sermon on the Mount taught disciples how to **behave**, then, this Missions Discourse teaches them how to **testify**. *Read Matthew 9:35–10:42.*

In chapter 10, verses 2–4 identify the harvesters with the twelve apostles. Verses 5–15 tell them how to evangelize **Jews** living in Galilee. And verses 16–42 warn against persecution in a further mission that will embrace **Gentiles** as well. Thus, the present restriction to Jews in Galilee (10:5b–6) gives way to a future inclusion of Gentiles elsewhere (10:18), but not at the expense of discontinuing the Jewish mission (10:23). Against self-aggrandizement, Jesus prohibits acquisitions taken from ministry (10:9–10); and he prohibits moving around in a locality to find the most comfortable living quarters (10:11–15). As to persecution, Jesus says to beware of informers, not to worry about preparing statements for court, and to flee from one city to another rather than staying suicidally in a city that poses a threat to life and limb (10:16–23). He also gives a number of reasons not to fear persecution:

- His own sufferings (10:24–25)
- The impossibility of hiding the truth (10:26–27)
- The unimportance of physical martyrdom in comparison with the eternal punishment of a whole person (10:28)
- The value God puts on Jesus' disciples (10:29–31)
- The necessity of confessing Jesus before others if you are to be confessed by him before God the Father (10:32–33)
- The unworthiness of anyone who shrinks back through fear of personal abuse (10:34–39)
- The conveying of eternal life to others through self-sacrificial witness (10:40–42)

PERSECUTION Having quoted Jesus' **warning** against persecution, Matthew now gives **examples** of persecution in John the Baptist, Jesus, and the disciples (11:1–12:50). More specifically, the case of John the Baptist illustrates the violence suffered by the kingdom of heaven (11:1–24). The gentleness of Jesus toward his disciples contrasts with that violence and highlights it (11:25–30). The Pharisees plot the destruction of Jesus (12:1–21) and slander him (12:22–37), but he exposes their wickedness, pronounces judgment on them (12:38–45), and describes the disciples (those who do the will of his heavenly Father and therefore are persecuted for righteousness' sake; see also 5:10–11) as his true family (12:46–52). *Read Matthew 11:1–12:50.*

A Tribute to the Baptist

The mention of John the Baptist's imprisonment suggests that though "the works of the Christ" have excited John's hopes that Jesus is the Coming One predicted by John, the failure of Jesus to rescue him from prison has raised a doubt. Jesus' answer to his question seems to indicate that the works of the Christ are providing sufficient evidence (compare Isaiah 35:5–6; 61:1). Jesus' tribute to John includes a statement that the least in the kingdom of heaven is greater than John (11:11b). Since the violence suffered by that kingdom started with the persecution of John, he belongs in the kingdom; so Jesus is not saying that leastness inside the kingdom surpasses greatness outside it. Greatness in the kingdom will be explained in terms of humility at 18:4. Hence, Jesus is saying that the humblest disciple will exceed even John, thus far the greatest human being ever born. The Jews who have responded favorably neither to John nor to Jesus are like children who stubbornly reject each suggestion concerning what game they should play: mock wedding and mock funeral (11:16–19). The parallel between "the works of wisdom" (11:19b) and "the works of the Christ" (11:2) implies that Jesus the Christ is **Wisdom personified** (compare 23:34 with Luke 11:49). "Babies" (11:25) represents teachable disciples in contrast with the scribes and Pharisees.

JOHANNINE THUNDERBOLT Jesus' unique sonship to God the Father receives eloquent expression in 11:25–27 (paralleled in Luke 10:21–22), sometimes called "the Johannine thunderbolt" because it sounds much like statements in the Gospel of John concerning the relation of Jesus to God. In what way does Jesus give rest and a light load? Not by demanding less of his disciples than do the scribes and Pharisees, for he demands more (5:20). Rather, by humbly, meekly getting under the other side of the "yoke," a figure of speech for law, and pulling with his disciples (compare 1:23; 28:20).

BREAKING THE SABBATH The priests can break the Sabbath by working in the temple, because the temple is greater

---

The Johannine Thunderbolt

"All things have been given over to me by my Father, and no one knows the Son except the Father. Neither does anyone know the Father except the Son and anyone to whom the Son wills to reveal him" (Matthew 11:27).

"The Father loves the Son and has given all things into his hand" (John 3:35).

"Just as the Father knows me, I also know the Father" (John 10:15).

"I made your name known to them" (Jesus addressing the Father concerning the disciples; John 17:26).

than the Sabbath (Numbers 28:9–10). The temple is greater than the Sabbath, because the Sabbath was made for human beings, the temple for God. Jesus is greater than the temple, because the temple is God's dwelling, but Jesus is God's very person with us (again see 1:23). Another quotation of Hosea 6:6 ("I desire mercy and not sacrifice"; compare Matthew 12:7 with 9:13) makes the Pharisees' condemnation of the innocent disciples an instance of merciless persecution. The man with a withered hand is like a sheep fallen into a pit; mercy demands that the man be healed even on the Sabbath more than it demands that the sheep be lifted out of the pit on the Sabbath (12:11–12). Jesus' withdrawal to escape the Pharisees' plot shows him heeding his own command to flee persecution (10:23) and fulfills Isaiah 42:1–4: he does not seek justice for himself; he proclaims it to the nations and actualizes it for his persecuted disciples (represented by "a bruised reed" and "a smoldering wick," 12:17–21). The person who is against Jesus and scatters is a persecutor (12:30). People's words reveal their character. The Pharisees' speaking blasphemy against the Holy Spirit reveals their rottenness and seals their condemnation (12:22–37).

JONAH'S SIGN The sign of Jonah the prophet is Jesus' spending three days and three nights in a tomb just as Jonah spent three days and three nights in the belly of a sea monster (12:39–40). The limit of three implies the resurrection. Jesus' dying on Good Friday and rising on Easter Sunday might seem to belie "three days and three nights," but Jews often counted part of a twenty-four-hour period as a whole such period (see Genesis 42:17–18; 1 Samuel 30:1, 12–13; 2 Chronicles 10:5, 12; Esther 4:16–5:1). Thus part of Friday, all Saturday, and part of Sunday may count for three days and

Mustard plant

three nights. The last and worst state of the man in Jesus' parable whom an unclean spirit repossessed with seven other spirits more wicked than itself points ahead to the outburst of evil in the Pharisees' helping to engineer the passion (21:45–46; 22:15, 34, 41; 27:62). The Father in heaven completes the family of Jesus' persecuted disciples: brother, sister, and mother.

Parabolic Discourse

The bulk of chapter 13 contains the third great discourse of Jesus in Matthew, a parabolic one. If the Sermon on the Mount dealt with Christian **conduct** and the Missions Discourse with Christian **testimony**, the Parabolic Discourse deals with Christian **understanding**. The many crowds of Jesus' audience appear to represent the **mixed** church of Matthew's time. The disciples among those crowds appear to represent true believers as opposed to false within that church (13:1–2). As in Mark 4:3–9, the introductory parable of the sower is a parable

Parabolic Background

- Tares are ↓darnels, a weed resembling wheat. Ordinarily darnels are weeded out. But here they are so numerous that their roots have intertwined with those of the wheat.
- Leaven is a bit of fermenting dough inserted as yeast into fresh dough to ferment it too.
- Three measures of flour amount to about fifty pounds, an immense quantity making a huge lump of dough. Jesus is using hyperbole, exaggeration for emphasis. Some have interpreted the leaven as symbolic of the evil that corrupts Christendom. It is true that elsewhere leaven often stands for evil, but association with the parable of the mustard seed favors interpretation in terms of a contrast between a small beginning and large ending. Other figures of speech carry various meanings. For example, salt stands for the witness of good works (Matthew 5:13), judgment (Mark 9:49), peace (Mark 9:50), and graciousness (Colossians 4:6). Here, to drive home the point that God's rule is more active and powerful than the rule of Satan, Jesus may have purposefully chosen a figure that usually has an evil connotation.
- Some have thought that the birds in the parable of the mustard seed represent false teachers who invade the church. But the phraseology comes from Nebuchadnezzar's dream (Daniel 4:12, 21), where the nesting of birds in the branches of a tree indubitably points to the large size of the tree.
- Repeated invasions of Palestine caused fearful people to bury their treasures for safekeeping. Here the one who buried his treasure seems to have died or been killed. As a result, the treasure is ownerless. The law allowed the discoverer of a treasure to hide it again and purchase the field so as to obtain the treasure legally.
- ↓Seine nets, used to catch fish, are either dragged between two boats or laid out by one boat and drawn to shore with two long ropes. Bad fish consist of those prohibited by the Mosaic law because they lack scales or fins, and also of other marine life considered inedible by Jews.

about parables (13:3–9). Jesus then explains that he speaks in parables because those who lack understanding—that is, false disciples—fall under the judgment of losing understanding (the parables puzzle them) and because those who have understanding—that is, true disciples—get further understanding (the parables inform them; 13:10–23).

The middle six parables fall into pairs and all begin with a reference to the kingdom of heaven (13:24–50). The parable of the wheat and the tares emphasizes a **delay of separation** until the harvest (13:24–30). The parables of the grown mustard tree and leavened lump of dough form a pair emphasizing **magnitude**; the kingdom has grown and spread throughout the world (13:31–32, 33). A quotation of Psalm 78:2 as fulfilled interrupts the series of parables (13:34–35). A private explanation of the parable of the wheat and the tares identifies the wheat with true disciples, the tares with false disciples, and so on (13:36–43). Thus the true disciples in Jesus' audience gain more understanding through the explanation, and also through a second pair of parables concerning a treasure and a pearl, both teaching the joyful sacrifice of everything for the kingdom (13:44, 45–46), and through the sixth parable, concerning good and bad fish, which pairs up with the first of the six to teach the final judgment of false disciples and the

darnels: DAHR-nuhlz ■ seine: sayn

Farmer plowing his field

final reward of true ones (13:47–50). A concluding parable compares the fully informed, true disciple to a houseowner who pulls out of his closet treasures of new clothes (new understanding) and old clothes (old understanding, 13:51–52). *Read Matthew 13:1–52.*

Understanding

Preceding parables have stressed the contrast between understanding and lack of understanding. The following block of narratives carries forward this same contrast. Jesus' fellow townspeople misidentify him as the carpenter's son, whereas he is the Son of God (2:15; 3:17 et passim). *Read Matthew 13:53–58.* Herod the tetrarch (Antipas) misidentifies Jesus as John the Baptist risen from the dead. *Read Matthew 14:1–12.* Though the disciples have little faith in the feeding of the five thousand, at least they understand that Jesus wants them to distribute the provisions on hand; and to the five thousand men are added an indeterminate number of women and children to produce a church-like throng of families—husbands, wives, and children—eating in anticipation of the Lord's Supper. *Read Matthew 14:13–21.* To the story of Jesus' walking on the water is added the episode of **Peter's walking on the water** temporarily. This episode reaches its climax in a confessional display of the disciples' understanding Jesus to be God's Son. *Read Matthew 14:22–33.*

DEFILEMENT On arrival in Gennesaret, Jesus grants his disciples understanding with respect to true defilement. It is not any unclean thing going into the mouth (food) that defiles a person, says Jesus, but evil things coming out of the mouth (words). Thus Jesus transmutes the dietary taboos of the Old Testament into a prohibition of evil speech. *Read Matthew 14:34–15:20.* The figures of being uprooted and of falling into a pit, applied to the Pharisees, represent judgment at the hands of God (15:13–14).

With no concern for ritual purity, Jesus withdraws from his persecutors (Pharisees and scribes from Jerusalem, 15:1) and goes into Gentile territory. There a woman shows her understanding of Jesus'

Pairs of Parables

A. The sower (on understanding)

  B. Wheat and tares (on true and false disciples)

    C. Mustard tree (on magnitude)

    C'. Leaven (on magnitude)

    D. Treasure (on joyful sacrifice)

    D'. Pearl (on joyful sacrifice)

  B'. Good and bad fish (on true and false disciples)

A'. The houseowner (on understanding)

true identity by addressing him once with "Son of David" and three times with "Lord" and by worshiping him. In other words, she understands his **universal deity** as well as his **Jewish messiahship**. To be sure, "Lord" sometimes carries the weak meaning of "Sir"; but in Matthew's Gospel the portrayal of Jesus as "God with us" (1:23; compare 18:20; 28:20), the sandwiching of Jesus as the Son between God the Father and the Holy Spirit in a baptismal formula (28:19), and the substitution of Jesus' "I" for "God" (compare 28:20 with 1:23) all demand that when applied to Jesus, "Lord" connotes deity. Here the Gentile woman's understanding generates faith so strong that it surmounts the obstacles of his silence, the disciples' antagonism, the limitation of his commission to the Jews, and his refusal. *Read Matthew 15:21–28.*

GENTILES Jesus goes back to the Sea of Galilee, but apparently to the predominantly Gentile east side, so that the four thousand whom Jesus now feeds seem to be Gentiles. If so, with the preceding Gentile woman and, earlier, the centurion and the magi, they represent the great mass of Gentiles who are flocking into the church of Matthew's time. And the disciples understand Jesus' intention that they should distribute bread to the crowd. As in the feeding of the five thousand, wives and children are added to portray a church-like throng of families eating in anticipation of the Lord's Supper. *Read Matthew 15:29–39.* ↓Magadan is obscure but apparently located on the west side of the Sea of Galilee.

The Pharisees and Sadducees renew their persecution of Jesus. He excoriates them for their failure to understand the **signs of the times**, that is, his miracles and exorcisms. Then he grants his disciples understanding of the **evil teaching** of the Pharisees and Sadducees. *Read Matthew 16:1–12.*

Peter and the Rock

Near Caesarea Philippi, Peter displays his understanding of Jesus' identity as the Christ, the Son of the living God. Jesus attributes this understanding to a revelation by his heavenly Father to Peter. *Read Matthew 16:13–20.* Peter's "the Son of the living God" echoes the disciples' "the Son of God" in 14:33. "Barjonas" means "son of Jonah" and alludes to "the sign of Jonah," that is, Jesus' death, burial, and resurrection (12:39–40; 16:4). "Flesh and blood" (16:17) means human beings as characterized by ignorance, frailty, mortality, and so forth. "Peter" (Greek: ↓*petros*) means "stone." But Jesus' wordplaying statement, "and on this rock [Greek: ↓*petra*] I will build my church," has received a variety of interpretations. If the Aramaic ↓*Cephas* underlies Matthew's Greek, a distinction between *petros* and *petra* may not hold, and Jesus may be saying that he will make **Peter**, prince of the apostles, the rock foundation of his church (whether by himself or in conjunc-

---

Magadan: MAG-uh-dan ■ *petros:* PEH-traws ■ *petra:* PEH-trah ■ Cephas: SEE-fuhs tion with the other apostles [compare Ephesians 2:20], whether for the period of his lifetime alone or in perpetuity through papal successors). On the other hand, one might have expected to read, "You are Peter and on *you* I will build my church." The switch from "you" to "this rock" suggests that Peter himself is not the foundation, but that the meaning of his name points to another entity as the foundation—say, **Jesus** as the one whom Peter has just confessed him to be, the Christ and Son of the living God (compare 1 Corinthians 3:11), or the **truth** of that confession (compare 1 Timothy 3:15), or the **teachings** of Jesus (see 7:24–25, where "these words of mine" form the foundation-rock [*petra*, as here] on which a wise man builds his house).

GATES, KEYS, BINDING AND LOOSING "The gates of Hades [hell]" means the power of death. The prominence of persecution in Matthew suggests death by martyrdom: the slaying of Christians will not overpower the church. Keys represent **authority to open or close**; binding and loosing represent **forbidding and allowing**. But it is disputed what churchly activity these figures of speech refer to:

- Providing and denying entrance into the church according to people's response to the gospel
- Providing such entrance first to Jews and then to Gentiles, as Peter did on the day of ↓Pentecost and later in the house of ↓Cornelius (Acts 2, 10)
- Forgiving and not forgiving sins, as in the practice of Roman Catholic priests
- Establishing rules of conduct for church order and discipline, that is, closing the door against some behavior—binding it up as prohibited—and opening the door to other behavior—unbinding it as allowable
- Accepting and rejecting professing disciples who under persecution have denied Jesus and later want to reenter the church

PREDICTION OF PASSION AND RESURRECTION Next, Jesus increases the disciples' understanding by informing them of his coming death and resurrection and of the necessity that any would-be followers risk their lives by open discipleship. *Read Matthew 16:21–28.* Even in rebuking Jesus, Peter man-

Bronze keys

ages to address him with "Lord" and wish him God's mercy. As toward the close of the Sermon on the Mount, Jesus portrays himself as the final judge of all humanity; and the clause "before they see the Son of Man coming in his kingdom" makes the following transfiguration of Jesus a preview of the second coming.

Transfiguration

In Jesus' transfiguration and a following conversation with him, the disciples Peter, James, and John gain understanding of him as the **new and greater Moses** and of John the Baptist as **Elijah**. *Read Matthew 17:1–13.* Jesus' face shines as that of Moses shone in consequence of his meeting with God on Mount Sinai (Exodus 34:29–30). But as "God with us," Jesus is greater than Moses; so his face shines "like the sun." Peter again addresses him with "Lord," and the three disciples fall on their faces in extreme fear. On the way down the mountain the disciples also show that they already understand Jesus' coming death and resurrection; and they gain new understanding that although Elijah has yet to come and restore all things after Jesus' sufferings, Elijah has already come in the person of John the Baptist, whose sufferings previewed those of Jesus.

LITTLE FAITH The disciples' increased understanding needs supplementing by larger faith; so the following story of an exorcism at the base of the Mount of Transfiguration ends with Jesus' criticism of little faith. *Read Matthew 17:14–20.* Again Jesus predicts his death and resurrection. The disciples' deep grief at this prediction shows that they understand it. *Read Matthew 17:22–23.*

Double drachmas used to pay the temple tax

PETER'S PENNY An annual tax was levied on male Jews over nineteen years old, wherever they lived, even in the Diaspora, for upkeep of the temple and its services. *Read Matthew 17:24–27.* Peter understands that Jesus pays the tax but gains further understanding from him both that he and Jesus are exempt and that to avoid giving offense to other Jews he and Jesus will nevertheless pay the tax. The stater to be found in a fish's mouth is worth two double ↓drachmas and thus sufficient to pay the tax of Peter as well as of Jesus. The argument for exemption—namely, that kings do not

tax their princely sons—implies that Jesus and Peter (and other disciples) belong to the royalty of the kingdom, whose king owns the temple for which the present tax is being collected.

drachmas: DRAK-muhs

Discourse on Christian Community

The fourth of Jesus' discourses in Matthew deals with Christian community. The kingdom of heaven provides the framework for this community. Entry requires **childlikeness** (18:1–3). **Humility** defines childlikeness (18:4). **Acceptance** of childlike disciples entails the acceptance of Jesus himself (18:5), but **causing** one of these little people (that is, childlike disciples) **to stumble** (that is, probably, to apostatize, to forsake the Christian faith) brings judgment on oneself (18:6–7). One also needs **self-discipline** to keep from stumbling (again, probably from apostatizing, 18:8–9). The heavenly Father wants straying (that is, sinning) little people in the church not to be despised, but to be **restored** if possible through **personal reproof, church discipline,** and **prayer** (18:10–20; compare similar rules for community life at Qumran).

"No one should bring a charge against his fellow in the presence of the Many [a term for the Qumran community as a whole] unless he has rebuked him earlier in the presence of witnesses" (*Community Rule* 6:1).

And a wronged disciple must **forgive** an offending fellow disciple, repeatedly if necessary (18:21–35). *Read Matthew 18:1–35.* "Their angels in heaven" (18:10) has been used for the doctrine of guardian angels, but such angels would seemingly need to accompany their charges rather than staying in heaven.

FORGIVENESS "Seventy-seven times" (or, alternatively translated, "seventy times seven") means any number of times (contrast such forgiveness with the seventy-sevenfold vengeance of which ↓Lamech boasted in Genesis 4:24). "Ten thousand" is the highest number in Greek, "talent" the highest unit of money. Ten thousand talents translates into more than fifteen years of wages for a manual laborer. The unrealism of a king's loaning so much money to a slave emphasizes the enormity of a human being's debt of sin to God and makes the proposed repayment by a mere sale of the slave's wife and children ironic (as well as shocking, for Jews prohibited the sale of wives), his promise to repay everything (given the king's patience) absurd, the king's forgiveness of the debt extravagant, and the slave's throttling and imprisoning a fellow slave to get repayment of a comparatively small debt (one hundred denarii, amounting to about four months' wages) outrageous. The torture to which the king subjects the unforgiving slave stands for eternal punishment and implies the falsity of a disciple who does not genuinely forgive a fellow disciple. "Until he should repay all the debt" implies the eternality of the punishment, since the unforgiving slave cannot hope to pay all. People are not really sorry for their own sins against God if they do not forgive the sins of others against them. Forgiveness must be worked out as well as received. Not to work it out indicates a failure not only to appreciate God's mercy, but also a failure to appropriate it.

Lamech: LAY-mik

Divorce, Remarriage, and Eunuchry

On his way to Jerusalem, Jesus now arrives in southern Transjordan, where some Pharisees put him to the test on a question of interpretation disputed by their rabbis: Does the Mosaic law allow a man to divorce his wife for **any** reason at all (so Rabbi Hillel and his followers) or only for reason of **immorality** on her part (so Rabbi Shammai and his followers; see Deuteronomy 24:1, and especially the enigmatic phrase "something indecent about her"). Whereas the Pharisees say that Moses **commanded** divorce, Jesus says that Moses only **permitted** it. *Read Matthew 19:1–12.* The disciples' reaction that Jesus' teaching makes it better not to marry at all suggests that they understand him to allow an exception for immorality only with respect to divorce, not with respect to remarriage (compare 5:31–32, where remarriage of the husband goes unmentioned though the exception of his wife's immorality is mentioned). If so and if they understand Jesus correctly, he redefines divorce as a dissolution of marriage without the right to remarry. His following statement about eunuchs—those born such, those made such by their captors or masters, and those who make themselves such—seems to describe in terms of eunuchry the single life of a man who has divorced his wife because of her immorality and, for the sake of the kingdom, has not remarried. Otherwise, Jesus would be talking about self-castration.

PERFECTION Just as the preceding narrative carried on the theme of communal life to which the discourse in chapter 18 was devoted, so again a topic of communal life comes up in narrative: the acceptance of children into the church. The disciples' rebuke of the children who come to Jesus rests on a general disdain of children in antiquity. Acting as a foil to the children who come to Jesus is a rich young man who went away from him. "If you wish to be perfect" also means "if you wish to be mature" and alludes by contrast to the rich man's youth. This perfection or maturity refers to discipleship as such, not to a higher-than-usual level of discipleship. *Read Matthew 19:13–26.*

> Parents loved their children, but children occupied a low rung on the ladder of society. Six times the Mishnah classifies them with "deaf-mutes" and "imbeciles." (*Eruvin* 3:2; *Bava Qamma* 4:4; 6:2, 4), and three times with "women" and "slaves" (*Sukkah* 2:8; 3:10; *Sheqalim* 1:3, here in contrast with "levites, Israelites, proselytes, and freed slaves").

LATECOMERS In contrast with the departed rich young man, notes Peter, he and his fellow disciples have left everything to follow Jesus. Then Peter asks what will be their compensation. Jesus' answer contains no rebuke but takes Peter's note at face value and promises that at the renewal of Israel the Twelve will sit enthroned, judging the twelve tribes. *Read Matthew 19:27–20:16.* Jesus' promise to the Twelve casts them as "the first," that is, as the original **Jewish** disciples. "The last" would then seem to be **Gentiles** discipled at a later time (compare the expansion in chapter 10 of a Jewish mission to include Gentiles as well and in 28:18–20 Jesus' sending the apostles to disciple all the nations). As a whole, then, this section teaches the ungrudging acceptance of Gentile latecomers into Jesus' community by Jewish early comers.

LABORERS IN A VINEYARD "The third hour" in the parable of workers in a vineyard is the third after dawn (9:00 A.M.), the sixth hour is the sixth after dawn (noon), and so on. Those hired at the eleventh hour (5:00 P.M.) worked for only an hour. A denarius represents the normal daily wage of a manual worker. Since every day is payday, the employer instructs his foreman to give the workers their money—but to everyone a full day's wage and in reverse order, the last being paid first. Ordinarily those who worked all day would be paid first and would leave before seeing that the latecomers were receiving an equal amount. But Jesus introduces an unrealistic feature to bring out the point of the parable in an argument that ensues: just as the employer is not being unfair to those who worked all day (they receive a full wage according to contract), but only generous to the latecomers in order that they may receive a livable wage (any less would fall below subsistence), so God grants his grace to the undeserving out of **sheer munificence**.

The Triumphal Entry and Temple Cleansing

The theme of Christian community proceeds with narratives concerning acceptance of the **blind**, the **lame**, and **children**. The section starts with Jesus' ascent to Jerusalem and ends with arrival there. He again predicts his death and resurrection (20:17–19), answers a request for special honor by pointing to his service to others (20:20–28), and exemplifies such service by giving sight to two blind men (20:29–34) and by entering Jerusalem and the temple to heal the blind and the lame and to defend the children who praise him there. *Read Matthew 20:17–21:17.* Compare with the two blind men in 20:29–34 those in 9:27–31. Does Matthew repeat the story for emphasis? The earlier passage stressed Jesus' **ability**; the present passage, in tune with the overarching theme of Christian community, stresses his **compassion**. The story of the triumphal entry emphasizes his **gentleness**—again in tune with the overarching theme of Christian community—but also his **kingship**, as underscored by the quotation of Isaiah 62:11; Zechariah 9:9 as fulfilled by the doubling of the animals and by the crowd's acclaiming Jesus to be "the Son of David." There was an expecta-

A vineyard

tion that the messianic king would reveal himself as such at the Passover season, as here; and Zechariah 14:1–11 prophesies the Lord's establishing his kingdom from the Mount of Olives, the very starting point of Jesus' triumphal entry. It is as a **prophet** too that he cleanses the temple and heals blind and lame people right in the temple (contrast their exclusion from the palace in 2 Samuel 5:8). The episode contains further quotations of the Old Testament, more specifically, of Psalm 118:26–27; Isaiah 56:7; Jeremiah 7:11; Psalm 8:2 (all except the last contained also in one or more of the other Gospels).

JUDGMENT ON THE JEWISH LEADERS The sandwiching of the cursing and withering of a fig tree (21:18–22) between confrontations of Jesus with members of the Sanhedrin (21:15–17; 23:1–39) makes the fate of the fig tree symbolic of God's coming judgment on the Jewish leaders. In the following confrontation Jesus tells three parables condemning those leaders. They are like the son who says he will work for his father but does not (21:28–32), like the tenant farmers who kill the owner's son (21:33–46), and like those who refuse a wedding invitation, go about their own activities, mistreat and kill the invitation-bearers, and receive a due judgment of destruction (22:1–14). *Read Matthew 21:18–22:14.*

The impudence of the son who at first refuses to obey comes out in his nonuse of the respectful address, "Sir," whereas the son who says he will obey uses this address. Contrasting with the ultimately disobedient son, but taking after the repentant and finally obedient one, are the tax collectors and prostitutes who are entering the kingdom (21:32). The destruction of the tenant farmers is accompanied by the transfer of God's kingdom "to another nation producing its fruits" (21:43), that is, to the **church** portrayed as a **new chosen nation.** The evil and the good people who are gathered into the wedding feast represent **false and true disciples** (22:10), and the man not wearing a wedding garment stands out as representative of the false. A wedding garment is probably a newly washed garment symbolizing good works as proof that one's discipleship is true. The king's inspection represents the Last Judgment. The many who are called are the masses in a large, mixed church; the few who are chosen are those found to be true.

QUESTIONS The introduction to a question of paying tax to Caesar reveals Matthew's point of emphasis: the wicked purpose of the Pharisees to trap Jesus into saying something they can use against him. *Read Matthew 22:15–22.* The conclusion to the Sadducees' question concerning resurrection reveals Matthew's point of emphasis: the overwhelming impact of Jesus' teaching. *Read Matthew 22:23–33.* The introduction to a question of the greatest commandment in the law reveals Matthew's point of emphasis: the plotting of the Pharisees against Jesus and the satanic role of one of their lawyers in testing (that is, tempting) Jesus (compare Mark 1:13). *Read Matthew 22:34–40.*

PASSION WEEK Bethany, the Mount of Olives, and Jerusalem

4. Clearing of the temple
MONDAY
Mt 21:10—17
Mk 11:15—18
Lk 19:45—48

The next day he returned to the temple and found the court of the Gentiles full of traders and money changers making a large profit as they gave out Jewish coins in exchange for "pagan" money. Jesus drove them out and overturned their tables.

†††
Alternate "Gordon's Calvary"

NORTH

Present Damascus Gate

Traditional Crucifixion and Tomb Site

†††

Jerusalem

Hugh Claycombe

SOUTH

KIDRON VALLEY

Meters 100 200 300
Feet 500 1000

7. Passover
Last Supper
THURSDAY
Mt 26:17—30; Mk 14:12—26;
Lk 22:7—23; Jn 13:1—30

In an upper room Jesus prepared both himself and his disciples for his death. He gave the Passover meal a new meaning. The loaf of bread and cup of wine represented his body soon to be sacrificed and his blood soon to be shed. And so he instituted the "Lord's Supper." After singing a hymn they went to the Garden of Gethsemane, where Jesus prayed in agony, knowing what lay ahead for him.

8. Crucifixion—FRIDAY Mt 27:1—66; Mk 15:1—47; Lk 22:66—23:56; Jn 18:28—19:37
Following betrayal, arrest, desertion, false trials, denial, condemnation, beatings and mockery, Jesus was required to carry his cross to "The Place of the Skull," where he was crucified with two other prisoners.

9. In the tomb
Jesus' body was placed in the tomb before 6:00 P.M. Friday night, when the Sabbath began and all work stopped, and it lay in the tomb throughout the Sabbath.

10. Resurrection—SUNDAY Mt 28:1—13; Mk 16:1—20; Lk 24:1—49; Jn 20:1—31
Early in the morning, women went to the tomb and found that the stone closing the tomb's entrance had been rolled back. An angel told them Jesus was alive and gave them a message. Jesus appeared to Mary Magdalene in the garden, to Peter, to two disciples on the road to Emmaus, and later that day to all the disciples but Thomas. His resurrection was established as a fact.

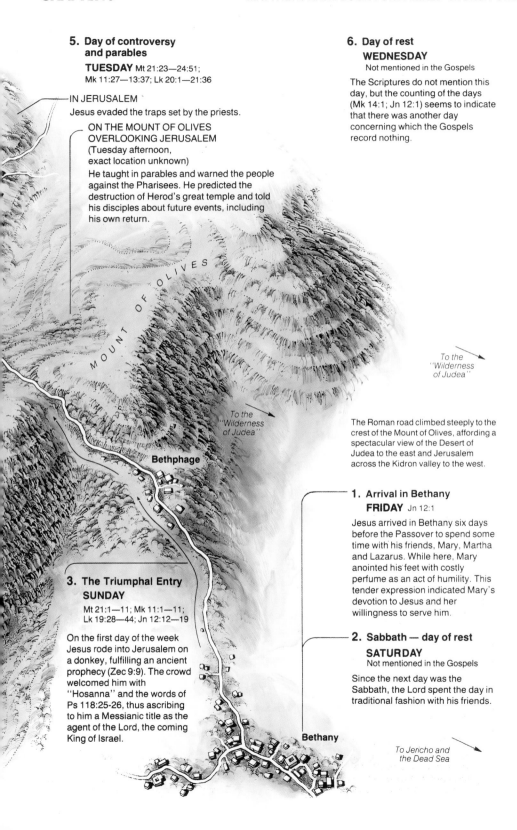

5. Day of controversy and parables

TUESDAY Mt 21:23—24:51;
Mk 11:27—13:37; Lk 20:1—21:36

IN JERUSALEM
Jesus evaded the traps set by the priests.

ON THE MOUNT OF OLIVES OVERLOOKING JERUSALEM
(Tuesday afternoon,
exact location unknown)

He taught in parables and warned the people against the Pharisees. He predicted the destruction of Herod's great temple and told his disciples about future events, including his own return.

6. Day of rest
WEDNESDAY
Not mentioned in the Gospels

The Scriptures do not mention this day, but the counting of the days (Mk 14:1; Jn 12:1) seems to indicate that there was another day concerning which the Gospels record nothing.

To the "Wilderness of Judea"

To the "Wilderness of Judea"

MOUNT OF OLIVES

Bethphage

The Roman road climbed steeply to the crest of the Mount of Olives, affording a spectacular view of the Desert of Judea to the east and Jerusalem across the Kidron valley to the west.

1. Arrival in Bethany
FRIDAY Jn 12:1

Jesus arrived in Bethany six days before the Passover to spend some time with his friends, Mary, Martha and Lazarus. While here, Mary anointed his feet with costly perfume as an act of humility. This tender expression indicated Mary's devotion to Jesus and her willingness to serve him.

3. The Triumphal Entry
SUNDAY

Mt 21:1—11; Mk 11:1—11;
Lk 19:28—44; Jn 12:12—19

On the first day of the week Jesus rode into Jerusalem on a donkey, fulfilling an ancient prophecy (Zec 9:9). The crowd welcomed him with "Hosanna" and the words of Ps 118:25-26, thus ascribing to him a Messianic title as the agent of the Lord, the coming King of Israel.

2. Sabbath — day of rest
SATURDAY
Not mentioned in the Gospels

Since the next day was the Sabbath, the Lord spent the day in traditional fashion with his friends.

Bethany

To Jericho and the Dead Sea

The conclusion to a question of the Christ's Davidic sonship reveals Matthew's point of emphasis: Jesus' victory in verbal combat. *Read Matthew 22:41–46.*

Last Discourse

Chapters 23–25 make up the fifth and last great discourse of Jesus in Matthew. It balances the first discourse, the Sermon on the Mount, in

- Its length
- Its association with a mountain
- Jesus' taking the seated position of a teacher (so also for the middle discourse, 13:1)
- The contrast between woes here and beatitudes there
- Closing judgmental scenes, each of which includes the addressing of Jesus as "Lord" by the condemned

Throughout the present discourse runs a note of warning. The discourse starts with a prohibition of honorific titles in the church. *Read Matthew 23:1–12.* That this prohibition has to do with church life is shown by references to the Christ as sole teacher of the addressed and to them as brothers in the family of the heavenly Father. The **seat of Moses** is the chair in the synagogue on which scribes sat when expounding the Mosaic law. To the extent they communicate that law, says Jesus, do what they say. But do not follow their example of disobeying the law. The heavy loads they lay on people's shoulders are not interpretations of the law, for Jesus has judged those interpretations too light (5:20; 15:3–9). The heavy loads consist of the scribes' and Pharisees' **demands for recognition** (23:5–7). The ↓phylacteries they broaden for religious show are amulets inscribed with Mosaic texts and worn on hand and forehead (compare Exodus 13:9, 16; Deuteronomy 6:8; 11:18). The tassels they lengthen for religious show are fringes of blue cord commanded by Moses to be sewn on the four corners of cloaks as reminders of the law (Numbers 15:38–39; Deuteronomy 22:12). As noted before, "rabbi" means "my great one."

AGAINST SCRIBES AND PHARISEES Next come **seven woes** against the scribes and Pharisees for their hypocrisy, which means acting in the sense of pretending, and a **lament** by Jesus

"The seat of Moses" in a synagogue at Chorazin

---

phylacteries: fi-LAK-tuh-reez

over Jerusalem. *Read Matthew 23:13–39.* Behind the scribes' and Pharisees' teaching on oaths lies the rationale that a creditor cannot place a lien on the temple or the altar because the temple and the altar belong to God. Therefore they provide no surety, so that if a debtor swears in their name to pay back his creditor, the oath is meaningless: it is not in the creditor's power to seize the temple or the altar if the debtor fails to pay. But if the debtor swears by the gold that he has dedicated for future offering to the temple or the altar and does not pay his debt, the creditor can seize that gold. According to Jesus, the making of such a distinction countenances untruthful oaths. Mint, anise, and cumin are small herbs used for seasoning and medicine. Gnats and camels are the smallest and largest of Palestinian animal life, both of them ritually unclean according to the law of Moses. The Pharisees strained wine through a piece of cloth or a fine wicker basket to ensure that they did not swallow an unclean insect when drinking the wine. Here straining out a gnat represents the doing of small duties to gain a reputation for piety; and swallowing a camel represents the neglect of large duties to avoid the sacrifice entailed by them. "Fill up the measure of your fathers!" (23:32) gives an ironic command: "Go ahead and kill me, as you are going to do. You will be imitating your murderous ancestors, not repudiating them as you now pretend to do."

Phylacteries

Since it is Jesus who sends the prophets, sages, and scribes in 23:34, they must be his disciples portrayed as such. "From the blood of righteous Abel to the blood of Zechariah" means "from the first martyr in the Old Testament to the last," because the Hebrew Bible starts with Genesis, which speaks of Abel's martyrdom, but ends with 2 Chronicles, which speaks of Zechariah's martyrdom (24:20–22). "Your house" (23:38) may refer to the temple in anticipation of Jesus' leaving it and predicting its destruction (24:1–2). Galilean pilgrims shouted, "Blessed is he who comes in the name of the Lord!" as Jesus rode toward Jerusalem (21:9); so the same shout by Jerusalemites is reserved for the second coming and may imply a happy reception (compare the regeneration of Israel in 19:28; see also Romans 11:25–27).

NON-SIGNS The narrative interruptions in 24:1, 3 are similar to those in 13:10; 18:21. *Read Matthew 24:1–14.* The disciples ask Jesus not only for the time of the destruction of the temple, but also for the sign of his coming (↓*parousia*, a Greek word often brought over into English for the second coming) and of the end of the age. His answer starts with a prediction of events that will *not* signal that coming and end. False Christs, wars, famines, earthquakes, and such like belong to the normal course of events. Particularly noteworthy are apostasy, treachery, laxity, and lovelessness in the church because of persecution. To save their necks, some will give up their Christian profession. Others will curry favor with persecutors by betraying fellow disciples to them. Others will live so loosely as to avoid being recognized as Christian. And mutual suspicion in the church will chill mutual love. Yet persecution will have the beneficial effect of scattering evangelists throughout the world.

SIGNS Now Jesus tells what *will* signal his coming and the end. *Read Matthew 24:15–31.* A necessity of fleeing the abomination of desolation on the Sabbath would pose difficulty and danger in the suspension of services to travelers and in exposure to capture because of others' not traveling. To counteract the claims of false prophets to have had private contacts with Christ in the isolation of the wilderness or in the secrecy of city hideouts, emphasis falls on the **universal visibility** of Jesus' coming. It will take place in the sky, where people will see him as easily as they see vultures circling over a carcass. "The sign of the Son of Man" (24:30) differs from the sign of his coming and of the end (24:3), which referred to the abomination of desolation (24:15), and refers to the universal visibility of Jesus at his coming.

READINESS AND UNREADINESS The emphasis on visibility carries over to the seeing of events predicted to signal Jesus' coming, events compared to the leafing of a fig tree. *Read Matthew 24:32–51.* "Eating and drinking, marry-

---

parousia: puh-ROO-zhee-uh (or, according to Greek pronunciation, pah´roo-SEE-ah)

ing [what men do] and giving in marriage [what fathers do with their daughters]" do not refer to gluttony, drunkenness, and serial marriages, but to usual human activity that shows unawareness of Jesus' coming soon. So also with respect to men's working in the field and women's grinding at the mill. Despite the danger of incurring persecution of themselves, true church leaders will feed refugees from persecution and get an appropriate reward. False church leaders will mistreat their fellow disciples, squander resources on their own and friends' selfish pleasures, and receive an appropriate punishment.

TEN VIRGINS *Read Matthew 25:1–13.* The bridegroom and his friends go to the bride's home to escort her to the groom's home, where the wedding festivities take place. The delay until midnight is probably due to insistence by the bride's family that the groom and his family give a larger dowry (wedding gift). Such insistence shows the reluctance of the bride's family to give up their daughter and compliments the groom, or rather his family, for choosing such an outstanding young woman, one who deserves the larger dowry. The lamps of the ten virgins are either torches wrapped with rags that have to be soaked repeatedly in oil, or copper fire vases filled with pitch, oil, and rags for burning, or clay bowls with spouts, a wick, and olive oil for fuel. The lamps need to be kept burning because it will not be easy to kindle them in a hurry when the procession arrives, but five of the virgins foolishly overlook the possibility of delay and run out of fuel.

- The ten virgins = professing disciples of Jesus
- The five foolish virgins = false disciples
- The five wise virgins = true disciples
- The lamp oil = good works of discipleship that show preparedness for Jesus' coming
- The bridegroom's arrival = Jesus' coming itself
- The foolish virgins' going off to buy more oil and returning too late for entrance into the wedding feast = the hopelessness of those caught unprepared
- The wedding feast = final salvation

TALENTS The following parable of talents also teaches good works as proof of true discipleship. Here talents are not abilities, but are the largest denomination of money (see 18:24), standing for opportunities given according to ability. *Read Matthew 25:14–30.* The slave who did not invest the one talent given him represents false disciples. His statement in 25:24 says in effect that the work of investment would not have profited him, because the master would have taken the profit as well as the principle. This slave did not consider the possibility of sharing the joy of his master (a figure of eternal reward) or of being cast out (a figure of eternal punishment).

A mixed flock of goats and sheep

SHEEP AND GOATS The discourse closes with yet another emphasis on good works as proof of genuine discipleship. *Read Matthew 25:31–46.* On account of the wool and meat they provide, sheep are more valuable than goats. Palestinian sheep and goats graze in mixed flocks during the day and then have to be separated from each other because sheep prefer open air at night but goats need the warmth of shelter. Here the separation of sheep from goats stands for the separation of true disciples from the rest of humanity at the Last Judgment. The charitable deeds of "the sheep" stand for care shown, not to needy people in general (as is often assumed), but to Jesus' persecuted disciples, called by him "these least brothers of mine" (see Jesus' use of "little" and "brother" only for his disciples in 5:22, 23, 24, 47; 7:3, 4, 5; 10:21, 42; 11:11; 12:48, 49, 50; 18:6, 10, 14, 15, 21, 35; 23:8, and also his identifying himself in 10:40 only with his needy disciples). Again, such care demonstrates genuineness of discipleship inasmuch as it exposes those who care to persecution (compare 24:10–12).

A Plotting and an Anointing

Matthew's passion account starts with Jesus' declaring that the disciples understand both the arrival of Passover after two days and the delivery of him to crucifixion. Then Matthew identifies as ↓**Caiaphas** the high priest in whose courtyard or palace the Sanhedrin plotted against Jesus. *Read Matthew 26:1–5.* In the story of Jesus' anointing, Matthew identifies the questioners of the anointing as the disciples, so that the answer of Jesus adds to their knowledge and the going of Judas Iscariot to strike a bargain with the Sanhedrin turns into a reaction against Jesus' answer. In Judas's bargain to deliver Jesus to the Sanhedrin, the Sanhedrists pay Judas on the spot. *Read Matthew 26:6–16.*

Passover

Read Matthew 26:17–25. By mentioning disciples without specifying only two of them (26:17), Matthew makes the obedience of those who followed Jesus' instructions in preparing the Passover an example of the obedience of true disciples in general. Emphasizing this obedience is 26:19a: "And the disciples did as Jesus had commanded them" (compare 21:6). On announcement that one of the Twelve will betray Jesus, the betrayer himself—Judas Iscariot—asks, "Rabbi, it isn't I, is it?" False disciple! The implied negative answer and the honorific address show his hypocrisy. The thirty pieces of

Caiaphas: KAY-uh-fuhs

silver are already jingling in his pocket. Jesus' answer, "*You* have said so," makes Judas self-condemned.

WORDS OF INSTITUTION *Read Matthew 26:26–29.* The commands to eat bread and drink from a cup stress the disciples' obligation and form the words of institution in that these commands established the Christian practice of eating the Lord's Supper, also called the holding of Communion or celebration of the ↓Eucharist ("thanksgiving"). Jesus does not say that the disciples should drink all the wine, but that all of them should drink from the cup. The interpretation of his blood-shedding as "for the forgiveness of sins" gives good reason for celebration. More particularly, the red wine in the cup represents his blood as the basis of a new covenant that contrasts with the Mosaic covenant, based on the blood of animal sacrifices capable only of covering up sins provisionally and temporarily. Jesus' blood **remits** sins, that is, takes them clean away.

Gethsemane

For the story of Jesus in Gethsemane, Matthew concentrates on Peter by leaving James and John unnamed (contrast Mark 14:33). Matthew is making Peter a **negative example of prayerlessness.** By contrast, Jesus stands out as a **positive example of prayerfulness.** Matthew counts out the number of Jesus' prayers—one, two, three—and specifies the content of all three of them. Correspondingly, Peter's three failures to pray will lead him to deny Jesus three times. *Read Matthew 26:30–46.*

ARREST When Judas Iscariot approaches Jesus for the arrest, Jesus addresses him with "Friend," the very address used in the parable of the wedding feast for the man without a wedding garment (22:12), and ironically tells him to do his dirty business. Thus the falsity of Judas's discipleship is underlined. *Read Matthew 26:47–56.* Matthew identifies the errant swordsman as "one of those with Jesus," and Jesus' command to put the sword away models the teaching of nonretaliation in the Sermon on the Mount (5:38–42). The twelve legions of angels that could be at his disposal would provide one legion apiece for him and the eleven apostles (Judas excepted, of course). As often in Matthew, emphasis falls on the fulfillment of Old Testament prophecy.

Caiaphas and Peter

Matthew portrays the Sanhedrin as seeking false testimony serious enough to sentence Jesus to death but as not finding any so serious. The later testimony of two witnesses (a number sufficient to establish truth, Deuteronomy 19:15) comes close to the words of Jesus in John 2:19. *Read Matthew 26:57–68.* Caiaphas puts Jesus under oath; but because Jesus prohibited oath-taking

Eucharist: YOO-kuh-rist

(5:33–37), he turns back Caiaphas's question whether he is the Christ, the Son of God, with the answer, "*You* have said so." Thus Jesus **models his own teaching**. But Peter disobeys it by denying Jesus with an oath. *Read Matthew 26:69–75*. Peter's threefold failure to pray in Gethsemane has caught up with him. In view of 10:32–33, his denying Jesus "before them all" poses a frightful fate. No wonder Peter shed bitter tears.

> "But whoever denies me before men, I also will deny him before my Father in heaven" (Matthew 10:33).

Judas Iscariot and Pilate

Back to back with the bitter weeping of Peter stands the **suicide** of Judas Iscariot. It warns against betrayals in the church during persecution (compare 24:10). As often, Matthew notes a fulfillment of Old Testament prophecy (see Jeremiah 19:1, 11; Zechariah 11:12–13). *Read Matthew 27:1–10*. In Jesus' interrogation before Pilate, Matthew emphasizes the **meekness** of Jesus as an example for his disciples to follow (compare 5:5; 11:29; 21:5). *Read Matthew 27:11–14*.

PILATE'S WIFE Before the unjust delivery of Jesus for crucifixion, Pilate's wife, declaring Jesus righteous, warns Pilate to have nothing to do with Jesus; and Pilate responds by washing his hands and declaring his **innocence** of Jesus' blood in a ceremony such as Moses commanded in Deuteronomy 21:1–9. All the people, who have demanded Jesus' crucifixion, accept responsibility for it and include their children with themselves.

Hinnom Valley, site of potter's field

Anti-Semites have taken this acceptance as grounds for persecuting the Jews, but such persecution goes against Jesus' prohibition of using a sword on his behalf (26:52–54). *Read Matthew 27:15–26.*

Crucifixion

Matthew's account of Jesus' crucifixion highlights the indignities done to Jesus as a **victim of persecution** and his **kingship** and **divine sonship**. Though Jesus' enemies mock the kingship and sonship, Matthew presents their mockery as ironically true: not only the robing of Jesus and the crowning of him with thorns, but also the putting of a reed in his right hand and the kneeling before him; not only the hailing of him as "king of the Jews," but also the wording of the inscription, "THIS IS JESUS, THE KING OF THE JEWS," and of the gibe, "He's the king of Israel!" plus two occurrences of "Son of God." *Read Matthew 27:27–44.* The spitting mocks Jesus' robe; the hitting of his head with a reed mocks his crown. The mixing of wine with gall gives the wine a bitter taste and insults Jesus with a drink that at first seems merciful but turns out cruel (compare Psalm 69:21, especially in the LXX [69:22]). The crucifixion itself is subordinated to the division of his garments.

> "Then all the elders of the town nearest the slain person shall wash their hands . . . , and they shall declare: 'Our hands did not shed this blood'" (Deuteronomy 21:6–7).

RESURRECTIONS OF SAINTS AND CONVERSIONS OF GENTILES As Jesus is dying, some bystanders thwart the effort of one of their number to aid him with a drink. Jesus dies with a second loud outcry. An earthquake splits rocks and opens tombs, so that many resurrections occur. These resurrections encourage Christians to endure persecution to the death, if necessary; for as Jesus was thus persecuted but then raised from the dead, so will his followers be raised (compare Ezekiel 37:7, 12–13; Daniel 12:2). Not only does the centurion confess Jesus' divine sonship; so also do his fellow soldiers. Together they, like the magi who came bearing gifts for the Christ child, represent the many Gentiles who later become disciples of Jesus. *Read Matthew 27:45–61.*

THE KINDNESSES OF WOMEN AND JOSEPH The ministry of women to Jesus on his way to Jerusalem provides a model of the way disciples are to care for fellow disciples under persecution; and the characterization of Joseph of Arimathea as a disciple of Jesus makes his burial of Jesus' corpse an act of loving remembrance, as further comes out in descriptions of Jesus' linen shroud as "clean" and of the tomb as "new" and Joseph's own.

BRIBING THE GUARDS "The next day, the one after Preparation Day," means "the Sabbath, which follows Friday." *Read Matthew 27:62–28:20.* The **reliability** of Jesus' predictions of his resurrection stands in contrast with the **deceitfulness** of the chief priests and of the Pharisees, who not only bribe the guards at the tomb to say that the disciples of Jesus stole his body but also promise to bribe Pilate into exercising leniency should he hear that the guards slept on duty, a dereliction punishable by death. What the chief priests and Pharisees call "the first deception" is belief in Jesus as the Christ and Son of God (27:64).

The Risen Jesus

As at the resurrection in 27:51–53, an **earthquake** occurs, only this time a big one befitting the identity of Jesus as the Christ and Son of God. Also befitting it is the descent of an angel of the Lord to roll away the stone and the guards' shaking with fear. For the women disciples, however, great joy mingles with fear until an appearance of the risen Jesus erases the fear. Their taking hold of his feet confirms his resurrection, and their worship of him again befits his identity. So also does that of the Eleven, except for some doubters who exemplify the **danger of little faith** in a persecuted church. Matthew has not mentioned Jesus' designation of a mountain before; so the inclusion of a mountain here combines with the mention of Jesus' commandments to suggest the mountain on which he gave commandments, that of the Sermon on the Mount. His universal authority makes all the nations the proper field of the disciples' mission, which is to last until the end of the age. In the meanwhile, his promise to be always with the disciples recalls "Immanuel, God with us" (1:23) and gives courage to endure the persecution incurred through carrying out the **Great Commission.**

Summary

Very early church tradition ascribes the Gospel of Matthew to the Apostle Matthew. Some features of the Gospel comport with this ascription. Many scholars put the date of writing in the last quarter of the first century; but distinctively Matthean material—for example, the business of the temple tax and the relative prominence of Sadducees—favors a date before A.D. 70. The introductory formula, "From that time on Jesus began to . . . ," divides Matthew's narrative into three sections (see 4:17; 16:21); and the concluding formula, "When Jesus had finished . . . ," gives a fivefold structure to Jesus' discourses (see 7:28; 11:1; 13:53; 19:1; 26:1). Lending a heavily Jewish Christian tone are such features as an emphasis on fulfillment of the Old Testament, the portrayal of Jesus as a lawgiver like Moses, and the necessity of good works in knowledgeable obedience to Jesus' commands. Given Matthew's emphases, we may infer that his intended audience consisted of a church or churches populated with false as well as true disciples of Jesus and tempted because of persecution to compromise their Christian testimony, to recant their Christian profession, and even to betray each other to their persecutors. So Matthew, writing perhaps in Antioch, Syria, warns against such compromise, recantation, and betrayal and urges the use of flight from persecution as an opportunity to make disciples of all the nations.

People to Remember

Abel	Elijah	Joseph	Peter
Abraham	Herod (the Great)	Judas Iscariot	Pilate
Archelaus	Herod the tetrarch	the magi	Pilate's wife
Caiaphas	(Antipas)	Mary	Zechariah
David	John the Baptist	Matthew	
C. H. Dodd	Jonah	Papias	

Places to Remember

Antioch, Syria	Egypt	Jerusalem
Bethlehem	Gennesaret	Nazareth
Caesarea Philippi	Gethsemane	Persia

Terms to Remember

antitheses	Johannine thunderbolt	seat of Moses
Barjonas	keys of the kingdom	Sermon on the Mount
Beatitudes	the Law and the Prophets	sign of Jonah
binding and loosing	leaven	slaughter of the innocents
blasphemy against the Holy	lex talionis	Son of David
Spirit	logia	star of David
Cephas/Peter/petros/petra	Lord's Prayer/Pater Noster	talent (as a unit of money)
denarius	Lord's Supper/ Communion/	tares/darnels
devil/Satan/accuser	Eucharist	temple tax
eunuch	magi	tempt/test
flesh and blood	mammon	Testimony Book
flight to Egypt	netzer/Nazareth/Nazarene	text-plot
gates of Hades	ossuary	typology
Great Commission	parousia	virgin birth
Immanuel	Peter's penny	words of institution
Jesus/Joshua	rabbi	Year of Jubilee

How Much Did You Learn?

- Evaluate the arguments for and against authorship by the Apostle Matthew and for and against a late date of writing.
- Identify the Jewish features of the Gospel of Matthew.
- How is this Gospel structured?
- Matthew's emphases imply what aims in the writing of this Gospel?
- How do these emphases differ from Mark's?

For Further Discussion

- How might Matthew's Gospel apply to contemporary megachurches? To Christians whose profession is mainly formal, inherited, or lapsed? To Christians suffering for their profession?
- How might Matthew's Gospel apply to contemporary questions of multiculturalism in the church?

For Further Investigation

Davies, W. D., and D. C. Allison Jr. *A Critical and Exegetical Commentary on the Gospel according to Saint Matthew.* Vols. 1–3. Edinburgh: T. & T. Clark, 1988, 1991, 1997. Advanced.

Garland, D. E. *Reading Matthew: A Literary and Theological Commentary on the First Gospel.* New York: Crossroad, 1995.

Gundry, R. H. *Matthew: A Commentary on His Handbook for a Mixed Church Under Persecution.* 2d ed. Grand Rapids: Eerdmans, 1993. Advanced.

Hagner, D. A. *Matthew 1–13* and *Matthew 14–28.* Dallas: Word, 1993, 1995. Advanced.

Keener, C. S. *A Commentary on the Gospel of Matthew.* Grand Rapids: Eerdmans, 1999.

Luz, U. *Matthew 1–7.* Philadelphia: Fortress Press, 1989. Advanced.

_____. *Matthew 8–20.* Minneapolis: Fortress Press, 2001. Advanced.

Morris, L. *The Gospel according to Matthew.* Grand Rapids: Eerdmans, 1992.

Ridderbos, H. N. *Matthew.* Grand Rapids: Zondervan, 1987.

Schnackenburg, R. *The Gospel of Matthew.* Grand Rapids: Eerdmans, 2002.

Stanton, G. N. *A Gospel for a New People: Studies in Matthew.* Louisville: Westminster John Knox, 1993.

CHAPTER
9

LUKE: A PROMOTION OF CHRISTIANITY IN THE GRECO-ROMAN WORLD AT LARGE

Overview:

- Introductory Issues
- An Outline of Luke
- Reading Luke with Interpretation
- Summary

Study Goals—Learn:

- Who wrote the Gospel of Luke
- The way we determine its authorship
- How the author went about writing
- The time this Gospel was written and what indications we have of its date
- For what audience, from what standpoint, and with what purpose the author wrote
- The features and emphases that distinguish this Gospel
- The overall plan that determines its movement

Ritual baths of the Temple of Jupiter built by the Roman Emperor Hadrian in Samaria

Introductory Issues

Sources and Purpose

The author of the Third Gospel begins with a reference to previous narratives of Christian beginnings based on reports of "**eyewitnesses and ministers of the word**" (1:1–2). He then defines his project as "an orderly account" of that tradition and states a purpose to convince his audience of its **reliability** (1:3–4).

Authorship

The Gospel of Luke and the Acts of the Apostles must come from the same author, for they both begin with dedications to Theophilus and exhibit common interests and a common style of writing. Moreover, Acts refers back to the "first account" (Acts 1:1). Since Luke and Acts must come from the same author, we deduce **Luke's** authorship of Luke-Acts from the fact that he is the only one of Paul's traveling companions mentioned in the Pauline Letters who could have written the "we"-sections of Acts. All others are excluded by the impossibility of harmonizing their geographical movements according to the Letters with the geographical movements in the "we"-sections of Acts (see page 300). Furthermore, Lucan authorship has the support of early tradition: the ↓Muratorian Canon, the anti-Marcionite prologue to Luke, Irenaeus (*Against Heresies* 3.1.1), plus later Christian writers.

THE EVANGELIST Luke was probably a Gentile (or at least a Hellenistic Jew) and may have been converted in Antioch, Syria (compare the anti-Marcionite prologue to Luke and "we" in Codex D at Acts 11:28, dealing with Antioch). Luke's name is Greek. In the farewells of Colossians 4:10–14, Paul seems to distinguish him from Jews, perhaps Hebraistic ones, and links him with Gentiles. His facility in using the Greek language also suggests that he was a Gentile (or a Hellenistic Jew), more at home in the Greek language than most Jews would have been. The Greek style of Luke, together with that in the Letter to the Hebrews, is the most refined in the New Testament. Exceptions occur where Luke appears to have been following Semitic oral or written sources, or adopting a Semitic style of Greek to sound "biblical," that is, Septuagintal (much as the use of thou, thee, thine, and associated verbal forms sounds biblical in English because of the influence of the King James Version). On the other hand, both of the books authored by Luke begin with a formal dedication in Greco-Roman literary style—the only New Testament books to do so. In Colossians 4:14, Paul

---

Example of a "We"-Passage in Acts

"And putting out to sea from Troas *we* ran a straight course to Samothrace, and the next day to Neapolis" (Acts 16:11). Luke's switching later to the third person pronoun, "*they* departed" (Acts 16:40), implies that he stayed in Philippi.

Muratorian: myoor´uh-TOR-ee-uhn

calls Luke "the beloved physician," a description supported by Luke's more than usual interest in sickness and by his frequent use of medical terms (see, for example, Luke 14:2: "a man suffering from dropsy"). This feature of his writing should not be overstressed, however.

↓*Theophilus and a Gentile Audience*

Luke dedicates his work to Theophilus, perhaps a potential or recent convert or a patron who sponsored the circulation of Luke-Acts, and slants both of his books toward Gentiles, especially those who have open-minded interest in the historical origins of Christianity—most probably **proselytes** and especially **God-fearers** who have renounced idolatry and immorality and attend Jewish synagogues. Luke's concern is to establish the **religious piety**, **moral purity**, and **political innocence** of Jesus and his followers (see especially Luke's account of Jesus' trial before Pilate in 23:1–25, where the Roman governor repeatedly absolves Jesus of guilt). Luke shows that the gospel is universal, that Jesus has broken down the barrier between Jews and Gentiles and inaugurated a **worldwide community** in which the old barriers between slaves and free and between men and women no longer exist. Because of his Gentile audience, Luke does not exhibit a narrowly Jewish interest in fulfilled messianic prophecy, as Matthew does, but a broader interest in **God's historical plan** as revealed by the Old Testament and in the **continuity** of Christianity with Judaism (compare the concern in 2 Maccabees 1:18–2:18 to establish the continuity of postexilic Judaism with preexilic Judaism through discovery of the ancient altar-fire and sacred books). Luke also modifies peculiarly Jewish expressions and allusions to Jewish customs in order that Gentiles may better understand. For example, "the abomination of desolation" (Mark 13:14 par.) becomes the encircling of Jerusalem with armies (21:20).

Universality

There are many specific indications of Luke's promotion of Christianity in the Greco-Roman world at large, indications largely missing in the other Gospels. Special interest attaches to dating Jesus' career by the **events of secular history** (1:5; 2:1; 3:1–2). Jesus is "a

> Pilate, speaking to the Sanhedrin, says about Jesus, "Having examined him in your presence, I have found not a single basis for the accusations you bring against him. Neither has Herod, for he sent him back to us. Look, he has done nothing to deserve death.... What evil has this man done? I have found in him no basis for the death penalty" (Luke 23:14–15, 22).

Tiberius Caesar. Compare Luke 3:1–2: "In the fifteenth year of the reign of Tiberius Caesar . . . the word of God came to John son of Zacharias in the desert."

Theophilus: thee-OF-uh-luhs

light . . . to the **Gentiles**" (2:32). A quotation of Isaiah 40 includes the statement that "**all** flesh will see God's salvation" (3:6). Jesus' genealogy goes back, not just to Abraham, father of the Jewish nation (as in Matthew 1:1–2), but to **Adam**, father of the whole human race, and ultimately to **God himself** (3:23–38). Jesus calls attention to Elijah's staying with a **Phoenician** widow instead of an Israelite and to Elisha's healing a **Syrian** leper (↓Naaman) rather than an Israelite (4:25–27). In common with Matthew, Luke contains the Great Commission to evangelize "**all nations**" (24:47; compare Matthew 28:19–20). But Matthew's is a universality in which Jewish Christianity has shed its parochialism, whereas Luke's is a Hellenistic universality which never knew Jewish parochialism.

Lucan universality includes not only Gentiles, but also **social outcasts**, such as the immoral woman who anointed Jesus' feet (7:36–50), ↓Zacchaeus the tax collector (19:1–10), the repentant criminal who died alongside Jesus (23:39–43), the prodigal son (15:11–32, parabolic), the repentant tax collector (18:9–14, parabolic), Samaritans, and poor people. James and John draw rebuke for wanting to call down fire from heaven on a Samaritan village (9:51–56). The good Samaritan of a parable appears in favorable light (10:29–37). The one leper out of ten who returns to thank Jesus for healing is a Samaritan, designated "this foreigner" (17:11–19). At Nazareth, Jesus preaches "good news to the poor" (4:16–22). Mary says that God "has exalted the lowly, filled the hungry with good things, and sent away the rich empty" (1:52b–53). The beatitude on the poor lacks Matthew's qualification "in spirit" (6:20; contrast Matthew 5:3), as also the beatitude on the hungry lacks Matthew's qualification "for righteousness" (6:21; contrast Matthew 5:6). And Luke balances the beatitudes on the poor and hungry with woes against the rich and full (6:24–25). He is the only evangelist to include Jesus' words: "When you give a dinner or a banquet, do not invite your friends or your brothers or your relatives or rich neighbors . . . . But when you give a feast, call poor people, crippled people, lame people, blind people" (14:12–13). It is Luke who calls the Pharisees "lovers of money" (16:14) and gives us the parables of the rich fool, the dishonest manager who acted charitably (and therefore shrewdly), and the rich man and Lazarus (12:13–21; 16:1–13, 19–31).

Lucan universality shows itself also in the special attention paid to **women**: Mary, Elizabeth, and Anna in the nativity story (1:5–2:39), the widow of ↓Nain (7:11–17), the women who supported Jesus financially (8:1–3), the immoral woman (7:36–50), Martha and Mary (10:38–42), the poor widow (21:1–4), and the women who lamented Jesus (23:27–31), watched his crucifixion (23:49), and intended to embalm him but witnessed the empty tomb instead and reported his resurrection (23:55–24:11).

Naaman: NAY-uh-muhn ■ Zacchaeus: za-KEE-uhs ■ Nain: nayn

Luke thus portrays Jesus as a **cosmopolitan** Savior with broad sympathies, one who mingles with all sorts of people, socializes with both Pharisees and tax collectors (5:27–32; 7:36; 11:37; 14:1; 19:1–10), and concerns himself with victims of personal calamity (7:11–17; 8:40–56; 9:37–43). Where Matthew concentrates on Jesus and the kingdom, Luke concentrates on Jesus and people, with resultant character sketches that are very vivid.

Prayer

On numerous occasions Jesus appears as a man of prayer: at his baptism (3:21), after ministering to crowds (5:16), before choosing the Twelve (6:12), before Peter's confession and Jesus' prediction of his own death and resurrection (9:18), at the time of his transfiguration (9:28–29), on the return of the Seventy-two from their mission (10:21), before teaching the disciples to pray (11:1), in Gethsemane (22:39–46), and twice on the cross (23:34, 46). Almost all these references to Jesus' prayers are distinctive of Luke's Gospel. Only Luke records two parables of Jesus about prayer (11:5–13; 18:1–8) and informs us that Jesus had prayed especially for Peter (22:31–32).

Holy Spirit

Luke similarly emphasizes the work of the Holy Spirit. He tells us that John the Baptist was to be filled with the Holy Spirit even from his mother's womb (1:15). The Holy Spirit comes on Mary in order that she may miraculously give birth to the Son of God (1:35). When Mary visits Elizabeth, Elizabeth is filled with the Holy Spirit to say, "Blessed are you among women, and blessed is the fruit of your womb" (1:42). When John the Baptist is born and then named, his father, ↓Zacharias (Zechariah), is filled with the Holy Spirit and prophesies (1:67). The Holy Spirit rests on ↓Simeon, informs him that before dying he will behold the Christ, and leads him to the temple to see the Christ child (2:25–27). After receiving the Spirit at his baptism, Jesus is "full of the Holy Spirit" and "led by the Spirit" in the wilderness (4:1). Following his temptation, he returns to Galilee "in the power of the Spirit" (4:14). When the seventy-two disciples return from their successful mission, he rejoices "in the Holy Spirit" (10:21). And before his ascension he promises that the Spirit will clothe the disciples "with power from on high" (24:49). Consequently, the Gospel of Luke (as later the book of Acts) throbs with the thrill of an irresistible movement of God's Spirit in human history—hence the many references to joy (1:14, 44, 47; 6:21, 23; 10:21; 15:5–7, 9, 10, 23–25, 32; 24:52–53). Luke writes with supreme confidence in the inevitably successful advance of the gospel inaugurated by Jesus "the Lord" (a favorite designation of Jesus in Luke) and carried on by his disciples in the energy of the Holy Spirit.

Zacharias: zak´ uh-RI/-uhs ■ Simeon: SIM-ee-uhn

Date and Provenance

Nothing prevents a fairly early date for the Third Gospel, slightly after that of Mark (and perhaps Matthew as well) under the assumption that Luke utilized Mark. Many scholars think that Luke's changing the abomination of desolation (Mark 13:14) to the siege of Jerusalem (Luke 21:20) proves that he wrote after A.D. 70. But this line of reasoning again overlooks or denies the possibility that Jesus really did predict the siege and destruction of Jerusalem. Luke may have omitted mentioning the abomination of desolation simply because he knew that his Gentile audience would not understand it. If he was conforming Jesus' words to the events in and around A.D. 70, why did he retain the command, "Flee to the mountains" (21:21), despite the fact that during the siege of Jerusalem Christians fled to Pella in an *un*mountainous part of Transjordan (if they fled to Pella at all—the evidence is disputed)?

Acts closes with Paul's awaiting trial in Rome, probably because events had progressed no further at the time of writing (see pages 302–3). If so, Acts dates from some time before A.D. 64–67, the most likely period of Paul's martyrdom. Then if Luke wrote his Gospel before Acts, as would seem likely, the Gospel must likewise date from a slightly earlier time (see page 128). The place of writing might be Rome, where Luke had gone with Paul for Paul's imprisonment (though early tradition is divided between Greece and Rome as the place of writing).

Plan and Materials

The Gospel of Luke is the most comprehensive of the Synoptics; indeed, it is the longest book of the New Testament. In the first two chapters Luke begins with a prologue and stories concerning Jesus' birth and boyhood. The baptism, genealogy, and temptation of Jesus follow in 3:1–4:13, the Galilean ministry in 4:14–9:50, the last journey to Jerusalem in 9:51–19:27, and finally Passion Week, Jesus' crucifixion, resurrection, postresurrection ministry, and ascension in 19:28–24:53. The **last journey to Jerusalem** makes the most distinctive contribution of Luke to our knowledge of Jesus' career. In that section he presents the ministry of Jesus in ↓Perea (see the map on page 126), gives many of the most famous parables not elsewhere recorded (the good Samaritan, the rich fool, the prodigal son, the rich man and Lazarus, the Pharisee and the tax collector, and others), and emphasizes the significance of Jerusalem as the goal of Jesus' ministry. (Later, in Acts, Jerusalem will turn into the place from which Christian witnesses go out to evangelize the world.) The nativity story in Luke contains much information not found in Matthew,

---

Paul in Rome

- "And when we came to Rome, Paul was allowed to stay by himself, with a soldier guarding him" (Luke in Acts 28:16).
- "Luke, the beloved physician, and Demas send you greetings" (Paul, writing Colossians 4:14 from his Roman imprisonment).

Perea: puh-REE-uh

including several **hymns** and an account of **John the Baptist's birth** as well as Jesus' birth. Finally, Luke gives material concerning Jesus' resurrection quite different from that in the other Gospels and becomes the only evangelist to describe Jesus' **ascension**.

An Outline of Luke

Prologue: Dedication to Theophilus and Statement of Purpose to Write an Orderly Account of Historical Trustworthiness (1:1–4)

I. The Nativity and Childhood of John the Baptist and Jesus (1:5–2:52)
  - A. The annunciation of John the Baptist's birth to Zacharias and Elizabeth (1:5–25)
  - B. The annunciation of Jesus' birth to Mary (1:26–38)
  - C. The visit of Mary to Elizabeth and Mary's *Magnificat* (1:39–56)
  - D. The birth, circumcision, and naming of John the Baptist, and the *Benedictus* of Zacharias (1:57–79)
  - E. John the Baptist's growing up in the wilderness (1:80)
  - F. The birth of Jesus (2:1–7)
  - G. The visit of the shepherds (2:8–20)
  - H. The circumcision and naming of Jesus (2:21)
  - I. The presentation in the temple, with the *Nunc Dimittis* of Simeon and the adoration of Anna (2:22–40)
  - J. Jesus' visit to the temple at the age of twelve (2:41–52)

II. The Prelude to Jesus' Ministry (3:1–4:13)
  - A. The preparatory ministry of John the Baptist (3:1–20)
  - B. The baptism of Jesus (3:21–22)
  - C. The genealogy of Jesus (3:23–38)
  - D. The temptation of Jesus (4:1–13)

III. The Galilean Ministry (4:14–9:50)
  - A. The rejection of Jesus in Nazareth (4:14–30)
  - B. An exorcism in the synagogue at Capernaum (4:31–37)
  - C. The healing of Peter's mother-in-law and further miracles and preaching (4:38–44)
  - D. A miraculous catch of fish and the call of Simon Peter, James, and John to discipleship (5:1–11)
  - E. The cleansing of a leper (5:12–16)
  - F. The forgiveness and healing of a paralytic (5:17–26)
  - G. The call of Levi and Jesus' eating with tax collectors and sinners (5:27–32)
  - H. Remarks about fasting (5:33–39)
  - I. Jesus' defense of his disciples' plucking and eating grain on the Sabbath (6:1–5)
  - J. The healing of a withered hand on the Sabbath (6:6–11)
  - K. The choice of the Twelve (6:12–16)

L. The Sermon on the Plain ("a level place," 6:17–49)

M. The healing of a centurion's servant (7:1–10)

N. The raising from the dead of a widow's son (7:11–17)

O. The question of John the Baptist and Jesus' answer and tribute to him (7:18–35)

P. Jesus' anointing by and forgiveness of a sinful woman (7:36–50)

Q. Preaching with financial support from certain women (8:1–3)

R. The parables of the seeds and the soils and of the lamp (8:4–18)

S. The attempt of Jesus' family to see him (8:19–21)

T. The stilling of a storm (8:22–25)

U. The deliverance of a demoniac (8:26–39)

V. The healing of the woman with a chronic flow of blood and the raising of Jairus's daughter from the dead (8:40–56)

W. The mission of the Twelve (9:1–6)

X. The guilty fear of Herod Antipas over the death of John the Baptist (9:7–9)

Y. The feeding of the five thousand (9:10–17)

Z. Peter's confession of Jesus' messiahship and the prediction by Jesus of his own death and resurrection, with a call to cross-taking discipleship (9:18–27)

AA. The transfiguration (9:28–36)

BB. The deliverance of a demonized boy (9:37–45)

CC. Remarks on humility (with a child as an example) and tolerance (9:46–50)

IV. **The Last Journey to Jerusalem (9:51–19:27)**

A. Jesus' determination to go to Jerusalem and the inhospitality of a Samaritan village (9:51–56)

B. Remarks on discipleship to would-be disciples (9:57–62)

C. The mission of the Seventy-two (10:1–24)

D. The parable of the good Samaritan (10:25–37)

E. Entertainment of Jesus by Mary and Martha (10:38–42)

F. Teaching about prayer, including the Lord's Prayer and the parable of the host whose guest arrived at midnight (11:1–13)

G. Polemical episodes (11:14–12:12)

   1. Defense against the charge of satanic empowerment, refusal to give any sign except that of Jonah, and the parable of the lamp (11:14–36)

   2. Exposé of the Pharisees and lawyers (11:37–54)

   3. Warning against Phariseeism (12:1–12)

H. Remarks on covetousness, anxiety, trust, and eschatological watchfulness, including the parable of a rich fool (12:13–59)

I. A call to repentance, including the parable of the fig tree (13:1–9)

J. The healing on a Sabbath of a woman bent over (13:10–17)

K. The parables of the mustard seed, leaven, and narrow door (13:18–30)

L. Jesus' refusal to be panicked in the face of Herod Antipas, and a lamentation over Jerusalem (13:31–35)

M. The Sabbath healing of a man with dropsy (14:1–6)

N. A parable about invitations to a marriage feast (14:7–14)
O. The parable of a great banquet (14:15–24)
P. The parables of a tower builder and of a king who goes to war (14:25–35)
Q. Three parables in defense of welcoming sinners (15:1–32)
    1. The parable of a lost sheep (15:1–7)
    2. The parable of a lost coin (15:8–10)
    3. The parable of the prodigal son and his elder brother (15:11–32)
R. Two parables about the use of money (16:1–31)
    1. The parable of the unjust steward, with further comments to the Pharisees (16:1–18)
    2. The parable of the rich man and Lazarus (16:19–31)
S. Remarks on forgiveness, faith, and a sense of duty (17:1–10)
T. The healing of ten lepers and the gratitude of one, a Samaritan (17:11–19)
U. The coming of God's kingdom and the Son of Man, including the parable of a widow and an unjust judge (17:20–18:8)
V. The parable of the Pharisee and the tax collector (18:9–14)
W. Jesus' welcoming little children (18:15–17)
X. The rich ruler (18:18–30)
Y. Prediction by Jesus of his death and resurrection (18:31–34)
Z. The healing of a blind man near Jericho (18:35–43)
AA. The conversion of Zacchaeus (19:1–10)
BB. The parable of the ten minas (19:11–27)

V. **Passion Week and the Death, Resurrection, Postresurrection Ministry, and Ascension of Jesus in and Around Jerusalem (19:28–24:53)**
    A. Passion Week and the death of Jesus (19:28–23:56)
        1. Jesus' triumphal entry, including his cleansing of the temple (19:28–48)
        2. Theological debate in the temple precincts (20:1–21:38)
            a. The challenge to Jesus' authority (20:1–8)
            b. A parable about the wicked tenants of a vineyard (20:9–18)
            c. A question about paying taxes to Caesar (20:19–26)
            d. The Sadducees' question about resurrection (20:27–40)
            e. Jesus' question about the Christ's Davidic ancestry and lordship (20:41–44)
            f. Warning against the scribes (20:45–47)
            g. A widow's two copper coins (21:1–4)
            h. Prophetic teaching (21:5–36)
            i. Further teaching (21:37–38)
        3. The Sanhedrin's plot to kill Jesus and the bargain with Judas Iscariot (22:1–6)
        4. The Last Supper (22:7–38)
        5. Jesus' praying in Gethsemane (22:39–46)
        6. The arrest (22:47–53)

7. The trials (22:54–23:25)
   a. A nighttime hearing in the high priest's house, with Peter's denials of Jesus (22:54–65)
   b. An early morning condemnation by the Sanhedrin (22:66–71)
   c. The first hearing before Pilate (23:1–5)
   d. The hearing before Herod Antipas (23:6–12)
   e. The second hearing before Pilate, with his grudging release of Barabbas and delivering up of Jesus for crucifixion (23:13–25)
8. Jesus' crucifixion (23:26–49)
   a. The carrying of Jesus' cross by Simon of Cyrene and the lament of the women (23:26–31)
   b. The crucifixion and mocking of Jesus (23:32–38)
   c. The repentant criminal (23:39–43)
   d. Jesus' death (23:44–49)
9. Jesus' burial (23:50–56)
B. Jesus' resurrection (24:1–12)
C. Jesus' postresurrection ministry (24:13–49)
   1. A walk to Emmaus with Cleopas and another disciple (24:13–35)
   2. An appearance in Jerusalem (24:36–43)
   3. Jesus' teaching about himself from the Old Testament, and the Great Commission (24:44–49)
D. Jesus' ascension (24:50–53)

Reading Luke with Interpretation

PROLOGUE In his prologue, Luke mentions earlier written accounts of Jesus' life, oral testimonies by eyewitnesses, his own investigation of these accounts and testimonies, and his purpose to present this tradition as reliable. *Read Luke 1:1–4.* The earlier accounts may include Mark and Matthew. The orderliness of Luke's account consists in careful arrangement, yet topical and geographical arrangements may sometimes override chronological arrangement. Though "most excellent" describes Theophilus loftily, nothing more is known about him. Perhaps he is Luke's literary patron, but other possibilities exist.

Dice for casting lots

Annunciation to Zacharias and Mary

Immediately after his prologue, Luke provides a **historical frame of reference**: "in the days of Herod, king of Judea." There follow the annunciation to Zacharias of John the Baptist's birth, the conception of John by Zacharias's wife, Elizabeth, the annunciation to Mary of Jesus' birth, and Mary's visit to Elizabeth. *Read Luke 1:5–56.* "The division of

↓Abijah" (1:5) was one of the twenty-four platoons of priests that served at the temple twice a year, a week each time. In line with his appeal to the **highest religious and moral ideals** of Hellenistic culture, Luke describes Elizabeth as descended from Aaron, elder brother of Moses in the tribe of Levi, just as her husband, Zacharias, had to be for priestly service, and emphasizes the righteousness of both of them. A casting of lots determined which priest gained the privilege of burning incense in the temple; and once privileged to do so, a priest was disqualified in order that other priests might have a better chance. But for Luke, the choice of Zacharias by lot was due to **divine providence**, not chance (compare Acts 1:24–26). Again in line with Luke's appeal to the highest religious and moral ideals, the coming abstinence of John from alcoholic beverages, his filling with the Holy Spirit even before birth, his reformative ministry to Israel, and his playing the role of Elijah all emphasize a special holiness (compare Leviticus 10:9; Numbers 6:2–4; Judges 13:4; 1 Samuel 1:11; Malachi 4:5). So also do the virginity of Mary, her having found favor with God, her coming virginal conception by the Holy Spirit, the consequent holiness and divine sonship of her son, whom she is to name Jesus, and her believing acquiescence. Notably, Luke is telling the story from her standpoint. "The sixth month" when the annunciation to her takes place is the sixth month of Elizabeth's pregnancy (1:26). The filling of Elizabeth with the Holy Spirit gives authority to her blessing of Mary and Jesus and to her calling Jesus "Lord." Mary's hymn of praise, traditionally called the ↓*Magnificat* (after the opening word for "magnifies" in the Latin Vulgate),[1] draws much of its phraseology from the song of Hannah (1 Samuel 2:1–10) and brings out the theme of **justice** for the poor, hungry, and oppressed.

The Annunciation to Mary by Gabriel, a painting in the Greek Orthodox church in Nazareth

1. The Latin Vulgate was a translation by Jerome in the fourth century and for many centuries afterward the standard text of the Bible for Roman Catholics.

JOHN THE BAPTIST'S BIRTH *Read Luke 1:57–80.* The Mosaic law prescribes circumcision on the eighth day (Genesis 17:12–14; 21:4; Leviticus 12:3; compare Philippians 3:5). The use of sign language in 1:62 shows that Zacharias was struck deaf as well as mute. His prophecy of praise is traditionally called the ↓*Benedictus* (after the opening word for "blessed" in the Latin Vulgate) and brings out the themes of fulfillment, deliverance from oppression, forgiveness of sins, and peaceful service to God—yet again in line with the highest religious and moral ideals, and social and political ones as well.

Abijah: uh-BI-juh ■ *Magnificat:* mag-NIF-uh-kat ■ *Benedictus:* ben´uh-DIK-toohs

Nativity of Jesus

For Jesus' birth Luke again provides a historical frame of reference, this time a much broader one suitable to the universality of the salvation brought by Jesus. *Read Luke 2:1–20.* A problem arises out of Luke's reference to the Syrian governorship of ↓Quirinius. According to Matthew, Herod the Great was still ruling Judea when Jesus was born. Herod died in 4 B.C. Yet outside the New Testament, Quirinius is said to have governed Syria over a decade later in A.D. 6–7. There is the possibility of an earlier governorship as well, however. (The sixth-century Christian monk ↓Dionysius Exiguus miscalculated the year of Jesus' birth when setting up the system of dating B.C. and A.D., in which Jesus is supposed to have been born on December 25, 1 B.C., and circumcised eight days later on January 1, A.D. 1, there being no year zero.)

The **census** of Caesar Augustus has traditionally been thought to have the purpose of levying taxes, but it may rather have had the purpose of declaring allegiance to Augustus. **Swaddling clothes** (KJV) are cloths wrapped tightly around an infant, as customarily done at the time. A **manger** is a feeding trough. The shepherds suit the birth of Jesus in Bethlehem, home town of David the **shepherd-king.** Their staying in the fields overnight disfavors winter as the season of Jesus' birth. The people for whom an angel of the Lord brings good news are the people of Israel, the Jews. The song of the angelic choir is traditionally called the ↓*Gloria in Excelsis Deo* (after the opening words for "glory to God in the highest" in the Latin Vulgate). "Peace" refers to the manifold blessings of salvation, and the traditional "good will to men" (KJV) refers to the goodwill *God* directs toward his people, not their goodwill toward each other. Mary's treasuring and pondering all these events hints that she is Luke's source (compare 2:51), and "all that they [the shepherds] had heard and seen, just as it had been told them" appeals to eyewitness testimony combined with heavenly revelation (compare 1:1–4).

Census papyrus

PRESENTATION IN THE TEMPLE Emphasis continues to fall on the moral and religious excellence of the players in this drama of the nativity: obedience to the angelic command to name Mary's son Jesus, obedience to the law of Moses in performing a ritual of purification (Leviticus 12), righteousness, devoutness, expectancy, enduement with the Holy Spirit, reception of divine revelation, the prophetic

A stone manger

gift, lengthy devotion to the temple, and constant fasting and prayer—and these of women as well as men. *Read Luke 2:21–40.* Simeon's praise of God is called the ↓*Nunc Dimittis* (after the opening words in the Latin Vulgate for "Now dismiss"). The directing of salvation to the Gentiles as well as Israel (2:32) contributes to Luke's cosmopolitanism. "The falling and rising of many in Israel" (2:34) probably refers to the judgment on Jews who will reject Jesus and the salvation of those who will accept him. He himself is the sign that some will oppose (2:34). And the sword that will pierce Mary's soul may stand for the coming crucifixion of Jesus as her firstborn son (2:35), whose physical and mental development and divine favor mark him out as the **ideal human being** (2:40).

VISIT TO THE TEMPLE Luke now relates a particular instance of Jesus' precociousness and concludes with another statement of Jesus' perfect progress **mentally** ("in wisdom"), **physically** ("in stature"), **spiritually** ("in favor with God"), and **socially** ("in favor with human beings"). In between, Luke notes the devotion of Jesus to God his Father and his obedience to Joseph and Mary. *Read Luke 2:41–52.* Since Jewish boys assumed adult responsibilities in Judaism at the age of thirteen, this visit to the temple may have had the purpose of preparing Jesus for those responsibilities.

The Baptist's Ministry

For John the Baptist's ministry of preparation, Luke provides a historical frame of reference yet again. *Read Luke 3:1–20.* Luke continues the quota-

Nunc Dimittis: noonk di-MIT-is

tion of Isaiah long enough to get the universalism of "all flesh will see God's salvation." In his preaching, John addresses the crowds; and Luke includes a section on the **social ideals** of charity, honesty, justice, and contentment. As a foil to these ideals stands the wickedness of John's nemesis Herod (Antipas), which according to Luke includes more than the imprisonment of John. The contrast enhances the admirability of the Christian movement, beginning as it does with John.

JESUS' BAPTISM AND GENEALOGY Luke's account of Jesus' baptism brings out the piety of Jesus: he is praying. The bodily form of the Holy Spirit that descends on him makes the descent open to eyewitness (again compare 1:1–4). The notation of Jesus' age lends a historical touch. And the tracing of Jesus' genealogy further back than Abraham, and even Adam, to God highlights the **divine sonship** of Jesus and the **universality** of the salvation he brings. *Read Luke 3:21–38.* For discussion of the many differences between the genealogies of Jesus in Matthew and Luke, see commentaries on these Gospels and books on Jesus' birth.

THE TEMPTATION The story of Jesus' temptation portrays him as filled with the Holy Spirit, constantly led by the Spirit, and refusing to serve himself by taking advantage of his divine sonship. *Read Luke 4:1–13.* The last placement of the temptation in Jerusalem links with Luke's emphasis on that city

Judean wilderness, where Jesus' first temptation occurred

as the point of destination in Jesus' ministry and the starting point of Christian witness afterwards. The devil's finishing every temptation and departing from Jesus until an opportune time highlight Jesus' moral victory.

In the Synagogue at Nazareth

The power of the Holy Spirit characterizes the return of Jesus to Galilee for the start of his teaching. The results are widespread publicity and universal admiration. The customariness of his attending synagogue evidences his piety. The application to himself of Isaiah 61:1–2 carries on Luke's portrayal of him as **endued with the Spirit** and adds the socially admirable element of ministry to the poor, the captive, the blind, and the oppressed. *Read Luke 4:14–30.* The question, "This is Joseph's son, isn't it?" illustrates the popular ignorance of Jesus' virgin birth (see 3:23) and leads him to anticipate ultimate rejection by his fellow townspeople. The reference to his deeds in Capernaum, when those deeds have yet to be narrated in the next paragraph, shows that Luke has advanced this visit to Nazareth to make it programmatic of Jesus' reception as a whole: **admiration followed by rejection.** The notation of Elijah's and ↓Elisha's ministries to Gentiles looks forward to Gentile salvation. Strikingly, Jesus stops his scriptural reading just before a reference to "the day of vengeance" (Isaiah 61:2), a central theme in the nationalistic messianism of first-century Jews, who interpreted the phrase in terms of their revenge on Gentile nations. Luke's notation of murderous rage on the part of all in the synagogue attributes the rejection of Jesus to a moral fault in them, not to any in him.

IN THE SYNAGOGUE AT CAPERNAUM Jesus continues to teach in the synagogue at Capernaum (compare 4:15), where a demoniac confronts him. The loudness of the demoniac's voice and his initial "Leave us alone!" (or "Ha!" [NIV]) heighten the conflict with Jesus. The demon's throwing of the man into the middle of the congregation makes the exorcism visible to all (compare Luke's emphasis on eyewitness testimony, 1:1–4), and the demon's doing the man no harm on exit heightens the power as well as the authority of Jesus' word of rebuke to the demon. So also the extremity of the fever of Peter's mother-in-law and the

Cliff near Nazareth

Elisha: i-LI-shuh

immediacy of her standing up and serving when healed heighten the power as well as the authority of Jesus' word of rebuke to her fever—and similarly with respect to the variety of the diseases afflicting others brought to Jesus and his nevertheless healing each one of them with the mere application of his hands. He displays his authority and power by even keeping the demons quiet after they have come out shouting that he is God's Son. *Read Luke 4:31–44.* Luke uses "the Christ" as a synonym for "the Son of God" (compare 9:20; 22:67 with 22:70; 23:35). The crowd's searching Jesus out and trying to keep him from leaving demonstrate his attractiveness, and his going off to preach the good news of God's rule in the synagogues of Judean cities demonstrates fidelity to his mission.

FISHING Jesus' preaching of God's word proves so attractive that a crowd presses in on him, so that he commandeers the boat of Simon (Peter) from which to teach them offshore. *Read Luke 5:1–11.* The failure of a whole night's fishing without Jesus makes the almost unmanageable success of fishing with him all the more impressive. Attraction of the crowd now transmutes into attraction of disciples; so Simon and his partners end up following Jesus instead of Jesus' departing from them, as Simon in fear has asked him to do.

Healing a Leper and a Paralytic

The fullness of a man's leprosy now makes its miraculous departure so astounding that the word concerning Jesus draws crowds from increasing distances. Uncorrupted by this popularity, he continues to slip away for prayer. *Read Luke 5:12–16.* In the story of the paralytic's healing, Luke continues to emphasize the extent of Jesus' attractiveness and the power that he has from God to heal. A further emphasis on the failure to wedge through the crowd with the paralytic enhances Jesus' **popularity**. Letting the paralytic down through the roof tiles "into the middle" of the crowd makes the healing **verifiable** by eyewitnesses, as the immediacy of his standing up heightens the miracle. The glorification of God by the healed man as well as by the eyewitnesses puts on exhibit the **religious validity** of Jesus' activity and erases the charge that Jesus is blaspheming God by forgiving sins. *Read Luke 5:17–26.*

CALL OF LEVI Levi's "leaving everything behind" to follow Jesus and holding "a big banquet for him in his [own] house" magnify the attractiveness of Jesus yet again. *Read Luke 5:27–39.* The question to the disciples, "Why do you eat and drink with the tax collectors and sinners?" paints a picture of social harmony at meal that appeals to Luke's Hellenistic audience; and "to repentance" shows that underlying this harmony is personal reformation. Since Jesus has answered their question to the disciples, the Pharisees and their scribes turn their questioning to Jesus.

Field of grain at harvest time

FEASTING INSTEAD OF FASTING The frequency of fasting by the disciples of John the Baptist and of the Pharisees and their praying while fasting point up their social withdrawal. The eating and drinking of Jesus' disciples refers to what they are doing at the moment in Levi's house. Using the figures of a bridegroom and groomsmen (or wedding guests), Jesus tells the Pharisees and their scribes that they cannot make his disciples fast, that is, cannot make them stop eating and drinking in Levi's house. Using further figures, Jesus says that stopping the enjoyment of social harmony at meal in Levi's house would be like tearing up a new garment to get a patch for an old one, a patch that would not match the old anyway, and like losing new wine by putting it in old wineskins, which would also be lost by bursting. But like wine-drinkers, who prefer old wine to new, the Pharisees and their scribes prefer the social isolation of their frequent fasting and praying to the social harmony of the disciples' meal with repentant tax collectors and sinners.

THE SABBATH QUESTION *Read Luke 6:1–11.* The disciples rub the heads of wheat in their hands to separate the edible kernels from the inedible chaff. As in 5:30–31, the Pharisees direct their question to Jesus' disciples, but it is he who answers. "Except for the priests alone" (6:4) emphasizes the illegality of David's and his men's eating the sacred bread of presence and thus emphasizes the kindness of Jesus in using his lordship over the Sabbath to let the disciples satisfy their hunger by breaking the Sabbath. The designation of the withered hand as a right hand and therefore presumably the most needful (since the vast majority of people are right-handed) likewise emphasizes Jesus' kindness in restoring it. The fury incurred by the restoration acts

Beatitudes	Woes
"Blessed are you who are poor . . . ."	"Woe to you who are rich . . . ."
"Blessed are you who hunger now . . . ."	"Woe to you who are well fed now . . . ."
"Blessed are you who weep now . . . ."	"Woe to you who laugh now . . . ."
"Blessed are you when people hate you . . . ."	"Woe to you when all people speak well of you . . . ."

as a foil to play up this kindness all the more, and the repeated reference to the patient's standing up in the middle of the synagogue congregation makes the restoration an object of eyewitness.

Sermon on the Plain

Read Luke 6:12–49. Luke introduces Jesus' Sermon on the Plain with the choice of the twelve apostles. Jesus' praying all night on a mountain before choosing them makes him a model of piety. His naming them apostles highlights their authority as eyewitnesses of his ministry (compare Acts 1:21–22). The great throng awaiting Jesus at the base of the mountain is a reminder of his attractiveness, and the exorcisms and other healings that occur by merely touching him are reminders of his power. Four beatitudes are balanced by four woes. Both sets deal with the **economic and social conditions** of Jesus' disciples and their persecutors. The following instructions tell the disciples how to live under these conditions, that is, to overcome evil with good, with love and mercy, generosity and helpfulness.

A Centurion and the Widow of Nain

With an eye to his Gentile audience, Luke stresses the worthiness and humility as well as great faith of a centurion (Gentile, of course) who seeks and gets from Jesus the healing of his highly esteemed slave. *Read Luke 7:1–10.* In a male-dominated society, the death of a widow's only son puts her in desperate straits (she has no man to support her); so Luke emphasizes Jesus' **compassion** in raising the son of the widow of Nain and in giving him back to her. The awestruck crowd's glorification of God and recognition of Jesus as his spokesman (the meaning of "prophet") add a religious benefit to the social benefit of Jesus' miracle. *Read Luke 7:11–17.*

Sandals found at Masada

JOHN THE BAPTIST In the episode concerning John the Baptist's question, Luke highlights Jesus' working of miracles on the spot, as John's two messengers are watching, so as to bring out the reliability of this eyewitness tradition (compare 1:1–4). Jesus' tribute to John underscores the contrast between John's more-than-prophetic ruggedness and the luxurious lifestyle of self-indulgent royalty. A similar contrast between the repentant masses and tax collectors, on the one hand, and the self-righteous Pharisees and experts in the Mosaic law, on the other hand, underscores God's justice in rejecting the latter and accepting the former, who are the children of wisdom, those who by their submission to John's baptism proved themselves to be wise in contrast with the others. *Read Luke 7:18–35.*

A SINFUL WOMAN The story of a sinful woman's forgiveness gives a particular instance of the loving effect of Jesus' forgiveness. *Read Luke 7:36–50.* Walking on dirt paths in open sandals made the offering of water for foot washing a courtesy. Also included among courtesies were a kiss of greeting and the rubbing of olive oil on the head so that it might glisten with the joy of the occasion. At formal meals diners stretched out in a reclining position on cushions with their feet away from table; so the woman had easy access to Jesus' feet. It was customary for uninvited people to enter and watch a dinner party.

Mosaic of a woman, dubbed "Mona Lisa," at Sepphoris near Nazareth

Support by Women

Read Luke 8:1–21. Jesus' itineration appeals to Luke's Hellenistic audience, fascinated as they are with **travel**. The proclamation of good news concerning God's rule strikes a happy note. Accompaniment by the Twelve provides eyewitness testimony. The women's support of Jesus and the Twelve exemplifies the Hellenistic ideal of **sharing goods**. Description of the women's prior maladies calls attention to the benefits of Jesus' ministry to women.

Parables

The gathering of crowds in one city after another exemplifies the attractiveness of Jesus. In his first parable, the trampling of the seed on a path intensifies the exposure of the seed by stressing a location on the edge of the path, not beside it. "On rock" (not "on rocky soil") stresses lack of moisture; for even thin soil holds some moisture above the underlying rocks, but a rock holds none. Identification of the seed as God's word equates it with Jesus' message (see 5:1). The issue raised by the parable is believing for salvation, as opposed to apostasy under trial and the preoccupations of worry, wealth, and pleasure. The faith that perseveres reveals a heart of moral beauty. The command to be careful how you hear therefore interprets the shining lamp and the manifest secret as the beautiful fruit of persevering faith. The inability of Jesus' mother and brothers to get to him because of the crowd comes back to his attractiveness. And hearing and doing the word of God, characteristics that define Jesus' family of followers, come back to persevering faith in his message.

STILLING A STORM AND EXORCISING LEGION The story of Jesus' stilling a storm revives the question of faith. *Read Luke 8:22–25.* The story concerning the exorcism of Legion gives another example of Jesus' saving power, magnified by a large number of items:

- The length of time the demoniac went naked and homeless
- His falling before Jesus
- His begging Jesus
- Legion's urging Jesus not to command them to depart into the abyss (another word for hell—compare Matthew 25:41; 2 Peter 2:4; Revelation 20:3)
- Jesus' permitting them to enter a herd of pigs
- The civilized condition and position of the delivered demoniac at Jesus' feet
- The great fear that grips the local inhabitants

Read Luke 8:26–39. The herders' seeing (8:34) provides testimony by eyewitnesses. The ex-demoniac's proclamation provides first-person testimony throughout the whole city from which he came (compare 8:27).

Jairus's Daughter and the Woman with a Chronic Blood Flow

A crowd's expectant welcome contrasts with the request in 8:37. *Read Luke 8:40–56.* That Jairus has only one daughter heightens the pathos of his request. As Jesus is on his way to Jairus's house, he recognizes that power has gone out from him and asks, "Who touched me?" Jesus' repetition of the question and the woman's seeing that she cannot stay hidden enhance his **prophetic clairvoyance.** Her declaration "in the presence of all the people" again provides both first-person and eyewitness testimony. Each in its own way, the command not to trouble Jesus and his command to stop weeping highlight the raising of the dead. So also does the breast-beating, in addition to weeping, and the mourners' knowledge that the child has died. The returning of her breath ("spirit") enables her to stand up and signals her salvation from death.

MISSION OF THE TWELVE Luke's version of the mission of the Twelve brings out the power as well as the authority that Jesus gave them, plus the elements of his sending them, which corresponds to the meaning of "apostle" (compare 6:13), and of their evangelistic and therapeutic itineration through one village after another, in accordance with the Hellenistic interest in travel. *Read Luke 9:1–6.* The doings of the Twelve come to the ears of Herod (Antipas), whose perplexity and desire to see Jesus (who gave the Twelve their power and authority) Luke uses to deride Herod, the high and mighty doer of evil (3:19–20), and to ennoble Jesus, the gracious doer of good. *Read Luke 9:7–9.* Testifying to Jesus' graciousness is his welcoming the crowds who followed him to Bethsaida even though he had retreated there for some privacy with his disciples. The same is true with respect to his talking to the crowds about God's rule, healing the sick, and feeding about five thousand men. *Read Luke 9:10–17.*

PETER'S CONFESSION Jesus' piety comes out again in his praying alone at the time of Peter's confessing him to be "the Christ of God," that is, "God's Anointed One." By

Gerasa

equating Jesus' instruction that the disciples not tell anyone with the first passion prediction, Luke indicates that as the Christ of God, Jesus and the rule of God that he brings are *not* politically dangerous: Jesus comes for rejection, not for revolution. Likewise, his followers must risk their lives daily for personal gain hereafter, not for political gain here and now. *Read Luke 9:18–27.*

Transfiguration

Luke's introduction to the transfiguration, "And it happened approximately eight days after these words," makes clear the fulfillment by that event of Jesus' preceding prediction that some of the audience would not die before seeing God's rule. The specification of eight days instead of Mark's and Matthew's six days appears to reflect a Roman week of eight days, but "approximately" forestalls a contradiction of Mark and Matthew. Again the praying of Jesus evidences his piety. The glorification of Moses and Elijah as well as of Jesus and their talking about his departure, which he is about to accomplish in Jerusalem, show the kingdom of God to be heavenly, **unthreatening** to the present Roman Empire; for Jesus' departure will turn out to be an ascension to heaven (9:51; 24:50–51; Acts 1:9–11). *Read Luke 9:28–36.* The linking of Peter's ill-considered suggestion with his and the other disciples' grogginess sympathetically lightens his blame. Their fear explains their later silence, and the addition of "the chosen one" to "my Son" distinguishes Jesus from Moses and Elijah as the one the disciples should listen to.

A HARD EXORCISM AND THE STRANGE EXORCIST The following episode happens "the next day" inasmuch as the disciples' sleepiness implied an overnight stay on the Mount of Transfiguration. *Read Luke 9:37–43a.* The father's begging Jesus and the son's being an only son heighten the pathos and thus the kindness of Jesus in giving the son back to his father healed from the unclean spirit. The amazement of all at God's greatness saves Jesus from any charge of self-promotion even though everybody marvels at all that Jesus is doing. Another passion prediction and the emphasis with which it is introduced also help save him from such a charge. *Read Luke 9:43b–50.* The hiddenness of Jesus' meaning again sympathetically lightens blame in the disciples' arguing who of them might be greatest. "Knowing the speculation of their heart" shows Jesus' prophetic insight, and standing a little child "beside himself" and the following sayings make the small great. Similarly, Jesus validates an exorcist who uses Jesus' name but does not follow with the Twelve. Thus the wide-ranging appeal of Jesus in Luke.

Journey to Jerusalem

Now begins a Hellenistically appealing **travelogue** of Jesus' journey to Jerusalem to be taken up in the ascension. That he "sets his face" shows **bravery** in view of the preceding passion predictions. The sending of messengers to make advance preparations turns this journey into one of royal visitations (see especially 10:1; 19:28–38, 44c), and most of it provides a narrative framework for extensive teaching by Jesus. Even the few miracle stories issue in his teaching. *Read Luke 9:51–62.* As residents of central Palestine and offspring from intermarriages of northern Israelites not taken into exile by the Assyrians and of Gentiles imported to northern Israel by those same Assyrians, the Samaritans hated Jews and vice versa—hence the refusal of a Samaritan village to receive Jesus, and James' and John's question whether to call down fire from heaven to annihilate the village. Jesus' rebuke of James and John and going to another village exhibit **magnanimity**.

"Hatred also arose between the Samaritans and the Jews for the following reason. It was the custom of the Galileans at the time of a festival to pass through the Samaritan territory on their way to the Holy City. On one occasion, while they were passing through, certain of the inhabitants of a village called Ginaë ... joined battle with the Galileans and slew a great number of them.... The ['Jewish'] masses ... taking up arms ... fired and sacked certain villages of the Samaritans" (Josephus, *Jewish Antiquities* 20.6.1 §§118–24).

The last three episodes in the chapter emphasize **itineration** ("the Son of Man has nowhere to lay his head"), **proclamation** ("come away [from your father] and announce far and wide the rule of God"), and **perseverance** ("No one putting his hand on a plow and looking back is useful for the rule of God").

MISSION OF THE SEVENTY-TWO Since ancient Jews counted the number of nations in the world at seventy-two, Jesus' appointment and sending of seventy-two other messengers ahead of him probably symbolize the worldwide evangelistic mission of the church (compare 24:27; Acts 1:8). *Read Luke 10:1–16.* Some ancient texts of Luke read the round number "seventy," but they tend to be inferior to those that read "seventy-two." The prohibitions of greetings along the road and of moving from house to house in a locality and the command to eat what is served are due to the need for haste, for Jesus is soon to arrive. "Peace" (↓*shalom* in Hebrew) is a normal Semitic greeting, but here it connotes the blessings of salvation that Jesus is bringing. "A son of peace" (10:6) is a person receptive of those blessings. Because Jesus is soon to arrive, the rule of God has come near.

A scorpion

Read Luke 10:17–24. Jesus equates the exorcisms reported by the Seventy-two with a lightning-like fall from heaven of Satan, ruler of the demons. The promise of protection has to do with travel in evangelistic endeavor (serpents and scorpions along the way), not with contrived demonstrations of supernatural power. To guard against arrogance, Jesus substitutes joy in **privilege** (the recording of names in heaven) for joy in **performance** (the exorcism of demons). Similarly, his own joy, inspired by the Holy Spirit always active in his life, lies in God the Father's revelation through him to **babies** in learning, such as the Seventy-two, rather than to the learned. The privilege of his revelation exceeds anything enjoyed by prophets and kings.

The Good Samaritan

Next, Jesus shows graciousness to a lawyer by commending his answer despite his testing of Jesus. The good answer of the lawyer sets out religious and social ideals. Read Luke 10:25–37. The parable of the good Samaritan robs the lawyer of his attempted self-justification by indicating that to love your neighbor obediently as you love yourself naturally, you must be a neighbor yourself rather than defining who else is or is not your neighbor.

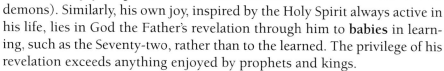

shalom: shah-LOHM

The canyon through which much of the road from Jerusalem to Jericho ran

Being a neighbor means treating any needy person near you as your neighbor without laboring over a definition, whereas laboring over the definition of a neighbor keeps you from helping the needy person. Jesus shocks the lawyer by making the helper a Samaritan. A Jew such as the lawyer would expect Jesus at most to have made the Samaritan a person in need of help, so that the lesson would run: A Jew should help even a Samaritan in need. Instead, it runs: Even a Samaritan helps a Jew in need. End of ethnic pride in Jesus' ideal society!

MARTHA AND MARY The travelogue continues with an episode that invites women into the privileges of discipleship heretofore reserved for males: sitting at the feet of Jesus and listening to his words. It is unnecessary for women to serve the meal. *Read Luke 10:38–42.*

PRAYER Again the piety of Jesus comes out in his praying, but this time his praying leads to instruction on praying. The Lord's Prayer, shorter here than in Matthew, tells the disciples **what** to pray. The following parable and sayings tell them **how** to pray: with perseverance. As beggars know, if you keep on asking, people will give. If you look long enough, you will find. If you do not stop knocking, the person inside will finally open the door. Given a fatherly relation to the disciples, how much more will God answer their persistent prayers! *Read Luke 11:1–13.* Both long and scaly, fish and snakes look alike. So too do eggs and scorpions if the latter have their

Background for the Parable of the Good Samaritan

The road from Jerusalem to Jericho descends over 3,000 feet in less than 15 miles through gorges and ravines infested with bandits. The priest and the Levite may fear ritual defilement from what could well be a corpse. Such defilement would cost them the purchase of ashes of a red heifer for purification, the loss of temple privileges (such as eating from sacrifices) during a week of defilement, the arrangement of burial for the corpse, and the rending of a perfectly good garment as a sign of grief. The priest and the Levite quite clearly see in the victim a threat of personal loss and inconvenience. The Samaritan has equal reason to bypass the injured and possibly dead man, however, because Samaritans likewise avoid defilement from the dead—and perhaps even more reason, because chances are that the victim is a detestable Jew. But not only does the Samaritan stop to investigate; he treats the wounds with wine to disinfect them and with olive oil to soothe them, tears bandages from his own turban or linen undergarment to wrap up the lesions, goes on foot as the victim rides his donkey (the slower pace exposing them to greater danger of further attack by bandits), pays enough money to an innkeeper for two weeks of convalescence, and pledges unlimited credit for any additional expense—all without hope of reimbursement, since Samaritans have no legal rights in Jewish courts. When asked to identify the true neighbor in the parable, the lawyer cannot bring himself to say, "The Samaritan," but uses a circumlocution, "The one who had mercy on him."

claws and tails rolled up. Apparently, the traveler in Jesus' parable journeys during the evening to avoid the heat of afternoon and so arrives at midnight, very late by the standards of ancient Orientals, who retire early. The oriental "law of hospitality" causes the traveler's host to wake a neighbor for provisions of food. The three small loaves of bread for which he asks are considered a meal for one person. The reluctance of the neighbor is aggravated by the fact that Palestinian families slept close together on mats in the same room, so that to rise and unbolt the door would wake up the whole family. In the neighbor's reply, the absence of a polite address, such as "Friend" in the request to him, shows annoyance.

DISBELIEF The setting back to back of the accusation that Jesus exorcises demons by their ruler, Satan, and the demand that Jesus produce a sign from heaven expose a disbelief unreasonable in its refusal to be satisfied by what should count as adequate evidence. *Read Luke 11:14–36.* The finger of God stands for his power, the fully armed strong man and his castle and possessions for Satan and his kingdom and demoniacs, and the stronger man and his victory for Jesus and his exorcisms. His beatitude on those who hear the word and do it shows him to be a teacher of high morals. The condemnation of his contemporaries as evil shows him to be impatient with low morals. Coming as it does right after Jesus as the sign of Jonah, the lamp on the lampstand seems likewise to represent Jesus. But "the lamp of your body" represents a person's perception of Jesus.

Pharisees and Lawyers

Next comes some **table talk** such as Luke's Hellenistic audience delighted in. *Read Luke 11:37–52.* The verb usually translated "washed" in 11:38 literally means "baptized" and may refer to bodily immersion, practiced by Pharisees among others, not just to hand washing. Ever the teacher of ethics and religion, Jesus contrasts the evil of rapacity and the good of generosity and pairs the social virtue of justice with the religious virtue of love for God. The wisdom of God that will send prophets and apostles appears to be God's wisdom personified, or perhaps a now lost book called "The Wisdom of God," or Jesus speaking of himself as God's wisdom.

The increasing attractiveness of Jesus to thousands contrasts with the hostile reaction of a few scribes and Pharisees. *Read Luke 11:53–12:59.* Jesus speaks to his disciples about speech (12:1b–12). First he warns them against hypocrisy in speech (12:1b–3). Calling his disciples "my friends," an address that projects a social ideal, he warns next against speaking in fear of other human beings and encourages speaking in fear of God and in dependence on the Holy Spirit, against which Spirit the disciples' opponents will blaspheme to their eternal loss (12:4–12). To a member of the crowd and then to the crowd, Jesus warns against **greed** (12:13–14, 15–21). To his disciples again, he warns against **anxiety** (12:22–32) and commands **charitable giving** (12:33–34) and **readiness** for the second coming (12:35–40). When Peter asks whether Jesus is speaking to the crowd as well as to the disciples, Jesus keeps right on speaking to the disciples by defining their readiness for the second coming in terms of **civility** and **moderation** (12:41–48), and by describing his first coming in terms of dividing disciples from nondisciples—at great cost to himself (12:49–53). Finally turning back to the crowds, he tells them to settle up with God before time runs out (12:54–59).

> **The Kaddish,** an ancient Jewish prayer that may have provided a base for the Lord's Prayer taught by Jesus: "Exalted and hallowed be his great name in the world that he created according to his will. May he let his kingdom rule in your lifetime and in your days and in the lifetime of the whole house of Israel, speedily and soon. Praised be his great name from eternity to eternity. And to this, say: Amen."

REPENTANCE To settle up with God means to repent and bear the fruit of good behavior, but time is limited. *Read Luke 13:1–9.* Nothing more is known about Pilate's having some Galilean pilgrims killed in Jerusalem as they were offering sacrifices in the temple, or about the fall of the tower in ↓Siloam (perhaps a tower in the wall of Jerusalem near the Pool of Siloam).

Siloam: *si*-LOH-uhm

To those who report the first of these incidents, Jesus speaks about the need for repentance (13:1–5) and, by parable, about the limited time available for it. Fig trees deprive surrounding vines and other plants by absorbing an extraordinary amount of nourishment from the soil. Therefore the fig tree in question is given only one more year's chance to bear fruit before being chopped down (13:6–9).

HEALING Time for repentance is followed by time for healing. Jesus' healing a woman on the Sabbath displays both his **humanitarianism**, in contrast with the legalistic indignation of a synagogue ruler, and Jesus' **esteem** for the woman as "a daughter of Abraham." Two parables follow. These interpret the humiliation of Jesus' opponents and the whole crowd's rejoicing over all the splendid things done by him as God's rule grown large, like a mustard seed grown into a tree,

A fig tree

and extensive, like leaven—that is, yeast—having permeated a huge lump of dough. The "therefore" that introduces the parables of a mustard seed and yeast relates them to the immediately preceding effect of Jesus' miracle. *Read Luke 13:10–21.*

Salvation

Now Luke reminds his audience of the character of the present narrative as a travelogue and relates Jesus' bypassing a question on the number of those being saved to teach the **avoidance of evil** as evidence of salvation, a salvation that on the grounds of such evidence will include many Gentiles, such as Luke writes for, but excludes many Jews. *Read Luke 13:22–30.* The last who will be first are Gentiles, the first who will be last are Jews. Final firstness means salvation, final lastness means damnation.

HEROD THE FOX Herod Antipas, too, is going to Jerusalem (see 23:8–12), but Jesus refuses to let that fact deter him from his own journey to Jerusalem. *Read Luke 13:31–35.* "That fox" is feminine in the Greek text and alludes caustically to Herod's insignificance: a vixen makes no lion and may hint at the domination of Herod by his unlawful wife Herodias.

HEALING AND TABLE TALK At Sabbath meal in the house of a leading Pharisee, Jesus heals a man afflicted with dropsy (14:1–6). This healing illustrates Jesus' humanitarianism again (compare 13:10–17) and leads to table talk

Aqueduct and ascent to Machaerus, where Herod Antipas had John the Baptist beheaded at the instigation of Herodias

(compare 7:36–50). The first part of the table talk, entailed in the healing, shames into silence the lawyers and Pharisees present (compare 13:17). The second part deals with honor and shame in the receiving of hospitality (14:7–11) and in the giving of hospitality (14:12–14). In the third part of the table talk (14:15–24), the universality of the gospel issues out of the offended honor of a man whose dinner invitations were refused by those whom he invited first. They represent **self-righteous Jews,** such as the lawyers and Pharisees at table with Jesus. The poor, crippled, blind, and lame who are brought to the dinner represent **social outcasts**; and those brought in from outside town represent **Gentiles**. *Read Luke 14:1–24.*

DISCIPLESHIP After reminding his audience again of Jesus' popularity and of the character of the narrative as a travelogue, Luke quotes sayings of Jesus that use the possibility of shame to spur his fellow travelers into true—that is, self-sacrificial—discipleship. *Read Luke 14:25–35.* Salt that has lost its saltiness (literally translated, "has become foolish") is subject to the shame of being thrown out as useless.

A Trio of Parables

Three parables follow to defend Jesus against the grumbling of the Pharisees and the scribes that he has table fellowship with tax collectors and sinners.

In all three, the element of **joy** over finding the lost contrasts with that grumbling; and in the third parable, the anger of an older brother represents the grumbling. *Read Luke 15:1–32.*

THE LOST SHEEP In connection with the parable of a lost sheep, the righteous who need no repentance do not really exist. Jesus is speaking sarcastically about the self-righteous who only think that they do not need to repent.

THE LOST COIN As part of the dowry given them at marriage, Palestinian wives often wore a headdress bedecked with coins. The lost coin may have belonged to such a headdress. The woman who lost the coin lights a candle, not because it is nighttime, but because the typical Palestinian house lacks windows and has only one low door, which lets in very little light. Apparently the coin has fallen on the lower level of a one-room house. There it lies hidden underneath some straw scattered over the lower level because of domestic animals. The housewife sweeps with a broom, probably a small palm branch, not to uncover the coin, but to make it tinkle on the hard earthen floor in order that she may determine its whereabouts. Her joy on discovering the coin represents "joy in the presence of the angels of God over one sinner who repents." Jesus is not referring to the joy of angels, but to the joy of God himself in the presence of the angels. Forming a stark contrast is the rabbinic saying, "There is joy before God when those who provoke him perish from the world" (*Sifra* Numbers 18, 8 §117 [37a]).

A coin-bedecked headdress

THE PRODIGAL SON According to the law of ↓primogeniture, a younger son receives much less by inheritance than an older son receives. "Gathering everything together" means converting into cash, presumably by sale. Since pigs are ritually unclean for Jews, feeding pigs because of employment to a Gentile and wanting to satisfy hunger with the carob pods fed to the pigs exhibit the desperate straits of the prodigal son. Repentance grows out of the prodigal's sense of misery and need and makes him resolve to return home with the confession, "Father [a respectful address], I have sinned against heaven [a reverential Jewish substitute for 'God'] and in your sight [an admission of guilt in relation to the father after such an admission in relation to God]," and with the plea to be restored only as a hired servant. Denying any claim on his father, he will ask for mercy.

THE FATHER But the prodigal underestimates his father's love, just as the Pharisees and the scribes are underestimating God's love. On seeing his son

---

primogeniture: pri´muh-JEN-i-chuhr

Ancient signet rings

returning, the father runs to meet him. Running is unusual and undignified for an aged oriental man, but the father's love and joy overpower his sense of decorum, as though to say that even God forgets his dignity in a burst of joy when a sinner turns in repentance to him. The father's kiss signifies forgiveness. The son begins to blurt out his prepared confession, but before he comes to the part about being taken back as a hired servant, the father interrupts with commands to clothe him with the best robe as a sign of honor, to place on his finger a signet ring for sealing legal documents as a sign of restored filial authority, to put shoes on his feet as a sign that he is no longer a hired laborer, and to kill the fattened calf for a banquet of celebration. Since meat did not form part of the daily diet, its presence on the menu denotes festivity.

THE OLDER BROTHER Here the parable might have ended. But it is double-edged. The words of the older brother to his father are revealing. He rudely omits the respectful address, "Father." He avoids calling the prodigal his brother but refers to him as "this son of yours." He complains that his father has never given him so much as a young goat, much less a fattened calf, for a party with his friends. (One could query how many friends such a person has.) The older brother follows a sense of duty without a balancing sense of freedom, serves his father without fellowship, and prides himself on his own merits. No wonder he feels resentful of his father's grace toward the prodigal. (There is a rabbinic parable in which a son is redeemed from slavery but brought back as a slave rather than as a son in order that obedience might be forced from him.) The father's reply to the older brother graciously begins with an affectionate "My child," reminds him that all the family estate is now deeded to him, and explains the appropriateness of festivity in that "this brother of yours" (not "my son") was (as good as) dead and lost, but is now alive and found. What is the older brother's response? Jesus does not say, but leaves the parable open-ended because the Pharisees and the scribes and all others who trust in their own merits finish the parable themselves, either by renouncing their self-righteousness to join in the messianic feast of salvation or by shutting themselves out through maintaining their self-righteousness. Finally, the older brother shows that a person does not have to feel lost to be lost. One can be estranged from God right on home territory. But everyone is invited—both flagrant sinner and decent older brother—on the same terms, God's forgiving grace.

The Unjust Steward

Jesus addresses his next parable to the disciples. Like the preceding parable of the prodigal son, it illustrates the shortsightedness of squandering wealth: by trying to serve wealth as well as his master, a household manager succumbs to the love of wealth, squanders his master's estate, and loses his position just as people in general who succumb to the love of wealth squander their heavenly reward and lose their position in God's household. By way of contrast with the prodigal's foolish shortsightedness, however, the present parable also shows a prudently foresighted way to use wealth, that is, to make friends with it through **generosity**. *Read Luke 16:1–13.*

The manager has his master's debtors dispose of their old bills and write new, smaller ones in their own handwriting. The manager hopes that if the ruse is discovered, the absence of his handwriting will keep him from blame. Since elsewhere Jesus compares God to an unjust judge without attributing injustice to God, and his own return to the housebreaking of a thief without attributing thievery to himself, the dishonesty of a manager does not destroy the positive point of the present comparison. Specifically, the manager uses money to help other people and thus to make friends for the period of his unemployment. Similarly, disciples of Jesus ought to use money in charitable enterprises, for such action will be to their own advantage in the eternal future. "The sons of this age" means worldly people. "The sons of light" means disciples of Jesus. "The mammon of unrigheousness" means wealth in its capacity of leading people who have it to *act* unrighteously, not wealth *gained* unrighteously; for one could hardly be "faithful" with regard to ill-gotten wealth. The making of **friends** with mammon points up a social ideal such as Luke uses to appeal to his Hellenistic audience.

A description of the Pharisees as **lovers of money** links the following section to the preceding one on wealth. Their scoffing at Jesus leads him to expose them as detested by God even though admired by their fellow human beings, in contrast with the tax collectors and sinners who, though detested by the Pharisees, are forcing their way by repentance into the kingdom of God. The Pharisees' practice of divorce and remarriage and of marrying divorcees offers an example of their violating the law through committing adultery despite their self-justification and despite the validity of the Law and the Prophets. *Read Luke 16:14–18.*

The Rich Man ("↓*Dives*") and Lazarus

Read Luke 16:19–31. The money-loving Pharisees resemble the rich man, who selfishly and shortsightedly disregards Lazarus, a helpless, poor man. The rich man is therefore the obverse of the foresighted manager in 16:1–8. "Lazarus" is Greek for the Hebrew ↓*Eleazar,* which means "God is (his) help." No one else helps him. The crumbs from the rich man's table, which

Dives: DI-veez ■ Eleazar: el´ee-AY-zuhr

Beggars

Lazarus would like to eat, may be pieces of bread used as napkins to wipe the hands and then discarded beneath the table. The phrase "Abraham's bosom" implies a **heavenly** banquet with Lazarus as a recently arrived guest reclining on a cushion immediately in front of Abraham. The banquet scene makes appropriate the rich man's request that Lazarus dip his finger in water. The address of the rich man, "Father Abraham," appeals to his Jewish descent from Abraham. But Abraham's response, beginning with "Son," indicates that although as a Jew the rich man has enjoyed every advantage, Hebrew ancestry does not guarantee heavenly bliss. The closing statement that someone's resurrection from the dead will not persuade the rich who disobey Mosaic and prophetic injunctions to help the poor hints at Jesus' resurrection.

CHRISTIAN COMMUNITY Now Jesus turns back to the disciples and speaks about their communal relations:

- The inevitability that some ("stumbling blocks") will lead others ("little ones") to sin ("stumble")
- The need to rebuke a sinning fellow disciple ("your brother") and forgive a repentant one repeatedly if necessary
- Obedience to the command to forgive as requiring only a small amount of faith and a mere sense of obligation

A reference to the uprooting of a sycamine (mulberry or sycamore) tree grows out of the extraordinary strength and depth of its roots. *Read Luke 17:1–10.*

THE HEALING OF TEN LEPERS A reminder of Jesus' journey to Jerusalem renews the narrative. Ten lepers' standing at a distance reflects a demand of the Mosaic law that lepers live apart from other people (Leviticus 13:45–46; Numbers 5:2–4). Emphasis falls not so much on Jesus' healing the ten lepers as on the glorifying of God, thanksgiving to Jesus, and saving faith of the one leper who is a Samaritan; for Luke is appealing to Gentiles. *Read Luke 17:11–19.* "Between Samaria and Galilee" contains two puzzles: (1) the border between these two regions runs east and west, whereas "the way to Jerusalem" runs from north to south; (2) going to Jerusalem would take Jesus from Galilee through Samaria, whereas Luke mentions Samaria before Galilee. Possibly but not certainly, Luke's original text read "through

Samaria and Galilee" and mentioned Samaria first, not because of geographical order but out of interest in the Samaritan who figures in the following story.

LOT'S WIFE Answering a question of the Pharisees, Jesus deters them from thinking that the rule of God is yet to come with observable signs. Though the Pharisees have not recognized its presence, it is already among them. Then turning to the disciples, Jesus speaks of the future: the time just preceding and including his unmistakably recognizable return ("the days of the Son of Man" culminating in "his day"), a time not to follow the example of Lot's wife, who turned into a pillar of salt for looking back toward the city of Sodom when she should have been fleeing its destruction without hesitation (Genesis 19:26). For Luke, however, the important point lies in the **futurity** of those days ("you will long to see one of the days of the Son of Man and will not see it") and therefore in the **political innocence** of the rule of God brought by Jesus here and now. Christianity does not threaten Roman society, but improves it. *Read Luke 17:20–37.*

A Widow and an Unjust Judge

Continuing Jesus' speech to the disciples is a parable that teaches them to pray patiently but persistently for justice at the second coming. *Read Luke 18:1–8.* In ancient Jewish society the marrying of girls thirteen or fourteen years old resulted in a large class of young widows. A widow's bringing her case to one judge instead of a tribunal implies a matter of money, such as an unpaid debt or part of an inheritance withheld from her. A judge's not fearing God means that he lacks honesty; his not regarding people means that he lacks sympathy. Apparently a rich and influential opponent of the widow in Jesus' parable has bribed the judge, but she is too poor to do so.

Her only weapon consists in a tenacious faith that justice will be done if she exasperates the judge with her persistence. The widow represents disciples, unjustly persecuted by their enemies and therefore unsubversive of the Roman government. The delay in her reception of justice represents a delay in the second coming. But the delay will not last long, for God has much greater concern for justice than the judge in the parable does. The only question, then, is whether Jesus' disciples will maintain their faith during the delay.

A sycamore tree

A Pharisee and a Tax Collector

The preceding parable dealt with praying for justice in relation to one's persecution; a follow-up parable deals with praying for justification in relation to one's sins. Directed to people who regard themselves as righteous and others as sinful, this parable teaches **humility**. Infants, the smallest of children, then become Jesus' example of humility. *Read Luke 18:9–17.* With the Pharisee's prayer may be compared an excerpt from the Jewish Prayer Book:

"Blessed are you, O Lord our God, King of the Universe, who have not made me a Gentile . . . who have not made me a slave . . . who have not made me a woman." But modern stereotyping of the Pharisee and the tax collector has taken away the force of this parable. Pharisees served God seriously by going without food from sunrise to sunset on Mondays and Thursdays and by tithing all their possessions as well as keeping the moral and ritual commandments of the law. Common people admired them greatly. Tax collectors, on the other hand, collaborated with the hated Roman oppressors, fleeced their fellow Jews, and practiced all sorts of fraud. The common people detested them. Jesus' audience must have been shocked to hear him put the Pharisee in a bad light, the tax collector in a good light. But the very unexpectedness in the reversal of good and bad roles underscores the nature of forgiveness as God's gift, ill-merited and granted solely on the basis of **repentant faith.**

> "And your fasts are not to be with the hypocrites, for they fast on Mondays and Fridays; you [Christians], on the contrary, fast on Wednesdays and Fridays [!]" (*Didache* 8:1).

While the self-righteous need to learn humility for entrance into God's kingdom, an extremely wealthy ruler needs to learn **charity** to the extent of selling all his property and distributing the proceeds to the poor, plus **following Jesus.** *Read Luke 18:18–30.* A second prediction of the passion and the resurrection (compare 9:22) puts emphasis on their carrying out prophetic passages in the Old Testament and on the hiding of Jesus' prediction from the disciples' comprehension. Luke is excusing their incomprehension so as to portray the Christian community in the most attractive light possible. *Read Luke 18:31–34.* The healing of a blind beggar issues in his glorifying God and in the eyewitnesses' giving praise to God—a **religious** success in addition to the **therapeutic** one. *Read Luke 18:35–43.*

ZACCHAEUS The episodes in Luke 19 are replete with notations of Jesus' progress to Jerusalem. The travelogue is nearing completion. *Read Luke 19:1–10.* In itself, the story of Zacchaeus shows that salvation can come even to a rich man if he repents. By promising to give half his possessions to the poor and pay back those he has defrauded four times the original amount, Zacchaeus far exceeds the normal boundaries of charity and restitution. For in cases of financial fraud, such as Zacchaeus's, the Mosaic law prescribes a restitution of the original amount plus only 20 percent. In Luke's larger picture, the excess of Zacchaeus's charity and restitution exhibits the social benefits of Christianity.

> "He shall make full restitution for his wrong, add one fifth to it, and give it to the person he has wronged" (Numbers 5:6–7; also Leviticus 6:1–5).

THE MINAS *Read Luke 19:11–27.* The practice of local leaders' going to Rome to gain imperial support for their claims to rulership forms a background for the parable of the minas (each one the equivalent of about three months' wages for a manual worker). The parable shows that neither the Hellenistic world in general nor the Roman government in particular has anything to fear from Christianity, for Christians regard themselves as individually subject to strict standards of judgment by their own Lord, as required to live productively, and as awaiting God's rule rather than fomenting rebellion against Rome.

- The nobleman = Jesus
- His going to a distant country = Jesus' ascension to heaven
- His receiving royal power there = Jesus' heavenly exaltation to the right hand of God (compare Acts 2:32–36)
- The citizens' expressed desire not to have him rule over them = the Jewish leaders' rejection of Jesus (compare 23:13–25)
- His return = the second coming of Jesus
- The calling of his servants to account = the Last Judgment
- The execution of his enemies = the Jewish leaders' final punishment

The case of the servant who wrapped up his mina teaches the impossibility of safe discipleship. To truly follow Jesus entails the risk of life-investment as opposed to the security of life-preserving.

In the Temple

Read Luke 19:28–48. The episodes of Jesus' triumphal entry and cleansing of the temple show his kingship to be heavenly and peaceful, not earthly and seditious. It features miracles of healing, not acts of rebellion, and issues in joyful praise to God and in religious reformation. Jesus does not fight; he weeps. Only the corrupt chieftans of the temple oppose him; the general populace applaud his teaching.

The next two chapters, Luke 20–21, tell of Jesus' teaching, preaching the gospel, and answering questions in the temple. *Read Luke 20:1–26.* The Sanhedrin's fear that all the people will stone them if they say that the baptism of John had a merely human origin points up the success of John's Spirit-empowered testimony to Jesus. Though the parable of the vineyard refers to God (the owner), Israel (the vineyard), Jewish leaders (the tenant farmers), Old Testament prophets (the slaves), and Jesus (the beloved son), the long time for which the owner goes away would seem to remind Luke's audience that Jesus too has been away for a long time (compare 17:22; 19:11–12). The members of the Sanhedrin correspond to the builders who reject the cap- or cornerstone and who will therefore be broken to pieces and crushed in judgment. Their wickedness, exposed in their trying to seize Jesus "that very hour," in their fear of the people, in their watching

Jesus, in their tricky sending of spies who pretend to be righteous, and in their intention to trap Jesus and hand him over to the governor—this wickedness sets Jesus by contrast in a good moral and political light.

Read Luke 20:27–44. Jesus' putdown of the Sadducees contrasts "the sons of this age" with those "considered worthy to attain that age [the coming age] and the resurrection from the dead" and brings out both the immortality of those worthy ones because "they are God's children, being children of the resurrection," and their living for God. Thus Jesus' disciples as well as he himself appear in a good light. The commendation of him by some of the scribes gives further testimony to the power of his putdown and prepares for his asking them a question, criticizing them in public, and contrasting their detestable behavior with the admirable behavior of a poor widow. As usual in Luke, Jesus looks the part of a **good moral teacher.** *Read Luke 20:45–21:4.*

Presence in the temple at or near the treasury leads some to remark the beautiful stones and votive gifts (tapestries, gold grape clusters, and so on) that decorate the temple. Jesus responds with a prediction of its destruction. When asked for the time and portent of this destruction, he stresses delay and avoidance of claims to immediacy: Do not go after those who say that the time is near; wars and revolutions must take place **first,** and even then the end does not follow right away; persecution and Christian testimony will precede large earthquakes, plagues, famines, terrors, and great heavenly signs; and Gentiles will trample Jerusalem for a while after its destruction. The exhortation not to be terrified by wars and revolutions distances Jesus' disciples from such fighting. Irresistible **wisdom** will char-

Inner relief of the Arch of Titus, celebrating in Rome the destruction of Jerusalem and the temple. Note the menorah taken as a trophy.

acterize their speaking and **perseverance** their suffering of persecution, which will include treachery of the worst kind and will fall due to the name of Christ, not to any misbehavior on the part of his disciples. They should flee Jerusalem and the Judean countryside rather than staying and joining in rebellion. It is nondisciples who will get their comeuppance. The disciples are to avoid dissipation, drunkenness, and worldly worries, and to keep alert by praying. Nothing to fear from Christians here! Their speech and conduct will be admirable, as is that of Jesus, who draws so much admiration that everybody gets up early to hear him in the temple. *Read Luke 21:5–38.*

Passion Narrative

Read Luke 22:1–6. The introduction to Luke's passion narrative features the Sanhedrin's fear of the people because of Jesus' popularity. Apparently the Sanhedrin fear that the people will stone them for killing Jesus just as they feared that the people would stone them for denying the heavenly origin of John's baptism (compare 20:1–8). The contrast between their fear and Jesus' popularity puts them in a bad light and him in a good light. **Satan's** entering Judas Iscariot makes Jesus' arrest, trial, and death due to influence from the archdemon himself rather than to any misdeed on the part of Jesus. This entry also explains how such a dastardly deed could have been done by one of the twelve apóstles. Otherwise, the deed would ruin Luke's portrayal of Jesus and the disciples as an ideal community.

PASSOVER PREPARATION *Read Luke 22:7–13.* The necessity of slaughtering a Passover lamb on the Day of Unleavened Bread combines with Jesus' taking the initiative in sending Peter and John to prepare the Passover meal. This combination portrays Jesus as a law-abiding Jew rather than as a renegade (compare 2:21–24, 39, 41–52). His including the apostles with himself as those for whom the meal is to be prepared highlights the fellowship of friends and family at table, a kind of fellowship that figures prominently in Hellenistic culture.

TABLE FELLOWSHIP *Read Luke 22:14–23.* The apostles' reclining with Jesus renews the emphasis on table fellowship among friends and family (compare 8:19–21). So also does Jesus' saying that he has eagerly desired to eat the Passover with the apostles before he suffers. This desire is due to his coming inability to eat the Passover with the apostles until the Passover reaches its fulfillment at the messianic banquet in God's kingdom. Yet again emphasizing table fellowship are a command that the disciples divide the cup among themselves, the description of Jesus' body (represented by bread) as "given" for them, and the further command to carry on this table fellowship in memory of him when he is gone. Double emphasis on the cup and a placement of the cup after dinner as well as before make for a **symposium** ("drinking together," accompanied by table talk) such as followed

Golden cup from the Roman period

a banquet in the Greco-Roman culture to which Luke is appealing. "Until the rule of God comes" is a reminder that the present interim poses no political threat to Rome. The setting of table fellowship makes the betrayer's presence as dastardly as possible. The going of Jesus "as it has been determined" makes his death a matter of **prior planning** on God's part instead of present human failure on Jesus' part. And the apostles' beginning to discuss among themselves which one of them might be the betrayer puts them in the good light of accepting Jesus' exclamation that the betrayer's hand is with him at table.

A DISPUTE Not so flattering to the apostles is their dispute over which of them seems to be the greatest. But some comments of Jesus, which carry on the table talk at this symposium, negate the dispute immediately. *Read Luke 22:24–30.* Jesus' comments do not redefine greatness in terms of a slave's service, but tell the greatest person to become like the youngest person, the leader to become like a waiter at table, just as Jesus himself, great though he is, has become like a waiter at table. Thus the theme of table fellowship is maintained, and service is taught without a denial of greatness. Again putting the apostles in a good light is Jesus' mentioning their loyalty to him in hard times and conferring on them the privilege of further table fellowship with him in his kingdom, just as God his Father has conferred rulership on him. Greatness indeed!

SATAN AND SIMON *Read Luke 22:31–34.* Sifting like wheat stands for an attempt to shake loyalty. Emphasizing that Peter's three denials of Jesus will hold the danger of apostasy are Jesus' using the old name "Simon" rather than the new name "Peter," doubling that old name "Simon," addressing Simon alone despite the plural number of "you" whom Satan has demanded to sift (as in the Greek text), praying that Simon's faith not fail, and indicating the need of Simon's fellow disciples that he strengthen them. Much as in Judas's case, the activity of Satan explains how Simon could be so disloyal as to verge on apostasy with his denials, how such disloyalty could show itself in the ideal community of Jesus and his disciples. The turning back of Simon to the extent of strengthening his fellow disciples illustrates the restorative possibilities in this community. Simon's response exhibits reverence for Jesus ("Lord") and expresses without any self-exalting comparison with the other apostles a readiness to travel with Jesus both to prison and to death. Though Simon will deny that he knows Jesus, he will not deny Jesus himself. Thus Luke continues to portray Christian community, as represented by the apostles, in the best possible light.

NORMALCY The next dialogue in this symposium indicates that the apostles should return to the taking of normal provisions now that Jesus will die the death of a criminal in fulfillment of Isaiah 53:12. By implication, he is not a criminal even though he will be treated as such; and the apostles will carry on an **itinerant** ministry in his absence. The presentation of two swords implies that the apostles think of defending Jesus and prepare for just such an effort in Gethsemane—even explains in advance how it can be that a disciple of the peace-loving Jesus will draw a sword and strike off the right ear of a servant of the high priest—whereas Jesus' answer, "It is enough," implies that he thinks of no such effort, much less of armed rebellion against the powers that be, but of their defending themselves from the dangers of travel. *Read Luke 22:35–38.*

SORROW AND SLEEP The symposium has ended. Luke's account of the episode in Gethsemane, for which he substitutes a less specific reference to the Mount of Olives in accordance with 21:37, now emphasizes the disciples' need to pray just as Jesus prays. A reference to their sorrow explains their sleeping, answers in advance his question, "Why are you sleeping?" and thus puts them and their community with Jesus yet again in the best possible light. *Read Luke 22:39–46.*

It is highly debatable whether Luke wrote 22:43–44 or a scribe added these verses later, for most of the very best manuscripts and early versions lack the verses. If authentic, they add to Luke's emphasis on Jesus' praying; and whether or not authentic, they do *not* say that Jesus sweat drops of blood (as is often misstated), but that the beads of his sweat that fell to the ground were *like* blood drops, presumably in their size and profusion.

ARREST *Read Luke 22:47–53.* Judas's kiss slips from the realm of actuality to that of intention so as to leave more room for the question of armed conflict. A description of the cut-off ear as the slave's right one adds to the seriousness of the swordman's act of violence, for the righthandedness of most people makes the right more useful and favorable than the left. Jesus' answer, "Enough of this!" and healing of the ear answer the question of armed conflict negatively. From now on, governmental authorities have nothing of this sort to fear from the disciples. That the ones around Jesus see what is going to happen lends the credibility of eyewitness to the episode (compare 1:1–4). And references to the hour of his enemies and the power of darkness attribute his arrest to the most evil of influences rather than to any misbehavior on his part.

Jesus' Trials

BEFORE THE SANHEDRIN Luke goes directly to Peter's denials of Jesus in the courtyard of the high priest's house. Jesus' turning and looking intently at Peter after the third denial and cockcrow trigger Peter's memory and bitter weeping. A description of Jesus' mockers as blaspheming, that is, as engaging in slander, shows him **innocent**. His trial before the Sanhedrin takes place with the coming of day. The questions of Christhood and divine sonship are divided. Jesus' answer to the first exposes the Sanhedrin's unbelief and fear (compare 20:3–8), projects a heavenly rule unthreatening to Caesar, and raises the second question. *Read Luke 22:54–71.*

BEFORE PILATE *Read Luke 23:1–5.* A description of the Sanhedrin as "all their multitude" (literal translation in 23:1) prepares for their overwhelming of Pilate's desire to release Jesus. The claim that they have found him forbidding people to pay taxes to Caesar and calling himself Christ, a king (and therefore a rival of Caesar), spells out the ways in which he is purported to have been perverting the Jewish nation. Refusal to pay taxes is considered an act of rebellion. Luke's audience can easily see the **falsity** of these charges in Jesus' having said to pay taxes to Caesar (20:19–26), in his having strictly ordered the disciples not to tell anyone that he is the Christ (9:20–21; compare 4:41), in his never having told the people himself that he is the Christ, a king (though they themselves called him a king at his triumphal entry, 19:38), and in his having refused to answer the Sanhedrin's own question whether he is the Christ (22:66–68). On interrogation, Pilate himself finds him innocent, but the Sanhedrin only expand their charge so as to say that in his teaching Jesus has been inciting the people to rebel all the way from Galilee to Jerusalem, whereas Luke's audience knows that Jesus has been teaching morality and religious devotion.

BEFORE HEROD ANTIPAS The Sanhedrin's mention of Galilee leads Pilate to ask whether Jesus is a Galilean. Learning that he is leads Pilate to send him to Herod Antipas, who has jurisdiction over Galilee. *Read Luke 23:6–12.* Herod's desire to see Jesus started as far back as 9:9. **Vehemence** substitutes

Pontius Pilate inscription in Caesarea: "Tiberius [Po]ntius Pilate [Pref]ect of Judea"

for truth in the Sanhedrin's accusations against Jesus before Herod. In view of Jesus' innocence, the ridicule to which Herod and his soldiers subject him is supposed to draw the sympathy of Luke's audience (though in view of Acts 12:21, where a future Herod will dress up in a bright robe, it is barely possible that the present Herod pridefully puts a bright robe on himself rather than mockingly on Jesus).

BACK TO PILATE *Read Luke 23:13–25.* Suddenly "the people" turn up on the side of the Sanhedrin against Jesus. Yet since they have joined the Sanhedrin in charging him with turning "the people" away from Roman rule, the people who accuse him must differ from those purportedly misled by him. Perhaps the accusatory people are the same as "the council of elders of the people" (22:66), but called simply "the people" to link up with Luke's having referred to the Sanhedrin as "all their multitude" (23:1). Pilate **repeats** his earlier declaration of Jesus' innocence, **underlines** its validity by noting that he interrogated him in the Sanhedrin's presence, **adds** to his own declaration a like one by Herod, and **indicates** that he will release Jesus after a good whipping just to teach him not to get in trouble with the Sanhedrin again. The thought of Jesus' release triggers a wholesale outcry for the release of Barabbas instead. The description of Barabbas as a prisoner who committed **murder** and participated in a **rebellion** right under the Sanhedrin's noses in Jerusalem exposes the gross injustice of the requested exchange: a life-giving **pacifist** for a murderous **rebel**. Pilate's second indication of desire to release Jesus draws forth a demand, doubled and put in the present tense for emphasis (so the Greek text), that Pilate crucify Jesus, that is, give him a criminal's death. Yet a third indication by Pilate that he will release Jesus after a good whipping because Jesus has not committed a capital crime seals the innocence of Jesus, supports the political innocence of his followers in Luke's time, and puts Roman officialdom in a comparatively good light and Jewish officialdom in an incomparably bad light. The voices of the latter prevail: insistence overcomes justice; loudness substitutes for evidence. Pilate never does declare Jesus guilty, but orders that the Sanhedrin's demand be carried out. Another mention of Barabbas's imprisonment for rebellion and murder renews attention to the gross injustice perpetrated by the Sanhedrin.

↓**VIA DOLOROSA** Luke now describes the leading of Jesus away as a procession in which Simon the Cyrenian carries the cross behind Jesus and a large multitude of the people and of mourning women follow. The loyalty of these people to the bitter end displays their recognition of Jesus' truly good character over against the false charges leveled at him by the Sanhedrin. Selflessly, he brushes aside a lamentation for him and warns of disasters to fall on the people. "Daughters of Jerusalem" implies that he is speaking about the

Via Dolorosa: VEE-uh doh´luh-ROH-suh, meaning "The Way of Sorrow"

destruction of Jerusalem (compare 19:41–44; 21:5–6). *Read Luke 23:26–31.* The green tree stands for a favorable time, the dry tree for an unfavorable time. Hence, if an event so bad as Jesus' crucifixion takes place during the present period of peace, how much worse will be the disaster to befall Jerusalem during the coming period of war (again compare 19:41–44).

Crucifixion with Criminals

Read Luke 23:32–43. The crucifixion of two criminals with Jesus further highlights the **injustice** of his crucifixion. The meaning of criminals, "doers of evil," contrasts with Jesus' having done good (compare Acts 10:38: "he went around doing good"). Luke avoids the word *bandits, revolutionaries* (so Mark and Matthew), perhaps to keep his audience from even associating Jesus with insurrection against Rome. Jesus' praying forgiveness for his enemies and excusing their injustice as due to ignorance show him pious to the end and boundlessly magnanimous. The rulers' sneering contrasts with the people's watching. So also does the soldiers' mockery. (Is Luke playing on public dislike of soldiers for their bullying, as in 3:14?) The blaspheming of Jesus by one of the criminals crucified with him forms a foil against which stands out the statement of the other criminal, who in contrast says Jesus has done nothing wrong. In the conversation between the second criminal and Jesus, the replacement of Jesus' kingdom with paradise makes that kingdom a heavenly state **unthreatening** to earthly Rome.

A crucified man's heel bone, pierced by a nail that fastened him to the wood—found in an ossuary in Jerusalem

PRAYING IN THE DARK *Read Luke 23:44–49.* Luke explains the darkness of early afternoon as due to the sun's failing to shine. Suitably to his emphasis on Jesus' piety as shown in prayer, the last word from the cross consists of a prayer, one that expresses trust in God the Father with the last breath drawn by Jesus. The centurion, an eyewitness of this event, reacts by glorifying God with an affirmation of Jesus' righteousness. And all the crowds, having viewed the whole series of events, react by lamenting his death as they leave the scene. But his acquaintances and female followers linger, seeing also things that now transpire.

A GOOD MAN AND FAITHFUL WOMEN *Read Luke 23:50–24:12.* Even in his death Jesus attracts the best: Joseph of Arimathea is a good and righteous man and a holdout against the Sanhedrin's machination. His interring of Jesus' body in a tomb never used before pays special tribute to Jesus' innocence (compare 19:30). The women disciples continue to play the role of eyewitnesses by following Joseph to the tomb and observing the interment. Their resting on the Sabbath after returning and preparing spices and perfumes with which to anoint Jesus' body shows them to be law-abiding Jews.

Given the suspicion of novelty and the legal standing of Judaism in the Greco-Roman world, Luke stresses the linkage of Christianity with Judaism. On Sunday morning the women's finding the stone rolled away from the tomb combines with their not finding the body of Jesus inside to cause them perplexity. The standing of two men to announce his resurrection provides sufficient testimony and erases their fear. The dazzling apparel of the men enhances their testimony by pointing to its divine source (compare 9:30, 32 and the identification in 24:23 of these two men as angels, that is, messengers from God). A reminder of Jesus' having predicted the very events of passion and resurrection that have now taken place erases the women's perplexity. The nonsensical and incredible impression made by their own testimony on the eleven apostles and Peter's confirmation of the emptiness of the tomb show that the apostles will believe in Jesus' resurrection only on sure and certain grounds (compare 1:1–4).

The Emmaus Disciples

The testimony of two disciples outside the circle of the Eleven now **supplements** that of the two angels who appeared as men at the empty tomb. This new testimony arises out of a personal encounter with the risen Jesus. The occurrence of this encounter on the very day that the angels have explained the emptiness of the tomb as due to his resurrection underlines the truth of their explanation. The naming of one of the disciples (↓Cleopas) and of the village to which they are traveling from Jerusalem (Emmaus) and the specification of distance (sixty stadia, or about seven miles) provide circumstantial data supporting the reliability of the two disciples' testimony. By matching Jesus' habit of talking with his disciples during travel and at table, his doing the same here likewise supports the testimony of the two. Their sadness and initial failure to recognize him disfavor fabrication of the testimony out of an expectation that he would rise from the dead. His scriptural explanation to the two of his passion and resurrection again supports their testimony by linking its subject matter with a divine plan already evident in **ancient tradition**. Their inward feeling of warmth as he gives this explanation supplements scriptural tradition with **existential impact**. The opening of their eyes to recognize him makes them eyewitnesses. And an appearance of him to Simon (Peter) adds to their **eyewitness testimony** a second such testimony. *Read Luke 24:13–35.*

Roman milestone

Cleopas: KLEE-oh-puhs

Bodily Resurrection and Ascension

A third appearance of the risen Jesus occurs in the midst of all the disciples as the travelers to Emmaus are giving their testimony. *Read Luke 24:36–53.* Alarm, fear, and long-lasting doubt again disfavor a fabrication of the account out of an expectation that Jesus would rise from the dead. The visibility and tangibility of his body link with his eating of food to define the resurrection as **physical** and make the disciples eyewitnesses. The reminder of his passion and resurrection predictions and his further explanation of the Old Testament (according to its Hebrew division into the Mosaic Law, the Prophets, and miscellaneous writings headed by the Psalms) confirm what they see and lead to his commissioning them to preach in his name to all the nations. The subject matter of their preaching—that is, repentance issuing in the forgiveness of sins—will carry on the **social reform** begun by John the Baptist and enlarged by Jesus. The promise of God the Father that he will "clothe" them with "power from on high" refers to the Holy Spirit's coming (Acts 1:4–5; 2:1–4). No one can criticize the effect of Jesus' appearance, actions, words, blessing, and departure through ascension into heaven; for the disciples praise God continually in the temple. Thus Luke ends volume one of his two-part work by evoking admiration for the piety of the Christian community.

Summary

Luke writes his Gospel, the first volume of a two-volume work, to assure his audience of the reliability of the Jesus-tradition, based as it is on the reports of eyewitnesses. This Gospel presents the Jewish Jesus in ways that would appeal to an audience of high-minded Gentiles. So emphasis falls on his broad sympathies, deep piety, moral attractiveness, political innocence, and on the same characteristics of his followers. The Holy Spirit's activity comes in for repeated mention, and Jerusalem appears prominently as the topographical goal of Jesus' itineration, especially his journey there for Passion Week. Luke puts a good deal of material distinctive to his Gospel—including some of Jesus' most famous parables, such as that of the prodigal son—in the course of this journey. Among other distinctives are an account of John the Baptist's birth, the standpoint of Mary in the story of Jesus' birth, his visit to the temple during boyhood, a mission of seventy-two disciples in addition to that of the Twelve, Jesus' being tried before Herod Antipas as well as the Sanhedrin and Pilate, the repentance of one of the two criminals crucified with Jesus, the risen Jesus' traveling to Emmaus with two nonapostolic disciples, an emphasis on the physicality of his resurrection, and his ascension.

People to Remember

Anna	Joseph of Arimathea	Simeon
Barabbas	Levi	Theophilus
Caesar Augustus	Lot's wife	widow of Nain
Cleopas	Luke	woman with a chronic
Elizabeth	Martha and Mary (sisters)	blood flow
Herod Antipas	Mary the mother of Jesus	Zacchaeus
Jairus's daughter	Pilate	Zacharias/Zechariah
Jerome	Quirinius	
John the Baptist	repentant criminal	

Places to Remember

Bethlehem	Galilee	Mount of Olives
Capernaum	Jerusalem	Nazareth
Emmaus	Judea	Perea

Terms to Remember

annunciation	the Kaddish	Sermon on the Plain
Benedictus	Latin Vulgate	symposium
"Dives" and Lazarus	law of primogeniture	the unjust steward
Gloria in Excelsis Deo	Magnificat	Via Dolorosa
the good Samaritan	Nunc Dimittis	"we"-sections of Acts

How Much Did You Learn?

- How do we deduce Luke's authorship of the Third Gospel?
- Discuss possible indications of Luke's ethnic and cultural background.
- To whom does Luke dedicate his Gospel?
- What purpose and emphases characterize it?
- List some of the items found only in Luke's Gospel.

For Further Discussion

- To what class of people in the modern world is Luke's Gospel best suited? Or is Luke's classless?
- How would you describe the personality of Jesus if you had only Luke's Gospel for evidence?

For Further Investigation

Bock, D. L. *Luke 1:1–9:50* and *Luke 9:51–24:53.* 2 vols. Grand Rapids: Baker, 1994, 1996. Advanced.

Evans, C. A. *Luke.* Peabody, Mass.: Hendrickson, 1990.

Fitzmyer, J. A. *The Gospel according to Luke.* 2 vols. Garden City, N.Y.: Doubleday, 1981, 1985. Advanced.

Kurz, W. S. *Reading Luke-Acts: Dynamics of Biblical Narrative.* Louisville: Westminster John Knox, 1993.

Nolland, J. *Luke 1–9:20; Luke 9:21–18:34;* and *Luke18:35–24:53.* 3 vols. Dallas: Word, 1989, 1993. Advanced.

Stein, R. H. *Luke.* Nashville: Broadman, 1992.

Tannehill, R. C. *Luke.* Nashville: Abingdon, 1996.

CHAPTER 10

JOHN: BELIEVING IN JESUS FOR ETERNAL LIFE

Overview:

- Introductory Issues
- An Outline of John
- Reading John with Interpretation
- Summary

Study Goals—Learn:

- Who wrote John, when, where, and why we think so
- How John compares and contrasts with the Synoptics
- Jesus' words as a development of John's portrayal of him as the Word
- Prominent theological themes distinctive of John
- Circumstances that led John to write the way he did
- John's arrangement of material
- What the text of John means

Saint John's Basilica in Ephesus

Introductory Issues

Authorship

Written in a simple style, the last of the Gospels exhibits a theological profundity beyond that of the Synoptics. Early church tradition favors that the **Apostle John** wrote this Gospel toward the close of the first century in ↓Ephesus, a city of Asia Minor. Especially important is the testimony of **Irenaeus**, a disciple of **Polycarp**, who was in turn a disciple of the Apostle John himself—a direct line of tradition with only one link between Irenaeus and John.

> **The Link Between John and Irenaeus**
>
> - "John himself, the disciple of the Lord, who also had leaned back on Jesus' chest—he, too, published the Gospel while he was staying at Ephesus in Asia" (Irenaeus, *Against Heresies* 3.1.1).
> - "I can remember the events of that time . . . so that I am able to describe the very place where the blessed Polycarp sat . . . and the accounts he gave of his conversation with John and with others who had seen the Lord" (Irenaeus as quoted by Eusebius, *Church History* 5.20.5–6).

RYLANDS FRAGMENT OF JOHN In the past some scholars insisted that the Fourth Gospel was not written until the mid-second century and therefore long after the Apostle John had died. But discovery of the Rylands Fragment of John forced abandonment of that view. This papyrus fragment dates from about A.D. 135 and requires several previous decades for the writing, copying, and circulation of John as far as the Egyptian hinterland, where the fragment was discovered. Other early papyri containing the text of John support this implication of the Rylands Fragment.

But many scholars are still unconvinced that the Apostle John wrote the Fourth Gospel. Some suggest that a disciple of the Apostle John, perhaps the **Elder John** mentioned very early by **Papias**, wrote it and was later confused with the apostle of the same name. But closer inspection of Papias's statement shows that he probably used the term *elder* in an apostolic sense, and so his statement becomes a primary witness for authorship by the Apostle John himself.

EYEWITNESS The writer of the Fourth Gospel claims to have been an eyewitness of Jesus' ministry (1:14; compare 19:35; 21:24–25) and as such exhibits a Semitic style of writing (seen especially in parallel statements) and an accurate knowledge of Jewish customs (for example, the customs of water-pouring and illumination by candelabra during the Festival of Tabernacles, presupposed in

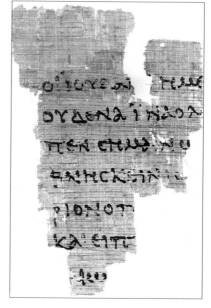

The Papyrus Rylands Greek 475, a fragment of John's Gospel that dates back to the first half of the second century

The Elder John

"But if anyone came who had followed the elders, I inquired into the words of the elders, what Andrew or Peter or Philip or Thomas or James or John or Matthew or any other of the Lord's disciples had said, and what Aristion and the Elder John, the Lord's disciples, were saying [literally, 'are saying,' with reference to the time present when Papias made his inquiry]" (Papias as quoted by Eusebius, *Church History* 3.39.4). Both times that the name John appears, it appears with both the designations "elder" and "Lord's disciple." By contrast, Aristion—even though designated a "Lord's disciple"— lacks the title "elder" when mentioned alongside John. This contrast points toward a single individual named John. Papias wanted to make plain the single identity of John by repeating the designation "elder," just used for the apostles but omitted with Aristion; and Papias mentioned John a second time because John was the only one of the Lord's disciples still living and speaking who was also an apostle. Admittedly, Eusebius interpreted Papias as referring to two different men named John and even claimed a tradition of two men named John and having different memorials in Ephesus. But one and the same person may have more than one memorial and sometimes does. Because Eusebius disliked the book of Revelation, he wanted to find a way around its apostolic authorship. So he conjured up an Elder John allegedly distinct from the Apostle John to enable an ascription of Revelation to someone lacking apostolic authority.

7:37–39; 8:12) and of Palestinian topography as it was before the destruction of Jerusalem and the temple in A.D. 70 (for example, the pool with five porches near the Sheep Gate [5:2] and the paved area outside the praetorium [19:13], both in Jerusalem). (Some scholars therefore date the Fourth Gospel three decades or so earlier than the closing years of the first century.) In addition, details such as one would expect from an eyewitness, yet incidental to the story, appear everywhere—numbers (six water jars [2:6], three or four miles [6:19], one hundred yards [21:8], 153 fish [21:11]), names (Nathanael [1:45–51], ↓Nicodemus [3:1–21; 7:50; 19:39], Lazarus [11:1–44; 12:9–11], ↓Malchus [18:10], and others), plus many similarly vivid touches. These traits substantiate both the early tradition of apostolic authorship and its corollary that the Gospel represents trustworthy historical tradition.

Ruins of the Pool of Bethzatha (Bethesda)

THE BELOVED DISCIPLE Moreover, the author writes as "the disciple whom Jesus loved," not out of egotism (he never identifies himself by name), but to emphasize that the contents of the Gospel merit belief since they come from the man in whom Jesus confided. Still further, the beloved disciple repeatedly appears in close association with Peter (13:23– 24; 20:2–10; 21:2, 7, 20–24). The synoptists tell us

Nicodemus: nik´uh-DEE-muhs ■ Malchus: MAL-kuhs

> **An Example of Parallelism in John 3:31**
>
> a. "The one who comes from above is above all;
>   b. the one who is from the earth belongs to the earth,
>   b'. and speaks as one from the earth.
> a'. The one who comes from heaven is above all."

that James and John, the sons of Zebedee, worked at fishing with Peter and with him formed an inner circle among the Twelve. Since James died as a martyr long before the time of writing (Acts 12:1–5) and since Peter appears as a different person from the beloved disciple, only John is left to be the beloved disciple and author of the Fourth Gospel. For if someone other than the beloved disciple wrote it, why did he not attach the name of John to "the disciple whom Jesus loved"? The anonymity of the beloved disciple can hardly be explained unless he himself wrote the Gospel, and the process of elimination identifies him with John the apostle.

John's Relation to the Synoptics

SUPPLEMENTATION OF THE SYNOPTICS John supplements the Synoptics and possibly reworks them at a number of points, though many think he did not know them. The Synoptics emphasize the Galilean ministry of Jesus, his parables, and the theme of God's kingdom. John emphasizes Jesus' Judean ministry, omits the parables and—for the most part—the kingdom, and substitutes long discourses and the theme of eternal life. John also supplements the Synoptics by making clear that Jesus' public ministry lasted considerably longer than a reading of the Synoptics alone would indicate. The Synoptics mention only the last Passover, when Jesus died. But John locates three Passovers, probably four, during Jesus' ministry, so that it lasted at least more than two years and probably from three to three and a half years.

JESUS' SPEECH IN JOHN With the partial exception of Matthew, the Fourth Gospel contains more extended discourses by Jesus than the Synoptics do. The discourses tend to curtail narrative. Questions and objections from the audiences often punctuate these discourses, and John regularly reports Jesus as speaking in a style different in many respects from what the Synoptists report. The differences may stem partly from John's way of translating into Greek the teaching that Jesus originally spoke in Aramaic, and

---

The Process of Elimination
That Points to the Apostle John as the Beloved Disciple and Author

Synoptics	Fourth Gospel
Peter	Peter (distinguished from the beloved disciple)
James	(deceased)
John	beloved disciple ("who wrote these things"—John 21:24)

perhaps occasionally in Hebrew, and partly from John's habit of elaborative paraphrasing, with the result that the vocabulary, style, and theological concerns of the evangelist often appear in his record of Jesus' teaching. The vocabulary and style of John himself are recognizable from those parts of the Fourth Gospel where Jesus is not speaking and from 1–3 John. In the Synoptics, translation is apparently more literal and elaborative paraphrasing less extensive. Often, loose translation and elaborative paraphrasing can communicate the intended meaning of a speaker and the larger implications of what he said even more effectively than direct quotation does, so that John's procedure is not at all illegitimate.

Synoptic Emphases	Johannine Emphases
Jesus in Galilee	Jesus in Judea
parables	long discourses
God's kingdom	eternal life

On the other hand, we must not overestimate the degree of Johannine elaboration or looseness in translation, for the two famous parallel passages in Matthew 11:25–27 and Luke 10:21–22 favor that Jesus could and did speak in the style represented by the Fourth Gospel. Prominent in those passages are the Father-Son relationship and emphasis on divine revelation, knowledge, and election—all typical of John's Gospel. It is also possible that he preserves the more formal aspects of Jesus' teaching, such as sermons in synagogues and disputes with Jewish theologians.

Johannine Theology

STYLE Throughout the Fourth Gospel, many important theological themes appear and reappear in different combinations and often crop up in 1–3 John and Revelation as well. John expounds these themes by skillfully alternating narratives and discourses, so that the **words** of Jesus bring out the inner meaning of his works (see the outline below). Thus, much of the action becomes **symbolic**. For example, Jesus' washing the disciples' feet represents cleansing from sin. There is also frequent **irony**, such as that which tinges his question, "I have shown you many good works from the Father. For which of these do you stone me?" (10:32). And just as the works of Jesus bear a symbolic meaning, so also his words often carry **multiple meanings**. "Born again [or anew]" also means "born from above" (3:3–7), and the reference to Jesus' being "lifted up" alludes not only to his crucifixion as such, but also to his crucifixion as an exaltation, a glorification (12:20–36, especially verse 32).

THEMES The theological themes in John begin under the category of **revelation**. Jesus is the revelatory **Word** (↓*logos*) of God. As such he reveals the **truth**, which is more than

Possible Elaborations in John and First John of a Synoptic Saying of Jesus

Matthew 18:3: "Truly I tell you, unless you are converted and become like little children, you will never enter the kingdom of heaven."

John 3:3: "Truly, truly I tell you, unless a person is born from above, he cannot see the kingdom of God."

John 3:5: "Truly, truly I tell you, unless a person is born of water and the Spirit, he cannot enter the kingdom of God.."

1 John 3:9: "No one born of God practices sin."

logos: LAW-gaws

A Reminder of the Johannine Thunderbolt in the Synoptics

"No one knows the Son except the Father; neither does anyone know the Father except the Son and the person to whom the Son wills to reveal him" (Matthew 11:25–27, excerpt; similarly Luke 10:21–22).

veracity. It is the reality of God's own person and character, to which Jesus bears **witness**, as do also the Father himself, the Spirit, Scripture, and others. The **light** of this revelation illumines those who believe and drives back the **darkness** of evil. The repulsion of darkness is the **judgment** of the world. Not that Jesus came to condemn the world, but he did come to discriminate between those who belong to the light and those who belong to the darkness. The darklings stand already self-condemned by their unbelief. The **world**, human society dominated by Satan, opposes the light and thereby becomes the object of God's wrath. This fact makes it all the more remarkable that God "loved the world" (3:16). His **love** came through Jesus Christ and continues to manifest itself through the love of Jesus' disciples for one another.

To demonstrate God's love, Jesus descended from the Father and worked toward his "**hour**," the time of his suffering and death on behalf of the world. For revealing the Father's **glory** in this way, the Father in turn glorified the Son with heavenly exaltation. By God's election and their own believing (John lets stand the antinomy between divine and human choices) some people experience **rebirth** by the Holy Spirit, so that they come to **know** God through Jesus Christ. But though election and believing characterize only some, **universality** characterizes the invitation. Those who do accept the invitation receive **eternal life** (qualitatively divine as well as quantitatively everlasting), an **abiding place** in Christ, and the ↓**Paraclete**, or Holy Spirit in his roles as Comforter, Counselor, and Prosecutor. To mention these themes is but to skim the surface of Johannine theology. Each theme has nuances that deserve a full elaboration.

Purposes of Writing

Preeminently, John writes to engender **believing**:

"Therefore Jesus performed in the presence of his disciples many other signs, too, that are not written in this book. But these have been written that you may *believe that the Christ, the Son of God, is Jesus,* and that by believing you may have life in his name" (John 20:30–31).

JESUS' ↓DEITY AND HUMANITY Christological in content, this believing highlights the deity of Jesus as the unique and preexistent Son of God who in obedience to his Father became a real human being to die sacrificially for the salvation of other human beings. Such an emphasis went against the

---

Paraclete: PAIR-uh-kleet ■ deity: DEE-uh-tee (= divine nature, state of being God)

denial of his humanity and death by Gnostics, early Christian heretics who thought anything material or physical to be inherently evil (see page 50). Thus, not only does the deity of Jesus receive emphasis (beginning with "the Word was God" [1:1] and many times throughout the Gospel); so also his humanity: "the Word became flesh" (1:14), grew tired and thirsty (4:6–7; 19:28), wept (11:35), and physically died and rose again (19:30–42; 20:12, 17, 20, 27–28).

"I AM . . ." Jesus himself demands this christological belief by making a series of "I am . . ." claims in the Fourth Gospel:

- "I am the bread of life" (6:35, 48; compare 6:41, 51).
- "I am the light of the world" (8:12).
- "I am the door" (10:7, 9).
- "I am the good shepherd" (10:11, 14).
- "I am the resurrection and the life" (11:25).
- "I am the way and the truth and the life" (14:6).
- "I am the true vine" (15:1, 5).

In addition, there are "I am" claims not followed by a complement. These suggest the claim to be the "I AM-YAHWEH" of the Old Testament (4:25–26; 8:24, 28, 58; 13:19; compare 6:20; 7:34, 36; 14:3; 17:24; Exodus 3:14).

REALIZED ESCHATOLOGY When people believe, they receive eternal life immediately—hence C. H. Dodd's phrase "realized eschatology," though "inaugurated eschatology" would be better, since 5:25–29 refers to resurrection and judgment yet to come, and 21:22 to Jesus' return. Full enjoyment awaits in the future, but every believer savors a foretaste in the present. (Perhaps some Christians were perturbed and some non-Christians incredulous over the delay in Jesus' return; thus the Johannine emphasis on salvation now.) With this emphasis John seeks to evangelize unbelievers with the gospel or to establish Christians in their faith. (It is disputed whether he wrote for unbelievers, believers, or both.)

ANTI-BAPTIST POLEMIC? The correction of a cult that had grown up around the figure of John the Baptist provides a possible subsidiary purpose behind the writing of the Fourth Gospel (compare the present-day ↓Mandeans in Iraq, who look back to the Baptist as their object of veneration). Acts 19:1–7 reveals the presence of Baptists in Ephesus some decades earlier, during

---

Examples of Universal Appeal in John's Gospel

- "Look, the Lamb of God, who takes away the sin of the world!" (1:29).
- "[Many Samaritans said,] 'We know that this is truly the Savior of the world'" (4:42).
- "[Jesus said,] 'I have other sheep that are not of this fold. I must bring them too'" (10:16).

Exodus 3:14	John 8:58
"God said to Moses,	"[Jesus said,] 'Before Abraham came into existence,
'I AM WHO I AM.'"	I am.'"

Mandeans: man-DEE-uhnz

the time of Paul; and according to early tradition, John the apostle wrote his Gospel in Ephesus. Moreover, John takes great pains to show that

- Jesus surpassed the Baptist.
- The Baptist had to decrease and Jesus increase.
- Through his disciples Jesus baptized more followers than the Baptist did.
- The Baptist testified on Jesus' behalf.
- Jesus had testimony even greater than what the Baptist gave him (1:15–37; 3:25–30; 4:1–2; 5:33–40).

The matter hangs in doubt, however, because these phenomena may reflect instead the Apostle John's own experience of conversion from the Baptist to Jesus.

ANTI-JEWISH POLEMIC? Some have thought that John wrote his Gospel as a polemic against Jews, who toward the end of the first century had incorporated into the liturgy of their synagogue services a Benediction against Heretics to root out all Jewish Christians who might still be participating in those services. This benediction could have occasioned the Fourth Gospel as an encouragement to Jewish Christians to endure ostracism from the synagogue without hiding their Christian identity or recanting their Christian profession (compare 9:22 and 16:2, which mention the expulsion of Jesus' disciples from synagogues). But although "the Jews" appear in a bad light throughout John, "the world" appears in an equally bad light—and for the same reason: unbelief (see, e.g., 15:18–19). Furthermore, there is no suppression of Jesus' Jewishness; and the Dead Sea Scrolls have shown that the religious vocabulary of John's Gospel is characteristic of first-century Judaism.

> **Benediction against Heretics**
> "For the excommunicated let there be no hope, and quickly root out the kingdom of pride in our days, and let the Christians and the heretics perish as in a moment. Let them be blotted out of the book of life, and with the righteous let them not be written."

Some Common Religious Vocabulary in the Dead Sea Scrolls and John

- "light"
- "light of life"
- "light" versus "darkness"
- "loving children of light/one another"
- "knowledge"/"knowing"
- "truth"

Materials

Theories of literary sources behind the Fourth Gospel stumble against the unity of style that pervades the entire book. Theories of disarrangement solve some problems of interpretation only to create others; and with one minor exception they lack manuscript evidence.

John 1:11–12 summarizes three lines of material included in the Fourth Gospel: (1) **"His own did not receive him"**—the dark backdrop of the Gospel consists in repeated rejections of Jesus by the Jews; (2) **"But as many as received him"**—as bright exceptions a number of individuals did receive Jesus through personal encounter with him; (3) "**To them he gave authority to become children of God**"—John details a number of miracles performed by Jesus but calls them "**signs**" and "**works**" because of their value in symbolizing the

Synoptics	John
Jesus' "miracles" as acts of supernatural power that astound people	Jesus' "signs" as symbols of salvation, and Jesus' "works" as the accomplishing of salvation

transformation that took place in those who received Jesus. All three lines converge in the story of his death and resurrection: "Those who were his own did not receive him"—crucifixion at the hands of the Jews; "but as many as received him"—the three Marys and the beloved disciple standing beside the cross; "to them he gave authority to become children of God"— transformation through the power of Jesus' resurrection.

An Outline of John

Prologue: Jesus Christ the Revelatory Word [Logos] of God (1:1–18)
I. The Faith-Producing Impact of Jesus' Initial Ministry (1:19–4:42)
    A. Narrative (1:19–2:25)
        1. The testimony of John the Baptist and the making of the first disciples (1:19–51)
        2. The turning of water to wine at a wedding in Cana (2:1–12)
        3. The cleansing of the temple and the performing of signs in Jerusalem (2:13–25)
    B. Discourse (3:1–4:42)
        1. The new birth in conversation with Nicodemus (3:1–21)
        2. The superiority of Jesus according to John the Baptist's testimony during their concurrent ministries of baptism (3:22–36)
        3. The water of life in conversation with the Samaritan woman, plus her conversion and that of her fellow townspeople (4:1–42)
II. The Authority of Jesus' Life-Giving Words (4:43–5:47)
    A. Narrative (4:43–5:9a)
        1. The healing of an official's son (4:43–54)
        2. The healing on a Sabbath of the invalid by a pool in Jerusalem (5:1–9a)
    B. Discourse: the authority of Jesus' words (5:9b–47)
III. The Giving of Jesus' Flesh and Blood for the Life of the World (6:1–71)
    A. Narrative: the feeding of the five thousand and the walking on water (6:1–21)
    B. Discourse: the bread of life (6:22–71)
IV. The Illumination of People by Jesus with Their Resultant Division into Unbelievers, Destined for Judgment, and Believers, Destined for Eternal Life (7:1–8:59)
    A. Narrative: the attendance of Jesus at the Festival of Tabernacles and a division of opinion about him (7:1–52)

B. Discourse: the light of the world and the true children of Abraham (8:12–59)

V. Jesus' Kindness in Contrast with Mistreatment by the Jewish Religious Authorities (9:1–10:39)

   A. Narrative: a blind man's healing and excommunication from the synagogue (9:1–41)

   B. Discourse: the Good Shepherd, hirelings, thieves, and robbers (10:1–39)

VI. The Gift of Life Through Jesus' Death (10:40–12:50)

   A. Narrative (10:40–12:19)

     1. The raising of Lazarus with the Sanhedrin's consequent plot to kill Jesus (10:40–11:57)

     2. The anointing of Jesus by Mary of Bethany and the Sanhedrin's plot to kill Lazarus (12:1–11)

     3. The triumphal entry (12:12–19)

   B. Discourse: the grain of wheat that dies and springs to fruitful life (12:20–50)

VII. The Departure and Return of Jesus (13:1–20:29)

   A. Discourse (13:1–17:26)

     1. The cleansing of the disciples and their menial service to one another as signified by Jesus' washing their feet (13:1–20)

     2. The announcement of betrayal and the dismissal of Judas Iscariot (13:21–30)

     3. The advantages to the disciples of Jesus' departure and of the Holy Spirit's coming (13:31–16:33)

     4. The prayer of Jesus for his disciples (17:1–26)

   B. Narrative (18:1–20:29)

     1. The arrest of Jesus (18:1–11)

     2. The hearings before Annas and Caiaphas with Peter's denials (18:12–27)

     3. The hearing before Pilate (18:28–19:16)

     4. The crucifixion and burial (19:17–42)

     5. The empty tomb and resurrection appearances to Mary Magdalene and the disciples (20:1–29)

Conclusion: The Purpose of the Fourth Gospel to Evoke Life-Bringing Faith in Jesus as the Christ, the Son of God (20:30–31)

Epilogue (21:1–25)

   A. Narrative: another resurrection appearance to the disciples, with a miraculous catch of fish and breakfast on the shore of the Sea of Tiberias [Galilee] (21:1–14)

   B. Discourse: the recommission of Peter (21:15–23)

Final Authentication (21:24–25)

Reading John with Interpretation

Prologue

THE WORD (GREEK: LOGOS) ↓INCARNATE The Fourth Gospel opens with a prologue. *Read John 1:1–18.* Some scholars think that in this prologue the evangelist works over an earlier existing hymn, others that he composes on his own against the background of the Old Testament stories of creation and the giving of the law on Mount Sinai. "In the beginning" recalls Genesis 1:1. "Was the Word" recalls God's speaking created order out of chaos (for example: "and God *said*, 'Let there be light,' and there was light"), only this speaking has turned into a personal being who preexisted with God, shared God's own identity, acted as God's agent in the creation, and in Jesus Christ became incarnate ("enfleshed")—that is, became a human being complete with a physical body so as to communicate to the human race the glory of God, not in a show of lightning and thunder as at Mount Sinai, but in a revelation of God's grace and truth, which have replaced the Mosaic law given at Sinai. Inasmuch as the verb for the Word's dwelling among us means to live in a ↓tabernacle, a tent (1:14), this glory of God's grace and truth likewise replaces the divine glory that settled on the tabernacle, or tent-sanctuary, when Moses had completed its construction according to the

---

incarnate: in-KAHR-nit ■ tabernacle: TAB-uhr-nak´uhl

Sunrise from Mount Sinai

blueprint given him on Mount Sinai. As God's visible speech, the Word contrasts with the Hellenistic divine title "Silence" and equates with the light of the knowledge of God, which in turn contrasts with the darkness of ignorance concerning God. This knowledge brings life to those who receive the Word, that is, believe in his name, believe him to be the one who his name says he is, the divine Word. Unlike the world (the society of unbelievers), believers have gained this life not by way of human procreation ("born neither of bloods nor of the will of the flesh nor of the will of a male") but by way of divine (re)generation ("born of God"; compare 3:3–8) and thus become God's children regardless of ancestry. By and large, not even the Word's own people, with whom he shared Jewish ancestry, received him so as to become the children of God. But they did not fail to receive him through any lack of testimony, for John the Baptist bore witness to him even to the extent of declaring him prior in rank because of his priority in time, his **preexistence**.

> "Immediately put your right [fore-]finger on your mouth and say, 'Silence! Silence!' (a symbol of the living, incorruptible god). 'Guard me, Silence!'"
> (Paris Papyrus 574).

Wisdom-Christology in John?

In Sirach 24:9 personified wisdom claims preexistence: "Before the ages, in the beginning, he [God] created me." The parallel with the preexistence of the Word in John 1:1 and a number of similar parallels have made many scholars think that John portrays Jesus as wisdom incarnate and—perhaps because Jesus was a male—substitutes "Word," which is masculine in Greek, for "wisdom," which is feminine in Greek. On the other hand, John uses a number of other Greek feminines for Jesus ("way," "truth," and "life," for instance) but never uses "wisdom" for him despite a heavy use of synonyms, which in this case would have paired "wisdom" with "Word." Note too the contrast between the Word as creator and wisdom as a creature. Is John pitting the Word *against* wisdom, then?

Though "in the beginning" relates the Word immediately to Genesis 1:1, other uses may also have influenced the evangelist's application of the term to Jesus Christ: (1) the use of "the word of the LORD" in the Old Testament; (2) the use of "the Word of the LORD" or "the Word of God" as a surrogate for God in the Old Testament Targums; (3) the description in the Old Testament and intertestamental Jewish literature of personified wisdom in terms very like the fourth evangelist's description of the Word; (4) the New Testament use of "the word" for the gospel; and (5) the use of *logos* by philosophers such as the Stoics and the first-century Alexandrian Jew, Philo, for the rational principle (Reason), which they thought governs the universe. Against influence from this philosophical use, however, the fourth evangelist writes of divine communication, not of divine thought; and differently from all possible influences, he identifies the *logos* with a human being of recent history.

The uniqueness of this *logos* or Word comes out in the adjective "only," traditionally translated "only begotten" (KJV). There is a text critical question whether 1:18 should read "(the) only God," looking back to the equation of the Word with God in 1:1 and requiring in the next phrase of 1:18 a switch from "God" to "the Father." Or should it read "the only Son," looking forward to "the Father" in the following phrase and to the emphasis on

Jesus' divine sonship throughout the remainder of the Gospel? The earliest and best manuscripts read "God" instead of "Son." The fourth evangelist's identification of the creative Word with the only God seems to strike against the Gnostic teaching of ↓Cerinthus that the Creator differs from the supreme God. Similarly, the incarnation of God the Word in the one human being Jesus Christ seems to strike against the Gnostic teaching of Cerinthus that distinguishes between a divine spirit, Christ, and a fleshly human being, Jesus, and makes Christ leave Jesus before the passion even though Christ descended on Jesus at Jesus' baptism.

> "The General Law, which is Right Reason [*logos*], pervading everything, is the same as Zeus, the Supreme Head of the government of the universe" (Zeno, *Fragment* 162).

The Baptist's Witness

LAMB OF GOD The fourth evangelist now spells out the witness of John the Baptist to Jesus. Clearing the ground for this witness is John's denial to "the Jews" (not the whole people, but their leaders living in Jerusalem, Judea) that he himself is the Christ, or Elijah come back to earth, or the prophet whom many Jews expected to appear in the end time. Also clearing the ground is John's self-identification with a mere voice. The witness itself identifies Jesus as the one whom John's Jewish questioners do not know (compare 1:10–11), the one whose sandal thong John is unworthy to loosen, the sacrificial lamb who not only is provided by God but who as God (1:1c) takes away the world's sin, the one who outranks John inasmuch as he existed before John, the one on whom John saw the Holy Spirit descend

Cerinthus: suh-RIN-thuhs

Jordan River

"Cerinthus . . . represented Jesus as having not been born of a virgin . . . . Moreover, Christ descended on him after his baptism . . . . But at last Christ departed from Jesus . . . . Jesus suffered and rose again, while Christ remained incapable of suffering since he was a spiritual being" (Cerinthus according to Irenaeus, *Against Heresies* 1.26.1; see also 3.11.1, 3).

and stay that he might baptize people in the Holy Spirit rather than in mere water, and the one who is God's Son. Thus John's preaching of repentance turns into a testimony to Jesus, and John's baptism into an occasion for the manifestation of Jesus to Israel. *Read John 1:19–34.*

FIRST DISCIPLES A repetition of John's witness leads two of his disciples, **Andrew** and an unnamed one (probably John the apostle and fourth evangelist), to follow Jesus and abide with him. Thus spatial abiding seems to symbolize the spiritual abiding in Christ spoken of later (15:1–7). The two disciples have addressed Jesus as a rabbi, or teacher; but in speaking to his brother **Simon**, Andrew identifies Jesus as the Messiah, or Christ. On seeing Simon, Jesus displays omniscience of Simon's present name, the name of Simon's father, and Simon's future name **Cephas** (Aramaic for the Greek name **Peter**, both meaning "stone" or, more traditionally but less accurately, "rock"). *Read John 1:35–42.* Counted from sunrise, "the tenth hour" would be 4:00 P.M.; but then so little of the day remains that the statement, "They abode with him that day," turns vapid. Better then to count from midnight for an abiding with Jesus from 10:00 A.M. onward.

Read John 1:43–51. Jesus takes the initiative in calling **Philip**. The description of Philip as "from Bethsaida" sets the stage for a description of Jesus as "from Nazareth," which in turn sets the stage for **Nathanael's** question whether anything good can come from Nazareth (see the map on page 126 for the locations of Bethsaida and Nazareth). This question and the additional description of Jesus as "son of Joseph" are ironic, for John the evangelist has located Jesus' origin "in the bosom of the Father" (1:18) and John the Baptist has described Jesus as "the Son of God" (1:34). But Philip's description of Jesus as the one about whom Moses and the prophets wrote rings true. Again Jesus displays omniscience, this time of Nathanael's character and activity. And this time "**Rabbi**" escalates to "**the Son of God**," which corrects "the son of Joseph," and to "**the King of Israel**," which suits Nathanael's being "truly an Israelite." Correcting Philip's description of Jesus as "from Nazareth" is Jesus' describing himself, "the Son of Man," as a ladder, like Jacob's (Genesis 28:12), connecting heaven with earth. Since "angels" means "messengers," the angels that ascend and descend on the Son of Man portray him as carrying a heavenly message. Deity is many-named and many-titled, and Jesus is deity—therefore the piling up of names and titles for him throughout this chapter.

Jesus' First Sign

Read John 2:1–12. Identification of the day on which Jesus performed his first sign as "the third day" may anticipate the climactic sign of his resurrection on the third day (compare 2:19). A wedding suggests the festivity of salvation (compare Revelation 19:6–9; Matthew 22:1–14; 25:1–13). Jesus' changing **water to wine at ↓Cana** symbolizes the replacement of Judaism with the gospel; for John describes the water in terms of Jewish rites of purification, and the keeping of the good wine until last can hardly fail to recall John's earlier statement that "the law was given through Moses, but grace and truth came through Jesus Christ" (1:17; see the map on page 126 for the location of Cana). Jesus' declaration of independence from his mother implies that he will act only in accord with the timetable of God his Father. This timetable will lead up to the **hour** of Jesus, that is, the climactic week of his death and resurrection (7:30; 8:20; 12:23, 27; 13:1; 17:1). The imperviousness of stone keeps the water inside from ritual defilement. The huge capacity of the stone pots, twenty or thirty gallons each, magnifies the coming sign. So also does the filling of the pots up to their brims. The steward's remark rests on an effect of drunkenness, namely, the inability to distinguish between good wine and inferior wine. "**This beginning of signs**" implies more signs to come, and the use of "signs" rather than "miracles" (which means "acts of power") shows that John is directing his audience's attention to the symbolic significance of Jesus' actions, not to their physical effect.

> ### A Question about Wine
>
> In his account of the Last Supper, John will not mention the wine that Jesus said represents his blood. Does the wine that Jesus produced from water at Cana anticipate and replace in John's Gospel the wine of the Lord's Supper?

Cleansing the Temple

John mentions Jesus' cleansing of the temple early, the synoptists not until Passion Week. Some think Jesus cleansed the temple twice to open and close his public ministry, others that the synoptists delay the cleansing through omission of all his visits to Jerusalem except the last one, and yet others that in line with a habit of anticipating the future John advances the cleansing to link it closely with the Baptist's identification of Jesus as the Lamb of God (1:29, 36) and to make room for Jesus' raising of Lazarus instead of the temple cleansing as the event that triggers a plot by the Sanhedrin to kill Jesus (compare John 11:1–57; 12:9–19; with Mark 11:15–19). As is fitting for the one whom John has identified as God, Jesus takes initiative. His finding sellers in the temple, his making a whip, his driving out the cattle and sheep, his pouring out the coins of the money changers, his telling the sellers of doves to take them away and stop making his Father's house a marketplace—none of these actions is mentioned in the Synoptics, and they all highlight the divine initiative of Jesus, which also gets emphasis from an Old Testament reference to zeal for God's house (Psalm 69:9). The driving out of animals being sold for sacrifice and the sending out of sacrificial doves symbolize the outmodedness of these sacrifices now that the Lamb of God has appeared on the scene. In a cryptic reference to his

Cana: KAY-nuh

own body, Jesus' ironic calling on the Jews to destroy "this temple" alludes to his sacrificial death at their hands (see 19:16–18); and his prediction that he will raise the temple in three days alludes to his raising that body from the dead by his own divine power. Since by definition a temple is the dwelling place of deity, Jesus' being God (1:1–18) makes his body a new temple replacing the old one in Jerusalem. *Read John 2:13–22.* The forty-six years of building the old temple refers to a renovation initiated by Herod the Great.

Nicodemus and Rebirth from Above

Read John 2:23–3:21. The story of Jesus and Nicodemus, a member of the Sanhedrin, illustrates Jesus' omniscience of the interior state of human beings. Nicodemus is an example of those who believe in the name of Jesus solely because of the signs he performs (compare 2:23 with 3:1–2) but whom Jesus knows to be still in need of a renewal so radical as to constitute a new birth, one that originates in heaven above (compare 2:24–25 with 3:3–8) and happens through belief in Jesus as God's unique Son who descended from heaven and ascended back to heaven by way of being lifted up on the cross (3:11–21). Coming at night to Jesus, who is the true light, symbolizes exit from the darkness of ignorance, evil, and death and entrance into the light of knowledge, truth, and life. Water and wind are figures of speech for the Holy Spirit, the agent of rebirth from above (compare 7:37–39; Ezekiel 36:25–27; Titus 3:5). One Greek adverb means both "**again, anew**" and "**from above.**" Likewise, one Greek noun means both "**wind**" and "**Spirit.**" The blowing of the wind "wherever it wishes" stands for the sovereignty of the Holy Spirit in causing rebirth to occur (compare 6:44). The inadequacy of fleshly birth means the inadequacy of Jewish ancestry.

> "[Jesus said,] 'I lay down my life in order that I may take it up again. No one takes it from me; rather, I lay it down of my own accord. I have authority to lay it down, and I have authority to take it up again'" (John 10:17–18).

Hearing the sound of the wind without knowing its origin and destination represents hearing the voice of the Spirit without understanding the mystery of the Spirit's movement (compare 10:16, 27; Revelation 2:7, 11, 17, 29). "Earthly things" means the metaphors of water and wind, "heavenly things" the realities of new birth from above by the Spirit's movement. For Moses' lifting up a bronze snake for the salvation of Israel, see Numbers 21:8–9. Jesus' being lifted up is for everyone in the world. God's lifting him up by way of the cross defines the way God loved the world. Just as believers enjoy eternal life in

> "I will sprinkle clean water on you.... I will put my Spirit in you" (Ezekiel 36:25, 27).

advance of the age to come, so unbelievers stand under the sentence of condemnation in advance of the Last Judgment. But judgment not only means condemnation; it also means discrimination, here between evildoers and

"So Moses made a bronze snake and put it up on a pole. And when it happened that a snake bit someone, when he looked at the bronze snake, he lived" (Numbers 21:9).

those who practice the truth, that is, the truth of God in Jesus Christ.

BAPTISM The way back to Galilee leads first through the countryside of Judea along the Jordan River, where Jesus spends some time with his disciples. A reference to their baptizing people prepares for 4:1–2 but more immediately calls attention to Jesus' achievement of a success greater than John the Baptist's and gives occasion for a renewal of the Baptist's testimony to Jesus' superiority. Does all this emphasis on the Baptist's testimony to Jesus' superiority take aim at diehard followers of the Baptist in Ephesus, where John the apostle is reputed to be writing the Fourth Gospel (compare Acts 18:24–19:7)? *Read John 3:22–4:42.*

The Woman of Samaria

God's love for the world, not only for the Jews, shows itself in the necessity that Jesus go through Samaria for the salvation of people there, hated though they are by the Jews. Out of this necessity he takes the initiative in striking up a conversation with the Samaritan woman at Jacob's well. Counting from sunrise, the sixth hour would be noon. But the disciples' having gone into ↓Sychar to buy food combines with the Jewish practice of eating two meals a day, one in the

> ### Double Meanings
> Born
> - again (temporal meaning)
> - from above (spatial meaning)
>
> ↓*pneuma* (Greek)
> - wind (surface meaning)
> - Spirit (deep meaning)

pneuma: NYOO-mah ■ Sychar: SI-kahr

Mount Gerizim and Mount Ebal, near Jacob's well

morning and another in late afternoon or evening, to favor the sixth hour from noon (compare the comments on 1:39; see the map on page 126 for the location of Sychar). Superficially, "**living water**" means flowing water, always fresh. But such water symbolizes the life-giving Spirit (compare 7:37–39). Like the water of purification in stone pots (2:6), the water in Jacob's well stands for Judaism, now to be replaced with water that brings eternal life. ("Will never thirst" refers, not to psychological—much less physical—satisfaction, but to everlasting salvation.) Do the woman's five husbands stand for the five books of Moses, the Pentateuch shared by Samaritans and Jews as the basis for their beliefs and practices, and the woman's present paramour for Samaritan apostasy from Judaism? "This mountain" is nearby ↓Gerizim, where the Samaritan temple lies in ruins.

We should not think of the human spirit and sincerity as the spirit and truth in which true worship of God the Father takes place; rather, of the Holy Spirit (3:5–8 and again 7:37–39) and Jesus the Truth (1:14, 17; 14:6). They provide the new locale of worship. The harvest of which Jesus speaks to his returned disciples is eternal life for the Samaritans who come out to hear him and believe in him. He sows; he starts the process. The disciples will reap, will finish it in their work of evangelism.

Healing an Official's Son

When Jesus does not find trustworthy faith in Judea—called his "own country" because he should have found such faith there at the center of Judaism (see 2:23–25)—he proceeds onward to Galilee, where the Galileans receive him (compare 1:11–13). *Read John 4:43–54.* The emphasis on a nearness to death so great that the *healing* translates into *living* makes this second sign of Jesus symbolize salvation from eternal death to eternal life through believing his word. If counted from noon, "the seventh hour" (7:00 P.M.) allows for a day's walking journey of twenty miles (from Capernaum to Cana) by the royal official (see the map on page 126 for the location of Capernaum in relation to Cana).

> **The Locale of Worship**
>
> With the arrival of Jesus the incarnate Word, the worship of God shifted its locale from a physical building in Jerusalem (the temple) to the physical body of Jesus, from whose pierced side flowed the water of the Spirit as a gift to believers (see John 7:37–39 with 19:34).

Healing a Lame Man on the Sabbath

As earlier, Jesus now goes to Jerusalem for a religious festival, this one unnamed, and there heals a sick man unable to walk. *Read John 5:1–47.* Like earlier mentions of Jewish water of purification, the water of Jacob's well, and the Samaritan woman's five husbands, the mention of five porches enclosing the water at the Pool of ↓Bethzatha (or ↓Bethesda or Bethsaida) combines with the issue of the Sabbath to suggest a symbolic allusion to the five books of Moses, the Law, which is unable to give salvation, whereas Jesus is able to do so—and does (again compare

---

Gerizim: GER-uh-zim ■ Bethzatha: beth-ZAY-thuh ■ Bethesda: buh-THEZ-duh

> "Now the time it took for us to come from Kadesh Barnea till we crossed the brook Zered was thirty-eight years" (Deuteronomy 2:14).

1:17). (Modern archaeologists appear to have discovered the five porches, so that John would not be dealing in symbolism alone.) It may even be that the thirty-eight years of sickness symbolically allude to Israel's thirty-eight years of wandering in the wilderness (Deuteronomy 2:14). In any case, Jesus' giving the man strength in place of weakness (the Greek word for "sickness" in 5:5 means "weakness") symbolizes the life-giving power of Jesus. The man's rising, picking up his mat, and walking when he hears Jesus' word symbolize the passing from death to eternal life both presently, at conversion, and in the future, at the resurrection, about which Jesus goes on to speak. Rabbinic law allows a physician to treat sickness on the Sabbath only if the patient's life is in danger. So Jesus' healing of this sickness, hardly a life-threatening emergency, as well as the carrying of a mat by the healed man breaches rabbinic law and brings persecution. Jesus equates his own work of healing on the Sabbath with the work of God his Father up to and including the present moment, Sabbath though it is. In such an equation, the calling of God his Father amounts to a claim of equality with God. But sonship to God also implies watching and doing what the Father does, just as an ordinary son, learning a trade, watches and does what his father does. The **witness of Jesus** on his own behalf is inadmissible, because Jewish courts treated people's testimony on their own behalf as possibly corrupted by self-interest. So Jesus appeals to the testimonies of John the Baptist, of the works that the Father has given Jesus to do, such as the preceding work of healing on the Sabbath, and of

> "But no one is to be believed when he testifies about himself" (Mishnah, *Ketubbot* 2:9).

the Father himself in the form of his Word, Jesus the Logos, abiding in believers. Jesus is often thought to mean that Moses wrote about him in Deuteronomy 18:15, 18. But the allusion may refer at least as much to the Mosaic story of God's giving manna to feed the Israelites on their way from Egypt to Canaan, for in the next chapter (John 6) Jesus will compare himself as the bread of life to that manna.

Feeding of the Five Thousand

Read John 6:1–71. John's linking the feeding of the five thousand to the Passover combines with Jesus'

Model of the Pool of Bethzatha (Bethesda)

> "Jesus answered [those who had come to arrest him], 'If then you are looking for me, let these men [my disciples] go.' This happened in order that the word he had spoken would be fulfilled: 'I did not lose even one of those you have given me'" (John 18:8–9).

comments about eating his flesh and drinking his blood to make the bread with which he feeds the crowd symbolic of his sacrificial death as the true Passover lamb (see 1:29, 36 with 19:34–36; Exodus 12:43–46; Numbers 9:12). The locale on a mountain reinforces the symbolism by recalling Moses on Mount Sinai. As God incarnate, Jesus takes the initiative and exhibits his omniscience. The specification of barley bread recalls attention to the Passover symbolism, for Passover coincides with the barley harvest. No groupings of the five thousand are mentioned (contrast the synoptic accounts), and the grass is described as "much"; so John appears to portray the crowd as the "one flock" of Jesus the Good Shepherd who leads out his sheep to feed in verdant pastures (10:1–16). He gives the bread and the fish just as he gives his flesh as the bread of life. "**That nothing be lost**" makes the gathering of leftovers symbolize Jesus' losing none of those people whom the Father has given him. The identification of Jesus with "the prophet who is coming into the world" probably alludes to the prophet like Moses in Deuteronomy 18:15 (though that text originally referred with a collective singular to a whole line of Moses-like prophets whom God would raise up). Jesus will not be made king by those who recognize no sign but only like the feeling of a full belly. Believing in him is the work that God requires in the sense that saving faith is active and persevering. Yet equal stress falls on the necessity of God's drawing people to Jesus.

BREAD OF LIFE As the bread of life Jesus is both living and life-giving. The heavenly origin of manna represents the heavenly origin of Jesus, the Word who in the beginning was with God and was God (1:1). Jesus' comments on eating his flesh and drinking his blood come so close to the words of institution at the Last Supper that John will omit those words in his account of that supper. The thought of cannibalism repulses the Jews, and Leviticus 17:10–14 prohibits the drinking of blood. But Jesus uses eating and drinking as metaphors of believing, that is, believing in the benefit of his sacrificial death; for the separation of flesh and blood denotes the violence of such a death. The flesh that contrasts with the Spirit and profits nothing is not Jesus' sacrificial flesh, but the useless flesh of ordinary human beings, as in 3:6. The turning away by many of Jesus' disciples previews the apostasy of professing Christians like the Gnostics at the time of John's writing.

> "The people of Israel called the bread manna. It was white like coriander seed, and its taste was like wafers with honey" (Exodus 16:31).

Festival of Tabernacles

The Jewish authorities in Judea are still seeking to kill Jesus (compare 5:18); so for the time being he stays in Galilee. Not even the sarcastic urging of his unbelieving brothers induces him to go along with other pilgrims to the Festival of Tabernacles, though its being the most popular of the Jew-

"None of you may eat blood" (Leviticus 17:12).

ish religious festivals would give him the best of opportunities to display his supernatural powers. *Read John 7:1–9.* Jesus follows a different timetable from that of his brothers, whom the world cannot hate because they belong to the world, whereas the hatred of the world for Jesus because he exposes its evil deeds means that he must regulate his travels in a way that avoids a premature death.

Read John 7:10–52. The delay and the secrecy of Jesus' journey to the Festival of Tabernacles and his remaining incognito until the middle of the festival keep him from exposure to arrest. By the time he does make a public appearance, he has become so lively a topic of discussion that the marvelousness and boldness of his teaching dumbfound some of the multitude and even immobilize the officers sent by the chief priests and Pharisees to arrest him. Having learned from God his Father more than compensates for his lack of a rabbinic education. By contrast, the teachings of a rabbi come from himself, a transgressor of the Mosaic law. When Jesus asks the Jewish authorities why they are seeking to kill him, the multitude from Galilee scoff. They do not know of the authorities' seeking to kill him (though for fear of the authorities they do not speak openly about him). Since the desire to kill him goes back to his healing a sick man at the Pool of Bethzatha on a Sabbath (5:1–18), he defends that healing by noting that the Mosaic law makes circumcision, the mutilation of one part of the body, more important than the Sabbath: circumcision must be performed on the eighth day after birth even though that day is a Sabbath (Leviticus 12:3). How much more should the **healing** of a man's **whole** body override the Sabbath law, Jesus argues. Unlike the multitude from Galilee, some of the Jerusalemites know about the authorities' seeking to kill him, ask whether they do not kill him because they know him to be the Christ, and themselves deny his messiahship because they know he comes from Galilee, whereas they believe the origin of the Christ should be unknown. Jesus retorts with a claim to have come from God as well as from Galilee. Divinely invincible against arrest until "his hour" comes, he now says that he will go away. The Jewish authorities think of a teaching mission to Gentiles ("Greeks") living alongside Jews outside Palestine ("the Dispersion"), but he means a return to his Father in heaven.

Pool of Siloam

"Messiah, even if he has been born and actually exists somewhere, is an unknown" (Jewish teachers according to Justin Martyr, *Dialogue with Trypho* 110.1).

During the first seven days of the Festival of Tabernacles, priests bring water in a gold vessel from the Pool of Siloam to the temple and ceremoniously pour it out. On the climactic eighth (or seventh) day of the festival, Jesus shouts that he is the source of the **true water**, the **life-giving Spirit**. But some of the multitude, thinking of him as only a Galilean, object that he cannot be the Christ because he comes from Galilee rather than from Bethlehem (see Micah 5:2). Thus in this one passage are reflected the apparently contradictory views that the origin of the Christ will be unknown and that he will be known to have been born in Bethlehem.

LIGHT OF THE WORLD The dialogue continues. *Read John 8:12–59*. Throughout the week-long Festival of Tabernacles the Jews keep four huge candelabra burning in the temple area to commemorate the pillar of fire that led and guarded Israel in the wilderness. That custom forms the background for Jesus' claim to be the light of the world, which in the first instance means the sun but ultimately means Jesus as the light of eternal life for all who believe in him. (Because in those days people kept a fire burning to avoid the laborious task of rekindling it, light came to be associated with life, darkness with death; for the dying of a person meant the dying out of the fire that he or she had kept going.) But light brings judgment on darkness. So Jesus plays on several possible meanings of **judgment**: (1) formation of an opinion, here in a superficial way; (2) discrimination; and (3) condem-

The Story of an Adulterer

The story of the woman taken in adultery (John 7:53–8:11) does not belong here or anywhere else in the Bible. The earliest and best manuscripts, undiscovered when the King James Version was published in 1611, omit it entirely. Later, inferior manuscripts have it inserted at various locations, some here, others after John 7:36, 21:24, or Luke 21:38. The very principles of textual criticism that assure the reliability of the rest of the New Testament text rule out this passage. Conversely, to insist on the originality of this passage in the text of the New Testament is to undermine the basis of our assurance that we have a substantially accurate text elsewhere in the New Testament. The story itself may be historically true, however, having been preserved in Christian tradition before interpolation into the canonical text.

In the story, Jesus' accusers try to put him on the horns of a dilemma. If he recommends the death penalty in accordance with the Mosaic law, they can accuse him of going against Roman authority, which forbids Jews to impose the death penalty. If he does not recommend the death penalty, they can destroy his reputation by telling people that he does not hold to the Mosaic law. It is customary for the eldest accuser to throw the first stone. The center of attention, therefore, shifts to the eldest when Jesus challenges them, "Let him who is sinless among you throw a stone at her." Each accuser leaves as he becomes the eldest in the group through the exit of someone older. Various suggestions concerning what Jesus writes on the ground are inconclusive. The final "sin no more" keeps Jesus from teaching an easygoing attitude toward sexual immorality.

"But as for you, Bethle-
hem Ephrathah, . . . out
of you will come for me
one who is to be ruler in
Israel" (Micah 5:2).

nation. When the Pharisees ask, "Where is your father?" (verse 19), they are not only challenging Jesus to produce his father as a witness. They are also insinuating that he was born out of wedlock. The claim of Jewish unbelievers to be free overlooks their political servitude to Rome and to preceding world powers. To their boast of descent from Abraham Jesus replies that moral descent outclasses physical descent. The Jews have subjected themselves to the slavery of sin; thus they are more like the slaveborn ↓Ishmael, who had to leave Abraham's household, than the freeborn Isaac, who remained in it. The statement, "Before Abraham came into existence, **I am**," presents a claim to be the eternal God of redemption, Yahweh, I AM WHO I AM (Exodus 3:14).

Healing of a Man Born Blind

Some Jews thought that a man could commit sin in a previous existence or in his mother's womb and be punished for it in this life. Others thought that children suffer for the sins of their parents. The disciples consider these possibilities when they see a blind man whom Jesus proceeds to heal. *Read John 9:1–41.* This healing brings light to a blind man and thus carries forward the theme of Jesus as the light of the world. That the man has been blind from birth makes his healing a kind of new birth (compare 3:3–8). Jesus makes clay with spittle and applies it to the blind man's eyes to elicit faith, because spittle is popularly thought to have curative power, and also to set the stage for washing, which symbolizes a moral cleansing by the Holy Spirit. The meaning of **Siloam**, "Sent," points to Jesus as the one whom God has sent to give the Spirit, represented by the water from Siloam in the background to 7:37–39. Once again Jesus breaks the rabbinic rule that cures are not to be performed on the Sabbath unless life is in danger. Addi-

"And Antoninus said to Rabbi, 'At what point does the impulse to do evil take hold of a man? Is it from the moment of creation [fertilization] or from the moment of parturition [birth]?' He said to him, 'It is from the moment of creation'" (Babylonian Talmud, *Sanhedrin* 91b).

tionally, the making of clay constitutes kneading and therefore work. The fear of the Jewish leaders (Pharisees) on the part of the formerly blind man's parents probably represents fear of Jewish persecution on the part of Christians in John's community. The casting out in 9:34 refers to excommunication of the former blind man from the synagogue and appears to foreshadow the later excommunication of Jewish Christians from synagogues. Counteracting this move, Jesus pronounces judgment on the Pharisees by saying that if they were blind, they would realize their need, repent, believe, and have their sins removed. But since they see, they feel self-sufficient and therefore remain unrepentant and unforgiven.

Ishmael: ISH-may-uhl

Menorah carved on stone from a first-century synagogue in Ostia, Italy

THE GOOD SHEPHERD The allegory of the good (or noble) shepherd comments on the blind man (a sheep), Jesus (the Good Shepherd), and the Pharisees (thieves and robbers). Shepherds leave their sheep overnight in a walled enclosure (fold) in charge of a porter. In the morning the shepherds come to the porter and call out their sheep, who recognize the shepherd's voice and their own names. In contrast, thieves and robbers climb over the wall of the sheepfold and thereby cause the sheep to panic. In other words, the shepherd is known by his kindness and the favorable response of the sheep, as in the story of the blind man and Jesus. Thieves and robbers are known by their savage treatment of the sheep and by the unfavorable response of the sheep, as in the altercation between the blind man and the Pharisees. *Read John 10:1–21.* When Jesus claims to be the door of the sheep, he changes the metaphor slightly, in accordance with the necessity that shepherds themselves guard the opening of the sheepfold with their sleeping bodies when a porter is unavailable. This exposure of a shepherd to danger develops into Jesus' reference to laying down his life for the sheep, but with emphasis on his authority not only to lay it down on his own initiative but also to take it up on his own initiative. His death and resurrection will not *happen* to him. As God incarnate and in obedience to his Father, he will *make* them happen. The "other sheep" that he must bring into the one flock, the undivided church of true believers (heretics like the Gnostics do not count), represent Gentiles.

> ## John 9–10
>
> Man born blind = Jesus' sheep
> Pharisees = thieves and robbers
> Jesus = the Good Shepherd who cares for his sheep and the door that leads into the protection of a sheepfold (salvation) and out to pasture (eternal life)

↓*Hanukkah*

The setting switches to the Festival of Dedication, also called Lights or Hanukkah, which is held in December to commemorate the rededication of the temple by Judas Maccabeus after Antiochus Epiphanes had desecrated it (see page 9). There, in the dead of winter and in the shelter of Solomon's porch at the temple, are no crowds of Galilean pilgrims sympathetic to Jesus. So when "the Jews," John's term here for the authorities in Jerusalem, encircle Jesus, they have him trapped for stoning or for arrest; and when he marches out from their hand, or grasp, he does so by the sheer force of his deity. *Read John 10:22–42.* According to Jesus, the unbelief of the Jewish authorities does not show *him* up as a false pretender; it shows *them* up as not belonging to the flock of his and God's people. When exception is taken to Jesus' claiming equality with God, Jesus

Doorway into a sheepfold

argues that if the Jews' own Scripture uses "gods" for those to whom the Word of God has come (see Psalm 82:6), no one should object to the claim of Jesus, who is that Word (1:1), to be God's Son. His **sanctification** does not refer to a cleansing from sin, but to consecration for his task of doing the Father's works in the world.

Raising of Lazarus

In a reference to **Lazarus, Mary,** and **Martha,** the description of Mary as the one "who anointed the Lord with perfume and wiped [the perfume] off his feet with her hair" anticipates a story in 12:1–8 and makes Jesus' raising of Lazarus from the dead symbolize Jesus' raising himself from the dead, for the anointing will prepare Jesus for burial and the wiping of his feet will signify that because of resurrection the perfume will not be needed for long (compare also in both the story of Lazarus and that of Jesus the mention of a mourning woman, grave clothes with the separate mention of a facecloth, a stone closing the mouth of the tomb, and Thomas's doubt). *Read John 11:1–44.* Being himself the resurrection, Jesus not only raises Lazarus and will raise himself from the dead; he will also raise to eternal life believers in him who die before the last day. Believers who have not yet died by then will never die (compare 1 Thessalonians 4:16–18). Jesus' groaning with indignation shows him working up his divine power. His weeping for Lazarus shows love for the deceased and provides an

Lazarus's Graveclothes

Concerning Lazarus's graveclothes, Jewish custom was to lay a corpse on a sheet of linen twice as long as the corpse, its feet at one end of the sheet, to fold the remainder of the sheet over the head and cover the corpse with it, to tie the feet together and the arms to the body with strips of linen, and to tie another cloth over the face.

"For three days the spirit returns to the tomb. It intends to reinhabit the corpse. But when it sees that the color of the corpse's face has changed, then it goes off and leaves the corpse" (*Genesis Rabbah* 100 [64a]).

occasion for the onlookers' asking whether Jesus could not have kept Lazarus from dying. That question, in turn, makes Jesus' raising of Lazarus go one better than preservation from death. The raising of Lazarus proves all the more remarkable in that Jews believed a deceased person's spirit hovers over the corpse for three days and then leaves, despairing of a resuscitation, whereas Lazarus has been dead four days, one day beyond hope, as evident from the stench that has developed. Notably, it is at the word of Jesus the Word that Lazarus comes out of his tomb (compare 5:25, 28–29).

The Sanhedrin

The Sanhedrin gets scared that by reviving his popularity this latest of Jesus' signs might bring about a messianic revolt that would draw Roman reprisal. Caiaphas the high priest brushes aside the Sanhedrin's hesitancy by recommending the death penalty for Jesus, so that the death of one man might save the whole nation from destruction at the hands of Rome. His words carry a deeper meaning than he himself understands, however, for he is unconsciously predicting the death of Jesus to bring salvation from sin— and that not only for the Jewish nation, but also for all God's people, both Jews and Gentiles in the one church. *Read John 11:45–54.*

Mary's Anointing of Jesus

Pilgrims are now arriving in Jerusalem from Galilee and elsewhere for the Passover festival. The Sanhedrin therefore issues a decree seeking information on Jesus' whereabouts in order that they may arrest and execute him. They also plot the death of Lazarus because of the convincing force of his being brought back to life by Jesus. *Read John 11:55–12:11.* Enhancing the dignity of Jesus as God incarnate are the large amount of perfume used for ointment (a pound = half a pint), its exoticness (pure nard), its expensiveness (300 denarii come to nearly a full year's wages for a manual laborer), and its application to Jesus' feet (which you would expect to be washed with water, not with even cheap perfume—compare 13:1–11). Since Mary has already expended the perfume on Jesus' feet, 12:7 should be translated, "Leave her alone; it was intended that she keep the perfume for the day of my burial-preparation." *This* day is that day; and Mary's keeping the perfume means that she has not sold it to benefit the poor, as Judas suggested it should have been sold, but has kept it to prepare Jesus' body for burial in advance of death.

Lazarus	Jesus
Death	Death
Graveclothes and facecloth	Graveclothes and facecloth
Stone-closed tomb	Stone-closed tomb
Mourning by Mary of Bethany	Mourning by Mary Magdalene
Jesus' raising of Lazarus	Jesus' raising of himself
Thomas's doubt	Thomas's doubt

Triumphal Entry on Palm Sunday

John's account of Jesus' triumphal entry repeatedly stresses the large size of the crowd that comes out from Jerusalem to greet and acclaim Jesus and escort him into their city as a visiting dignitary, the king of Israel, symbolized by palm branches such as were imprinted on Jewish coins of the period. To the exasperated Pharisees it looks as though the whole world has gone after him; and, indeed, the large size of the crowd previews the coming success of the gospel throughout the world, Gentiles included, as confirmed by the immediate request of some Greeks to see Jesus. *Read John 12:12–19.*

Perfume bottles

GREEKS AND A GRAIN OF WHEAT *Read John 12:12–50.* The Greeks are Gentile proselytes or God-fearers. As Greeks they direct their request to Philip, whose name is Greek; and Philip tells Andrew, whose name is likewise Greek. Jesus responds that his hour of suffering and exaltation has finally come; and he compares his death, burial, and resurrection, and the resultant eternal life for all who believe in him, to a grain of wheat that falls into the earth, germinates, and springs up into multiplied life. To this talk about dying the Jews object that he cannot then be the Christ. According to their view the Christ will not die. They therefore conclude that the dying Son of Man of whom Jesus speaks must differ from the immortal Christ, and that Jesus must be claiming to be the Son of Man rather than the Christ. On the other hand, Jesus portrays death and rising as a glorification of his Father's name (not a disgrace to it), as a judgment against the world (not its judgment against him), as an exorcism of Satan (not Satan's getting rid of Jesus), and as an uplifting from the earth (not a stoning, a knocking down, as was earlier attempted in 8:59; 10:31–33; 11:8, but a crucifixion that becomes the first step in a return to heavenly exaltation with the Father). The unbelief of some is due to a prophecy in Isaiah 6:10, and the secrecy of others' belief draws criticism so as to warn John's community against a failure of Christian witness through fear of persecution. The command of the Father which Jesus equates with eternal life is that Jesus lay down his life that he might take it again (10:17–18), for eternal life is based on his death and resurrection.

> ### The Omnibus Exorcism
>
> John omits the many exorcisms of run-of-the-mill demons that the Synoptics tell about and concentrates on the omnibus exorcism of Satan from the world, portrayed as collectively possessed by him.

Washing the Disciples' Feet

Read John 13:1–20. "Before the Passover" leaves Jesus' death to be itself the Passover (compare 1:29, 36; 18:28; and 19:33 with Exodus 12:43–46; Numbers 9:12). His laying down his garments and taking them again symbolize

"He [a Jewish slave] does not have to wash the feet of his master" (*Midrash Mekilta* on Exodus 21:2).

his laying down his life and taking it again (see 10:17–18). His washing the disciples' feet symbolizes cleansing from sin by the Holy Spirit, represented by water (3:5; 7:37–39) and released to the disciples by Jesus' death and resurrection (19:30, 34; 20:22), but a cleansing that goes beyond the bath of regeneration, which takes place at conversion. His washing the disciples' feet also sets a pattern for humble service to one another in the church. Only slaves have to wash the feet of others, though Jewish slaves did not have to wash the feet of their masters. So although the pupils of a rabbi had to perform the other duties of a slave for him, they did not have to wash his feet. Here the rabbi (Jesus) does for his pupils (the disciples) what was considered too menial even for them to do for him.

THE BETRAYER *Read John 13:21–30.* The beloved disciple (presumably John) is reclining on his left side with his back toward Jesus, so that to speak with Jesus privately he has only to lean backward onto Jesus' chest. The sop or morsel that Jesus gives to Judas Iscariot is a piece of bread dipped in the common dish of broth and customarily presented to the honored guest. Taking the initiative as he usually does in John's Gospel, Jesus commands Judas to do quickly what he is going to do. Not even under Satan's control, then, can Judas betray Jesus apart from Jesus' command. The "quickly" of that command and the "immediately" of Judas's exit ensure that the betrayal will take place on schedule. Jesus' hour has come, and he will not let it pass without seeing to it that the Father's will is accomplished. The notation that it was night when Judas went out contrasts with the earlier notation of Nicodemus's having come to Jesus by night (3:2) and calls attention to the symbolism of entering the darkness of sin and judgment on leaving Jesus, the light of salvation.

Upper Room Discourse

LOVING ONE ANOTHER After Judas's exit, Jesus speaks of his impending death and resurrection as a glorification of himself and of God. "Immediately" stresses the quickness with which the glorification in resurrection will follow glorification through the uplifting on a cross. *Read John 13:31–38.* The disciples' loving one another is designed to help make up for Jesus' coming absence. The description of the love commandment as "new" relates to the earlier part of John's Gospel, in which Jesus has given no commandments to his disciples. This new commandment rests on the commandment to love your neighbor as you love yourself (Leviticus 19:18; compare Mark 12:31 par.); but your neighbor has changed to your fellow believer in Jesus, and "as [you love] yourself" has changed to "as I [Jesus] have loved you," that is, to the extent of sacrificing your own life when necessary. The truth is just the reverse of Peter's statement, "I will lay down my life for you." Jesus will lay down his life for Peter (see 10:11).

Peter has asked where Jesus is going. Jesus now answers that question: He is going to the Father. *Read John 14:1–31.* The Father's house is a household, not a building. "Many dwellings" means **abiding places** in the very person of Jesus, just as he and the Father make their abode with the persons of believers, those who abide in Christ (14:23). It is by his death, resurrection, and ascension that he prepares those abiding places in himself. And his coming to receive the disciples to himself means his reunion with them after the resurrection; for in contrast with the Synoptics, John repeatedly uses the verb "come" for Jesus' coming in resurrection appearances to the disciples (20:19, 24, 26; 21:13). These comings look forward to a final coming at the end (21:22, 23). The disciples know the **way** to the Father because they know Jesus, who is that way; and he is that way because he is also the **truth**, the very manifestation of God in human flesh (1:14); and as the truth of God incarnate he is the **life**, for in him believers find the eternal life of God himself. The works they do will not be greater than those of Jesus in the sense of exhibiting more power (John never uses the term *miracles*, which means "acts of power"), but greater in the sense of extending throughout the world. Jesus has confined himself to Palestine; his disciples will carry the gospel far and wide. **Asking in his name** means appealing to his authority. Asking *him* in his own name (14:14) implies his oneness with the Father, since prayers are normally directed to the Father (15:16; 16:23).

THE PARACLETE A Greek word transliterated as "Paraclete" stands behind various English translations, such as "Comforter," "Counselor," and "Prosecutor" (or "Advocate"), and refers to the Holy Spirit, though "another Paraclete" implies that Jesus too is a paraclete. Just as in these roles Jesus has represented the Father, so from now on the Holy Spirit will represent him and the Father in these roles. Through the Spirit, in fact, Jesus and the Father will abide with believers just as they will abide in Jesus. The Spirit's

The Old Commandment	The New Commandment
Love	Love
your neighbor	one another
as [you love] yourself.	as I have loved you.

Note: "Your neighbor" (whoever is near you, whether believer or unbeliever) shrinks to "one another" (your fellow believers), but the standard escalates from self-love to Jesus' self-sacrificial love.

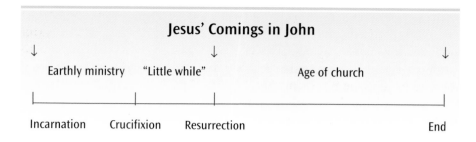

Jesus' Comings in John

Earthly ministry	"Little while"	Age of church
Incarnation	Crucifixion Resurrection	End

teaching the disciples everything by reminding them of everything that Jesus has said gives the lie to revelations purporting to go beyond him, as in the case of Gnostic revelations. As God incarnate, Jesus provides the complete revelation of God. The Spirit can only expound that revelation. More immediately, the ruler of the world (Satan) is coming in the person of Judas Iscariot, whom he has entered (13:27) and who is making his way to the Garden of Gethsemane. So Jesus' saying, "Get up, let's go from here," shows him determined to be there for his arrest. He will not miss his hour.

ALLEGORY OF THE VINE In the Old Testament a vine symbolized Israel (Psalm 80:8–18; Isaiah 5:1–7; Jeremiah 2:21; Ezekiel 19:10–14; Hosea 10:1). Now that Israel has been set aside because of their rejection of Jesus, he and those who abide in him become the new and true vine of God's planting. Jesus is the whole vine, not just the stem, so that as branches those who abide in him are not merely connected to him; they are absorbed by him. The **fruitbearing** of branches represents obedience to Jesus' commands, most especially the one that believers should love one another. The **removal** and **burning** of branches that do not bear fruit represents the doom of apostates, false believers. The **pruning** of branches that do bear fruit represents the cleansing of true believers, more particularly, ongoing cleansing after an initial cleansing at conversion, just as did Jesus' washing of the disciples' feet in relation to

A grapevine with grape clusters
carved on a stone at Gerasa

the disciples' having been bathed already (13:10). By way of contrast with Gnostic secessionists who despise the human Jesus, who deny the incarnation, and who consequently fall into disobedience to Jesus' commandments (most especially the disobedience of haughtily failing to love true believers), abiding in the vine represents abiding in Jesus by adherence to orthodox Christian belief and practice. *Read John 15:1–27.* The figure changes from that of a vine with branches to that of friends. Though in other respects the relation of Jesus' disciples to him is one of slavery, his revelation of the Father to them has resembled the free and open communication of friend to friend. And now, despite incurring the world's hatred, disciples are to join the Paraclete, the Spirit of truth, in bearing witness to this revelation.

> The Lord to Israel: "I planted you as a choice vine of sound, reliable stock" (Jeremiah 2:21).

Read John 16:1–33. "The hour" (16:4) is the time of Jesus' physical absence and of his enemies' persecution of the disciples. Since Peter has asked Jesus where he is going (13:36; compare 14:5), Jesus' statement, "None of you is asking me, 'Where are you going?'" implies that he should be asked again. Instead, sorrow over their coming persecution has crowded out curiosity about his destination. But the coming of the Paraclete more than makes up for Jesus' departure and the subsequent persecution of those who truly believe in him. For the Paraclete will bring to light the sin of the world's **unbelief** in Jesus, the **righteousness** of Jesus as seen in his return to the Father so that not even the disciples can see him, and the **judgment** inflicted on Satan at the cross. The Paraclete's disclosure to the disciples of coming events (16:13) will still center on Jesus (compare the book of Revelation). The "little while" of Jesus' absence will be the interval of the disciples' sorrow between his death and resurrection, a sorrow like the pain of childbirth both in its intensity and in its replacement by joy, here the joy of Easter, a joy so secure as to overcome the trauma of persecution. And the joy of Easter is made full by the joy of receiving answers to prayer offered in Jesus' name, for those answers provide continuing, repeated proof that he is risen indeed.

Prayer for the Disciples

Now Jesus directs his words away from the disciples to his Father in heaven and first takes up the subject of his and the Father's glorification, already broached in 13:31–32, and then the safekeeping, sanctification, and unity of believers, that is, their being kept from apostasy and its results: worldliness and division in the church. *Read John 17:1–26.* Jesus prays for his

The Holy Spirit as Paraclete	Translation
Consoles believers in Jesus' absence	Comforter
Teaches believers what Jesus has said and will yet say	Counselor
Convicts unbelievers of their rejection of Jesus	Prosecutor

disciples, but not for the world, because the disciples belong to the Father but the world does not, because they belong to Jesus but the world does not, and because Jesus has been glorified in them but not in the world. His going out of the world to the Father leaves them exposed to satanic danger—hence his prayer for their protection. **Sanctification** means a setting apart from the world. "**The son of perdition**" (17:12 according to its traditional translation) refers to Judas Iscariot and describes him as destined to be lost. Jesus' prayer for the disciples culminates in a request that they may join him in his heavenly glory.

> "Son of . . ." is a Semitic way of noting a person's characteristics or fate.

Arrest

Though Jesus told the disciples to get up and go with him as far back as 14:31b, only now do he and they leave supper and go across the Kidron Valley, immediately east of Jerusalem and the temple, to Gethsemane, which John calls a garden to match the garden where Jesus will lay down his life and take it again (see 19:41; 20:15). His gathering the disciples in this garden therefore symbolizes the larger gathering of God's children on the basis of Jesus' death and resurrection (the Greek verb for gathering occurs in both 18:2b and 11:52). He has already prayed at length; so the narrative moves right to his arrest. Indeed, he goes to the garden to get arrested. When his

An olive tree in the Garden of Gethsemane

arresters fall back on the ground at his self-identification, "I am [Jesus the Nazarene]," which carries connotations of the divine title "I AM" (compare 8:58; Exodus 3:14), he insists on getting arrested, but on condition that his disciples be let free as a symbol of their salvation through his suffering. He is laying down his life on his own initiative (10:17–18). Peter's swordplay in defense of Jesus provides a foil against which Jesus' will to die stands out. *Read John 18:1–11.*

Jesus' Trial and Peter's Denials

Though Caiaphas is high priest during the year of Jesus' death, Jesus is taken first to Caiaphas's father-in-law ↓**Annas**, formerly the high priest, still called such, and still the dominant political force in Jewish hierarchy. *Read John 18:12–27.* Since Jesus has insisted on his own arrest, the binding of him produces irony. The disciple known to the high priest Annas and following Jesus, as Peter follows him, is probably the beloved disciple (John the apostle). So when Annas questions Jesus about his disciples and his teaching, he is questioning Jesus about Peter and the disciple with whom Annas is acquainted and about what Jesus has taught them. Not at all silent, Jesus the Word answers so vociferously that Annas can only send him to **Caiaphas**. The "also" in the first two questions to Peter alludes to the presence of the disciple known to Annas. Peter's denials of Jesus offer a dramatic foil to Jesus' unapologetic outspokenness.

Irony appears again in the Jewish leaders' staying outside the praetorium, or palace, of the pagan governor to avoid a defilement that would keep them from eating the Passover. But by engineering the death of Jesus, they become instruments in the offering of Jesus and miss this true Passover. In particular, Caiaphas becomes a tool in the fulfillment of his own unconscious prophecy at 11:49–52. *Read John 18:28–40.* Jewish custom would have dictated death by stoning. The reservation of capital punishment to Roman authority (in fact, Annas had lost the high priesthood for violating this reservation) ensures Jesus' death by crucifixion, a lifting up by means of a cross rather than a knocking down by means of stones, and thus—in a divine reversal—an exaltation, as befits God incarnate, rather than a humbling. Jesus' statement, "Everyone who is of the truth hears my voice," assumes the Greek principle that like understands like (compare the modern American saying, "It takes one to know one"). The question of **Pilate**, "What is truth?" strikes another ironic note, since he who is the Truth is standing right in front of Pilate. Pilate's verdict, "I find nothing to accuse him of," indicates Jesus' qualification to die as the sinless Lamb of God who takes away the sin of others, of the world (1:29).

> ### Hearings During Jesus' Trial according to John
> - Before Annas, ex–high priest
> - Before Caiaphas, current high priest and son-in-law of Annas
> - Before Pilate, Roman governor

Annas: AN-uhs

Read John 19:1–16a. Twice more Pilate affirms Jesus' innocence and tries to satisfy Jesus' enemies by having him flogged and mocked. When they let slip that Jesus has claimed to be the Son of God, Pilate, whose pagan mythology includes stories of gods becoming angry with human beings for not recognizing them when they masqueraded among them, interrogates Jesus further out of fear that Jesus may be a god masquerading as a human being. But Jesus refuses to answer a question about his origin lest the answer, "From heaven," scare Pilate from letting Jesus be crucified. Jesus wills his crucifixion. Pilate succumbs to a threat of blackmail contained in the Jewish leaders' statement that as a king Jesus rivals Caesar. The implication: They will tattle on Pilate if he releases Jesus, and Caesar will get rid of Pilate. Counting from sunrise, the sixth hour of Pilate's delivering Jesus to the Jewish leaders for crucifixion would be 12:00 noon. But as earlier in John, counting from midnight produces a better hour, 6:00 A.M.; for Roman governors held court very early in the morning (compare the comments on 1:39; 4:6, 52; also 20:19, where John's description of the first Easter Sunday evening as the evening of "the first day of the week" most certainly represents a counting from midnight and noon, for a counting from sunset and sunrise would make that evening the first half of the *second* day of the week). "**Preparation of the Passover**" means the **Friday** when the Passover was sacrificed and roasted for eating in the evening. As the true Passover sacrifice, then, Jesus the Lamb of God will die at just the right time.

> **The Greek Basis of Knowledge**
> "For like is akin to like" (Plato, *Protagoras* 337D).

> "Antonoos, you did not do well to hit a hapless vagabond. You are cursed if he is in fact some heavenly god. And the gods, seeming like foreigners from another land and taking all sorts of shapes, do visit cities, looking on both the violence and the orderliness of human beings" (Homer, *Odyssey* 17.483–87).

The Lifting Up of Jesus

It is "the Jews," the very leaders to whom Jesus said, "Destroy this temple [his body] . . ." (2:19), who take and crucify Jesus. But true to no one's taking his life from him and his laying it down on his own initiative (10:17–18), he carries his cross by himself. The omission of Simon of Cyrene also keeps anyone from thinking, as some Gnostics did, that Simon rather than Jesus died on the cross. Since Pilate has repeatedly declared Jesus guiltless, the inscription that Pilate writes and puts on the cross presents in this context an affirmation of Jesus' kingship over the Jews, not an accusation of insurrection against Caesar. Pilate's refusal to alter the inscription underlines the affirmation. John's listing the three languages of the inscription—Hebrew (probably meaning Aramaic), Latin, and Greek—alludes to the universality of this Jewish king's death as the Lamb of God to take away the sin of the world, not just of the Jews (1:29). *Read John 19:16b–22.*

Through association with the four corners of the earth (compare Revelation 7:1), the division of Jesus' outer clothes into four portions may likewise allude to the universal benefit of the crucifixion as well as fulfill Psalm 22:18. The seamlessness of Jesus' tunic, or undergarment, can hardly allude to the seamless robe worn by Jewish high priests; for that was an outer garment. Rather, seamlessness provides the reason for lot-casting (in avoidance of spoiling such a fine tunic by tearing it up), which helps fulfill Psalm 22:18 exactly. Ever in control, even on the cross, the Word who is God calmly commits the beloved disciple to his (Jesus') mother, and her to the beloved disciple, and by so making this disciple his adoptive brother enhances the testimony of the beloved disciple, author of the Fourth Gospel (19:35; 21:24). *Read John 19:23–27.*

"Jesus did not himself suffer death, but Simon, a certain man of Cyrene, being forced, carried the cross in Jesus' stead, so that Simon, being transfigured by Jesus that he might be thought to be Jesus, was crucified through ignorance and error while Jesus himself received the form of Simon and, standing by, laughed at them" (the Gnostic heretic Basilides according to Irenaeus, *Against Heresies* 1.24.4; some pronouns replaced with personal names for clarity).

BLOOD AND WATER Still in full possession of his divine powers, Jesus orchestrates the manner of his death to fulfill Scripture. *Read John 19:28–37.* Not only does "I am thirsty" recall Psalm 22:15; 69:21. It also recalls Jesus' thirst at 4:6, which issues in his offering to give the living water of the Holy Spirit (compare 4:10, 13–14 with 7:37–39) just as here water flows from Jesus' pierced side. Therefore he breathes the Holy Spirit on the disciples as soon as he sees them after his resurrection (compare 19:34 with 20:22). ↓Hyssop has association with the blood of the Passover sacrifice (Exodus 12:22), and the outflow of Jesus' blood makes him just such a sacrifice. It is the work of salvation given him by his Father that Jesus pronounces finished (compare 19:30 with 4:34; 17:4; 19:28). "He bowed his head" shows him laying down his life by his own initiative: God incarnate dies with all deliberation. "He gave over his spirit" carries the double meaning of expiration and the coming gift of the Spirit to Jesus' disciples.

Hyssop

Burial

Read John 19:38–42. The notation that **Joseph of Arimathea** was a secret disciple because he feared the Jews may serve to criticize disciples who remain secret for the same reason in the circumstances within which John writes his Gospel. On the other hand, Joseph's burial of Jesus may provide the good example of a secret disciple's coming out of the closet, as did Nicodemus in 7:50–51. Supporting this view are their present pairing and the

reminder that at first Nicodemus came to Jesus at night, though now he comes by day carrying a load of spices weighing about 100 litras (about 75 pounds, since one litra equals 12 ounces). The hugeness of this amount befits the burial of God incarnate and forestalls any stench of decay such as characterized the corpse of Lazarus (11:39). Thus, Jesus' burial adds to his glorification rather than robbing him of it.

> "And you shall take a bunch of hyssop and dip it in the blood that is in the basin, and apply some of the blood . . . on the top and both sides of the door frame . . . . For the Lord will go through the land to strike down the Egyptians, and when he sees the blood . . . the Lord will pass over that doorway" (Exodus 12:22–23).

Resurrection

Read John 20:1–31. **Mary ↓Magdalene**'s coming to Jesus' tomb so early that it is still dark makes his subsequent appearance to her a reshining of him as the light of the world (compare 8:12). The beloved disciple's not entering the empty tomb though he arrives before Peter favors historicity, because bias for the beloved disciple would have led to fictionalizing his entrance as first. Again historically, thieves would hardly have unwrapped Jesus' corpse before carrying it away, or have

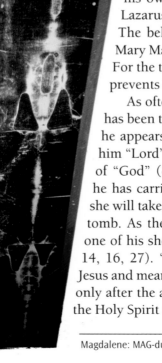

Shroud of Turin, in which some suppose Jesus was buried—but which is probably inauthentic

rolled up his facecloth and placed it aside. Theologically, the lying there of the linen wrappings and facecloth shows that Jesus has taken up his life by his own initiative, under his own divine power; nobody has had to unwrap him as Lazarus had to be unwrapped (11:44; compare 2:19; 10:18). The beloved disciple's seeing and believing has to do with Mary Magdalene's false report that Jesus' body has been stolen. For the time being, ignorance of Scripture (the Old Testament) prevents belief in Jesus' resurrection.

As often in John, ironies abound. Mary thinks Jesus' corpse has been transferred elsewhere. She fails to recognize him when he appears to her, and she thinks he is the gardener. She calls him "Lord" in the sense of "Sir" though he is "Lord" in the sense of "God" (compare 20:28). She supposes that as the gardener he has carried Jesus off and laid him somewhere, and says that she will take Jesus up, whereas he has taken himself up and left the tomb. As the Good Shepherd, he calls her by name: "Mary." As one of his sheep, she then recognizes his voice (compare 10:3–4, 14, 16, 27). "Stop clutching me" implies that Mary has grabbed Jesus and means that she must now release him for his ascension, for only after the ascension has completed his glorification can he give the Holy Spirit to his disciples, as he does on the evening of this first

Magdalene: MAG-duh-leen

Easter Sunday. The "therefore" in 20:19 indicates that the ascension has taken place by evening (compare 7:39 with 20:17, 19–22).

Against Gnostic denials of the divine Word's physical death and resurrection, John mentions the risen Jesus' exhibition of his hands and side, scarred by crucifixion, and stresses the disciples' recognition of Jesus as the Lord. Especially prominent is the exclamation of **doubting Thomas**, "My Lord and my God." Jesus' pronouncing peace on disciples who equate the Crucified One with the risen Lord God and commissioning them with the gift of the Holy Spirit and with the authority to **forgive and retain sins** leave Gnostic deniers out in the cold. Forgiving and retaining sins means declaring sins forgiven or unforgiven according to belief and unbelief in the orthodox gospel (that is, the *only* gospel). John even uses Thomas, a Gnostic hero (compare the Gnostically tinged, so-called *Gospel of Thomas*), against the Gnostics. Though at first skeptical of Jesus as the physically risen Lord and God, Thomas comes around to this orthodox belief. Thus, like other signs performed by Jesus in such abundance that John's Gospel cannot include them all, the resurrection is a sign performed by Jesus and written up by John to induce people to equate the divine Christ with the human Jesus and by this kind of believing to gain life in his name—that is, eternal life through believing that "the Christ, the Son of God" is none other than Jesus, as indicated by his name "Word" (compare 1:1, 12–14, 17).

The Ascension, from a 12th-century manuscript

Epilogue

Because 20:30–31 contains a statement of purpose for "this book," 21:1–25 looks like an epilogue added by the book's author, who at the very end finally switches from speaking of himself as the beloved disciple to speaking *as* himself, "I." The epilogue subdivides into a third appearance of the risen Jesus to his disciples, a conversation between him and Peter, and a conclusion similar to the one in 20:30–31. *Read John 21:1–25.*

FISHING Night and darkness go together with Jesus' absence and the disciples' failure to catch any fish. His standing on the beach as the light of the world goes together with daybreak and overwhelming success in catching fish. The catching of fish stands for evangelism, and the putting together of fish caught by the disciples with fish that Jesus already has on a charcoal fire stands for the one church or, to repeat an earlier metaphor, the one flock (10:16; 11:51–52). The charcoal fire prepares for Peter's compensating for three denials of Jesus with three affirmations of love for him, for it was over a charcoal fire that Peter denied Jesus (18:17–18, 25–27). The comment that the net did not tear combines with a notation of the large number of fish caught (153) to symbolize Jesus' not losing any of those whom the Father has given him (compare 6:12, 39; 10:28–30; 17:11–15; 18:8–9). The mention of bread as well as fish recalls the feeding of the five thousand, and Jesus' giving the disciples bread represents his giving them himself, his sacrificial flesh, as the bread of life (6:1–50).

> "Jesus said to them, 'Come, follow me, and I will make you become fishers of human beings'" (Mark 1:17).

SHEPHERDING The distinction in meaning that is often seen between two Greek verbs used for "love" in Jesus' conversation with Peter does not survive scrutiny. The verb usually considered inferior (↓*philein*) occurs elsewhere in John for the Father's loving the Son and the disciples (5:20; 16:27) and for Jesus' loving Lazarus (11:3, 36) and the beloved disciple (20:2), as well as for destructive self-love (12:25) and worldly love (15:19). And the verb usually considered superior (↓*agapan*) occurs elsewhere in John for people's loving darkness rather than light (3:19) and for their loving human glory (12:43), as well as for the Father's loving the Son (3:35; 10:17; 15:9; 17:23, 24, 26) and the disciples (14:21, 23; 17:23), for God's loving the world (3:16), and for Jesus' loving the Father (14:31), the disciples (13:1; 15:9, 12), Martha, Mary, and Lazarus (11:5), and the beloved disciple (13:23; 19:26; 21:7). John is fond of using pairs of words as synonyms, as in this very same passage for shepherding and sheep (see the Greek text). "More than these" means "more than the other disciples on hand [see 21:2] love me [Jesus]." As catching fish represents evangelism, shepherding sheep represents pastoral care of the converted.

Verbs for Loving in Jesus' Conversation with Simon Peter

Jesus' Questions	Simon's Answers
agapan	*philein*
agapan	*philein*
philein	*philein*

The well-known noun ↓*agapē* is cognate to the verb *agapan*.

THE FATES OF PETER AND THE BELOVED DISCIPLE Jesus predicts for Peter a death by crucifixion in old age (hands stretched out to carry his cross while being led to the unwanted site of crucifixion), as has almost certainly happened by the time John writes. (Nothing hints at crucifixion upside down, the first mention of this probably legendary detail about Peter's martyrdom appear-

---

philein: fee-LAYN ▪ *agapan:* ah-gah-PAHN ▪ *agapē:* ah-GAH-pay ing in the apocryphal *Acts of Peter* 33–41, late in the second century.) But against a popular misunderstanding, Jesus does not say that the beloved disciple will survive until the second coming. The denial that Jesus said so does not imply the beloved disciple's death by the time the Fourth Gospel is written, for that disciple "testifies" (present tense) at the time of writing. Only his old age and possibly the imminence of his death are implied. Though many regard at least 21:24 (if not more or the whole of chapter 21) as added by the Christian community centered around the beloved disciple John, the "we" who bear witness to the truth of the beloved disciple's testimony may include that disciple himself, just as earlier in this Gospel Jesus joined others in bearing witness to himself (5:31–47; 8:12–20).

> "So I ask you, executioners, to crucify me head-downwards" (Peter according to the *Acts of Peter* 37 [8]).

Summary

Evidence points to authorship of the Fourth Gospel by the Apostle John, probably in Ephesus toward the end of the first century. To a large extent John's Gospel contains material not in the Synoptics and therefore supplements them, with special emphasis on Jesus' ministry in Judea and on its profound theological meaning. Prominent among the themes that make up this meaning is Jesus as the preexistent divine Word who became a human being so as to speak the words of God, reveal the glory of God's grace and truth, separate the children of light from the children of darkness, judge the world of unbelievers, and provide eternal life through the gift of the Holy Spirit to all who believe and abide in Jesus. After a prologue that presents Jesus as the Word, John arranges his material in alternating blocks of narrative concerning Jesus' signs and works and discourses that interpret the salvific significance of those signs and works.

People to Remember

Andrew	Irenaeus	Nicodemus
Annas	Lazarus	Philip
Baptists	Mandeans	Polycarp
Caiaphas	Martha	Simon Peter/Cephas
Cerinthus	Mary of Bethany	Simonians
Elder John/Apostle	Mary Magdalene	Thomas
John/Beloved Disciple	Mary the mother of Jesus	
Gnostics	Nathanael	

Places to Remember

Cana	Kidron Valley	Pool of Siloam
Ephesus	Mount Gerizim	Samaria
Jacob's well	Pool of Bethzatha	Sychar

Terms to Remember

abiding	Jesus' lifting up	realized eschatology
believing	judgment	Rylands Fragment of John
born again/from above	knowing	signs
deity	Lamb of God	truth
eternal life	light versus darkness	wind/Spirit
Good Shepherd	logos/Word	witness/testimony
I AM	new commandment	works
incarnation	Paraclete/Comforter/	world
Jesus' hour	Counselor/Prosecutor	

How Much Did You Learn?

- How does John differ from the Synoptics?
- What prompted the writing of John?
- How is John arranged?
- What are John's emphases?
- How does John portray Jesus?
- What do early church tradition and internal evidence say about the authorship of the Fourth Gospel?

For Further Discussion

- Besides what is mentioned above, what other symbolism might be legitimately found in the Fourth Gospel?
- Is this Gospel simple or complex? Give evidence supporting your answer.
- Does John write to convince unbelievers to believe in Jesus or to convince believers to abide in Christian faith?

For Further Investigation

Beasley-Murray, G. R. *Gospel of Life*. Peabody, Mass.: Hendrickson, 1991.

Burge, Gary M. *The NIV Application Commentary: John*. Grand Rapids: Zondervan, 2000.

The Interpretation of John. Edited by John Ashton. 2d ed. Edinburgh: T. & T. Clark, 1997.

Morris, L. *The Gospel according to John*. 2d ed. Grand Rapids: Eerdmans, 1995.

Smith, D. Moody. *The Theology of John*. Cambridge: Cambridge University Press, 1994.

Stibbe, Mark W. G. *John*. Sheffield: Sheffield Academic Press, 1993.

Talbert, C. H. *Reading John*. New York: Crossroad, 1992.

Whiteacre, R. A. *John*. Downers Grove, Ill.: InterVarsity Press, 1999.

A COMPARISION OF THE FOUR GOSPELS

The Gospels	Mark	Matthew	Luke	John
Probable date of writing	50s	50s or 60s	60s	80s or 90s
Probable place of writing	Rome	Antioch, Syria	Rome	Ephesus
Intended audience	Nonchristian Gentiles	Mixed church under persecution	Gentile inquirers	Those threatened by Gnostic heresy
Thematic emphasis	Jesus' power as counteracting the shame of his crucifixion	Jesus as builder and purifier of the church	Historical reliability of the gospel	Believing in Jesus the Word as the Christ, God's Son, for eternal life

For Yet Further Discussion

- Which of the Gospels is best suited to the following modern audiences, and why?

  Poor people
  Middle class
  Wealthy people
  Whites
  People of color
  Children
  Teenagers
  Adults
  The elderly
  Skeptics
  People who have never heard the gospel

- How much editing of Jesus' deeds and words by the evangelists is compatible with a trustworthy account?
- To what extent is Christian faith dependent on history and historical research?

For Yet Further Investigation

(The literature on the Gospels is very extensive; the following general treatments refer to many specialized discussions.)

Blomberg, Craig L. *Jesus and the Gospels*. Nashville: Broadman & Holman, 1997.

Dictionary of Jesus and the Gospels. Edited by Joel B. Green and Scot McKnight. Downers Grove, Ill.: InterVarsity Press, 1992.

Powell, Mark Allan. *Fortress Introduction to the Gospels*. Minneapolis: Fortress Press, 1998.

ACTS: A PROMOTION OF CHRISTIANITY IN THE GRECO-ROMAN WORLD AT LARGE

(Continued from the Gospel of Luke)

Overview:

- Introductory Issues
- An Outline of Acts
- Reading Acts with Interpretation
- Excursus on Saul-Paul
- Summary

Study Goals—Learn:

- The relation of Acts to the Gospel of Luke as to authorship, style, date, and purpose of writing
- Where Luke got the information he records in Acts, and the historical value of that information
- Why Acts ends abruptly
- The geographical and theological developments of Christianity in relation to the Roman Empire, Judaism, and pagan religions—and the leaders in those developments
- The legal status of Christianity and source or sources of the first persecutions
- How and why Paul was very important to the history of the early church

Columns of the temple of Apollo in ancient Corinth

Introductory Issues

Authorship

According to early church tradition, **Luke** wrote the book of Acts. If he did, the book is a **sequel** to the Gospel of Luke. Evidence within Acts supports authorship by Luke. Just as his Gospel opens with a dedication to Theophilus, so also does Acts.

> "Luke, the beloved physician, greets you" (Colossians 4:14).

Vocabulary and style are very similar in the two books. Though it does not prove that he wrote Luke-Acts, frequent use of medical terms agrees with Luke's being a physician. By his use of "**we**" in narrating parts of Paul's journeys, the author of Acts implies that he was a **traveling companion** of Paul. Other traveling companions do not fit the data of the text. For example, Timothy and several lesser-known ones are mentioned apart from the "we" and "us" of Acts 20:4–6. According to Paul's letters, neither Titus nor ↓Silas (still other traveling companions unmentioned in Acts 20:4–6) accompanied him to Rome or stayed with him there. Yet the narrative of his voyage to Rome makes up one of the "we"-sections. By such processes of elimination Luke remains the only likely candidate for the authorship of Acts.

> "When it was decided that *we* would sail for Italy, . . . *we* put out to sea. . . . And so *we* came to Rome" (Acts 27:1–2; 28:14, skipping many "we"-statements in between).

LITERARY TECHNIQUE Together with the Gospel of Luke and the Letter to the Hebrews, the book of Acts contains

Silas: SI-luhs

A Roman road

some of the most cultured Greek writing in the New Testament. On the other hand, roughness of Greek style turns up where Luke appears to be following Semitic sources or imitating the Septuagint (compare page 208). Some scholars regard the speeches and sermons in Acts as literary devices improvised by Luke himself to fill out his stories. That some ancient historians followed such a practice is true, but not to the extent that has sometimes been claimed.

Although Luke need not have given verbatim reports of speeches and sermons, it does seem that he accurately gives the gist of what was said. Support for such accuracy comes from striking **parallels** of expression between Peter's sermons in Acts and 1 Peter and between Paul's sermons in Acts and his letters. These parallels can hardly have arisen by chance; and no other evidence exists to indicate that Luke imitated or used in any other way the letters, or that Peter and Paul imitated Acts when writing their letters. The only adequate explanation: Luke did not make up the speeches and sermons, but summarized their contents so accurately that the characteristic phraseology of Peter and Paul is evident in Luke's reporting as well as in their letters.

> "As to the speeches that were made . . . , it was hard for me, and for others who reported them to me, to recollect the exact words. I have therefore put into the mouth of each speaker the sentiments proper to the occasion, expressed as I thought he would be likely to express them, while at the same time I endeavored, as nearly as I could, to give the general sense of what was actually said" (Thucydides, *Histories* 1.22.1).

Sources

For the material in Acts, Luke drew on his own recollections where possible. He may have put some of these in a diary at the time of the events. Doubtless, additional information came to him from Paul, from Christians in Jerusalem, Syrian Antioch, and other places that he visited with and without Paul, from other traveling companions of Paul, such as Silas and Timothy, and from Philip the deacon and evangelist and an early disciple

Examples of Parallels Between the Sermons of Peter and Paul in Acts and Their Letters

- Peter according to Acts 2:23: "This man [Jesus] was delivered up by God's set plan and foreknowledge."

- Peter in 1 Peter 1:20: "For he [Jesus] was foreknown before the founding of the world, but was manifested in these last times for your sake."

- Paul according to Acts 13:38–39: "Through him [Jesus] everyone who believes is justified from all the things that you could not be justified from by the law of Moses."

- Paul in Romans 3:28: "For we maintain that a person is justified by faith apart from works of the law."

named ↓Mnason, in whose homes he stayed (Acts 21:8, 16). Also available were written sources, such as the decree of the Jerusalem Council (Acts 15:23–29) and perhaps Aramaic or Hebrew documents relating the early events of Christianity in and around Jerusalem.

HISTORICAL ACCURACY To a large degree, archaeological discoveries have supported Luke's historical accuracy. For example, we now know that his use of titles for various kinds of local and provincial governmental officials—procurators, consuls, ↓praetors, ↓politarchs, ↓Asiarchs, and others—was exactly correct for the times and localities about which he was writing. This accuracy is doubly remarkable in that the use of these terms was in a constant state of flux because the political status of various communities was constantly changing.

Ending and Date

The book of Acts ends **abruptly**. Luke brings the story of Paul to the point where Paul, imprisoned in Rome, has been waiting for two years to be tried before Caesar. But we read no more. What happened to Paul? Did he ever appear before Caesar? If so, was he condemned? Martyred? Acquitted? Released? Luke does not tell. Many suggestions are offered to explain the abruptness of this ending:

- Perhaps Luke intended a third volume that would answer the lingering questions. But his first volume, the Gospel of Luke, closes with a sense of completeness even though he probably intended already to write Acts.

Mnason: NAY-suhn ■ praetors: PREE-tuhrz ■ politarchs: POL-i-tahrks ■ Asiarchs: AY-zhee-ahrks

Asiarch inscription

- Maybe Luke came to the end of his papyrus scroll. But presumably he would have seen that space was running out and formed an appropriate conclusion.
- Personal catastrophe may have prevented Luke from finishing the book. But it is already long enough to fill a lengthy papyrus scroll.
- Perhaps Acts 20:22–25; 21:4, 10–14 imply well enough that Paul was martyred in Rome. But those passages set out the possibility of martyrdom at the hands of hostile Jews in Jerusalem, not at the hands of Caesar in Rome; and the remainder of Acts tells of Paul's escaping martyrdom at the hands of such Jews and of his exoneration by Roman officialdom.
- Perhaps Luke accomplished a purpose of showing the progress of Christianity from Jerusalem, the place of origin, to Rome, capital of the empire. But Paul's prison ministry in Rome makes a disappointing climax; a Christian community already existed there; and the problem remains why Luke did not tell what happened to Paul, the dominant character in Acts 13–28.
- The best solution is to say that Luke wrote up to the events so far as they had happened; that is, at the time of writing Paul was **still awaiting trial** before the Caesar, Nero. Surely it would have been irrelevant for Luke to prove the political innocence of Christianity, as he does throughout the book, if he were writing after Nero had turned against Christians (A.D. 64). Too late then to appeal to the favorable decisions of lesser officials! Luke wrote Acts, therefore, when Paul had been in Rome for two years (about A.D. 63). Also favoring an early date is the lack of allusions to the Neronic persecution, to the martyrdom of James the Lord's brother, again in the 60s, and to the destruction of Jerusalem in A.D. 70. Relatively undeveloped theology and controversy over the status of Gentile Christians possibly point in the same direction, but may instead reflect Luke's accuracy in describing the primitive church, without implications for the date of writing.

> ### The Tübingen Hypothesis
>
> Confirmation of the historical accuracy of Acts has outmoded the "↓Tübingen Hypothesis" of the nineteenth century that a second-century author wrote Acts to reconcile the supposedly conflicting standpoints of Petrine and Pauline Christianity. Evidence is lacking for such a division, and a late author could hardly have written so accurately as Luke does about first-century conditions. F. C. ↓Baur of the University of Tübingen, Germany, led the Tübingen school of thought. According to his hypothesis, Petrine Christianity was legalistic, Pauline Christianity antilegalistic.

ϰ   Theologically, the abruptness with which Acts ends suggests the unfinished task of worldwide evangelism. What the early church began, the later church is to finish.

Purpose

As in his Gospel, Luke slants the book of Acts toward **Gentiles**, especially those with open-minded interest in the historical origins of Christianity. In

---

so doing, he continues to emphasize the **religious piety**, **moral purity**, and **political innocence** of believers in Jesus, and to portray Christianity as **universal**, a traditional religion rooted in Judaism but open to all. In Luke the narrative progressed to Jerusalem, the center of Judaism. In Acts the narrative progresses to **Rome**, center of the world. The **power of the Holy Spirit** makes possible this progress. Luke does not write about the spread of Christianity to Egypt or to the East, but we do read recurring statements that summarize the success of the gospel wherever Christians proclaimed it: "And the word of God kept growing, and the number of the disciples in Jerusalem kept multiplying greatly" (Acts 6:7; see also 9:31; 12:24; 16:5; 19:20; 28:30–31).

Special attention goes to showing that Christianity deserves continued freedom because it derives from Judaism, which has legal standing, and because it does not pose any threat to the Roman government. Repeatedly, Luke describes Christianity as a kind of **fulfilled Judaism** and cites **favorable judgments** concerning Christianity and its proponents by various kinds of local and provincial officials. Such an apology was needed, because Christianity had started with the handicap that its founder had died by crucifixion, the Roman means of executing criminals, and because disturbance arose wherever Christianity spread. Already in his Gospel, Luke has shown that both Pilate and Herod Antipas pronounced Jesus innocent and that mob pressure led to a miscarriage of justice. In Acts, too, Luke shows that disturbances over Christianity arose from the violence of mobs and from false accusations, often by unbelieving Jews, not through any misdeeds of the Christians themselves. In this way Luke hopes to dispel prejudice against Christianity and to win sympathy from the likes of Theophilus, whose designation "most excellent" in Luke 1:3 may indicate influential political position as well as aristocratic, or at least middle-class, social standing (compare the address, "most excellent Festus," to a Roman governor in Acts 26:25).

An Outline of Acts

I. **The Acts of the Spirit of Christ in and out from Jerusalem (1:1–12:25)**
    A. In Jerusalem (1:1–8:3)
        1. The postresurrection ministry and ascension of Jesus (1:1–11)
        2. The replacement of Judas Iscariot with Matthias (1:12–26)
        3. The Day of Pentecost: an outpouring of the Holy Spirit, speaking in tongues, Peter's sermon, mass conversion, and Christian community (2:1–47)
        4. The healing of a lame man and Peter's sermon (3:1–26)
        5. The imprisonment and release of Peter and John (4:1–31)
        6. The community of goods in the Jerusalem church and the death of Ananias and Sapphira (4:32–5:11)

      7. Miracles, conversions, imprisonment of the apostles, and release (5:12–42)

      8. A dispute over food rations and the choice of seven "deacons" (6:1–7)

      9. The sermon and martyrdom of Stephen and a general persecution following (6:8–8:3)

   B. Out from Jerusalem (8:4–12:25)

      1. Philip's evangelization of Samaria, the Samaritan reception of the Spirit, and the story of Simon the magician (8:4–25)

      2. Philip's conversion of the Ethiopian eunuch (8:26–40)

      3. The conversion of Saul (Paul), his preaching in and escape from Damascus, return to Jerusalem, and flight to Tarsus (9:1–31)

      4. Peter's healing of Aeneas and raising of Tabitha (9:32–43)

      5. The salvation of Cornelius and his Gentile household, including Peter's vision of a sheet, a sermon by him, and Gentile reception of the Spirit (10:1–11:18)

      6. The spread of the gospel to Antioch in Syria (11:19–26)

      7. The bringing of famine relief from Antioch to Jerusalem by Barnabas and Saul (Paul) (11:27–30)

      8. Herod Agrippa I's execution of James the apostle and imprisonment of Peter, Peter's miraculous release, and Herod's horrible death (12:1–25)

II. The Acts of the Spirit of Christ Far and Wide through the Apostle Paul (13:1–28:31)

   A. Paul's first missionary journey (13:1–14:28)

      1. The sending from Antioch, Syria (13:1–3)

      2. Cyprus: the blinding of Elymas and conversion of Sergius Paulus (13:4–12)

      3. Perga: the departure of John Mark (13:13)

      4. Antioch of Pisidia: Paul's sermon in the synagogue (13:14–52)

      5. Iconium, Lystra, and Derbe: the healing of a crippled beggar, worship of Barnabas and Paul as Zeus and Hermes, and stoning of Paul at Lystra (14:1–18)

      6. The return to Antioch, Syria, with preaching in Perga (14:19–28)

   B. The Judaizing controversy (15:1–35)

      1. Debate in Antioch, Syria (15:1–2)

      2. The Jerusalem Council: a decision for Gentile freedom from the Mosaic law and considerateness toward Jewish Christians (15:3–35)

   C. Paul's second missionary journey (15:36–18:21)

      1. A dispute with Barnabas over John Mark and the departure from Antioch, Syria, with Silas (15:36–41)

      2. A journey through South Galatia and the selection of Timothy (16:1–5)

      3. Troas: a vision of the man of Macedonia (16:6–10)

      4. Philippi: the conversion of Lydia, deliverance of a demon-possessed girl, jailing of Paul and Silas, earthquake, and conversion of the jailer and his household (16:11–40)

5. Thessalonica: a Jewish assault on the house of Jason, Paul's host (17:1–9)
6. Berea: the verifying of Paul's message with the Old Testament (17:10–15)
7. Athens: Paul's sermon on Mars' Hill (17:16–34)
8. Corinth: Paul's tentmaking with Aquila and Priscilla, a favorable decision by the Roman proconsul Gallio, and general success (18:1–17)
9. The return to Antioch, Syria, via Cenchrea (18:18–21)
D. Paul's third missionary journey (18:22–21:16)
1. A journey through Galatia and Phrygia (18:22–23)
2. The preparatory ministry of Apollos in Ephesus (18:24–28)
3. Ephesus: the Christian baptism of disciples of John the Baptist, successful evangelism, and a riot led by Demetrius (19:1–41)
4. A journey through Macedonia to Greece and back through Macedonia (20:1–5)
5. Troas: Eutychus's fall from a window during Paul's sermon (20:6–12)
6. A journey to Miletus and Paul's farewell speech to the Ephesian elders (20:13–38)
7. A voyage to Caesarea and predictions of misfortune for Paul in Jerusalem (21:1–14)
8. A journey to Jerusalem (21:15–16)
E. Events in Jerusalem (21:17–23:35)
1. Paul's involvement in a Jewish vow (21:17–26)
2. A riot in the temple area, Paul's arrest, defense before a mob, and conversation with Claudius Lysias (21:27–22:29)
3. Paul's defense before the Sanhedrin (22:30–23:11)
4. A Jewish plot against Paul and his transfer to Caesarea (23:12–35)
F. Events in Caesarea (24:1–26:32)
1. Paul's trial before Felix (24:1–23)
2. Paul's private hearing before Felix and Drusilla (24:24–27)
3. Paul's trial before Festus and appeal to Caesar (25:1–12)
4. Paul's hearing before Festus and Herod Agrippa II (25:13–26:32)
G. Paul's voyage to Rome, including a shipwreck on Malta (27:1–28:16)
H. The preaching of Paul to Jews and Gentiles in his Roman house-prison (28:17–31)

Reading Acts with Interpretation

Awaiting the Spirit

Read Acts 1:1–8. "The first treatise" is the Gospel of Luke. Emphasis falls on Jesus' choice and instruction of the apostles as the link between him in the past and Christians in the present, and on the persuasive force of his resurrection appearances. "Not many days from now" looks forward to the outpouring of the Holy Spirit on the Day of Pentecost (2:1–4). The apostles then wonder whether Jesus will now restore the kingdom to Israel, that is, whether he will immediately establish the messianic kingdom on earth with Israel occupying the favored, central position. They think of this possibility because the Old Testament associates the outpouring of God's Spirit with the messianic age.

THE GREAT COMMISSION Jesus' answer turns the disciples' attention from messianic chronology, dealing with the nation of Israel, to universal evangelism, dealing with all nations. Harmoniously with 1:8, then, the gospel will spread

> ## On the Outpouring of God's Spirit in the Messianic Age
>
> "I will pour out my Spirit on your offspring" (Isaiah 44:3).
>
> "I will put my Spirit in you" (Ezekiel 36:27).
>
> "I will pour out my Spirit on the house of Israel" (Ezekiel 39:29).
>
> "I will pour out my Spirit on all flesh.... I will pour out my Spirit in those days" (Joel 2:28–29).

- Throughout **Jerusalem and Judea** in chapters 1–7
- To **Samaria** and other outlying regions in chapters 8–12
- To **distant parts** in chapters 13–28

And as **Peter** will be the leading figure in evangelizing Jews for the most part in chapters 1–12, so **Paul** will be the leading figure in evangelizing Gentiles for the most part in chapters 13–28.

The Ascension and Choice of ↓Matthias

Read Acts 1:9–26. The two men at Jesus' ascension recall the two at his transfiguration and resurrection (Luke 9:30–31 [Moses and Elijah]; 24:4–7). The cloud into which he ascends represents the presence of God the Father, as at Jesus' baptism, transfiguration, and second coming. "A Sabbath day's journey" amounted to three-fifths of a mile (see page 64). So Jesus and the disciples have not traveled farther away from their residence than allowed on the Sabbath. They are **law-keepers** rather than law-breakers. They are pious, too, devoting themselves constantly to **prayer**—but not in exclusion of others; for women, including the mother of Jesus, and his brothers belong to the same company, an **ideal religious community**. Not even the betrayal of Jesus by Judas Iscariot can spoil this community; for that betrayal fulfilled a Spirit-inspired Scripture, received its just and well-publicized punishment, and left a vacancy soon filled with a thoroughly qualified replacement. As did all the apostles, Matthias followed Jesus from the time of John the Baptist's ministry to Jesus' ascension; and the falling of the lot on Matthias indicates that as the exalted Lord, Jesus chooses him for apostleship just as he chose the other apostles.

Pentecost

The Day of Pentecost (see pages 57–58) brings the promised **baptism in the Spirit**, here called a **filling** and an **outpouring**. All these figures stress

---

Matthias: muh-TH*I*-uhs

abundance. The accompanying noise, like that of a violently blowing wind, stresses **power** and plays on the use of cognate Greek words for "wind" (↓*pnoē*) and "Spirit" (*pneuma*). The appearance on each disciple of a tongue-shaped flame of fire represents the ability to speak in **tongues,** that is, in foreign languages—a sign of the universality of the gospel. Non-Palestinian pilgrims attending the festival, both Jews of the Diaspora and Gentile proselytes, are amazed to recognize the languages of their homelands being spoken by Palestinian Jews who have never learned those languages. But the Palestinian Jews in the audience do not understand them and so make a false and foolish charge of drunken babbling. *Read Acts 2:1–47.*

PETER'S SERMON Peter equates what has happened with a prophecy in Joel 2:28–32. Though the predicted celestial and earthly signs (blood, fire, smoke, darkened sun, reddened moon) await fulfillment at the second coming, he continues his quotation so as to include the universalistic statement that "everyone who calls on the name of the Lord will be saved." For Peter, Jesus is the Lord whose name spells salvation. Peter's sermon goes on to stress God's attestation of Jesus with miracles, God's plan and the Jews' guilt in Jesus' death, God's raising Jesus from death in fulfillment of Scripture, and the heavenly and therefore politically unthreatening character of Jesus' kingship. Baptism signals repentance, and the gift of the Spirit signals forgiveness. "For all who are far away" stresses God's calling of Gentiles as well as Jews. Numerous conversions enlarge the Christian community, so that its piety and power, its unselfishness and harmony, become so conspicuous as to earn both universal admiration and universal awe.

> "And the proverb says, 'The possessions of friends are shared'—and says this correctly, for friendship consists in sharing, and brothers and comrades have all things shared" (Aristotle, *Nicomachean Ethics* 8.9.1–2).

Healing a Crippled Beggar

Read Acts 3:1–4:31. Peter's and John's going to the temple at the hour of prayer, the ninth hour (3:00 P.M.), shows them living out their Christianity **within Judaism.** The miracle of healing that they perform produces praise of God, and with true piety Peter takes no credit. Instead, he describes Jesus as the holy, righteous, and resurrected one to whom all credit is due. Another emphasis on Jewish guilt in Jesus' death is balanced by **Peter's magnanimity** ("I know that you acted in ignorance, as did also your rulers") and **God's plan** ("In this way God fulfilled what he had foretold through the mouth of all the prophets"). An emphasis on repentance makes Christianity a movement of **moral reform.** "The restoration of all things" makes it **universal,** as does also the quotation of God's promise that in Abraham's descendants *all* the families of the earth will be blessed. And so despite an arrest by the Sadducees, who believe in no resurrection at all, much less in

---

pnoē: naw-AY

Jesus' resurrection, believers multiply by the thousands, the Holy Spirit fills Peter, and he calls the miracle of healing for what it is, "**a good deed**" such as the Hellenistic world admires. His declaration that there is **salvation in no one besides Jesus** puts forward a gospel for all as much as it excludes any other way of salvation. And the **bravery** and **boldness** of Peter, John, and the whole Christian community exhibit their devotion to God, loyalty to truth, and empowerment by the Holy Spirit.

COMMUNAL LIVING Once again the sharing of goods comes into Luke's description of this ideal community (compare 2:44–45); and just as the betrayal of Jesus by Judas Iscariot received a just and swift punishment in 1:15–20, so also the dishonesty and incomplete charity of ↓Ananias and ↓Sapphira contrast with the unstinting charity of Barnabas and receive a just and swift punishment. The ideal is thus maintained (compare the disciplinary deaths of ↓Nadab and ↓Abihu in Israel's early history). *Read Acts 4:32–5:11.*

SUCCESS AND OPPOSITION Signs, wonders, and conversions increase. The converted include women as well as men. Unity reigns. Solomon's portico locates believers at the cultic center of Judaism, the temple. Admiration and awe of them continue. *Read Acts 5:12–42.* Opposition arises out of envy, not out of any legitimate complaint. Angelic intervention and popular favor

> "Aaron's sons Nadab and Abihu . . . offered before the LORD unauthorized fire that he had not commanded them to offer. So fire came out from the presence of the LORD and consumed them, and they died before the LORD. . . . So they [Mishael and Elzaphan] came and carried them, still in their tunics, outside the camp, as Moses had ordered" (Leviticus 10:1–2, 5).

Ananias: an´uh-N*I*-uhs ■ Sapphira: suh-F*I*-ruh ■ Nadab: NAY-dab ■ Abihu: uh-B*I*-hy*oo*

Temple Scroll from Qumran

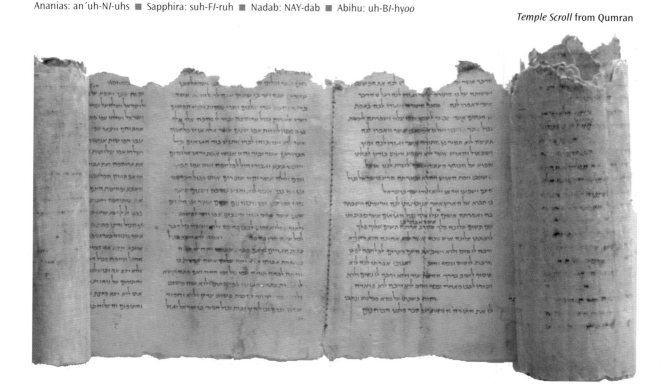

frustrate the Sanhedrin; and right within the Sanhedrin a voice of reason prevails, that of the universally respected teacher of the law, Gamaliel.

WIDOWS When Hellenistic believers complain that their widows are being neglected in the doling out of food rations, Hebraistic believers graciously choose seven Hellenistic men to supervise the dole, as shown by these men's Greek rather than Hebrew or Aramaic names. Perhaps the later church office of deacon ("servant, helper"), having to do with mundane matters of church life and especially with the dispensing of charity, developed out of this incident. *Read Acts 6:1–8:1a.*

Stephen

The conversion of many priests strengthens the ties of Christianity to Judaism. Stephen, one of the Seven, not only waits on tables; he also performs wonders and signs and preaches. It takes the action of a lynch mob and the testimony of false witnesses to bring about his **martyrdom**. The Romans reserved almost entirely to themselves the right to impose capital punishment, but the stoning of Stephen starts and proceeds as a lynching. Even the Sanhedrin turn into a lynch mob. They do not so much as bother to reach a verdict. The angelic look on Stephen's face, his vision of God's glory and of Jesus standing at the right hand of God, and his prayers of trust and forgiveness exonerate him, whereas the rage, teeth-gnashing, and impulsiveness of the Sanhedrin condemn their stoning of him. Saul, at whose feet they lay their robes for ease of throwing stones, will become the Apostle Paul, as he is better known. (But the man's two names do not represent the unbelieving and believing phases of his life, respectively; for Saul is simply his Hebrew name, and Paul his similar-sounding and common Greco-Roman ↓cognomen, or surname.)

Stephen's **sermon** exposes the falsity of the charge that he blasphemed Moses and God, the law and the temple. Rather, it is his accusers who committed such blasphemy by following the example of their ancestors' rejection of God's messengers, including Moses, in their own murder of Jesus. As for the temple, they have corrupted its legitimacy by failure to recognize that God dwells in the universe of his own making, not in the humanly made temple, just as one of their own prophets said (Isaiah 66:1–2).

Saul, Philip, and Simon ↓Magus

The stoning of Stephen triggers a persecution in Jerusalem of believing Jews by unbelieving ones, led by Saul. The resultant scattering of believers leads to the evangelization of Judea and Samaria, as in the stories of Philip's preaching in Samaria and elsewhere. *Read Acts 8:1b–40.* The baptism of Samaritans, women as well as men, broadens the inclusiveness of the

cognomen: kog-NOH-men ■ Magus: MAY-guhs

church. The belief and baptism of Samaritans who have previously adulated Simon Magus (that is, Simon the magician) for his practice of magic show the superiority of Philip's signs and miracles. So also do the belief, baptism, and amazement of Simon himself.

SAMARITAN RECEPTION OF THE SPIRIT The Holy Spirit does not come on the Samaritan believers until Peter and John come, pray, and lay their hands on them as a sign of solidarity between Jewish and Samaritan believers. This delay enables apostolic representatives of Jewish believers to see for themselves that God has equally accepted Samaritan believers, as shown by their receiving the Spirit in the apostles' presence. The apostles' horrified refusal to sell Simon authority for bestowing the Spirit exhibits their pecuniary purity; and his request that they pray for him exalts their superiority over this magician, and therefore their gospel over his magic. The attempt by Simon to buy authority for bestowing the Spirit has turned his name into the nouns *simony* and *simonism*, the crime of buying or selling ecclesiastical preferment. Some early Christian tradition traces the heretical movement of Gnosticism to Simon.

> "Now this Simon of Samaria, from whom all sorts of heresies derive their origin . . . conferred salvation on men by making himself known to them. For . . . he had descended, transfigured and assimilated to powers and principalities and angels, so that he might appear among men to be a man, while as yet he was not a man; and that thus he was thought to have suffered in Judea, when he had not suffered" (Irenaeus, *Against Heresies* 1.26.2–3; compare page 50 on Gnosticism).

ETHIOPIAN EUNUCH The story of an Ethiopian eunuch foreshadows the Gentile missions of Paul (Acts 13–28). The eunuch has been attending a Jew-

Possible site of the Ethiopian eunuch's baptism

A chariot, such as the Ethiopian eunuch was riding

ish religious festival in Jerusalem. He is therefore at least a God-fearer, perhaps a full proselyte. Eunuchs lack religious privileges in Judaism according to Deuteronomy 23:1, but the law may have been relaxed (compare Isaiah 56:3–5); or in Acts "eunuch" may be an official title, not a physical description. It was customary for lone travelers like Philip to attach themselves to caravans like the eunuch's. Reading aloud, as the eunuch was doing, was customary in ancient times, even for private study. The baptism of an Ethiopian, a high governmental official no less, broadens the inclusiveness of the church yet further. Luke is appealing to the cosmopolitanism of his Hellenistically minded audience. And Philip's interpreting Isaiah 53:7–8 as a reference to Jesus roots the gospel in ancient tradition. Christianity is no "Johnny-come-lately."

Conversion of Saul the Persecutor

Luke comes back to Saul's persecution of "**the Way**" (the first name used for Christianity, though we do not know why: as a reference to the way of the Lord prepared by John the Baptist in accordance with Isaiah 40:3? as a reference to the way of the cross? as a reference to the way of righteousness? as a reference to Jesus, the way of salvation?). But on the **road to Damascus** in Syria, Saul the persecutor of Jesus turns into Saul the preacher of Jesus. *Read Acts 9:1–31.* Saul's persecution of *Jesus* in the persecution of Jesus' *disciples* implies a **union** of them on earth with him in heaven, a theme to become prominent in Pauline theology, where "in Christ" and "with Christ" occur over and over again for this union. According to 9:7, Paul's companions hear Jesus' voice; according to a parallel account in 22:9 they do not hear his voice. But the underlying Greek constructions differ in such a way as to suggest that in 9:7 the companions hear his voice as a sound, and that in 22:9 they do not hear it as meaningful words. Saul's conversion makes him pray, see a vision, enjoy acceptance as a brother in the community of Jesus' disciples, receive the Holy Spirit, proclaim Jesus to be God's Son and the Christ, and suffer the kind of persecution he once perpetrated.

EXCURSUS
Saul-Paul

Saul was born a Roman citizen in ↓**Tarsus,** a city of southeastern Asia Minor (see the map on page 317), and therefore must have had a ↓*praenomen* (first name, distinguishing a family member from others in the family) and a ↓*nomen gentile* (middle name, distinguishing one's clan from other clans) as well as his *cognomen* Paul (a last name, distinguishing the

Tarsus: TAHR-suhs ■ praenomen: pri-NOH-men ■ nomen gentile: NOH-men gen-TEE-leh family from other families), but the first two have not survived. How his father had obtained Roman citizenship—whether through purchase, service to the state, or some other means—we do not know. But Roman citizenship gave **legal privileges** and **protection** that served Saul well in his later endeavors as a Christian missionary. He, his father, and at least his grandfather too were **Pharisees** (note the plural "fathers" in Acts 26:5–6) and, resisting Hellenism as much as possible, lived **Hebraistically** (Philippians 3:5–6). Most of his young manhood Saul spent in Jerusalem, where he studied under the famous rabbi Gamaliel (Acts 22:3). We do not know whether Saul ever saw Jesus in person or whether he ever married. He does not mention a wife in his letters; but since bachelorhood was rare among Jews, some have surmised that he lived as a widower.

Peter's Miracles and Visions, and the Salvation of Gentiles in Cornelius's House

Read Acts 9:32–11:18. Peter's miraculous healing of ↓**Aeneas** and raising of ↓**Tabitha** (or ↓**Dorcas**), whose many charitable deeds typify the behavior of believers, demonstrate an enjoyment of the presence and power of God during the very period that Peter preaches to Gentiles and accepts them into the church, actions for which narrow-minded Jewish Christians later censure him. The fact that he is lodging with a **tanner** named **Simon** shows that he has already shed some of his Judaistic scruples, for tanners are ritually unclean through ongoing contact with dead animals and are therefore to be

Aeneas: i-NEE-uhs ■ Tabitha: TAB-i-thuh ■ Dorcas: DOR-kuhs

Straight Street in Damascus, where Saul stayed

A street, gutter, and colonnade in Tarsus, Saul's home-city

avoided. It takes a threefold vision to convince Peter, a threefold denier of Jesus, that contact with Gentiles is permissible. He sees a **sheet**, perhaps suggested by an awning under which he may have been taking a midday nap on the rooftop. The sheet is full of ritually impure creatures. God's command to kill and eat indicates that the Mosaic dietary restrictions, and indeed all other ritual restrictions, are now lifted. Finally persuaded, Peter goes on a preaching mission to Gentiles in the house of Cornelius, a Roman centurion, God-fearer, almsgiver to the Jews, man of perpetual prayer, and—most recently—a visionary. That such a man will believe the gospel recommends it. Peter's sermon to the household of Cornelius offers C. H. Dodd's prime example of the **kerygma** (see page 101). Appropriately to a Gentile audience, the sermon sounds a note of universality again and again: "from **every** nation . . . Lord of **all** . . . **everyone** who believes in him." The portrayal of Jesus as a **doer of good** appeals to high-minded Gentiles like Cornelius, himself a man of good deeds. A mention of the risen Jesus' eating and drinking with the disciples revives the picture of **table fellowship** dear to the hearts of Luke's Hellenistic audience. In contrast to what happened in Samaria, an apostle is already present as witness. Therefore God gives his Spirit to the Gentiles **immediately** on their exercise of faith, even before Peter finishes preaching and before baptism or the laying on of hands can be administered. In this way God dramatically demonstrates his accepting Gentile believers into the church on **equal** terms with Jewish and Samaritan believers. Peter is then able to use God's sudden action to defend himself against parochially minded Jewish believers in Jerusalem who criticize his going to the Gentiles. It takes much longer for these believers to understand the far-reaching implications that the Mosaic law is repealed in its entirety (though many of its moral precepts are repromulgated for Christians), that the synagogues and the temple are no longer required places for worship, and that Gentile converts do not need circumcision.

Evangelizing Gentiles in Antioch

With the further scattering of disciples as far as Antioch, Syria, comes a concerted and highly successful effort to evangelize Gentiles ("Greeks"). Thus the episode of Gentile conversions in Cornelius's house turns into a wholesale program in the third largest city of the Roman Empire. This city is about to become the base of extensive Gentile evangelism throughout the empire. Luke's emphasis on inclusiveness is growing, and he shows how Saul comes to be linked with the church in Antioch and with Barnabas as a traveling companion (compare 9:27: "But Barnabas took him [Saul/Paul] and brought him to the apostles"). *Read Acts 11:19–30.*

> ### Hellenists or Greeks?
>
> At Acts 11:20 some of the earliest textual tradition reads "Hellenists," that is, Hellenistic Jews, instead of "Greeks." But Hellenistic Jews would not make the needed contextual contrast with Jews (compare 14:1; 16:1; 17:4–5; 18:4; 19:10, 17; 20:21; 21:27–28), so that "Hellenists" looks like influence on a copyist from 6:1; 9:29, in the former of which Hellenistic Jews contrast with Hebraistic Jews, a contrast lacking in 11:20 because of the use of "Jews" rather than "Hebrews" in 11:19.

"CHRISTIANS" The concern of the church in Jerusalem for the religious well-being of Gentile believers in Antioch and the concern of the church in Antioch for the economic well-being of Jewish believers in Jerusalem and Judea illustrate the social benefit of Christianity: it heals divisions. The description of Barnabas as "a good man, full of the Holy Spirit and faith" puts him forward as an example of the virtues characteristic of individual Christians. So Luke is able to offer without embarrassment—on the contrary, with pride—the historical note that disciples were called "Christians" first in Antioch, though originally the designation may have carried a derisive connotation (as in a present-day epithet like "Jesus-freaks," used sneeringly by opponents).

HEROD AGRIPPA I *Read Acts 12:1– 25.* The Herod who figures in this passage is Herod Agrippa I, grandson of Herod the Great. Posing as a champion of Judaism, he martyrs James the apostle and brother of John and imprisons Peter. Luke describes these actions as mistreatment and the currying of political

The cave-church of St. Peter at Antioch of Syria (modern-day Antakya in Turkey), the city that had the first Christians outside of Palestine

favor. God's estimate is seen in the contrast between the angel of the Lord's rescuing Peter from prison and that same angel's striking Herod with a disease that kills him. Luke's description of the disease makes one think of intestinal cancer. The death of this Herod occurred about A.D. 44, so that the whole account represents a chronological stepping back from the famine relief visit (11:27–30; about A.D. 47). Since James the apostle has died as a martyr, the James to whom Peter sends a report must be James the brother of Jesus.

> "Clad in a garment woven completely of silver, so that its texture was wondrous indeed, he [Herod Agrippa I] entered the theatre at daybreak. There the silver, illumined by the first rays of the sun, was wondrously radiant and by its glitter inspired fear and awe in those who gazed intently on it. Immediately his flatterers raised their voices . . . addressing him as a god. . . . The king did not rebuke them, nor did he reject their flattery as impious. . . . At once . . . he felt a stab of pain in his heart. He was also gripped in his stomach by an ache . . . . He was overcome by more intense pain. . . . Exhausted after five straight days by the pain in his abdomen, he departed this life" (Josephus, *Jewish Antiquities* 19.8.2 §§344–50).

Saul's First Missionary Journey

Now Luke starts to narrate the more extensive missionary endeavors of Saul. As a skillful author Luke has prepared his audience by describing the spread of the gospel through Stephen's preaching to Hellenistic Jews in Jerusalem; the scattering of Christians through persecution with a resultant expansion of the Christian witness; Philip's evangelizing Samaria and converting the Ethiopian eunuch; Saul's preaching in Damascus and to Hellenists in Jerusalem; Peter's going to ↓Lydda and ↓Joppa and to Caesarea, where he converted a houseful of Gentiles; and the spread of Christianity to Antioch, Syria, where numerous Gentiles have become Christians. Furthermore, Barnabas and Saul have already appeared as partners, Barnabas having introduced Saul to the church in Jerusalem and both of them having ministered in Antioch and traveled together to take famine relief from the church there to the church in Jerusalem. Finally, the failure of Herod Agrippa I to stem the rising tide of Christianity has set up a foil for the wide-ranging evangelistic successes of Saul. *Read Acts 13:1–14:28 and follow Saul's journey on the map (page 317).*

SYRIAN ANTIOCH AND ↓CYPRUS Luke attributes the sending of Barnabas and Saul both to the **church** at Antioch and to the **Holy Spirit**, who inspires the church to send them. The laying on of hands does not constitute an induction or ordination into the Christian ministry (Barnabas and Saul have been preaching for a long time), but indicates that the church is supporting this particular mission of Barnabas and Saul. It is natural for them to go first to the island of Cyprus, because Barnabas hails from there.

↓BAR-JESUS AND ↓SERGIUS PAULUS Paul takes the initiative when a Jewish magician named Bar-Jesus, or ↓Elymas, tries to dissuade the Roman proconsul Sergius Paulus from believing (doubtless because the magician can see that a converted Sergius Paulus will no longer buy his magical services).

Lydda: LID-uh ■ Joppa: JOP-uh ■ Cyprus: SI-pruhs ■ Bar-Jesus: bahr-JEE-zuhs ■ Sergius Paulus: SUHR´jee-uhs PAW-luhs ■ Elymas: EL-uh-muhs

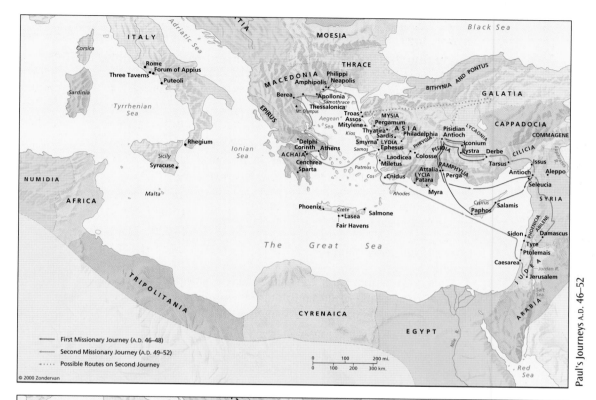

First Missionary Journey (A.D. 46–48)

Second Missionary Journey (A.D. 49–52)

Possible Routes on Second Journey

Paul's Journeys A.D. 46–52

Third Missionary Journey (A.D. 53–57)

Trip to Rome (A.D. 59–60)

Paul's Journeys A.D. 53–63

PAUL'S JOURNEYS

A Summary of Main Stopping Places and Events Synchronized with the Pauline Epistles
(All dates approximate)

A.D. 33   Jesus died and rose.

34

Paul was converted, preached in Damascus, and escaped a Jewish plot by being let
     down in a basket through an opening in the wall at Damascus.
Barnabas introduced Paul to the church in Jerusalem.
Paul returned to Tarsus.
Barnabas brought Paul to Antioch in Syria.

47   Barnabas and Paul took famine relief to Jerusalem.

I. The First Missionary Journey
     Antioch in Syria
     Cyprus—Bar-Jesus (Elymas) was blinded and the proconsul Sergius Paulus converted.
     Perga in Pamphylia—John Mark returned.
     Antioch of Pisidia—Paul preached in the synagogue.
     Iconium
     Lystra—Paul healed a cripple; Barnabas and Paul were worshiped as Zeus and
         Hermes; Paul was stoned.
     Derbe
     Lystra
     Iconium
     Antioch of Pisidia
     Perga in Pamphylia
     Antioch in Syria

49   GALATIANS
       (under early date
       of South Galatian   The Jerusalem Council (Acts 15)
50–51   theory)

II. The Second Missionary Journey
     (Paul and Barnabas disagreed whether to take John Mark; Paul took Silas.)
     Antioch in Syria
     Derbe
     Lystra—Paul took Timothy.
     Iconium   }   Phrygia and South Galatia
     Antioch of Pisidia
     Troas—Paul saw the man of Macedonia in a vision.
     Philippi—Lydia was converted, a demon-possessed girl was delivered; Paul and
         Silas were jailed; an earthquake occurred at midnight; the jailer was converted.
     Thessalonica—A Jewish-inspired mob assaulted the house of Jason, where
         Paul was staying.
     Berea—The Bereans "searched the [Old Testament] scriptures" to verify
         Paul's message.
     Athens—Paul was alone; he preached his sermon on Mars' Hill; Timothy and Silas
         rejoined Paul, but Paul sent Timothy back to Thessalonica and Silas elsewhere.

1 AND 2
THESSALONIANS

Corinth—Paul made tents with Priscilla and Aquila; Timothy and Silas rejoined Paul; Paul moved his preaching from the synagogue to the house of Titius Justus; Crispus the synagogue ruler was converted; in a vision Jesus told Paul to stay; the Roman proconsul Gallio refused to condemn Paul for preaching; Paul spent one and a half years in Corinth.

Cenchrea—Paul shaved his head.

Ephesus—Priscilla and Aquila accompanied Paul this far, but stayed in Ephesus.

Caesarea

Jerusalem

Antioch in Syria

III. The Third Missionary Journey

Antioch in Syria

Galatia and Phrygia

1 CORINTHIANS

Ephesus—Disciples of John the Baptist received the Spirit; Paul preached in the school of Tyrannus; the seven sons of Sceva (unbelieving Jews) tried to use Jesus' name in exorcising demons; converts burned their books of magic; Demetrius led a riot in behalf of the goddess Artemis (Diana); Paul spent two years and three months in Ephesus.

2 CORINTHIANS
ROMANS

Macedonia (Philippi, Thessalonica, Berea)

Greece, or Achaia (Athens and Corinth)—Jews plotted to kill Paul on a voyage to Palestine.

Macedonia

Troas—Eutychus fell out of a window during Paul's sermon.

Miletus—Paul bade farewell to the Ephesian elders.

Tyre—Paul was warned not to go to Jerusalem.

Caesarea—Paul stayed in the house of Philip; Agabus warned Paul with a symbolic girdle about what would happen in Jerusalem.

57

Jerusalem—Paul reported to the church; involved himself in a Jewish vow to show he was not against the Mosaic law; was seized in the temple; was rescued by Roman soldiers; spoke to the Jews from the castle stairway; spoke to the Sanhedrin; Jews plotted to ambush him; Claudius Lysias sent him to Felix in Caesarea.

Caesarea—Paul stood trial before Felix, Festus, and Agrippa and appealed his case to Caesar.

IV. The Journey to Rome

Caesarea

Crete—Paul's advice not to sail was rejected.

60

Storm on the Mediterranean Sea

Malta (Melita)—Shipwreck occurred; Paul shook a viper off his hand and suffered no ill effects.

PHILEMON

61   COLOSSIANS
      EPHESIANS
      PHILIPPIANS

Rome—Paul rented a house-prison; preached to Jews and Gentiles; and for two years awaited trial before Nero.

63

Paul was released from prison; did further traveling.

1 TIMOTHY
TITUS   Reimprisonment
2 TIMOTHY   Martyrdom

Sergius Paulus inscription

The description of Sergius Paulus as "intelligent" contrasts with the description of the magician as "full of all deceit and of all fraud" and "an enemy of all righteousness." This contrast argues to Luke's Hellenistic audience that it is intelligent to believe the gospel, ignorant not to. From this point onward, Luke mentions Paul *before* Barnabas. The only exceptions appear at 14:12, where the mention of Barnabas before Paul will depend on the hierarchy of the Greek gods Zeus and ↓Hermes, with whom they are misidentified, and at 15:12, where in the setting of Jerusalem Luke will mention Barnabas before Paul because in the minds of Christians there Barnabas enjoys seniority over Paul. Luke switches from "Saul" to "Paul" for the first time in 13:9 and sticks with "Paul" for the rest of Acts. The mission to Gentiles makes this Greco-Roman name more appropriate than the Hebrew name "Saul."

↓**PERGA: JOHN MARK** At Perga in ↓Pamphylia, John Mark, a cousin of Barnabas and helper to both Paul and Barnabas and later the author of a gospel, turns back. Luke does not say why. Suggestions range from homesickness to fear. Whatever the reason, Paul considers it invalid, Barnabas at least excusable (15:36–41). Paul now adopts a twofold strategy: (1) preaching in **cities**, from which the gospel will reverberate through the surrounding villages and countryside; and (2) preaching first in the local Jewish **synagogue**, if one is there. The letters of Paul will display a deep concern for his fellow Jews and a conviction that as the chosen people of God they should hear the gospel first. And the synagogue provides a ready-made opportunity to preach, since it is customary for synagogues to offer qualified visitors like Paul a platform. Furthermore, audiences at synagogue include large numbers of Gentile proselytes and God-fearers as well as Jews. In fact, Paul usually enjoys his greatest success among these Gentiles, for their interest in Judaism has prepared them for his message. As a result, unbelieving Jews come to regard Paul as a poacher who seduces Gentiles from Judaism to Christianity by offering them salvation on easier terms than observance of the Mosaic law.

↓**PISIDIAN ANTIOCH** This Antioch, smaller and less important than Antioch in Syria, is located near Pisidia but not quite within it; hence Antioch *of* Pisidia but not Antioch *in*

Examples of Paul's Concern for His Fellow Jews

"For I am not ashamed of the gospel, for it is the power of God for salvation to everyone who believes, to the Jew first and also to the Greek" (Romans 1:16).

"I have great sorrow and unceasing anguish in my heart. For I could wish that I myself were cursed and cut off from Christ on behalf of my brothers and sisters, my kinsfolk according to the flesh, . . . Israelites" (Romans 9:2–4).

Hermes: HUHR-meez ■ Perga: PUHR-guh ■ Pamphylia: pam-FIL-ee-uh ■ Pisidian: pi-SID-ee-uhn ■

Pisidia. Paul's sermon in the synagogue at Pisidian Antioch reviews the history of Israel to proclaim that the messianic promise has found its **fulfillment** in Jesus Christ, but also strikes the note of **justification** from the sins from which the law of Moses cannot provide justification, a justification open to everyone who believes in Jesus. This will become a familiar theme in Paul's letters. He also stresses the innocence of Jesus and the testimony of eyewitnesses to Jesus' appearances after his resurrection. When the Jews come to their synagogue the next Sabbath, they find crowds of Gentiles occupying the pews and eagerly awaiting another sermon from Paul. Jealous, the Jews instigate persecution; and Paul and Barnabas leave after ministering briefly to the Gentiles. Thus a pattern develops:

- Preaching in the synagogue
- Success especially among Gentile proselytes and God-fearers
- Jewish hostility
- Withdrawal from the synagogue
- Further successful ministry among Gentiles
- Persecution
- Flight

> "A person is not justified by works of the law; a person is not justified except through faith in Jesus Christ" (Galatians 2:16).

Luke highlights the universality of the gospel by paying special attention to the large numbers of Gentiles converted, to Paul and Barnabas's turning from unbelieving Jews to the Gentiles, and to the rejoicing of Gentiles because a door of faith has been opened to them.

A main street in Antioch of Pisidia

"In the Phrygian hill-country . . . . Hither came Jupiter in the guise of a mortal, and with his father came Atlas's grandson . . . . To a thousand houses they came, seeking a place for rest. A thousand houses were barred against them. Still one house received them, humble indeed, thatched with straw and reeds from the marsh. But pious old Baucis and Philemon, of equal age, were in that cottage . . . . And so when the heavenly ones came to his humble house and, stooping, entered in at the lowly door, the old man set out a bench and bade them rest their limbs [there follows an account of further hospitality and a surprise ending]" (Ovid, *Metamorphoses* 8.620–724).

A LEGAL QUESTION Luke blames persecution on the jealousy of unbelieving Jews. Even when some Gentiles join in the persecution, it is jealous Jews who have stirred them up to do so. Persecution does not yet come from the Roman government, whose policy is one of granting freedom to traditional religions but banning new ones for fear of social disruption and consequent difficulties of administration. Only at a later date, when the Romans come to view Christianity as distinct from Judaism and socially disruptive, will they begin to persecute Christians. Meanwhile, Luke emphasizes the linkage of Christianity with Judaism, portrays Christians as victims rather than culprits, and drums up admiration for the bravery of Paul and Barnabas in their persisting to evangelize Gentiles despite antagonistic Jews' persecuting them nearly to death.

✂ ↓**LYSTRA** A legend has it that in this region an elderly couple named ↓Baucis and ↓Philemon (no relation to the Philemon who appears later in the New Testament) gave hospitality unawares to Zeus and Hermes, visiting incognito. This legend probably leads the people of Lystra to misidentify Barnabas and Paul with these same two gods. Refusal to accept worship shows the genuineness of Paul's and Barnabas's piety. On the return trip from ↓Derbe through Lystra, ↓Iconium, and Pisidian Antioch, they avoid open preaching (they have just recently been driven out of those cities) and concentrate on strengthening believers and organizing churches by the appointment of **elders** to take charge. In this way and as another Lucan link between Christianity and Judaism, churches look like synagogues, each of which has a board of elders. Paul and Barnabas do preach openly on the way back through Perga, however; for apparently they passed through this city very quickly the first time.

Judaizing Controversy

The report of Paul and Barnabas to their home church in Syrian Antioch emphasizes the successful evangelization of Gentiles; so the stage is set for a dispute over the status of Gentile believers. Jewish believers come from Judea to Antioch and teach that Gentile believers must submit to **circumcision**, as prescribed by Moses, else they cannot be saved. In other words, Gentile believers must come into the church under the same terms that govern the entrance of Gentile proselytes into Judaism. Jewish believers and their Gentile followers who hold to such teaching are called **Judaizers**. The

Lystra: LIS-truh ■ Baucis: BAW-kis ■ Philemon: fi-LEE-muhn ■ Derbe: DUHR-bee ■ Iconium: i-KOH-nee-uhm

disagreement of Paul and Barnabas with the Judaizers leads the church in Antioch to refer this issue to the mother church in Jerusalem. **Historically**, the stakes can hardly be higher: Set up the requirement of circumcision, and Gentiles—for whom the rite mars the Greek ideal of beauty in the human body, especially that of the male—will convert to Christianity in fewer and fewer numbers, so that it will turn into a small Jewish sect; or Gentiles will develop their own form of Christianity, un-Jewish and therefore uninoculated against paganism and degenerating into it. **Theologically**, too, the stakes can hardly be higher: Set up the requirement of circumcision, and the whole of the Mosaic law follows as a way of establishing one's own righteousness instead of trusting in Jesus alone for the righteousness of God. *Read Acts 15:1–35.*

JERUSALEM COUNCIL Luke paints a picture of Christian conciliation, a family of religious brothers and sisters who iron out their differences to the benefit of the Gentiles concerned. The report by Paul and Barnabas of Gentile conversions "brings great joy to all the brothers and sisters" in ↓Phoenicia and Samaria. The church in Jerusalem, including the apostles and the elders, "welcomes" Paul and Barnabas. None less than Peter notes that God himself has not treated believing but uncircumcised Gentiles differently from circumcised Jews who believe, and even says that Jews too are saved by grace through faith rather than by the unbearable yoke of the Mosaic law. The whole multitude of Jewish believers listen in respectful silence as Barnabas and Paul speak of God's work among the Gentiles. James, a brother of Jesus, supports the freedom of Gentile believers from the law by citing Amos 9:11–12 and Isaiah 45:21. The decree of the Jerusalem Council tells Gentile Christians that to avoid setting up barriers to social interchange with Jewish believers, they should

The god Hermes, with whom the Lystrans identified Paul

- Not eat meat that has been dedicated to an idol before sale
- Not marry close relatives (as Gentiles often did but Jews did not—compare Leviticus 18:6–18; 1 Corinthians 5:1 for the incestuous meaning of "fornication")
- Not eat meat that comes from a strangled animal
- Not eat meat that still contains the animal's blood

But these restrictions do not burden Gentile believers so much as they enjoin reciprocal consideration on their part. Luke goes out of his way to emphasize that the apostles, elders, and church issue the Gentile believers

Phoenicia: fi-NISH-uh

Cilician Gates

"But Paul said to them, '. . . we are Romans . . . .' And when they heard that they [Paul and Silas] were Romans . . ." (Acts 16:37–38).

a favorable decree **unanimously**, and lard it with a commendation of Barnabas and Paul, with an accompanying oral report by two of their own number, Judas (or ↓Barsabbas) and Silas, so that no one will be able to think that Barnabas and Paul forged the decree to their own advantage, and with an appeal to the Holy Spirit. Joy and encouragement are spread all around. The ideal community stays intact.

Paul's Second Missionary Journey

TIMOTHY After a while Paul's second missionary journey begins. Alas, a dispute over John Mark breaks up the partnership of Paul and Barnabas, but Luke makes the best of it by noting the justification of Paul's position in Mark's having deserted Paul and Barnabas, the replacement of Barnabas with Silas (who along with Paul will turn out to be a Roman citizen), the commendation of Paul to the Lord's grace by the church in Syrian Antioch, and the replacement of Mark with Timothy on arrival in Lystra. A good report concerning Timothy contrasts with Mark's earlier desertion (though see Colossians 4:10; 2 Timothy 4:11; Philemon 24 for Mark's restored companionship with Paul and a favorable comment about him by Paul himself).

Barsabbas: bahr-SAB-uhs

The circumcision of Timothy displays Paul's desire to avoid giving offense to the local Jews. Having won freedom from the law for Gentile believers, he regularizes the religious status of Timothy, half Jew and half Greek by birth, to that of a Jew so as to keep him from being regarded as an apostate Jew and therefore excluded from synagogues. *Read Acts 15:36–18:22 and follow Paul's journey on the map (page 317).*

THE MAN OF ↓MACEDONIA AND CITY OF ↓PHILIPPI "Asia" means a Roman province in western Asia Minor, not the whole of Asia Minor, much less the continent of Asia (see the map on page 352). Some identify the man of Macedonia in Paul's vision with Luke. Against this identification, Luke writes "we" in narrating the departure from Troas for Macedonia; yet the man of Macedonia calls from the other side of the ↓Dardanelles, "Come over . . . ." Philippi is a city of the first of the four administrative districts in Macedonia. Antony and Octavian (later known as Augustus) settled a number of Roman army veterans in Philippi and made the city a Roman colony after Antony's and Octavian's victory in 42 B.C. over ↓Brutus and ↓Cassius, assassins of Julius Caesar. Octavian settled more colonists there after defeating Antony and Cleopatra at Actium (31 B.C.). Jews in the city pray beside

Macedonia: mas´uh-DOH-nee-uh ■ Philippi: FIL-i-p*i* ■ Dardanelles: dahr´duh-NEHLZ, the strait joining the Aegean and the Sea of Marmara ■ Brutus: BROO-tuhs ■ Cassius: KASH-uhs

Gangites River near Philippi. Compare Paul's evangelizing women such as Lydia at this riverside.

On the assassination of Julius Caesar, see the account in Suetonius, *The Deified Julius* 82.1–4, and a dramatized version in Shakespeare, "Julius Caesar," Act III, Scene I.

a nearby river, apparently because their number does not rise to the level required for establishing a synagogue. Only women are mentioned.

↓**LYDIA AND THE PHILIPPIAN JAILER** Lydia's hospitality following baptism contributes to the communitarian ideal emphasized by Luke. On the one hand, the crying out of a spirit of divination gives supernatural attestation to Paul, his companions, and their message. On the other hand, Paul's patience in tolerating this annoyance day after day robs of any justification the arrest, disrobing, beating, and imprisonment of him and Silas for Paul's exorcism of the spirit. Similarly exposing the injustice are their accusers' pecuniary motive, appeal to anti-Jewish sentiment, and false charge that Paul and Silas are advocating anti-Roman customs, whereas it turns out that Paul and Silas are Romans being robbed of their rights as citizens. Their passing up an opportunity to escape demonstrates good citizenship, as does also their influencing through prayers and hymns other prisoners not to escape. The kindness and hospitality of the newly believing and baptized jailer, who nearly commits suicide because he knows himself responsible on pain of death not to let any prisoners escape yet thinks that all of them have escaped, revives the communitarian ideal. So also does the baptism of all his

Lydia: LID-ee-uh

The city of Athens

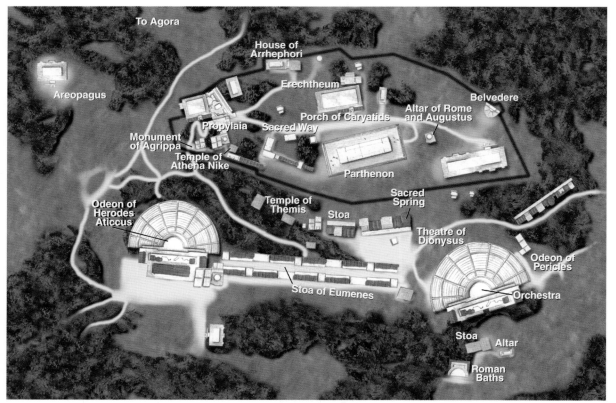

English	Greek	Pronunciation of the Greek
Jesus	*iēsous*	ee-ay-SOOS
healing	*iēsis* or	EE-ay-sis *or*
	iasis	EE-ah-sis

Compare the genitive of the Greek goddess of healing—*iasous*, pronounced ee-ah-SOOS—which sounds even more like the Greek for "Jesus."

household. Finally, a frightened plea by the city magistrates exonerates Paul and Silas. Since a "we"-section ends after the Philippi narrative and resumes with the return of Paul to Philippi at a later date, Luke must have stayed in Philippi, perhaps as a pastor and evangelist.

↓**THESSALONICA, ↓BEREA, AND ATHENS** The jealousy of unbelieving Jews in Thessalonica and their engagement of ruffians from the marketplace, formation of a mob, and assault on the house of Jason, Paul's host, all expose the falsity of their charge that Paul and Silas are teaching insurrection against Caesar. Showing the gospel's attractiveness to high-minded people, by contrast, are the large number of Thessalonian God-fearers who believe, the leading positions of quite a few Thessalonian women who believe, the nobility and eagerness with which Berean Jews search the Old Testament to confirm Paul's and Silas's message, the large number of conversions among the Berean Jews, and the lofty social standings of quite a few Berean Gentiles who believe. The same point is to be drawn from the conversion in Athens of Dionysius the ↓Areopagite, that is, member of the Athenian city council, and of the apparently prominent woman ↓Damaris. The recording of Paul's attack on Athenian idolatry appeals to the high-mindedness of those Gentiles in Luke's audience who see through idolatry. The Athenians who hear Paul think that he is teaching Jesus and "resurrection" as two gods unfamiliar to them. They may confuse "Jesus" with the similar-sounding Greek word for "healing" and thus misunderstand Paul to refer to related gods of healing and resurrection.

MARS' HILL Either Paul has to present his teaching on Mars' Hill before the ↓**Areopagus**, the city council, which licenses teachers; or he preaches to a general audience who have withdrawn to Mars' Hill to escape the din of the marketplace. His portrayals of God as the universal creator and sustainer and the object of human groping, and of all humanity as having a single origin in God, appeal to the cosmopolitanism of Hellenistic culture represented in Luke's audience as well as Paul's. Underlining this appeal are

---

Thessalonica: thes´uh-luh-N*I*-kuh ■ Berea: bi-REE-uh ■ Areopagite: air´ee-OP-uh-g*it* ■ Damaris: DAM-uh-ris ■ Areopagus: air´ee-OP-uh-guhs

Mars' Hill as seen from the acropolis in Athens

quotations from two Greek poets, ↓**Epimenides** and ↓**Aratus**, called by Paul "some of your own poets." But despite mocking by most of the Athenians, neither Paul nor Luke will back down on the point of Jesus' bodily resurrection. The Greeks' best hope lay in immortality of the soul, but most of them remained skeptical even of that. We may question whether they would have so much as wanted to believe in bodily resurrection, for to them the body encumbers the soul. Paul and Luke represent biblical anthropology, according to which God created the body as well as the soul, so that they belong together—hence the sacredness of the body and its resurrection.

↓**CORINTH, ↓AQUILA AND PRISCILLA, ↓GALLIO** Earlier Corinth was noted for its debauchery: "to act like a Corinthian" meant to practice immorality, and "Corinthian girl" meant the same as "prostitute." Apparently short of funds on arrival in Corinth, Paul makes tents with his fellow Jews, Aquila and Aquila's wife Priscilla. Since Luke does not relate their conversion, they may have already become Christians. Around A.D. 49 or 50 Emperor Claudius expelled them and other Jews from Rome because of rioting in the Jewish quarter over "↓Chrestus," probably intra-Jewish strife over the preaching of "↓Christus," Latin for "Christ" but misspelled

On Zeus

"All the streets and all the market places of humanity are full of Zeus. Also full of him are the sea and the harbors, and everywhere we all have need of Zeus. **For we are also his offspring**" (Aratus of Soli in Cilicia, *Phaenomena* 2–5). Compare Cleanthes, *Fragment* 537, "Hymn to Zeus": "The beginning of the world was from you, and with law you rule over all things. To you all flesh may speak, **for we are your offspring.** Therefore I will lift a hymn to you and will sing of your power." The text of Epimenides has not survived apart from Paul's quotation of it.

Epimenides: epʹi-MEN-uh-deez ■ Aratus: AIR-uh-tuhs ■ Corinth: KOR-inth ■ Aquila: AK-wi-luh ■ Gallio: GAL-ee-oh ■ *Chrestus*: KRES-tuhs ■ *Christus*: KRIS-tuhs

"Chrestus," a common slave's name because it rests on the Greek ↓*chrēstos*, which means "useful," as slaves are to their masters. (Suetonius seems to think that Chrestus himself instigated the rioting, but writing seventy years afterward he probably mistakes preaching *about* Christ for preaching, or rabble-rousing, *by* Christ.) Lukes' emphasis falls on

- The seriousness of Paul's attempt to convert the Corinthian Jews
- The blasphemy of those who refuse to believe
- Paul's turning to Gentiles
- The conversion of the synagogue leader ↓Crispus and his household and a large number of resultant other conversions
- The length of Paul's stay
- The Roman proconsul Gallio's dismissal of charges against Paul on the grounds that they have to do with intra-Jewish disputes rather than with crimes against Roman law

chrēstos: KRAYS-taws ■ Crispus: KRIS-puhs

"For the body keeps us constantly busy by reason of its need of sustenance; and, moreover, if diseases come upon it, they hinder our pursuit of the truth. And the body fills us with passions and desires and fears, and all sorts of fancies and foolishness . . . . The body is constantly breaking in on our studies . . . so that it prevents our beholding the truth, and in the fact we perceive that, if we are ever to know anything absolutely, we must be free from the body . . . . When we are dead we are likely to possess the wisdom that we desire and claim to be enamored of, but not while we live . . . . For then the soul will be by itself apart from the body" (Socrates according to Plato, *Phaedo* 66).

Ancient Corinth

- Gallio's being so unimpressed with the Jewish charges against Paul that he does not stop the beating of a new synagogue leader named ↓Sosthenes right in front of the judgment seat (an open air platform still visible in Corinth)

Apparently it is others besides Paul's unbelieving Jewish accusers who take advantage of Gallio's snub to the Jews by beating up Sosthenes (though some think that unbelieving Jews beat up their own new leader for a lack of forcefulness in his pressing of charges against Paul, so that in accordance with 1 Corinthians 1:1 Sosthenes becomes the second synagogue leader in a row to turn Christian). A Latin inscription found at Delphi, Greece, indicates that the proconsulship of Gallio lasted from about A.D. 51 to 53. The importance of his decision to allow Christian evangelism lies in the **breadth** of his jurisdiction (it covered the whole province of ↓Achaia, or Greece) and in its setting a **precedent** to be followed in other provinces making up the Roman Empire. Paul's shaving his head in ↓Cenchrea, a port town serving Corinth, points up his piety, for such a shave indicates the completion of a religious vow (but in this case not a Nazirite vow, for that kind cannot be observed or completed outside the land of Israel; compare Numbers 6:1–21).

> "Since the Jews constantly made disturbances at the instigation of Chrestus, he [Claudius] expelled them from Rome" (Suetonius, *Lives of the Caesars,* "Claudius" 25.4).

Sosthenes: SOS-thuh-neez ■ Achaia: uh-KAY-yuh ■ Cenchrea: SEN-kree-uh

A street and the civic agora in Ephesus

Paul's Third Missionary Journey

Paul's third missionary journey begins again in Antioch, Syria. As on the second journey, he first revisits the region of ↓**Galatia** and ↓**Phrygia** and thus the churches in Derbe, Lystra, Iconium, and Pisidian Antioch. Then he goes to **Ephesus,** where after a brief visit he left Priscilla and Aquila on his second journey. *Read Acts 18:23–19:41 and follow Paul's journey on the map (page 317).*

Gallio inscription

↓**APOLLOS AND BAPTISTS IN EPHESUS** By emphasizing Apollos's learning (or eloquence or culturedness) and powerful use of the Old Testament to refute unbelieving Jews in public, Luke furthers his portrayal of Christianity as **fulfilled Judaism.** The episode concerning Apollos also prepares for Paul's finding in Ephesus some disciples who know only John the Baptist's teaching about Jesus as the Coming One and John's baptism of repentance, both apparently passed on to them by Apollos before his fuller instruction by Priscilla and Aquila (Priscilla's name being mentioned first in the present Ephesian context probably because she took the instructional lead [contrast 18:2]). Since these disciples received only the baptism of repentance despite Jesus' and then the Holy Spirit's having come in the meantime, Paul baptizes them in the name of Jesus and they receive the Holy Spirit, as demonstrated by their speaking in tongues and prophesying. (If they had received the baptism of repentance *before* the comings of Jesus and the Holy Spirit, by implication they would not need rebaptizing in Jesus' name.) Notably, each of the spectacular bestowals of the Holy Spirit in Acts has to do with the entrance of different groups into the church:

- The original Jewish believers (chapter 2)
- Samaritans (chapter 8)
- Gentiles (chapter 10)
- Followers of the Baptist (chapter 19)

This special evidence of God's approval contributes further to Luke's emphasis on universality.

DEMETRIUS AND ALEXANDER For the rest of Paul's ministry in Ephesus, Luke emphasizes its boldness and persuasiveness (both admired in Hellenistic as well as classical Greek culture); its extension in time (two years) and reach (echoing throughout the whole province of Asia); its accompaniment by extraordinary miracles (counteracting the influence of Ephesus as a center

Galatia: guh-LAY-shuh ■ Phrygia: FRIJ-ee-uh ■ Apollos: uh-POL-uhs

for the practice of magic and publication of magical formulas); an evil spirit's testimony to Jesus and Paul (causing fear and conversions); and the origination of social unrest not in any actions of Paul and his missionary companions but in the self-aggrandizing concerns of Demetrius and his fellow craftsmen and in the appearance of an unbelieving Jew, Alexander—as opposed to the friendship and friendly advice given Paul by some high officials called Asiarchs, and as opposed to the town clerk's exoneration of Paul and his fellow missionaries as neither robbers of temples nor blasphemers of ↓Artemis and the town clerk's rebuke of Demetrius and company.

BOOK-BURNING According to an early tradition, Paul uses the school of ↓Tyrannus from 11:00 A.M. until 4:00 P.M. Paul may spend his mornings making tents, his afternoons teaching people interested enough in the gospel to forgo their midday siesta. The Jewish exorcist ↓Sceva is a high priest only by his own claim. Jews were highly regarded as exorcists because it was thought they alone could pronounce the potent name Yahweh correctly, and success in casting out demons supposedly required a correct pronunciation of the proper formulas. Sceva's seven sons, apprentices in the exorcising trade, try to use the name "Jesus" but find the results discon-

---

Artemis: AHR-tuh-mis ■ Tyrannus: t*i*-RAN-uhs ■ Sceva: SEE-vuh

The theater at Ephesus

The Temple of Artemis

"I have set eyes on the wall of lofty Babylon, on which is a road for chariots; and the statue of Zeus by the Alpheus; and the hanging gardens; and the colossus of the Sun; and the huge labor of the high pyramids; and the vast tomb of Mausolus. But when I saw the house of Artemis that mounted to the clouds, those other marvels lost their brilliance; and I said, 'Lo, apart from Olympus [the mountain on which the gods were believed to dwell], the Sun never looked on anything so grand" (Antipater the epigrammist, *Greek Anthology* 9.58). The temple of Artemis rested on a platform over 400 feet long and almost 240 feet wide. The building itself was 360 feet long and 180 feet wide (that is, considerably larger than a football field) and had over 100 columns more than 55 feet high (that is, as high as a six-story building, plus a peaked roof resting on the columns).

certing, for Christian exorcism does not depend on the recitation of magical names. When the converts in Ephesus burn their books of magical formulas, they also divulge those formulas to make them useless to the pagan onlookers, who believe secrecy as well as correct pronunciation to be necessary for success.

RIOTING OVER ARTEMIS The people of Ephesus had identified a local goddess with the Greek virgin goddess of the hunt, Artemis (Roman name: Diana). Her image in the Ephesian temple apparently consisted of a meteorite thought by the Ephesians to resemble a many-breasted female. The temple itself, one of the seven wonders of the ancient world, had a floor area of almost 10,000 square feet. When a rioting mob fills the amphitheater, which accommodated about 25,000 people, unbelieving Jews fear they will suffer by association with the Christians because the Jews too preach against idolatry. So they put up Alexander to tell the mob that the Jews have nothing to do with the Christians, but his voice is no match for the uproar.

FURTHER TRAVEL AND AN EPHESIAN FAREWELL After two years and three months in Ephesus, Paul travels to Macedonia and Achaia and, as he himself says in Romans 15:25–27; 1 Corinthians 16:1–5; and 2 Corinthians 8–9 (see also Acts 24:17), takes up a **collection** for the church in Jerusalem as he proceeds. He intends to go to Rome after delivering the collection to Jerusalem. And go to Rome he will, but under circumstances different from those presently envisioned; for he will go in chains as a prisoner.

Artemis

"Just as Xenophon believes that a bride should have seen as little and heard as little as possible before she proceeds to her husband's house, so this girl, inexperienced and uninformed about practically everything, a pure, virgin soul, becomes the associate of the god. . . . the voice and language of the prophetic priestess" (Plutarch, *Moralia*, "The Oracles at Delphi" 405C–D).

Meanwhile, his plan is to take a Jewish pilgrim ship from Greece to Palestine for the upcoming Passover. Unbelieving Jews plot to do away with him during the voyage, however; so changing plans, he goes back through Macedonia. Then on his way down the west coast of Asia Minor he bids farewell to the Ephesian elders, who meet him at ↓Miletus. As his journey progresses toward Jerusalem, repeated warnings come that he will be arrested and persecuted there; but he presses on. *Read Acts 20:1–21:16 and follow Paul's journey on the map (p. 317).*

TO JERUSALEM This section reads even more like a travelogue than preceding sections. In most of it Luke includes himself—thus the use of "we," "our," and "us." He is capitalizing on the popularity of travelogues in the Greco-Roman world. His communitarian emphasis resurfaces in the description of a meal at Troas, of Paul's extensive table talk afterward, in the restoration of ↓Eutychus, in the farewell scene with the Ephesian elders at Miletus, and in the Christian concern for Paul's welfare as expressed in Tyre and Caesarea—all of these in contrast with the foul plot that made him change his travel plans. And proving that Paul is no charlatan, like a good many of the traveling teachers who criss-cross the Greco-Roman world, are his humility, tears, endurance of trials, refusal to pander, industriousness in private as well as public teaching and in supporting by manual labor his fellow missionaries as well as himself, concern for the well-being of converts after his departure, and life-risking venture to Jerusalem. The notation that Philip has four virgin daughters who are prophetesses appeals to the Hellenistic fascination with virgin prophetesses.

Paul's Arrest in Jerusalem

According to rumor, Paul tells Jewish Christians of the Diaspora not to keep the Old Testament law. When he arrives in Jerusalem, four Jewish Christians have contracted ceremonial defilement during the period of a temporary Nazirite vow and are undergoing a seven-day period of purification. The law says that these men are required to shave their heads on the seventh day and bring offerings on the eighth before they can resume their vow (Numbers 6:9–12). Since the week of purification is soon to be completed, the elders of the church suggest that Paul join these men in the purificatory rites and pay the expenses of their offerings to demonstrate that he does not teach against the Mosaic law. He cooperates, but certain Jews from Asia Minor have previously seen that with him in Jerusalem is a Gentile companion named ↓Trophimus, an Ephesian. They mistakenly suppose that Paul has brought him into the inner courts of the temple, where only Jews are allowed. On pain of death even for Roman citizens, Gentiles are forbidden to enter these courts. The outcry of the Jews causes a **riot**, from which the

Miletus: m*i*-LEE-tuhs ■ Eutychus: YOO-tuh-kuhs ■ Trophimus: TROF-uh-muhs

soldiers of the Roman tribune **Claudius ↓Lysias** rescue Paul. The fortress of ↓Antonia, into which Paul is taken, lies northwest of the temple precincts. Roman soldiers garrison the fortress, and a double flight of stairs connects it with the outer court of the temple. Three years before this incident an Egyptian Jew appeared in Jerusalem claiming to be a prophet. He led a large group to the Mount of Olives and told them to wait until the walls of Jerusalem fell at his command. Then they would march into the city and overthrow the Roman garrison. The governor Felix sent troops, killed a number of the Jews, and imprisoned others. But the Egyptian Jew escaped. At first Claudius Lysias thinks Paul might be that same impostor, on whom the Jews are now trying to take revenge for his having duped them. *Read Acts 21:17–23:35.*

Luke's portrayal of Christianity as an ideal community revives in the **gladness** with which the Jewish Christians in Jerusalem welcome Paul and his fellow missionaries, in James's and the church elders' **glorification of God** for widespread salvation among the Gentiles, and in Paul's **acceding** to the request that he engage in and pay for the purificatory rites of certain Jewish Christians. The riot in the temple and the attempt to kill Paul show *unbelieving* Jews, not believing ones, to be the cause of social unrest. Rescue by a cohort (one thousand strong) puts the Romans in a good light.

> "At this time there came to Jerusalem from Egypt a man who declared that he was a prophet and advised the masses of the common people to go out with him to the mountain called the Mount of Olives, which lies opposite the city at a distance of five furlongs. For he asserted . . . that at his command Jerusalem's walls would fall down, through which he promised to provide them an entrance into the city. When Felix heard of this he ordered his soldiers to take up their arms. Setting out from Jerusalem with a large force of cavalry and infantry, he fell upon the Egyptian and his followers, slaying four hundred of them and taking two hundred prisoners. The Egyptian himself escaped from the battle and disappeared" (Josephus, *Jewish Antiquities* 20.8.6 §§169–72).

Lysias: LIS-ee-uhs ■ Antonia: an-TOH-nee-uh

Aqueduct at Caesarea

PAUL'S DEFENSE In his defense before the Jewish mob, Paul stresses what a zealous Jew he has been and what a devout Jew Ananias, the Christian who helped him in Damascus, was. He also emphasizes his miraculous vision of Christ on the road to Damascus and another vision at prayer in the temple. The unbelieving Jews listen until Paul says that God has told him to preach to the Gentiles. Unable to tolerate pro-Gentilism, the Jews cry out for Paul's blood just as they demanded the death of Jesus. This prejudice against Gentiles makes Paul and his gospel look all the more attractive to Luke's Gentile audience.

ROMAN CITIZENSHIP A subsequent conversation between Paul and Claudius Lysias reveals that Paul is a free-born Roman citizen, whereas Claudius Lysias had to purchase his citizenship "for a large sum," which may have constituted a bribe. Paul's citizenship by birth is superior in status. The names of citizens were registered in Rome and in places of residence. The citizens themselves possessed wax, wooden, or metal certificates inscribed with the names of witnesses as well as their own name. Execution was the penalty for a false claim to citizenship. If a citizen was not carrying his certificate or if his certificate was suspected of forgery, the authorities might ask for witnesses. Possibly for this reason Paul, who traveled far away from Tarsus (the location of his witnesses), did not appeal to his Roman citizenship very often.

CAESAREA To determine a reason for the riot, Claudius Lysias brings Paul before the Sanhedrin; but the session ends in confusion. When Paul's young nephew hears of a plot to ambush and kill Paul as Paul is being taken from place to place within Jerusalem, he informs Claudius Lysias. The tribune immediately sends Paul to Caesarea under cover of night and with a large contingent of soldiers for protection. According to his letter to Felix, the governor in Caesarea, Claudius Lysias rescued Paul on discovery that he was a Roman citizen. Actually, he did not discover Paul's Roman citizenship until Paul was about to be scourged for the purpose of extracting information from him. To be scourged was to be beaten with a ↓*flagellum* (Latin), which consisted of leather thongs attached to a wooden handle and weighted with sharp bits of bone and metal. Victims often died from the ordeal. It was illegal to scourge an uncondemned Roman citizen.

In these episodes a number of items contribute to Luke's defense and promotion of Christianity:

- The good conscience of Paul right up to his present Christian moment
- The unlawful mistreatment of him by the high priest
- Paul's respectful apology for unknowingly rebuking the high priest

---

flagellum: flah-GEL-uhm

- The division between Pharisees and Sadducees, which argues that since unbelieving Jews disagree among themselves, their disagreement with Christians does not rule Christians out of Judaism
- The support of Paul by some of the Pharisaic scribes
- The unbelieving Jews' verging on physical violence
- The conspiracy to assassinate Paul, including an attempt to deceive the Roman tribune
- The tribune's finding Paul innocent of any crime deserving of death—or even of imprisonment

BEFORE FELIX A man named ↓**Tertullus** acts as prosecutor for the Sanhedrin in pressing charges against Paul in Caesarea. His flattery of Felix and promise of brevity are traditional ways to begin speeches. The charges against Paul are that he has disturbed the peace and tried to desecrate the temple. Disturbing the peace was an elastically defined crime that tyrannical emperors used as a weapon of political terror. Almost anything could be put in this category. By way of defense, Paul answers that he has nowhere agitated the people. In fact, he came to Jerusalem, not in a spirit of contention, but for worship in a state of ritual purity and with charity for the aid of Jews who reside in Jerusalem. He particularly notes that the Jews from Asia who

Tertullus: tuhr-TUHL-uhs

Promontory at Caesarea
by the Mediterranean Sea

provoked a riot in the temple and originally accused him have not appeared in court against him. As a Christian, he does not oppose Judaism, but serves the God of the Jewish patriarchs and believes everything written in the Old Testament Law and Prophets. Before the Sanhedrin in Jerusalem his only "crime" was to declare a belief in the resurrection, and even the Pharisaic faction of the Sanhedrin supported his position (though of course they do not believe in the resurrection of Jesus, as Paul does). Putting off an immediate decision concerning Paul, Felix keeps him in custody but hears him again in a private audience with ↓**Drusilla.** She is a girl bride not yet twenty years old. As a small child she was engaged to a crown prince in Asia Minor; but the marriage did not take place, because the prince refused to embrace Judaism. Later she married the king of a petty state in Syria. When she was sixteen, Felix, with the help of a magician from Cyprus, lured her from her husband to become his third wife. Quite understandably, then, when Paul discusses **righteousness, self-control,** and the **coming judgment,** Felix thinks the discussion uncomfortably pointed and personal, and dismisses Paul. *Read Acts 24:1–27.*

The fear of Felix at Paul's preaching combines with his hoping for a bribe from Paul to explain why he keeps Paul in custody for so long as two years. The length of time has nothing to do with any suspicion that Paul is guilty. Otherwise Felix would not give him some privileges, such as allowing the friends of Paul to take care of his needs. But hope for a bribe is not the only factor that prevents Felix from releasing Paul. Though unmentioned by Luke, Felix's offending the Jews on a number of earlier occasions and a change of administration in the central government at Rome have made his political position precarious. Even on leaving the governorship he dares not risk offending the Jews again and facing a complaint against him in Rome.

BEFORE FESTUS A man named Festus succeeds Felix in the governorship and immediately visits Jerusalem to make acquaintance with the leading Jews, members of the Sanhedrin. They renew charges against Paul and ask Festus to bring Paul to Jerusalem for trial. As before, they plan to assassinate Paul en route. Since Festus does not intend to stay very long in Jerusalem, he tells them to send a delegation of accusers to Caesarea. They do, but Luke notes that they cannot prove their accusations, whereas Paul can say truthfully that he has done nothing against the Jewish law, the temple, or Caesar. It does not matter to Festus whether Paul's trial takes place in Caesarea or in Jerusalem, however, and friendly relations with the Sanhedrin would ease the governorship of Festus; so he suggests to Paul that the trial be held in Jerusalem. Paul may fear assassination en route; or perhaps he thinks the Sanhedrin may convince Festus, a novice in Jewish affairs, that they should have jurisdiction over Paul. They could support such a claim

---

Drusilla: DROO-sil-uh

by arguing that Paul is supposed to have committed a sacrilege against the temple, the kind of crime over which the Romans often gave jurisdiction to the Jews. Paul could easily guess the verdict should Festus turn him over to the Sanhedrin for trial. Whatever his reasoning, Paul exercises his right as a Roman citizen to appeal to the Caesar in Rome. *Read Acts 25:1–12.*

Before Herod Agrippa II with Festus

Herod Agrippa II is a **great-grandson** of Herod the Great, a **brother** of Drusilla (the wife of the ex-governor Felix), and the **king** of a small district near Lebanon. His younger sister Bernice is living with him at Caesarea Philippi during this time. While Agrippa is paying Festus an official visit of welcome to his new governorship, Festus decides to take advantage of the visit by having Agrippa, an expert in Jewish affairs, hear Paul and help draw

Appian Way, the oldest Roman road connecting Rome with cities to the south

up a list of charges against him; for Festus has discovered in Paul no capital crime, but only some theological differences with other Jews. The list of charges will accompany Paul when he goes to Rome for an appearance before Caesar. *Read Acts 25:13–27.*

To prove the reality of his vision on the Damascus road, Paul stresses his **leading part** in the persecution of Christians. He also underscores his **strict upbringing** as a Pharisee who believed in resurrection. Now he is preposterously being charged for preaching a fulfillment in Jesus Christ of the very doctrine he always believed as a Pharisee. And of all people, those accusing him are the Jews who, except for Sadducees, likewise believe in the resurrection. Festus, the host, rudely interrupts Paul's speech with the charge that he has gone insane through excessive study. But Paul appeals to Agrippa, the guest, by noting that the things about Jesus are matters of public knowledge and by asking Agrippa whether or not he believes in messianic prophecy. *Read Acts 26:1–32.* Paul's appeal embarrasses Agrippa, who can hardly say that he agrees with Paul right after Agrippa's host, Festus, has charged Paul with insanity. Neither can Agrippa say that he does not believe in the prophets without damaging his reputation among the Jews. Wryly, then, he says that Paul is trying to make him act like a Christian. Luke's purpose in narrating this episode is to show that the **expert Jewish opinion** of Agrippa agrees with the **official Roman opinion** of Felix and Festus that Paul has committed no real crime. In this respect, Paul represents Christianity as a whole.

The Colosseum in Rome as seen from the Arch of Titus

Paul's Voyage to Rome

STORM AND SHIPWRECK *Read Acts 27:1–28:31 and follow the journey of Paul from Caesarea to Rome on the map (page 317).* Again Luke treats his Hellenistic audience to a travelogue, this time almost entirely a voyage. Despite being a prisoner, Paul gets good treatment, proves correct in his predictions, manages the salvation of all on board, suffers no harm from a snake bite, and performs miraculous healings. The hoisting up of a boat during the storm at sea refers to the hauling aboard of a small lifeboat, which in fair weather is towed behind the large ship. The sailors pass cables underneath and around the ship and tighten them to keep the timbers from breaking apart under the leverage of the mast. Lowering the gear means dropping a drift anchor or taking down the top sails, which are used only in fair weather, though storm sails are still set. Next, the cargo is jettisoned and, finally, all the spare gear. Throughout eleven dreary days and nights the ship is doubtless leaking badly. The only hope lies in making for shore, but the sailors do not know in what direction to steer the ship. Storm clouds have blotted out the sun and stars, and compasses have yet to be invented. Despair grips those on board. Seasickness keeps them from eating. But in the end, God's purpose for Paul results in the safety of all. The hospitality of Christians in ↓Puteoli and a welcoming party of Christians from Rome revive Luke's portrayal of the church as an ideal community.

ROME To the Jewish leaders in Rome, Paul emphasizes that he is there purely in self-defense. He does not intend to accuse the Jewish nation or its

Puteoli: Py*oo*-TEE-oh-lee

leaders. The Roman Jews deny knowledge of Paul and any direct knowledge of Christianity, though they admit to having heard negative reports about it. Nevertheless, news of Paul may have already reached the Jews in Rome; and surely they have come in contact with Christians at Rome, for the church there is long and strongly established. Paul wrote a letter to it; and even earlier, as we have seen, the Emperor Claudius banished Jews from Rome, probably because of unrest among them over the preaching of Christ. So it appears that the representatives of non-Christian Jews in Rome are feigning ignorance. Later, on a prearranged day, a large number of these Jews hear Paul explain the gospel. Some believe, but most do not. As usual, then, Paul turns his attention to the evangelization of Gentiles.

The **delay** of at least two years in Paul's trial may be due to one or more of several factors: (1) the necessity for accusers to come from Palestine; (2) the loss in shipwreck of Festus's list of charges against Paul, with the consequent need for a duplicate to be sent from Caesarea; and (3) the crowdedness of Nero's court calendar. During the period of delay Paul enjoys considerable freedom for a prisoner. Though chained to a Roman soldier and confined to the house he rents, he can receive visitors and any kind of attention from his friends. The reason for this laxity is that he is a Roman citizen against whom no charge has yet been proved. He takes advantage of this semifreedom by preaching. Luke wants his readers to note that even in Rome, capital of the empire, the gospel is not banned as illegal. Thus he has traced its spread from Jerusalem to Rome.

Summary

As a follow-up on Luke's Gospel, the book of Acts traces the Spirit-powered progress of the gospel from Jerusalem to Rome. Luke himself participated in many of the events that contributed to this progress. Its tracing gives him opportunity to highlight items that would appeal to a Hellenistic audience, items such as the rootage of Christianity in the ancient religion of Judaism, the openness of Christianity to Gentiles, the exemplary religious, moral, and political behavior of Christians, and the failure of Roman officialdom to find any truth in accusations brought against them. Peter and Paul loom large in Luke's narrative. In particular, Paul's three missionary journeys and voyage to Rome occupy more than half the last chapters of Acts. Sermons and speeches dot the whole of the narrative. Acts ends with Paul's awaiting trial before Caesar in Rome, probably because nothing more had happened at the time of writing.

People to Remember

Aeneas	Dionysius the Areopagite	Mnason
Alexander	Drusilla	Philip the deacon
Ananias and Sapphira	Epimenides	Philippian jailer
Ananias of Damascus	Ethiopian eunuch	Priscilla
Apollos	Eutychus	Saul/Paul
Aquila	Felix	Sceva
Aratus	Festus	Sergius Paulus
Artemis	Gallio	Silas
Bar-Jesus/Elymas	Herod Agrippa I	Simon Magus
Barnabas	Herod Agrippa II	Simon Peter
F. C. Baur	James the apostle	Simon the tanner
Bernice	James the Lord's brother	Sosthenes
Caesar Nero	Jason	Stephen
Chrestus	John the apostle	Tabitha/Dorcas
Claudius the emperor	John Mark	Tertullus
Claudius Lysias	Judas/Barsabbas	Theophilus
Cornelius	Judas Iscariot	Timothy
Crispus	Lydia	Titus
Damaris	man of Macedonia	Trophimus
Demetrius	Matthias	Tyrannus

Places to Remember

See the place-names listed in the summary of Paul's journeys on pages 318–19. In addition:

Damascus	The road from Jerusalem	Tarsus
Joppa	to Gaza	
Lydda	Samaria	

Terms to Remember

Areopagus	Great Commission	Tübingen hypothesis
Asiarchs	Jerusalem Council	The Way
"Christians"	Judaizers	"we"-sections
Day of Pentecost	simony/simonism	
"The first treatise"	speaking in tongues	

How Much Did You Learn?

- List similarities between Acts and Luke's Gospel.
- List differences between Acts and Luke's Gospel.
- Compare and contrast the leading characters in Acts.
- Identify evidences of the Holy Spirit's activity in the history of the early church as told by Luke.
- Trace on a map the four extensive journeys of Paul and identify the events that took place at the locations he visited.
- Discuss the theological and historical importance of the Judaizing controversy.

For Further Discussion

- What prompted Luke but no other evangelist to add a volume on church history to his volume on Jesus' earthly life?
- Compare the tensions and disagreements that arose in the early church with those in contemporary Christendom as to source, kind, and attempted solution.
- Identify similarities and differences between the structure of the early church and that of modern churches. What accounts for the differences?
- Trace the development of the church from a Jewish to a transethnic and international body. Are today's churches truly transethnic in character? Is today's church truly international?
- Do current methods of evangelism, missionary endeavor, and church building follow Paul's methods or diverge from them, and in what ways?
- Does the activity of the present-day church lack the visible evidence of the Holy Spirit that receives repeated mention in Acts?
- Would the church in Acts be counted successful by contemporary standards?

For Further Investigation

The Book of Acts in Its First-Century Setting. 6 vols. Various editors. Grand Rapids: Eerdmans, 1993–1996. Advanced.

Bruce, F. F. *The Acts of the Apostles.* 3d ed. Grand Rapids: Eerdmans, 1990. Advanced.

_____. *The Book of Acts.* 2d ed. Grand Rapids: Eerdmans, 1988.

Dunn, J. D. G. *The Acts of the Apostles.* Valley Forge, Pa.: Trinity Press International, 1996.

Fernando, A. *The NIV Application Commentary: Acts.* Grand Rapids: Zondervan, 1998.

Fitzmyer, J. A. *The Acts of the Apostles.* New York: Doubleday, 1998.

Larkin, W. J. *Acts.* Downers Grove, Ill.: InterVarsity Press, 1995.

Talbert, C. H. *Reading Acts: A Literary and Theological Commentary on the Acts of the Apostles.* New York: Crossroad, 1997.

Witherington, B., III. *The Acts of the Apostles: A Socio-Rhetorical Commentary.* Grand Rapids: Eerdmans, 1998.

PART 4

The Letters

CHAPTER
12

THE EARLY LETTERS OF PAUL

Overview:

- Paul's Letters and Letter-Writing in the Greco-Roman World
- Galatians: Against the Judaizers
- Excursus on "Works of the Law" and "Faith of Jesus Christ"
- First Thessalonians: Congratulations and Comfort
- Second Thessalonians: Correction on the Second Coming
- Summary

Study Goals—Learn:

- The style, contents, and techniques typically used in the writing of ancient letters
- How Paul's letters compare with other ancient letters
- Why Paul's Letter to the Galatians is crucial in the history of Christianity
- The addresses, dates, occasions, purposes, and contents of Paul's early letters

Remains of Byzantine church at Pisidian Antioch built on the foundations of a structure identified as a first-century Jewish synagogue

347

Paul's Letters and Letter-Writing in the Greco-Roman World

Length, Contents, Address

In the Greco-Roman world private letters averaged close to 90 words in length. Literary letters, such as those written by the Roman orator and statesman ↓Cicero and by ↓Seneca the philosopher, averaged around 200 words. Since the usual papyrus sheet measured about 9-1/2 inches by 11-1/2 inches (approximately the size of modern notebook paper) and could accommodate 150 to 250 words, depending on the size of writing, most ancient letters occupied no more than one papyrus page. But the average length of Paul's letters runs to about 1,300 words, ranging from 335 words in Philemon to 7,114 words in Romans, that is, several times longer than the average letter of ancient times. From one standpoint, then, Paul invented a new literary form—and new not only in its prolongation as a letter but also in the theological character of its contents and usually in the communal nature of its address—something like an ancient literary "epistle" containing a political, philosophical, or similar essay. From another standpoint, however, Paul's letters count as true letters in that they have genuine and specific addresses, whereas ancient literary epistles were written for a broad

Cicero: SIS-uh-roh ■ Seneca: SEN-uh-kuh

An Example of Broken Grammar in Paul

"But from the ones seeming to be something—of what sort they once were makes no difference to me; God does not show partiality—for the ones seeming [to be something] added nothing to me" (a fairly literal translation of Galatians 2:6, whose grammatical roughness is sometimes smoothed out in English translations).

An Example of Broken Thought in Paul

"The ministering of this service is not only supplying fully the needs of the saints but is also overflowing through many thanksgivings to God. . . . because of the surpassing grace of God on you. Thanks to God for his indescribable gift! But by the meekness and gentleness of Christ . . . I beg you that when I come I may not have to be as bold as I propose to be toward some who regard us as behaving according to the flesh. . . . And we are ready to punish every disobedience, once your obedience is complete. You are looking at things superficially" (2 Corinthians 9:12–10:7, excerpts; note the sudden switch from thanks to warning).

The Cameo Appearance of an Amanuensis in Paul

"I, Tertius, who wrote down this letter, greet you in the Lord" (Romans 16:22).

A Final Word in Paul's Penmanship

"The greeting is in my own hand—Paul's" (1 Corinthians 16:21).

readership despite their fictitiously narrow addresses (compare modern "Letters to the Editor" intended for readers in general rather than for an editor in particular).

Amanuenses

For long documents like Paul's Letters, single papyrus sheets were joined edge to edge and rolled to form a scroll. Since the coarse grain of papyrus made writing tedious, authors usually dictated their letters to a professional scribe, called an *amanuensis* (plural, *-es*), who used shorthand during rapid dictation. The ruggedness of Paul's literary style—seen, for example, in numerous incomplete and otherwise broken sentences—suggests that at times he dictated too rapidly for close attention to careful sentence structure and that his amanuenses found it difficult to keep up. Sudden

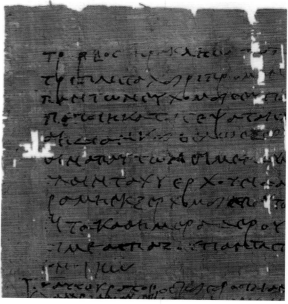

An ancient Greek letter on papyrus

breaks in thought similarly suggest temporary suspension of dictation, perhaps overnight, or for shorter or longer periods. Sometimes authors simply left oral instructions, a rough draft, or notes for their amanuenses to follow. Under such circumstances the amanuenses themselves molded the exact phraseology, a factor that may account for some of the stylistic differences among letters by the same author. The author finally edited the letter. We know for certain of Paul's using amanuenses from the fact that one of them identifies himself by name. Also, Paul's frequent statements that he is writing the final greeting with his own hand imply that the rest was written with the help of amanuenses (1 Corinthians 16:21; Galatians 6:11; Colossians 4:18; 2 Thessalonians 3:17; compare Philemon 19).

Format

Ancient letters opened with a **greeting**, which included the name of the sender and that of the recipient and usually wishes for good health and success and an assurance of the sender's prayers. The **main body** of the letter followed, and finally the **farewell** and sometimes a **signature**. Many times the farewell included greetings from others besides the author and further good wishes. Through fear that documents were being or might be forged in his

To Be Compared with Paul's Instructions to Various Social Classes in the Church:

"For parents belong to the superior class of the above-mentioned pairs, that which comprises seniors, rulers, benefactors, and masters, while children occupy the lower position with juniors, subjects, receivers of benefits, and slaves. And there are many other instructions given: to the young on courtesy to the old; to the old on taking care of the young; to subjects on obeying their rulers; to rulers on promoting the welfare of their subjects; to receivers of benefits on requiting them with gratitude . . . ; to servants on rendering an affectionate loyalty to their masters; to masters on showing the gentleness and kindness by which inequality is equalized" (Philo, *The Decalogue* 166–67).

name, Paul adopted the practice of writing the farewell lines as well as a signature with his own hand to guarantee authenticity. Usually letters carried no date. The lack of public postal service made it necessary to send letters with travelers.

↓*Parenesis*

Paul closes several of his letters with a section containing **ethical instructions**. Such instructions appear scattered throughout his other letters and letters by other writers of the New Testament. Scholars have noted striking similarities to Jewish and Stoic ethical codes of the same historical period. Nevertheless, the New Testament writers root Christian conduct in the dynamics of faith in Jesus rather than throwing out a lofty but lifeless set of precepts without power to effect their own fulfillment. The similarities of exhortations in the letters suggests that the authors draw from a common stock of parenetic (hortatory, instructional) tradition in the church, originally designed for catechizing newly converted candidates for baptism. On

---

parenesis: pair´uh-NEE-sis

**An Example of Similarities between New Testament
Letters in Ethical Instructions**

Romans 5:3–4	1 Peter 1:6–7	James 1:2–3
"And not only this, but we also exult in our tribulations, knowing that tribulation produces perseverance; and perseverance, tested genuineness; and tested genuineness, hope."	"In this you greatly rejoice, though now for a little while, if necessary, you may have suffered grief in various trials in order that the tested genuiness of your faith . . . ."	"Consider it all joy, my brothers and sisters, whenever you fall into various trials, knowing that the tested genuineness of your faith produces perseverance.'

Peter on Paul's letters

". . . just as our beloved brother Paul also wrote you . . . . as also in all his letters . . . . in which are some things hard to understand" (2 Peter 3:15–16).

**An Example of Similarities between Jesus
and New Testament Letters in Ethical Teaching**

Matthew 5:37	James 5:12
"But let your word 'Yes' be yes, and your 'No,' no."	"But let your word 'Yes' be yes, and your 'No,' no."

the other hand, Paul may simply develop his own set of ethical instructions for converts and influence later writers, such as Peter, who knew Paul's Letters. One further element needs mention, a drawing on Jesus' ethical teaching, preserved in oral and written tradition and often reflected in the phraseology and concepts of the letters.

Order

In our present New Testament, the order of Paul's letters written to churches depends on length, beginning with the longest (Romans) and ending with the shortest (2 Thessalonians). The same principle of arrangement holds for his letters written to individuals (1 and 2 Timothy, Titus, and Philemon). We will consider these letters in the chronological order of their writing so far as that order can be determined with some probability.

GALATIANS: AGAINST THE JUDAIZERS

Introductory Issues

The Judaizing Controversy

Though a few scholars think that Paul's opponents in Galatia were semipagan, semi-Jewish syncretists, perhaps of a Gnostic sort, it is far more likely that the letter to the Galatians has to do with the Judaizing controversy about which the Jerusalem Council met (Acts 15). As with that council, so

Galatia

also with Galatians it is almost impossible to overestimate how **historically crucial** were the theological issues at stake. Many of the first Christians, being Jewish, continued in large measure their Jewish mode of life, including attendance at the synagogue and temple, offering of sacrifices, observance of Mosaic rituals and dietary taboos, and social aloofness from Gentiles. Conversion of Gentiles forced the church to face several important questions:

- Should Gentile Christians be required to submit to circumcision and practice the Jewish way of life, as Gentile proselytes to Judaism were required to do?
- To those Gentile Christians unwilling to become wholly Jewish, should the church grant a second-class citizenship, as for Gentile "God-fearers" in Judaism?
- Most importantly, what makes a person Christian—faith in Christ **solely**, or faith in Christ **plus** adherence to the principles and practices of Judaism?

See again the discussion of Acts 15 (page 322–24).

Themes and Address

Galatians insists on **Christian liberty** from any doctrine of salvation that requires human effort in addition to divine grace, and on the **unity** of all believers in Jesus Christ. Paul writes this letter to believers residing in the region known as Galatia, but his use of the term *Galatia* has caused a debate

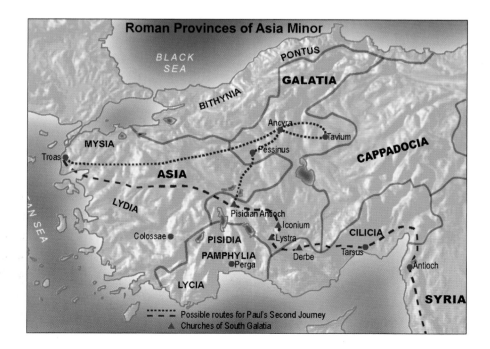

Roman Provinces of Asia Minor

Possible routes for Paul's Second Journey
▲ Churches of South Galatia

that affects our dating of the letter. In agreement with its original meaning, the term may refer exclusively to territory north of the cities of Pisidian Antioch, Iconium, and Lystra. Or it may also include those cities, for the Romans added southern districts when they made Galatia a province.

NORTH GALATIA According to the North Galatian theory, Paul addresses the letter to Christians in North Galatia, which he did not visit until his second journey on his way from Pisidian Antioch to ↓Troas. Under this view the letter could not have been written until some time after the beginning stage of the second journey and therefore after the Jerusalem Council of Acts 15, which preceded the second journey. Then the visit to Jerusalem that Paul describes in Galatians 2 probably has to do with the Jerusalem Council, recently held. Perhaps the strongest arguments for the North Galatian theory, with its late dating, are the original restriction of the term *Galatia* to the northern territory and the similarity of the statements by Paul concerning justification by faith to what he says in Romans, which he certainly wrote at a later date (see page 394).

Against the North Galatian theory, Luke nowhere suggests that Paul evangelized North Galatia. It is even doubtful that Paul visited that territory on his second journey, for "the region of Phrygia and Galatia" in Acts 16:6 more naturally refers to the southern territory. A traversing of North Galatia would have required an unlikely wide detour to the northeast. And elsewhere in his letters Paul consistently uses geographical terms in an imperial sense, which would allow South Galatia in his Letter to the Galatians.

SOUTH GALATIA According to the usual form of the South Galatian theory, Paul addresses his first letter to the churches in South Galatia just after the first missionary journey but before the Jerusalem Council. Then the visit to Jerusalem described in Galatians 2 has nothing to do with the Jerusalem Council, but refers instead to the famine relief visit mentioned in Acts 11:27–30. An argument in favor of the South Galatian address and early date is that if Paul wrote the letter after the Jerusalem Council, he would probably have capitalized on that council's decree favoring Gentile Christian freedom from the Mosaic law, the main topic under discussion in Galatians. But he makes no mention of the decree. This unlikely omission implies that the letter was written before the council met and therefore at a time when Paul had as yet visited only South Galatia. It is also doubtful that Peter would have vacillated, as he did according to Galatians 2:11–14, after the

> ## A Sample of Similarity Between Galatians and Romans
>
> - "A person is not justified by works of the law; a person is not justified except through faith in Jesus Christ" (Galatians 2:16).
> - "A person is justified by faith apart from works of the law" (Romans 3:28).

> "Before certain men came from James, he [Peter] used to eat with the Gentiles. But when they came, he started drawing back and separating himself because he was afraid of the circumcision party" (Galatians 2:12).

Troas: TROH-az

North Galatian Theory	South Galatian Theory
Paul's first missionary journey	Paul's first missionary journey
Jerusalem Council	Writing of Galatians
Paul's second missionary journey	Jerusalem Council
Writing of Galatians	Paul's second missionary journey

Jerusalem Council, where he strongly supported the position of freedom from the Mosaic law. By the time Paul went through North Galatia—if he did so at all on his second journey—Peter had declared that not even Jews were able to keep the law ("a yoke that neither our fathers nor we were able to bear," Acts 15:10). It remains possible to adopt a South Galatian address and, despite Paul's failure to mention the decree of the Jerusalem Council, a late date (say, shortly before Romans). Such a hybrid view pays homage to the most likely route of Paul's travels and to the similarity of Galatians to Romans, though that similarity may depend on an identity of issue without requiring proximity in time.

An Outline of Galatians

Introduction: A Greeting to the Galatians and an Anathema on the Judaizing Per-verters of the True Gospel (1:1–10)
I. An Autobiographical Argument for the Gospel of God's Free Grace (1:11–2:21)
    A. The direct revelation of that gospel by Jesus to Paul (1:11–12)
    B. The impossibility of its originating from Paul's own very Judaistic past (1:13)
    C. The impossibility of Paul's having learned it from merely human sources, the apostles, whom Paul met not until three years after his conversion and then only for a brief time (1:14–24)
    D. The later acknowledgment of Paul's gospel by the ecclesiastical leaders in Jerusalem (2:1–10)
    E. Paul's rebuke of Peter for his yielding to Judaizing pressure in Antioch, Syria (2:11–21)
II. A Theological Argument for the Gospel of God's Free Grace (3:1–5:12)
    A. The sufficiency of faith (3:1–5)
    B. The example of Abraham (3:6–9)
    C. The curse of the law (3:10–14)
    D. The divine covenant of promise to Abraham and his offspring, or seed (Christ and those united to him by faith), prior to the law of works (3:15–18)
    E. The purpose of the law, not to provide a way of salvation through human merit, but to demonstrate the necessity of divine grace through faith in Christ (3:19–4:7)

Reading Galatians with Interpretation

Introduction

The letter opens with a greeting in which Paul stresses his apostleship, for he wishes to establish his authority against the Judaizers. In place of the usual thanksgiving for his audience, Paul immediately and violently intro-duces the reason for his writing. He is shocked that the Galatian Christians are deserting to another gospel, which is not really a gospel ("good news") at all. *Read Galatians 1:1–10.*

Autobiographical Argument

Now Paul puts forward an autobiographical argument for the gospel of God's grace over against the Judaizing message, which requires adherence to the Mosaic law for salvation. He states that this gospel came to him by **direct rev-elation** from Jesus Christ. It certainly could not have come from his past, he argues, for before his divine call he had been zealous for Judaism. Nor did he learn it from the apostles in Jerusalem, for he did not even meet them until three years after his conversion. And when he did visit Jerusalem, he saw only Peter (whom Paul calls by the Aramaic equivalent and original Cephas) and James (Jesus' brother), stayed only fifteen days, and did not become acquainted with the Judean Christians at large. Since the gospel of grace could not have come from his Jewish past or from his Christian contacts in Jerusalem, it must have come from God. When he visited Jerusalem again after fourteen years (figured either from his call or from his first visit to Jerusalem), the leaders there—James, Peter, and John—formally **acknowl-edged** the correctness of the gospel of grace that he had been preaching to the Gentiles. They did so by giving him the right hand of fellowship. Further-more, they did not require Titus, his Gentile companion, to be circumcised.

Peter in Syrian Antioch

On coming to Antioch, Syria, Peter at first ate with Gentile Christians but then yielded to pressure from the Judaizers. Paul rebuked him publicly.

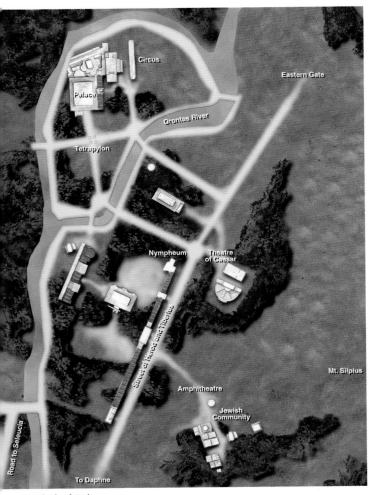

Antioch of Syria

Despite much present opinion to the contrary, the implication seems to be that Peter yielded to the rebuke. If not, Paul would hardly have brought up the incident as an argument in his favor. The fact that even Peter stood rebuked by Paul demonstrates the authority of Paul's gospel of grace. *Read Galatians 1:11–2:21.*

"Justify"

Paul's summary of his reprimand to Peter contains the germ of his theological argument to follow. Here Paul uses the term *justify,* which appears repeatedly, for God's treating believers in Christ as just—that is, righteous—even though they are sinners. In Classical Greek the term meant almost the opposite: to treat people justly, especially to secure justice for the righteous by punishing the wicked. (Our English words *just* and *righteous* go back to the same Greek adjective, as also *justice* and *righteousness* go back to the same Greek noun—and, for that matter, *faith* and *belief* go back to the same Greek noun.) Paul's use of "justify" echoes Old Testament usage, especially in Isaiah, where God graciously intervenes to set things right between himself and human beings. God's gracious intervention remains just, however, for Christ suffered the penalty for others' sins, a penalty necessitated by God's holiness, and the imputation—that is, crediting—of God's righteousness to the believer in Christ would make it unjust for God to condemn that believer.

EXCURSUS
"Works of the Law" and
"Faith of Jesus Christ"

More or less literally translated, Galatians 2:16a reads, "but knowing that a person is not justified by works of the law, but through faith of Jesus

Christ." The contextual references to circumcision and the religious calendar (2:3, 12; 4:10, 12–13; 5:2–6, 11; 6:12) highlight particular regulations in the Mosaic law that mark out Jews from Gentiles and cause social problems in the racially mixed churches of Galatia. But are "works of the law" restricted to such regulations? No, for throughout the rest of chapter 2 and the whole of chapter 3, Paul speaks of the Mosaic law in general; and elsewhere he lists as an element in his own law-righteousness prior to Christian conversion the zeal he showed in persecuting the church—hardly a Jewish identity marker on the order of circumcision (compare Numbers 24:6–18; Psalm 106:28–31). Therefore "works of the law" means obedience to the Mosaic law without restriction as a way of adding one's own righteousness to the righteousness of God for salvation. In the Judaism represented by the Dead Sea Scrolls, for example, justification is ascribed to God's goodness and abundant compassion: "Only by your goodness is a person justified, and by your abundant compassion . . ." (*Thanksgivng Hymns* [1QH] 5:22–23).

> ## Justification as Punishment in Classical Greek
>
> "He was a hard man in the observance of justice. . . . For when he heard that a man was doing violence, he would send for him and punish him [literally, 'justify him'] as befitted each offence" (Herodotus 1.100).
>
> ## Justification as Amnesty in Isaiah
>
> "All the offspring of the sons of Israel will be justified by the Lord, and they will be glorified by God" (Isaiah 45:25 LXX).

But to God's goodness and compassion are added works of the law: "Now we have written to you some of the works of the law . . . . And to your own benefit and that of Israel, it will be credited to you as righteousness when you do what is right and good before him [God]" (*Sectarian Manifesto* [4QMMT] C, 26–32). Paul tolerates no such addition, whether of ritual or of moral works of the law, as in his quotation of Genesis 15:6 concerning Abraham: "He *believed* God [in opposition to doing 'works of the law' as part of justification; 3:2–5], and it was credited to him as righteousness" (3:6).

The phrase "faith of Jesus Christ" in 2:16a raises another question of interpretation (similarly 2:16c; 3:22; Romans 3:22, 26; Ephesians 3:12; Philippians 3:12). Lately, some scholars have interpreted this phrase as referring to faith, or faithfulness, that Jesus Christ exercised rather than as faith of which he is the object. The English preposition "of" may make it sound as though Jesus Christ exercised faith or faithfulness, but the underlying Greek remains completely neutral on the question whether he is the subject or object of faith. Neither here nor elsewhere, however, does Paul say that Jesus "believes" or "is faithful." On the other hand, both here and elsewhere Paul repeatedly makes Jesus the object of people's believing (see, for example, the middle part of this very same verse: "even we have believed in Christ Jesus"). Therefore, the traditional interpretation that "faith of Jesus Christ" means "faith *in* Jesus Christ" stands firm.

A paraphrase may aid the understanding of 2:17–21: "If we have to forsake the law to be justified by faith in Christ, does Christ encourage sin? No; rather, if I go back to the law, I imply that I was sinning in abandoning it. But I did not sin in abandoning the law, for Christ died under the judgment of the law against sin. As a believer, I died with Christ in the sense that God counts Christ's death as mine too. Now the law has no authority over a dead person, especially one who has died under its penalty. So having died with Christ, I am no longer obligated to keep the law. But he rose and lives in me; and just as I died in Christ when he died and thus became free from the law, I likewise rose in Christ to a new life of righteousness in which the law plays no part. Therefore, if human beings could become righteous through keeping the law, Christ did not need to die."

Theological Arguments

Paul now develops his theological argument. It features three oppositions:

- **Law** versus **grace** and **promise**
- **Works** versus **faith**
- **Flesh** versus the **Spirit**

On the basis of these oppositions, Paul argues that if we are justified by faith at the start, we should continue by faith rather than by the law. Abraham was justified long before the law was given; so even in the Old Testament righteousness came by faith, not by the law. The law can only curse or condemn, because no one obeys it entirely. Christ died to deliver us from the law and its inevitable curse. God's making a covenant with Abraham before giving the law through Moses indicates that the Abrahamic covenant is more basic than the law. The law, then, did not annul it. On God's side, the Abrahamic covenant consisted of a promise to bless Abraham's seed; on the side of human beings, an acceptance of God's promise by faith. Abraham's **seed** consists of Christ plus all those incorporated into him by following Abraham's example of faith.

The law of Moses did have a purpose, but only a temporary one. It was to lead people to Christ as ancient slave-tutors led children to school. The law accomplished this purpose by making people keenly aware of their **inability** to make themselves righteous. Being under the law, therefore, was like being minors or slaves. But in Christ people live as free adults, adopted into God's family as sons and heirs with grown-up privileges and responsibilities. Why revert to an inferior status?

Paul then recalls how the Galatians accepted his message at their conversion and pleads with them to accept his present message as they did his first. He further supports his argument in rabbinic style by allegorizing an Old Testament story. ↓**Hagar** the slave woman stands for Mount Sinai,

Hagar: HAY-gahr

which in turn stands for the Mosaic law and its headquarters in Jerusalem, Palestine. **Ishmael** her slaveborn son stands for those who are enslaved to the law. **Sarah** stands for Christianity and its capital, the heavenly Jerusalem. **Isaac** her promised and freeborn son stands for all the spiritual children of Abraham, that is, those who follow Abraham's example of faith and are therefore freed in Christ from the law. *Read Galatians 3:1–5:12.*

A Warning

The last main section of the letter warns against ↓*libertinism,* or ↓*antinomianism* (literally, "against-law-ism"), the attitude that freedom from the law means license to sin. Not so, writes Paul. Christians must conduct themselves according to the Holy Spirit rather than according to the flesh (the sinful urge). Moreover, they must lovingly help others, especially their fellow Christians, and give liberally to those who minister the gospel. *Read Galatians 5:13–6:10.*

The contradiction between 6:2, "Bear one another's burdens," and 6:5, "For each shall bear his or her own load," is only apparent. In the first, Paul means that Christians should help one another in their **present** difficulties; in the second, that at the **future** judgment each person will answer to God for his or her own conduct alone.

To his prolonged attack on the Judaizers' legalism, Paul appends numerous precepts governing Christian conduct. These show that legalism does not consist merely in having rules. The books of the New Testament contain many rules of behavior. Legalism is rather the imposition of wrong rules, and particularly more rules than a situation warrants, so that in a

libertinism: LIB-uhr-tin-iz´uhm ■ antinomianism: an´ti-NOH-mee-uh-niz´uhm

Mount Sinai

maze of minutiae people lose their ability to distinguish the more important from the less important, the principle from its application. Legalism also includes a striving for merit in one's obedience, over against a recognition that obedience is nothing more than one's duty. The personal dimension of enjoying fellowship with God on the basis of his grace alone is consequently lost.

Paul adds a conclusion in his own handwriting. The "large letters" that he uses may be for emphasis, though some think that poor eyesight necessitated them. He charges that the Judaizers are motivated by a desire to avoid persecution from unbelieving Jews and by an ambition to boast that they are able to steal converts from him. By way of contrast, he calls attention to the sufferings he has gladly endured for his message and appeals to the Galatians that they themselves judge who has the purer motives, he or the Judaizers. *Read Galatians 6:11–18.*

FIRST THESSALONIANS: CONGRATULATIONS AND COMFORT

Introductory Issues

Themes

Paul's letters to the church in Thessalonica are best known for their teaching about the **second coming** of Jesus Christ and associated events. These two letters, the Olivet Discourse of Jesus, and the Apocalypse of John (the book of Revelation) form the three main predictively prophetic portions of the New Testament. In 1 Thessalonians this eschatological note belongs to the second of the two overall themes:

- Congratulations to the Thessalonian believers on their conversion and progress in the Christian faith
- Exhortations toward further progress, with particular emphasis on comfort from and expectancy toward the second coming

Background

Thessalonica, the capital city of Macedonia, lay on the ↓**Via Egnatia**, the main highway connecting Rome with the East. The city had its own government, led by politarchs, and a Jewish settlement. Paul evangelized the city on his second missionary journey. Some Jews and many Greeks and prominent women embraced the Christian faith. Paul's statement, "You

---

Via Egnatia: VEE-uh eg-NAH-tee-uh

Ruins of Roman Thessalonica

turned to God from idols" (1 Thessalonians 1:9), implies that the majority of Christians there were **Gentiles**, for Jews of that era did not practice idolatry. (The Assyro-Babylonian exile had cured them of it.) Unbelieving Jews in Thessalonica violently opposed the gospel by assaulting the house of Jason, Paul's host, and later traveled to Berea to drive Paul out of that city too.

According to Acts 17:2, Paul spent three Sabbaths preaching in the synagogue at Thessalonica. Luke's narrative seems to imply that the riot which forced Paul to leave occurred immediately following his ministry in the synagogue, and Acts 17:10 indicates that the Christians sent Paul away right after the riot. Some scholars have nevertheless put a gap between the ministry in the synagogue and the riot, because Paul mentions having worked for his own living in Thessalonica (1 Thessalonians 2:7–11) and having received one or two gifts from Philippi during his stay in Thessalonica (Philippians 4:16). But he may have begun working immediately on arrival in Thessalonica and continued for three or four weeks. Likewise, two offerings could have arrived from Philippi within a month.

Another argument for a longer stay in Thessalonica is that 1 and 2 Thessalonians presuppose more doctrinal teaching than Paul could have given in a month or so. But Paul probably taught his converts outside the synagogue on weekdays; and Timothy, who stayed longer in Thessalonica and after leaving returned again, must have taught them yet more. Therefore we should probably limit Paul's ministry in Thessalonica to about a month.

Occasion

Timothy rejoined Paul in Athens, went back to Thessalonica, and then rejoined Paul in Corinth. His report provided the occasion for Paul's writing of 1 Thessalonians (compare 3:1–2 with Acts 18:5). We infer, then, that Paul wrote 1 Thessalonians from **Corinth** during his **second journey**, not very many weeks after evangelizing the addressees.

An Outline of First Thessalonians

Introduction: Greeting (1:1)
I. Congratulations (1:2–3:13)
    A. Thanksgiving for the exemplary conversion of the Thessalonian believers (1:2–10)
    B. Paul's reminiscences concerning his ministry in Thessalonica (2:1–16)
    C. Timothy's glowing report about the progress of the Thessalonian Christians (2:17–3:10)
    D. A prayer for the Thessalonian believers (3:11–13)
II. Exhortations (4:1–5:22)
    A. To morality (4:1–8)
    B. To mutual love (4:9–12)
    C. To consolation over deceased fellow Christians because of their participation in the Parousia (4:13–18)
    D. To expectant readiness for the Day of the Lord (5:1–11)
    E. Miscellaneous exhortations (5:12–22)
Conclusion: A Benediction and Final Instructions (5:23–28)

Reading First Thessalonians with Interpretation

Congratulations

The first main section of 1 Thessalonians consists of congratulations to the Thessalonian believers on their conversion and on their progress in the Christian life. Their fidelity even in the midst of persecution is providing a good example to other Christians in Macedonia and Greece (Achaia). Timothy's report about them has been very favorable. *Read 1 Thessalonians 1:1–3:13.*

As usual, Paul combines the typical Greek greeting in a transmuted Christian form, "grace," with the typical Semitic greeting, "peace." The form of the word *grace* that non-Christian Greeks used carries the simple meaning of "hello," but Paul changes the term to

---

Christian Virtues and Their Effects

Faith → Good works
Love → Labor
Hope → Steadfastness

carry overtones of **divine favor** bestowed through Jesus Christ on ill-deserving sinners. "Peace" means more than the absence of warfare; it also carries the positive connotation of **prosperity** and **blessing**. A well-known triad of Christian virtues appears in 1:3: **faith, love,** and **hope.** Faith produces good works. Love results in labor, which means deeds of kindness and mercy. And hope, an eschatological term referring to confident expectation of Jesus' return, generates steadfastness under trial and persecution. In the middle of this congratulatory section, Paul reminds the Thessalonians of his loving, self-sacrificial ministry among them. Some have thought that he defends himself here against slander intended to destroy his influence. More probably, he stresses that in view of his laboring fervently among the Thessalonians, it gratifies him that they have responded well to the gospel.

Exhortations

Read 1 Thessalonians 4:1–5:28. Paul expertly passes from congratulation to exhortation by telling the Thessalonian Christians to continue their progress. The commands to live quietly and keep working may rebuke those who believe so strongly in the immediacy of Jesus' return that they are leaving their jobs. Paul's unblushing advocacy of manual labor contrasts with the view typical of Greeks, who held that sort of work in contempt.

Via Egnatia

Rapture is the term commonly used to designate the **catching up** of Christians at the second coming, as described in 4:16–17. *Translation* designates the **immortalizing** and **glorifying** of the bodies of Christians alive on earth when Jesus returns. Lack of need for a resurrection will necessitate such a change in their still-living but mortal bodies. The Thessalonian Christians have been sorrowing over the decease of fellow Christians, apparently because they do not realize that these fellow Christians will share in the joy of Jesus' return. Perhaps they think of death before the Parousia as chastisement for sin, or even as an indication of lost salvation. Paul reassures his audience by explaining that deceased Christians will be resurrected just before the rapture in order that they may be taken up **along with** Christians who are still alive on earth.

Then Paul shifts from **comfort** to **warning.** Christians must watch for the Day of the Lord (the second coming and following events) lest they be taken by surprise. Failure to watch is to put oneself in the category of the wicked, who *will* be caught unexpectedly. On the other hand, preparedness for the Day of the Lord consists of more than mental awareness. It includes also a mode of conduct characterized by obedience to commands such as those with which the letter closes.

SECOND THESSALONIANS: CORRECTION ON THE SECOND COMING

Introductory Issues

OCCASION AND THEME Some scholars reverse the order of 1 and 2 Thessalonians; but that view lacks support in ancient manuscripts and, among other considerations, 2 Thessalonians 2:15 ("you were taught through our letter") seems to presuppose 1 Thessalonians. So Paul writes 2 Thessalonians from **Corinth** on his **second missionary journey**, shortly after writing 1 Thessalonians. During the interval between writings, fanaticism increased in the church at Thessalonica. The fanaticism arose out of a belief in the immediacy of Jesus' return. Apparently that belief arose in turn out of a desire for deliverance from persecution. (The wish was the father of the thought.) Paul therefore writes this second letter to the Thessalonians to quiet the fanaticism by correcting the eschatology that gave rise to it.

An Outline of Second Thessalonians

Introduction: Greeting (1:1–2)
I. Persecution (1:3–12)
    A. Thanksgiving for the Thessalonian believers' progress in the midst of persecution (1:3–4)
    B. Assurance of deliverance from persecution and of divine judgment on persecutors at the Parousia (1:5–10)
    C. Prayer for the Thessalonian believers (1:11–12)
II. The Parousia, Rapture, and Day of the Lord (2:1–17)
    A. Denial that the Day of the Lord has arrived (2:1–2)
    B. Affirmation of necessary precedents (2:3–15)
        1. The rebellion (2:3a)
        2. The man of lawlessness (2:3b–15)
            a. His divine claim (2:3b–5)
            b. The present restraint of his appearance (2:6–7)
            c. His doom (2:8)
            d. His deceitfulness (2:9–12)

       e. The protection of Thessalonian Christians from his deceitfulness and
         doom (2:13–15)
   C. Benediction (2:16–17)
III. Exhortations (3:1–15)
   A. To prayer, love, and stability (3:1–5)
   B. To industrious labor (3:6–13)
   C. To disciplinary ostracism of disobedient church members (3:14–15)
Conclusion: A Further Benediction and a Final Greeting, with Emphasis on Paul's
   Own Handwriting in the Last Few Lines to Guarantee the Authenticity of This
   Letter (3:16–18)

Reading Second Thessalonians with Interpretation

Encouragement

After an initial greeting, Paul again thanks God for the progress of the
Thessalonian believers in their Christian life and for their patient endurance
of persecution; but the commendation is much shorter than in 1 Thessalonians. Passing quickly to the subject of eschatology, Paul vividly describes
the second coming, when persecutors will be judged and the persecuted
relieved of their sufferings. His purpose is to encourage the Thessalonians
to continued endurance by pointing forward to the turning of the tables
when Christ comes back. Then Paul begins to deal with their misunderstanding of the Parousia by saying that it is not immediate. Therefore, they
should return to their jobs and businesses. Looking for Christ's return does
not mean cessation of normal living. He may not return for some length of
time. *Read 2 Thessalonians 1:1–3:18.*

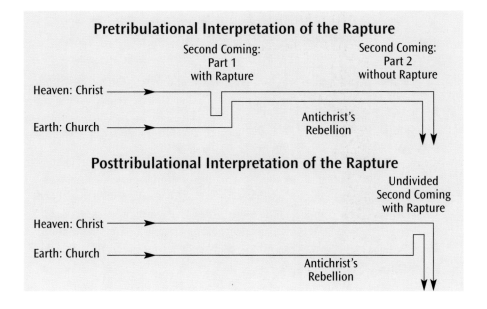

Correction

Paul's warning not to be deceived by a false prophecy or by an oral or written report forged in his name suggests that the leaders of the fanaticism in Thessalonica claimed his support. The phrase "man of lawlessness" (2:3) refers to the antichrist, a world leader of wickedness and persecution in the last days. This evil figure will demand worship of himself in the temple of God; that is, he will try to force the Jewish people to worship his image, which he will place in the temple at Jerusalem (compare Mark 13:14; Matthew 24:15; Revelation 13:1–18). The suggestion that this concept of an antichrist originates in the myth that Nero had not really died but would return to Rome with a vengeance stumbles against the pre-Neronian date of the concept or would require us to reject without sufficient reason the authenticity of 2 Thessalonians by dating the letter after Paul's martyrdom and after Nero's death. It is also suggested that Paul has in mind the unfulfilled order of Emperor Caligula in A.D. 40 that a statue of himself be erected for worship in the temple at Jerusalem. Perhaps so, but Daniel's prophecy concerning the abomination of desolation (9:27; 11:31; 12:11), the desecration of the temple by Antiochus Epiphanes in 168 B.C., and Jesus' allusion to a still future abomination of desolation (see the references above) provide the primary background for Paul's statements.

Restraint-Restrainer

Paul feels it unnecessary to identify what or who restrains the antichrist from appearing until the proper time, for the Thessalonians already know from his oral teaching. According to the two most probable suggestions, the

A Myth about Nero

- "He met his death in the thirty-second year of his age .... Yet there were some who for a long time ... produced his edicts as if he were still alive and would shortly return and deal destruction to his enemies" (Suetonius, *Lives of the Caesars*, "Nero" 57).
- "About this time Achaia and Asia were terrified by a false rumor of Nero's arrival. The reports with regard to his death had been varied, and therefore many people imagined and believed that he was alive" (Tacitus, *Histories* 2.8).
- "Beliar will descend ... from his firmament in the form of a man, a king of iniquity, a murderer of his mother.... He will say, 'I am the Lord, and before me there was no one.' And all men in the world will believe in him. They will sacrifice to him and will serve him .... And after 1,332 days the Lord will come with his angels ... and will drag Beliar, and his hosts also, into Gehenna. And he will give rest to the pious whom he finds in the body of this world" (Martyrdom and Ascension of Isaiah 4:2–15, excerpts).

restraint consists (1) in the institution of **human government**, personified in rulers such as the Roman emperor and his underlings and ordained by God for the protection of law and order (the antichrist will be "lawless") or (2) in the activity of the **Holy Spirit**, keeping back the antichrist either directly or through the medium of the church. Others think that Paul refers to missionary preaching as the restraint and to himself, the leading missionary, as the restrainer; but it is difficult to think that he anticipated his own special removal as a condition of the antichrist's appearance, for elsewhere he looks for the Parousia just as other Christians do. Finally, the emphasis on Paul's own handwriting as an indication of the genuineness of this letter may imply that a letter has been forged in Paul's name to support the fanaticism at Thessalonica.

Summary

By and large, Paul's letters are hybrids of a private letter and a literary epistle. Like other authors, he employed the services of amanuenses. The bulk of his letters contain theological and parenetic materials, sometimes in succession, sometimes mixed. The letters to churches come first in the New Testament, then those to individuals; and within each group the order is one of decreasing length.

Galatians probably comes first in the order of writing, postdates Paul's first missionary journey, antedates the Jerusalem Council and second missionary journey, and has a South Galatian address. The letter takes aim against the Judaizing heresy, according to which salvation requires adherence to the Mosaic law, beginning with circumcision. Both autobiographically and theologically, Paul argues for justification by faith alone—from beginning to end—a justification made possible by God's viewing believers in Christ as so united to Christ that when he died and rose again, they too died and rose again. At the same time Paul warns against misconstruing liberty from the Mosaic law as license to sin. The exercise of such license would betray an absence of the Holy Spirit, without whom the union with Christ that makes justification by faith possible does not take place.

Paul writes 1 Thessalonians from Corinth during Paul's second missionary journey. The letter responds to a report by Timothy concerning the state of the church in Thessalonica. The good progress of recent converts there draws Paul's praise, and their sorrow over the decease of some in their number draws words of comfort from him. The comfort consists of an assurance that deceased Christians will share in the event of the Lord's return. In the meantime, says Paul, living believers should remain alert so as not to be taken by surprise.

Paul writes 2 Thessalonians a little later than 1 Thessalonians during his stay in Corinth on the second missionary journey. Between the two letters, there has arisen among Thessalonian believers a belief in the immediacy of Jesus' return to destroy their persecutors. Not so fast, says Paul. The end-of-the-age rebellion against God—a rebellion led by "the man of lawlessness" (Paul's term for the antichrist)—must take place first. So go back to normal Christian living.

People to Remember

For Galatians	Ishmael	**For 1 and 2 Thessalonians**
Abraham	James the Lord's brother	Caligula
Cephas/Peter	John the apostle	Nero
Hagar	Sarah	Timothy
Isaac	Titus	

Places to Remember

For Galatians	North Galatia	**For 1 and 2 Thessalonians**
earthly Jerusalem	Phrygia and Galatia	Corinth
heavenly Jerusalem	South Galatia	Via Egnatia
Mount Sinai		

Terms to Remember

amanuensis	imputation	**For 1 and 2 Thessalonians**
epistle	justify/justification	Day of the Lord
letter	law/works/flesh	man of lawlessness
parenesis	legalism	Parousia
For Galatians	libertinism/antinomianism	peace
Abraham's seed	union with Christ	rapture
grace or promise/faith/Spirit		restraint/restrainer
		translation

How Much Did You Learn?

- Distinguish between ancient letters and literary epistles. Compare and contrast Paul's letters with them.
- Of what significance is Paul's use of amanuenses for questions of authorship?
- Outline the format of a typical ancient letter.
- Distinguish the canonical and chronological orders of Paul's Letters.

- Rehearse some arguments for and against the North and South Galatian addresses of Galatians.
- Interrelate the contents of Galatians and the decree of the Jerusalem Council.
- Interrelate justification by faith alone and believers' union with Christ.
- How does the information in Acts about Paul's ministry in Thessalonica aid an understanding of the situations Paul addresses in 1 and 2 Thessalonians?
- Contrast the main problem addressed by Paul in 1 Thessalonians with the one addressed by him in 2 Thessalonians—also his solutions to them.

GALATIANS

For Further Discussion

- What manifestations of legalism exist within contemporary Christendom?
- What modern forms does antinomianism take?
- Compare Paul's concept of Christian freedom with current situational ethics, and the Christian ethic of love with the secular ethic of love.
- How does Paul's emphasis on love tally with his anathema on the Judaizers?
- How can Christian parents avoid both legalism and permissiveness in rearing their children?
- How can Christian educational institutions, churches, and missionary agencies avoid both legalism and libertinism?
- Compare Paul's account of his visit to Jerusalem (Galatians 2:1–10) with Luke's account of the Jerusalem Council (Acts 15:1–29). How are they similar? How do they differ? Are they readily harmonized?

For Further Investigation

Bunyan, J. *Grace Abounding to the Chief of Sinners.*

Chafer, L. S. *Grace.* Grand Rapids: Zondervan, 1922.

Danby, H. *The Mishnah.* London: Oxford, 1933. Almost any part of this translation of the Mishnah will give the flavor of rabbinic legalism.

Dunn, J. D. G. *The Theology of Paul's Letter to the Galatians.* Cambridge: Cambridge University Press, 1993.

Genesis 15–17; 21:1–21. For Old Testament passages referred to by Paul.

Hansen, G. W. *Galatians.* Downers Grove, Ill.: InterVarsity Press, 1994.

Jervis, L. A. *Galatians.* Peabody, Mass.: Hendrickson, 1999.

Lührmann, D. *Galatians A Continental Commentary.* Minneapolis: Fortress Press, 1992.

Luther, M. "The Argument of St. Paul's Epistle to the Galatians." In *Luther's Works*. Vol. 26. St. Louis: Concordia, 1963. Pp. 4–12.

_____. "The Freedom of a Christian." In *Luther's Works*. Vol. 31. Philadelphia: Muhlenberg, 1957. Pp. 328–77.

Martyn, J. L. *Galatians*. New York: Doubleday, 1997. Advanced.

McKnight, S. *The NIV Application Commentary: Galatians*. Grand Rapids: Zondervan, 1995.

Silva, M. *Interpreting Galatians: Explorations in Exegetical Method*. 2d ed. Grand Rapids: Baker, 2001. Advanced.

Stowers, S. K. *Letter-Writing in Greco-Roman Antiquity*. Philadelphia: Westminster, 1986.

FIRST AND SECOND THESSALONIANS

For Further Discussion

- What doctrines and how much insight from Paul's previous oral ministry do the Thessalonian letters presuppose? Compare these doctrines with the level of evangelistic preaching today.
- From the Thessalonian letters construct an outline of future eschatological events. Why is it sketchy? Attempt to fit it with Jesus' Olivet Discourse (Mark 13; Matthew 24–25; Luke 21) and the book of Revelation.
- Infer the Thessalonians' reaction to 1 Thessalonians from what Paul writes in 2 Thessalonians. Then imagine what their response to 2 Thessalonians might have been.

For Further Investigation

Best, E. *The First and Second Epistles to the Thessalonians*. Peabody, Mass.: Hendrickson, 1987.

Donfried, K. P., and I. H. Marshall. *The Theology of the Shorter Pauline Letters*. Cambridge: Cambridge University Press, 1993.

Gaventa, B. R. *First and Second Thessalonians*. Louisville: Westminster John Knox, 1998.

Green, G. L. *The Letters to the Thessalonians*. Grand Rapids: Eerdmans, 2002.

Gundry, R. H. *First the Antichrist*. Grand Rapids: Baker, 1997. For the view that the rapture of the church will not occur until after the tribulation.

Holmes, M. W. *The NIV Application Commentary: 1 and 2 Thessalonians*. Grand Rapids: Zondervan, 1998.

Morris, L. *The First and Second Epistles to the Thessalonians*. 2d ed. Grand Rapids: Eerdmans, 1991. Advanced.

Walvoord, J. F. *The Rapture Question*. Revised and enlarged edition. Grand Rapids: Zondervan, 1979. For the view that the rapture of the church will occur before the tribulation.

THE MAJOR LETTERS OF PAUL

Overview:

- First Corinthians: Church Problems
- Second Corinthians: Paul's Conception of His Ministry
- Romans: The Gift of God's Righteousness through Faith in Christ
- Summary

Study Goals—Learn:

- Paul's connections and communications with the Corinthian church prior to the writing of 1 Corinthians
- How and why the church in Corinth had sunk into the deplorable condition reflected in 1 Corinthians
- The specific problems in the church at Corinth and Paul's remedies for them

Ancient Corinth

FIRST CORINTHIANS: CHURCH PROBLEMS

Introductory Issues

Purpose

The First Letter of Paul to the Corinthians demonstrates that lamentable conditions in the church do not characterize the postapostolic church alone. Aberrant beliefs and practices of astonishing variety and vulgarism flourished in the Corinthian church. It is to solve those problems that Paul writes this letter.

Previous Ministry in Corinth

On first arriving in Corinth, according to Acts 18:1–18a, Paul made tents with Aquila and Priscilla. Sabbath days he preached in the synagogue. After Silas and Timothy rejoined him, he wrote 1 and 2 Thessalonians; moved his preaching activity next door to the house of ↓Titius Justus; converted Crispus, ruler of the synagogue; received from the Roman proconsul Gallio a dismissal of Jewish accusations against him; and ministered altogether one and a half years in the city.

Titius Justus: TISH-ee-uhs JUHS-tuhs

Sunset over the Gulf of Corinth

A Lost Earlier Letter

The statement in 1 Corinthians 5:9, "I wrote you in my letter not to associate with immoral people," implies that Paul wrote to the church in Corinth an earlier letter, which has since been lost. The Corinthians misunderstood that letter to mean they were to dissociate themselves from *all* immoral people. Now Paul explains that he had in mind dissociation only from *professing Christians* who live in flagrant sin.

Time and Place of Writing

First Corinthians, then, is really the second letter written by Paul to the church in Corinth. He writes it from the city of **Ephesus** during his **third missionary journey.** The end of his stay there has nearly come, for he is already planning to leave (16:5–8). Some have translated 16:10, "*when* Timothy comes," and inferred that Timothy will carry the letter to Corinth. But Acts 19:22 says that Paul "sent two of his helpers, Timothy and ↓Erastus, to Macedonia, while he stayed in the province of Asia [where Ephesus was located] a little longer." This statement suggests that Timothy has gone to Macedonia by the time of writing and supports a better translation of 1 Corinthians 16:10: "*if* Timothy comes [from Macedonia to you in Corinth]." Were Timothy carrying the letter, Paul would hardly write "if." Paul tried to induce Apollos, a very important figure, to visit Corinth and probably intended to send 1 Corinthians with him. But Apollos refused (16:12), so that the carrier remains unknown.

Occasion

Two events prompted the writing of 1 Corinthians: (1) the bringing of **oral reports** by the household of ↓Chloe regarding contentions in the Corinthian church (1:11); (2) the coming of a delegation from the Corinthian church—↓Stephanas, ↓Fortunatus, and ↓Achaicus—both with an **offering** (16:17) and with a **letter asking Paul's judgment** on various problems, which he takes up successively with the introductory phrase, "Now concerning . . . ," or simply, "Now . . . ." At least this understanding seems to follow from 16:17 ("these men have supplied what was lacking on your part") and 7:1 ("now concerning the things you wrote about"). Otherwise, Stephanas, Fortunatus, and Achaicus merely assuaged Paul's desire to see all the Corinthian Christians in person and the letter from Corinth arrived through other hands. Chloe is a feminine name. The members of her household were probably slaves. It remains uncertain whether they visited Paul in Ephesus,

---

Persistent Problems in Corinth

"The more things change, the more they stay the same":

Around fifty years after Paul wrote concerning problems in the church at Corinth, a bishop of the church in Rome wrote to the church in Corinth about a further problem: "It is a shameful report, beloved, extremely shameful and unworthy of your training in Christ, that on account of one or two persons the steadfast and ancient church of the Corinthians is being disloyal to the elders" (*1 Clement* 47:6).

Erastus: i-RAS-tuhs ■ Chloe: KLOH-ee ■ Stephanus: STEF-uh-nuhs ■ Fortunatus: for´chuh-NAY-tuhs ■ Achaicus: uh-KAY-uh-kuhs

> "Corinth is called 'wealthy' because of its commerce, since it is situated on the Isthmus and is master of two harbors, of which the one leads straight to Asia and the other to Italy; and it makes easy the exchange of merchandise from both countries that are so far distant from each other. . . . The Isthmian Games, which were celebrated there, regularly drew crowds of people. . . . And the temple of Aphrodite was so rich that it owned more than a thousand temple-slaves, courtesans [a probably exaggerated figure in regard to Corinth at an earlier period] . . . . The ship-captains freely squandered their money, and hence the proverb, 'Not for every man is the voyage to Corinth' [with the implication, 'If you get the chance, don't miss it']. Moreover, it is recorded that a certain courtesan said. . . , 'Yet . . . in this short time I have lowered three masts'" (Strabo, *Geography* 8.6.20).

having come from Corinth, or visited Corinth from Ephesus and reported back to Paul.

Municipal Background

The city of Corinth was located on a narrow isthmus between the ↓Aegean Sea and the ↓Adriatic Sea. The voyage around the southern tip of Greece was dangerous. Many ships were therefore carried or dragged on rollers across the isthmus and put to sea again. For various reasons several attempts to dig a canal were abandoned. As a juncture for commerce and travel, Corinth was quite cosmopolitan. The athletic games that used to be held there had ranked second only to the Olympics. The outdoor theater accommodated twenty thousand people; the roofed theater, three thousand. Temples, shrines, and altars dotted the city. Prostitution flourished. The south side of the marketplace was lined with taverns equipped with underground cisterns for cooling the drinks. Archaeologists have discovered numerous drinking vessels in these liquor lockers; some bear inscriptions, such as "Health," "Security," "Love," and the names of gods. It is natural that a church set in such extreme paganism should bristle with problems. First Corinthians deals with them almost entirely.

> ### "Now . . ."
>
> "Now concerning the things you wrote about" (7:1)
> "Now concerning virgins" (7:25)
> "Now concerning food sacrificed to idols" (8:1)
> "Now I praise you" (11:2)
> "Now concerning spiritual gifts" (12:1)
> "Now I make known to you, brothers and sisters, the gospel that I preached to you" (15:1)
> "Now concerning the collection for the saints" (16:1)

An Outline of First Corinthians

Introduction: Greeting to and Thanksgiving for the Corinthian Church (1:1–9)
I. Reproofs in Response to Reports by the Household of Chloe (1:10–6:20)

Aegean: ee-JEE-uhn ■ Adriatic: ay´dree-AT-ik

A. Divisions and the necessity of their healing by recognition of the weak humanity of Christian leaders and their followers over against the power of God in the gospel of the cross (1:10–4:21)

B. The case of a man cohabiting with his stepmother and the necessity of disciplining the offender by ostracism from Christian fellowship (5:1–13)

C. Lawsuits between Christians and the necessity of their settlement by the church outside secular courts (6:1–8)

D. Immorality in general and the necessity that Christians live virtuously by the indwelling Holy Spirit (6:9–20)

II. Replies to Questions Raised in a Letter from the Corinthians (7:1–16:9)

A. Marriage, its essential goodness, but the advantage to some of an unmarried state; restriction of divorce; and exhortation to reconciliation (7:1–40)

B. Food, especially meat, offered to idols and its allowance for Christians provided they neither abuse their freedom by injuring the consciences of the theologically ignorant nor join in idolatrous banquets (8:1–11:1)

C. Order of public worship (11:2–14:40)

1. The requirement of a head-covering for women who pray and prophesy in church services (11:2–16)

2. The Lord's Supper, its desecration in the Corinthian church by disunity and overindulgence, and the requirements of reverence and discontinuance of love feasts (11:17–34)

3. Spiritual gifts (12:1–14:40)

a. Diversity of function within the unity of the church as the body of Christ (12:1–31)

b. The supremacy of love (13:1–13)

c. The superiority of prophesying and inferiority of speaking in tongues, with rules for orderliness (14:1–40)

D. The resurrection, from Christ's in the past to believers' in the future (15:1–58)

E. The collection for the church in Jerusalem, its manner of gathering and delivery (16:1–9)

Conclusion: Timothy's Coming Visit to Corinth, Apollos's Failure to Visit, Miscellaneous Exhortations, Final Greetings, and a Benediction (16:10–24)

Corinthian canal, dug in modern times

Reading First Corinthians with Interpretation

Disunity

Read 1 Corinthians 1:1–4:21. Corinthian factionalism has derived from **hero worship**. The admirers of **Paul** are loyal to him because he founded the church in Corinth, but he does not side even with his own admirers. The admirers of **Apollos** are apparently spellbound by his learning and eloquence. The followers of **Cephas** (Peter) may be a Jewish segment of the church or traditionalists who rest on the authority of the foremost original apostle. The admirers of **Christ** are sometimes regarded as those who want to avoid squabbles and therefore withdraw in an attitude of superior spirituality. More probably, though, "I belong to Christ" represents Paul's own position in condemnation of those who admire merely human leaders (see 3:21–23). Doctrinal differences seem not to underlie the personality cults. At least the factions are still meeting together, for Paul addresses a single letter to them.

> "But the fact is, gentlemen, it is likely that the god ['of Delphi'] is really wise and by his oracle means this: 'Human wisdom is of little or no value'" (Socrates according to Plato, *Apology* 23A).

In writing that he is glad for not having baptized very many of the Corinthians, Paul is not denying the validity of baptism (he admits to the baptism of some) but is strongly denying that he or any other Christian evangelist should baptize converts to gain a personal following. On the contrary, the proper task of Christian evangelists is hardly popular, for the preaching of a Savior who died as a criminal—that is, by crucifixion—offends human pride and worldly wisdom. Consequently, most believers come from the lower strata of society. But what they lack by way of background and attainment Christ more than makes up: he is their wisdom, righteousness, sanctification, and redemption, for all of which God is the source.

Paul recalls that on coming to Corinth from Athens, where the worldly wise philosophers had rejected him, he preached the **cross of Christ** in weakness and trembling, not with the rhetorical methods of sophistic philosophers. Alternatively, he did not preach that salvation comes through embracing wisdom, religiously and philosophically conceived and limited to the spiritually elite. Nevertheless, he claims to teach **genuine wisdom**, the kind that comes from the **Holy Spirit**, who alone knows the mind of God.

Because of the factionalism in Corinth, Paul charges the Christians there with **carnality**, or **fleshliness** in the sense of **sinfulness**. Boasting in human leaders is wrong, he

Different Meanings of "Flesh" in the New Testament

- The soft tissues of the body, as distinguished from bones
- The body as a whole
- An individual person
- Humanity in general
- Human ancestry
- External appearance
- Physical conditions
- The sexual urge (legitimate within bounds)
- The sinful urge (illegitimate by definition)

says, because they are only human beings. Furthermore, they are fellow workers, not rivals. The section closes with an admonition to **unity**. By implication, Christians can achieve unity if they want it and work for it.

Immorality

Read 1 Corinthians 5:1–7:40. Paul brings up the case of a man living immorally with his father's wife. Presumably she is his stepmother, since Paul does not identify her as the man's own mother. And apparently she is a non-Christian and therefore outside the jurisdiction of the church, since Paul does not prescribe any punishment for her. He rebukes the Corinthians for their arrogant pride in condoning such flagrant sin within their number and commands **discipline** in the form of dismissal from the fellowship of the church, that is, social ostracism and exclusion from the Lord's Supper. The problem of **Christians going to court against one another** may have some connection with the case of immorality, for the discussion of this problem occurs in the middle of Paul's reproof concerning immorality. He cautions that ceremonial freedom does not imply moral freedom and stresses that as a **temple of the Holy Spirit** the body is sacred.

> "Union with one's stepmother ... is viewed with abhorrence as an outrageous crime" (Josephus, *Jewish Antiquities* 3.12.1 §274).

Celibacy

Voluntary celibacy is good, writes Paul, but because of sexual desire God has provided marriage for the avoidance of illicit unions. Within marriage, then, spouses should give themselves sexually to each other. Paul wishes that all might be free from marital responsibilities, as he is, because of the single person's ability to devote full energy to preaching the gospel. Nevertheless, Paul concedes that in this respect God's will varies for different Christians.

Marriage and Divorce

On the question of divorce, Paul does not show so much flexibility. Divorce reached epidemic proportions in some classes of Greco-Roman society. Paul repeats **Jesus' teaching against divorce** so far as Christian couples are concerned and at most allows them separation with the possibility of reconciliation. But Jesus' words do not cover the case of husbands or wives who have converted after marriage but whose spouses have not. Therefore Paul advises the Christian spouse to **stay** with the non-Christian spouse, if at all possible, at least partly because the non-Christian and any children in the family are consecrated by

The Body as a Temple

Compare the following with Paul's statement that the Christian's body is a temple of the Holy Spirit: "You are a fragment of God; you have within you a part of him. ... It is within yourself that you bear him and do not perceive that you are defiling him with impure thoughts and filthy actions" (Epictetus, *Discourses* 2.8.11, 13). But note that for Epictetus a human being bears deity as a part of that deity, whereas for Paul a Christian bears deity as a redeemed creature distinct from deity.

the close range of Christian witness in the home. If the non-Christian insists on breaking up a marriage, however, the Christian is "not enslaved." It is debatable whether this phrase means only that the Christian is not obligated to seek reconciliation, or also that the Christian is free to remarry within the Christian fellowship (the so-called "Pauline privilege"). Paul's indication that these instructions are his own rather than the Lord's does not imply that they lack authority, but only that Jesus said nothing on these points, and therefore Paul must give his own teaching as one who is "trustworthy" and possesses the Spirit.

> "You must not get married or rear children, since our race is weak and marriage and children burden human weakness with troubles" (Diogenes, *Letter 47* [to Zeno]).

The last part of chapter 7, especially verses 36–38, poses difficult problems of interpretation. Is Paul referring to spiritual marriages, never physically consummated? To engaged couples? To unengaged sweethearts? Or to a Christian father, his daughter, and her suitor? The main lessons, however, are clear. On the one hand, marriage is not to be condemned on the basis of asceticism. On the other hand, marriage is not to be contracted out of social pressure. Single Christians can often lead fuller, richer, and more productive lives than married Christians. Throughout, Paul stresses the critical nature of the period in which Christians are living. He probably has in mind the possibility of the Lord's return, a possibility that should lend a sense of urgency to Christian work and witness.

Food Dedicated to Idols

It is important to understand the background of Paul's discussion concerning food associated with the worship of idols. In the ancient world pagan shrines were the main suppliers of meat for human consumption. Thus, most of the meat in butcher shops had come from animals sacrificed to idols. The gods received a token portion—usually not a choice cut—burned on the altar. After priests and priestesses took their portions and the worshiper and family consumed further portions, the remainder of meat went up for sale to the general public. But Jews purchased their meat in Jewish shops, where they could be sure that it had not come from an animal sacrificed to a pagan god. Should Christians be as scrupulous as the Jews? *Read 1 Corinthians 8:1–11:1.*

Serving False Gods

- "While Israel was staying in Shittim, the men began to indulge in sexual immorality with Moabite women, who invited them to the sacrifices to their gods; and the men ate and bowed down before their gods" (Numbers 25:1–2).
- "Chaeremon requests your company at dinner at the table of the lord Sarapis [a god] in the Serapaeum [the god's temple] tomorrow, the 15th, at 9 o'clock" (Oxyrhynchus Papyrus 110).

Christian Freedom and the Law of Love

Paul advocates freedom to eat but cautions his audience lest their exercise of that freedom inflict spiritual damage on people with uninformed consciences. In other words, Christians who understand that an idol has no real divine existence may eat meat dedicated to the idol without damage to their conscience. But if people who mistakenly think that idols have real divine existence happen to be observing, better-informed Christians should then refrain from eating such meat, lest they damage the Christian life of uninformed, recently converted Christians and lest they mar their witness to uninformed, idolatrous non-Christians.

↓Adiaphora

The balance between freedom and the "law of love" covers only adiaphora, that is, ritual and other questions that are **morally neutral**. So Paul warns that though he allows the judicious eating of meat dedicated to idols, by no means does he allow participation in idolatrous feasts associated with pagan worship. It would be blatant inconsistency for a Christian to partake both of the Lord's Supper and of suppers demonically designed to foster the worship of false gods. When in Old Testament times the people of Israel joined in such pagan feasts, Paul notes, they also fell into forms of pagan worship that led to immoralities.

Head-Covering

Paul's instructions on the head-covering of women are traditionally understood in terms of veiling (though not with the kind of veil that covers the face as well as the head). On the other hand, he never uses the specific Greek word for a veil; and he says that a woman's long hair is given her for a covering. In either case, his concern is to maintain a visible distinction between women and men with respect to long and short hair. *Read 1 Corinthians 11:2–16.*

Long hair as a woman's head-covering

The Lord's Supper and Love Feasts

Read 1 Corinthians 11:17–34. Paul states that factionalism among the Corinthians makes mockery of their communion services, which are to be times of Christian fellowship. The Corinthians are celebrating the Lord's Supper in conjunction with a love feast, a kind of church potluck corresponding in a way to the Passover meal, during which Jesus instituted the Lord's Supper. Some of the Corinthians are coming early to the meeting place, eating their meal, and taking communion before the arrival of others who have longer working hours. Some are even getting drunk. Maybe they take so sacramental a view of the Lord's Supper that they think the more bread and more wine, the more divine grace. In any case, Paul commands **discontinuance** of the love feasts, **delay** of the Lord's Supper until the arrival of latecomers, **introspection**, and **reverence**. His rehearsal of the institution

adiaphora: ad´i-AF-uh-rah

of the Lord's Supper comes from **presynoptic tradition**, which originated in the action of the Lord Jesus himself. "I received . . ." (11:23) is technical for the reception of tradition that has been handed down.

Speaking in Tongues

↓*Charismata* ("gifts") and ↓*glossolalia* ("speaking in tongues") make up the subject matter of chapters 12–14. Many hold that the speaking in tongues discussed here by Paul consists of speaking ecstatically, perhaps in a heavenly or angelic language, but not in human languages. He does indeed state that apart from the gift of interpretation not even a speaker in tongues knows what he or she is saying. But "interpretation" usually means *translation*. It would therefore seem that in Paul's usage, tongues-speaking consists in the **miraculous speaking of unlearned human languages**. The tongues are sometimes unintelligible, then, not because they are ecstatic nonlanguages, but because on some occasions neither the speaker nor anyone else present in the audience happens to possess the equally miraculous gift of translation.[1]

1. See further R. H. Gundry, "'Ecstatic Utterance' (N.E.B.)?" *Journal of Theological Studies,* new series 17 (1966): 299–307.

Love and Spiritual Gifts

Through valuing tongues-speaking too highly, the Corinthians have been overusing the gift. Paul devalues it and insists that its use be orderly and limited. At the expense of tongues-speaking, he magnifies superior gifts, in particular, prophecy, which communicates direct revelation from God, needed especially though not necessarily exclusively in the early church in

charismata: kuh-RIZ-muh-tah ■ *glossolalia:* glos´uh-LAY-lee-uh

Spiritual Gifts in Paul's Letters

1 Corinthians 12:8–10	1 Corinthians 12:28–30	Romans 12:6–8	Ephesians 4:11
word of wisdom	apostles	prophecy	apostles
word of knowledge	prophets	service	prophets
faith	teachers	teaching	evangelists
healings	miracles	exhortation	pastor-teachers
miracles	healings	giving	
prophecy	helps	leading	
distinguishing of spirits	administrations	mercy-showing	
kinds of tongues	kinds of tongues		
interpretation of tongues	interpretation		

lieu of the New Testament Scriptures. Above all, Paul celebrates the Christian ethic of love in the prose poem of the famous thirteenth chapter. There is no proper exercise of the spiritual gifts apart from love; there is no love in the church apart from the exercise of spiritual gifts. *Read 1 Corinthians 12:1–14:40.*

Paul's concept of **the church as the body of Christ** stands out prominently in chapter 12 and emphasizes respect for the **variety** of spiritual gifts. The prohibition against women's speaking in church (14:34–35) can hardly be absolute, for Paul has just given instructions in chapter 11 for the head-covering of women so that they may pray and prophesy in public worship. "If they want to learn anything, let them ask their own husbands at home" suggests that he is prohibiting the interruption of church services by women with outspoken questions and—if women sat separately from men, as in synagogues—perhaps also by disruptive conversation among women.

> "Not only the arm of the virtuous woman, but her speech as well, ought not to be for the public" (Plutarch, *Moralia,* "Advice to Bride and Groom" 31).

Resurrection

Paul now takes up the topic of bodily resurrection, a concept foreign to Greek thought. Some Athenians, entirely skeptical or hoping at best for immortality of the soul, mocked Paul when he spoke of such resurrection (see Acts 17:32 and page 328). This skepticism may also be causing some Christians in Corinth to doubt and deny a future resurrection of the body. But they are not denying the past resurrection of Christ, as would be expected of skepticism. So they may be denying a future resurrection under the view that Christ's is the only resurrection. Paul then argues from the

The Body's Parts Need to Work Together

Compare with Paul's figure of the body for the church:

"In the days when man's members did not all agree among themselves, as is now the case, but had each its own ideas and a voice of its own, the other parts thought it unfair that they should have the worry and the trouble and the labor of providing everything for the belly, while the belly remained quietly in their midst with nothing to do but to enjoy the good things that they bestowed on it. Therefore they conspired together that the hands should carry no food to the mouth, nor the mouth accept anything that was given it, nor the teeth grind up what they received. While they sought in this angry spirit to starve the belly into submission, the members themselves and the whole body were reduced to the utmost weakness. Hence it had become clear that even the belly had no idle task to perform, and was no more nourished than it nourished the rest by giving out to all parts of the body that by which we live and thrive, when it has been divided equally among the veins and is enriched with digested food—that is, the blood" (Livy 2.32.9–12).

common ground of belief in Christ's **past** resurrection to the disputed belief in a **future** resurrection of others: Christ is the **firstfruits** of resurrection, its initial stage, not the whole harvest.

The great chapter on resurrection opens with a summary of the gospel and a list of those to whom the risen Christ appeared, a list that Paul would not have dared to include with such reckless confidence unless the eyewitnesses were in fact available. "I received" indicates that he is quoting a confessional statement from Christian tradition even more ancient than the dates of his writing and of his first preaching in Corinth. He continues with a description of the resurrected body and an analogy between **death in Adam** and **life in Christ**. Some rabbis taught that the resurrected body will match the present body exactly, even to the extent of rising fully clothed. No, says Paul; the resurrected body will have continuity with the present body but be suited to the conditions of eternal life. The chapter comes to climax in a burst of triumphant praise. *Read 1 Corinthians 15:1–58.*

Baptism for the Dead

Various explanations have been devised for the reference in 15:29 to baptism for the dead. Perhaps Paul refers merely to those who have been converted and baptized out of a desire to be reunited with their Christian loved ones and friends at the resurrection. More likely he is referring to vicarious baptism in the full sense but using it as a point of argument without supporting the practice ("What will *they* do. . . ?" and "Why are *they* getting baptized for them?" as opposed to "we" in the next verse). In other words, he is pointing out the inconsistency of those who undergo baptism for the very dead people whose future resurrection they deny. Just as an overly sacramental view of the bread and wine of the Lord's Supper may have contributed to eating and drinking too much, so an overly sacramental view of baptismal water may be contributing to baptism for dead people as well as for themselves. A "spiritual body" (15:44) is not a nonphysical body, but a body made alive by the Spirit of Christ. So we should capitalize the adjective "Spiritual," for "the last Adam [Christ] became a life-giving Spirit" (15:45). Nor does the inability of "flesh and blood" to inherit the kingdom of God (15:50) deny the physicality of resurrected bodies; it denies only their perishability, their mortality: "for the perishable must clothe itself with the imperishable, and the mortal with immortality" (15:53). The fighting with "wild beasts" (15:32) is probably metaphorical.

An Inscription
Often Found on Tombs in the Greco-Roman Period

"I didn't exist. I did exist. I don't exist. I don't care."

"Queen Cleopatra [not the earlier Cleopatra allied with Mark Antony] asked R. Meir [about A.D. 150], saying, 'I know that the dead will live . . . . But when they rise, will they rise naked or in their clothing?' He said to her, '. . .Now if a grain of wheat, which is buried naked, comes forth in many garments, the righteous, who are buried in their garments, all the more so [will rise in many garments]'" (Babylonian Talmud, *Sanhedrin* 90b).

Earthly Man, Heavenly Man

Contrast as well as compare the following with Paul's distinction between the first and the last Adams:

"There are two types of men; the one a heavenly man, the other an earthly. The heavenly man, being made after the image of God, is altogether without part or lot in corruptible and terrestrial substance; but the earthly one was compacted out of the matter scattered here and there, which Moses calls 'clay'" (Philo, *Allegorical Interpretation of Genesis* 1.31).

The Offering and Miscellany

Paul's concluding chapter contains various exhortations, such as the one to lay aside money for the offering he will collect on his arrival and take to Jerusalem with accredited companions. Appearing in 16:22 is the important Aramaic phrase, "↓Maranatha," which means "O [our] Lord, come!" (compare Revelation 22:20). It shows that the designation of Jesus as Lord dates from early times in Aramaic-speaking circles and is therefore not attributable to later, Greek-speaking Christianity—against the claim of some modern scholars that the view of Jesus as a divine figure was a rather tardy development, original neither to Jesus nor to the earliest church. *Read 1 Corinthians 16:1–24.*

SECOND CORINTHIANS: PAUL'S CONCEPTION OF HIS MINISTRY

Introductory Issues

Tone

More than any other letter of Paul, 2 Corinthians allows us a glimpse into his inner feelings about himself, about his apostolic ministry, and about his relation to the churches he founded and nurtured. This letter is autobiographical in tone, then, though not in framework or substance.

The Painful Visit

After writing 1 Corinthians from Ephesus, Paul found it necessary to make a "painful visit" to Corinth and back—painful because of the strained relationship between him and the Corinthians at the time. Luke does not record

---

Maranatha: mair´uh-NATH-uh

Corinthian columns

this visit in Acts. It is to be inferred, however, from 2 Corinthians 12:14; 13:1–2, where Paul describes his coming visit as the "third." Apart from the inferred painful visit, he has visited Corinth only once before. The statement in 2 Corinthians 2:1, "For I decided not to make *another* painful visit to you," implies a past painful visit that can hardly be identified with his first coming to give them the joyful tidings of salvation through Jesus Christ.

The Lost "Sorrowful Letter"

Whatever the reason for Paul's making the short, painful visit, he was unsuccessful in bringing the church into line. On returning to Ephesus, therefore, he wrote a now lost "sorrowful letter" to Corinth, which at first he regretted having sent (2 Corinthians 2:4; 7:8). Despite frequent attempts at identification, his descriptions of the sorrowful letter do not fit 1 Corinthians, which exhibits considerable criticism on Paul's part, but hardly sorrow. So the sorrowful letter is his second lost one to Corinth. It commanded the church to discipline an obstreperous individual who was leading the opposition against Paul (2 Corinthians 2:5–10). Titus carried the letter to Corinth. Meanwhile, knowing that Titus would return via Macedonia and Troas and being anxious to hear from Titus the reaction of the Corinthians, Paul left Ephesus and waited in Troas. When Titus failed to arrive quickly, Paul went on to Macedonia, where Titus finally met him and reported the good news that the majority in the church had repented of their rebellion against Paul and had disciplined the leader of opposition to him (2 Corinthians 2:12–13; 7:4–16).

Occasion

Paul wrote 2 Corinthians from **Macedonia** on his **third missionary journey**, then, (1) to express **relief and joy** at the favorable response of the majority of Corinthian Christians (chapters 1–7); (2) to stress **the collection** that he wants to gather from the church for the Christians in Jerusalem (chapters

8–9); and (3) to defend **his apostolic authority** to the still recalcitrant minority (chapters 10–13).

A Summary of Paul's Relationships with the Corinthian Church

- Paul evangelizes Corinth during his second journey.
- Paul writes a lost letter in which he commands the Corinthian church to dissociate from professing Christians who live immorally.
- Paul writes 1 Corinthians from Ephesus during his third journey to deal with a variety of problems in the church.
- Paul makes a quick, "painful" visit from Ephesus to Corinth and back to straighten out the problems at Corinth but fails to accomplish his purpose.
- Paul sends another lost letter, called the "sorrowful letter," in which he commands the Corinthians to discipline his leading opponent in the church.
- Paul leaves Ephesus and anxiously waits for Titus, first at Troas and then in Macedonia.
- Titus finally arrives with good news that the church has disciplined Paul's opponent and that most of the Corinthians have submitted to Paul's authority.
- Paul writes 2 Corinthians from Macedonia (still on the third journey) in response to Titus's favorable report.

The Integrity of 2 Corinthians

It has been argued that 2 Corinthians 10–13 is at least part of the otherwise-lost sorrowful letter, because Paul changes his tone from happiness in chapters 1–9 to self-defense in chapters 10–13. But the distinction does not entirely hold true, for self-defense crops up also in chapters 1–9 (see 1:17–2:4, 17; 4:2–5; 5:12–13). The difference in emphasis may be due to Paul's addressing primarily the repentant majority in chapters 1–9, primarily the still-recalcitrant minority in chapters 10–13. Or fresh news of revived opposition may force him to change his tone from the tenth chapter onward.

Several considerations militate against dividing 2 Corinthians into two originally separate letters: (1) if written earlier as the sorrowful letter, chapters 10–13 would likely precede chapters 1–9; (2) though firm in tone, chapters 10–13 do not exhibit sorrow; (3) chapters 10–13 contain nothing about insulting behavior by the leader of Paul's opposition, yet that was the subject matter of the sorrowful letter according to 2:5; (4) 12:18 mentions a *previous* visit of Titus, which must have been for delivering the sorrowful letter; but according to the theory of partition, 12:18 is itself part of the sorrowful letter!

An Outline of Second Corinthians

Introduction: Greeting (1:1–2)

I. The Relationship Between Paul and the Corinthian Church with Special Reference to the Now-Agreeable Majority (1:3–7:16)

    A. Thanksgiving for divine comfort and protection (1:3–11)

    B. Explanation of Paul's failure to visit Corinth again, not fearful vacillation but desire to avoid another painful visit (1:12–2:4)

    C. Instruction to restore the disciplined, penitent leader of opposition to Paul, with a statement of forgiveness by Paul (2:5–11)

    D. Inner description of Paul's ministry (2:12–6:10)

        1. Anxiety over Titus's failure to come to Troas (2:12–13)

        2. Thanksgiving for triumphant confidence in Christ (2:14–17)

        3. The living recommendation of Paul's ministry in the Corinthian converts themselves (3:1–3)

        4. The superiority of the new covenant over the old (3:4–18)

        5. The determination of Paul to carry out his ministry (4:1–6:10)

    E. Plea for mutual affection and separation from unbelievers (6:11–7:4)

    F. Joy over Titus's report in Macedonia that the majority of Corinthian Christians have repented of their opposition to Paul (7:5–16)

II. Exhortation to Contribute to the Collection for the Church in Jerusalem (8:1–9:15)

    A. The example of Christians in Macedonia (8:1–7)

    B. The example of Jesus (8:8–9)

The Arch of Severus, with the Arch of Titus in the distance

    C. The ideal of equality (8:10–15)
    D. The coming of Titus and others to receive the collection (8:16–9:5)
    E. The divine reward for liberality (9:6–15)
  III. The Relationship Between Paul and the Corinthian Church with Special Reference to a Still-Recalcitrant Minority (10:1–13:10)
    A. The defense of Paul against charges of weakness and cowardice (10:1–11)
    B. The rightful claim of Paul over the Corinthians as his converts (10:12–18)
    C. Paul's concern over the danger of false teachers at Corinth (11:1–6)
    D. Paul's refusal to take financial support from the Corinthians (11:7–15)
    E. Paul's pedigrees of Jewish ancestry and Christian service, including the suffering of persecution (11:16–33)
    F. Paul's visions and thorn in the flesh (12:1–10)
    G. The apostolic miracles of Paul (12:11–13)
    H. The coming visit of Paul to Corinth, with a threat of harshness and an appeal for repentance (12:14–13:10)
  Conclusion: Farewell Exhortations and Greeting and a Benediction (13:11–14)

Reading Second Corinthians with Interpretation

Review of Past and Present Relationships

The letter opens with a greeting and thanksgiving for **comfort** from God in persecutions and hardships. Paul then begins to describe his ministry as sincere and holy and defends himself against the charge of vacillation—failure to carry out a threatened further visit—by claiming that his words are just as affirmative as the promises of God in Christ and by explaining that he has delayed his visit to give the Corinthians time for repentance. Their repentance would make for an arrival under happier circumstances than otherwise. Pleased that the Corinthian church has disciplined his leading opponent, Paul advises **restoration** of the man into churchly fellowship. This would be shown especially by allowing him to participate again in the Lord's Supper. The section closes with a metaphor of Christ as a victorious general entering Rome in **triumphal procession**, and another metaphor in which the Corinthian Christians, as Paul's converts, are a **letter of recommendation** for Paul written by Christ himself. *Read 2 Corinthians 1:1–3:3.*

Ministry of the Gospel

Paul now describes the superiority of his gospel over the Mosaic law. The fading of God's glory from the face of Moses when he descended from Mount Sinai represents the **temporariness** of the Mosaic covenant. Christians are now free from the law and its condemnation. But just as Moses reflected the fading glory of the old covenant, Christians should reflect the **permanent, greater,** and **increasing glory** of the new covenant. How amazing that God should entrust the preaching of this glorious gospel of the new

"What does a wolf have in common with a lamb? No more has a sinner with the devout" (Sirach 13:17).

covenant to poor, weak human beings! But although we feel our inadequacy, writes Paul, we do not despair. The hope of resurrection makes us overlook our present physical dangers in preaching the gospel. With awareness of tremendous privilege and responsibility as a minister of the new covenant, Paul claims **conscientiousness** and **integrity** no matter how adverse or favorable the conditions of his ministry. *Read 2 Corinthians 3:4–7:16.*

Separation

In the digression of 6:11–7:1 Paul portrays the life of separation from unbelievers as enlarging rather than confining. Some have thought that this digression formed part of his first lost letter to Corinth, referred to in 1 Corinthians 5:9: "I wrote to you in my letter not to associate with immoral people." But why an excerpt from that letter should have been inserted here is difficult to say; and manuscript evidence is lacking to indicate that 6:11–7:1 did not originally belong to 2 Corinthians—a fact that also militates against the theory that 6:14–7:1 has been interpolated from a non-Pauline source.

The Offering

Pleading for a generous offering to the church in Jerusalem, Paul presents the **liberality of Macedonian Christians** as worthy of Corinthian imitation.

The judgment seat at Corinth, where Paul stood trial before Gallio with Acrocorinth in the background. Compare Paul's statement in 2 Corinthians 5:10 that we must all stand before the judgment seat of Christ.

Even more so is the **self-sacrifice of Christ**. Sometime *you* may need help, Paul argues. Furthermore, you eagerly seized on the idea of such an offering when I first mentioned it some time ago. Do not prove that my bragging to the Macedonians about your zeal was unfounded. *Read 2 Corinthians 8:1–9:15.*

↓*Apologia*

The opponents of Paul have accused him of boldness when absent, cowardice when present. He therefore reminds the Corinthians that **meekness** is a virtue of Christ. But like Christ he can be **bold** in their presence if he wants—and will be, if necessary, though in the Lord, not in himself. *Read 2 Corinthians 10:1–13:13.* In these chapters Paul presents the **credentials** of his apostolic ministry:

- His sincerity as a preacher (he did not even accept wages from the Corinthians)
- His extensive sufferings
- Special revelations from God
- Miracle-working powers

But Paul carefully guards against boastful pride by repeatedly insisting that the recalcitrants are forcing him to write in this vein and also by mentioning his weakness, particularly his "thorn in the flesh" (12:7–10). Among the suggested identifications of this thorn in the flesh are epilepsy, eye disease, malaria, leprosy, migraine headaches, depression, stammering, and false teachers. The letter closes with an appeal that Paul's next visit may not have to be an occasion for rebuking the Corinthians again.

> ### On Commending Oneself
>
> How well does Paul's self-defense conform to the following advice?
>
> "But those who are forced to speak in their own praise are made more endurable by another procedure as well: not to lay claim to everything, but to unburden themselves, as it were, of honor, letting part of it rest with chance and part with God" (Plutarch, *Moralia*, "On Inoffensive Self-Praise" 11).

ROMANS: THE GIFT OF GOD'S RIGHTEOUS THROUGH FAITH IN CHRIST

Introductory Issues

Theme

Justification by God's grace through faith in Jesus Christ makes up the great theme of Paul's Letter to the Romans. Jesus himself implied something

apologia: ap´uh-loh-JEE-uh

similar in his parables of the prodigal son, the Pharisee and the tax collector, the laborers in the vineyard, and the great supper. The same implication lies behind his statement, "I did not come to call righteous people but sinful people to repentance" (Mark 2:17), and behind his dealings with Zacchaeus (Luke 19:1–10). Thus Paul did not invent a doctrine of free forgiveness; rather, he developed it in his own distinctive way. The doctrine receives its most systematic treatment in his letter to the churches at Rome (see 16:5, 14, 15 for the presence of more than one church there).

Founding of the Churches in Rome

Toward the end of the first century, ↓Clement of Rome suggested that Paul and Peter were martyred in his city. By the time of ↓Tertullian (early third century) the church at large had generally accepted this tradition. The churches in Rome, however, were probably not founded by an apostle, certainly not by Paul and almost certainly not by Peter. As noted before, the Roman historian Suetonius wrote that the emperor Claudius banished Jews from Rome in A.D. 49 or 50 because of rioting at the instigation of one called

Clement: KLEM-uhnt ■ Tertullian: tuhr-TUHL-ee-uhn

The forum of ancient Rome

"Chrestus," probably a misspelling of "Christus" (Latin for Christ), accompanied by a misunderstanding of preaching *about* Christ as preaching *by* him (see pages 12, 328–29). If so, Christianity had already gone to Rome. But Peter was still in Jerusalem at the Jerusalem Council, about A.D. 49. In Romans, moreover, Paul makes no reference and sends no greeting to the Apostle Peter. Perhaps then some of the Jews and proselytes from Rome who were visiting Jerusalem on the Day of Pentecost converted to Christ and carried the gospel back to Rome at the very dawn of church history (Acts 2:10).

Jewish or Gentile?

Some scholars maintain that the Roman churches consisted mainly of Jewish Christians. In favor of this view they cite Paul's emphasis on the Jewish nation in chapters 9–11, appeal to the example of Abraham, quotations of the Old Testament, and passages in which Paul appears to be arguing against Jewish objections (2:17–3:8; 3:21–31; 6:1–7:6; 14:1–15:3). But according to chapters 9–11, God has temporarily turned his attention from the Jewish nation to the Gentiles; so these chapters may rather indicate that the original audience of the letter consisted mainly of Gentile Christians. The appeals of Paul to Abraham and to the Old Testament may reflect his own Jewish background, not the background of his audience—or if theirs, Gentile proselytes' and God-fearers' knowledge of the Old Testament gained through attendance at synagogues prior to Christian conversion. Paul appeals to Abraham, moreover, to include Gentile believers alongside Jewish believers. And the answering of typically Jewish objections may stem from Paul's frequent debates with unbelieving Jews and with Judaizers, the latter of whom tried to proselytize Gentile Christians, rather than from a Jewish Christian address for the letter.

A number of passages demonstrate the **predominantly Gentile composition** of the Roman churches:

- Paul writes in 1:5–6, "among all the Gentiles ... among whom are you also."
- In 1:13 he writes, "among you just as also among the *rest* of the Gentiles."
- His statement, "I am speaking to you Gentiles" (11:13), characterizes the Roman churches as a whole, not a minority within them; for in 11:28–31 the audience is said to have obtained mercy because of Jewish unbelief.
- In 15:15–16 he speaks of his writing to them in conjunction with his ministry "to the Gentiles."

Peter's and Paul's Martyrdoms

- "Peter, ... having thus given his testimony, went to the glorious place which was his due. ... And when he ['Paul'] had reached the limits of the West, he gave his testimony before the rulers, and thus passed from the world and was taken up into the Holy Place" (*1 Clement* 5:4, 7).
- "At Rome, Nero was the first who stained with blood the rising faith. Then is Peter girded by another, when he is fixed to the cross. Then does Paul obtain a birth suited to Roman citizenship, when in Rome he springs to life again ennobled by martyrdom" (Tertullian, *Scorpiace* 15).

Erastus inscription

Time and Place of Writing

Paul has just completed collecting an offering for Christians in Jerusalem during his **third missionary journey** (15:25–26). He writes from **Corinth**, for ↓Gaius the Corinthian is hosting him at the time (16:23; 1 Corinthians 1:14). The mention of Erastus, a city treasurer (16:23), supports Corinth as the place of writing, for an inscription discovered in Corinth and dating from the first century reads, "Erastus, the commissioner of public works, laid this pavement at his own expense." Strictly, "commissioner of public works" represents a lower office than that of "city treasurer," but it is natural to think either that Erastus advanced from commissioner to treasurer or that he was demoted from treasurer to commissioner. It also remains possible that the two titles are roughly synonymous. Further support for Paul's writing from Corinth is found in the commendation of ↓Phoebe, who belongs to the church at Cenchrea right by Corinth. This commendation probably indicates that she will carry the letter from Corinth to Rome (16:1–2).

Purpose

Paul writes Romans to prepare believers living in Rome for his first visit to their city. For a long time he has been intending to visit but has been prevented (1:13; 15:22–24a). He purposes to **strengthen** the Roman Christians in their faith (1:11, 15) and to **win their financial support** for his projected mission to Spain after visiting Rome (15:24, 28). For the most part, what he writes seems to be what he has on his mind to tell Jewish Christians in Jerusalem when he arrives there with the offering he has been collecting for them. He fears that the tension between Jewish and Gentile Christians in the East may have reached such proportions that the Jewish Christians in Jerusalem will refuse the offering because of its having been collected largely from Gentile Christians in Macedonia and Achaia and delivered personally by himself as the apostle to Gentiles (15:30–31). He also knows enough about the churches in Rome to **warn** Gentile Christians against boasting of superiority over Jewish Christians (11:17–32) and against despising them for their ritual observances (14:1–23). Claudius's banishment from Rome of Jews, including Jewish Christians, must have left the churches there in the charge of Gentile Christians who very likely are trying to maintain control even now that Jewish Christians are returning to Rome, along with other Jews, after the death of Claudius. Paul's warnings signal the **fear of a full-scale rupture** between Jewish and Gentile Christians in Rome as well as in the East. So he presents in Romans what he will present in Jerusalem, the gospel of justification by faith for Jews and Gentiles alike as the **basis of Christian unity**—but unity not for its own sake; rather, for the sake of **further evangelism** such as he plans to pursue in Spain. A rupture in Rome would spoil his chances of getting much support for the Spanish mission.

Personal Greetings

Because Paul knows only certain of the Christians in Rome, those who have moved there since he became acquainted with them elsewhere, Romans is more formal than any of Paul's other letters. Nevertheless, chapter 16 contains many personal greetings; and he sends them even though he has never visited Rome. Some scholars have thought the chapter originally belonged to a letter sent to Ephesus, where Paul had certainly become acquainted with many people. But the chapter does not make up a whole letter (it consists almost entirely of greetings); and there is no manuscript evidence that it ever circulated independently, either as a whole letter or as part of one. The only other long series of greetings in Paul's letters appears in ↓Colossians, sent to another city he had never visited. Probably to establish friendly relations with

Colossians: kuh-LOSH-uhnz

Harbor at Cenchrea with a temple of Isis in the foreground

churches he has never visited, then, Paul emphasizes his previous acquaintance with Christians who have moved to such churches; and to avoid favoritism he omits individual greetings in letters to churches he has founded (↓Ephesians offering the special case of a circular letter to churches that he has neither founded nor visited).

Textual Confusion

Ancient manuscripts vary widely on the position of the doxology at 16:25–27 in English Bibles and on the position of the benediction in 16:20. The confusion may derive from Marcion, a Gnostic who possibly omitted chapters 15–16 because they contain Old Testament and Jewish references disagreeable to his anti-Judaistic way of thinking. The confusion may be compounded by a truncated form of the letter lacking chapter 16, for which there is ancient textual evidence. Because of the personal greetings in that chapter, some editions probably omitted it to adapt the letter for circulation throughout the Christian world.

The Development of Thought in Romans

Introduction

In the opening part of this letter Paul greets his audience and mentions his hope of visiting them in order that he may preach the gospel in Rome as elsewhere (1:1–15). He then states his theme in 1:16–17: the good news of deliverance from sin by the giving of God's righteousness to everyone who believes in Jesus Christ.

The Plight: Sinfulness

The first main section delineates the need for justification because of human sinfulness (1:18–3:20). The latter half of chapter 1 describes the wickedness of the Gentile world, chapter 2 describes the self-righteousness and sin of the Jewish world, and the first half of chapter 3 summarizes the guilt of all humanity. It should be noted that for Paul, sins in the plural symptomize the root problem of sin in the singular as a dominating force in non-Christian existence.

The Remedy: Justification

As a remedy for the sinful plight of humanity, according to the second main section (3:21–5:21), God has provided justification. The latter half of chapter 3 presents the sacrificial death of Christ as the basis of justification and faith as the means of appropriating the benefits of his death. Chapter 4 portrays Abraham as the great example of faith, against the rabbinic doctrine

Ephesians: i-FEE-zhuhnz

of Abraham's store of merit so excessive that other Jews can draw on it. Chapter 5 lists the manifold blessings of justification—peace, joy, hope, the gift of the Holy Spirit, and others—and contrasts the unbeliever's position in Adam, where sin and death take effect, and the believer's position in Christ, where righteousness and life eternal take effect.

The Outcome: Sanctification

In the third main section the discussion progresses to the topic of sanctification, or holy living (chapters 6–8). Should believers sin in order that God may exercise his grace all the more and thus gain more praise for himself? No! Baptism illustrates death to sin and coming alive to righteousness (chapter 6). This kind of sanctification does not consist in self-generated attempts to keep the Old Testament law, which can give only a sense of defeat, or in any human ability to surmount the demonic control of sin over human conduct (chapter 7). Rather, the Spirit of Christ gives overcoming power. Thus chapter 8 climaxes in a burst of praise: "Who will separate us from the love of Christ?" Paul lists the possibilities and denies them all.

A Problem: Israel's Unbelief

But despite divine covenants and other privileges, Israel appears to be separated from the love of Christ. So Paul's discussion turns to the problem of Israel in the fourth main section (chapters 9–11). Because of his own Jewishness, he is keenly concerned about the fate of his fellow Jews. All along he has been claiming that the gospel is no innovation, but a derivative from the Old Testament and a fulfillment of all that Abraham, David, and the prophets stood for. But if so, why have Jews by and large failed to accept the truth of this claim? Does rejection of the gospel by a Jewish majority imply a flaw in Paul's claim? By way of answer, chapter 9 stresses the doctrine of election, God's right to choose whomever he wishes. It is perfectly legitimate, argues Paul, for the sovereign God to do with Israel and the Gentiles what he wants to do. And it is as much God's prerogative to choose the Gentiles now as it was for him to choose the Jews earlier. But his current turn from Israel is not capricious, for Israel deserves it on account of her self-righteousness and refusal to believe what she has both heard and understood in the gospel (chapter 10). Furthermore, God's turning from Israel is only temporary and partial. By believing in Christ, a Jew may gain salvation as easily as a Gentile does; and in the future God will restore the whole nation to his favor. Meanwhile, Gentiles enjoy equality with Jews (chapter 11).

Jewish Views of Abraham

- "Therefore you, O Lord, God of the righteous, have not appointed repentance for the righteous, for Abraham and Isaac and Jacob, who did not sin against you" (Prayer of Manasseh 8).

- "For Abraham was perfect in all of his actions with the Lord and was pleasing through righteousness all the days of his life" (*Jubilees* 23:10).

- "And we find that Abraham our ancestor had performed the whole law before it was given" (Mishnah, *Qiddushin* 4:14).

- "The faith with which their [the Israelites'] ancestor Abraham believed in me [God] merits that I should divide the sea for them" (*Mekilta* on Exodus 14.15 [35b]; note the contrast between this rabbinic view of faith as a meritorious work and Paul's view of faith as the opposite of a meritorious work).

The Obligation: Christian Precepts

The fifth main section contains practical exhortations for Christian living, including commands to obey governmental authorities and to allow freedom on ritual issues (chapters 12–14).

Conclusion

Paul concludes the letter by stating his plans in detail and sending greetings at length (chapters 15–16).

An Outline of Romans

Introduction (1:1–17)
 A. Greeting (1:1–7)
 B. Paul's plan to visit Rome (1:8–15)
 C. Statement of theme (1:16–17)
I. The Sinfulness of All Human Beings (1:18–3:20)
 A. The sinfulness of Gentiles (1:18–32)
 B. The sinfulness of Jews (2:1–3:8)
 C. The sinfulness of Jews and Gentiles together (3:9–20)
II. The Justification of Sinners Who Believe in Jesus Christ (3:21–5:21)
 A. The basis of justification in the propitiatory death of Jesus (3:21–26)
 B. Faith as the means of obtaining justification (3:27–4:25)
  1. Its exclusion of boasting in one's work (3:27–31)
  2. Its Old Testament examples in Abraham (especially) and David (4:1–25)
 C. The many blessings of justification (5:1–11)
 D. A contrast between Adam, in whom there is sin and death, and Christ, in whom there is righteousness and life (5:12–21)
III. The Sanctification of Sinners Justified by Faith in Jesus Christ (6:1–8:39)
 A. Baptism as a representation of believers' union with Christ in his death with reference to sin and in his coming alive with reference to righteousness (6:1–14)
 B. Slavery to sin and freedom from righteousness versus slavery to righteousness and freedom from sin (6:15–23)
 C. Death to the law through union with Christ in his death, as illustrated by the cancellation of marriage through the death of one's spouse (7:1–6)
 D. The failure of the law to produce righteousness as due to the inability of human beings to overcome their own sinful bent (7:7–25)
 E. Righteous living through the Spirit by those who are justified through faith in Jesus Christ (8:1–27)
 F. A statement of confidence and triumph (8:28–39)
IV. The Unbelief of Israel (9:1–11:36)
 A. The concern of Paul for Israel (9:1–5)
 B. The unbelief of Israel as a matter of God's predetermined plan (9:6–33)

Reading Romans with Interpretation

Righteousness by Faith

Read Romans 1:1–3:20. With a quotation of Habakkuk 2:4, Paul highlights **Old Testament support** for the fundamental truth that righteousness comes through faith (1:17). Since the traditional translation, "The righteous will live by faith," sounds as though Paul is using this text with regard to a righteous person's exercising faith in **daily** life, we might prefer the translation, "The person who is righteous by faith will live," and understand Paul to be using the text in regard to **eternal** life. He also states that nature itself reveals the power and deity of God; therefore, pagans have **no excuse** (1:19–20). The rest of chapter 1 describes the retrograde nature of sin. Three times throughout the passage the statement, "God gave them over," tolls like a death knell (1:24, 26, 28).

Human Guilt

In chapter 2 Paul describes self-righteous Jews who delight in pointing out the sins of pagans but are just as guilty in their own proud way. Furthermore, he argues, genuine Jewishness does not consist in physical ancestry or in the rite of circumcision, but in a proper spiritual relation to God. In fact, Gentiles who follow God's law written in their consciences demonstrate a right relation to him that many Jews lack. The word "**Jew**" means "**praise**." Therefore, the true Jew is the one whose life is praiseworthy by divine criteria (2:17).

In 3:1 Paul anticipates a Jewish objection: If Jews are no better than Gentiles, why did God choose the Jewish nation? Does not the whole Old Testament imply that God has specially favored the Jews? Yet you, Paul, are saying that God treats Jews and Gentiles in the same way! Paul freely admits that Jews do have the advantage of standing closest to divine revelation in the Scriptures. But higher privilege does not imply less sinfulness. With a string of Old Testament quotations, Paul concludes the section by charging the entire human race with guilt before God.

↓*Propitiation*

The next paragraph forms the core of this letter. "The law and the prophets" refers to the Old Testament. Paul emphasizes that though righteousness comes through faith in Jesus Christ rather than through keeping the law, yet the law and the rest of the Old Testament do attest righteousness by faith. "The glory of God," which human beings lack (3:23), is the splendor of God's character. The term "propitiation" (3:25) describes Jesus' death as a sacrifice that appeased the anger of God against human wickedness. The alternative translation "↓expiation" fails to imply that anger, though Paul

---

propitiation: pruh-pish´i-AY-shuhn ■ expiation: ek´spi-AY-shuhn

---

The Results of Idolatry according to Wisdom of Solomon 14:22–26

"Then it was not enough for them to err about the knowledge of God . . . . For whether they kill children in their initiations, or celebrate secret mysteries, or hold frenzied revels with strange customs, they no longer keep either their lives or their marriages pure, but they either treacherously kill one another, or grieve one another by adultery, and all is a raging riot of blood and murder, theft and deceit, corruption, faithlessness, tumult, perjury, confusion over what is good, forgetfulness of favors, defiling of souls, sexual perversion, disorder in marriages, adultery, and debauchery."

A Pagan Condemnation of Homosexual Behavior

"In the beginning . . . human life . . . obeyed the laws made by nature; and men, linking themselves to women . . . became fathers of children. But gradually the passing years degenerated from such nobility to the lowest depths of hedonism . . . . The same sex entered the same bed. Though they saw themselves embracing each other, they were ashamed neither at what they did nor at what they had done *to* them. And sowing their seed on barren rocks, to quote the proverb, they bought a little pleasure at the cost of great disgrace" (Pseudo-Lucian, *Affairs of the Heart* 20).

has emphasized it (1:18). The term may also allude to the **mercy seat**, a gold lid over the ark of the covenant. On this lid the Jewish high priest sprinkled sacrificial blood once a year to atone for the sins of Israel. Paul indicates that God forgave sins during the Old Testament period only in anticipation of Christ's death. When he states that God is both "just and the justifier of the person who has faith in Jesus," he means that God's anger has been satisfied in that Jesus paid the penalty for human guilt, and that God's love has likewise been satisfied in that Jesus' death provided a way by which the guilty can be forgiven. Divine righteousness is inflexible enough to demand the imposition of a penalty for the upholding of justice but flexible enough to allow the righteous God to exercise mercy on unrighteous but believing human beings. *Read Romans 3:21–31.*

Stone replica of the ark of the covenant from Capernaum

Examples of Faith

Again Paul anticipates a Jewish objection: If a person gains righteousness merely by faith in Christ, there is no advantage in being a Jew or in keeping the law as a Jew. Essentially, Paul agrees with this conclusion; but, he argues, the Old Testament itself indicates that righteousness comes by faith, not by works, as in the examples of Abraham and David. *Read Romans 4:1–5:21.*

Blessings

In the first verses of chapter 5, Paul lists the blessings that accompany justification:

- Peace with God through Jesus Christ
- Introduction into the sphere of God's grace
- Joy in the hope of God's glory ("hope" meaning confident expectation that Jesus will return and "the glory of God" here meaning the divine splendor that Christians will enter at the second coming)
- Joy in present persecution
- Perseverance
- Tested genuineness
- Hope (again)
- An interior experience of God's love as ministered by the Holy Spirit

The terms "reconcile" and "reconciliation" in verses 10 and 11 refer to the turning of sinners from hatred against God to love for God.

Adam versus Christ

In 5:12–14 Paul argues that the reign of death before God gave the law through Moses proves that the whole human race was affected by Adam's **original sin**; for before Moses' time there was no written law to break. A contrast between "the one" and "the many" follows: One man (Adam) sinned in Eden, with the result that the many (a Semitic expression for "all") sinned and died; one man (Jesus Christ) performed an act of righteousness on the cross, with the result that the many (all who believe in Jesus Christ) are regarded as righteous and will live eternally.

> "O Adam, what have you done? For though it was you who sinned, the fall was not yours alone, but ours also who are your descendants" (2 Esdras 7:48 *118*).

Union with Christ

The primary objection to this easy way of salvation, of justification by faith alone, is that it implies a patently false line of reasoning with a ridiculous conclusion: the more sin, the more God exercises his grace and gains greater glory for so doing—therefore, sin as much as possible for the glory of God! Paul's horrified repudiation of such reasoning rests on the doctrine of believers' union with Christ as dramatized through **Christian baptism.** In baptism, believers confess their death to sin through identification with Christ in his death and also confess their coming alive to righteousness through identification with Christ in his resurrection. So far as God is concerned, then, they died when Christ died and rose when Christ rose. These events put believers under obligation to live as people who are dead to sin and alive to righteousness. They must form their self-image according to God's way of looking at them. *Read Romans 6:1–8:39.*

Freedom and Slavery

> "Though the body is enslaved, yet the mind is free" (Sophocles, Fragments 940).

In the last part of chapter 6, Paul writes that freedom from the law does not imply freedom to sin, because freedom and slavery are relative terms. An unbeliever is free from the restrictions of Christian holiness but enslaved to the control of sin. On the other hand, a believer is free from the control of sin but enslaved to the restrictions of Christian holiness. In reality, captivity to Christian holiness brings the truest kind of freedom, freedom not to sin, freedom to live righteously.

Purpose of the Law

In chapter 7 Paul illustrates his argument from marriage law. A spouse is free to marry another person when the other spouse has died, because death has broken the marital bond. Similarly, the death of Christ and the union of believers with him in his death have broken their bond to the Mosaic law and freed them to belong to the risen Christ and bear fruit for God. Why then was the law given? It was given to prompt a total dependence on Christ for righteousness by increasing the awareness of human beings con-

The Power of Desire and Pleasure

- "So great then and transcendent an evil is desire [the same word in Greek that Paul uses, sometimes translated 'lust,' though not always limited to sexual lust] or rather, it may be truly said, the fountain of all evils! For plunderings and robberies and repudiations of debts and false accusations and outrages, also seductions, adulteries, murders, and all wrongful actions, whether private or public, whether in things sacred or things profane—from what other source [than 'desire'] do they flow?" (Philo, *Special Laws* 4.84).
- "But there is another battle more terrible and a struggle not slight but much greater . . . and fraught with greater danger. I mean the fight against pleasure. . . . For pleasure uses no open force, but deceives and casts a spell . . . . Yes, such is this thing pleasure that it hatches no single plot, but all kinds of plots, and aims to undo men through sight, sound, smell, taste, and touch—with food, too, and drink and carnal lust—tempting the waking and the sleeping alike. . . . for it is impossible to dwell with pleasure, or even to dally with her for any length of time, without being completely enslaved. . . . For pleasure, after overpowering and taking possession of her victims, delivers them over to hardships, the most hateful and most difficult to endure" (Dio Chrysostom 8.20–26, excerpts).

cerning their sin and moral incapability. Paul does not deny that God intended the Mosaic law to guide the conduct of Old Testament believers. But so far as justification is concerned, he does deny that God gave the law to be a means of achieving merit before him; rather, as a means of inducing people to cast themselves solely on his grace.

From Frustration to Triumph

The last part of chapter 7 classically describes the frustration of a person who wants to do good but cannot because of the demonic power of sin aggravated by the law. Frustration changes to triumph for believers, however, because they have the Spirit of Christ (chapter 8). As in Galatians, Paul contrasts the flesh and the Spirit. The Spirit of Christ empowers believers to **conquer** the sinful urge, **assures** them of salvation, will someday **glorify** them, and in the meantime **prays** for them. Chapter 8 climaxes with a burst of praise and confidence. The only one who has a right to accuse believers, because he is holy, is the very one who justifies them. God would not be righteous if he *did* condemn them now that they are in Christ.

The Election, Rejection, and Restoration of Israel

Read Romans 9:1–11:36. In discussing the problem of Israel, Paul maintains that God has a right to choose some and reject others as he wants. Sinners have no claim on God. He does not exercise his prerogative arbitrarily, however. He has turned to Gentiles because Israel sought their own righteousness rather than his. But the invitation to salvation stands open to all, Jews and Gentiles alike. The outcomes:

- A remnant of Jews believe.
- Gentiles have a better opportunity than they had before.

The Progress of Salvation According to Romans 8:30

Predestined $\rightarrow$ Called $\rightarrow$ Justified $\rightarrow$ Glorified

- Jealousy over the widespread salvation of Gentiles will induce the Jews to repent.
- All Israel will yet be saved; that is, those Jews who are still living at the return of Christ will accept his messiahship and, as a result, receive salvation.
- Gentile believers should not self-righteously exalt themselves over Jewish believers, lest they suffer the judgment that Jewish unbelievers have suffered.

Christian Commitment

Practical exhortations occupy the next main section of the letter. For Paul, theology always affects life; and to maintain a high level of Christian conduct in the churches he never leaves his audience to guess the practical import of his doctrinal teaching. After an appeal that believers offer themselves to God as "**living** [as opposed to slain] **sacrifices**," Paul exhorts his audience not to imitate the outward conduct of non-Christians, but to live pleasingly before God out of renewed mental attitudes (12:1–2).

Individual consecration leads to the social ministries of preaching, teaching, serving, giving, and leading—all according to the various abilities God

An olive tree

has given to believers, and all to be performed modestly and harmoniously (12:3–8). Harmony within a church depends, however, on mutual love, which includes sincerity, hatred of evil, retention of right standards (goodness), affection, respect, industriousness, devotion to God, joy in hope, patience, prayer, generosity, and hospitality (12:9–13).

Similarly, believers should maintain good relations with unbelievers through prayer for their welfare, empathy with their joys, sympathy with their sorrows, and respectful and forgiving attitudes toward them. If the unbelievers still practice persecution, God himself will judge them and vindicate his own (12:14–21). Paul also commands submission to governmental authority by obedience and payment of taxes; but his words must not be taken as blind support of totalitarianism. The stated presupposition is that governing authorities are carrying out justice by punishing wrongdoers and praising rightdoers. Thus resistance for purely political or selfish reasons deserves censure, but not resistance for moral and religious reasons (13:1–7). God requires love not only for one's fellow believers, but also for humanity in general. This includes payment of debts and avoidance of adultery, murder, theft, and covetousness (13:8–10). The prospect of Jesus' return sharpens these commands (13:11–14). As in 1 Corinthians, finally, Paul indicates that believers must allow one another freedom to differ on ritual questions so long as damage is not done to weaker, uninformed people (14:1–15:3). *Read Romans 12:1–15:13.*

> ### Good Governance
>
> - "The government of the earth is in the hand of the Lord, and over it he will raise up the right leader for the time" (Sirach 10:4).
> - "To no one will I return evil for evil. I will pursue a man only for good. For to God belongs the judgment of every living being, and he will pay each one his recompense. . . . I will not maintain anger against those who repent of their sin, but I will show no mercy to those who deviate from the Way. I will not console the smitten until their way is perfect" (*Community Rule* [1QS] 10:17–18, 20–21).

Concluding Remarks

Stating his plans with more detail than in chapter 1, Paul now relates his hopes to deliver an offering to the church in Jerusalem and to evangelize Spain after visiting Rome. The commendation of Phoebe in 16:1–2 reflects the Christian practice in which a home church recommends one of its members to a church in the locality to which that member is moving or paying a visit. The greeting to ↓Prisca (a shortened form of Priscilla) and Aquila in 16:3 implies that they have returned to Rome. We know from secular sources too that Claudius's edict expelling the Jews from Rome lapsed after he died. Greetings, a warning against false teachers, a benediction, further greetings, and a doxology complete the letter. *Read Romans 15:14–16:27.*

Summary

Paul writes 1 Corinthians to solve problems that have arisen in the church at Corinth. At the time he is staying in Ephesus during his third missionary journey. An oral report has reached him concerning some of those problems, and a letter of inquiry from the Corinthian church had alerted him to others. The problems consist of factionalism, sexual immorality, lawsuits, marriage and divorce issues, food dedicated to idols, the bareheadedness of women praying and prophesying in church meetings, desecration of the Lord's Supper, uncontrolled tongues-speaking, denial of a future resurrection, and the business of collecting money for an offering to the church in Jerusalem. With apostolic authority Paul commands a halt to the hero

Prisca: PRIS-kuh

worship that gave rise to factionalism; discipline of a particularly immoral church member; the settlement of lawsuits between Christians within the church rather than in outside courts; sexual morality; sexual satisfaction within marriage; celibacy as a possibility for those with a gift for it; no divorce and remarriage for Christian couples, but at most separation and the single life with a preference for reconciliation; the maintenance of marriages to non-Christians, given their willingness; marriage only to a fellow Christian on the part of a widow; freedom to eat anything so long as the eating does not do spiritual harm to someone with a theologically uninformed conscience; nonparticipation in pagan banquets; head-coverings for women praying and prophesying in church meetings; discontinuance of love feasts; celebration of the Lord's Supper in unison and with self-examination; tight controls on speaking in tongues; the exercise of spiritual gifts out of communal love rather than private enjoyment; belief in a future resurrection of the body after the pattern of Christ's bodily resurrection in the past; and a regular laying aside of money prior to Paul's arrival to take the collection to Jerusalem.

Paul writes 2 Corinthians from Macedonia on his third missionary journey. The letter exhibits three purposes. The first is to commend the majority in the church at Corinth for their having disciplined an opponent of Paul, and to command the restoration of that opponent in view of his repentance. The second is to urge liberality in the laying aside of money that Paul is coming to collect for the church in Jerusalem. And the third purpose is to defend his apostleship against a minority in the church who seem still opposed to him. Throughout, but especially in its first and third sections, this letter sounds a heavily autobiographical note.

In Corinth on his third missionary journey, Paul writes Romans to churches he has neither founded nor visited. He wants to prepare them for his upcoming visit and solicitation of financial help for a subsequent mission to Spain. But tension between Jewish and Gentile Christians threatens this and the wider missionary endeavor; so Paul discusses at length God's impartiality. God justifies Jews and Gentiles alike, that is, solely on the basis of their faith in Christ as the propitiation that satisfied God's righteous anger aroused by their sins. Paul's discussion looks like what he has in mind to say in Jerusalem, where Jewish Christians harbor suspicions against him and his Gentile converts just as Gentile Christians in Rome harbor the same against Jewish Christians there. After preliminaries, Paul establishes the sinfulness of all human beings; provides the one and only remedy in God's righteousness; indicates the outcome in holy living by Spirit-filled believers; outlines the temporary rejection and ultimate restoration of Israel as a benefit to Gentiles; spells out a batch of precepts for Christian conduct; and concludes with his plans, a commendation of Phoebe, greetings, a warning against false teachers, a benediction, and a doxology.

People to Remember

Abraham	David	Silas
Adam	Erastus	Stephanus, Fortunatus,
Apollos	Gaius	and Achaicus
Aquila	Gallio	Suetonius
Cephas/Peter	Marcion	Tertullian
Chloe	Moses	Timothy
Clement of Rome	Phoebe	Titius Justus
Crispus	Priscilla/Prisca	Titus

Places to Remember

Achaia	Cenchrea	Macedonia
Adriatic Sea	Corinth	Spain
Aegean Sea	Ephesus	Troas
Athens	Jerusalem	

Terms to Remember

adiaphora	gift of tongues	original sin
apologia	glossolalia	painful visit
baptism for the dead	hope	Pauline privilege
body of Christ	justification	propitiation
carnality	law of love	reconcile/reconciliation
charismata	letter of recommendation	sanctification
Christian freedom	Lord's Supper	sorrowful letter
election	love feast	spiritual body
expiation	"the many"	thorn in the flesh
food dedicated to idols	Maranatha	union with Christ
gift of interpretation	mercy seat	

How Much Did You Learn?

- For each of Paul's three major letters, identify the time, place, and purpose of writing.
- List as many of the church problems discussed in 1 Corinthians as you can remember and Paul's solutions to them.
- Outline the three main sections of 2 Corinthians.
- Trace Paul's relations to the Corinthian church from its establishment onward.
- Rehearse the progress of thought in Romans.

FIRST CORINTHIANS

For Further Discussion

- How is it possible to strike the proper balance between the unity and the purity of the church without making one cancel the other?
- How are we to evaluate the modern ecumenical movement toward church unity?
- How do Paul's strictures against immorality and emphasis on love compare with "the new morality"?
- How is church discipline of erring members possible when today a Christian excluded from one church can easily gain admittance to another? How "serious" a sin requires discipline?
- What current questions of Christian conduct validly fall within the area of private freedom and public responsibility?
- Why do most churches not require women speaking in public services to wear a head-covering?
- Does the Holy Spirit still grant the gifts of prophecy and tongues? If so, do their recipients exercise them in the manner prescribed by Paul?
- From the standpoint of modern science, how could there be a continuity between the mortal body and the resurrected body?

For Further Investigation

Blomberg, C. L. *The NIV Application Commentary: 1 Corinthians.* Grand Rapids: Zondervan, 1994.

Collins, R. F. *First Corinthians.* Collegeville, Minn.: Glazier/Liturgical Press, 1999.

Fee, G. D. *The First Epistle to the Corinthians.* Grand Rapids: Eerdmans, 1987. Advanced.

Furnish, V. P. *The Theology of the First Letter to the Corinthians.* Cambridge: Cambridge University Press, 1999.

Hays, R. B. *First Corinthians.* Louisville: Westminster John Knox, 1997.

Soards, M. L. *1 Corinthians.* Peabody, Mass.: Hendrickson, 1999.

Thiselton, A. C. *The First Epistle to the Corinthians: A Commentary on the Greek Text.* Grand Rapids: Eerdmans, 2000. Advanced.

Witherington, B., III. *Conflict and Community in Corinth: A Socio-Rhetorical Commentary on 1 and 2 Corinthians.* Grand Rapids: Eerdmans, 1995.

SECOND CORINTHIANS

For Further Discussion

- For what historical and theological reasons might two of Paul's letters to the Corinthian church have been lost? Is it likely that had they been preserved, the church would have accepted them into the canon? How should they now be received if somehow discovered?
- How do Paul's remarks about Christian stewardship of money compare with the Old Testament law of tithing?
- Why did Paul not "turn the other cheek" rather than defend himself from personal attack?
- Construct a profile of Paul's personality from this most self-revealing of his letters.

For Further Investigation

Barnett, P. *The Second Epistle to the Corinthians.* Grand Rapids: Eerdmans, 1997. Advanced.

Hafemann, S. J. *The NIV Application Commentary: 2 Corinthians.* Grand Rapids: Zondervan, 2000.

Kistemaker, S. J. *New Testament Commentary: II Corinthians.* Grand Rapids: Baker, 1997.

Lambrecht, J. *Second Corinthians.* Collegeville, Minn.: Liturgical Press, 1999.

Murphy-O'Conner, J. *The Theology of the Second Letter to the Corinthians.* Cambridge: Cambridge University Press, 1991.

Scott, J. M. *2 Corinthians.* Peabody, Mass.: Hendrickson, 1998.

ROMANS

For Further Discussion

- Does Paul's doctrine of human sinfulness degrade the dignity and nobility of the human race?

- Does Paul contradict himself in appealing to the Gentiles' good works performed out of conscience (2:12–16) and contending for the total depravity of Jews and Gentiles alike (3:9–20)? Or does he mean Christian Gentiles in 2:12–16?
- Is transferring a penalty from a guilty to an innocent party morally and legally defensible?
- Is justification possible without sanctification?
- Does the inner struggle between right and wrong depicted in Romans 7:7–25 characterize Christians or non-Christians? (Compare Romans 8.)
- How can God maintain his sovereignty and yet allow human beings enough freedom to be held responsible?
- Are people saved because they decide to believe in Christ or because God decides to make them believe? Is there another alternative?
- Do Paul's statements about the future of Israel relate to current events in the Middle East?
- What should be the attitude of Christians toward government in the face of current social problems and international disputes?

For Further Investigation

Cranfield, C. E. B. *A Critical and Exegetical Commentary on the Epistle to the Romans.* 2 vols. Edinburgh: T. & T. Clark, 1975, 1979. Advanced.

_____. *Romans.* Grand Rapids: Eerdmans, 1985.

Dunn, J. D. G. *Romans.* 2 vols. Dallas: Word, 1988. Advanced.

Johnson, L. T. *Reading Romans: A Literary and Theological Commentary.* New York: Crossroad, 1997.

Moo, D. J. *The Epistle to the Romans.* Grand Rapids: Eerdmans, 1996. Advanced.

_____. *The NIV Application Commentary: Romans.* Grand Rapids: Zondervan, 2000.

Schreiner, T. R. *Romans.* Grand Rapids: Baker, 1998.

Stuhlmacher, P. *Paul's Letter to the Romans.* Louisville: Westminster John Knox, 1994.

Books on Topics Appearing in Romans

Arminius, J. *Declaration of Sentiments,* I–IV, and *Apology Against Thirty-One Defamatory Articles,* Articles I, IV–VIII, XIII–XVII. For the Arminian view of divine sovereignty and human free will.

Augustine. *Confessions.* Especially the first several "books" for the problem of guilt.

Calvin, J. *Institutes of the Christian Religion,* Book I, chapter 15; Book II, chapters 1–5; Book III, chapters 21–24. For the Calvinistic view of divine sovereignty and human free will.

Calvin, J., and J. Sadoleto. *Reformation Debate: Sadoleto's Letter to the Genevans and Calvin's Reply.* Edited by J. C. Olin. New York: Harper & Row, 1966. For justification by faith as a disputed point during the Reformation.

Chafer, L. S. *He That Is Spiritual.* Grand Rapids: Zondervan [Dunham], 1918. On sanctification.

Lewis, C. S. *The Case for Christianity.* Part 1. New York: Macmillan, 1950. Or *Mere Christianity.* Book 1. London: G. Bles, 1952; reprint, San Francisco: HarperSanFrancisco, 2001. On human moral consciousness.

Luther, M. *Commentary* [or *Lectures*] *on Romans.* On 3:21–31.

Walvoord, J. F. *Israel in Prophecy.* Grand Rapids: Zondervan, 1962. For comparison with Paul's discussion of Israel in Romans 9–11.

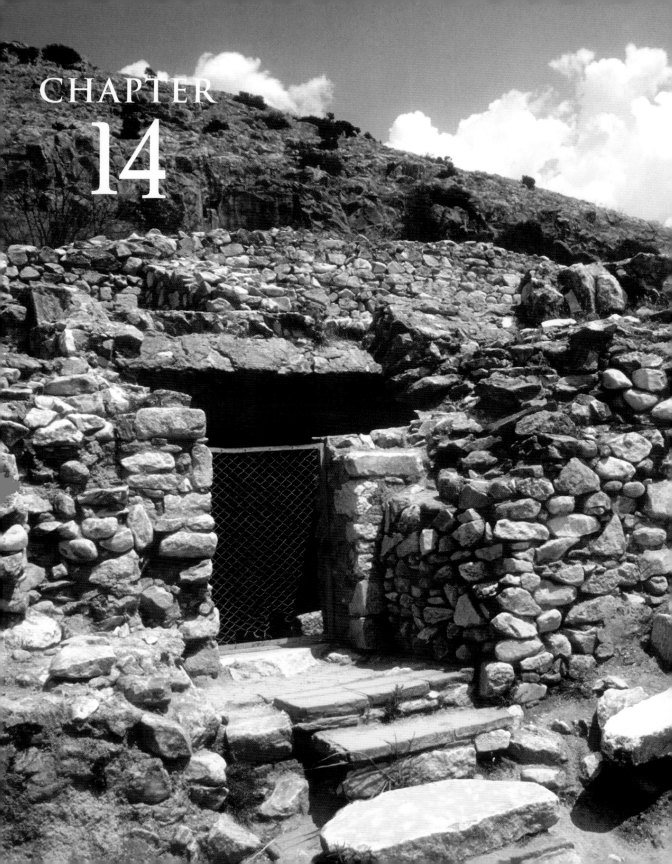

CHAPTER
14

THE PRISON LETTERS OF PAUL

Overview:

- Paul's Imprisonment
- Philemon: Plea for a Runaway Slave
- Colossians: Christ as the Head of the Church
- Ephesians: The Church as the Body of Christ
- Philippians: A Friendly Note of Thanks
- Summary

Study Goals—Learn:

- The various imprisonments from which Paul probably writes his Prison Letters
- The interrelations of the Prison Letters
- The circumstances that lead Paul to plead with Philemon on behalf of a runaway slave
- Why Paul writes to the church in Colossae though he is unacquainted with them
- The nature of the "Colossian heresy" as inferred from Paul's correctives
- The destination of the probably misnamed "Ephesians"
- How the structure and distinctive theological emphasis of Ephesians compare with those of Colossians
- What prompts the writing of Philippians
- The attitudes and prospects of Paul when he writes Philippians and his concerns for the church in Philippi

Entrance to a Greco-Roman jail

Paul's Imprisonment

Ephesians, ↓Philippians, Colossians, and Philemon constitute the Prison (or Captivity) Letters, so called because Paul is in prison (that is, captivity) when he writes them. There are two known imprisonments of Paul, one in Caesarea under the governorships of Felix and Festus (Acts 23:23–26:32), another in Rome while Paul awaits trial before Caesar (Acts 28:30–31). Supported by a small amount of early church tradition, some scholars have conjectured yet another imprisonment in Ephesus during Paul's extended ministry there. Paul does mention "frequent" imprisonments in 2 Corinthians 11:23, but these probably refer to overnight stays in jail, as at Philippi (Acts 16:19–40). The traditional view assigns all the Prison Letters to Paul's Roman imprisonment, but the Ephesian and Caesarean possibilities must at least be kept in mind for each of the Prison Letters.

Books of One Chapter

When citing a passage in a biblical book like Philemon that is undivided into chapters, only the verse number or numbers are indicated. It would be wrong, in other words, to cite Philemon 1:2, 19, as though the book had a first chapter as well as verses in that chapter; rather, Philemon 2, 19, referring only to verses.

PHILEMON: PLEA FOR A RUNAWAY SLAVE

Introductory Issues

Address

In the Letter to Philemon, Paul asks a Christian slavemaster named Philemon to receive kindly, perhaps even to release, his recently converted runaway slave ↓Onesimus, now returning. A resident of ↓Colossae, Philemon became a Christian through Paul ("you owe me your very self," verse 19). This conversion probably took place in nearby Ephesus during Paul's ministry there. A church meets in the house of Philemon (verse 2). Early Christians had no church buildings and therefore met in homes. If the number of believers grew too large for one home to accommodate them, they used several homes (hence the expression "house-churches").

An Outline of Philemon

Introduction: Greeting (1–3)
  I. Thanksgiving for Philemon (4–7)
  II. Plea for Onesimus (8–22)
Conclusion: Greetings and Benediction (23–25)

Philippians: fi-LIP-ee-uhnz ■ Onesimus: oh-NES-uh-muhs ■ Colossae: kuh-LOS-ee

Onesimus: Slave or Free Man?

It has recently been argued that Onesimus was not a slave, much less a runaway slave, but a free man—perhaps even Philemon's biological brother—who sought out Paul for the purpose of getting him as Philemon's friend and patron to settle a financial dispute between himself (Onesimus) and Philemon. But it is unlikely that "as a slave" in verse 16 means "as *if* a slave"; and in that same verse "a brother in the Lord" is more easily understood to mean "a brother through shared relationship with the Lord," as in Paul's calling Timothy "our brother" (verse 1), than to mean "a biological brother who also happens to be a Christian." Furthermore, under Roman law a slave could seek the help of his owner's friend to reestablish a good relationship with the owner.

Reading Philemon with Interpretation

Background

Onesimus absconded with some of his master's money and fled to Rome, perhaps to seek Paul's help as well as to escape (see the following discussions of the place of origin for Colossians and Ephesians, written and sent at the same time as Philemon). The apostle converted Onesimus and convinced him that now as a Christian he should return to his master and live up to the meaning of his name, for "Onesimus" means "profitable" (verses 10–12). With great tact and Christian courtesy, therefore, Paul writes to persuade Philemon not only to take back Onesimus without punishing him or putting him to death (a common treatment of runaway slaves) but also to welcome Onesimus "as a beloved brother . . . in the Lord" (verse 16).

Prospects

Paul wants to retain Onesimus as a helper (verse 13). It has been suggested that the confident "you will do even more than I say" (verse 21) broadly hints that Philemon should liberate Onesimus; but perhaps Paul is suggesting only that Philemon loan Onesimus for missionary work. Paul promises to pay Philemon the financial loss caused by Onesimus's theft. On the other hand, the immediate mention of Philemon's greater spiritual debt to Paul invites Philemon to cancel the financial debt that Paul has just assumed (verses 18–20). *Read Philemon 1–25.*

Comic actor playing the part of a runaway slave

COLOSSIANS: CHRIST AS THE HEAD OF THE CHURCH

Introductory Issues

Theme

In his Letter to the Colossians, Paul highlights the divine person and creative and redemptive work of Christ against devaluation of Christ by a particular brand of heresy that threatens the church in Colossae. Then Paul draws out the practical implications of this high Christology for everyday life and conduct.

Ephesian Origin?

The ancient Marcionite prologue to Colossians (see pages 80–81 on Marcion's Gnosticism) says that Paul writes this letter from Ephesus. The tradition is doubtful, however, because it also says that Paul writes Philemon from Rome. Yet Colossians and Philemon are inseparably linked—both letters mention Timothy, ↓Aristarchus, Mark, ↓Epaphras, Luke, ↓Demas, ↓Archippus, and Onesimus. The duplication of so many names must indicate that Paul writes and sends both letters at the same time and from the same place.

Furthermore, if Paul writes Colossians and Philemon from an Ephesian imprisonment, the slave Onesimus absconded with his master's money only 100 miles west to Ephesus. The shortness of this distance seems improbable, for Onesimus would have known that he might easily be captured so close to home. More likely, he fled far away to the larger city of Rome to hide himself among the crowds there. Moreover, Luke is with Paul when Paul writes Colossians (Colossians 4:14); but the description of Paul's Ephesian ministry is not one of Luke's "we"-sections in Acts. Despite partial support from the Marcionite tradition, then, we should reject an Ephesian imprisonment as the place of origin for Colossians.

Caesarean Origin?

It is even more improbable that Colossians comes from the Caesarean imprisonment. Caesarea was much smaller than Rome and therefore a less likely destination for a runaway slave seeking to escape detection. Onesimus would

Colossians

- "Paul . . . and Timothy our brother" (1:1).
- "He [Tychicus] is coming with Onesimus, our faithful and beloved brother, who is one of you" (4:9).
- "My fellow prisoner Aristarchus sends you his greetings, and so does Mark . . . . Epaphras . . . sends greetings. . . . Luke, the beloved physician, sends greetings, and so does Demas" (4:10–14).
- "And say to Archippus . . ." (4:17).

Philemon

- "Paul . . . and Timothy our brother" (1).
- "I appeal to you for my son Onesimus . . ." (10).
- "Epaphras, my fellow prisoner in Christ Jesus, sends you greetings, and so do Mark, Aristarchus, Demas and Luke, my fellow workers" (23–24).
- "And to Archippus" (2).

Aristarchus: air´is-TAHR-kuhs ■ Epaphras: EP-uh-fras ■ Demas: DEE-muhs ■ Archippus: ahr-KIP-uhs

scarcely have come in contact with Paul at Caesarea, for only Paul's friends could see him there (Acts 24:23). Also, the expectation of Paul that he will soon be released (he asks Philemon to prepare lodging for him, Philemon 22) does not tally with the Caesarean imprisonment, where Paul came to realize that his only hope lay in appealing to Caesar.

Roman Origin

Several considerations favor the Roman imprisonment:

- It is most likely that to hide his identity Onesimus fled to Rome, the most populous city in the empire.
- Luke's presence with Paul at the writing of Colossians agrees with Luke's accompanying Paul to Rome in Acts.
- The difference in doctrinal emphases between Colossians, where Paul is not preoccupied with the Judaizing controversy, and the Letters to the Galatians, Romans, and Corinthians, where he strongly emphasizes freedom from the Mosaic law, suggests that he writes Colossians during a later period, such as his Roman imprisonment, when the Judaizing controversy no longer dominates his thinking (though the attack on Judaizers in Philippians 3, probably written later, weakens this third argument).

The mound (tell) on which ancient Colossae was located

Occasion

The city of Colossae lay in the valley of the ↓Lycus River in a mountainous district about 100 miles east of Ephesus (see the map on page 317). The neighboring cities of ↓Laodicea and ↓Hierapolis overshadowed Colossae in importance. The distant way in which Paul writes that he has "heard" of his audience's faith (1:4) and his inclusion of them among those "who have never seen [his] face in the flesh" (2:1) imply that he neither founded the church in Colossae nor has visited it. Since the Colossians learned God's grace from **Epaphras** (1:6–7), Epaphras must have founded the church. Yet he is with Paul at the time of writing (4:12–13). We may surmise that Epaphras became a Christian through Paul's Ephesian ministry, evangelized the neighboring region of Colossae, Laodicea, and Hierapolis, and is now visiting Paul in prison to solicit his advice concerning a dangerous heresy threatening the Colossian church. Apparently **Archippus** has been left in charge of the church (4:17). Under this hypothesis we can understand why Paul assumes authority over the Colossian church even though he has never been there: since he is "grandfather" of the church through his convert Epaphras, his judgment has been sought.

A Gentile Church

The Christians in Colossae are predominantly Gentile. Paul talks about "the uncircumcision" of their "flesh" (2:13). In 1:27 the phrases "among the Gentiles" and "in you" seem to be synonymous. And the description of the Colossians as "once estranged and hostile in mind" (1:21) matches similar phraseology in Ephesians 2:11–13, where Paul refers explicitly to "Gentiles by birth."

The Colossian Heresy

The Letter to the Colossians centers on the so-called Colossian heresy. We can infer certain features of this false teaching from the counteremphases of Paul. In fact, he may borrow the false teachers' favorite terms, such as *knowledge* and *fullness,* and turn them against the heresy by filling them with orthodox content. The heresy

- Diminishes the person of Christ, so that Paul stresses the preeminence of Christ (1:15–19)
- Emphasizes human philosophy, that is, human speculations divorced from divine revelation (2:8)
- Contains elements of Judaism, such as circumcision (2:11; 3:11), rabbinic tradition (2:8), dietary regulations and Sabbath and festival observances (2:16)

Lycus: LIK-uhs ■ Laodicea: lay-od´i-SEE-uh ■ Hierapolis: hi´uh-RAP-uh-lis

- Includes the worship of angels as intermediaries keeping the highest God (pure Spirit) unsullied through contact with the physical universe (a pagan feature, since although orthodox Jews have constructed a hierarchy of angels, they do not worship them or regard the materiality of the universe as evil [2:18])
- Flaunts an exclusivist air of secrecy and superiority, against which Paul stresses the all-inclusiveness and publicity of the gospel (1:20, 23, 28; 3:11).

The Colossian heresy, then, blends together **Jewish legalism, Greek philosophic speculation,** and **oriental mysticism.** Perhaps the location of Colossae on an important trade route linking East and West has contributed to the mixed character of the false teaching. Most of its features will appear full-blown in later Gnosticism and in the Greek and oriental mystery religions. But the presence of Judaistic features points to a syncretistic Judaism lacking the redeemer motif of later, anti-Judaistic Gnosticism.

An Outline of Colossians

Introduction (1:1–12)
    A. Greeting (1:1–2)
    B. Thanksgiving (1:3–8)
    C. Prayer (1:9–12)
I. The Preeminence of Christ in Christian Doctrine (1:13–2:23)
    A. His creative and redemptive work (1:13–23)
    B. His proclamation by Paul (1:24–2:7)
    C. His sufficiency over against the Colossian heresy (2:8–23)
II. The Preeminence of Christ in Christian Conduct (3:1–4:6)
    A. Union with Christ in his death, resurrection, and exaltation (3:1–4)
    B. Application of death with Christ to sinful actions (3:5–11)
    C. Application of resurrection with Christ to righteous actions (3:12–4:6)
Conclusion (4:7–18)
    A. The coming of Tychicus and Onesimus (4:7–9)
    B. Greetings and final instructions (4:10–17)
    C. Farewell and benediction (4:18)

Fellow Servants with Paul

- "The word of truth, the gospel . . . just as you learned it from Epaphras, our beloved fellow servant, who is a faithful minister of Christ on your behalf, who also informed us of your love in the Spirit" (Colossians 1:5–8).
- "Epaphras, who is one of you . . . , sends greetings. . . . I vouch for him that he has much concern for you and those in Laodicea and Hierapolis" (Colossians 4:12–13).
- "And say to Archippus, 'See to the ministry that you have received in the Lord, that you fulfill it'" (Colossians 4:17).

Reading Colossians with Interpretation

Doctrine, Especially Christology

As seen in the outline, Colossians divides into two main sections: doctrine (chapters 1–2) and exhortation (chapters 3–4). Paul puts the doctrinal accent on Christology. The letter opens with a greeting, thanksgiving, and prayer. Then begins the great christological discussion. *Read Colossians 1:1–2:23.*

Paul's laudatory statements about Christ mention

- His kingdom (1:13)
- His redemptive work (1:14)
- His being the outward representation ("image") of God in human form (1:15)
- His supremacy over creation as its master and heir (since firstborn sons received more inheritance than other sons, "firstborn of all creation" [1:15] need not imply that Jesus was the first to be created)
- His creatorship (1:16)
- His preexistence and cohesion of the universe (1:17)
- His headship over the new creation, the church (1:18)
- His primacy in rising from the dead never to die again (1:18)

A number of scholars take 1:15–20 as a quotation from some early hymn. "The fullness of God" dwelling in Christ is the **totality of divine nature.** When Paul writes that his own sufferings complete "what is lacking in Christ's afflictions" (1:24), there is no implication that Christ suffered too little to provide a full atonement for sins. Paul means that sufferings endured in spreading the gospel are also necessary if people are to be saved and that Christ continues to suffer with his persecuted witnesses because of their union, or solidarity, with him (compare Jesus' statement to Paul when Paul was still persecuting the church, "Saul, Saul, why do you persecute *me*?" Acts 9:4). The term **"mystery"** ("this mystery, which is Christ in you," 1:27) refers to theological truth hidden from unbelievers but revealed to believers.

In his polemic against the Colossian heresy (2:8–23), Paul charges that this false teaching obscures the preeminence of Christ; that its ritual observances, taken from Judaism, only foreshadow spiritual realities in Christ; and that its asceticism and angel-worship foster pride and detract from the glory of Christ.

Exhortation

The union of believers with Christ in his death, resurrection, and ascension forms the basis for practical exhortations. Believers are to adopt God's point of view by regarding themselves as dead in Christ to sin and alive in him to righteousness. *Read Colossians 3:1–4:18.* "↓Scythians" (3:11) were regarded as particularly uncouth barbarians. Since salt retards corruption, speech "seasoned with salt" (4:6) probably means speech that is not corrupt or obscene.

Scythians: SITH-ee-uhnz

EPHESIANS: THE CHURCH AS THE BODY OF CHRIST

Introductory Issues

Theme

Unlike most of Paul's letters, Ephesians seems not to have been written in response to a particular circumstance or controversy. It has an almost meditative quality. In the theme shared with Colossians—Christ the head of the church his body—Ephesians emphasizes the church as Christ's body, whereas Colossians emphasizes the headship of Christ. Colossians warns against a false doctrine that diminishes Christ; Ephesians expresses praise for the unity and blessings shared by all believers in Christ.

↓Tychicus

Paul must have written Ephesians and Colossians at approximately the same time, because the subject matter in the two letters looks related and because some verses about Tychicus appear in almost identical form in both letters. The indication that by word of mouth Tychicus will add further details about Paul's circumstances implies that Tychicus will carry both letters at once to their destinations. Paul's self-identification as "a prisoner of the Lord" indicates his imprisonment at the time of writing and his awareness of the Lord's purpose in that imprisonment.

Though Ephesians may be directed to the region around Ephesus rather than to Ephesus itself (see the discussion below), it is hardly probable that Paul writes from an Ephesian imprisonment. So far as the Caesarean imprisonment is concerned, his reference to preaching "boldly" as "an ambassador in chains" implies that he is still proclaiming the gospel in spite of his imprisonment (Ephesians 6:20); yet in Caesarea only his friends could visit him (Acts 24:22–23). In Rome, however, he preached to a steady stream of visitors who came to his house-prison (Acts 28:30–31). Like the closely related letters to the Colossians and Philemon, therefore, Ephesians seems to have been written during the Roman imprisonment.

Goodspeed's Theory

The American scholar E. J. Goodspeed theorized that an admirer of Paul wrote Ephesians toward the end of the first century. Goodspeed went so far as to suggest that the admirer was Onesimus, the converted slave about

Ephesians 6:21–22

"Tychicus, our beloved brother and faithful minister in the Lord, will make known to you everything, so that you also may know the news about me, what I am doing. I am sending him to you for this very purpose, that you may know the news concerning us, and that he may encourage your hearts."

Colossians 4:7–9

"Tychicus, our beloved brother and faithful minister and fellow servant in the Lord, will make known to you all the news about me. I am sending him to you for this very purpose, that you may know the news concerning us and that he may encourage your hearts. He is coming with Onesimus, our faithful and beloved brother, who is one of you. They will make known to you everything that is happening here."

Tychicus: TIK-uh-kuhs

whom Paul wrote to Philemon. According to this theory, the writer designed Ephesians to introduce a collection of Paul's genuine letters by way of summarizing their theology. The collection was prompted by the prominence of Paul in Acts, written just recently.[1] To the contrary, however, manuscript evidence is lacking that Ephesians ever stood first in the collection of his letters, against expectation if Goodspeed's hypothesis were true. Moreover, very early church tradition assigns Ephesians to Paul himself.

Destination Not Ephesus

The phrase "in Ephesus," which refers to the locale of the addressees (1:1), is missing in the most ancient manuscripts. Thus Paul omits the geographical location of the addressees altogether. Furthermore, the distant way in which he speaks of his having "heard" about their faith (1:15) and of their having "heard" about his ministry (3:2) combines with the absence of his usual terms of endearment to rule out Ephesus as the destination; for Paul labored there for more than two years and knew the Ephesian Christians intimately, as they also knew him (Acts 19:1–20:1, 10–38).

LAODICEANS? Some early tradition identifies the church in Laodicea as the recipients of this letter. The German scholar Adolf von Harnack suggested that early copyists suppressed the name Laodicea because of the condem-

1. E. J. Goodspeed, *The Key to Ephesians* (Chicago: University of Chicago Press, 1956), and other works by Goodspeed and those following his lead.

The stadium at Laodicea

nation of the Laodicean church in Revelation 3:14–22 and that later copyists substituted the name Ephesus because of Paul's close association with the church in that city. Paul does mention a letter to Laodicea; but since no manuscript mentions Laodicea in Ephesians 1:1, the making of "Ephesians" into "Laodiceans" in early tradition probably represents an attempt to identify the letter to Laodicea mentioned in Colossians.

> "And when this letter [Colossians] has been read to you, have it read also in the church of the Laodiceans; and you in turn **read the letter from Laodicea**" (Colossians 4:16).

A CIRCULAR LETTER More likely, "Ephesians" is a circular letter addressed to various churches in the vicinity of Ephesus. Under this view, Paul's mention of the letter to Laodicea in Colossians 4:16 may refer to "Ephesians" but would not imply that the letter is addressed only to the church of Laodicea. Rather, in its circulation to the churches throughout the region the letter has reached Laodicea and is about to go to nearby Colossae. A circular destination for the letter then explains the omission of a city name in the address. If a single copy of the letter circulated from Ephesus and came back to Ephesus, the name of that city could easily have become linked to the letter, as happened.

Structure
Like Colossians, Ephesians falls into two parts. Ephesians 1–3 contains doctrine and discusses the spiritual privileges of the church. Ephesians 4–6 contains exhortation and discusses the spiritual responsibilities of Christians.

An Outline of Ephesians

Introduction: Greeting (1:1–2)
I. The Spiritual Privileges of the Church (1:3–3:21)
  A. Praise for spiritual blessings planned by the Father, accomplished by the Son, and applied by the Spirit (1:3–14)
  B. Thanksgiving and prayer for increased comprehension of divine grace (1:15–23)
  C. The regeneration of sinners by divine grace alone (2:1–10)
  D. The reconciliation of Gentiles with God and with Jews in the church (2:11–22)
  E. Paul's sense of privilege in proclaiming the gospel (3:1–13)
  F. Prayer for stability through increased comprehension (3:14–19)
  G. Doxology (3:20–21)
II. The Spiritual Responsibilities of the Church (4:1–6:20)
  A. Maintenance of unity through diversity of edifying ministry (4:1–16)
  B. Moral conduct (4:17–5:14)
  C. The filling with the Spirit (5:15–21)
  D. A code for Christian households (5:22–6:9)
    1. Submission of wives to husbands (5:22–24)

Reading Ephesians with Interpretation

Heavenly Blessings

After a greeting (1:1–2) Paul launches into a doxology of praise to God for spiritual blessings in Christ "in the heavenly realms" (1:3–14). That is to say, the union of believers with Christ entails a share in his heavenly exaltation as well as in his earthly death, burial, and resurrection. The doxology delineates the parts played in salvation by all three members of the Trinity:

- The Father **chose** believers (the doctrine of election, 1:4).
- The Son **redeemed** them (1:7).
- The Holy Spirit "**sealed**" them; that is, the gift of the Spirit is God's down payment, or guarantee, that he will complete their salvation at the return of Christ (1:13–14).

Following the doxology is a thanksgiving and prayer that believers may comprehend and appreciate the immensity of God's grace and wisdom (1:15–23). *Read Ephesians 1:1–23.*

Divine Grace

To help his audience appreciate the immensity of God's grace, Paul contrasts their domination by sin before conversion and their freedom from that tyranny after conversion. He also emphasizes that salvation is wholly unearned; it comes by God's grace, through faith, and apart from meritorious good works. God's action does produce good works, but they are a consequence rather than a means of salvation. His grace reveals itself especially in the redemption of Gentiles from paganism and in their unity with Jews in the church. The dividing wall of hostility between the two groups, symbolized by the wall in the temple courtyards beyond which Gentiles were not allowed to go, does not exist in the church. Alternatively, the dividing wall represents the old barrier between God and human beings, now broken down by Christ. But

> **Election and Nonelection**
>
> Paul writes of divine election to salvation *regardless* of human works, whereas the following speaks of divine nonelection to salvation *because of* human works:
> "For God did not choose them ['those who turn from the Way and shun the ordinance'] from eternity past. He knew their deeds before they were created and abhorred their generations" (*Damascus Document* 2:7–8).

however grand the plan of salvation, Paul and his audience face the unpleasant reality of present persecution. He writes that his awareness of divine grace and of his privilege in spreading the good news prevents discouragement. Similar awareness on the part of his audience will also prevent their discouragement. The section therefore closes with another doxology and prayer that the audience may be stabilized by increased spiritual knowledge. *Read Ephesians 2:1–3:21.*

> ### The Structure of Ephesians 2:8–10
> You have been saved:
> - by grace;
> - through faith.
>
> Your having been saved is:
> - not from yourselves;
> - God's gift;
> - not by works;
> - God's work for us to do good works.

Unity and Diversity

The practical exhortations begin with a plea for outward unity growing out of the already existing spiritual unity of the church. Yet this unity includes a diversity of function for the growth of the body, or church. Each believer has a ministerial function. Leaders in the church are to equip other believers for the carrying out of their various functions. *Read Ephesians 4:1–16.*

Holy Conduct

Miscellaneous instructions on holiness follow:

- Tell the truth.
- Be righteously indignant when necessary, but do not sin by failing to control your anger.
- Do not steal.
- Avoid obscene speech and risqué humor.

The section closes with a metrical triplet that may have come from an early baptismal hymn, sung at the moment of rising from the water:

> Awake, sleeper,
> And rise from the dead,
> And the Christ will shine on you.

Read Ephesians 4:17–5:14.

Filling with the Spirit

Paul's exhortation to be filled with the Holy Spirit indicates that such a filling will show itself in avoiding drunkenness (contrast the drunken orgies of Hellenistic cults) and in joyful singing, witnessing, and submission to one another. In particular, **wives** should submit themselves to their husbands as the church is submissive to Christ its head. **Husbands** should love their wives as Christ loved the church his body. **Children** should obey their parents. **Fathers** should be reasonable with their children. **Slaves** should obey their masters. And **masters** should be kind to their slaves.

Paul unites the metaphors of head and body with a picture of the church as the **bride** and **wife** of Christ, who is the groom and husband. Just as husband and wife become physically one ("one flesh") in the relationship of marriage, so Christ and the church are **one in the Spirit**. Scholars have suggested different sources for Paul's metaphor of the church as Christ's body:

- The Stoic notion that the universe is a body with many different parts
- The rabbinic idea that human beings are the members of Adam's body in a literal sense
- The symbolic or sacramental union of believers with Christ's body when they eat the bread of the Lord's Supper
- A Hebrew concept of corporate personality
- Paul's own doctrine of the union between believers and Christ

A soldier in full armor

The Armor of God

Before saying farewell, Paul urges his audience to don the spiritual armor provided by God and to fight the satanic powers that dominate the world. Perhaps the sight of the soldier to whom Paul is chained while dictating Ephesians in his house-prison suggests "the full armor of God." The word for "shield" denotes the large kind that covers the whole body, not the small circular shield used by Greeks. "Flaming arrows" refers to darts and arrows dipped in pitch or some other combustible material, set aflame, and hurled or shot toward the enemy. *Read Ephesians 5:15–6:24.*

"And one could find no other fellowship more necessary or more pleasant than that of husbands and wives. For what man is so devoted to his companion as an ardent wife is to the man she has married? What brother to his brother? What son to his parents? Who is so longed for when absent as a husband by his wife, and a wife by her husband? Whose presence would do more to lighten grief or increase joy or straighten out a calamity? To whom are all things regarded to be shared—both bodies, souls, and possessions—except husband and wife? For these reasons, too, all men regard the love of husband and wife to be the most venerable of all loves" (Musonius Rufus, "Is Marriage a Handicap for the Pursuit of Philosophy?" 2–11).

PHILIPPIANS: A FRIENDLY NOTE OF THANKS

Introductory Issues

Theme and Occasion

The church at Philippi appears to be Paul's favorite. He has received regular assistance from it (Philippians 4:15–20; 2 Corinthians 11:7–9). The Letter to the Philippians is thus the most personal of any that he wrote to a church. In fact, it is a thank-you for their most recent financial gift (4:10, 14), which they sent through ↓Epaphroditus (2:25).

Epaphroditus

During his trip or after his arrival with the offering, Epaphroditus fell almost fatally ill (2:27). Back home the Philippians heard of his illness, and word came to Epaphroditus that they were concerned about him. Paul senses that Epaphroditus wants to return to Philippi and therefore sends him with the letter (2:25–30).

Purposes

The return of Epaphroditus not only enables Paul to write his gratitude for the **financial assistance** given by believers in Philippi. It also gives him opportunity to counteract a tendency toward **divisiveness** in their church (2:2; 4:2), to warn against **Judaizers** (chapter 3), and to prepare the church for **approaching visits** by Timothy and, God willing, by Paul himself (2:19–24). "Epaphroditus" is the full form of the name "Epaphras," which appears in Colossians. But we do not have enough evidence to identify Epaphras, founder of the church in Colossae, with Epaphroditus, messenger of the church in Philippi.

Caesarean Origin?

Paul is in prison at the time of writing ("my chains," 1:7, 13). But to which of his imprisonments does he refer? Probably not the Caesarean, because there he would not be able to preach so freely as is implied in 1:12–13 (compare Acts 24:23). Also, he would know that release in Caesarea would mean almost instant lynching by Jews in the territory; his only prospect of safety would lie in appealing to Caesar and thus going to Rome under guard. Yet in Philippians 1:25; 2:24 the hope for release (Philemon 22) has turned into confidence that the release will occur "soon."

Epaphroditus: i-paf´ruh-D/-tuhs

Ephesian Origin?

Presenting a better possibility is an imprisonment in Ephesus. Paul writes that he hopes to send Timothy to Philippi (2:19, 23); and Luke writes that Paul sent Timothy and Erastus to Philippi from Ephesus (Acts 19:22). (But if the two passages are really parallel, why does Paul omit mentioning Erastus in Philippians 2:19–24?) The polemic against Judaizers in chapter 3 looks like Paul's earlier polemics around the time he spent in Ephesus. (It remains possible, however, that a later Judaizing threat revives his earlier polemics.)

Furthermore, inscriptions testify that a detachment of the ↓Praetorian Guard was once stationed in Ephesus, and Paul mentions the Praetorian Guard in 1:13. Similarly, "Caesar's household" (4:22) might refer to imperial civil servants at Ephesus. According to Acts, Luke accompanied Paul to Rome but not to Ephesus. Paul does not mention Luke in Philippians as he does in Colossians 4:14 and Philemon 24. This nonmention therefore suggests that Paul writes Philippians from an Ephesian imprisonment. (But if he writes toward the end of his Roman imprisonment, which lasted at least two years, Luke might have left Paul by then, so that this argument from silence is not decisive.)

Another argument for an Ephesian imprisonment is that if Paul writes Philippians from Rome at a later date, he could hardly state that his readers have for some time "lacked opportunity" to support him financially (4:10). So much time has elapsed by the time of the Roman imprisonment that they would have had prolonged opportunity; but an earlier Ephesian imprisonment allows for such a statement. (On the other hand, we do not know all the financial circumstances of Paul and the Philippians. To avoid the charge of embezzlement, Paul may have refused personal gifts during the period he was collecting money for the church in Jerusalem. Such a refusal may be the reason the Philippians have "lacked opportunity.")

Generally considered the strongest argument in favor of an Ephesian imprisonment over against the Roman is that Philippians presupposes too many **journeys between Rome and Philippi** (about a month's journey apart), whereas the short distance between Ephesus and Philippi makes the numerous journeys more

A game scratched on stone in ancient Philippi

conceivable within a short period of time. The journeys presupposed in Philippians are as follows:

- The carrying of a message from Rome to Philippi that Paul has been imprisoned in Rome
- Epaphroditus's bringing of a gift from Philippi to Rome
- The delivery back to Philippi of word that Epaphroditus has fallen ill
- The return of a report that the Philippians are concerned about Epaphroditus

In reality, however, this argument for Ephesus and against Rome lacks substance. Time for the journeys between Rome and Philippi would require only four to six months in toto. Allowance for intervals between the journeys still keeps the whole amount of required time well within the two years that we know Paul spent in Rome (Acts 28:30). And he almost certainly spent more than two years there; for even by their end his trial had not yet started, but a transfer from his own rented house (Acts 28:16, 23, 30) to the barracks of the Praetorian Guard on the ↓Palatine Hill (Philippians 1:13) and his confidence of soon release and of a subsequent visit to Philippi (1:19–26; 2:23–24) would favor that his trial is finally in progress and near conclusion and therefore that he is writing after the two years mentioned in Acts.

Moreover, the Philippians may have known before Paul arrived in Rome that he was going there as a prisoner, so that Epaphroditus already could have started toward Rome. Or, since the shipwreck delayed Paul at Malta, Epaphroditus may even have arrived in Rome before Paul. The Christians in Rome knew beforehand of Paul's coming, for they met Paul outside the city and escorted him the rest of the way (Acts 28:15–16). Had Epaphroditus informed them? Only the second, third, and fourth journeys are necessarily presupposed, then; and the temporal factor does not at all hinder the view that Paul writes to the Philippians from Rome.

Against an Ephesian imprisonment, Paul fails to mention the offering for Jerusalem, though it was very much on his mind throughout his third missionary journey, during which he ministered in Ephesus; and his writing about monetary matters in Philippians would have made a reference to the offering almost certain had he been writing from Ephesus during that period. Also, we must bear in mind that an Ephesian imprisonment of Paul is largely conjectural and not at all mentioned in Acts even though Luke goes into great detail about Paul's ministry in Ephesus (Acts 19).

Roman Origin

In favor of Rome, "**Praetorian Guard**" (literally, "the whole praetorium," 1:13) and "**Caesar's household**" (4:22) most likely point to Rome. According to 1:19–27, Paul's life is at stake in the trial ("whether by life or by

---

Palatine: PAL-uh-tin´

2. Since the Praetorian Guard in Rome numbered about nine thousand, but in Ephesus far fewer, the fact that "the whole" have heard of Paul's imprisonment for Christ (1:13) is thought by some to favor Ephesus over Rome. But the success of Paul's witness elsewhere suggests that the whole guard may indeed have heard, especially if Paul has converted some of them. Or "praetorium" may refer to the emperor's palace rather than to a large group of soldiers making up the guard.

death," for instance). The trial must therefore be before Caesar in Rome, for in any other location Paul could always exercise his right of appeal to Caesar. The early tradition of the Marcionite prologue likewise assigns the letter to Rome. For all these reasons and because of the weakness of arguments to the contrary, the traditional view that Paul writes Philippians from Rome remains the best.[2]

An Outline of Philippians

Introduction: Greeting (1:1–2)
I. Personal Matters (1:3–26)
    A. Paul's thanksgiving, prayer, and affection for the Christians in Philippi (1:3–11)
    B. Paul's preaching in prison, prospect of release, and readiness to die (1:12–26)
II. Exhortations (1:27–2:18)
    A. To worthy conduct (1:27–30)
    B. To unity by humility, with the example of Christ's self-emptying (2:1–18)
III. The Sending of Timothy and Epaphroditus to Philippi (2:19–30)
IV. Warning Against the Judaizers, with a Famous Autobiographical Passage (3:1–21)
V. Exhortations (4:1–9)
    A. To unity between Euodia and Syntyche (4:1–3)
    B. To joy and trust (4:4–7)
    C. To nobility of thought (4:8–9)
VI. Thanks for Financial Assistance (4:10–20)
Conclusion: Greetings and a Benediction (4:21–23)

The Next Life

Compare and contrast the following with Paul's "desire to depart and be with Christ, which is better by far" (Philippians 1:23): "But if my body should become water-logged beforehand, it will sink into its fate. Yet my soul will not sink; rather, being a deathless entity, it will fly up on high into heaven.... I will not be a citizen among human beings, but among gods. I will not erect others' statues; rather, others will erect statues to me" (Letter of Heraclitus to Amphidamas, number 5, lines 15–21).

Reading Philippians with Interpretation

Joy in Hardship

The character of Philippians as a letter of thanks makes for some informality. Throughout, the dominant emotional note is one of joy. In the first chapter—after the customary greeting, thanksgiving, and prayer—Paul describes the ministry he is carrying on despite his imprisonment, even because of it. The palace guard and Roman officialdom in general are hearing the gospel. Moreover, the boldness of Paul's witness has inspired other Christians, even those who do not like him. The latter are not false teachers, however, for he calls them "brothers." *Read Philippians 1:1–30.*

↓*Kenosis*

Read Philippians 2:1–30. This chapter is famous for the passage on Jesus' **self-emptying**, or humiliation, and **exaltation** (2:6–11). Many scholars think Paul is quoting an early Christian hymn. Whether or not a hymn, however, the passage is incidental to an exhortation to ecclesiastical **unity through humility**, of which Jesus provides the great example. The ancient Greco-Roman world despised humility; Christian teaching makes it a virtue. The passage mentions the existence of Christ before his incarnation—that is, his preexistence— and the emptying of himself. The Greek verb "to empty," ↓*kenoun*, has given rise to the *kenosis*-theory of the incarnation, the incarnation as an emptying (*kenosis* being a noun cognate to the verb). But of what did Christ empty himself? Of divine metaphysical attributes, such as omnipotence, omniscience, and omnipresence (though not of divine moral attributes, such as love and justice)? But he often displayed these metaphysical attributes according to the gospel accounts of his earthly ministry. Of the independent exercise of those attributes (compare John 5:19)? But had he ever acted independently of the Father? Or simply of the outward

> Epictetus describes a person as "humble" in the sense of "petty," as shown by the further descriptions "hypercritical, quick-tempered, cowardly, finding fault with everything, blaming everybody, never quiet, vain-glorious" (*Discourses* 3.2.14).

kenosis: ki-NOH-sis ■ *kenoun:* keh-NOON

The Structure and Meaning of Philippians 2:6–11

A Who existing in the form of God did not consider being equal with God something to be taken advantage of,

   B but emptied himself by having taken the form of a slave,

      C having come to be in the likeness of human beings;
      and having been found as a human being in constitution,

   B' he humbled himself by becoming obedient to the extent of death, even death on a cross.

A' Therefore also God has highly exalted him and granted him the name above every name, that in Jesus' name should bow every knee of heavenly and earthly and subterranean beings and every tongue confess, "Jesus Christ is Lord," for the glory of God the Father.

• A and A' refer to Christ's pre-earthly existence and postearthly existence, respectively.
• B and B' refer synonymously to Christ's death on a cross, a slave's kind of death.
• C alone refers to Christ's incarnation, which enabled his self-emptying, self-humbling in death.
• The greater length of A' puts emphasis on Christ's exaltation.
• Jesus' name is probably not the name which *is* "Jesus," but the name which he *has,* that is, "Lord."

Philippians 2:12b–13

"Work out your own salvation with fear and trembling, for it is God working in you to will and to work according to his good purpose."

Mishnah, *Avot* 3:16

"Everything is foreseen, but freedom of choice is granted; and the world is judged with goodness, yet everything is according to the preponderance of works."

glory of his deity? But does not "himself" require something inward? Perhaps then the self-emptying does not refer to incarnation at all, but to Jesus' **expiring on the cross**. If so, there is synonymous parallelism with a reference to death in the following verse and a possible allusion to Isaiah 53:12: "he poured out [that is, emptied] his soul [a Hebrew equivalent of 'himself'] to death."

"Finally, my brothers and sisters" (3:1) sounds so much like the closing part of a letter (yet two more chapters follow) and Paul changes tone so suddenly that some scholars posit a long interpolation, beginning in 3:2, from another letter. But the theory lacks manuscript evidence. It is better to suppose a break in dictation, perhaps with fresh news from Philippi about a threat of false teachers there. Paul intended to close but now thinks it necessary to prolong the letter with a warning against the Judaizers.

Against Judaizers

Chapter 3 contains another famous passage: Paul's autobiographical review of his Jewish background and the revolution in his scale of values when Christ became the goal of his life (3:3–14). Again, however, the passage is incidental—this time to a warning against the Judaizers, who practice, according to Paul's sarcastic term, "mutilation" instead of circumcision (3:2). Paul also calls them "dogs," regarded then as despicable creatures, the very term by which Jews often referred to Gentiles. Still another designation is "evil-workers," an ironic counterthrust at their belief in salvation at least partly by good works. Contrastingly, circumcision consists of inward faith in Christ Jesus alone, no reliance on one's own merit mixed in.

Pauline Autobiography

Paul's Jewish background was impeccable:

- Circumcision on the eighth day after birth, exactly as prescribed by the Mosaic law (Leviticus 12:3)
- Israelite ancestry
- Tribal origin in Benjamin, from which came the first king of Israel, Saul (another name of Paul)
- Hebraistic rather than Hellenistic practice and heritage (compare page 68)
- Phariseeism
- Zealousness to the point of persecuting the church
- Observance of the law so scrupulous that others could find nothing to fault

But the entrance of Christ into his life caused Paul not merely to dismiss, but to renounce as liabilities, all his former assets as such a Jew. And he continues to do so, growing to regard them as "**rubbish**" (3:8), that he might experience increasing union with Christ in Christ's **resurrection, sufferings,** and **death.** Realizing that his audience might misunderstand him to claim perfection, Paul disclaims it and expresses the ardor with which, forgetting the past, he is pursuing a **heavenly goal** (3:12–16). "Forgetting" does not mean banishing from memory (if that were possible), but disregarding as to present potency.

The discussion comes back to the **Judaizers,** who oppose the cross of Christ by requiring works of the law, who worship their belly by insisting on adherence to the dietary restrictions of the law, who glory in their shame by exposing nakedness for the rite of circumcision, and who set their minds on earthly things by occupying themselves with outward forms and ceremonies (3:17–19). Some scholars see antinomian and perfectionist Gnostics as the target of these remarks; but Paul's appeal to his own Judaistic, indeed Pharisaical, background favors identification with the Judaizers. Chapter 3 closes with a reference to the Christians' "commonwealth" or "citizenship" in heaven, a figure of speech particularly meaningful to the Philippians, whose own city was a colony populated mainly with Roman citizens living away from their true home in Italy. *Read Philippians 3:1–4:23.*

Exhortations

The various exhortations in chapter 4 include a plea for unity between two women of the church, ↓Euodia and ↓Syntyche, former helpers of Paul. The man who is to aid their reconciliation is a "true yokefellow," unknown by name unless that is his name with a play on its meaning: "↓*Syzygos* [Greek for 'yokefellow, comrade'], truly so called" (4:3). At any rate, Paul asks him to live up to his name or description by promoting the reconciliation. Exhortations to joy, patience, trust, prayer, thanksgiving, and nobility of thought follow with promises of God's presence and peace and of Jesus' return.

Thanks and Conclusion

Then Paul expresses thanks for the Philippians' recent gift to him as well as for previous contributions. Throughout this section he maintains disinterest in money for its own sake and for his personal benefit but indicates a concern for and confidence in the reward of the Philippians for having given so generously. Finally, greetings and a benediction conclude the letter.

A running athlete

Euodia: yoo-OH-dee-uh ■ Syntyche: SIN-ti-kee ■ *Syzygos:* SYOO-dzyoo-gaws

Summary

Paul writes Ephesians, Philippians, Colossians, and Philemon while in prison—hence the designation "Prison Letters." Traditionally and probably, it is from his imprisonment in Rome that he writes; but his imprisonments in Caesarea and possibly in Ephesus offer other possibilities.

Paul writes to Philemon on behalf of Philemon's slave Onesimus, who has stolen from Philemon, run away, become a Christian through Paul, and is returning to Philemon. Paul's letter urges Philemon to receive Onesimus forgivingly and welcome him into Philemon's house-church. Paul also assumes Onesimus's financial debt but hints that Philemon cancel it and loan Onesimus to help Paul, possibly even to free him for that purpose.

Epaphras founded the largely Gentile church in Colossae; but a heresy of mixed legalistic, philosophic, and mystical ingredients is infecting the church there, so that he has left it in charge of Archippus and has been seeking Paul's help against the heresy. Paul's antidote exalts Christ over against ritualism, Greek speculation, and asceticism. After two chapters of doctrine, the letter closes with two chapters of instructions on Christian living.

Like Colossians, Ephesians divides into halves, doctrinal and hortatory—only each half has three chapters instead of two. Whereas Colossians highlights Christ as the head of his body the church, Ephesians highlights the church as the body whose head he is. As such, the church enjoys heavenly blessings and a unity in Christ that destroys the old antipathy between Jews and Gentiles. And though the demonic powers of evil attack the church, it can withstand in the Lord's might. A man named Tychicus is to deliver Ephesians along with Colossians and Philemon; but though misnamed after the city of Ephesus, the letter called Ephesians circulated to churches in the outlying region.

Paul writes Philippians toward the end of his imprisonment and expects to be released soon and visit the church in Philippi. Through one of their members, Epaphroditus, they have sent him financial help; so he thanks them for it in this letter, which Epaphroditus will carry with him on his return. Paul takes advantage of the opportunity to include also a correction of division in the church and a warning against Judaizers. A note of joy sounds throughout the letter, and the letter contains famous passages on Christ's self-emptying and exaltation and on Paul's transformation from a self-righteous persecutor of the church to a pursuer of God's high calling in Christ.

People to Remember

Archippus	Goodspeed, E. J.	Syntyche
Epaphras	Harnack, Adolf von	Timothy
Epaphroditus	Onesimus	Tychicus
Euodia	Philemon	

Places to Remember

Caesarea	Hierapolis	Philippi
Colossae	Laodicea	praetorium
Ephesus	Palatine Hill	Rome

Terms to Remember

Caesar's household	kenosis	Prison Letters
Colossian heresy	Marcionite prologue	Scythians
fullness of God	mystery	
house-churches	Praetorian Guard	

How Much Did You Learn?

- List the Prison Letters of Paul.
- Discuss the pros and cons of possible imprisonments from which Paul wrote.
- Identify the occasions for Paul's writing of the Prison Letters and the purposes for which he wrote. Which of these letters lacks a knowable occasion?
- Which of these letters has a circular address, and how do we deduce it does?
- What two of these letters share a structure and theme though they differ in length and emphasis?
- Identify the famous christological and Pauline autobiographical passages in these letters.

For Further Discussion

- Should Paul and the early Christians have crusaded against slavery? Why did they not? What should be the involvement or noninvolvement of the church in curing social ills—within the church, outside the church, officially, individually?
- Compare current neo-mysticism and intellectualism with the Colossian heresy.
- Why do people tend to react against the Ephesian emphasis on salvation through the sheer grace of God by constructing their own systems of salvation by meritorious works?
- What was the key to Paul's joy in hardship, as expressed in Philippians?

PHILEMON

For Further Investigation

Barth, M., and H. Blanke. *The Letter to Philemon.* Grand Rapids: Eerdmans, 2000.
Fitzmyer, J. A. *The Letter to Philemon.* New York: Doubleday, 2000.
See also the bibliography under the following subsection on Colossians.

COLOSSIANS

For Further Investigation

Barth, M., and H. Blanke. *Colossians.* New York: Doubleday, 1994. Advanced.
Dunn, J. D. G. *The Epistles to the Colossians and to Philemon: A Commentary on the Greek Text.* Grand Rapids: Eerdmans, 1996. Advanced.
Garland, D. E. *The NIV Application Commentary: Colossians and Philemon.* Grand Rapids: Zondervan, 1998.
O'Brien, P. T. *Colossians, Philemon.* Waco: Word, 1982. Advanced.
Wall, R. W. *Colossians and Philemon.* Downers Grove, Ill.: InterVarsity Press, 1993.

EPHESIANS

For Further Investigation

Best, E. *A Critical and Exegetical Commentary on Ephesians.* Edinburgh: T. & T. Clark, 1998. Advanced.
Lincoln, A. T. *Ephesians.* Dallas: Word, 1990. Advanced.
Morris, L. *Expository Reflections on the Letter to the Ephesians.* Grand Rapids: Baker, 1994.

O'Brien, P. T. *The Letter to the Ephesians.* Grand Rapids: Eerdmans, 1999.

Schnackenburg, R. *Ephesians: A Commentary.* Edinburgh: T. & T. Clark, 1991. Advanced.

Snodgrass, K. *The NIV Application Commentary: Ephesians.* Grand Rapids: Zondervan, 1996.

PHILIPPIANS

For Further Investigation

Bruce, F. F. *Philippians.* Peabody, Mass.: Hendrickson, 1989.

Fee, G. D. *Paul's Letter to the Philippians.* Grand Rapids: Eerdmans, 1995.

O'Brien, P. T. *The Epistle to the Philippians.* Grand Rapids: Eerdmans, 1991.

Silva, M. *Philippians.* Chicago: Moody, 1989.

Thielman, F. *The NIV Application Commentary: Philippians.* Grand Rapids: Zondervan, 1995.

Witherington, B., III. *Friendship and Finances in Philippi: The Letter of Paul to the Philippians.* Valley Forge, Pa.: Trinity Press International, 1994.

CHAPTER
15

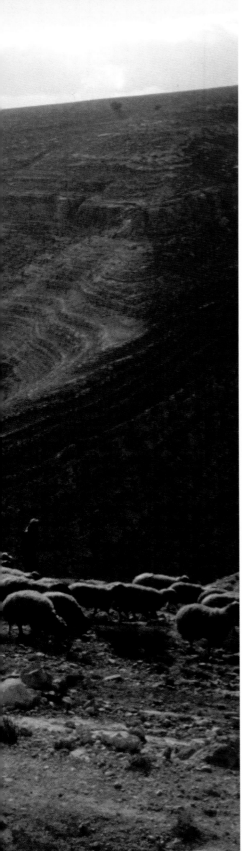

THE PASTORAL LETTERS OF PAUL

Overview:

- Introductory Issues
- First Timothy
- Titus
- Second Timothy
- Summary
- Excursus: A Resumé of Paul's Theology

Study Goals—Learn:

- What the Pastoral Letters are and why they are so called
- The pros and cons of Pauline authorship of the Pastorals
- Where the Pastorals fit in the chronology of Paul's life if he wrote them
- The instructions that the Pastorals give for the church's ongoing life and the maintenance of Christian belief

Pastoral life in the Judean Desert

Introductory Issues

Theme

First and **Second Timothy** and **Titus** constitute the Pastoral Letters, so called because Paul writes them to young pastors (literally, "shepherds"). They contain instructions concerning the administrative responsibilities of Timothy and Titus in churches, plus warnings against heresy and personal matters.

SUBSIDIARY PURPOSES In addition to the administrative instructions, Paul summons Titus to come to him in ↓Nicopolis on the west coast of Greece. And in 2 Timothy, Paul, reminiscing over his past career and expecting his execution soon, asks Timothy to come to him in Rome before winter (1:17; 4:6–9, 21). Paul fears that otherwise he may never see Timothy again, for navigation ceases during winter and the execution might occur in the meantime.

The Question of Authenticity

Modern higher critical scholarship casts more doubt on the authenticity of these letters than on any of the others claiming authorship by Paul. According to the view that denies his authorship, a ↓pseudonymous writer of the second century is using the authority of Paul's name to combat the rising tide of Gnosticism. It is said either that the Pastorals are wholly pseudonymous (but why then the presence of very personal items about Paul which have the ring of authenticity?) or, more often, that an admirer of Paul incorporates authentically Pauline fragments in writing the letters after Paul's lifetime.

FRAGMENTARY THEORY Disagreement exists concerning what sections of the Pastorals contain the supposed fragments written by Paul. Moreover, it is unlikely that mere fragments of genuinely Pauline letters would be preserved, especially since most of them are of a personal nature and lack theological attractiveness. It is still more unlikely that they would later be incorporated into longer pseudonymous letters in a haphazard way. And why would a forger concentrate almost all the fragments in 2 Timothy instead of distributing them evenly throughout the Pastorals? For that matter, why does he write three Pastorals? Their contents do not differ enough to indicate why he should be writing three instead of one.

Examples of Pastoral Fragments Claimed to Be Authentically Pauline

- "May the Lord grant mercy to the household of ↓Onesiphorus, because he often refreshed me and was not ashamed of my chains; rather, on coming to Rome, he very quickly searched for me and found me. May the Lord grant that he will find mercy from the Lord on that day! And you know quite well how many ways he helped me in Ephesus" (2 Timothy 1:16–18).
- "When I send ↓Artemas or Tychicus to you, be quick to come to me at Nicopolis, for I have decided to winter there. Send ↓Zenas the lawyer and Apollos on their way quickly; see that they lack nothing. And our people must also learn to devote themselves to good works in order that they may meet urgent needs and not be unfruitful. All those who are with me send you greetings. Greet those who love us in the faith. Grace be with you all" (Titus 3:12–15).
- See also 2 Timothy 3:10–11; 4:1–2a, 5b–22.

Nicopolis: ni-KOP-uh-lis ■ pseudonymous: soo-DON-uh-muhs ■ Onesiphorus: on´uh-SIF-uh-ruhs ■ Artemas: AHR-tuh-muhs ■ Zenas: ZEE-nuhs

PAULINE AUTHORSHIP In favor of authorship by Paul stands the claim in the first verse of each pastoral that he is writing. Against this claim it is argued that in ancient times and in the early church pseudonymous writing was an accepted literary practice ("pious forgery"). But 2 Thessalonians 2:2 and 3:17 warn against forgeries in Paul's name, and the early church expelled an elder from ecclesiastical office for writing pseudonymously and exercised itself over questions of authorship, as shown, for example, by debate on the authorship of Hebrews and by hesitancy in adopting a book of unknown authorship into the New Testament canon.

> "In Asia, the elder who composed that writing [The Acts of Paul and Thecla], as if he were augmenting Paul's fame from his own store [by writing 'under Paul's name'], after being convicted and confessing that he had done it from love of Paul, was removed from his office" (Tertullian, *On Baptism* 17).

Furthermore, it is very improbable that a late admirer of Paul would have called him "the **foremost** of sinners" (1 Timothy 1:16). The Pastorals are much closer in style and content to Paul's other letters than are noncanonical and indubitably pseudonymous books to the authentic writings of those in whose names they were forged. Added to the claim of the Pastorals themselves that Paul is writing them and to the concern of the early church over questions of authorship is the very strong and **early tradition** of Pauline authorship. Only Romans and 1 Corinthians have stronger attestation.

VOCABULARY AND STYLE Doubt about Paul's authorship stems primarily from differences in vocabulary and grammatical style that appear when the Pastorals are compared with other Pauline letters. Comparisons consist of statistical tables, sometimes drawn up with the aid of computers. But this scientific-sounding objection to Pauline authorship does not take sufficient account of differences in vocabulary and style as caused by differences in subject matter and addressees and by changes in a person's writing style because of environment, age, experience, and the sheer passage of time. Perhaps even more significant is the possibility that stylistic differences stem from different amanuenses and from Paul's giving greater freedom to his amanuenses in the exact wording of his thoughts at some times than at other times. An appeal to amanuenses is sometimes scorned as too easy and scientifically uncontrollable. But it is historically realistic, for we know positively that Paul dictated his letters and that ancient authors gave their amanuenses varying amounts of freedom.

Yet again, the generally accepted Pauline letters, or extended passages within them, sometimes exhibit the same kinds of differences that assertedly disprove Paul's authorship of the Pastorals. For example, the verb "to examine" (↓*anakrinein* in Greek) occurs ten times throughout 1 Corinthians and nowhere else in Paul's letters, yet Pauline authorship of 1 Corinthians is undoubted. Likewise regarding the verb "to gather together" (↓*synerchesthai* in Greek), which occurs seven times in 1 Corinthians but nowhere else in the

---

anakrinein: ah´nah-KREE-nayn ■ *synerchesthai:* syoon-ER-kuhs-thi

letters of Paul. And most of the words occurring only in the Pastorals among his letters also occur in the Septuagint and in extrabiblical Greek literature of the first century, so that the words must have belonged to his and his amanuenses' vocabulary.

MARCION'S OMISSION Doubters of Pauline authorship also contend that the Gnostic heretic Marcion omitted the Pastorals from his New Testament canon because Paul did not write them. But Marcion had a propensity for rejecting parts of the New Testament accepted by orthodox Christians. He rejected Matthew, Mark, and John, for example, and excised portions of Luke. The statement that "the law is good" (1 Timothy 1:8) must have offended Marcion's radical rejection of the Old Testament, and the disparaging reference to "what is falsely called knowledge [Greek: *gnōsis*]" (1 Timothy 6:20) must also have offended him because of his calling his own system of doctrine *gnōsis*—ample reasons from his standpoint for omitting the Pastorals without any implication that they are pseudonymous.

GNOSTICISM Some also assert that the Pastorals attack a kind of Gnosticism that arose only after Paul's lifetime. To be sure, the asceticism criticized in 1 Timothy 4:3 ("forbidding people to marry and teaching them to abstain from foods") sounds like a branch of later Gnosticism. Nevertheless, the prominent Jewish element in the false teaching—"those of the circumcision," "Jewish myths," "disputes about the law" (Titus 1:10, 14; 3:9)—disproves that the Pastorals necessarily attack later Gnosticism; for later Gnosticism, though it borrowed its cosmological myth from Judaism, was opposed to the other features of Judaism.

The Pastorals strike rather at the mixed kind of heresy rebutted earlier in Colossians and now known to have originated in syncretistic Judaism of a pre-Christian variety. Thus, an early date for the Pastorals is preferable; and an early date favors authorship by Paul, since a pious forger would not likely have succeeded in using Paul's name so close to Paul's lifetime.

ECCLESIASTICAL STRUCTURE It is claimed that the Pastorals reflect a more highly organized ecclesiastical structure than had developed during the lifetime of Paul. But they mention only **elders** (or **bishops**), **deacons**, and **widows**, all of whom figure earlier in the New Testament period as distinct classes within the church (see, for example, Acts 6:1; 9:39, 41; 1 Corinthians 7:8; Philippians 1:1). Moreover, the pre-Christian Dead Sea Scrolls describe an officer in the Qumran community who bears remarkable similarity to the bishops (literally, "overseers, superintendents") who appear in the Pastorals.

Instructions for the appointment of elders by Timothy and Titus (1 Timothy 5:22; Titus 1:5) are due, not to advanced, hierarchical church government, but to

"And this is the regulation for the camp overseer. He shall instruct the Many in the works of God and make them consider his marvelously mighty deeds. . . . And he shall pity them as a father pities his sons, and shall bring back all those that have strayed, as a shepherd does with his flock" (*Damascus Document* 13:7–9).

the starting of new churches under missionary conditions, just as Paul and Barnabas at a very early date appointed elders for the new churches in South Galatia (Acts 14:23).

ORTHODOXY In the same way it is argued that the Pastorals' emphasis on orthodoxy of doctrine implies a post-Pauline stage of theological development when Christian doctrine was considered complete and therefore to be defended from corruption rather than widened in scope. But the defense of traditional Christian orthodoxy characterized Paul's letters from the very earliest. Galatians as a whole and the fifteenth chapter of 1 Corinthians provide outstanding examples.

CONFLICTING DATA Finally, some maintain that the Pastorals give historical and geographical data which do not harmonize with Paul's career as recorded in Acts and the other letters. These are supposed to be the telltale mistakes of a pious forger. The conflicting data are that Paul left Timothy in Ephesus when he traveled on to Macedonia (1 Timothy 1:3; contrast Acts 20:4–6), that Demas has deserted Paul (2 Timothy 4:10—yet Demas is still with Paul in Philemon 24), and that Paul left Titus in Crete (Titus 1:5) and went to Nicopolis (Titus 3:12) while Titus proceeded to ↓Dalmatia (2 Timothy 4:10—whereas in Acts, Paul visits neither Crete nor Nicopolis; see the map on page 317).

Dalmatia: dal-MAY-shee-uh

Harbor at Phoenix, Crete

TWO ROMAN IMPRISONMENTS Answering the foregoing argument is the hypothesis that Paul was acquitted and released from his first Roman imprisonment; that he enjoyed a period of freedom, into which the travel data of the Pastorals fit; and that he was later reimprisoned and condemned to die as a martyr for the Christian faith. Thus the historical and geographical data of the Pastorals refer to events that took place after the close of Acts. The Pastorals themselves constitute evidence favoring this hypothesis, but independent support comes from Paul's expectation of being released in Philippians 1:19, 25; 2:24, written most likely during the first Roman imprisonment, in contrast with Paul's failure to entertain any possibility of release in 2 Timothy 4:6–8, written during the hypothesized second Roman imprisonment.

ORDER OF WRITING We may conclude that Paul wrote 1 Timothy and Titus between the imprisonments and 2 Timothy during the second imprisonment, just before his martyrdom. Whether or not he ever reached Spain, as planned in Romans 15:24, 28, remains unknown. *First Clement* 5:7 says that he "reached the limits of the West," a statement that may be interpreted as a reference either to Rome or to Spain at the far western end of the Mediterranean Basin.

FIRST TIMOTHY

An Outline of First Timothy

Introduction: Greeting (1:1–2)
 I. Warning Against Heresy, with Personal Reminiscences (1:3–20)
 II. The Organization of the Church by Timothy (2:1–3:13)
   A. Public prayer (2:1–8)
   B. Modesty and subordination of women (2:9–15)
   C. Qualifications for bishops (3:1–7)
   D. Qualifications for deacons (3:8–13)
 III. The Administration of the Church by Timothy (3:14–6:19)
   A. Preserving the church as the bastion of orthodoxy against heterodoxy (3:14–4:16)
   B. Pastoring members of the church (5:1–6:2b)
     1. Men and women, young and old (5:1–2)
     2. Widows (5:3–16)
     3. Elders, with an aside regarding Timothy (5:17–25)
     4. Slaves (6:1–2b)
   C. Teaching and urging of Christian duties (6:2c–10)
   D. Leading by example (6:11–16)
   E. Warning the wealthy (6:17–19)
 Conclusion: A Final Charge to Timothy and a Benediction (6:20–21)

Reading First Timothy with Interpretation

First Timothy proceeds from a **greeting** to a **warning** against false teachers who mishandle the law. Paul then recalls his own experience of **conversion** and **commission to apostleship** and charges Timothy to cling tenaciously to **orthodox** Christian faith.

↓*Hymenaeus and Alexander*

Timothy must take warning from two false teachers whom Paul has ejected from the church into the world, which he calls Satan's territory ("whom I have given over to Satan that they may learn not to blaspheme," 1:20). *Read 1 Timothy 1:1–20.* The clause "Trustworthy is the statement" is a formula that introduces and caps early Christian confessions, slogans, and hymns.

Prayer and Moderation

Chapter 2 begins with an exhortation to public prayer for all people, especially for governmental authorities. There follow instructions that Christian women dress moderately rather than extravagantly and that in the church they not occupy authoritative teaching positions over men. It is disputed whether Paul means the prohibition to be taken universally, as he has been traditionally understood, or only locally because of the influence of false teachers on Christian women in Ephesus (compare 1:3–7). The statement,

Gold earring from the Hellenistic period

Hymenaeus: hi´muh-NEE-uhs

A Trustworthy Saying

- "**Trustworthy is the statement** and worthy of full acceptance: Christ Jesus came into the world to save sinners" (1 Timothy 1:15).
- "**Trustworthy is the statement:** If anyone aspires to overseership, he desires a noble task" (1 Timothy 3:1).
- "**Trustworthy is the statement** and worthy of full acceptance . . . : We have put our hope in the living God, who is the Savior of all human beings, particularly believers" (1 Timothy 4:9–10).
- "**Trustworthy is the statement:** If we died with him ['Christ Jesus'], we will also live with him; if we endure, we will also reign with him. If we deny him, he also will deny us; if we are faithless, he will remain faithful, for he cannot deny himself" (2 Timothy 2:11–13).
- "But when the kindness of God our Savior and his love for humankind appeared, he saved us, not because of righteous things that we had done, but according to his mercy through the washing of regeneration and renewal by the Holy Spirit, whom he poured out on us abundantly through Jesus Christ our Savior, so that having been justified by his grace we might become heirs according to the hope of eternal life: **Trustworthy is the statement**" (Titus 3:4–8a).

"Yet she will be saved through childbearing" (2:15), probably means that despite her suffering of birthpangs, a lingering result of the original curse on human sin (Genesis 3:16), the Christian woman is still saved from the eternal judgment of God against sin; in other words, the continuation of pain in giving birth to children does not contradict the salvation of Christian mothers. Under this view "through" means "through the midst of" rather than "by means of (bearing children)." Other interpretations are that

- Believing women are saved through the supreme childbirth, that of Christ.
- Christian women work out their salvation by bearing and rearing children in a godly manner.
- Paul does not promise eternal salvation, but deliverance from the physical dangers of childbearing.

Bishops and Deacons

Paul now lists the qualifications for bishops and deacons. *Bishop* (Greek: ↓*episkopos,* from which comes "Episcopalian") alludes to the office filled by an *elder* (↓*presbyter,* from which comes "Presbyterian"). Thus, though *bishop* and *elder* go back to different Greek words, they are largely synonymous. *Deacon* means "servant, helper" and refers to the bishops' assistants, who take care of the mundane matters of church life, particularly the distribution of charity. The listing of qualifications for women in 3:11 may imply a female order of deaconesses or may refer to deacons' wives, expected to help in the charitable work of their husbands. Closing the section is a quotation from an early Christian hymn or creed that traces the career of Christ from incarnation to ascension ("who was revealed in flesh . . . taken up in glory," 3:16). *Read 1 Timothy 2:1–3:16.*

Forms of Church Government

- Episcopalians have a church government that invests great authority in a bishop over many local churches.
- Presbyterians have a church government that invests great authority in a board of elders in each local church.

Propriety

A further warning against false doctrine is followed in chapter 5 by discussions of Timothy's proper relation to different age groups in the church, the status of widows, and the treatment of elders. As a young man, Timothy is to treat other young men as brothers, older men as fathers, older women as mothers, and young ladies as sisters.

Widows

Families should support their widows. But godly widows sixty or more years old and unsupported by a family should receive economic assistance

---

episkopos: eh-PIS-kuh-paws ■ *presbyter:* PRES-bi-tuhr

An Early Christian Hymn or Creed

Note in 1 Timothy 3:16 the complementary pairs of verbs and the equally complementary pairs of prepositional phrases:

"Who

     — was manifested   in flesh, ——————
     — was vindicated   by the Spirit, ————
     — was seen   by angels, ————
     — was proclaimed   among the nations, —
     — was believed on   in the world, ————
     — was taken up   in glory." ————

- What is said about "Who" makes obvious a reference to Christ.
- Manifestation in flesh refers to the incarnation.
- Vindication by the Spirit refers to the Holy Spirit's raising Jesus from the dead.
- Being seen by angels refers to the risen Jesus' appearance to the angelic world (compare the angelic presence at Jesus' empty tomb).
- Proclamation and belief refer to worldwide evangelism and resultant conversions.
- Being taken up in glory refers to Jesus' ascension and, with the initial reference to incarnation, frames the intervening items.

from the church. Younger widows should marry lest they fall into the temptation of resorting to an immoral life as means of support.

Elders

Faithful elders, especially those who preach and teach, merit financial support. Elders are not to be impeached except on the testimony of two or three witnesses, but those who are duly convicted must be rebuked publicly. Timothy is not to ordain ("lay hands on") a man to eldership hastily, that is, without first proving his character over a period of time (unless the reference is to restoring disciplined members of the church). The letter closes with miscellaneous instructions about Christian slaves, false teachers, wealthy Christians, and Timothy's own spiritual responsibilities. *Read 1 Timothy 4:1–6:21.*

"Bion the sophist said, 'The love of money is the mother city [the literal meaning of "metropolis"] of all evils'" (Stobaeus, *Anthologium* 3, 417 = III 10, 37).

TITUS

An Outline of Titus

Introduction: Greeting (1:1–4)
  I. The Appointment and Qualifications of Bishops (1:5–9)
  II. The Suppression of False Teachers (1:10–16)

III. The Teaching of Good Conduct (2:1–3:8a)
Conclusion (3:8b–15)
> A. Summary (3:8b–11)
> B. Request for Titus to come to Nicopolis and other instructions (3:12–14)
> C. Greetings and a benediction (3:15)

Reading Titus with Interpretation

Place and Purpose

Paul writes this letter from Nicopolis, on the west coast of Greece, to Titus, whom he has left on the island of Crete to organize the church there. As in 1 Timothy, he warns against false teachers and issues instructions to various classes of Christians on proper conduct. The doctrinal basis for these instructions is **God's grace**, which brings salvation, leads to godly living, and offers the "blessed hope" of Jesus' return (2:11–14). The experiential basis for these instructions is **regeneration by the Holy Spirit** (3:3–7). *Read Titus 1:1–3:15.*

SECOND TIMOTHY

An Outline of Second Timothy

Introduction: Greeting (1:1–2)
I. Exhortation to Strength of Ministry, Against Timothy's Tendency to Timidity (1:3–2:7)
II. Exhortation to Orthodoxy, Against False Teaching and Practice (2:8–4:8)
Conclusion (4:9–22)
> A. A request for Timothy to come soon (4:9–13)
> B. News about Paul's trial (4:14–18)
> C. Greetings, with a further plea for Timothy to come and a benediction (4:19–22)

Reading Second Timothy with Interpretation

Reminiscence and Exhortation

This last letter of Paul opens with reminiscences of God's call to Timothy and to Paul interspersed with exhortations and a sidelight on some who have forsaken Paul in prison and others who have stood by him. Further directions to Timothy draw comparisons with the hard work and self-discipline required of soldiers, athletes, and farmers. Against heretical teaching, Paul stresses that "all Scripture is inspired by God [that is, 'God-breathed'] and profitable" (3:16). A final charge to preach the word of

God, a statement of readiness to die, and personal news and requests conclude Paul's farewell letter. *Read 2 Timothy 1:1–4:22.*

↓*Jannes and* ↓*Jambres*

According to Targum Jonathan on Exodus 7:11 and early Christian literature outside the New Testament, Jannes and Jambres (3:8) were two of Pharaoh's magicians who opposed Moses. The parchments that Paul asks Timothy to bring (4:13) must have had important contents, for parchment was expensive. Perhaps they included Paul's legal papers, such as his certificate of Roman citizenship, copies of the Old Testament Scriptures, and records of Jesus' life and teachings.

A Lion

We are probably to understand the deliverance of Paul "from the lion's mouth" figuratively rather than literally, for the lion was a common metaphor for extreme danger (4:17; compare Psalm 22:21). More specifically, the lion has been taken as a symbol for the Emperor Nero, or for the devil, as in 1 Peter 5:8: "Like a roaring lion, your enemy the devil prowls around looking for someone to devour."

> "Jannes and Jambres, magicians of Egypt, did the same by their burnings of divination. Each man threw down his rod, and they became serpents but were immediately changed back to what they were at first. And the rod of Aaron swallowed up their rods" (Targum Pseudo-Jonathan on Exodus 7:11).

Summary

The Pastoral Letters—1 and 2 Timothy and Titus—have disputed authorship, mainly because of differences from other letters whose authorship by Paul is undisputed. But similar differences within those undisputed letters, changing circumstances, and Paul's use of various amanuenses support the early church tradition of Pauline authorship. Under this view Paul suffered two imprisonments in Rome, wrote 1 Timothy and Titus between them, and wrote 2 Timothy during the second one shortly before his martyrdom.

The overarching purpose of the Pastorals is to instruct Timothy and Titus on the administration of church life. The instructions deal by and large with orthodoxy (right belief) and ↓orthopraxy (right conduct) over against ↓heterodoxy (wrong belief) and ↓heteropraxy (wrong conduct); and with the proper organization of the church; the qualifications of bishops/elders, deacons, deaconesses or deacons' wives, and widows; the roles of these and others, both men and women, in the church; and the behavior of Timothy and Titus toward various classes in the church. Personal details concerning the last phase of Paul's life, plus reminiscences of earlier phases, come up here and there in the Pastorals.

A victorious Roman athlete wearing his crown. Compare Paul's confidence that the Lord will give him "a crown of righteousness."

Jannes: JAN-iz ■ Jambres: JAM-briz ■ orthopraxy: OR-thuh-prak´see ■ heterodoxy: HEH-tuhr-uh-dahk´see ■ heteropraxy: HEH-tuhr-uh-prak´see

EXCURSUS
A Resumé of Paul's Theology

ORIGINS Since Paul's theology is distributed throughout a number of letters written in a variety of missionary circumstances, it remains for us to summarize his thought. Some early scholars believed that for the content and form of his theology Paul borrows extensively from Greek concepts and from the mystery religions. There is general agreement now, however, that his debt to the **Old Testament** and **Second Temple Judaism** far exceeds his debt to Greek and mystical sources.

Those same early scholars also believed that Paul is the great innovator, who transforms Jesus from what he actually was, a prophet, teacher, and martyr, into a cosmic Savior with divine attributes. But closer study has shown that Paul draws on **earlier Christian tradition**: hymns, creeds, baptismal confessions, catechetical instructions concerning Christian conduct, and oral and written traditions about Jesus' life and teaching prior to the writing of the Gospels. A study of the Gospels, Acts, and the non-Pauline letters leads to this same conclusion: Paul develops an already existing Christian theology that originated with Jesus and grew out of the Scriptures of the Old Testament.

GOD AND CREATION From Judaism and the Old Testament comes Paul's belief in one true God who is omnipotent, holy, and gracious. This God is a person. Those who know him through Christ may address him affectionately as Father (*Abba*). But there is multiplicity within the person of the one God; so Paul writes in the trinitarian terms of Father, Son, and Holy Spirit (though philosophical development of the doctrine of the Trinity will not come until after the writing of the New Testament). God the Father created the universe and all beings in it through and for his Son. In all its materiality, then, the universe is inherently good. But sin intruded through Adam and has gained such a firm grip on human beings that the good law of God provokes transgression rather than obedience. In the wake of sin followed death, both physical and spiritual. As part of the material creation, the human body is inherently good; but because sin works itself out through the body, Paul calls the sinful urge "the flesh."

CHRIST AND REDEMPTION Jesus, the eternally preexistent Son of God, came from heaven to rescue human beings from sin and death. Thus he became a human being himself and died to satisfy both God's anger against sin and God's love for sinners. To demonstrate his satisfaction, God raised Jesus from the dead and exalted him as Lord in heaven. Now the "call" of God comes to those people whom he has elected, or chosen, beforehand. Yet his election of some for salvation does not contradict the open invitation to all. People accept this invitation by sincere sorrow for sin (repentance) and faith in Jesus Christ, which includes mental assent to what Christianity says about his identity, exclusive trust in his death and resurrection for the remission (removal) of sins, and moral commitment to the kind of life he demands. Repentant believers immediately come to be "in Christ," so that their sin is transferred to Christ, and God's righteousness is transferred to them. Solidarity with Christ replaces solidarity with Adam. In this way God can lovingly treat believers as righteous (the doctrine of justification) while still upholding his own standard of justice. As Lord, Jesus redeems believers, that is, sets them free from slavery to sin by paying a price, just as the LORD redeemed Israel from bondage in Egypt at the exodus. God and believers are reconciled, their broken fellowship restored. All these events happen by divine grace, the favor of God toward ill-deserving human beings, without meritorious good works on their part.

THE SPIRIT, CHRISTIANS, AND THE CHURCH To believers God gives his Spirit as a guarantee of future and eternal glory and as an aid to individual and corporate Christian living. The Spirit enables them to conquer the sinful urge ("the flesh"), to live virtuously, to pray, and to minister to others. The body, once dominated by the flesh, becomes a temple of the Spirit and is destined for the resurrection to life eternal. But just as the body of an individual Christian is a temple of the Holy Spirit, so also is the church as a whole. Indeed, the body with its various parts becomes Paul's grand metaphor for the church in its organic unity, diversity of function, and subordination to Christ the head. And churches (from the Greek word ↓*ekklēsia*) are not buildings, but local assemblies of those who belong to the kingdom of God. These people are the holy ones ("saints"), the brothers and sisters into whose hearts have shone the open secrets ("mysteries") of the gospel. By baptism they confess their union with Christ in his death, burial, and resurrection, and the continuance of that union by the Lord's Supper, which looks forward to a messianic banquet at the second coming as well as backward to the death of Christ.

ESCHATOLOGY The forces of evil—Satan, demonic spirits, and human beings dominated by them—control this present age. But their domination will not last forever; for the Day of the Lord is coming. Then *he* will take control. When the man of lawlessness (antichrist) leads a great rebellion against God, Christ the Lord will return to judge the wicked, vindicate the godly, and restore the nation of Israel. For this event Christians must watch; it is their confident "hope." After the Day of the Lord, the age to come begins, a never-ending succession of ages called eternity, in which God will enjoy his people and they him—forever.[1]

1. Paul draws the three terms, "this (present) age," "the Day of the Lord," and "that [or, 'the coming'] age," from rabbinic parlance and fills them with Christian content.

ekklēsia: i-KLEE-zhee-uh

People to Remember

Alexander	Jambres	Nero
Demas	Jannes	Timothy
Hymenaeus	Marcion	Titus

Places to Remember

Crete	"the limits of the West"	Rome
Dalmatia	Macedonia	Spain
Ephesus	Nicopolis	

Terms to Remember

amanuensis/-es	Gnosticism	the Pastorals
asceticism	heterodoxy	pastors
authenticity	heteropraxy	pious forgery
bishops	inspiration of Scripture	pseudonymity
deacons	"the lion's mouth"	Septuagint
elders	ordain	syncretistic Judaism
fragmentary theory	orthodoxy	widows
gnōsis	orthopraxy	

How Much Did You Learn?

- Why are 1 and 2 Timothy and Titus called the Pastorals?
- What are the arguments for and against Pauline authorship of the Pastorals?
- When and where were the Pastorals written? Where were Timothy and Titus at the time? And what are they asked to do for Paul?
- Detail the ecclesiastical concerns the Pastorals take up and the ways those concerns are dealt with.
- List the church officers and their qualifications as outlined in the Pastorals.
- List other classes of church members concerning whom the Pastorals give instructions. What are those instructions?

For Further Discussion

- What differences are noticeable between the structure of modern churches and the early church as reflected in the Pastorals? How do we account for these differences?

- How binding on the modern church are the ecclesiastical structure and functional style of the ancient church? Conversely, do changing circumstances and different cultures allow the church freedom of operation and innovation—and if so, within what limits, provided there are limits?

- Evaluate the charge that Paul's concern for orthodoxy in the Pastorals sounds negative and overly defensive.

For Further Investigation

Barrett, C. K. *The Pastoral Epistles in the New English Bible.* Oxford: Clarendon, 1963.

Fee, G. D. *First and Second Timothy, Titus.* Peabody, Mass.: Hendrickson, 1989.

Guthrie, D. *The Pastoral Epistles.* 2d ed. Grand Rapids: Eerdmans, 1991.

Knight, G. W., III. *The Pastoral Epistles: A Commentary on the Greek Text.* Grand Rapids: Eerdmans, 1992. Advanced.

Liefeld, W. L. *The NIV Application Commentary: 1 and 2 Timothy, Titus.* Grand Rapids: Zondervan, 1999.

Marshall, I. H., with P. H. Towner. *A Critical and Exegetical Commentary on the Pastoral Epistles.* Edinburgh: T. & T. Clark, 1999. Advanced.

Mounce, W. D. *Pastoral Epistles.* Nashville: Thomas Nelson, 2000. Advanced.

Quinn, J. D., and W. C. Wacker. *The First and Second Letters to Timothy.* Grand Rapids: Eerdmans, 2000.

For a summary chart of the Pauline letters, see "A Chart of the Books in the New Testament," pages 530–31.

EXCURSUS

For Further Discussion

- Why did Paul and other early Christian authors not write systematic theological books rather than occasional letters and tracts?
- What particular aspects of his theology kept Paul from becoming an armchair theologian and for the sake of evangelism compelled him to travel far and wide at great personal cost?

For Further Investigation

Barrett, C. K. *Paul: An Introduction to His Thought.* Louisville: Westminster John Knox, 1994.

Becker, J. C. *Paul: Apostle to the Gentiles.* Louisville: Westminster John Knox, 1993. Advanced.

Bruce, F. F. *Paul.* Grand Rapids: Eerdmans, 1977.

Dunn, J. D. G. *The Theology of Paul the Apostle.* Grand Rapids: Eerdmans, 1998. Advanced.

Fitzmyer, J. A. *Paul and His Theology: A Brief Sketch.* 2d ed. Englewood Cliffs, N.J.: Prentice-Hall, 1989.

Machen, J. G. *The Origin of Paul's Religion.* Grand Rapids: Eerdmans, 1925.

Murphy-O'Conner, J. *Paul: A Critical Life.* Oxford: Clarendon, 1996.

Ridderbos, H. *Paul.* Grand Rapids: Eerdmans, 1975.

Sanders, E. P. *Paul and Palestinian Judaism.* Philadelphia: Fortress Press, 1977.

Schweitzer, A. *The Mysticism of Paul the Apostle.* New York: Seabury, 1968.

Wenham, D. *Paul: Follower of Jesus or Founder of Christianity?* Grand Rapids: Eerdmans, 1995.

Witherington, B., III. *Paul's Narrative Thought World: The Tapestry of Tragedy and Triumph.* Louisville: Westminster John Knox, 1994.

Wright, N. T. *What Saint Paul Really Said: Was Paul of Tarsus the Real Founder of Christianity?* Grand Rapids: Eerdmans, 1997.

CHAPTER
16

HEBREWS: JESUS AS PRIEST

Overview:

- Introductory Issues
- An Outline of Hebrews
- Reading Hebrews with Interpretation
- Excursus: The Theological Debate over 6:1–12
- Summary

Study Goals—Learn:

- The leading candidates for the authorship of Hebrews
- What people Hebrews was written to, where they lived, and their spiritual state
- The distinctive christological emphasis in Hebrews and how it relates to the dissuasion of the addressees from apostasy

The forum at the House of the Vestal Virgins in Rome, the probable destination of the Letter to the Hebrews

Introductory Issues

Theme

The author of Hebrews portrays Jesus Christ distinctively as a priest who, having offered none other than himself as the completely sufficient sacrifice for sins, now ministers in the heavenly sanctuary. The purpose of this portrayal, which emphasizes the **superiority of Christ** over every aspect and hero of Old Testament religion, is to ensure that the recipients of the letter do not apostatize from Christianity back to Judaism.

Authorship

Early church tradition exhibits uncertainty over the authorship of this anonymous letter. Nevertheless, at a very early date Hebrews was known and used in *1 Clement* (about A.D. 95); and right up to the present time guesswork has flourished on the question of authorship.

PAUL In the eastern part of the Roman Empire, Paul was usually regarded as author of Hebrews. Its theology does resemble his when we compare the preexistence and creatorship of Christ in Hebrews 1:1–4 with Colossians 1:15–17, the humiliation of Christ in Hebrews 2:14–17 with Philippians 2:5–8, the new covenant in Hebrews 8:6 with 2 Corinthians 3:4–11, and the distribution of gifts by the Holy Spirit in Hebrews 2:4 with 1 Corinthians 12:11. The western segment of the church doubted Paul's authorship, however, and at first even excluded Hebrews from the canon because of the uncertain authorship. This fact shows that the early church did not gullibly accept books into the canon without first examining their credentials as to authorship, trustworthiness, and doctrinal purity.

A horned altar

The western church had good reasons to doubt authorship by Paul. None of his acknowledged letters are anonymous, as Hebrews is. The polished Greek style of Hebrews differs radically from Paul's rugged style, more than can be reasonably explained by a difference in amanuenses. And Paul constantly appeals to his own apostolic authority, but the author of Hebrews appeals to the authority of **others**, those who were eyewitnesses to Jesus' ministry (Hebrews 2:3; but compare Acts 13:31).

BARNABAS Some have suggested Barnabas, whose Levitical background (Acts 4:36) fits the interest in priestly functions evident throughout Hebrews and whose association with Paul would explain the similarities to Pauline theology. But as a resident of Jerusalem

(Acts 4:36–37), Barnabas probably heard and saw Jesus, whereas the author of Hebrews includes himself among those who had to depend on others for eyewitness testimony (Hebrews 2:3 again).

LUKE As another companion of Paul, Luke is also a candidate for the authorship of Hebrews because of similarities between the polished Greek style of Hebrews and that of Luke-Acts. But Luke-Acts is Gentile in outlook, Hebrews very Jewish.

APOLLOS Martin Luther suggested Apollos, whose acquaintance with Paul (1 Corinthians 16:12) and being tutored by Priscilla and Aquila (Acts 18:26) would account for the likenesses in Hebrews to Pauline theology. Apollos's learning or eloquence (Acts 18:24, 27–28) could have produced the refined literary style of Hebrews. And his Alexandrian background fits Hebrews' frequent and nearly exclusive use of the Septuagint in Old Testament quotations, for the Septuagint was produced in Alexandria, Egypt. Some scholars also draw a parallel between the allegorical interpretation of the Old Testament by the Jewish philosopher Philo, a contemporary of Apollos and fellow native of Alexandria, and the treatment of the Old Testament in Hebrews. But Hebrews treats the Old Testament as typological history rather than as allegory, and the lack of early tradition favoring Apollos leaves doubt.

↓**SILVANUS** To suppose that Paul's companion Silvanus (Silas) authored the letter would again explain the similarities to Pauline theology. Not much more can be said for or against authorship by Silvanus.

PHILIP The same is true of the suggestion that Philip wrote Hebrews.

PRISCILLA Adolf von Harnack suggested Priscilla because of her close association with Paul and her teaching of Apollos. Harnack ingeniously argued that she left the book anonymous because of the cultural unacceptability of female authorship.

CLEMENT Likenesses between Hebrews and *1 Clement* make Clement of Rome a possibility. But there are also many differences in outlook; and Clement probably borrowed from Hebrews. So like the early church father Origen, we may conclude that only God knows who wrote Hebrews.

> ## An Example of Hebrews' Style as Compared with Paul's
>
> "He [Christ] sat down at the right hand of the Majesty in the heights" (Hebrews 1:3).
>
> "Christ Jesus . . . is at the right hand of God" (Romans 8:34).
>
> Note the floweriness of Hebrews' phraseology as compared with the simplicity of Paul's (compare Psalm 110:1).

> "If I were to give my opinion, I should say that the thoughts are those of the apostle [Paul], but the diction and phraseology are those of someone who remembered the apostle's teachings and wrote down at his leisure what had been said by his teacher. . . . But who wrote the letter—well, God knows the truth" (Origen according to Eusebius, *Church History* 6.25.13).

Addressees

Despite the traditional heading, "To the Hebrews," some have thought that Hebrews was originally addressed to **Gentile Christians**. For support, an appeal is made to the polished Greek style of the letter and its extensive use of the Septuagint, with only an occasional departure from that Greek translation of the Old Testament. But these phenomena imply nothing about the original addressees; they indicate only the background of the author. The frequent appeal to the Old Testament, the presupposed knowledge of Jewish ritual, the warning not to apostatize back to Judaism, and the early traditional title all point to **Jewish Christians** as the original recipients. Some scholars go so far as to identify them with converted Jewish priests in Jerusalem (Acts 6:7) or with converts from the sect at Qumran, where the Dead Sea Scrolls were produced (but see the following two paragraphs).

DESTINATION At first blush it might seem most likely that these Jewish Christians lived in Palestine. But according to 2:3 they neither saw nor heard Jesus for themselves during his earthly ministry, as many Palestinian Christians doubtless did; and according to 6:10 they materially assisted other Christians, whereas Palestinian Christians were poor and had to receive aid (Acts 11:27–30; Romans 15:26; 2 Corinthians 8:1–9:15). Furthermore, the addressees' knowledge of Jewish ritual appears to have come from the Old Testament in its Septuagintal version rather than from attendance at the temple services in Jerusalem; and the statement, "Those from Italy greet you" (13:24), sounds as though Italians away from Italy are sending greetings back home. If so, **Rome** is the probable destination. Supporting this conclusion is the fact that evidence for the knowledge of Hebrews surfaces first in Rome (*1 Clement*).[1]

Alternatively, it has been proposed that Apollos wrote Hebrews in A.D. 52–54 at **Ephesus** and sent it to the church in **Corinth**, especially to its Jewish Christian members. This proposal draws many parallels between Hebrews and Paul's Corinthian correspondence and identifies "those from Italy" (13:24) as Priscilla and Aquila, who originally moved to Corinth from Rome but subsequently accompanied Paul from Corinth to Ephesus.[2] It remains a difficulty, however, that the author of Hebrews does not mention Priscilla and Aquila by name rather than by a generalizing phrase, especially since he has just mentioned Timothy by name.

PURPOSE Wherever the addressees lived, they are well known to the author. He writes about their generosity (6:10), their persecution (10:32–34; 12:4), their immaturity (5:11–6:12), and his hope of revisiting them soon (13:19, 23). Two additional details may be significant: (1) the addressees are exhorted to greet not only the leaders and fellow Christians in their own assembly, but also "**all** the saints" (13:24); (2) they are rebuked for **not meeting together often enough** (10:25). Possibly, then, they are a Jewish

1. See further W. Manson, *The Epistle to the Hebrews* (London: Hodder & Stoughton, 1951).

2. See H. Montefiore, *A Commentary on the Epistle to the Hebrews* (London: Black, 1964).

Christian group or house-church who have broken away from the main body of Christians in their locality and who stand in danger of lapsing back into Judaism to avoid persecution. The main purpose of the letter is to **prevent such apostasy** and restore them into mainstream Christian fellowship. The immediate fading of a sure tradition concerning authorship may be due to separatism on the part of the addressees.

Date

The use of Hebrews in *1 Clement* requires a date of writing before A.D. 95 or so, the date of *1 Clement*. It is sometimes argued further that the present tense of verbs in Hebrews describing sacrificial rituals implies a date before A.D. 70, when Titus destroyed the temple and sacrifices ceased to be offered. But other writings that most certainly date from after A.D. 70 continue to use the present tense about Mosaic rituals (*1 Clement*, Josephus, Justin Martyr, the Talmud). Furthermore, Hebrews does not describe the ritual of the

Model of Rome showing the city center

Life-size model of the Old
Testament tabernacle

temple, but the ritual of the pre-Solomonic tabernacle (a portable tent-sanctuary that the Israelites used on their way from Mount Sinai to the land of Canaan). Therefore the present tense may represent only a vivid literary style and cannot settle the question of Hebrews' date. What does favor a date before A.D. 70, however, is the lack of any reference in Hebrews to the destruction of the temple as a divine indication that the Old Testament sacrificial system has been outmoded. The author would probably have used such a historical argument were he writing after that event.

Literary Form
As do other letters, Hebrews concludes with personal allusions; but unlike other letters, it has no introductory greeting. The oratorical style and remarks such as "time would fail me to tell" (11:32) might seem to indicate a sermon. But the statement, "I have written you briefly" (13:22), requires us to acknowledge that Hebrews is a letter after all, written in sermonic style.

Christ's Superiority
To keep his audience from lapsing back into Judaism, the author of Hebrews emphasizes the superiority of Christ over all else, especially over various features of Judaism arising out of the Old Testament. The phrase "**better than**" epitomizes this dominant theme of Christ's superiority, a theme punctuated throughout the book by exhortations not to apostatize.

An Outline of Hebrews

I. The Superiority of Christ over the Old Testament Prophets (1:1–3a)
II. The Superiority of Christ over Angels (1:3b–2:18) and a Warning against Apostasy (2:1–4)
III. The Superiority of Christ over Moses (3:1–6) and a Warning against Apostasy (3:7–19)
IV. The Superiority of Christ over Joshua (4:1–10) and a Warning against Apostasy (4:11–16)
V. The Superiority of Christ over the Aaronites (Aaron and His Priestly Descendants) and Warnings against Apostasy (5:1–12:29)
    A. Christ's human sympathy and divine appointment to priesthood (5:1–10)
    B. Warning against apostasy with exhortation to maturation (5:11–6:20)
    C. The Melchizedek pattern of Christ's priesthood (7:1–10)
    D. The transitoriness of the Aaronic priesthood (7:11–28)
    E. The heavenly realities of Christ's priesthood (8:1–10:18)
    F. Warning against apostasy (10:19–39)
    G. Encouragement from Old Testament heroes of faith (11:1–40)
    H. Encouragement from the example of Christ (12:1–11)
    I. Warning against apostasy with the example of Esau (12:12–29)
VI. Practical Exhortations (13:1–19)
Conclusion: Greetings, News of Timothy's Release, and Benedictions (13:20–25)

Reading Hebrews with Interpretation

OVER THE PROPHETS Christ is better than the Old Testament prophets because he is the Son of God, the heir of the universe, the creator, the exact representation of divine nature, the sustainer of the world, the purifier from sins, the exalted one—and therefore God's last and best word to the human race (1:1–3a).

OVER THE ANGELS Christ is also better than the angels, whom Jews regarded as agents through whom God gave the Mosaic law on Mount Sinai; for Christ is the divine Son and eternal creator, but angels are mere servants and created beings (1:3b–2:18). Even his becoming lower than the angels through incarnation and death was only temporary. He had to become a human being to qualify as the one who by his death could lift fallen humanity to the dignity in which God originally created them. For that sacrificial act, Christ has received great honor. In the middle of this discussion occurs an exhortation not to drift away from Christian profession (2:1–4). *Read Hebrews 1:1–2:18.*

> "The law ... was put into effect through angels" (Acts 7:53).
>
> "The law was put into effect through angels" (Galatians 3:19).

OVER MOSES As the divine Son over God's household, Christ is better than Moses, a mere servant in God's household (3:1–6). The exhortation, therefore, is to avoid incurring God's judgment as a result of unbelief. Providing a warning example is the generation of Israelites who came out of Egypt under Moses but died in the wilderness because of God's anger against their rebellion (3:7–19).

OVER JOSHUA Christ is better than Joshua; for though Joshua brought Israel into Canaan, Christ will bring believers into the eternal resting place of heaven,

> Transliteration of the Hebrew for Joshua/Jesus: *yĕhôšuaʿ*, pronounced yuh-HOH´shoo-a
>
> Transliteration of the Greek for Joshua/Jesus: *iēsous*, pronounced eeay-SOOS"

where God rests from his work of creation (4:1–10). It is obvious that Joshua did not bring Israel into this heavenly rest, for long after Joshua lived and died, David spoke of Israel's resting place as yet to be entered (Psalm 95:7–11). The comparison between Jesus and Joshua is all the more pointed in the Greek text because the Hebrew name *Joshua* has *Jesus* as its Greek form. In other words, the Greek text knows no distinction between the names of the Old Testament Joshua and the New Testament Jesus.

The author now exhorts his audience to enter the heavenly rest by fidelity to their Christian profession (4:11–16). Later emphasis on the all-sufficiency of Jesus' sacrifice eliminates any implication that continuance of good works in the Christian life merits salvation. Good works and the avoidance of apostasy are necessary, however, to demonstrate genuineness of Christian profession. We find in 4:12 the famous comparison of God's word to a double-edged sword that pierces and lays bare a person's innermost being. Christians must therefore prove that their outward profession springs from inward reality. *Read Hebrews 3:1–4:16.*

OVER AARON Christ is better than Aaron and his successors in the priesthood (5:1–12:29). The author of Hebrews first indicates two points of similarity between the Aaronic priests and Christ: (1) Like Aaron, Christ was **divinely appointed** to priesthood; and (2) by sharing our human experiences, Christ

According to another interpretation, the "rest" into which Jesus leads Christians is not future heavenly rest from the good works of Christian living, but present spiritual rest or cessation from self-righteous works of the law, because Christ has already accomplished redemption. Yet the closely connected warning against apostasy, with its dire consequences, and the parallel between God's resting from his good work of creation and our resting from work both favor the interpretation given above. According to still another view, the rest is not salvation itself (whether present or future), but successful Christian living as typified by the conquest of Canaan under Joshua. But this interpretation also tends to cut the connection with the parallel between God's resting and our resting.

Stone anchors. Compare the statement in Hebrews 6:19 that the Christian hope is "a sure and steadfast anchor of the soul."

has a **sympathy** for us at least equal to that of Aaron (5:1–10). The outstanding example of Jesus' human feelings is his instinctive shrinking from death while praying in Gethsemane. Next comes a lengthy exhortation (5:11–6:20) to grow out of spiritual infancy into maturity by advancing beyond elementary doctrines of the Jewish faith that form the foundation for Christian belief but gain new significance in their Christian context. Failure to grow increases the danger of apostasy; and if a Christian apostatizes—that is, renounces Christ willfully and utterly—all possibility of salvation forever ceases to exist. The author describes his audience as Christians from the standpoint of their present profession (not knowing their hearts, how else can he describe them?) but goes on to point out that apostasy would both demonstrate the unreality of that profession and incur an irrevocable judgment for false profession. Apostasy, it should be noted, carries a much stronger meaning than temporary disobedience. *Read Hebrews 5:1–6:20.*

"Then the Lord will raise up a new priest, to whom all the words of the Lord will be revealed.... And his star will arise in heaven, as a king [arises] .... And he will have no successor throughout all generations forever.... In his priesthood all sin will come to an end; and the lawless will stop doing evil things. But the righteous will rest in him" (*Testaments of the Twelve Patriarchs,* "Levi" 18:1–14, excerpts).

Here are the points of Christ's superiority over Aaron:

- Christ became priest with a **divine oath**, but the Aaronites did not.
- Christ is **eternal**, whereas the Aaronites died and had to be succeeded.
- Christ is **sinless**, but the Aaronites were not.
- The priestly functions of Christ deal with **heavenly realities**, those of the Aaronites only with earthly symbols.

- Christ offered himself voluntarily as a sacrifice that will **never need to be repeated**, whereas the repetition of animal offerings exposes their ineffectiveness as inferior creatures to take away sins.
- The Old Testament itself, written during the period of the Aaronic priesthood, predicted a **new covenant** that would make obsolete the old covenant under which the Aaronites have functioned (Jeremiah 31:31–34).

EXCURSUS
The Theological Debate over 6:1–12

Interpretive dispute has raged around the warning in 6:1–12:

- Those who believe that the passage teaches the terrifying possibility of a true Christian's reverting to a lost condition struggle against the stated **impossibility of restoration** (6:4), against those New Testament passages that assure believers, the elect, of **eternal security** (John 6:39–40; 10:27–29; Romans 11:29; Philippians 1:6; 1 Peter 1:5; 1 John 2:1), and against the entire doctrine of **regeneration**, according to which a believer has become a new creature in Christ.
- Those who tone down the impossibility of restoration by saying that that impossibility lasts only as long as the apostate continues in apostasy run up against the later statement that Esau "found no place for repentance even though he sought it ['the blessing'] with tears" (12:17).
- Those who think that the author of Hebrews poses a hypothetical rather than realistic possibility find the repetition, severity, and urgency of this warning here and elsewhere in Hebrews (especially 10:26–31) embarrassing.
- Those who soften the severity of the threatened judgment from loss of salvation to loss of reward (with a bare retention of salvation; compare 1 Corinthians 3:12–15) go against the implication of 6:9 that the threatened judgment is the **opposite of salvation**: "Even though we speak this way, yet concerning you, beloved, we are persuaded of better things that belong to salvation" (compare 10:27: "a fearful prospect of judgment and a fury of fire that is going to consume the adversaries").
- Those who view the warning as addressed to near Christians rather than to full Christians must minimize the force of the phrases "those who have once been enlightened [compare 10:32; 2 Corinthians 4:4, 6; 1 Peter 2:9 et passim], who have tasted the heavenly gift [compare

Christ's tasting death for every person (2:9), certainly a full experience of death] and become partakers of the Holy Spirit [compare Christ's partaking of human nature (2:14), surely not a partial incarnation] and tasted the good word of God and the powers of the coming age [compare 1 Peter 2:3]." They also find difficult the appeal for **maturity** instead of conversion, the warning against **apostasy** (6:6) instead of failure to confess Christ initially, and the distinctively Christian address "**beloved**" (6:9; compare 10:30: "The Lord will judge *his people*").

- Perhaps the most promising interpretation takes the warning as directed to professing Christians, with the implication that they must show the genuineness of their profession by withstanding pressure to apostatize. Whereas assurances of eternal security assume a true profession of faith in which the saints persevere, warnings like this one take into account the phenomenon of false professions and the fact that only God knows in advance the difference between true professions and false.

MELCHIZEDEK Taking his cue from the statement in Psalm 110:4 that the messianic king will be a priest after the pattern of Melchizedek, the author of Hebrews draws several parallels between Christ and that shadowy Old Testament figure, to whom Abraham gave a tenth of the spoils of battle after rescuing Lot (Genesis 14:1–24):

- Melchizedek was a **priest of God**; so also is Christ.
- The name Melchizedek means "king of **righteousness**" (more literally, "my king is righteous"); the man by that name was king of "Salem" (perhaps a short form of "Jerusalem"), which means "**peace**" (in the sense of full divine blessing); and righteousness and peace are characteristics and results of Christ's priestly ministry.
- Absence in the Old Testament of a recorded genealogy for Melchizedek and of accounts of his birth and death typifies the **eternality** of Christ as God's Son, in contrast with the dying of all Aaronic priests.
- The superiority of Christ over Aaron is further symbolized by Melchizedek's receiving a **tenth** of the spoils of battle from Abraham, whose descendant Aaron was. Solidarity with one's ancestors is here presupposed.
- The same superiority appears again in Melchizedek's **blessing** Abraham, rather than vice versa; for the greater person blesses the lesser.

Read Hebrews 7:1–10:18.

The Two Old Testament Passages Mentioning Melchizedek

"Then Melchizedek king of Salem brought out bread and wine. He was priest of God Most High, and he blessed Abram . . . . Then Abram gave him a tenth of everything" (Genesis 14:18–20).

"The Lord has sworn and will not change his mind: 'You are a priest forever, in the order of Melchizedek'" (Psalm 110:4).

A Passage in the Dead Sea Scrolls Mentioning Melchizedek

"Just as Isaiah said: 'To proclaim liberty to the captives' [Isaiah 61:1]. . . . Melchizedek . . . will make them return. He will proclaim liberty to them so as to free them from the debt of all their sins. . . . And following the tenth jubilee will be the Day of Atonement, when atonement will be made for all the Sons of Light, even for the people predestined to Melchizedek. . . . For this will be the time for 'the year of Melchizedek's favor' . . . . But [against the wicked] Melchizedek will prosecute the vengeance required by God's judgments" (*Melchizedek Text* 1–26, excerpts).

EXHORTATION AND GREETINGS Hebrews closes with a long hortatory section and final greetings (10:19–13:25). The author urges his audience to use the superior method of approaching God through Christ rather than the outdated Old Testament method, especially in collective worship, which they have been neglecting (10:19–25). He warns them again, as in chapter 6, of the **terrifying judgment** that comes on those who willfully and utterly repudiate their Christian profession, but he states his confidence, based on their previous endurance of persecution, that they will not fall into apostasy (10:23–31). Then he encourages them to continued steadfastness by citing as examples the Old Testament **heroes of faith**, by linking his audience with them, and finally by citing Jesus as the most outstanding example of **patient endurance** of suffering and ultimate reception of reward (10:32–12:3). Suffering is good discipline and a sign of sonship (12:4–13). **Esau** becomes a warning example of the faithless apostate (12:14–17). And finally, the writer stresses again the superiority of the new covenant, based on the blood of Christ (12:18–29), and exhorts his audience to mutual love, hospitality (especially needed in those days by itinerant preachers), sympathy, the healthy and moral use of sex within marriage, avoidance of avarice, imitation of godly church leaders, avoidance of false teaching, acceptance of persecution, thanksgiving, generosity, obedience to ecclesiastical leaders, and prayer. *Read Hebrews 10:19–13:25.* Chapter 11 is sometimes considered the great chapter on faith in the New Testament, just as 1 Corinthians 13 is considered the great chapter on love and 1 Corinthians 15 the great chapter on resurrection.

Summary

We do not know who wrote Hebrews. The author wrote anonymously but exhibits theological influence from Paul. The letter appears to have been written to Jewish Christians in Italy, probably Rome, who had suffered persecution but were neglecting to meet with other Christians, probably to hide their Christian identity. The author fears they will apostatize back into their prior Jewish faith; so he warns that apostasy will incur God's judgment and stresses the superiority of Jesus over the Old Testament prophets, over the angels through whom the Jews believed God gave them the Mosaic law, over Moses himself, over Joshua, and over Aaron and his priestly descendants. Particular emphasis falls on Christ's human sympathy, divine appointment, eternality, heavenly locale, and likeness to Melchizedek—all within a portrayal of Christ as our great high priest.

"And they seized Isaiah the son of Amoz and sawed him in half with a wooden saw. . . . And while Isaiah was being sawed in half, he did not cry out or weep; but his mouth spoke through the Holy Spirit until he was sawed in two" (*Martyrdom and Ascension of Isaiah* 5:1–16, excerpt).

People to Remember

Aaron

Abraham

Apollos

Barnabas

Clement

Esau

Joshua

Luke

Melchizedek

Moses

Paul

Philip

Priscilla (and Aquila)

Silvanus

Places to Remember

Canaan

Corinth

Ephesus

Italy

Jerusalem

Mount Sinai

Qumran

Rome

Salem

the wilderness

Terms to Remember

Aaronic priesthood

Aaronites

apostasy

eternal security

Melchizedek (according to its meaning rather than as a personal name)

perseverance of the saints

priesthood according to the pattern of Melchizedek

Salem (according to its meaning rather than as a place name)

tabernacle

How Much Did You Learn?

- List the nominees for the authorship of Hebrews and the pros and cons of their authorship.
- List the figures associated with Old Testament Judaism over whom Christ is portrayed as superior and the points of his superiority.
- Contrast Aaron and Melchizedek in relation to Christ.
- Outline the theological issues in Hebrews' warning about the consequence of apostasy.
- Identify as many as you can of the heroes of faith in Hebrews 11, and tell how they demonstrated their faith.

For Further Discussion

- How important is it to determine the authorship of Hebrews and the date, geographical destination, and original audience of the letter?
- What would be a likely apology by the author of Hebrews to the modern charge that salvation by sacrificial blood is a primitive religious concept?
- If God accurately sees the inward state of a professing Christian but other people judge with only relative certainty by observing outward profession, in what ways do Christians know their own individual state, and with what degree of certainty?

For Further Investigation

Bruce, F. F. *The Epistle to the Hebrews*. 2d ed. Grand Rapids: Eerdmans, 1990.

deSilva, D. A. *Perseverance in Gratitude: A Socio-Rhetorical Commentary on the Epistle "to the Hebrews."* Grand Rapids: Eerdmans, 2000.

Ellingworth, P. *The Epistle to the Hebrews: A Commentary on the Greek Text*. Grand Rapids: Eerdmans, 1993. Advanced.

Guthrie, G. *NIV Application Commentary: Hebrews*. Grand Rapids: Zondervan, 1998.

Hagner, D. A. *Hebrews*. Peabody, Mass.: Hendrickson, 1990.

Lane, W. L. *Hebrews*. 2 vols. Dallas: Word, 1991. Advanced.

THE CATHOLIC, OR GENERAL, LETTERS

Overview:

- James: Salvation by Works
- First Peter: Salvation and Suffering
- Second Peter: In Defense of Orthodoxy
- Jude: Danger! False Teachers!
- First John: Fatherly Instruction to "Little Children"
- Second and Third John: Fatherly Instruction to Christians
- Summary

Study Goals—Learn:

- Why the Catholic, or General, Letters are so called
- Which James writes the letter bearing this name, whom he addresses, what the practical value of his letter is, and how his doctrine of works compares with Paul's doctrine of faith
- The nature of the persecution being suffered by the addressees of 1 Peter, how Peter encourages them, and where the "Babylon" is from which he writes
- How we are to evaluate modern doubts over the Petrine authorship and canonicity of 2 Peter, the theme that the letter shares with Jude, and the relation between these two letters
- Who Jude is, why he changes his mind regarding the contents of his letter, and how we are to understand his quotations of pseudepigraphal literature
- To whom and against whom John addresses his first letter, and his criteria of genuine Christianity
- Who "the elect lady and her children" are whom John warns in his second letter not to entertain false teachers
- The roles Gaius, Diotrephes, and Demetrius play in the ecclesiastical dispute around which 3 John revolves

Remains of the Circus Maximus in Rome

473

Catholic

The term *catholic,* meaning "general, universal," came to be applied by the early church to James, 1–2 Peter, 1–3 John, and Jude, because these letters (with the exceptions of 2–3 John) lack indications of limited address to a single locality. They are titled according to their traditional authors, like the Gospels, but unlike Paul's letters and Hebrews, which take their titles after the traditional addressees.

JAMES: SALVATION BY WORKS

Introductory Issues

The Letter of James is the least doctrinal and most practical book in the New Testament. We are dealing, then, with a **manual of Christian conduct** that assumes a foundation of faith.

Authorship

Harvest time, one of the many images from nature used in the Letter of James (see 3:18)

This letter bears the name of its author, James (Greek for the Hebrew name "Jacob"), a leader in the early Jerusalem church (Acts 15:12–21.; 21:18; Galatians 2:9, 12) and usually considered to be a **brother of Jesus,** but only a half brother because of the virgin birth. It is possible, however, that James is an older stepbrother of Jesus by a conjectural marriage of Joseph preceding his marriage to Mary. This view, which excludes any blood relationship to Jesus, might better explain the failure of Jesus' brothers to believe in him during his lifetime (Mark 3:21; John 7:2–8). And a lack of concern for Mary because she was only their stepmother might also better explain why Jesus, while hanging on a cross, committed his mother to the beloved disciple (John 19:25–27). But the reason may have been that Mary's discipleship alienated her from her other children, who still did not believe in Jesus.

To maintain the doctrine of Mary's perpetual virginity, the traditional Roman Catholic view is that "brother" means "cousin." But the associations between Jesus and his brothers in Matthew 13:55; Mark 6:3; and John 2:12; 7:2–10 imply a closer relation than that of cousins and probably also closer than that of stepbrothers. The view that the James who wrote this letter was Jesus' half brother therefore remains the most probable.

Though not a believer in Jesus during his public ministry, James saw the risen Christ (1 Corinthians 15:7) and was among those who were awaiting the Holy Spirit on the Day of Pentecost (Acts 1:14). Therefore James (and the other brothers of Jesus) must have come to belief some time during the last stage of Jesus' time on earth. Though James himself carefully practiced the Mosaic law (Acts 21:17–26; Galatians 2:12), at the Jerusalem Council he supported Paul's position that Gentile converts should not have to keep the law (Acts 15:12–21; compare Galatians 2:1–10).

Jewishness

The subject matter of James and its Jewish tone, especially its **stress on God's law**, harmonize with what we know of James the Lord's brother from Acts, Galatians, and other sources. Though often obscured by varying translations in English, there are also some significant **verbal parallels** between the Letter of James and the words of James in Acts 15, such as the term "greeting" (Greek: ↓chairein, used at the start of letters only in James 1:1 and Acts 15:23, the decree drafted under James's leadership), the term "visit" (Greek: ↓episkepsesthai, used in James 1:27 and Acts 15:14, the speech of James before the Jerusalem Council), and others (compare James 2:5, 7 with Acts 15:13, 17). Those who regard the letter as a late first- or early second-century pseudonymous work maintain that a simple Galilean, such as James, could not have written its well-styled Greek. But this objection overestimates the literary quality of the Greek style in James and, more importantly, fails to consider the mounting evidence that Palestinian Jews knew and used Greek along with Aramaic and Hebrew.[1]

The Jameses of the New Testament

- James the brother of Jesus
- James the son of Zebedee and one of the twelve apostles, brother of John the apostle, and a martyr at such an early date (A.D. 44; Acts 12:2) that it is unlikely he wrote the Letter of James
- James the son of ↓Alphaeus and one of the twelve apostles
- James the father of Judas (not Iscariot)

Some would add a James the son of a Mary different from Jesus' mother. The tone of authority in the Letter of James makes unlikely its authorship by one of the lesser known Jameses, that is, the son of Alphaeus and the father of Judas. See a concordance for references.

1. See S. E. Porter, "Did Jesus Ever Teach in Greek?" *Tyndale Bulletin* 44 (1993): 199–235.

Alphaeus: al-FEE-uhs ■ *chairein:* khi-RAYN ■ *episkepsesthai:* eh´pi-SKEP-ses-th*i*

"James, the brother of the Lord, . . . has been called the Just by all from the time of our Savior till the present day; for there were many who bore the name of James. He was holy from his mother's womb; and he drank no wine or strong drink; nor did he eat flesh. No razor came on his head. He did not anoint himself with oil, and he did not use the bath. . . . And he was in the habit of entering alone into the temple, and was often found on his knees begging forgiveness for the people, so that his knees became hard [= calloused] like those of a camel" (Hegesippus according to Eusebius, *Church History* 2.23.4–6).

"Saint John's gospel and his first letter, Saint Paul's letters, especially those to the Romans, Galatians, Ephesians, and Saint Peter's first letter—these are the books that show Christ to you and teach you everything needed and blessed for you to know even though you never see or hear any other book or doctrine. Therefore Saint James's letter is a right strawy epistle in comparison with them, for it has no gospel character to it. Therefore I will not have it in my Bible in the number of the proper chief books, but do not intend by this to forbid anyone to place and exalt it as he pleases, for there is many a good saying in it" (Martin Luther in the introduction to the first edition of his German New Testament, September 1522).

Canonicity

The Letter of James encountered some difficulty in gaining canonical status. Several factors explain the hesitancy of the early church: the **brevity** of the letter; its dominantly **practical** rather than doctrinal character; and the **limitation** of its address to Jewish Christians—all of which doubtless retarded wide circulation. An **uncertainty** about the identity of James in 1:1 (for several men by that name appear in the New Testament) also cast initial doubt on the letter's canonicity. The mistaken impression (voiced by Martin Luther among others) that the doctrine of works in James contradicts Paul's doctrine of faith did not seriously disturb the early church so far as we can tell. When it came to be realized that the author was almost surely James the Lord's brother, the final verdict proved favorable to canonicity.

Addresses

James writes "to the twelve tribes in the Diaspora" (1:1). This designation may be taken metaphorically, as in 1 Peter 1:1 (see pages 483–84), for the predominantly Gentile church scattered throughout the Roman Empire. In James, however, the reference is more likely to **Jewish Christians living outside Palestine,** as favored by a number of items:

- The specificity of reference to "the twelve tribes"
- The use in 2:2 of the Greek word for a synagogue, usually translated here in its untechnical sense of "assembly"
- The five quotations of and numerous allusions to the Old Testament
- Jewish idioms, such as "Lord of ↓sabaoth [hosts]" (5:4)
- Stress on several permanent principles of the Jewish law (2:8–13; 4:11–12) and on monotheism (2:19)
- The omission of any polemic against idolatry, for idolatry did not characterize Jews of the first century and had not characterized them since the Babylonian exile but was commonly practiced by Gentiles

sabaoth: SAB-ay-oth

Date

Josephus puts the martyrdom of James in A.D. 62; so the Letter of James must be dated earlier.[2] Some scholars advance arguments for a date so early (A.D. 45–50) that the letter could be considered the first New Testament book to have been written. For example, the lack of any reference to the Judaizing controversy is said to imply a date before that controversy arose just prior to the Jerusalem Council of about A.D. 49; and the Jewish tone of this letter is said to imply a date before Christianity had expanded to include Gentiles. But a limitation of the address to Jewish Christians and the strongly Jewish outlook of James himself can account for both phenomena. We should therefore content ourselves with an indeterminate date before James's martyrdom.

Allusions to Jesus' Sayings

Notably, James contains numerous allusions to sayings of Jesus recorded in the Gospels, especially material associated with the Sermon on the Mount. For example, the contrast in 1:22 between hearers and doers of the word recalls the parable of the wise person, who builds on a solid foundation by hearing and doing the words of Jesus, and the foolish person, who builds on the sand by hearing but failing to do his words (Matthew 7:24–27; Luke 6:47–49).

2. Josephus, *Jewish Antiquities* 20.9.1 §§197–203. Less likely is the date A.D. 68 given by the early church father Hegesippus according to Eusebius, *Church History* 2.23.18.

A Stanza from Martin Luther's Hymn, "A Mighty Fortress Is Our God"

Did we in our own strength confide,
Our striving would be losing,
Were not the right man on our side,
The Man of God's own choosing.
Dost ask who that may be?
Christ Jesus, it is He—
Lord Sabaoth His name,
From age to age the same,
And He must win the battle.

Note: "Sabaoth" is Hebrew for "hosts" and refers in this expression to the Lord's armies of angels, so that Luther and James 5:4 use it to assure the persecuted people of God that he will overwhelm their oppressors with his heavenly forces.

On the Martyrdom of James the Lord's Brother

- "And so he [↓Ananus the high priest] convened the judges of the Sanhedrin and brought before them a man named James, the brother of Jesus who was called the Christ, and certain others. He accused them of having transgressed the law and delivered them up to be stoned. Those of the inhabitants of the city [Jerusalem] who were considered the most fair-minded and who were strict in observance of the law were offended at this" (Josephus, *Jewish Antiquities* 20.9.1 §§200–201).

- "So they went up and threw down [from 'the pinnacle of the temple'] the just man and said to each other, 'Let us stone James the Just.' And they began to stone him, for he was not killed by the fall. . . . And one of them, who was a laundryman, took the club with which he beat out clothes and struck the just man on the head. And thus he suffered martyrdom" (Hegesippus according to Eusebius, *Church History* 2.23.16–18).

Reading James with Interpretation

Topics

It is difficult to outline James. On the one hand, the letter has the rambling and moralistic style of Proverbs and other wisdom literature. On the other hand, its precepts are delivered with the fire and passion of a prophetic sermon. After the initial greeting (1:1), one can only list a series of practical exhortations on various topics dealing with Christian conduct in church meetings and everyday life.

- Rejoice in trials (1:2–4).
- Believingly ask God for wisdom (1:5–8).
- Do not desire wealth (1:9–11).
- Distinguish between trials, which come from God, and temptations, which come from human lusts, for God gives only good gifts (1:12–18).
- Be doers of the word in speech and action, not mere hearers (1:19–27).
- Do not show partiality toward the rich, but love all equally and as yourselves (2:1–13). As in the Old Testament, the emphasis in "the rich" lies as much on their wicked persecution of the righteous as on their wealth, just as "poor" often means "pious and persecuted" as well as "poverty stricken."
- Demonstrate the genuineness of your **faith** by **good works** (2:14–26). James writes of justification by works *before other human beings*, who need outward evidence because they *cannot* see into the heart. He is not contradicting Paul, who writes of justification by faith *before God*, who does not need outward evidence because he *can* see into the heart. Some scholars who think that James wrote the letter

---

Ananus: AN-uh-nuhs

late in his lifetime argue for his correcting an antinomian perversion of Paul's doctrine of justification by faith. Others, failing to see that James and Paul complement each other (but Paul, too, emphasizes good works as a consequence of true faith), hold that James or a later forger is attacking not merely a distortion of Paul's doctrine, but that doctrine itself. *Read James 1:1–2:26.*

- Exhibit the characteristics of genuine wisdom required of Christian teachers: **control of the tongue**, that is, of its speech; **meekness**, which avoids quarrelsomeness; and **purity**, which avoids worldliness (3:1–4:10).
- Do not slander one another (4:11–12).
- Do not plan overconfidently by failing to take into account God's will and the possibility of death (4:13–17).
- Be patient until Jesus returns, for then God will punish your rich and powerful persecutors (5:1–11).
- Do not use oaths, but speak straightforwardly and honestly (5:12).
- Share your concerns and joys with one another (5:13–18). In particular, let the elders of the church believingly **pray** for the healing of the sick as they **anoint** them with oil in the name of the Lord. If a sick person has sinned and confesses, healing will demonstrate that God has forgiven. (The reverse—that sickness is always a direct chastisement for sin and that failure to recover always implies unforgiveness by God—does not logically follow.) Olive oil was a common household remedy. The good Samaritan, for example, poured "oil and wine" on the wounds of a waylaid traveler (Luke 10:34). So James may have its medicinal properties in mind, as though to say, "Treat with medicine and pray for recovery." The command to anoint with oil underlies the Roman Catholic sacrament of **extreme unction**, in which a priest anoints the eyes, ears, nostrils, hands, and feet of a person about to die as a medium of forgiveness if the person cannot consciously engage in confession to receive priestly absolution. But James speaks of "elders," not priests. Nor does he speak of people already in the throes of death. Similarly, the command, "Confess your sins to each another" (5:16), is a Roman Catholic proof text for **auricular confession**. But James writes "to each other" and may refer to resolving differences among Christians rather than to exposing one's private sins either to a priest or to the whole church.
- Keep fellow professing Christians from apostatizing and incurring eternal judgment (5:19–20).

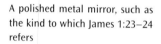

A polished metal mirror, such as the kind to which James 1:23–24 refers

> "Was not Abraham found faithful when tested, and it was reckoned to him as righteousness?" (1 Maccabees 2:52).

> "The Lord created small persons and great persons. Whoever insults a person's face insults the Lord's face. Whoever treats with contempt the face of any person treats with contempt the face of the Lord" (2 Enoch 44:1–2).

"And of all the virtues, is not wisdom the one to which people in general lay claim, thereby filling themselves with strife and false conceit of wisdom?" (Socrates according to Plato *Philebus* 49A).

Read James 3:1–5:20. The sinners who are to be turned from the error of their ways are fellow Christians whose straying tends toward apostasy. The death of their soul means eternal death, should they apostatize (see the remarks on pages 466–67 concerning apostasy in Hebrews). And covering a multitude of sins means God's forgiveness of strayers' sins when others have induced them to repent.

FIRST PETER: SALVATION AND SUFFERING

Introductory Issues

Themes

The audience to whom this letter was first directed were suffering **persecution.** The emphasis therefore falls on **proper Christian conduct** in the face of anti-Christian hostility and on the compensatory **gift of salvation** that will reach completion in the future.

Authorship

The author identifies himself as **Peter** (1:1). This identification agrees remarkably with two phenomena: (1) A number of phrases in 1 Peter recall the phraseology of Peter's sermons as recorded in Acts, and (2) allusions to Jesus' sayings and deeds as recorded in the Gospels come from stories in which Peter played a special part or from sayings in which he would have taken a special interest. Therefore, though some modern scholars have theorized that 1 Peter is a baptismal sermon or liturgy (1:3–4:11) transformed into a letter by the addition of 1:1–2 and 4:12–5:14 and hence probably non-Petrine, we should accept the letter's own claim to have been written by the Apostle Peter, a claim supported by early church tradition.

Date

The element of persecution, which pervades the letter, suggests that Peter wrote it around A.D. **63–64,** shortly before his martyrdom in Rome under Nero about A.D. 65. But the persecution lying behind 1 Peter seems not to have originated from an imperial ban on Christianity, for Peter still speaks of the government as a protector (2:13–17; 3:13). The empire-wide ban came later. The present persecution rather takes the forms of **slanderous accusations, social ostracism, mob riots,** and **local police action.** Scholars who deny Petrine authorship usually date the letter during the persecutions under Domitian (A.D. 81–96) or ↓Trajan (A.D. 98–117). But in these later persecutions the dominant issue was Christians' refusal to sacrifice to the emperor. Since this issue does not come up in 1 Peter, the early date, with Petrine authorship, is preferable.

Silvanus's Role

Either Silvanus acts as Peter's amanuensis for this letter ("I have written . . . through Silvanus," 5:12) and so may produce the fair style of its Greek or, since we must not think of Palestinian Jews like Peter as incapable of handling that language well, Silvanus simply carries the letter (hence Peter's commending him as a "faithful brother"). Or Silvanus performs both of these services. His name, a Latin one, sounds like the Aramaic "Silas" and probably refers to the Silas who accompanied Paul on his second missionary journey; for Paul mentions a "Silvanus" as his companion during that journey (2 Corinthians 1:19; 1 Thessalonians 1:1; 2 Thessalonians 1:1), and Luke's narrative of the same journey uses "Silas" (nine times in Acts 15:40–18:5). The similarity of Peter's ethical exhortations to those in Pauline literature (for examples, see page 350) suggests that Peter is influenced by Paul's letters, perhaps known to him through Silvanus, or that both apostles draw from a common stock of more or less stereotyped catechetical instruction—oral or written, prebaptismal or postbaptismal.

Trajan: TRAY-juhn

Cappadocia, one of the provinces named in the address of 1 Peter

Roman Origin

Peter writes from "Babylon" (5:13), but almost certainly not the city by that name in ↓Mesopotamia—rather, Rome. For Mesopotamian Babylon had lost almost all its inhabitants by the beginning of the Christian era, and "Babylon" occurs as a symbolic name for Rome in Revelation 17:4–6, 9, 18 inasmuch as Rome was the ruling city in the New Testament period (verse 18), the city of seven hills whereas Mesopotamian Babylon was situated on a plain, its ruins still visible today (verse 9), and the persecutor of the church (verse 6). Rome is called "Babylon" because it is the world capital of idolatry, a position once held by the Mesopotamian city (compare the

Mesopotamia: mes´uh-puh-TAY-mee-uh

Examples of Similar Phraseology in 1 Peter and Peter's Sermons in Acts

"You were redeemed . . . with the precious blood of Christ; he was **foreknown** before the **founding** of the world" (1 Peter 1:18–20)	"This man [Jesus] was delivered up by God's set purpose and **foreknowledge**; and you . . . put him to death" (Acts 2:23).
"He himself bore our sins in his body on the **tree**" (1 Peter 2:24).	"Whom you had killed by hanging him on a **tree**" (Acts 5:30; similarly 10:39).
"They will have to give account to him who is ready to **judge the living and the dead**" (1 Peter 4:5).	"He is the one appointed by God to be **judge of the living and the dead**" (Acts 10:42).

An Example of Allusion to a Saying of Jesus Specially Associated with Peter

"Submit yourselves for the Lord's sake to every human institution, whether to the **king** as the supreme authority or to governors as those sent by him . . . . Live as **free** men, but do not use your freedom as a cover-up for evil . . . . Honor the **king**" (1 Peter 2:13–17).	"And when Peter came into the house, Jesus anticipated him by saying, 'What do you think, Simon? From whom do the **kings** of the earth take customs duties and poll-tax? From their sons or from foreigners?' And when he said, 'From foreigners,' Jesus said to him, 'As a matter of fact, then, the sons are **free**. But in order that we not offend them, go to the sea, throw in a hook, take the first fish that comes up, and opening its mouth you will find a stater [= four drachmas]. Take that and give it to them for me and you'" (Matthew 17:25–27).

For further examples, see R. H. Gundry, "'Verba Christi' in 1 Peter: Their Implications Concerning the Authorship of 1 Peter and the Authenticity of the Gospel Tradition," *New Testament Studies* 13 (1967): 336–50.

calling of Jerusalem "↓Sodom and Egypt" because of Jesus' crucifixion there—Revelation 11:8). Extrabiblical references to Rome as "Babylon" also suggest that Peter is using a well-known designation, and the early church fathers understood "Babylon" as a reference to Rome.

Tradition knows of no church in Mesopotamian Babylon or of Peter's ever going there, but tradition does indicate that Peter died in Rome. When John Mark's presence in Rome during Paul's imprisonment there (Colossians 4:10) is connected with his presence with Peter at the writing of 1 Peter (1 Peter 5:13), another formidable argument for the Roman origin of this letter appears. Finally, the order of provinces in the address (1:1) suggests that the bearer of the letter comes from Rome in the West, makes a circuit of certain provinces in Asia Minor with the letter, and returns westward to Rome. The route can be traced on a map through ↓Pontus, Galatia, ↓Cappadocia, Asia, and ↓Bithynia (see page 352).

Addressees

At first glance the phrases "exiles of the Dispersion" (1:1), "among the Gentiles" (2:12), and "the Gentiles" (as a third party, 4:3) seem to imply that the original addressees were Jewish Christians. But references to their idolatry prior to conversion (4:3; Jews of the first century did not practice idolatry) and "passions of your former ignorance" and "futile way of life" (1:14, 18; compare Ephesians 4:17, where similar phraseology applies to Gentiles) clearly indicate the predominantly **Gentile** background of the intended audience. This conclusion is confirmed by 2:10: "Once you were not a

---

Sodom: SOD-uhm ■ Pontus: PON-tuhs ■ Cappadocia: kap′uh-DOH-shee-uh ■ Bithynia: bi-THIN-ee-uh

Saint Peter's Square in Rome with the Basilica in the background

people [this could hardly be said of the Jews, God's covenant nation], but now you are the people of God." Just as Peter uses the term "Babylon" figuratively for Rome, then, he also uses the term "Gentiles" figuratively for non-Christians and the phrase "exiles of the Dispersion" for Gentile Christians scattered throughout the world. Because the church has for the time being displaced Israel, Jewish designations can apply to the predominantly Gentile church.

An Outline of First Peter

Introduction: Greeting (1:1–2)
 I. Praise for the Heavenly Inheritance of Persecuted Christians (1:3–12)
 II. Exhortation to Personal Holiness (1:13–21)
 III. Exhortation to Mutual Love (1:22–25)
 IV. Exhortation to Advancement in Salvation (2:1–10)
 V. Exhortation to Christian Conduct in Non-Christian Society (2:11–4:19)
     A. Good deeds (2:11–12)
     B. Good citizenship (2:13–17)
     C. Submission of slaves, with the example of Christ (2:18–25)
     D. Submission of wives (3:1–6)
     E. Considerateness of husbands (3:7)
     F. Sympathetic and loving unity (3:8–12)
     G. Innocent suffering, with the example of Christ and his vindication in hell (3:13–4:6)
     H. Loving Service (4:7–11)
     I. Joyful suffering (4:12–19)
 VI. Exhortation to Humility in the Church and Resistance to Persecution (5:1–11)
Conclusion: Silvanus's Function as Amanuensis or Carrier or Both, Greetings, and Benediction (5:12–14)

Reading First Peter with Interpretation

Suffering and Reward

After his greeting, Peter praises God for the prospect of a glorious heavenly inheritance that makes present persecution bearable. Christ also had to suffer before glorification, something the Old Testament prophets did not understand because they did not discern the distinction between Jesus' first coming, for death, and his second coming, for dominion. *Read 1 Peter 1:1–12.*

Good Conduct

In view of future glory, it is imperative for Christians to be **holy** in conduct. They have been liberated ("redeemed") from slavery to sin by Jesus' blood, which is the evidence of his life sacrificed for sinners. It is imperative for Christians also to **love** one another, because they have all been born into the family of God through his word, and to **grow** like newborn infants and be **built up** like a temple, with Christ as the corner- or capstone. Furthermore, Christians are to make a favorable impression on the unbelieving world by **good behavior.** This entails exemplary citizenship, obedience of slaves to masters without talking back, Christian wives' adorning themselves with obedience to their husbands rather than with gaudy fashions, the honoring of wives by their husbands, and, once again, mutual love in the Christian fellowship. *Read 1 Peter 1:13–3:22.*

Woman with braided hair

Descent into Hell

The preaching of Christ to the spirits in prison (3:18–20) most probably means that during the time between his death and resurrection he descended in disembodied form into hell to proclaim his triumph over the demonic spirits whom God had imprisoned there because of their corrupting the human race at the time of Noah, just before the flood. A slight variation is that the prison is not hell, but the atmosphere of the earth, to which demons are now confined (compare Ephesians 2:2; 6:12; but in favor of hell see 2 Peter 2:4; Jude 6). The preaching need not refer to an offer of salvation. The point of the passage is that just as God vindicated Christ before the very spirits who had tried to thwart the history of redemption, so also God will someday vindicate Christians before their persecutors.

An alternative interpretation is that the preincarnate Christ offered salvation through Noah's preaching to members of the antediluvian generation, who are now confined to hell because they rejected the message. In this interpretation the point of the passage lies in the parallel between God's past vindication of Noah (rather than of Christ) and his future vindication of Christians. But when unqualified, the term *spirits* refers in the Bible to supernatural beings, not to departed human spirits; and the succession of mainly verbal phrases about Christ—"put to death," "made alive in spirit," "went," "preached," "the resurrection of Jesus Christ," "has gone into heaven," "is at God's right hand"—makes a back reference to the activity of Christ millennia before his incarnation very awkward.

Baptism

In comparing baptism to the flood, Peter carefully indicates that contact with baptismal water does not remove sin ("not the removal of dirt from the flesh"); rather, the inward attitude of repentance and faith, which shows itself by submission to the baptismal rite ("an appeal to God for a good conscience," 3:21), leads to remission.

Compare the following with 1 Peter 3:19–20: "He [Christ] went and preached to the spirits in prison who once disobeyed when God waited patiently in the days of Noah while the ark was being constructed."

- "The ↓Nephilim were on the earth in those days—and also afterward—when the sons of God went to the daughters of men and had children by them. Those were the mighty men of old, men of renown" (Genesis 6:4).
- "For what reason have you ['the Watchers of heaven'] abandoned the high, holy, and eternal heaven and slept with women and defiled yourselves with the daughters of the people by taking wives, acting like children of the earth, and begetting giant sons?" (*1 Enoch* 15:3).
- "Jesus Christ . . . who was conceived by the Holy Ghost, born of the Virgin Mary, suffered under Pontius Pilate, was crucified, dead, and buried; **He descended into hell;** the third day He rose again from the dead . . ." (The Apostle's Creed).

Exhortations

The next section begins with a summary exhortation not to sin. Suffering in the flesh (4:1) refers to physical persecution. Since Christ suffered such persecution, his followers should be prepared to do so too. This suffering does not cause a person to stop sinning; rather, it is ceasing to sin that causes the suffering of persecution. Ceasing to sin means not pursuing "debaucheries, lusts, drunkenness, orgies, drinking parties, and forbidden idolatries" (4:3). The **surprise** of unbelievers that Christians no longer join them in such activities turns into taking **offense** that the Christians no longer do so. The result is persecution: malignment that leads to physical suffering. "The dead" to whom the gospel was preached (4:6) are not "the spirits in prison" of 3:18–20. They are Christians who have been **martyred** ("judged in the flesh according to human beings [their persecutors]") and consequently enjoy heavenly life as **disembodied** spirits ("live in spirit according to God"). The final exhortations are to rejoice in suffering for Christ, to make sure that suffering is incurred by Christian testimony rather than by bad conduct, to show humility, and to resist with courage satanically instigated persecution. *Read 1 Peter 4:1–5:14.*

SECOND PETER: IN DEFENSE OF ORTHODOXY

Introductory Issues

Theme

Heretical teachers who peddled **false doctrine** and practiced **immorality** were beginning to make serious inroads into the church. Second Peter

---

Nephilim: NEF-uh-lim

polemicizes against them, particularly against their denial of Jesus' return, and affirms the true knowledge of Christian belief to counter their heretical teaching.

Authenticity and Canonicity

Widespread doubt exists among modern scholars that the Apostle Peter wrote this letter. The early church exhibited some **hesitancy** in accepting it into the canon. This hesitancy can be explained by the comparative brevity of the letter, however; and such brevity may have curtailed its distribution and limited people's acquaintance with it. The early church did finally accept it as a genuine and canonical writing of Peter. We should note, moreover, that two books of the New Testament apocrypha, the *Gospel of Truth* and the *Apocryphon of John,* contain possible and probable quotations from or allusions to 2 Peter and thus show an acceptance of 2 Peter as authoritative already in the second century. Similarly, the third-century Bodmer papyrus designated P[72] shows acceptance of 2 Peter as canonical; for in that manuscript 2 Peter shares with 1 Peter and Jude a blessing on readers of

Possible and Probable Reflections of 2 Peter in Early Gnostic Literature

2 Peter 1:16–18 We were **eyewitnesses** of his majesty. For he received honor and glory from God **the Father** when the voice came to him from the Majestic Glory, saying, 'This is my **beloved Son**; with him I am well pleased.' We ourselves **heard** this voice."	*Gospel of Truth* 30:24–32 "He gave them the means of knowing the knowledge of **the Father** and the revelation of his Son. For when they had **seen** him and had **heard** him, he granted them to taste him and to smell him and to touch the **beloved Son**."
2 Peter 2:2 "The **way** of **truth** will be slandered."	*Gospel of Truth* 18:19–21 "He showed (them) a **way**; and the **way** is the **truth** that he taught them."
2 Peter 2:4–5 "God did not spare **the angels** when they sinned, but gave them over to pits of darkness to be **kept for judgment**. And he did not spare the ancient world, but preserved **Noah**, a **proclaimer** of righteousness, along with seven others, when he brought a flood on the world of the ungodly. "	*Apocryphon of John* 27:24–30; 29:1–4 "To that place where **the angels** of poverty go they will be taken, the place where there is no repentance. And they will be **kept for** the day on which those who have blasphemed the spirit will be tortured, and they will be punished with **eternal punishment**. . . . But the greatness of the light of the foreknowledge informed **Noah**, and he **proclaimed** (it) to all the offspring that are the sons of men."

A frieze depicting Peter being crucified upside down, based on an unfounded legend (see pages 292–93)

these sacred books and gets even more elaborate ornamentation than the other two letters.

The **style** of 2 Peter differs from that of 1 Peter. But a difference in amanuenses may provide the reason. Remarkable similarities of phraseology between 2 Peter and 1 Peter and the Petrine speeches in Acts point to a common source, the Apostle Peter.

Relation to Jude

It is also argued that 2 Peter borrows from Jude, especially in description of false teachers, and that a man of Peter's apostolic stature would not have borrowed from a comparatively insignificant writer, such as Jude. But we may question the last part of this argument, for literary history is filled with examples of prominent writers who borrowed from obscure ones. Shakespeare did, and the practice was especially common in the ancient world. Furthermore, a number of scholars have argued that Jude wrote his letter later and borrowed from 2 Peter. For example, the fact that 2 Peter speaks of the coming of the false teachers predominantly in the future tense and Jude in the past tense might indicate that 2 Peter was written before the spread of heresy, Jude afterward. It is also possible that their similar phraseology comes from a common source unknown to us.

Allusion to Paul's Letters

In further objection to Petrine authorship, the reference to Paul's letters in 2 Peter 3:15–16 is said to imply that all of them had been written, collected, and published; yet these things could have happened only after the martyrdoms of Peter and Paul, for Paul was writing up to the very end of his life.

Examples of Similarities of Phraseology Between 2 Peter and 1 Peter

1:1: "equally precious faith"

1:7: "the tested genuineness of your faith, more precious than gold"

1:16: "having become eyewitnesses"

2:12; 3:2: " being/having become eyewitnesses"

2:7; 3:17: "wanton men"

4:3: "wanton idolatries"

2:14: "unceasing from sin"

4:1: "have ceased from sin"

3:14: "spotless and unblemished"
(cf. 2:13: "spots and blemishes")

1:19: "unblemished and spotless"

3:17: "your own stability"
(cf. 2:14: "unstable souls")

5:10: "will stabilize you"

But the reference to his letters need imply the existence of only those letters he had written up to the time that Peter wrote his second letter. Peter's
knowledge of them probably came from his travels, from the circulation of
Paul's letters, and from Silvanus (or Silas), who was both Paul's missionary
companion and Peter's helper (1 Peter 5:12). The description of Paul as "our
beloved brother" (2 Peter 3:15) is what an apostolic contemporary and
equal would write, not what a later pseudonymous author would write
about an ecclesiastical hero of a bygone generation. Despite modern doubt,
then, we may accept the final verdict of the early church that shortly after
the Apostle Peter wrote his first letter and shortly before his martyrdom
about A.D. 65, he wrote this second letter which bears his name.[3]

3. For full defenses of Petrine
authorship, see E. M. B. Green, *2
Peter Reconsidered* (London: Tyn-
dale, 1961), 12–14; D. Guthrie,
New Testament Introduction (Down-
ers Grove, Ill.: InterVarsity Press,
1971), 814–63; and for con-
ceptual similarities to the pre-
Christian Dead Sea Scrolls, see W.
F. Albright, *From the Stone Age to
Christianity*, 2d ed. (Garden City,
N.Y.: Doubleday, 1957), 22–23.

An Outline of Second Peter

Introduction: Greeting (1:1–2)
I. The True Knowledge of Christian Belief (1:3–21)
    A. The moral undergirding of Christian belief with correct conduct (1:3–11)
    B. The historical reliability of Christian belief, supported by eyewitness testi-
       mony and fulfilled prophecy (1:12–21)
II. False Teachers (2:1–22)
    A. Their coming appearance in the church (2:1–3)
    B. Their future judgment (2:4–10a)
    C. Their immoral ways (2:10b–22)
III. The Parousia and Final Dissolution (3:1–18a)
    A. Its certainty in spite of delay and denials by false teachers (3:1–10)
    B. Its call to godliness (3:11–18a)
Conclusion: Doxology (3:18b)

Reading Second Peter with Interpretation

Reliability of Orthodoxy

Second Peter affirms the true knowledge of Christian belief in opposition to
false teaching. After the greeting, Peter glories in the magnitude of God's
promises to believers, by which they come to share the divine nature, and
points out the resultant necessity of nurturing Christian virtues. Correct
conduct must undergird correct belief. He reminds his audience of the reliability of the Christian faith, as supported by eyewitness testimony to the
events of Jesus' life (Peter singles out his own observation of the transfiguration, 1:16–18) and as proved by the fulfillment of divinely inspired
prophecy. *Read 2 Peter 1:1–21.* "No prophecy of Scripture is a matter of one's
own interpretation" (1:20) probably means that the Old Testament predictions of messianic events did not arise out of the prophets' own interpretation of the future, but from the influence of the Holy Spirit. Compare 1:21:

"For no prophecy was ever brought about by the will of a human being; but human beings spoke from God as they were carried along by the Holy Spirit." Other interpretations are that

- Prophetic predictions should not be interpreted in isolation from other Scriptures.
- Prophetic predictions were not addressed exclusively to the generation contemporary with their issuance.
- The Holy Spirit interprets prophecy as well as inspires it.
- By themselves Christians do not have the ability or right to interpret Scripture, but need ecclesiastical direction.

Judgment on Heterodoxy

The mention of true prophecy at the end of chapter 1 leads to a condemnation of false prophecy. Current and future false teachers stand in the tradition of false prophets in the Old Testament and will incur the same judgment from God on themselves. Though they promise freedom, their licentious living demonstrates their depravity and slavery to lust. True Christians, however, should recall the predictions of judgment at the second coming—a judgment after the pattern of the flood, but with fire instead of water. The delay in Jesus' return should not be misinterpreted as cancellation. It is due, rather, to God's patience in giving each generation more time for repentance. After all, what is a thousand years to the eternal God? Since the present scheme of things will be destroyed, Christians should live uprightly, that is, according to the eternal values that are fostered by anticipating Jesus' return. The classification of Paul's letters among "the other Scriptures" (3:15–16) shows that they are already regarded as inspired. *Read 2 Peter 2:1–3:18.*

> "God . . . distinguishes whether the passions of the sick soul to which he administers justice will in any way yield and make room for repentance, and for those in whose nature vice is not unrelieved or intractable, he fixes a period of grace. . . . As for the gods, any length of human life is but nothing" (Plutarch, *Moralia,* "On the Delays of the Divine Vengeance" 6, 9).

JUDE: DANGER! FALSE TEACHERS!

Introductory Issues

Theme

Like 2 Peter, the Letter of Jude polemicizes against false teachers who have penetrated the church—in greater numbers, it would appear, than at the time 2 Peter was written (but the point is disputed; see page 488). The particular heresies receive no detailed description or rebuttal, but the heretics themselves draw vehement castigation.

Authorship

The author of this letter identifies himself as Jude, "a brother of James" (verse 1). He is probably not referring to the Apostle James of the well-known trio, Peter, James, and John. Herod Agrippa I martyred the Apostle James at an early date (Acts 12:1–2). The writer refers instead to James the leader of the church in Jerusalem (Acts 15:12–21; 21:18; Galatians 1:18–2:13) and the half brother of Jesus. Thus Jude too is a half brother of Jesus but modestly describes himself as "a servant of Jesus Christ" (verse 1). The date of this letter is uncertain, but it is late enough for heretics to have made serious inroads into the church.

An Outline of Jude

Introduction: Greeting (1–2)
  I. The Entrance of False Teachers into the Church (3–4)
  II. The Ungodly Character and Coming Judgment of the False Teachers (5–16)
  III. Resistance Against the False Teachers (17–23)
Conclusion: Benediction (24–25)

Reading Jude with Interpretation

False Teachers

Jude intended to write a doctrinal treatise, but the infiltration of false teachers into the church has compelled him to change his letter into an exhortation to fight vigorously for the truth of the gospel. In vivid terms he describes both the wickedness of the false teachers and their doom by citing past examples of divine judgment: the generation of Israel that perished in the wilderness for their faithless ways, the fallen angels (probably the demonic spirits who corrupted the human race just before the flood [Genesis 6:1–4; 1 Peter 3:18–20]), and Sodom and ↓Gomorrah. The false teachers' lack of reverence for spiritual things and for superhuman beings stands in contrast to the care that Michael the archangel exercised when disputing with Satan over Moses' corpse. The letter closes with a stirring doxology. *Read Jude 1–25.*

Pseudepigraphal References

In verses 14–15 Jude quotes the pseudepigraphal apocalypse of *1 Enoch* ("Enoch . . . prophesied, saying, 'Behold, the Lord came with myriads of his holy ones . . . ,'" *1 Enoch* 1:9). In an allusion to the dispute between Michael

Gomorrah: guh-MOR-uh

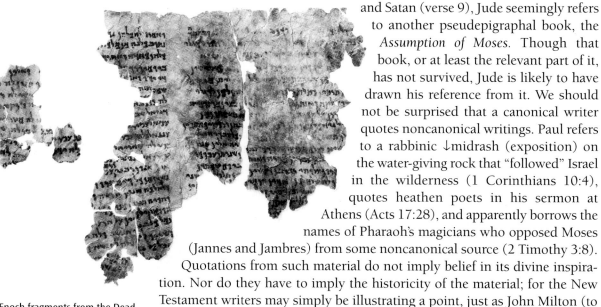

Enoch fragments from the Dead
Sea Scrolls

and Satan (verse 9), Jude seemingly refers to another pseudepigraphal book, the *Assumption of Moses*. Though that book, or at least the relevant part of it, has not survived, Jude is likely to have drawn his reference from it. We should not be surprised that a canonical writer quotes noncanonical writings. Paul refers to a rabbinic ↓midrash (exposition) on the water-giving rock that "followed" Israel in the wilderness (1 Corinthians 10:4), quotes heathen poets in his sermon at Athens (Acts 17:28), and apparently borrows the names of Pharaoh's magicians who opposed Moses (Jannes and Jambres) from some noncanonical source (2 Timothy 3:8). Quotations from such material do not imply belief in its divine inspiration. Nor do they have to imply the historicity of the material; for the New Testament writers may simply be illustrating a point, just as John Milton (to take one of many possible examples) utilizes Greek myths without implying a belief in the historicity of their contents.

FIRST JOHN: FATHERLY INSTRUCTION TO "LITTLE CHILDREN"

Introductory Issues

Theme
For early Christians, heresy in the church posed the problem of distinguishing orthodoxy from heterodoxy, faithful ministers of the word from false teachers. The Letter of 1 John formulates several criteria—**righteousness, love of fellow believers**, and **correct Christology**—for testing the Christian profession of teachers and of oneself.

Literary Form, Address, and Purpose
Written probably toward the end of the first century by the Apostle John, 1 John has no introduction, author's greetings, or concluding salutations. Yet the statements, "I am writing" (2:1) and "These things I have written to you" (2:26), show that originally 1 John was not an oral sermon, but a written composition. It might have been a general tract for the whole church. But the affectionate **"my little children,"** by which the writer repeatedly

---

midrash: MID-rash

addresses his audience, implies a limited circle of Christians with whom he is closely acquainted. According to early church tradition, John lived in Ephesus during his old age. Therefore, 1 John is probably a general letter written in sermonic style to Christians he came to know in Asia Minor in the region surrounding Ephesus (compare Paul's circular letter to the "Ephesians" and the sermonic style of Hebrews). It is also possible that 1 John represents a western Asiatic letter form that lacked an opening address and a closing greeting. John clearly states his purpose in writing to strengthen the addressees' **knowledge, joy,** and **assurance** in the Christian faith (1:3–4; 5:13) over against false teaching (2:1–29; 4:1–21).

Antignostic Polemic

CERINTHIANISM The heresy of Gnosticism was probably growing in Christendom by the time John wrote. According to early tradition, John hurriedly left a public bath in Ephesus when he heard that the Gnostic leader Cerinthus had entered: "There are also those who heard from him [Polycarp] that John, the Lord's disciple, going to bathe at Ephesus, and perceiving Cerinthus inside, rushed out of the bath house without bathing [and] exclaiming, 'Let us flee, lest even the bath house fall down, because Cerinthus, the enemy of the truth, is inside'" (Irenaeus, *Against Heresies* 3.34). Building on the notion that matter is inherently evil, Cerinthus distinguished between an immaterial, divine Christ-spirit and a human Jesus with a physical body, and said that the Christ-spirit came on the human Jesus right after Jesus' baptism and left just before the crucifixion.

Against this Cerinthian doctrine John stresses that it was the **one** person "Jesus Christ" who began his public manifestation by being baptized and finished it by being crucified: "This is the one who came by water and blood—Jesus Christ; not by the water only, but by the water and by the blood" (5:6). That is, Jesus Christ really died as well as entered his ministry by the water of baptism. The water may also refer to the watery fluid that flowed with blood from his pierced side and proved the reality of his death (John 19:34).

↓**DOCETISM** Working on the same presupposition that anything material and physical must necessarily be evil, other Gnostics tried to avoid the incarnation and bodily death of Jesus Christ by saying that he only seemed to be human (so-called docetism, from the Greek verb ↓*dokein*, "to seem"). Therefore John emphasizes the reality of the incarnation: "What we have heard, what we have seen with our eyes, what we observed and our hands felt . . . and we have seen" (1:1–2). Ironically from the modern standpoint, the first christological heresy attacked the humanity of Jesus rather than his deity.

---

docetism: DOH-suh-tiz´uhm ■ *dokein:* daw-KAYN

Criteria of True Christian Profession

To accomplish the purpose of strengthening his audience by combating heresy with truth, John discusses three criteria for determining genuine Christian profession: (1) righteous living; (2) love for other believers; (3) belief in Jesus as the incarnate Christ. Just as the criterion of belief in Jesus as the incarnate Christ is directed against the **christological errors** of Gnostics, so also is the criterion of righteous conduct directed against the **moral laxity** of Gnostics and the criterion of love toward fellow Christians directed against the **haughty exclusivism** of Gnostics.

An Outline of First John

Prologue: The Eye-Witnessed Incarnation of Christ as the Basis for Christian
     Fellowship (1:1–4)
  I. The Criterion of Righteous Conduct (1:5–2:6)
  II. The Criterion of Mutual Christian Love (2:7–17)
  III. The Criterion of Incarnational Christology (2:18–28)
  IV. The Criterion of Righteous Conduct (2:29–3:10a)
  V. The Criterion of Mutual Christian Love (3:10b–24a)
  VI. The Criterion of Incarnational Christology (3:24b–4:6)
  VII. The Criterion of Mutual Christian Love (4:7–5:3)
  VIII. The Criterion of Righteous Conduct (5:4–21)

Reading First John with Interpretation

After claiming firsthand knowledge of Jesus' life (1:1–4), John insists that true Christians, though not sinless, live righteously (1:5–2:6), love one another instead of the world (2:7–17), and believe the truth concerning Jesus Christ. Thus they reject false teachers, called "antichrists" because they are precursors of *the* antichrist, who will appear during the tribulation just before the end of this age (2:18–28). Then John discusses the criteria again and yet again. *Read 1 John 1:1–5:21.*

> 1 John 2:18: "You have heard that the antichrist is coming."
>
> 2 Thessalonians 2:8: "And then the lawless one will be revealed."
>
> Revelation 13:1, 4: "And I saw a beast coming out of the sea.... People worshiped the beast."
>
> *Didache* 16:4: "Then shall appear the deceiver of the world as a Son of God."

Sinlessness?

The strong language in chapter 3 about Christians' not sinning cannot denote flawlessness, for 1:8 reads: "If we say that we have no sin, we deceive ourselves and the truth is not in us" (compare 1:10; 2:1). The Greek present tense may indicate that the conduct of true Christians is not *predominantly* sinful. Or John may mean that Christians cannot sin *as* Christians. When they do sin, they temporarily deny their Christian identity. Not that they cease to be Christians, but they cease to act like the Christians they are. The

Gnostics pride themselves on their "Christian freedom" to do anything they please, including freedom to sin.

The Sin unto Death

The enigmatic mention of a sin leading to death, a sin undeserving of intercessory prayer (5:16–17), probably refers to the apostasy warned against in Hebrews, exhibited by the Gnostic heretics, and resulting in irrevocable condemnation. Alternatively, John refers to physical (not eternal) death as a chastisement for disobedient Christians (compare 1 Corinthians 5:5; 11:27–34).

SECOND AND THIRD JOHN: FATHERLY INSTRUCTION TO CHRISTIANS

Introductory Issues

Canonicity and Authorship

The attestation of 2 and 3 John in patristic writings is somewhat weak, doubtless because of the brevity of these letters. But the earliest church fathers exhibited no doubt that the Apostle John wrote them. In both letters John identifies himself as "the elder," not in the sense of an officer in a local church, but in the sense of an **elder statesman** of the church at large, that is, an **apostle** (compare 1 Peter 5:1). The term stands in contrast with John's favorite designation of his audience, "my dear children."

An Outline of Second John

Introduction: Greeting (1–3)
 I. Exhortation to Christian Love (4–6)
 II. Warning Against False Doctrine and Entertainment of False Teachers (7–11)
Conclusion: Hope for a Coming Visit and Another Greeting (12–13)

Reading Second John with Interpretation

Themes, Purpose, and Address

The themes of Christian **love** and **truth** dominate 2 John. The purpose is to warn against showing hospitality to any false teacher ("Do not take him into your house and do not say hello to him," verse 10). The addressees are "the elect ['chosen'] lady and her children" (verse 1). Some interpreters consider them to be personal acquaintances of the apostle or even treat the words "elect" and "lady" as proper names of a woman, giving "↓Electa" or "↓Kyria" or both. But "elect" can hardly be a proper name, for the lady's sister is also "elect" (verse 13). Two sisters would not have the same name. It is far more likely that "the elect lady" personifies a **local church** and that "her children" represent the **individual members** of that church, for the lady and her children are beloved by "all who know the truth" (verse 1). It is improbable that one family enjoyed such a wide reputation in Christendom but quite conceivable that a prominent church did. Furthermore, neither the lady's children nor her nephews (verse 13) are mentioned by personal names; and the pronoun "you" in verses 8, 10, and 12 is plural. These data, plus the warning against false teachers and the command to love one another, are more appropriate to a church than to a family (compare 1 John). Where the church was located we do not know. *Read 2 John 1–13.*

An Outline of Third John

Introduction: Greeting (1)
  I. Commendation of Gaius's Hospitality to Traveling Christian Workers (2–8)
  II. Condemnation of the Rebellion of Diotrephes Against Apostolic Authority and of His Refusal of Hospitality to Traveling Christian Workers (9–11)
  III. Commendation of Demetrius, Probable Carrier of the Letter and Envoy of John (12)
Conclusion: The Prospect of a Coming Visit and Final Greetings (13–14)

Reading Third John with Interpretation

Theme, Address, and Purpose

Third John focuses on an ecclesiastical dispute. The place where the recipient lives remains unknown, but it is most likely the region around Ephesus. John sends the letter to Gaius

- To **commend Gaius** for his hospitality to "the brothers" (probably itinerant teachers sent by John)
- To **rebuke ↓Diotrephes**, a self-assertive leader in the church, for his lack of hospitality toward "the brothers," for his dictatorial ways, and for his opposition to the apostolic authority of John
- To **recommend Demetrius**, who probably carries the letter

Demetrius may need a recommendation because he is moving from the Ephesian church, with which John is associated, to the church where Gaius lives (compare the recommendation of Phoebe in Romans 16:1–2) or because he is one of the itinerant teachers of the kind to whom Diotrephes has refused hospitality. Indeed, Diotrephes has expelled from the church

Electa: eh-LEK-tah ■ Kyria: KIHR-ee-uh ■ Diotrephes: di-OT-ruh-feez

those who dared to give them food and lodging. John indicates that he has written another letter to the whole church to which Gaius belongs (verse 9). This other letter may be 2 John, the circular 1 John, or a letter that has since been lost. Verse 10 contains the threat of a personal visit by John for a direct confrontation with Diotrephes. *Read 3 John 1–15.*

Summary

Named after their authors, the letters of James, Peter, John, and Jude lack specific addresses for the most part and are therefore called "catholic" in the sense of "general." James and Jude were written by half brothers of Jesus. James, addressed to Jewish Christians of the Diaspora, contains little doctrine but much practical instruction on proper behavior in church meetings and in everyday life. Of particular note are James's comments on the necessity of demonstrating faith by good works and on controlling the tongue, that is, your speech. First Peter portrays Gentile Christians as a new Diaspora suffering persecution but assured of salvation and urged to live in such a way as to expose the injustice of their persecution. In other words, imitate Christ in his righteous living, and you will enjoy a vindication like his. Peter writes from Rome, which he symbolically calls "Babylon," and uses Silvanus as his amanuensis or letter-carrier or both. Second Peter and Jude team up to attack heresy and defend orthodoxy in much the same language and with emphasis on the immorality of false teachers. It remains a question whether 2 Peter borrowed from Jude, vice versa, or both borrowed from a common source. And the authorship of 2 Peter by the Apostle Peter is often denied, though there are reasons to doubt the arguments for such a denial. Whereas the heretics attacked in 2 Peter denied the second coming of Jesus, those who are attacked in 1 John denied the incarnation in the one person Jesus Christ. They were Gnostics, against whose heresy, moral laxity, and exclusivism John pits the correct Christology, righteous conduct, and mutual love of true Christians. Second John warns a local church against extending hospitality to heretics, and 3 John commends a man named Gaius for extending hospitality to true ministers of the gospel. Third John also condemns a man named Diotrephes for refusing them hospitality and recommends John's envoy and probable carrier of the letter, a man named Demetrius.

People to Remember

Cerinthus

Demetrius

Diotrephes

Domitian

Enoch

Gaius

James the brother of Jesus, as
    distinguished from James

the apostle, brother of
John and son of Zebedee;
from James the son of
Alphaeus; and from James
the father of Judas (not
Iscariot)

John the apostle

John Mark

Jude

Moses

Nero

Noah

Paul

Peter

Sivanus/Silas

Trajan

Places to Remember

Asia

Asia Minor

Babylon

Bithynia

Cappadocia

Ephesus

Galatia

Gomorrah

Pontus

Rome

Sodom

Terms to Remember

antichrist

auricular confession

Catholic Letters

Cerinthianism

descent into hell

docetism

the elect lady and her
    children

extreme unction

Gnosticism

heterodoxy

Lord of sabaoth

orthodoxy

sin unto death

twelve tribes of the
    Dispersion

How Much Did You Learn?

- Tell how the Catholic Letters differ from the Pauline Letters in titles and addresses.
- How does the address of 1 Peter differ from that of James even though the phraseology is very much alike?
- Who was the James who wrote James?
- Distinguish the context and style of James from the context and style of, say, Galatians.
- Describe the situation of those to whom 1 Peter was written, and sketch Peter's consequent instructions.
- How are 2 Peter and Jude similar?
- Who was Jude, and what are the pros and cons of authorship of 2 Peter by Peter?
- Detail the kinds of Gnosticism refuted in 1 John, and cite the criteria of true Christianity that 1 John puts forward.
- Identify the elect lady and her children to whom 2 John is written. What message to them does 2 John contain?
- Name the players and describe their roles in the ecclesiastical dispute with which 3 John deals.

For Further Discussion

- Is there anything specifically Christian (rather than merely Jewish) about the Letter of James? If any, why so little?
- What relevance can a letter that arose out of persecution, as 1 Peter did, have for the church in a free society?
- How should false teachers in the church be treated? And how serious a deviation is required to merit the opprobrious epithet "false teacher" or "heretic"?
- What are the theological connections between righteousness, love, and orthodoxy in 1 John?

JAMES

For Further Investigation

Davids, P. H. *James.* Peabody, Mass.: Hendrickson, 1989.

Johnson, L. T. *The Letter of James.* New York: Doubleday, 1995.

Martin, R. P. *James.* Dallas: Word, 1988. Advanced.

Moo, D. J. *The Letter of James.* Grand Rapids: Eerdmans, 2000.

Perkins, P. *First and Second Peter, James, and Jude.* Louisville: Westminster John Knox, 1995.

Wall, R. W. *Community of the Wise: The Letter of James.* Valley Forge, Pa.: Trinity Press International, 1997.

Romans 4, for comparison with James 2:14–26 on faith and works.

FIRST PETER

For Further Investigation

Achtemeier, P. J. *First Peter.* Minneapolis: Fortress Press, 1996. Advanced.

Best, E. *First Peter.* Grand Rapids: Eerdmans, 1982.

Davids, P. H. *The First Epistle of Peter.* Grand Rapids: Eerdmans, 1990. Advanced.

Marshall, I. H. *First Peter.* Downers Grove, Ill.: InterVarsity Press, 1991.

Michaels, J. R. *1 Peter.* Waco: Word, 1988. Advanced.

1 Enoch 6–21, 67–69; *Jubilees* 10, in *The Old Testament Pseudepigrapha* (edited by J. H. Charlesworth; 2 vols.; Garden City, N.Y.: Doubleday, 1983–85), for comparison with Christ's preaching to the spirits in prison according to 1 Peter 3:19.

SECOND PETER

For Further Investigation

Bauckham, R. J. *Jude, 2 Peter.* Waco: Word, 1983. Advanced.

Green, E. M. B. *The Second Epistle of Peter and the Epistle of Jude.* Grand Rapids: Eerdmans, 1987.

Kelly, J. N. D. *The Epistles of Peter and Jude.* Peabody, Mass.: Hendrickson, 1988.

Moo, D. J. *The NIV Application Commentary: 2 Peter and Jude.* Grand Rapids: Zondervan, 1996.

Neyrey, J. H. *2 Peter, Jude.* New York: Doubleday, 1993.

JUDE

For Further Investigation

See the preceding bibliography for 2 Peter.

FIRST, SECOND, AND THIRD JOHN

For Further Investigation

Brown, R. E. *The Epistles of John.* Garden City, N.Y.: Doubleday, 1982. Advanced.

Burge, G. M. *The NIV Application Commentary: The Letters of John.* Grand Rapids: Zondervan, 1996.

Kruse, C. G. *The Letters of John.* Grand Rapids: Eerdmans, 2000.

Lieu, J. M. *The Theology of the Johannine Epistles.* Cambridge: Cambridge University Press, 1991.

Schackenburg, R. *The Johannine Epistles.* New York: Crossroad, 1992. Advanced.

Smalley, S. S. *1, 2, 3 John.* Waco: Word, 1984. Advanced.

Strecker, G. *The Johannine Letters.* Minneapolis: Fortress Press, 1996. Advanced.

Thompson, M. M. *1–3 John.* Downers Grove, Ill.: InterVarsity Press, 1992.

PART 5

The Apocalypse

REVELATION: JESUS IS COMING!

Overview:

- Introductory Issues
- An Outline of Revelation
- Reading Revelation with Interpretation
- Summary

Study Goals—Learn:

- Why the style of Revelation differs from that of the Gospel and Letters of John if John authored them all
- The historical circumstance that prompted the writing of Revelation
- The main interpretive approaches to Revelation, their strengths, and their weaknesses
- The local background that enlivens our understanding of the messages to seven churches in Asia
- The meanings of the apocalyptic symbols in Revelation
- The nature of the plagues described in Revelation
- The identities of the 144,000, the two witnesses, the woman, the male child, the beast, and the false prophet
- The events with which Revelation says present history will conclude and the eternal state begin

A beach on the island of Patmos

Introductory Issues

Theme

The Apocalypse (Greek for "uncovering"), or book of Revelation, contains more extended prophecies about the future than any other part of the New Testament. These prophecies focus on the eschatological triumph of Christ over the anti-Christian forces of the world—beginning with the **tribulation**, climaxing with the **second coming**, and reaching completion with the full realization of **God's kingdom**—all to the great encouragement of Christians who face worldly allurements and the antagonism of an unbelieving society.

Canonicity and Authorship

Revelation is strongly attested as canonical and apostolic in the earliest post–New Testament period of church history, from *The Shepherd of Hermas* in the early second century through Origen, a church father in the first half of the third century. Doubts arose later, largely because of Dionysius's argument that differences between Revelation and the Gospel and Letters of John exclude common authorship: The Apostle John cannot therefore have written Revelation. It is true that from a grammatical and literary standpoint the Greek style of Revelation is inferior to that of the Gospel and Letters. But in part the "bad grammar" may be **deliberate**, for purposes of emphasis and allusion to Old Testament passages in Hebraic style, rather than due to

Patmos and the Seven Churches of Asia

ignorance or blundering. In part the "bad grammar" may also stem from an **ecstatic** state of mind, due to John's having received prophecies in the form of visions. Or writing as a prisoner on the island of ↓Patmos in the Aegean Sea, he did not have the advantage of an amanuensis to smooth out his rough style, as he probably did have for his Gospel and Letters.

Date

Concerning the date of writing, one view maintains that Nero's persecution of Christians after the burning of Rome in A.D. 64 evoked Revelation as an encouragement to endure the persecution. Supporting this view is the observation that when added up, the numerical value of the Hebrew letters spelling **Nero Caesar** comes to **666**, the very number that appears in Revelation 13:18 as symbolic of "the beast." Technical problems cast some doubt on the numerical value of Nero's name and title; but more seriously, an allusion to Nero Caesar in 666 need not imply a writing at the time of Nero. It could refer back to him from a later date.

Another argument in favor of an early (Neronian) date is that the smoother **literary style** of the Gospel and Letters of John exhibits an improvement in his command of the Greek language and thus implies that Revelation dates from an earlier period when he was still struggling with Greek as a language not very familiar to him. But there are other explanations for the rough style in Revelation (as noted above); and archaeological discoveries and literary studies have recently demonstrated that along with Aramaic and Hebrew, Greek was commonly spoken among first-century Palestinians (see page 475). Thus John must have known and used Greek since his youth.

More often, Revelation has been dated during the reign of **Domitian** (A.D. 81–96). Though Domitian did not persecute Christians on a wide scale, his attempt to enforce emperor worship presaged the violent persecutions to come. Revelation is designed, then, to prepare Christians for resistance. The early church father Irenaeus explicitly dates the writing of Revelation during Domitian's emperorship. The testimony of Irenaeus gains importance from his having been a protégé of Polycarp (A.D. 60–155), the bishop of ↓Smyrna who had sat under the tutelage of John himself. On the other hand, if against the usual interpretation of Revelation 17:9–11 we start numbering the heads of the beast with Nero because he was the first emperor to persecute Christians, then the sixth, during whose reign John writes Revelation, is **Titus**, the predecessor of Domitian

Domitian's Sovereignty

• "The apocalyptic vision . . . was seen not long ago, but almost in our own day, toward the end of Domitian's reign" (Irenaeus, *Against Heresies* 5.30.3).

• "With no less arrogance he [Domitian] began as follows in issuing a circular letter in the name of his procurators: 'Our Master and our God bids that this be done.' And so from then on, the custom arose of addressing him in no other way even in writing or in conversation. He allowed no statues to be set up in his honor in the Capitol, except of gold and silver and of a fixed weight" (Suetonius, *Lives of the Caesars*, "Domitian" 13).

Patmos: PAT-muhs ■ Smyrna: SMUHR-nuh

(A.D. 79–81). Then Revelation reflects the Neronic persecution and anticipates later persecutions.

Apocalyptic Style

In a style typical of apocalyptic literature,
Revelation uses highly **symbolic language** for
the description of **visions**. The visions portray the **end of history** when evil will have
reached its limit and God will intervene to
commence his reign, judge the wicked, and

> "Five ['kings'] have fallen,
> one [the sixth] is, the other
> [the seventh] has not yet
> come" (Revelation 17:10).

reward the righteous. All this is presented, not to satisfy idle curiosity about
the future, but to encourage the people of God to **resist** and **endure** in a
world dominated by wickedness. Very often John borrows phraseology
from the Old Testament, especially from Daniel, Ezekiel, and Isaiah.

The extravagant figures of speech used throughout the Apocalypse may
sound strange to modern ears, but they convey the cosmic proportions of
the described events far more effectively than prosaic language could ever
do. The strange figures compare in style to the creations of our own contemporary cartoonists, which we readily accept and understand.

Schools of Interpretation

Interpreters follow one or more of four main approaches to Revelation:

1. IDEALISM, which strips the symbolic language of any predictive value and
reduces the prophecy to a picture of the continuous struggle between good
and evil, the church and the world, and of the eventual triumph of Christianity. This approach contains a kernel of truth but arises mainly from a
predisposition against genuinely predictive prophecy and from embarrassment over the extravagance of apocalyptic language.

2. ↓PRETERISM, which shares the predisposition behind idealism but limits
Revelation to describing the persecution of Christianity by ancient Rome
and to what was expected to happen by way of the destruction of the Roman
Empire and the vindication of Christians at the supposedly near return of
Christ. Of course, under this view Revelation turns out to be mistaken: Jesus
did not return quickly, though the Roman Empire did fall and Christianity
did survive. Consequently, preterists may try to salvage the significance of
the book for modern times by resorting also to idealism. Preterists are prone
to infer a use of pagan mythology throughout Revelation.

3. HISTORICISM, which interprets Revelation as a symbolic prenarration of
church history from apostolic times until the second coming and the last
judgment. Thus, the breaking of seven seals represents the fall of the Roman

---

preterism: PREH-tuhr-iz´uhm

> "Seventy weeks [of seven years, not days, apiece] have been decreed . . . . From the issuing of a decree to restore and rebuild Jerusalem until Messiah the Prince there will be seven weeks plus sixty-two weeks. . . . Then after the sixty-two weeks the Messiah will be cut off and have nothing, and the people of the prince who is to come will destroy the city and the sanctuary. And its end will come like a flood. War will continue even to the end. Desolations have been decreed. And he will make a firm covenant with the many for one week [the last of the seventy weeks], but in the middle of the week he will put a stop to sacrifice and grain offering. And one who causes desolation will place abominations on a wing of the temple until the complete destruction that is decreed is poured out on that one who causes desolation" (Daniel 9:24–27).

Empire, locusts from the bottomless pit stand for Islamic invaders, the beast represents the papacy (according to the Protestant Reformers), and so on. But the explanations of individual symbols vary so widely among interpreters of this school that doubt is cast on the interpretive method itself. For though prophetic language is somewhat opaque before the predicted events come to pass, the fulfilling events should clarify the language well enough to prevent the breadth of interpretive variation that exists among historicists. (Historicists have variously identified the locusts from the abyss in 9:1–11, for example, with the Vandals, Goths, Persians, Muslims, Christian heretics, and others.) Generally, historicists hold to postmillennialism, the belief that Christ will return *after* a lengthy golden age (the millennium) resulting from conversion of the world to Christianity (a view popular in the nineteenth century); or they hold to amillennialism (the more usual view today), which denies a future thousand years' reign of Christ over the earth and transmutes that reign into his present rulership while seated at God's right hand in heaven.

4. FUTURISM, which holds that Revelation describes a coming painful and chaotic time called "the tribulation" immediately followed by the return of Christ, the advent of God's kingdom, the Last Judgment, and the eternal state. Futurists usually calculate the tribulation, or Daniel's seventieth week, as seven years in length, with perhaps only the latter three and one-half years intensely distressing. Also, they usually hold to the premillennial view that on his return Christ will rule the world with the saints for one thousand years, crush a satanically inspired rebellion at the close of this millennium, and preside at the Last Judgment before the eternal state begins.

THE RAPTURE QUESTION Disagreement exists among futurists (or premillennialists) over whether the nation of Israel will enjoy restoration during the tribulation and the millennium (dispensationalism) and whether the church

Different Views of the Millennium (1000 Years)

	1000 years figurative of church age at present		Second Coming & Last Judgment		Eternal state
Amillennialism					

	Church age at present	Conversion of the world	1000 years of Christian rule	Second Coming & Last Judgment	Eternal state
Postmillennialism					

	Church age at present	Second Coming	1000 years of rule by Christ and saints	Last Judgment	Eternal state
Premillennialism					

will stay on earth throughout the tribulation (posttribulationism), will be evacuated from the earth by a preliminary coming of Christ before the tribulation (pretribulationism) or at its halfway mark (midtribulationism), or whether only the godly part of the church will be evacuated beforehand (partial rapturism; on the rapture, see page 363). Most futurists hold either to pretribulationism or to posttribulationism. Broadly speaking, the more strictly an interpreter separates God's dealings with the church from his dealings with Israel, the more inclined that interpreter is to see the church removed from earth before the tribulation. Entire loss (or nearly so) of a distinction between the church and Israel usually results in historicism, the denial that there will be a future period of seven years' tribulation, so that it becomes meaningless to ask whether the rapture will occur before, during, or after the tribulation. But some historicists believe in a millennium following Jesus' return.

PERSPECTIVE The view adopted here blends preterism with futurism: John writes for the Christians of his own time. They might have turned out to be the last generation. But since they did not, what John writes will apply to the generation that does turn out to be the last; and every generation of Christians should read Revelation with the possibility in mind that they will be that one. More particularly, the ancient struggle between Christianity and the Caesars corresponds to the struggle between God's people and the antichrist in the coming tribulation.

Origin, Address, and Contents

After an address, the first chapter of Revelation contains an account of John's **vision of Christ** on a certain Sunday ("Lord's Day," 1:10) while John was in exile on **Patmos** because of his Christian testimony. Early church tradition seems to imply that he was later released from Patmos and spent his last years in Ephesus. Chapters 2–3 contain **seven messages** dictated to John by Christ and addressed to seven churches in Asia in and around Ephesus. (As before in the New Testament, "Asia" refers to a Roman province in western Asia Minor.) These messages are somewhat incorrectly called "letters," since that designation implies separate communications to each church, whereas John is to write and send the entire contents of Revelation with the seven messages embedded in it (1:11). Then follows a vision of **God**, his **heavenly court**, and an appearance of **Christ** (chapters 4–5). For the most part, chapters 6–19 describe **plagues** that will take place during the tribulation and the subsequent **return** of Christ. Finally, John tells about the **reign** of Christ and the saints for a thousand years, the **Last Judgment**, and the **New Jerusalem** (chapters 20–22).

An Outline of Revelation

Introduction (1:1–8)
    A. Title and means of revelation (1:1–2)
    B. A blessing on the public reader and audience (1:3)
    C. Greeting (1:4–5a)
    D. Doxology (1:5b–6)
    E. Statement of theme (1:7–8)
  I. Christ the Royal Priest Tending Seven Lampstands (Churches) and Holding Seven Stars (Angels or Messengers of the Churches) (1:9–20)
  II. The Seven Messages to Churches in Asia (2:1–3:22)
    A. A message to the church in Ephesus (2:1–7)
    B. A message to the church in Smyrna (2:8–11)
    C. A message to the church in Pergamum (2:12–17)
    D. A message to the church in Thyatira (2:18–29)
    E. A message to the church in Sardis (3:1–6)
    F. A message to the church in Philadelphia (3:7–13)
    G. A message to the church in Laodicea (3:14–22)
  III. The Heavenly Court (4:1–5:14)
    A. The worship of God by four living creatures and twenty-four elders (4:1–11)
    B. The appearance of Christ the Lamb to take a scroll with seven seals, and further praise (5:1–14)
  IV. The Plagues of the Tribulation (6:1–16:21)
    A. The first six seals (6:1–17)

    1. The first seal: militarism (6:1–2)

    2. The second seal: warfare (6:3–4)

    3. The third seal: famine (6:5–6)

    4. The fourth seal: death (6:7–8)

    5. The fifth seal: persecution and martyrdom (6:9–11)

    6. The sixth seal: celestial phenomena (6:12–17)

B. The sealing of 144,000 for protection (7:1–8)

C. A white-robed multitude of saints who came out of the tribulation (7:9–17)

D. The seventh seal: silence in heaven, thunder, lightning, and an earthquake (8:1–5)

E. The first six trumpets (8:6–9:21)

    1. The first trumpet: hail, fire (or lightning), blood, and a burning of one-third of the earth (8:7)

    2. The second trumpet: the throwing of an erupting volcano into the sea, the turning into blood of one-third of the sea, and the destruction of one-third of life and ships at sea (8:8–9)

    3. The third trumpet: the falling of a meteorite on one-third of the water supply on land, turning it poisonous and causing widespread loss of life (8:10–11)

    4. The fourth trumpet: a darkening of sun, moon, and stars by one-third (8:12)

    5. Announcement that the last three trumpets constitute the three woes (8:13)

    6. The fifth trumpet: locusts from the bottomless pit (9:1–12)

    7. The sixth trumpet: the slaughter of one-third of human population by barbaric horsemen (9:13–21)

F. The canceling of seven thunders to avoid further delay (10:1–7)

G. John's eating a scroll of prophecies about the nations (10:8–11)

H. The two witnesses (11:1–13)

I. The seventh trumpet: a transfer of the world to Christ's rule, lightning, thunder, an earthquake, judgment, and reward (11:14–19)

J. Protection from the dragon of the woman who bears a male child (12:1–17)

K. Two beasts (13:1–18)

    1. The beast out of the sea with seven heads and ten diadems (13:1–10)

    2. The beast out of the earth with two horns (13:11–18)

L. The 144,000 with Christ the Lamb on Mount Zion (14:1–5)

M. Three angelic messages (14:6–12)

    1. The eternal gospel (14:6–7)

    2. The fall of Babylon (Rome) (14:8)

    3. A warning against worship of the beast (14:9–12)

N. Two harvests (14:14–20)

    1. By "one like a son of man" (14:14–16)

        2. By an angel, with much bloodshed (14:17–20)
    O. The seven bowls (15:1–16:21)
        1. Preparation (15:1–16:1)
        2. The first bowl: malignant sores (16:2)
        3. The second bowl: a turning of the sea into blood and death to all life
           at sea and in it (16:3)
        4. The third bowl: a turning of all rivers and springs into blood (16:4–7)
        5. The fourth bowl: scorching heat (16:8–9)
        6. The fifth bowl: darkness and pain (16:10–11)
        7. The sixth bowl: a gathering of Eastern hordes for the battle of
           Armageddon (16:12–16)
        8. The seventh bowl: "It is done," an earthquake, thunder, lightning, and
           the downfall of pagan powers (16:17–21)
  V. **The Fall of Babylon (Rome) and the Return of Christ (17:1–19:21)**
    A. A description of the harlot Babylon, with emphasis on her paganism and
      a prediction of her downfall (17:1–18)
    B. The destruction of Babylon, with emphasis on her commercialism
      (18:1–19:5)
    C. The marriage supper of the Lamb (19:6–10)
    D. The descent of Christ (19:11–16)
    E. The defeat of wicked hordes and the casting of the beast and the false
      prophet into a lake of fire (19:17–21)
  VI. **The Kingdom of Christ and of God (20:1–22:5)**
    A. The binding of Satan for one thousand years (20:1–3)
    B. The millennial reign of Christ and the saints (20:4–6)
    C. The loosing of Satan, a rebellion, and its defeat (20:7–10)
    D. Judgment at the great white throne (20:11–15)
    E. The new Jerusalem, new heaven, and new earth (21:1–22:5)
Conclusion (22:6–21)
    A. The trustworthiness of Revelation, with warnings and an invitation
      (22:6–20)
    B. Benediction (22:21)

Reading Revelation with Interpretation

Introduction and First Vision

Read Revelation 1:1–3:22. The seven spirits of God mentioned in the introductory remarks (1:4; compare 4:5) are probably not seven different spirits, but the one Holy Spirit parceled out in fullness to each of the seven
churches addressed. John does not intend his description of Christ to be
taken with strict literalness, which would prove grotesque. The figures of
speech are rather to be translated into the various characteristics and functions of Christ. His clothing represents royal priesthood, his white hair

eternal age, his flaming eyes the piercing gaze of omniscience, his bronze-like feet the judgmental activity of stamping down, his thunderous voice divine authority, the two-edged sword his word, and his shining face the glory of his deity.

The **seven golden lampstands** symbolize the seven addressed churches, for whom Christ cares. The **seven stars** in his hand represent the "angels" of the seven churches, either guardian angels for each local assembly or human "messengers" (another possible translation) sent from the churches to visit John on Patmos. The translation "messengers" is favored by their being addressed and exhorted throughout chapters 2–3. How could John write to angels and exhort them?

The command given to John, "Write the things that you have seen, and the things that are, and the things that are going to take place after these things" (1:19), is sometimes taken as a built-in, threefold outline of Revelation: (1) past things, or John's vision of Christ (chapter 1); (2) present things, or the messages to seven churches representing the entire age of the church (chapters 2–3); and (3) future things, or the return of Christ with preceding and following associated events (chapters 4–22). But at the time Christ speaks the words recorded in 1:19, "the things that are" still have to do with the vision of him; for dictation of the messages has not yet started. After the introduction, chapters 1–3 describe a single vision. The statement in 1:19 should not be taken as a formal outline of the book, then, but as a simple statement that John is to write the things he has **just** seen, **is** seeing, and will **yet** see.

The Seven Messages
Each of the seven messages contains

- An address
- A self-designation
- An analysis (with a commendation, a rebuke, or both)
- An exhortation
- A promise to those who "overcome," that is, those who by their conduct prove themselves to be true Christians

Christ carefully chooses his self-designating titles to suit the condition of each church. For example, to the suffering church at Smyrna he is the one "who died and came to life again" (2:8). On the other hand, most of the churches appear not to be suffering to the point of martyrdom at the time John writes. So although in reflection on the Neronic persecution and anticipation of later persecutions, the book of Revelation aims to steel Christians for martyrdom, it also aims to strengthen their resistance against compromises with worldly culture.

"They chose Stephen, a man full of faith and of the Holy Spirit; also Philip and Procorus and Nicanor and Timon and Parmenas and **Nicolaus**, a proselyte from Antioch" (Acts 6:5).

EPHESUS The ↓Nicolaitans were opposed by the Ephesian church and have been identified as heretical followers of ↓Nicolaus of Antioch (an identification perhaps based on a similarity of the names). This Nicolaus was one of the seven men chosen to wait on tables in the early church at Jerusalem. Did he turn apostate? We gather from scattered statements in Revelation 2–3 that the Nicolaitans participated in pagan worship and immorality. Perhaps the commendable opposition to them by the Ephesian church led to a divisiveness that made the orthodox Christians lose their former love ("first love") toward one another.

> "Please test your servants for ten days, and let us be given some vegetables to eat and water to drink. . . . So he listened to them and tested them for ten days" (Daniel 1:12, 14).

SMYRNA The "ten days" of persecution for the church in Smyrna (2:10) refers to a short period of testing, like the ten days of testing for Daniel and his three friends in Babylon.

↓**PERGAMUM** "Satan's throne" in Pergamum (2:13) alludes to the centrality of that city for emperor worship in Asia and to a huge altar to Zeus located on a nearby hill and dominating the city. The "manna" that is promised to overcomers symbolizes eternal life (2:17). Compare Jesus' self-designation as the "bread of life" in a typological fulfillment of the Old Testament manna (John 6:25–59). The symbolism of the "white stone" inscribed with a new name and given to overcomers (2:17 again) signifies their right to enter eternal life; for manna was compared to white stones, and they were used as a pass of admission and as a vote of acquittal or approval.

Nicolaitans: nik´uh-LAY-uh-tuhnz ▪ Nicolaus: nik´uh-LAY-uhs ▪ Pergamum: PUHR-guh-muhm

The acropolis and theater at Pergamum

"Pliny, governor of Bithynia, to Trajan the Emperor.... The method I have observed toward those who have been denounced to me as Christians is this: I interrogated them whether they were Christians. If they confessed they were, I have repeated the question a second and a third time, with a threat of the death penalty. If they have persisted in their confession, I have ordered them led away for execution.... Those who denied they were, or ever had been, Christians I thought it necessary to release, since they invoked our gods ... and since they offered sacrifices of wine and incense to your image, which I had ordered brought in for this purpose along with the images of our gods. I also had them curse Christ. It is said that real Christians cannot be induced to do any of these things" (Pliny the Younger, *Letters* 10.97).

↓**THYATIRA** Numerous trade guilds in the industrial city of Thyatira caused many Christian members of the guilds to participate in heathen festivities that formed part of the guilds' activities. It appears that a false prophetess, sarcastically called "↓Jezebel" after King Ahab's wicked Tyrian wife, was practicing and encouraging this licentious kind of freedom (2:20; compare 1 Kings 16–22; 2 Kings 9:30–37).

↓**SARDIS** The city of Sardis was noted for its immorality. The effect on the church: only "a few people in Sardis ... have not soiled their garments" (3:4). The city was noted also for its dyeing of woolen garments. Therefore Christ promises that overcomers will walk with him, by contrast, "in white garments" (3:4–5).

PHILADELPHIA Because of frequent earthquakes the population of Philadelphia was small. The church there was correspondingly small ("You have little power," 3:8). As the one who has authority to admit or deny entrance into the messianic kingdom ("him ... who has the key of David," 3:7), the Lord promises admittance to the Philadelphian Christians, whom he does not criticize at all. Pretribulationists take the promise to the church at Philadelphia, "I will also keep you from the hour of testing" (3:10), as an

Thyatira: thî´uh-TI-ruh ■ Jezebel: JEZ-uh-bel ■ Sardis: SAHR-dis

A temple of Artemis beneath the acropolis at Sardis

indication that true Christians will be removed from the world before the tribulation. Posttribulationists, comparing the phraseology of John 17:15 ("I do not ask that you should take them out of the world but that you should keep them from the evil one"), regard the promise as one of protection on earth from God's wrath.

LAODICEA The city of Laodicea was a prosperous center of banking, a place for the manufacture of clothing from the raven-black wool of sheep raised in the region, and a center for medical studies. In particular, a famous Phrygian powder used to cure eye diseases came from the region. So self-sufficient was Laodicea that after a destructive earthquake in A.D.

Ruins of the aqueduct at Laodicea

60, the city did not need the financial aid that Rome gave to neighboring cities for reconstruction. In allusion to these facts, Christ castigates the Laodicean Christians for their spiritual poverty and nakedness in the midst of material affluence and advises them to acquire spiritual wealth, to clothe themselves with *white* clothing (righteousness), and to treat their defective spiritual eyesight, or distorted sense of values, with spiritual medicine (3:18). Cold water is refreshing; hot water is useful. But the Laodiceans were like the water from nearby hot springs, which after flowing to Laodicea through an aqueduct was tepid and nauseating.

The Seven Churches and Church History

The churches addressed in the seven messages existed as **local** assemblies in Asia during the first century. They also represent **types** of churches that have existed throughout church history. It has been suggested even further, though not all agree, that the dominant characteristics of the seven churches in the order of their mention represent distinctive characteristics and developments within Christendom during successive **eras** of church history:

- Ephesus, the hardworking apostolic church
- Smyrna, the heavily persecuted postapostolic church
- Pergamum, the increasingly worldly church after Emperor Constantine made Christianity virtually the Roman state religion
- Thyatira, the corrupt church of the Middle Ages
- Sardis, the church of the Reformation with a reputation for orthodoxy but a lack of spiritual vitality

- Philadelphia, the church of modern revivals and global missionary enterprise
- Laodicea, the contemporary church made lukewarm by apostasy and affluence

This suggestion suffers, however, from the criticism that Thyatira receives some higher marks than are usually given to the church of the Middle Ages: "I know your deeds and love and faith and service and your perseverance, and that your most recent deeds are more than the first ones" (2:19). Also, the church of the Reformation hardly merits the message of almost total rebuke directed to Sardis; the open door mentioned in the message to Philadelphia probably refers to entrance into the messianic kingdom rather than to missionary enterprise; and the lengthening of church history demands frequent readjustments in the matching of the seven churches with church historical eras.

John's Rapture
A difference of opinion exists concerning John's being caught up to heaven in 4:1. Posttribulationists treat it as a purely personal experience for the reception of further visions, but many pretribulationists regard it as symbolizing a rapture of the entire church before the tribulation. Moreover, pretribulationists usually regard the twenty-four "elders" surrounding God's throne as representing the just-raptured church. To posttribulationists they are no more than human or angelic leaders in the heavenly worship of God and Christ. *Read Revelation 4:1–5:14.*

The Seven-Sealed Scroll
The scroll with seven seals that keep it rolled up along its exposed edge is a **title deed** to the world. Only the one who owns the world has the right to take the scroll, break its seals, open it, and claim his property. At first that one does not appear; so John weeps, for until the rightful owner appears the forces of wickedness, who have usurped control of the world, will persecute the saints. John hears mention of the **Lion** of the tribe of Judah, the messianic conqueror from David's tribe, but what he then sees is a **lamb**, Jesus, bearing the scars of crucifixion but standing in resurrection rather than lying slain on an altar (compare John 20:24–29). Jesus' taking the scroll, breaking its seals, and unrolling it will therefore represent his seizing control of the world from the persecutors of God's people. This activity peaks at the second coming and establishment of God's kingdom on earth.

Seals, Trumpets, and Bowls
Chapters 6–16 contain three series of seven plagues each: seals, trumpets, and bowls. Some interpreters think that their fulfillment will be **consecutive**, the plagues under the trumpets coming to pass after those under the seals, the

plagues in the bowls after those of the trumpets, and the second coming forming a climax. In this scheme the trumpets constitute the seventh seal; the bowls, the seventh trumpet; and the second coming, the seventh bowl:

Seals 1 2 3 4 5 6 7

     Trumpets 1 2 3 4 5 6 7

          Bowls 1 2 3 4 5 6 7

               Second Coming

But the fact that the contents of the seventh in each series are practically identical and seem to indicate finality—thunder, lightning, an earthquake, and various indications that the end has come—favors that the seals, trumpets, and bowls are at least partly **concurrent** in their fulfillment. Thus, the plagues of the seals will be spread out over the whole tribulation, those of the trumpets over its last part, and those of the bowls concentrated at the end, so that the seventh in each series is identical and encompasses the second coming and its immediate accompaniments:

						Second Coming	
Seals	1	2	3	4	5	6	7
Trumpets	1	2	3	4	5	6	7
Bowls	1	2	3	4	5	6	7

SEALS The majority of the seals have to do with **war** and its effects:

A horseman

Seal 1: militarism, perhaps on the part of the antichrist

Seal 2: warfare, resulting from militarism

Seal 3: famine, resulting from warfare

Seal 4: death, resulting from famine and other ravages of war (the first four seals represented by "the four horsemen of the Apocalypse")

Seal 5: persecution and martyrdom of the saints (the last generation of the church according to posttribulationism; others who have turned to God after the rapture of the church according to pretribulationism)

Seal 6: the celestial phenomena that Jesus said would immediately precede his return (Mark 13:24–26; Matthew 24:29–30; Luke 21:25–27)

Seal 7: silence in heaven, thunder, lightning, and an earthquake

Read Revelation 6:1–8:5.

144,000 Some interpreters regard the 144,000 as **orthodox Jews** whom God will protect during the tribulation, especially when they are being persecuted for refusal to worship an image of the antichrist placed in a rebuilt temple at Jerusalem, and who will thus survive to become the nucleus of a reestablished David kingdom during the millennium. Pretribulationists usually cast the 144,000 in the role of **Israelite evangelists** who spread the gospel throughout the world in the absence of the church, with the result that a vast multitude of Gentiles believe and are saved. Others regard the 144,000 as symbolizing the last generation of the **church** in that just as earlier John *heard* Jesus announced as a lion but *saw* him as a lamb, so now John *hears* the church announced as the tribes of Israel but *sees* them as an international multitude of redeemed people who have come out of the tribulation victoriously.

TRUMPETS The majority of the trumpets have to do with **ecological disasters**:

Trumpet 1: hail, fire (or lightning), and blood, resulting in wildfires that burn one-third of the earth

Trumpet 2: the throwing of an erupting volcano ("burning mountain") into the sea (the Mediterranean for John and his audience), resulting in the turning into blood of one-third of the sea and in death and destruction to one-third of life and ships at sea

Trumpet 3: the falling of a meteorite, described as a blazing star named "Wormwood," on one-third of the fresh water supply on land (rivers and springs), turning it bitter and poisonous with widespread loss of life

Trumpet 4: the darkening of the sun, moon, and stars by one-third

Trumpet 5: the opening of the bottomless pit by a star that has fallen from heaven to earth, resulting in the demonic torment of human beings, the demons being likened to locusts with the stinging tails of scorpions

Trumpet 6: the slaughtering of one-third of human population by barbaric horsemen

Trumpet 7: the turning of the kingdoms of the world into the kingdom of Christ, lightning, thunder, an earthquake, and the time of judgment and reward

Much of the language in these descriptions is meant to be taken symbolically. Nevertheless, symbolic language may point to literal reality, so an interpreter must avoid overspiritualization. The star that falls from heaven to earth under the fifth trumpet refers to Satan, who lets loose a horde of demons. *Read Revelation 8:6–11:19.*

THUNDERS In chapter 10 John hears seven thunders, apparently another series of plagues. But when he is about to write them down, the command comes to seal them up rather than write them down. Since *unsealing* has caused an earlier series of plagues to take place, sealing up the thunders must mean that they will not take place. In other words, these plagues have been canceled (compare the shortening of the days of the tribulation in Mark 13:20 par.).

TWO WITNESSES The two witnesses in the first part of chapter 11 probably minister during the latter three and one half years (1,260 days, or 42 lunar months of 30 days each) of the tribulation, because during the time of their preaching the Gentiles "will trample on the holy city" (11:2; compare Daniel 9:27). Futurists often identify the two witnesses with Moses and Elijah, who will reappear and represent the Law and the Prophets. Elijah's return for ministry to Israel was predicted in Malachi 4:5 and confirmed by Jesus (Matthew 17:11; Mark 9:12a). Moses and Elijah appeared together on the Mount of Transfiguration during Jesus' first advent; and the miracles of the two witnesses in Revelation 11:6 correspond to the Old Testament miracles of Moses (turning water to blood and smiting the earth with plagues—compare Exodus 7–12) and of Elijah (striking their enemies with lightning, or "fire"— compare 2 Kings 1:9–12—and producing drought—compare 1 Kings 17:1).

Sometimes the two witnesses are identified with Enoch and Elijah, the only biblical characters to avoid physical death (by translation to heaven) and therefore to be sent back during the tribulation to preach until martyred. But believers still alive at the second coming will all avoid physical death; so we need not suppose that both Enoch and Elijah must die to maintain an exceptionless rule of physical death as part of the curse on sin. Interpreted still differently by a large number of commentators, the two

---

The Pain of Childbirth as Grief Over Jesus' Death

"Jesus . . . said to them ['his disciples'], '. . . A little while and you will not see me. . . . Truly, truly I tell you that you will weep and mourn, but the world will rejoice. You will grieve . . . . A woman giving birth has pain because her hour has come . . . . So also you: now you have pain'" (John 16:19–22).

Catching Up to God as Jesus' Ascension

"I am going up to my Father and your Father, and to my God and your God" (John 20:17).

Refuge as an Abiding Place in Christ

"Your hearts are not to be troubled. Believe in God; believe also in me. In my Father's household are many abodes. . . . I will prepare a place for you. . . . Abide in me" (John 14:1–2 with 15:4).

Satan's Downfall as an Effect of the Cross

"Jesus answered and said [on the eve of his crucifixion], '. . . Now the ruler of this world will be cast out'" (John 12:30–31).

Comparison with Nero

With the beast's one head that is wounded and then healed, compare the following passage on Nero: "Then a great king will flee from Italy like a runaway slave unseen and unheard over the channel of the ↓Euphrates . . . . But even when he disappears he will be destructive. Then he will return declaring himself equal to God. But he [God] will prove that he [Nero] is not [equal to God]" (*Sibylline Oracles* 4:119–20; 5:33–34).

witnesses stand for the collective Moses- and Elijah-like testimony of all God's people on earth during the tribulation. Under this interpretation the number two symbolizes the sufficiency of their testimony, for "a matter must be established by the testimony of two or three witnesses" (Deuteronomy 19:15).

WOMAN AND MALE CHILD Chapter 12 poses uncertainties of interpretation. Perhaps it is best to understand the woman as representing **Jesus' first disciples**, and her pain in childbirth as their **grief** when he died. The catching up of the male child to God then represents Jesus' **ascension**. Since the saints are subject to severe persecution (13:7), the woman's refuge in the wilderness, "where she has a place prepared by God" (12:6), does not refer to protection from persecution, but to **salvation in Christ**. The wilderness represents the place of redemption, just as at the exodus; and Satan's downfall occurred at the cross. *Read Revelation 12:1–17.*

BEAST AND FALSE PROPHET The beast and the false prophet of chapter 13 have been interpreted to represent the Roman Empire (revived) and the antichrist, respectively. More probably, the beast represents the empire personified in its ruler the **antichrist**, and the false prophet represents a **minister of propaganda** in the idolatrous cult of antichrist (compare Daniel 9:27; Mark 13:14; Matthew 24:15; 2 Thessalonians 2:3–4, 9). In 19:20 both the beast and the false prophet appear to be individuals, because each is thrown into a lake of fire: "And the beast was seized, and with him the false prophet who had performed the signs

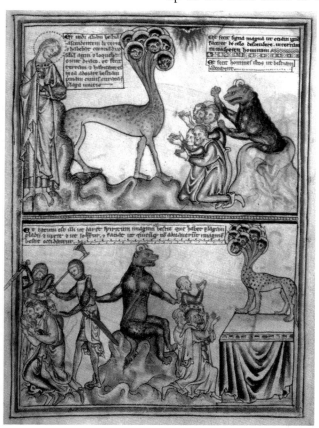

A medieval portrayal of the beasts of Revelation

Euphrates: *yoo-FRAY-teez*

in his presence by which he deceived . . . the ones worshiping his image. These two were thrown alive into the lake of fire burning with sulfur [that is, a lake of molten lava]." *Read Revelation 13:1–14:20.*

144,000 The 144,000 appear again in chapter 14, this time on Mount Zion with Christ the Lamb, and celebrate their triumphant passage through the tribulation. The celebration implies a time at the close of the tribulation, after Christ's return, and constitutes one indication among many that John's visions dart back and forth chronologically.

HARVESTS Both of the harvests reaped in 14:14–20 may symbolize judgment at the second coming. Or the first harvest, reaped by one "like a son of man" sitting on a white cloud, represents the **rapture** of the church at the coming of Christ after the tribulation; and because of the phrase mentioning "God's wrath," the second reaping represents the immediately following outburst of **judgment** at ↓Armageddon.

BOWLS John states that the bowls represent plagues originating in **God's wrath**, which is concentrated at the end of the tribulation ("seven plagues, which are last," 15:1):

Bowl 1: malignant sores
Bowl 2: the turning of the sea to blood, resulting in death to all life at sea and in it (an intensification of the second trumpet)

Armageddon: ahr´muh-GED-uhn

Temple of Roma in Ephesus

Bowl 3: the turning of all rivers and springs to blood (an intensification of the third trumpet)

Bowl 4: scorching heat

Bowl 5: darkness and pain

Bowl 6: the gathering of hordes to invade the Roman Empire from the East, the battle of Armageddon

Bowl 7: "It is done," an earthquake, thunder, lightning, and the downfall of pagan powers

Read Revelation 15:1–16:21.

Fall of Babylon

The collapse of the Roman Empire is now celebrated. "Babylon" is symbolic for Rome, since Rome has taken the place of that Mesopotamian city as the world's center of idolatry, immorality, and persecution of God's people (see pages 482–83 concerning the application of "Babylon" to Rome in 1 Peter 5:13). Chapter 17 puts emphasis on the **false religion** of pagan Rome, chapter 18 on her **commercialism** and **materialism**. Much of the phraseology in these chapters comes from prophecies against Babylon in Isaiah 13–14, 46–48 and especially Jeremiah 50–51 and the prophecy against Tyre in Ezekiel 26–28. *Read Revelation 17:1–18:24.*

Marriage Supper

The marriage supper of the Lamb represents a uniting of the saints with their Savior at the long-awaited **messianic banquet**. Many pretribulationists see the event as having taken place in heaven during the tribulation, since all the church will have been taken to heaven by that time. Posttribulationists see it as on the verge of taking place at the return of Christ following the tribulation, because until then the last generation of the church will remain on earth.

Parousia, Millennium, and Judgment

At his coming, Christ **destroys** the gathered armies of the wicked nations. The beast and the false prophet are thrown into the **lake of fire**. Satan is **confined** for one thousand years. The righteous dead rise and share in Christ's millennial **rule** over the earth. John makes special mention of the martyrs to encourage willingness on the part of God's people to undergo martyrdom, if necessary, in maintaining fidelity to Christ. Satan, loosed after the thousand years, instigates a **revolt** against the rule of Christ among the many who have had to submit outwardly to his political dominion but have not submitted in their hearts. The revolt is crushed, the wicked dead rise, and the **Last Judgment** takes place. *Read Revelation 19:1–20:15.* Amillennialists refer the binding of Satan to the work of Christ during his first advent, the first resurrection to the spiritual coming alive of those who believe in Christ,

the thousand years' reign with Christ to the present spiritual kingship of
Christ and the saints (one thousand being figurative for a long period of
time), the crushing of a revolt to the second coming, and the second resurrection to the bodily resurrection of both the righteous and the wicked at
the second coming.

New Jerusalem

The new Jerusalem, spotless bride and wife of the Lamb—in other words,
the **church**—contrasts sharply with the harlot Babylon (Rome) of preceding chapters.[1] That "the kings of the earth bring their glory into it" (21:24)
may indicate a descent of the New Jerusalem to earth at the beginning of the
millennial kingdom. But the abolishing of death, grief, crying, pain, and all
"the first things" associated with the world in which evil resides (21:4)
points to the eternal state after the millennium and the final elimination of
sin with all its results.

1. For an interpretation of the
new Jerusalem as the saints
themselves, not their eternal
habitat, see R. H. Gundry, "The
New Jerusalem: People as Place,
Not Place for People," *Novum
Testamentum* 29 (1987): 254–64.

Conclusion

And so the New Testament ends with the beatific vision of God ("they will
see his face," 22:4), an invitation to eternal life (22:17), a curse on anyone
who adds to or subtracts from the prophecies in Revelation (22:18–19), a
promise of and prayer for Jesus' return (22:20), and a benediction (22:21).
Read Revelation 21:1–22:21.

Summary

In the book of Revelation, also called the Apocalypse, John records visions
that he received as an exile on the island called Patmos. The visions contain
messages to local churches in seven cities of the province of Asia and information concerning what will happen during the tribulation and at the second coming and following. The visions shift back and forth between earth
and heaven, and chronologically forward and backward as well. The date of
writing is disputed, but it is generally agreed that the language is often symbolic. Disagreement persists, however, over the meaning of the symbols and
over larger questions of interpretation. It is nevertheless clear that emphasis falls on the need of Christians to resist the allurements of the world, to
suffer willingly for Christ's sake, and thus to gain a victorious reward in the
end—over against the temporal and eternal judgments to which the wicked
will fall prey.

People to Remember

Dionysius	Irenaeus	Nicolaus of Antioch
Domitian	Jezebel	Origen
Elijah	Moses	Polycarp
Enoch	Nero	Titus

Places to Remember

Aegean Sea	Mediterranean Sea	Sardis
Asia	Mount Zion	Smyrna
Babylon/Rome	Patmos	Thyatira
Ephesus	Pergamum	
Laodicea	Philadelphia	

Terms to Remember

144,000	idealism	pretribulationism
amillennialism	key of David	rapture
angels/messengers	Lamb	Satan's throne
Apocalypse	Lion of the tribe of Judah	seals
battle of Armageddon	Lord's Day	second coming/Parousia
beast	marriage supper of the Lamb	seven spirits of God
bowls	midtribulationism	seven-sealed scroll
dispensationalism	millennium	tribulation/Daniel's
dragon	new Jerusalem	seventieth week
false prophet	Nicolaitans	trumpets
four horsemen of the	partial rapturism	twenty-four elders
Apocalypse	postmillennialism	two witnesses
futurism	posttribulationism	white stone
historicism	premillennialism	woman and male child
hour of testing	preterism	

How Much Did You Learn?

- Discuss the different possible dates for the writing of Revelation.
- Show how Revelation fits into the category of apocalyptic literature.
- Identify the four main approaches to the interpretation of Revelation.
- Interpret Revelation from the standpoint of a pretribulationalist.
- Interpret Revelation from the standpoint of a posttribulationalist.
- Interpret Revelation from the standpoint of an amillennialist.
- Interpret Revelation from the standpoint of a premillennialist.
- List as many as you can of the churches addressed in Revelation 2–3, and characterize them.
- List the three series of known plagues, and detail some of the plagues.
- Depict the main players in the drama of Revelation.

For Further Discussion

- In view of almost two thousand years of church history, how are we to understand "what must soon take place" and "the time is near" (1:1, 3)?
- Why is predictive prophecy at least partly opaque in meaning until after its fulfillment?
- To which of the seven churches in Asia are the various branches of Christendom, including denominations, most comparable?
- What guidelines might help settle the question of literal versus figurative interpretation of the Apocalypse?
- What developments in recent and current history may be a stage-setting for events predicted in Revelation, or should we even attempt to engage in such speculation?
- Why are so few clearly understandable details about heaven and hell given us? Is the assumption of the question false?

For Further Investigation

Aune, D. E. *Revelation*. 3 vols. Dallas: Word, 1997–98. Advanced.

Bauckham, R. *The Theology of the Book of Revelation*. Cambridge: Cambridge University Press, 1993.

Beale, G. K. *The Book of Revelation: A Commentary on the Greek Text*. Grand Rapids: Eerdmans, 1999. Advanced.

Four Views on the Book of Revelation. Edited by C. M. Pate. Grand Rapids: Zondervan, 1998.

Hemer, C. J. *The Letters to the Seven Churches of Asia in Their Local Setting*. Sheffield: JSOT, 1986. Advanced.

Knight, J. *Revelation*. Sheffield: Sheffield Academic Press, 1999.

Morris, L. *Revelation*. 2d ed. Grand Rapids: Eerdmans, 1987.

Mounce, R. H. *The Book of Revelation*. 2d ed. Grand Rapids: Eerdmans, 1998.

Sandy, D. B. *Plowshares and Pruning Hooks: Rethinking the Language of Biblical Prophecy and Apocalyptic*. Downers Grove, Ill.: InterVarsity Press, 2002.

Thomas, R. L. *Revelation 1–7* and *Revelation 8–22*. Chicago: Moody, 1992, 1995.

IN RETROSPECT

Jesus Christ came into the world at a time of religious and philosophical malaise. Under the heel of Roman domination, his own people, the Jews, were looking for a political messiah. When for the most part he avoided the politically loaded term *Messiah* and presented himself as the Son of Man who must suffer and die as the Servant of the Lord before being exalted to dominion, not even his own disciples understood him. The Jews in general and the Sanhedrin in particular rejected him for Barabbas, a political revolutionary. Unjustly charged with sedition himself, Jesus died by Roman crucifixion.

But the resurrection vindicated Jesus before his disciples. After his ascension and the outpouring of the Holy Spirit on the Day of Pentecost, they began to proclaim him as Lord and Savior. Apparently they expected him to return within a short time, and in an ongoing spirit of Jewish nationalism they set about evangelizing their fellow Jews in preparation for a soon-to-be established kingdom in which Israel would dominate the Gentiles. The second coming was delayed, however, and converted Hellenistic Jews, having less anti-Gentile bias than most Hebraistic Jewish Christians, sent Barnabas and Paul from Antioch, Syria, on the first concerted effort to win Gentiles. Success inspired further missions, and the gospel eventually spread across the Roman Empire.

Evangelistic success necessitated the organization of local groups of converts for instruction and worship. The structure of the institutional church began to take shape. Doctrinal and ethical instruction was amplified by those elements in the Old Testament not outmoded through New Testament fulfillment and by the recall, application, and elaboration of Jesus' teaching and example. These led to deeper reflection on the person and work of Christ, on the significance of the church, and on the eschatological future.

Except for some scattered and now lost writings, the earliest communication of Christian doctrine and ethics was oral. The geographical spread of the gospel created the need for instruction from a distance, however; so the writing of the New Testament Letters started. Somewhat later the writing of the Gospels and Acts commenced as a literary means of evangelizing unbelievers, confirming the faith of believers, and providing an authoritative record of Jesus' life and ministry as the availability of eyewitnesses diminished through their deaths and through movement of the gospel away from Palestine, where most of the remaining eyewitnesses resided. Toward the close of the first century, the last surviving apostle, John, contributed the last of the New Testament writings with both the literary forms of gospel and letter, and added a book unique in form within the New Testament—the visionary, forward-looking Apocalypse. Then began the process of collection and canonization. For a final conspectus of New Testament literature, see the chart on pages 530–31.

BOOKS IN THE NEW TESTAMENT: A SUMMARY

Book	Author	Time of Writing (A.D.)*	Place of Writing	Addressees	Themes and Distinctive Emphases
Galatians	Paul	49, just after Paul's 1st missionary journey	Antioch in Syria	Christians in Pisidian Antioch, Iconium, Lystra, and Derbe, South Galatia	Justification by divine grace through faith in Jesus Christ—against the Judaizing doctrine of meritorius works of the law
1 Thessalonians	Paul	50–51, during the 2d missionary journey	Corinth	Christians in Thessalonica	Congratulations upon conversion and Christian growth and exhortations to further progress, with emphasis on comfort from and expectancy toward the Parousia
2 Thessalonians	Paul	50–51, during the 2d missionary journey	Corinth	Christians in Thessalonica	Quieting of a fanatical belief (engendered by persecution) in the immediacy of the Parousia
1 Corinthians	Paul	55, during the 3d missionary journey	Ephesus	Christians in Corinth	Problems of manners, morals, and beliefs within the church
2 Corinthians	Paul	56, during the 3d missionary journey	Macedonia	Christians in Corinth	Paul's inner feelings about his apostolic ministry; the offering for the church in Jerusalem
Romans	Paul	57, during the 3d missionary journey	Corinth	Christians in Rome	Justification by divine grace through faith in Jesus Christ
James	James the half-brother of Jesus	40s or 50s	Jerusalem	Jewish Christians of the Dispersion	Exhortations to Christian conduct in everyday life
Mark	John Mark	Late 50s or early 60s	Rome	Non-Christian Romans	Jesus as the powerful Son of God
Matthew	Matthew	Late 50s or early 60s	Antioch in Syria	Jewish Christians in Syria	Jesus as builder of the church
Philemon	Paul	61–62	Rome	Philemon, his family, and the church in his house—all in Colossae	Mercy for a runaway slave, Onesimus, who had become a Christian
Colossians	Paul	61–62	Rome	Christians in Colossae	The preeminence of Christ
Ephesians	Paul	61–62	Rome	Christians in the region around Ephesus	The spiritual privileges and responsibilities of the church
Luke	Luke	62	Rome	Non-Christian Gentiles, especially those with some culture and interest in Christianity	The historical reliability of the gospel

Book	Author	Date	Place of Writing	Audience	Purpose/Theme
Acts	Luke	62	Rome	Non-Christian Gentiles, especially those with some culture and interest in Christianity	The historical reliability of the gospel
Philippians	Paul	62	Rome	Christians in Philippi	Thanks for financial assistance, with personal news and exhortations
1 Timothy	Paul	63–64	Macedonia	Timothy in Ephesus	The organization and administration of churches by Timothy
Titus	Paul	63–64	Nicopolis	Titus in Crete	The organization and administration of the churches in Crete by Titus
1 Peter	Peter	63–64	Rome	Christians in Asia Minor	The salvation and conduct of suffering Christians
2 Peter	Peter	65	Rome	Christians in Asia Minor	The true knowledge of Christian belief versus false teachers and their denial of the Parousia
2 Timothy	Paul	65	Rome	Timothy in Ephesus	The commission of Timothy to carry on Paul's work
Hebrews	Unknown (Apollos?)	60s	Unknown	Jewish Christians in Rome	The superiority of Christ as a deterrent against apostasy from Christianity back to Judaism
Jude	Jude the half-brother of Jesus	60s or 70s	Unknown	Christians everywhere	Warnings against false teachers in the church
John	John	Late 80s or early 90s	Ephesus	Christians in the region around Ephesus	Believing in Jesus as the Christ and Son of God for eternal life
1 John	John	Late 80s or early 90s	Ephesus	Christians in the region around Ephesus	The criteria of true Christian belief and practice over against Gnosticism
2 John	John	Late 80s or early 90s	Ephesus	A church near Ephesus	Christian love and Christian truth
3 John	John	Late 80s or early 90s	Ephesus	Gaius, a Christian in the region around Ephesus	An ecclesiastical dispute involving Gaius, Diotrephes, Demetrius, and John himself
Revelation	John	Late 80s or early 90s	Patmos	Seven churches in western Asia Minor	Visions of the eschatological triumph of Christ over the anti-Christian forces of the world

*Datings are approximate and often disputed. They presuppose the discussions throughout this book. Places of writing and identification of authors are also disputed.

GLOSSARY OF
PRONUNCIATIONS

Aaronic   air-ON-ik
abba   AH-buh
Abihu   uh-B*I*-hy*oo*
Abijah   uh-B*I*-juh
Achaia   uh-KAY-yuh
Achaicus   uh-KAY-uh-kuhs
Actium   AK-ti-uhm
adiaphora   ad´i-AF-uh-rah
Adriatic   ay´dree-AT-ik
Aegean   ee-JEE-uhn
Aeneas   i-NEE-uhs
aeons   EE-uhns
agapan   ah-gah-PAHN
agapē   ah-GAH-pay
agrapha   AG-ruh-fuh
Agrippa   uh-GRIP-uh
Alphaeus   al-FEE-uhs
amanuensis   uh-man´y*oo*-EN-sis
    (plural -es, eez)
anakrinein   ah´nah-KREE-nayn
Ananias   an´uh-N*I*-uhs
Ananus   AN-uh-nuhs
Annas   AN-uhs
antilegomena   ahn´tee-leh-GAW-meh-nah
antinomianism   an´ti-NOH-mee-uh-niz´uhm
Antioch   AN-tee-ok
Antiochus   an-T*I*-uh-kuhs
Antipas   AN-tee-puhs
Antipater   an-TIP-uh-tuhr
Antitheses   an-TITH-uh-seez
Antonia   an-TOH-nee-uh
Aphrodite   af´ruh-D*I*-tee
apocalyptic   uh-pok´uh-LIP-tik
Apocrypha   uh-POK-ruh-fuh
apokalyptein   ah-paw´kah-LY*OO*P-tayn
Apollonius   ap´uh-LOH-nee-uhs
Apollo   uh-POL-oh
Apollos   uh-POL-uhs
apologia   ap´uh-loh-JEE-uh
apophthegm   AP-uhf-them´
Aquila   AK-wi-luh
Aramaic   air´uh-MAY-ik
Aratus   AIR-uh-tuhs
Archelaus   ahr´kuh-LAY-uhs
Archippus   ahr-KIP-uhs

Areopagite   air´ee-OP-uh-git
Areopagus   air´ee-OP-uh-guhs
Arimathea   air´uh-muh-THEE-uh
Aristarchus   air´is-TAHR-kuhs
Aristeas   air´is-TEE-uhs
Armageddon   ahr´muh-GED-uhn
Artemas   AHR-tuh-muhs
Artemis   AHR-tuh-mis
Asiarchs   AY-zhee-ahrks
atrium   AY-tree-uhm
Attis   AT-is
Augustus   aw-GUHS-tuhs
Azariah   az´uh-R*I*-uh
Bacchus   BAK-uhs
Bar Kokhba   bahr KOHK-buh
Barabbas   buh-RAB-uhs
Bar-Jesus   bahr-JEE-zuhs
Barnabas   BAHR-nuh-buhs
Barsabbas   bahr-SAB-uhs
Bartimaeus   bahr´tuh-MEE-uhs
Baruch   BAIR-uhk
Bathsheba   bath-SHEE-buh
Baucis   BAW-kis
Baur   BOU-uhr
beatitudes   bee-AT-uh-ty*oo*dz
Beelzebul   bee-EL-zi-buhl
Benedictus   ben´uh-DIK-toohs
Berea   bi-REE-uh
Bethany   BETH-uh-nee
Bethesda   buh-THEZ-duh
Bethphage   BETH-fuh-jee
Bethsaida   beth-SAY-uh-duh
Bethzatha   beth-ZAY-thuh
Bithynia   bi-THIN-ee-uh
Brutus   BROO-tuhs
Bultmann   BOOLT-mahn
Caesarea Philippi   ses´uh-REE-uh FIL-i-p*i*
Caiaphas   KAY-uh-fuhs
Caligula   kuh-LIG-yuh-luh
Cana   KAY-nuh
Canaan   KAY-nuhn
canon   KAN-uhn
Capernaum   kuh-PUHR-nay-uhm
Cappadocia   kap´uh-DOH-shee-uh
Carthage   KAHR-thij

532

Cassius   KASH-uhs
Cenchrea   SEN-kree-uh
Cephas   SEE-fuhs
Cerinthus   suh-RIN-thuhs
chairein   khi-RAYN
charismata   kuh-RIZ-muh-tah
Chloe   KLOH-ee
chrēstos   KRAYS-taws
Chrestus   KRES-tuhs
Christus   KRIS-tuhs
Cicero   SIS-uh-roh
Claudius   KLAW-dee-uhs
Clement   KLEM-uhnt
Cleopas   KLEE-oh-puhs
codices   KOH-duh-seez
cognomen   kog-NOH-men
Colossae   kuh-LOS-ee
Colossians   kuh-LOSH-uhnz
Conzelmann   KONT-suhl-mahn
Corinth   KOR-inth
Cornelius   kor-NEEL-yuhs
Crispus   KRIS-puhs
Cronus   KROH-nuhs
Cybele   SIB-uhl-ee´
Cynicism   SIN-uh-siz´uhm
Cyprus   SI-pruhs
Cyrene   si-REE-nee
Dalmanutha   dal´muh-NOO-thuh
Dalmatia   dal-MAY-shee-uh
Damaris   DAM-uh-ris
Dardanelles   dahr´duh-NEHLZ
darnels   DAHR-nuhlz
Decapolis   di-KAP-uh-lis
deity   DEE- uh-tee
Delphi   DEL-fi
Demas   DEE-muhs
Demetrius   di-MEE-tree-uhs
demythologize   dee´mith-OL-uh-jiz
denarii   di-NAIR-ee-i
Derbe   DUHR-bee
Diaspora   di-AS-puh-ruh
Dibelius   di-BAY-lee-uhs
Didache   DID-uh-kay
diadochi   dee-AH-doh-khi´
Diognetus   di-OG-ni-tuhs
Dionysius Exiguus
   di´uh-NISH-ee-uhs ek-SIG-yoo-uhs
Dionysus   di´uh-NI-suhs
Diotrephes   di-OT-ruh-feez
Dives   DI-veez
docetism   DOH-suh-tiz´uhm
dokein   daw-KAYN

dominical   duh-MIN-uh-kuhl
Domitian   duh-MISH-uhn
Dorcas   DOR-kuhs
Douay   DOO-ay
drachmas   DRAK-muhs
Drusilla   droo-SIL-uh
dyadic   di-AD-ik
Ecclesiasticus   i-klee´zee-AS-ti-kuhs
Edersheim   AY-duhr-shim
Edomite   EE-duh-mit
ekklēsia   i-KLEE-zhee-uh
Eleazar   el´ee-AY-zuhr
Electa   eh-LEK-tah
Eleusis   i-LOO-sis
Elian   EE-lee-ahn
Elijah   i-LI-juh
Elisha   i-LI-shuh
Eloi   EE-loh-i
Elymas   EL-uh-muhs
Emmaus   i-MAY-uhs
endogamy   en-DAW-guh-mee
Epaphras   EP-uh-fras
Epaphroditus   i-paf´ruh-DI-tuhs
Ephesians   i-FEE-zhuhn
Ephesus   EF-uh-suhs
Epicureanism   ep´uh-kyoo-REE-uhn-iz-uhm
Epimenides   ep´i-MEN-uh-deez
Epiphanes   i-PIF-uh-neez
episkepsesthai   eh´pi-SKEP-ses-thi
episkopos   eh-PIS-kuh-paws
Erastus   i-RAS-tuhs
Eratosthenes   er´uh-TOS-thuh-neez
Esau   EE-saw
eschatological   es´kat-uh-LOJ-i-kuhl
Esdras   EZ-druhs
Essenes   ES-eenz
Eucharist   YOO-kuh-rist
Euodia   yoo-OH-dee-uh
Euphrates   yoo-FRAY-teez
Eusebius   yoo-SEE-bee-uhs
Eutychus   YOO-tuh-kuhs
expiation   ek´spi-AY-shuhn
Festus   FES-tuhs
flagellum   flah-GEL-uhm
Florus   FLOR-uhs
Fortunatus   for´chuh-NAY-tuhs
Gadarenes   GAD-uh-reenz
Gaius   GAY-yuhs
Galatia   guh-LAY-shuh
Gallio   GAL-ee-oh
Gamaliel   guh-MAY-lee-uhl
Gaza   GAH-zuh

Gemarah   guh-MAH-ruh

Gennesaret   gi-NES-uh-ret

Gerasa   GER-uh-suh

Gerasenes   GER-uh-seenz

Gergasenes   GER-guh-seenz

Gerizim   GER-uh-zim

Gethsemane   geth-SEM-uh-nee

Gloria in Excelsis Deo
    GLOR-ee-uh in ex-SEL-sis DAY-oh

glossolalia   glos´uh-LAY-lee-uh

gnōsis   NOH-sis

Gnostic   NOS-tik

Gnosticism   NOS-tuh-siz´uhm

Gomorrah   guh-MOR-uh

Griesbach   GREES-bahkh

Habakkuk   huh-BAK-uhk

Hades   HAY-deez

Hadrian   HAY-dree-uhn

Hagar   HAY-gahr

haggadah   huh-GAH-duh

Haggai   HAG-*i*

halakah   hah´lah-KAH

Hallel   HAL-el

Hanukkah   HAH-nuh-kuh

Hasideans   has´uh-DEE-uhnz,
    also Hasidim, HAS-uh-dim

Hasmoneans   haz´muh-NEE-uhnz

Hebron   HEE-bruhn

Hellenism   HEL-uh-niz´uhm

Hellenization   hel´uh-ni-ZAY-shuhn

Hermas   HUHR-muhs

Hermes   HUHR-meez

Herodians   hi-ROH-dee-uhnz

Herodias   hi-ROH-dee-uhs

heterodoxy   HEH-tuhr-uh-dahk´see

heteropraxy   HEH-tuhr-uh-prak´see

Hierapolis   hi´uh-RAP-uh-lis

Hillel   HIL-uhl

homolegoumena   ho´muh-leh-GOO-meh-nah

hosanna   hoh-ZAN-uh

Hosea   hoh-ZAY-uh

huios   hyoo-ee-AWS

hus   hyoos

Hymenaeus   hi´muh-NEE-uhs

hyssop   HIS-uhp

iasis   EE-ah-sis

iasous   ee-ah-SOOS

Iconium   *i*-KOH-nee-uhm

iconography   *i*´kuh-NOG-ruh-fee

Idumean   id´yoo-MEE-uhn

iēsis   EE-ay-sis

iēsous   ee-ay-SOOS

Ignatius   ig-NAY-shuhs

Immanuel   i-MAN-*yoo*-uhl

incarnate   in-KAHR-nit

Irenaeus   *i*´ruh-NEE-uhs

Iscariot   is-KAIR-ee-uht

Ishmael   ISH-may-uhl

Isis   *I*-sis

Jairus   jay-*I*-ruhs

Jambres   JAM-briz

Jamnia   JAM-nee-uh

Jannes   JAN-iz

Jericho   JER-uh-koh

Jezebel   JEZ-uh-bel

Joppa   JOP-uh

Josephus   joh-SEE-fuhs

Judea   *joo*-DEE-uh

kenosis   ki-NOH-sis

kenoun   keh-n*oo*n

kerygma   ki-RIG-muh

Kidron   KID-ruhn

Kyria   KIHR-ree-uh

Lamech   LAY-mik

Laodicea   lay-od´i-SEE-uh

laver   LAY-vuhr

Lazarus   LAZ-uh-ruhs

leaven   LEV-uhn

Levirate   LEV-uh-rit

Levites   LEE-vits

lex talionis   leks tal-ee-OH-nis

libertinism   LIB-uhr-tin-iz´uhm

lingua franca   LING-gwuh FRANG-kuh

logia   LAW-gee-ah

logos   LAW-gaws

Lucian   L*OO*-shuhn

Lycus   LIK-uhs

Lydda   LID-uh

Lydia   LID-ee-uh

Lysias   LIS-ee-uhs

Lystra   LIS-truh

Maccabean   mak´uh-BEE-uhn

Macedonia   mas´uh-DOH-nee-uh

Magadan   MAG-uh-dan

Magdalene   MAG-duh-leen

Magi   MAY-ji

Magnificat   mag-NIF-uh-kat

Magus   MAY-guhs

majuscule   muh-JUHS-ky*oo*l

Malchus   MAL-kuhs

mammon   MAM-uhn

Manasseh   muh-NAS-uh

Mandeans   man-DEE-uhnz

manna   MAN-uh

Maranatha   mair´uh-NATH-uh
Marcion   MAHR-shuhn
Masada   muh-SAH-duh
Mattathias   mat´uh-THI-uhs
Matthias   muh-THI-uhs
Melchizedek   mel-KIZ-uh-dek
Menelaus   men´uh-LAY-uhs
menorah   muh-NOR-uh
Mesopotamia   mes´uh-puh-TAY-mee-uh
midrash   MID-rash
Miletus   mi-LEE-tuhs
minuscule   mi-NUHS-kyool
Mishnah   MISH-nuh
Mithra   MITH-ruh
Mnason   NAY-suhn
Modein   MOH-deen
Muratorian   myoor´uh-TOR-ee-uhn
myrrh   muhr
Naaman   NAY-uh-muhn
Nadab   NAY-dab
Nag Hammadi   nahg huh-MAH-dee
Nahum   NAY-huhm
Nain   nayn
Nebuchadnezzar   neb´uh-kuhd-NEZ-uhr
Nephilim   NEF-uh-lim
Nero   NIHR-oh
netzer   NAY-tser
Nicodemus   nik´uh-DEE-muhs
Nicolaitans   nik´uh-LAY-uh-tuhnz
Nicolaus   nik´uh-LAY-uhs
Nicopolis   ni-KOP-uh-lis
nomen gentile   NOH-men gen-TEE-leh
Nunc Dimittis   noonk di-MIT-is
Octavian   ok-TAY-vee-uhn
Onesimus   oh-NES-uh-muhs
Onesiphorus   on´uh-SIF-uh-ruhs
Onias   oh-NI-uhs
Origen   OR-uh-juhn
orthopraxy   OR-thuh-prak´see
Osiris   oh-SI-ruhs
ossuary   OS-yoo-er´ee
Oxyrhynchus   ok´si-RING-kuhs
Palatine   PAL-uh-tin´
Pamphylia   pam-FIL-ee-uh
Papias   PAY-pee-uhs
papyrus   puh-PI-ruhs
Paraclete   PAIR-uh-kleet
paradigms   PAIR-uh-dimz
Paralipomena   pair´uh-li-POM-uh-nuh
parenesis   pair´uh-NEE-sis
parousia   puh-ROO-zhee-uh
Pater Noster   PA-ter NOS-ter

Patmos   PAT-muhs
Pax Romana   pahks roh-MAH-nuh
Pella   PEL-uh
Pentateuch   PEN-tuh-tyook
Pentecost   PEN-ti-kost
Perea   puh-REE-uh
Perga   PUHR-guh
Pergamum   PUHR-guh-muhm
pericope   puh-RIK-uh-pee
peripatetic   per´i-puh-TET-ik
petra   PEH-trah
petros   PEH-traws
Pharisees   FAIR-uh-seez
philein   fee-LAYN
Philemon   fi-LEE-muhn
Philippi   FIL-i-pi
Philippians   fi-LIP-ee-uhnz
Philo   FI-loh
Phoebe   FEE-bee
Phoenicia   fi-NISH-uh
Phrygia   FRIJ-ee-uh
phylacteries   fi-LAK-tuh-reez
Pisidian   pi-SID-ee-uhn
Pliny   PLIN-ee
pneuma   NYOO-mah
pnoē   naw-AY
politarchs   POL-i-tahrks
Polycarp   POL-ee-kahrp
Pompeian   pom-PAY-uhn
Pompey   POM-pee
Pontius Pilate   PON-shuhs PI-luht
Pontus   PON-tuhs
Poseidon   poh-SI-duhn
praenomen   pri-NOH-men
Praetorian   pri-TOR-ee-uhn
praetorium   pri-TOR-ee-uhm
praetors   PREE-tuhrz
presbyter   PRES-bi-tuhr
preterism   PREH-tuhr-iz´uhm
primogeniture   pri´muh-JEN-i-chuhr
Prisca   PRIS-kuh
proconsuls   proh-KON-suhlz
procurators   PROK-yuh-ray´tuhrz
propitiation   pruh-pish´i-AY-shuhn
propraetors   proh-PREE-turz
Pseudepigrapha   soo´duh-PIG-ruh-fuh
pseudonymous   soo-DON-uh-muhs
Ptolemaic   tol´uh-MAY-ik
Purim   PYOO-rim
Puteoli   pyoo-TEE-oh-lee
Quelle   KVEL-eh
Quirinius   kwi-RIN-ee-uhs

Qumran   KOOM-rahn
Rahab   RAY-hab
Rylands   RI-luhndz
sabaoth   SAB-ay-oth
sacral manumission
        SAY-kruhl man´yoo-MI-shuhn
Sadducees   SAD-joo-seez
Samaria   suh-MAIR-ee-uh
Sanhedrin   san-HEE-druhn
Sapphira   suh-FI-ruh
Sardis   SAHR-dis
Sceva   SEE-vuh
Schweitzer   SHVIT-suhr
Scythians   SITH-ee-uhnz
seine   sayn
Seleucid   si-LOO-sid
Seleucus   si-LOO-kuhs
Seneca   SEN-uh-kuh
Septuagint   SEP-too-uh-jint
Sergius Paulus   SUHR-jee-uhs PAW-luhs
shalōm   shah-LOHM
Shammai   SHAM-i
Shema   SHEE-muh, or shuh-MAH
Shemone Esreh   sheh-MOH-neh ES-reh
Sibylline   SIB-uh-leen
Sicarii   si-KAHR-ee-i
Sidon   SI-duhn
Silas   SI-luhs
Siloam   si-LOH-uhm
Silvanus   sil-VAY-nuhs
Simeon   SIM-ee-uhn
Sinai   SI-ni
Sirach   SI-ruhk
Sitz im Leben   zits im LAY-buhn
Smyrna   SMUHR-nuh
Smyrnaeans   SMUHR-nee-uhnz
Sodom   SOD-uhm
Sosthenes   SOS-thuh-neez
Stephanus   STEF-uh-nuhs
Stoicism   STOH-i-siz´uhm
Suetonius   swi-TOH-nee-uhs
Sychar   SI-kahr
syncretism   SIN-kruh-tiz´uhm
synerchesthai   syoon-ER-kuhs-thi
synoptic   sin-OP-tik
Syntyche   SIN-ti-kee
Syro-Phoenician   si´roh-fi-NISH-uhn
Syzygos   SYOO-dzyoo-gaws
tabernacle   TAB-uhr-nak´uhl

Tabitha   TAB-i-thuh
Tacitus   TAS-uh-tuhs
Talmud   TAL-mood
Tamar   TAY-mahr
Targum   TAHR-guhm
Tarsus   TAHR-suhs
Tertullian   tuhr-TUHL-ee-uhn
Tertullus   tuhr-TUHL-uhs
Theophilus   thee-OF-uh-luhs
Thessalonica   thes´uh-luh-NI-kuh
Thyatira   thi´uh-TI-ruh
Tiberius   ti-BIHR-ee-uhs
Titius Justus   TISH-ee-uhs JUHS-tuhs
Titus   TI-tuhs
Tobias   toh-BI-uhs
Tobit   TOH-bit
Torah   TOH-ruh
Trajan   TRAY-juhn
Troas   TROH-az
Trophimus   TROF-uh-muhs
Tübingen   TYOO-bing-uhn
tunics   TOO-niks
Tychicus   TIK-uh-kuhs
Tyndale   TIN-duhl
Tyrannus   ti-RAN-uhs
Tyre   tir
uncial   UN-shuhl
Uranus   YOOR-uh-nuhs
Uriah   yoo-RI-uh
Vespasian   ves-PAY-zhuhn
Via Dolorosa   VEE-uh doh´luh-ROH-suh
Via Egnatia   VEE-uh eg-NAH-tee-uh
vicarious   vi-KAIR-ee-uhs
Wellhausen   VEHL-houz-en
Wrede   VRAY-duh
Wycliffe   WIK-lif
Yahweh   YAH-weh
yĕhôšuaᶜ   yuh-HOH-shoo-uh
Zacchaeus   za-KEE-uhs
Zacharias   zak´uh-RI-uhs
Zadok   ZAY-dok
Zadokite   ZAY-duh-kit
Zebedee   ZEB-uh-dee
Zechariah   zek´uh-RI-uh
Zenas   ZEE-nuhs
Zephaniah   zef´uh-NI-uh
Zerubbabel   zuh-RUHB-uh-buhl
Zeus   zoos

SELECTIVE INDEX
OF SUBJECTS